MACHINE LEARNING
FOR BUSINESS ANALYTICS

MACHINE LEARNING FOR BUSINESS ANALYTICS

Concepts, Techniques, and Applications with
Analytic Solver® Data Mining

Fourth Edition

GALIT SHMUELI
National Tsing Hua University
Taipei, Taiwan

PETER C. BRUCE
statistics.com
Arlington, USA

KUBER R. DEOKAR
UpThink Edutech Services Pvt. Ltd.
Pune, India

NITIN R. PATEL
Cytel, Inc.
Cambridge, USA

This edition first published 2023
© 2023 John Wiley & Sons, Inc.

The right of Galit Shmueli, Peter C. Bruce, Kuber R. Deokar, and Nitin R. Patel to be identified as the authors of this work has been asserted in accordance with law.

Registered Office

John Wiley & Sons, Inc., 111 River Street, Hoboken, NJ 07030, USA

For details of our global editorial offices, customer services, and more information about Wiley products visit us at www.wiley.com.

Wiley also publishes its books in a variety of electronic formats and by print-on-demand. Some content that appears in standard print versions of this book may not be available in other formats.

Trademarks: Wiley and the Wiley logo are trademarks or registered trademarks of John Wiley & Sons, Inc. and/or its affiliates in the United States and other countries and may not be used without written permission. All other trademarks are the property of their respective owners. John Wiley & Sons, Inc. is not associated with any product or vendor mentioned in this book.

Library of Congress Cataloging-in-Publication Data Applied for:

Hardback: 9781119829836

Cover Design: Wiley
Cover Image: © Suthat_Chaitaweesap/Getty Images

Set in 11.5/14.5pt Bembo Std by Straive, Chennai, India

SKY10043829_030223

ANALYTIC SOLVER DATA MINING (ASDM) FOR EDUCATION

Your new textbook, *Machine Learning for Business Analytics: Concepts, Techniques, and Applications with Analytic Solver® Data Mining*, Fourth Edition, uses this software throughout. Here's how to get it for your course.

For Instructors: Setting Up the Course Code

Students in your course will need to purchase their license for $25 (140 days in length), or the school itself may pre-purchase student licenses by contacting sales@solver.com and provide students with the course code. Course codes MUST be renewed each time you teach your course.

A pre-purchase will work in a similar fashion to the students purchasing themselves, course code and all, but at the purchase page students will see a charge of $0 and not need to enter any payment information, and will enable Frontline Systems to assist students with installation, and provide technical support to you during the course. Please give the course code, plus the instructions, to your students.

If you're evaluating the book for adoption, you can use the course code yourself to download and install the software as described below.

For Students: Installing Analytic Solver Data Mining (ASDM) for Education

1. To download and install ASDM for Education from Frontline Systems, to work with Microsoft Excel for Windows, please visit https://www.solver.com/welcome-students
2. **Fill out the registration form on this page**, supplying your name, school, email address (key information will be sent to this address), Course Code (obtain this from your instructor), and Textbook Code (enter **SDMBI4**).
3. **Click the download button**, and save the downloaded file SolverSetup.
4. **Close any Excel windows you have open**.
5. **Run SolverSetup to install the software.**

If you have problems downloading or installing, please email support@solver.com or call **775-831-0300** and press 4 (tech support). Say that you have Analytic Solver Data Mining for Education, and have your course code and textbook code available.

If you have problems setting up or solving your model, or interpreting the results, please ask your instructor for assistance. Frontline Systems cannot help you with homework problems.

- *If you purchase this textbook but you aren't enrolled in a course, call 775-831-0300 and press 0 for assistance with the software.*
- If you have a Mac, the best option is to use "Analytic Solver Cloud" or use Excel online via an office 365 by inserting the add-in from the Microsoft Store (see https://solver.zendesk.com/hc/en-us/articles/360024207754-Inserting-Analytic-Solver-Cloud-from-the-Microsoft-Store).

To our families
Boaz and Noa
Liz, Lisa, and Allison
Komal and Yash
Tehmi, Arjun, and in
memory of Aneesh

Contents

PART II DATA EXPLORATION AND DIMENSION REDUCTION

CHAPTER 3 Data Visualization   59

CHAPTER 10   Logistic Regression   229

CHAPTER 11   Neural Nets   257

CHAPTER 12 Discriminant Analysis   283

CHAPTER 13 Generating, Comparing, and Combining   303
Multiple Models

Smoothing Methods

DATA ANALYTICS

Social Network Analytics

Foreword

I was tasked to develop a course on statistical and machine learning for our new business analytics program at a major public university almost a decade ago. I quickly discovered that, unlike business statistics and management science, a legacy of textbooks on this subject appropriate for students without an extensive mathematical background did not exist. Fortunately, a colleague at another institution pointed me toward *Data Mining for Business Intelligence*, the 2nd edition of this book (now called *Machine Learning for Business Analytics*), and it has been the core text for my predictive analytics course ever since. My initial choice was validated, and the book is still the best choice for our students.

Universities are now offering a wide range of degrees, concentrations, and certificates in business analytics. Success with analytics is grounded in employees with the requisite skills to meet industry needs. The market for business analytics continues to expand rapidly as companies adopt new technologies to manage and understand business processes using enterprise, e-commerce, and sensor data. Numerous media and vendor reports have documented the contribution of predictive analytics to improved business outcomes. More recently, analytical solutions have been extended to incorporate artificial intelligence using advanced maching learning techniques, thereby reducing labor costs, enhancing customer experiences, and improving cybersecurity. Negotiating such a new constellation of developing frontiers requires good integrated learning resources. This book is certainly one of them.

The genesis of this book, now in its 4th edition with a revised title, was to make machine learning accessible to students outside of traditional STEM disciplines. It uses the Analytic Solver® add-in for Excel from Frontline Systems, Inc., to quickly introduce students to the machine learning process in a spreadsheet environment without the need for writing computer code. With the Data Mining module of Analytic Solver, students can gain hands-on skills with a broad range of data visualization, data handling utilities, and statistical and machine learning techniques, augmented by tools for data partitioning, variable transformation, feature selection, and model performance evaluation. As a result, both instructors and students are free to focus on conceptual learning using data sets that illustrate a variety of use cases for machine learning in the major functional areas of business.

While this book is also available in other editions based on alternative software platforms, I can speak firsthand as to how its content when used in conjunction with Analytic Solver facilitates a concrete understanding of how statistical and machine learning algorithms work. Students can interactively experiment with the effects of changing algorithmic settings and explore the detailed reports and charts generated by Analytic Solver to review intermediate calculations. By the end of each chapter, students can describe the primary mechanism being used by an algorithm for classification or prediction, articulate its requirements in terms of input variables and parameters, interpret its results, and identify its strengths and weaknesses. They are also exposed to carefully crafted business scenarios and associated real data for each topic. With this foundation, they will be well-prepared for a data analyst role in their respective domains, as well as further study of advanced analytics.

The authors of this book bring together a combination of extensive academic and industry experience that makes a unique contribution to the textbook landscape. In this new edition, they have updated the text and figures to correspond to the latest version of Analytic Solver, expanded coverage of metrics for assessing model performance, and added contemporary topics including deep learning and ethical considerations in the use of data science.

If you are a newcomer to teaching in this area of predictive analytics, *Machine Learning for Business Analytics* will support you and your students while you gain traction in the classroom. With more background, it will serve as a useful resource to guide your own discovery and acquisition of new knowledge and skills for machine learning.

SUSAN W. PALOCSAY
James Madison University 2023

Preface to the Fourth Edition

This textbook first appeared in early 2007 and has been used by numerous students and practitioners and in many courses, including our own experience teaching this material both online and in person for more than 15 years. The first edition, based on the Excel add-in Analytic Solver Data Mining (ASDM, previously XLMiner), was followed by two more Analytic Solver editions, a JMP edition, two R editions, a Python edition, a RapidMiner edition, and now this 4th edition with Analytic Solver, with its companion website, www.dataminingbook.com.

As in the previous Analytic Solver editions, the focus in this new edition is on machine learning concepts and how to implement the associated algorithms in Analytic Solver Data Mining.

For this new ASDM edition, a new co-author, Kuber Deokar, comes on board bringing extensive experience in online course design, development, and delivery, including using ASDM. He has taught courses using various editions of this book for over a decade and has helped shape the student experience in many ways.

The new edition provides significant updates both in terms of ASDM and in terms of new topics and content. In addition to updating software routines and outputs that have changed or become available since the 3rd edition, this edition also incorporates updates and new material based on feedback from instructors teaching MBA, MS, undergraduate, diploma, and executive courses, and from their students as well. Importantly, this edition includes several new topics:

- A new chapter on *Responsible Data Science* (Chapter 22) covering topics of fairness, transparency, model cards and datasheets, legal considerations, and more, with an illustrative example.

- A dedicated section on *deep learning* in Chapter 11.

- The *Performance Evaluation* exposition in Chapter 5 was expanded to include further metrics (precision and recall, F1).

- A new chapter on *Generating, Comparing, and Combining Multiple Models* (Chapter 13) that covers ensembles and AutoML.

- A new chapter dedicated to *Interventions and User Feedback* (Chapter 14) that covers A/B tests, uplift modeling, and reinforcement learning.
- A new case (Loan Approval) that touches on regulatory and ethical issues.

A note about the book's title: The first two editions of the book used the title *Data Mining for Business Intelligence*. Business Intelligence today refers mainly to reporting and data visualization ("what is happening now"), while Business Analytics has taken over the "advanced analytics," which include predictive analytics and data mining. Later editions were therefore renamed *Data Mining for Business Analytics*. However, the recent AI transformation has made the term *machine learning* more popularly associated with the methods in this textbook. In this new edition, we therefore use the updated terms *Machine Learning* and *Business Analytics*.

Since the appearance of the (Analytic Solver based) second edition, the landscape of the courses using the textbook has greatly expanded: whereas initially, the book was used mainly in semester-long elective MBA-level courses, it is now used in a variety of courses in Business Analytics degrees and certificate programs, ranging from undergraduate programs, to post-graduate and executive education programs. Courses in such programs also vary in their duration and coverage. In many cases, this textbook is used across multiple courses. The book is designed to continue supporting the general "Predictive Analytics" or "Data Mining" course as well as supporting a set of courses in dedicated business analytics programs.

A general "Business Analytics," "Predictive Analytics," or "Machine Learning" course, common in MBA and undergraduate programs as a one-semester elective, would cover Parts I–III, and choose a subset of methods from Parts IV and V. Instructors can choose to use cases as team assignments, class discussions, or projects. For a two-semester course, Part VII might be considered, and we recommend introducing Part VIII (Data Analytics).

For a set of courses in a dedicated business analytics program, here are a few courses that have been using our book:

Predictive Analytics—Supervised Learning: In a dedicated Business Analytics program, the topic of Predictive Analytics is typically instructed across a set of courses. The first course would cover Parts I–III and instructors typically choose a subset of methods from Part IV according to the course length. We recommend including "Part VIII: Data Analytics."

Predictive Analytics—Unsupervised Learning: This course introduces data exploration and visualization, dimension reduction, mining relationships, and clustering (Parts II and VI). If this course follows the Predictive Analytics: Supervised Learning course, then it is useful to examine examples and approaches that integrate unsupervised and supervised learning, such as Part VIII on Data Analytics.

Forecasting Analytics: A dedicated course on time series forecasting would rely on Part VI.

Advanced Analytics: A course that integrates the learnings from Predictive Analytics (supervised and unsupervised learning) can focus on Part VIII: Data Analytics, where social network analytics and text mining are introduced, and responsible data science is discussed. Such a course might also include Chapter 13, Generating, Comparing, and Combining Multiple Models and AutoML from Part IV, as well as Part V, which covers experiments, uplift, and reinforcement learning. Some instructors choose to use the Cases (Chapter 23) in such a course.

In all courses, we strongly recommend including a project component, where data are either collected by students according to their interest or provided by the instructor (e.g., from the many machine learning competition datasets available). From our experience and other instructors' experience, such projects enhance the learning and provide students with an excellent opportunity to understand the strengths of machine learning and the challenges that arise in the process.

GALIT SHMUELI, PETER C. BRUCE, KUBER R. DEOKAR, AND NITIN R. PATEL

2023

Acknowledgments

We thank the many people who assisted us in improving the book from its inception as *Data Mining for Business Intelligence* in 2006 (using XLMiner, now Analytic Solver), its reincarnation as *Data Mining for Business Analytics*, and now *Machine Learning for Business Analytics*, including translations in Chinese and Korean and versions supporting Analytic Solver Data Mining, R, Python, SAS JMP, and RapidMiner.

Anthony Babinec, who has been using earlier editions of this book for years in his data mining courses at Statistics.com, provided us with detailed and expert corrections. Dan Toy and John Elder IV greeted our project with early enthusiasm and provided detailed and useful comments on initial drafts. Ravi Bapna, who used an early draft in a data mining course at the Indian School of Business and later at University of Minnesota, has provided invaluable comments and helpful suggestions since the book's start.

Many of the instructors, teaching assistants, and students using earlier editions of the book have contributed invaluable feedback both directly and indirectly, through fruitful discussions, learning journeys, and interesting data mining projects that have helped shape and improve the book. These include MBA students from the University of Maryland, MIT, the Indian School of Business, National Tsing Hua University, and Statistics.com. Instructors from many universities and teaching programs, too numerous to list, have supported and helped improve the book since its inception.

At Statistics.com, Valerie Troiano has shepherded many instructors and students through the courses that have helped nurture the development of these books, and Janet Dobbins has helped bring them to the wider machine learning community. We also thank the many students who have used and commented on this text at Statistics.com. We thank assistant teachers (from UpThink Edutech Services Pvt Ltd) Anuja Kulkarni and Poonam Tribhuwan, and especially Shweta Jadhav for her hours of double checking the software (ASDM).

Colleagues and family members have been providing ongoing feedback and assistance with this book project. Vijay Kamble at UIC and Travis Greene at NTHU have provided valuable help with the section on reinforcement learning. Boaz Shmueli and Raquelle Azran gave detailed editorial comments and suggestions on the first two editions; Bruce McCullough and Adam Hughes did the same for the first edition. Noa Shmueli provided careful proofs of the third edition. Ran Shenberger offered design tips. Ken Strasma, founder of the microtargeting firm HaystaqDNA and director of targeting for the 2004 Kerry campaign and the 2008 Obama campaign, provided the scenario and data for the section on uplift modeling. We also thank Jen Golbeck, Professor in the College of Information Studies at the University of Maryland and author of *Analyzing the Social Web*, whose book inspired our presentation in the chapter on social network analytics. Randall Pruim contributed extensively to the chapter on visualization.

Marietta Tretter at Texas A&M shared comments and thoughts on the time series chapters, and Stephen Few and Ben Shneiderman provided feedback and suggestions on the data visualization chapter and overall design tips.

Susan Palocsay and Mia Stephens have provided suggestions and feedback on numerous occasions, as has Margret Bjarnadottir. We also thank Catherine Plaisant at the University of Maryland's Human–Computer Interaction Lab, who helped out in a major way by contributing exercises and illustrations to the data visualization chapter. Gregory Piatetsky-Shapiro, founder of KDNuggets.com, was generous with his time and counsel in the early years of this project.

We thank colleagues at the Sloan School of Management at MIT for their support during the formative stage of this book—Dimitris Bertsimas, James Orlin, Robert Freund, Roy Welsch, Gordon Kaufmann, and Gabriel Bitran. As teaching assistants for the data mining course at Sloan, Adam Mersereau gave detailed comments on the notes and cases that were the genesis of this book, Romy Shioda helped with the preparation of several cases and exercises used here, and Mahesh Kumar helped with the material on clustering.

Colleagues at the University of Maryland's Smith School of Business: Shrivardhan Lele, Wolfgang Jank, and Paul Zantek provided practical advice and comments. We thank Robert Windle, and University of Maryland MBA students Timothy Roach, Pablo Macouzet, and Nathan Birckhead for invaluable datasets. We also thank MBA students Rob Whitener and Daniel Curtis for the heatmap and map charts.

Anand Bodapati provided both data and advice. Jake Hofman from Microsoft Research and Sharad Borle assisted with data access. Suresh Ankolekar and Mayank Shah helped develop several cases and provided valuable pedagogical comments. Vinni Bhandari helped write the Charles Book Club case.

We are grateful to colleagues at UMass Lowell's Manning School of Business for their encouragement and support in developing data analytics courses at the undergraduate and graduate levels that led to the development of this edition: Luvai Motiwalla, Harry Zhu, Thomas Sloan, Bob Li, and Sandra Richtermeyer. We also thank Michael Goul (late), Dan Power (late), Ramesh Sharda, Babita Gupta, Ashish Gupta, and Haya Ajjan from the Association for Information

System's Decision Support and Analytics (SIGDSA) community for ideas and advice that helped the development of the book.

We would like to thank Marvin Zelen, L. J. Wei, and Cyrus Mehta at Harvard, as well as Anil Gore at Pune University, for thought-provoking discussions on the relationship between statistics and data mining. Our thanks to Richard Larson of the Engineering Systems Division, MIT, for sparking many stimulating ideas on the role of data mining in modeling complex systems. Over two decades ago, they helped us develop a balanced philosophical perspective on the emerging field of machine learning.

Lastly, we thank the folks at Wiley for this successful journey of nearly two decades. Steve Quigley at Wiley showed confidence in this book from the beginning and helped us navigate through the publishing process with great speed. Curt Hinrichs' vision, tips, and encouragement helped bring the first edition of this book to the starting gate. Jon Gurstelle guided us through additional editions and translations. Brett Kurzman has taken over the reins and is now shepherding the project. Becky Cowan, Sarah Lemore, and Kavya Ramu greatly assisted us in pushing ahead and finalizing this 4th edition. We are also especially grateful to Amy Hendrickson, who assisted with typesetting and making this book beautiful.

## PART I

Preliminaries

## CHAPTER 1

Introduction

1.1 WHAT IS BUSINESS ANALYTICS?

Business analytics (BA) is the practice and art of bringing quantitative data to bear on decision making. The term means different things to different organizations.

Consider the role of analytics in helping newspapers survive the transition to a digital world. One tabloid newspaper with a working-class readership in Britain had launched a web version of the paper, and did tests on its home page to determine which images produced more hits: cats, dogs, or monkeys. This simple application, for this company, was considered analytics. By contrast, the *Washington Post* has a highly influential audience that is of interest to big defense contractors: it is perhaps the only newspaper where you routinely see advertisements for aircraft carriers. In the digital environment, the *Post* can track readers by time of day, location, and user subscription information. In this fashion, the display of the aircraft carrier advertisement in the online paper may be focused on a very small group of individuals—say, the members of the House and Senate Armed Services Committees who will be voting on the Pentagon's budget.

Business analytics, or more generically, *analytics*, includes a range of data analysis methods. Many powerful applications involve little more than counting, rule checking, and basic arithmetic. For some organizations, this is what is meant by analytics.

The next level of business analytics, now termed *business intelligence* (BI), refers to data visualization and reporting for understanding "what happened and what is happening." This is done by use of charts, tables, and dashboards to display, examine, and explore data. BI, which earlier consisted mainly of generating static reports, has evolved into more user-friendly and effective tools and practices, such as creating interactive dashboards that allow the user not only to

Machine Learning for Business Analytics: Concepts, Techniques, and Applications with Analytic Solver® Data Mining, Fourth Edition. Galit Shmueli, Peter C. Bruce, Kuber R. Deokar, and Nitin R. Patel.
© 2023 John Wiley & Sons, Inc. Published 2023 by John Wiley & Sons, Inc.

access real-time data but also to directly interact with it. Effective dashboards are those that tie directly into company data, and give managers a tool to quickly see what might not readily be apparent in a large complex database. One such tool for industrial operations managers displays customer orders in a single two-dimensional display, using color and bubble size as added variables, showing customer name, type of product, size of order, and length of time to produce.

Business analytics now typically includes BI as well as sophisticated data analysis methods, such as statistical models and machine learning algorithms used for exploring data, quantifying and explaining relationships between measurements, and predicting new records. Methods like regression models are used to describe and quantify "on average" relationships (e.g., between advertising and sales), to predict new records (e.g., whether a new patient will react positively to a medication), and to forecast future values (e.g., next week's web traffic).

Readers familiar with earlier editions of this book might have noticed that the book title changed from *Data Mining for Business Intelligence* to *Data Mining for Business Analytics*, and finally, in this edition to *Machine Learning for Business Analytics*. The first change reflects the more recent term BA, which overtook the earlier term BI to denote advanced analytics. Today, BI is used to refer to data visualization and reporting. The change from *data mining* to *machine learning* reflects today's common use of *machine learning* to refer to algorithms that learn from data. This book uses primarily the term *machine learning*, except for specific references to the software *Analytic Solver Data Mining* and its menus.

WHO USES PREDICTIVE ANALYTICS?

The widespread adoption of predictive analytics, coupled with the accelerating availability of data, has increased organizations' capabilities throughout the economy. A few examples:

Credit scoring: One long-established use of predictive modeling techniques for business prediction is credit scoring. A credit score is not some arbitrary judgment of credit-worthiness; it is based mainly on a predictive model that uses prior data to predict repayment behavior.

Future purchases: A controversial example is Target's use of predictive modeling to classify sales prospects as "pregnant" or "not-pregnant." Those classified as pregnant could then be sent sales promotions at an early stage of pregnancy, giving Target a head start on a significant purchase stream.

Tax evasion: The US Internal Revenue Service found it was 25 times more likely to find tax evasion when enforcement activity was based on predictive models, allowing agents to focus on the most likely tax cheats (Siegel, 2013).

The business analytics toolkit also includes statistical experiments, the most common of which is known to marketers as A-B testing. These are often used for pricing decisions:

- Orbitz, the travel site, found that it could price hotel options higher for Mac users than Windows users.
- Staples online store found it could charge more for staplers if a customer lived far from a Staples store.

Beware the organizational setting where analytics is a solution in search of a problem: A manager, knowing that business analytics and machine learning are hot areas, decides that her organization must deploy them too, to capture that hidden value that must be lurking somewhere. Successful use of analytics and machine learning requires both an understanding of the business context where value is to be captured, and an understanding of exactly what the machine learning methods do.

1.2 WHAT IS MACHINE LEARNING?

In this book, machine learning (or data mining) refers to business analytics methods that go beyond counts, descriptive techniques, reporting, and methods based on business rules. While we do introduce data visualization, which is commonly the first step into more advanced analytics, the book focuses mostly on the more advanced data analytics tools. Specifically, it includes statistical and machine-learning methods that inform decision making, often in automated fashion. Prediction is typically an important component, often at the individual level. Rather than "what is the relationship between advertising and sales?" we might be interested in "what specific advertisement, or recommended product, should be shown to a given online shopper at this moment?" Or we might be interested in clustering customers into different "personas" that receive different marketing treatment, then assigning each new prospect to one of these personas.

The era of big data has accelerated the use of machine learning. Machine learning algorithms, with their power and automaticity, have the ability to cope with huge amounts of data and extract value.

1.3 MACHINE LEARNING, AI, AND RELATED TERMS

The field of analytics is growing rapidly, both in terms of the breadth of applications, and in terms of the number of organizations using advanced analytics. As a result there is considerable overlap and inconsistency of definitions. Terms have also changed over time.

The older term *data mining* means different things to different people. To the general public, it may have a general, somewhat hazy and pejorative meaning of digging through vast stores of (often personal) data in search of something interesting. *Data mining*, as it refers to analytic techniques, has largely been superceded by the term *machine learning*. Other terms that organizations use are *predictive analytics*, *predictive modeling*, and most recently *machine learning* and *Artificial Intelligence (AI)*.

Many practitioners, particularly those from the IT and computer science communities, use the term *AI* to refer to all the methods discussed in this book. AI originally referred to the general capability of a machine to act like a human, and, in its earlier days, existed mainly in the realm of science fiction and the unrealized ambitions of computer scientists. More recently, it has come to encompass the methods of statistical and machine learning discussed in this book, as the primary enablers of that grand vision, and sometimes the term is used loosely to mean the same thing as *machine learning*. More broadly, it includes generative capabilities such as the creation of images, audio, and video.

Statistical Modeling vs. Machine Learning

A variety of techniques for exploring data and building models have been around for a long time in the world of statistics: linear regression, logistic regression, discriminant analysis, and principal component analysis, for example. But the core tenets of classical statistics—computing is difficult and data are scarce—do not apply in machine learning applications where both data and computing power are plentiful.

This gives rise to Daryl Pregibon's description of "data mining" (in the sense of machine learning) as "statistics at scale and speed" (Pregibon, 1999). Another major difference between the fields of statistics and machine learning is the focus in statistics on inference from a sample to the population regarding an "average effect"—for example, "a $1 price increase will reduce average demand by 2 boxes." In contrast, the focus in machine learning is on predicting individual records—"the predicted demand for person i given a $1 price increase is 1 box, while for person j it is 3 boxes." The emphasis that classical statistics places on inference (determining whether a pattern or interesting result might have happened by chance in our sample) is absent from machine learning. Note also that the term *inference* is often used in the machine learning community to refer to the process of using a model to make predictions for new data, also called *scoring*, in contrast to its meaning in the statistical community.

In comparison to statistics, machine learning deals with large datasets in an open-ended fashion, making it impossible to put the strict limits around the question being addressed that classical statistical inference would require. As a result, the general approach to machine learning is vulnerable to the danger of *overfitting*, where a model is fit so closely to the available sample of data that it describes not merely structural characteristics of the data but random peculiarities as well. In engineering terms, the model is fitting the noise, not just the signal.

In this book, we use the term *machine learning algorithm* to refer to methods that learn directly from data, especially local patterns, often in layered or iterative fashion. In contrast, we use *statistical models* to refer to methods that apply global structure to the data that can be written as a simple mathematical equation. A simple example is a linear regression model (statistical) vs. a k-nearest-neighbors algorithm (machine learning). A given record would be treated by linear regression in accord with an overall linear equation that applies to *all* the records. In k-nearest-neighbors, that record would be classified in accord with the values of a small number of nearby records.

1.4 BIG DATA

Machine learning and big data go hand in hand. *Big data* is a relative term—data today are big by reference to the past, and to the methods and devices available to deal with them. The challenge big data presents is often characterized by the four V's—volume, velocity, variety, and veracity. *Volume* refers to the amount of data. *Velocity* refers to the flow rate—the speed at which it is being generated and changed. *Variety* refers to the different types of data being generated (time stamps, location, numbers, text, images, etc.). *Veracity* refers to the fact that data is being generated by organic distributed processes (e.g., millions of people signing up for services or free downloads) and not subject to the controls or quality checks that apply to data collected for a study.

Most large organizations face both the challenge and the opportunity of big data because most routine data processes now generate data that can be stored and, possibly, analyzed. The scale can be visualized by comparing the data in a traditional statistical analysis (e.g., 15 variables and 5000 records) to the Walmart database. If you consider the traditional statistical study to be the size of a period at the end of a sentence, then the Walmart database is the size of a football field. And that probably does not include other data associated with Walmart—social media data, for example, which comes in the form of unstructured text.

If the analytical challenge is substantial, so can be the reward:

- OKCupid, the online dating site, uses statistical models with their data to predict what forms of message content are most likely to produce a response.

- Telenor, a Norwegian mobile phone service company, was able to reduce subscriber turnover 37% by using models to predict which customers were most likely to leave, and then lavishing attention on them.

- Allstate, the insurance company, tripled the accuracy of predicting injury liability in auto claims by incorporating more information about vehicle type.

The examples above are from Eric Siegel's book *Predictive Analytics* (2013, Wiley).

Some extremely valuable tasks were not even feasible before the era of big data. Consider web searches, the technology on which Google was built. In early days, a search for "Ricky Ricardo Little Red Riding Hood" would have yielded various links to the *I Love Lucy* TV show, other links to Ricardo's career as a band leader, and links to the children's story of Little Red Riding Hood. Only once the Google database had accumulated sufficient data (including records of what users clicked on) would the search yield, in the top position, links to the specific *I Love Lucy* episode in which Ricky enacts, in a comic mixture of Spanish and English, Little Red Riding Hood for his infant son.

1.5 DATA SCIENCE

The ubiquity, size, value, and importance of big data has given rise to a new profession: the *data scientist*. *Data science* is a mix of skills in the areas of statistics, machine learning, math, programming, business, and IT. The term itself is thus broader than the other concepts we discussed above, and it is a rare individual who combines deep skills in all the constituent areas. In their book *Analyzing the Analyzers* (Harris et al., 2013), the authors describe the skillsets of most data scientists as resembling a "T"—deep in one area (the vertical bar of the T), and shallower in other areas (the top of the T).

At a large data science conference session (Strata-Hadoop World, October 2014) most attendees felt that programming was an essential skill, though there was a sizable minority who felt otherwise. And, although big data is the motivating power behind the growth of data science, most data scientists do not actually spend most of their time working with terabyte-size or larger data.

Data of the terabyte or larger size would be involved at the deployment stage of a model. There are manifold challenges at that stage, most of them IT and programming issues related to data handling and tying together different components of a system. Much work must precede that phase. It is that earlier piloting and prototyping phase on which this book focuses—developing the statistical and machine learning models that will eventually be plugged into a deployed system. What methods do you use with what sorts of data and problems? How do the methods work? What are their requirements, their strengths, their weaknesses? How do you assess their performance?

1.6 WHY ARE THERE SO MANY DIFFERENT METHODS?

As can be seen in this book or any other resource on machine learning, there are many different methods for prediction and classification. You might ask yourself why they coexist, and whether some are better than others. The answer is that each method has advantages and disadvantages. The usefulness of a method can depend on factors such as the size of the dataset, the types of patterns that exist in the data, whether the data meet some underlying assumptions of the method, how noisy the data are, and the particular goal of the analysis. A small illustration is shown in Figure 1.1, where the goal is to find a combination of *household income level* and *household lot size* that separates owners (solid circles) from nonowners (hollow circles) of riding mowers. The first method (left panel) looks only for horizontal and vertical lines to separate owners from nonowners; the second method (right panel) looks for a single diagonal line.

Different methods can lead to different results, and their performance can vary. It is therefore customary in machine learning to apply several different methods (and perhaps their combination) and select the one that appears most useful for the goal at hand.

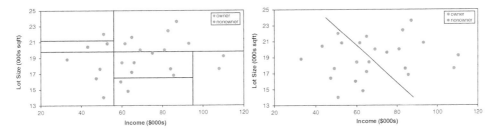

FIGURE 1.1   TWO METHODS FOR SEPARATING OWNERS FROM NONOWNERS

1.7 TERMINOLOGY AND NOTATION

Because of the hybrid parentry of data science, its practitioners often use multiple terms to refer to the same thing. For example, in the machine learning and artificial intelligence fields, the variable being predicted is the *output variable* or *target variable*. A categorical target variable is often called a *label*. To a statistician or social scientist, the variable being predicted is the *dependent variable* or the *response*. Here is a summary of terms used:

Algorithm   A specific procedure used to implement a particular machine learning technique: classification tree, discriminant analysis, and the like.

Attribute   See **Predictor**.

Case   See **Observation**.

Confidence   A performance measure in association rules of the type "IF A and B are purchased, THEN C is also purchased." Confidence is the conditional probability that C will be purchased IF A and B are purchased.

Confidence   Also has a broader meaning in statistics (*confidence interval*), concerning the degree of error in an estimate that results from selecting one sample as opposed to another.

Dependent variable   See **Response**.

Estimation   See **Prediction**.

Feature   See **Predictor**.

Holdout data   (or **holdout set**) A sample of data not used in fitting a model, but instead used to assess the performance of that model. This book uses the term *test set* instead of *holdout set*.

Inference   In statistics, the process of accounting for chance variation when making estimates or drawing conclusions based on samples; in machine learning the term often refers to the process of using a model to make predictions for new data (see **Score**).

Input variable   See **Predictor**.

Label   A categorical variable being predicted in supervised learning.

Model   An algorithm as applied to a dataset, complete with its settings (many of the algorithms have parameters that the user can adjust).

Observation   The unit of analysis on which the measurements are taken (a customer, a transaction, etc.); also called *instance, sample, example, case, record, pattern,* or *row*. In spreadsheets, each row typically represents a record; each column, a variable. Note that the use of the term "sample" here is different from its usual meaning in statistics, where it refers to a collection of observations.

Outcome variable   See **Response**.

Output variable   See **Response**.

$P\left(A|B\right)$ The conditional probability of event A occurring given that event B has occurred. Read as "the probability that A will occur given that B has occurred."

Profile   A set of measurements on an observation (e.g., the height, weight, and age of a person).

Prediction   The prediction of the numerical value of a continuous output variable; also called *estimation*.

Predictor   A variable, usually denoted by X, used as an input into a predictive model. Also called a *feature*, *input variable*, *independent variable*, or from a database perspective, a *field*.

Record   See **Observation**.

Response   A variable, usually denoted by Y, which is the variable being predicted in supervised learning; also called *dependent variable*, *output variable*, *target variable*, or *outcome variable*.

Sample   In the statistical community, "sample" means a collection of observations. In the machine learning community, "sample" means a single observation.

Score   A predicted value or class. *Scoring new data* means using a model developed with training data to predict output values in new data.

Success class   The class of interest in a binary outcome (e.g., *purchasers* in the outcome *purchase/no purchase*); the outcome need not be favorable.

Supervised learning   The process of providing an algorithm (logistic regression, classification tree, etc.) with records in which an output variable of interest is known and the algorithm "learns" how to predict this value for new records where the output is unknown.

Target   See **Response**.

Test data   (or **test set**) The portion of the data used only at the end of the model building and selection process to assess how well the final model might perform on new data. Also called "holdout data."

Training data   (or **training set**) The portion of the data used to fit a model.

Unsupervised learning   An analysis in which one attempts to learn patterns in the data other than predicting an output value of interest.

Validation data   (or **validation set**) The portion of the data used to assess how well the model fits, to adjust models, and to select the best model from among those that have been tried.

Variable   Any measurement on the records, including both the input (X) variables and the output (Y) variable.

1.8 ROAD MAPS TO THIS BOOK

The book covers many of the widely used predictive and classification methods as well as other machine learning tools. Figure 1.2 outlines machine learning from a process perspective and where the topics in this book fit in. Chapter numbers are indicated beside the topic. Table 1.1 provides a different perspective: it organizes supervised and unsupervised machine learning procedures according to the type and structure of the data.

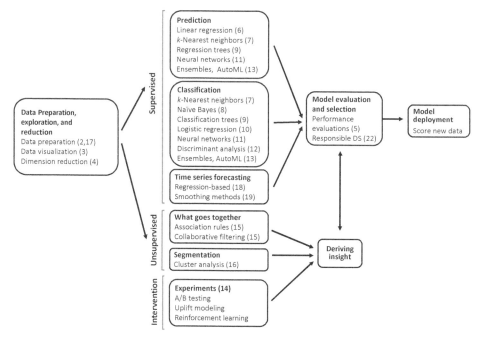

FIGURE 1.2   MACHINE LEARNING FROM A PROCESS PERSPECTIVE. NUMBERS IN PARENTHESES INDICATE CHAPTER NUMBERS

TABLE 1.1   ORGANIZATION OF MACHINE LEARNING METHODS IN THIS BOOK, ACCORDING TO THE NATURE OF THE DATA[a]

	Supervised		Unsupervised
	Continuous response	Categorical response	No response
Continuous predictors	Linear regression (6) Neural nets (11) k-Nearest neighbors (7) Ensembles (13)	Logistic regression (10) Neural nets (11) Discriminant analysis (12) k-Nearest neighbors (7) Ensembles (13)	Principal components (4) Cluster analysis (16) Collaborative filtering (15)
Categorical predictors	Linear regression (6) Neural nets (11) Regression trees (9) Ensembles (13)	Neural nets (11) Classification trees (9) Logistic regression (10) Naive Bayes (8) Ensembles (13)	Association rules (15) Collaborative filtering (15)

[a]Numbers in parentheses indicate chapter number.

Order of Topics

The book is divided into nine parts: Part I (Chapters 1–2) gives a general overview of machine learning and its components. Part II (Chapters 3–4) focuses on the early stages of data exploration and dimension reduction.

Part III (Chapter 5) discusses performance evaluation. Although it contains only one chapter, we discuss a variety of topics, from predictive performance metrics to misclassification costs. The principles covered in this part are crucial for the proper evaluation and comparison of supervised learning methods.

Part IV includes eight chapters (Chapters 6–13), covering a variety of popular supervised learning methods (for classification and/or prediction). Within this part, the topics are generally organized according to the level of sophistication of the algorithms, their popularity, and ease of understanding. The final chapter introduces ensembles and combinations of methods.

Part V (Chapter 14) introduces the notions of experiments, intervention, and user feedback. This single chapter starts with A/B testing, then its use in uplift modeling, and finally expands into reinforcement learning, explaining the basic ideas and formulations that utilize user feedback for learning best treatment assignments.

Part VI focuses on unsupervised learning of relationships. It presents association rules and collaborative filtering (Chapter 15) and cluster analysis (Chapter 16).

Part VII includes three chapters (Chapters 17–19), with the focus on forecasting time series. The first chapter covers general issues related to handling and understanding time series. The next two chapters present two popular forecasting approaches: regression-based forecasting and smoothing methods.

Part VIII presents two broad data analytics topics: social network analysis (Chapter 20) and text mining (Chapter 21). These methods apply machine learning to specialized data structures: social networks and text. The final chapter on responsible data science (Chapter 22) introduces key issues to consider for when carrying out a machine learning project in a responsible way.

Finally, part IX includes a set of cases.

Although the topics in the book can be covered in the order of the chapters, each chapter stands alone. We advise, however, to read parts I–III before proceeding to chapters in parts IV–VI. Similarly, Chapter 17 should precede other chapters in part VII.

USING ASDM SOFTWARE

To facilitate hands-on machine learning experience, this book comes with access to Analytic Solver Data Mining (ASDM), a comprehensive add-in for Excel, for nominal cost. For those familiar with Excel, the use of an Excel add-in dramatically shortens the software learning curve. ASDM helps you get started quickly on machine learning and offers a variety of methods for analyzing data. The illustrations, exercises, and cases in this book are written in relation to this software. ASDM has extensive coverage of machine learning techniques for classification, prediction, mining associations and text, forecasting, and data exploration and reduction. It offers a variety of supervised learning algorithms: neural nets, classification and regression trees, k-nearest-neighbor classification, naive Bayes, logistic regression, linear regression, and discriminant analysis, all for predictive modeling. It provides for automatic partitioning of data into training, validation, and test samples and for the deployment of the model to new data. It also offers unsupervised algorithms: association rules, principal component analysis, k-means clustering, and hierarchical clustering, as well as visualization tools and data-handling utilities. With its short learning curve, affordable price, and reliance on the familiar Excel platform, it is an ideal companion to a book on machine learning for the business student.

Download: To download the ASDM setup program, visit www.solver.com/welcome-students and follow the instructions there. Save the USERNAME/EMAIL and PASSWORD you used to Register to Download Analytic Solver Basic; you will need these at the time you start using the software.

Install: Close any Excel windows, then run the Solver-Setup program. Dialog boxes will guide you through the installation procedure. The final dialog box gives you an option to "start Excel and show me Analytic Solver." You'll see *Analytic Solver* and *Data Mining* Tabs on the Excel Ribbon.

Use: ASDM is loaded when you start Excel, and appears as an Excel Ribbon, as shown in Figure 1.3. By clicking Data Mining menu and choosing the appropriate menu item, you can run the machine learning procedures on the dataset that is open in your Excel worksheet.

ASDM's user interface, pictured in Figure 1.3, includes a custom Ribbon tab in Excel, and a Task Pane at the side of the spreadsheet where further tabs and menu options appear.

Note: The figures and images in this text are based on ASDM version 23.0.0.0. Depending on your ASDM version, you may see some variations in the user interface: For example, the location of the Text, Partition, and Chart menus in the Ribbon might vary depending on the Desktop and Cloud version used. Also, the *Generate Data* menu shown on the Ribbon in Figure 1.3, and a *Simulate* tab you may see on some dialog windows, were both slated for release after this book went to press. They do not appear in earlier ASDM versions and are not needed for the examples and exercises in this book edition.

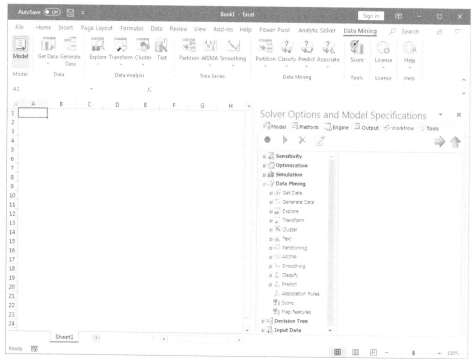

FIGURE 1.3   ANALYTIC SOLVER DATA MINING (ASDM) SCREEN: THE DATA MINING RIBBON PROVIDES VARIOUS MACHINE LEARNING MENUS

## CHAPTER 2

Overview of the Machine Learning Process

In this chapter, we give an overview of the steps involved in a machine learning (ML) solution, starting from a clear goal definition and ending with model deployment. The general steps are shown schematically in Figure 2.1. We also discuss issues related to data collection, cleaning, and preprocessing. We introduce the notion of *data partitioning*, where methods are trained on a set of training data and then their performance is evaluated on a separate set of validation data, as well as explain how this practice helps avoid overfitting. Finally, we illustrate the steps of model building by applying them to data.

Define purpose	Obtain data	Explore and clean data	Determine ML task	Choose ML methods	Apply methods, select final model	Evaluate performance	Deploy

FIGURE 2.1   SCHEMATIC OF THE DATA MODELING PROCESS

2.1 INTRODUCTION

In Chapter 1, we saw some very general definitions of business analytics and machine learning. In this chapter, we introduce a variety of machine learning methods. The core of this book focuses on what has come to be called *predictive analytics*, the tasks of classification and prediction as well as pattern discovery, which have become key elements of a "business analytics" function in most large firms. These terms are described and illustrated next.

Machine Learning for Business Analytics: Concepts, Techniques, and Applications with Analytic Solver® Data Mining, Fourth Edition. Galit Shmueli, Peter C. Bruce, Kuber R. Deokar, and Nitin R. Patel.
© 2023 John Wiley & Sons, Inc. Published 2023 by John Wiley & Sons, Inc.

2.2 CORE IDEAS IN MACHINE LEARNING

Classification

Classification is perhaps the most basic form of predictive analytics. The recipient of an offer can respond or not respond. An applicant for a loan can repay on time, repay late, or declare bankruptcy. A credit card transaction can be normal or fraudulent. A packet of data traveling on a network can be benign or threatening. A bus in a fleet can be available for service or unavailable. The victim of an illness can be recovered, still be ill, or be deceased.

A common task in machine learning is to examine data where the classification is unknown or will occur in the future, with the goal of predicting what that classification is or will be. Similar data where the classification is known are used to develop rules, which are then applied to the data with the unknown classification.

Prediction

Prediction is similar to classification, except that we are trying to predict the value of a numerical variable (e.g., amount of purchase) rather than a class (e.g., purchaser or nonpurchaser). Of course, in classification we are trying to predict a class, but the term *prediction* in this book refers to the prediction of the value of a continuous numerical variable.

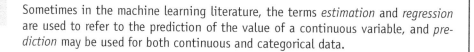

> Sometimes in the machine learning literature, the terms *estimation* and *regression* are used to refer to the prediction of the value of a continuous variable, and *prediction* may be used for both continuous and categorical data.

Association Rules and Recommendation Systems

Large databases of customer transactions lend themselves naturally to the analysis of associations among items purchased, or "what goes with what." *Association rules*, or *affinity analysis*, is designed to find such general associations patterns between items in large databases. The rules can then be used in a variety of ways. For example, grocery stores can use such information for product placement. They can use the rules for weekly promotional offers or for bundling products. Association rules derived from a hospital database on patients' symptoms during consecutive hospitalizations can help find "which symptom is followed by what other symptom" to help predict future symptoms for returning patients.

Online recommendation systems, such as those used on Amazon and Netflix, use *collaborative filtering*, a method that uses individual users' preferences and tastes given their historic purchase, rating, browsing, or any other measurable behavior indicative of preference, as well as other users' history. In contrast to *association rules* that generate rules general to an entire population, collaborative filtering generates "what goes with what" at the individual user level. Hence, collaborative filtering is used in many recommendation systems that aim to deliver personalized recommendations to users with a wide range of preferences.

Predictive Analytics

Classification, prediction, and, to some extent, association rules and collaborative filtering constitute the analytical methods employed in *predictive analytics*. The term predictive analytics is sometimes used to also include data pattern identification methods such as clustering.

Data Reduction and Dimension Reduction

The performance of some machine learning algorithms is often improved when the number of variables is limited, and when large numbers of records can be grouped into homogeneous groups. For example, rather than dealing with thousands of product types, an analyst might wish to group them into a smaller number of groups and build separate models for each group. Or a marketer might want to classify customers into different "personas" and must therefore group customers into homogeneous groups to define the personas. This process of consolidating a large number of records (or cases) into a smaller set is termed *data reduction*. Methods for reducing the number of cases are often called *clustering*.

Reducing the number of variables is typically called *dimension reduction*. Dimension reduction is a common initial step before deploying supervised learning methods, intended to improve predictive power, manageability, and interpretability.

Data Exploration and Visualization

One of the earliest stages of engaging with data is exploring it. Exploration is aimed at understanding the global landscape of the data and detecting unusual values. Exploration is used for data cleaning and manipulation as well as for visual discovery and "hypothesis generation."

Methods for exploring data include looking at various data aggregations and summaries, both numerically and graphically. This includes looking at each variable separately as well as looking at relationships between variables. The purpose is to discover patterns and exceptions. Exploration by creating charts and dashboards is called *data visualization* or *visual analytics*. For numerical variables, we use histograms and boxplots to learn about the distribution of their values, to detect outliers (extreme observations), and to find other information that is relevant to the analysis task. Similarly, for categorical variables, we use bar charts. We can also look at scatter plots of pairs of numerical variables to learn about possible relationships, the type of relationship, and, again, to detect outliers. Visualization can be greatly enhanced by adding features such as color and interactive navigation.

Supervised and Unsupervised Learning

A fundamental distinction among machine learning techniques is between supervised and unsupervised methods. *Supervised learning algorithms* are those used in classification and prediction. We must have data available in which the value of the outcome of interest (e.g., purchase or no purchase) is known. These *training data* are the data from which the classification or prediction algorithm "learns," or is "trained," about the relationship between predictor variables and the outcome variable. Once the algorithm has learned from the training data, it is then applied to another sample of data (the *validation data*) where the outcome is known, to see how well it does in comparison to other models. If many different models are being tried out, it is prudent to save a third sample, which also includes known outcomes (the *test data*) to use with the model finally selected to predict how well it will do. The model can then be used to classify or predict the outcome of interest in new cases where the outcome is unknown.

Simple linear regression is an example of a supervised learning algorithm (although rarely called that in the introductory statistics course where you probably first encountered it). The Y variable is the (known) outcome variable, and the X variable is a predictor variable. A regression line is drawn to minimize the sum of squared deviations between the actual Y values and the values predicted by this line. The regression line can now be used to predict Y values for new values of X for which we do not know the Y value.

Unsupervised learning algorithms are those used where there is no outcome variable to predict or classify. Hence, there is no "learning" from cases where such an outcome variable is known. Association rules, dimension reduction methods, and clustering techniques are all unsupervised learning methods.

Supervised and unsupervised methods are sometimes used in conjunction. For example, unsupervised clustering methods are used to separate loan applicants into several risk-level groups. Then, supervised algorithms are applied separately to each risk-level group for predicting loan default propensity.

SUPERVISED LEARNING REQUIRES GOOD SUPERVISION

In some cases, the value of the target variable is known because it is an inherent component of the data. Web logs will show whether a person clicked on a link or didn't click. Bank records will show whether a loan was paid on time or not. In other cases, the value of the known target must be supplied by a human labeling process to accumulate enough data to train a model. Email must be labeled as spam or legitimate, documents in legal discovery must be labeled as relevant or irrelevant. In either case, the machine learning algorithm can be led astray if the quality of the supervision is poor.

Gene Weingarten reported in the January 5, 2014, *Washington Post* magazine how the strange phrase "defiantly recommend" is making its way into English via auto-correction. "Defiantly" is closer to the common misspelling *definatly* than is *definitely*, so Google, in the early days, offered it as a correction when users typed the misspelled word "definatly" on http://google.com. In the ideal supervised learning model, humans guide the auto-correction process by rejecting *defiantly* and substituting *definitely*. Google's algorithm would then learn that this is the best first-choice correction of "definatly." The problem was that too many people were lazy, just accepting the first correction that Google presented. All these acceptances then cemented "defiantly" as the proper correction.

2.3 THE STEPS IN A MACHINE LEARNING PROJECT

This book focuses on understanding and using machine learning algorithms (steps 4–7 below). However, some of the most serious errors in analytics projects result from a poor understanding of the problem—an understanding that must be developed before we get into the details of algorithms to be used. Here is a list of steps to be taken in a typical machine learning effort:

1. *Develop an understanding of the purpose of the machine learning project.* How will the stakeholder use the results? Who will be affected by the results? Will the analysis be a one-shot effort or an ongoing procedure?

2. *Obtain the dataset to be used in the analysis.* This often involves random sampling from a large database to capture records to be used in an analysis. It may also involve pulling together data from different databases or sources. The databases could be internal (e.g., past purchases made by customers) or external (credit ratings). While machine learning deals with very large databases, usually the analysis to be done requires only thousands or tens of thousands of records.

3. *Explore, clean, and preprocess the data.* This step involves verifying that the data are in reasonable condition. How should missing data be handled? Are the values in a reasonable range, given what you would expect for each variable? Are there obvious outliers? The data are reviewed graphically: for example, a matrix of scatterplots showing the relationship of each

variable with every other variable. We also need to ensure consistency in the definitions of fields, units of measurement, time periods, and so on. In this step, new variables are also typically created from existing ones. For example, "duration" can be computed from start and end dates.

4. *Reduce the data dimension, if necessary.* Dimension reduction can involve operations such as eliminating unneeded variables, transforming variables (e.g., turning "money spent" into "spent $> \$100$" vs. "spent $\leq \$100$"), and creating new variables (e.g., a variable that records whether at least one of several products was purchased). Make sure that you know what each variable means and whether it is sensible to include it in the model.

5. *Determine the machine learning task* (classification, prediction, clustering, etc.). This involves translating the general question or problem of step 1 into a more specific machine learning question.

6. *Partition the data (for supervised tasks).* If the task is supervised (classification or prediction), randomly partition the dataset into three parts: training, validation, and test datasets.

7. *Choose the machine learning techniques to be used* (regression, neural nets, hierarchical clustering, etc.).

8. *Use algorithms to perform the task.* This is typically an iterative process—trying multiple variants, and often using multiple variants of the same algorithm (choosing different variables or parameter settings within the algorithm). Where appropriate, feedback from the algorithm's performance on validation data is used to refine the parameter settings.

9. *Interpret the results of the algorithms.* This involves making a choice as to the best algorithm to deploy and, where possible, testing the final choice on the test data to get an idea as to how well it will perform. (Recall that each algorithm may also be tested on the validation data for tuning purposes; in this way, the validation data become a part of the fitting process and are likely to underestimate the error in the deployment of the model that is finally chosen.)

10. *Deploy the model.* This step involves integrating the model into operational systems and running it on real records to produce decisions or actions. For example, the model might be applied to a purchased list of possible customers, and the action might be "include in the mailing if the predicted amount of purchase is >\$10." A key step here is "scoring" the new records, or using the chosen model to predict the target value for each new record.

The foregoing steps encompass the steps in SEMMA, a methodology developed by the software company SAS:

Sample: Take a sample from the dataset; partition into training, validation, and test datasets.

Explore: Examine the dataset statistically and graphically.

Modify: Transform the variables and impute missing values.

Model: Fit predictive models (e.g., regression tree, neural network).

Assess: Compare models using a validation dataset.

IBM SPSS Modeler (previously SPSS-Clementine) has a similar methodology, termed CRISP-DM (CRoss-Industry Standard Process for Data Mining). All these frameworks include the same main steps involved in predictive modeling.

2.4 PRELIMINARY STEPS

Organization of Data

Datasets are nearly always constructed and displayed so that variables are in columns and records are in rows. In the example shown in Section 2.6 (home values in West Roxbury, Boston, in 2014), 14 variables are recorded for over 5000 homes. The spreadsheet is organized so that each row represents a home—the first home's assessed value was $344,200, its tax was $4430, its size was 9965 ft^2, it was built in 1880, and so on. In supervised learning situations, one of these variables will be the outcome variable, typically listed in the first or last column (in this case it is TOTAL VALUE, in the first column).

Sampling from a Database

Quite often, we want to perform our modeling on less than the total number of records that are available. Machine learning algorithms will have varying limitations on what they can handle in terms of the numbers of records and variables, limitations that may be specific to computing power and capacity as well as software limitations. Even within those limits, many algorithms will execute faster with smaller samples.

Accurate models can often be built with as few as several hundred or thousand records. Hence, we will want to sample a subset of records for model building.

Oversampling Rare Events in Classification Tasks

If the event we are interested in classifying is rare, such as customers purchasing a product in response to a mailing, or fraudulent credit card transactions, sampling a random subset of records may yield so few events (e.g., purchases) that we have little information on them. We would end up with lots of data on nonpurchasers and nonfraudulent transactions but little on which to base a model that distinguishes purchasers from nonpurchasers or fraudulent from nonfraudulent. In such cases, we would want our sampling procedure to overweight the rare class (purchasers or frauds) relative to the majority class (nonpurchasers, nonfrauds) so that our sample would end up with a healthy complement of purchasers or frauds.

Assuring an adequate number of responder or "success" cases to train the model is just part of the picture. A more important factor is the costs of misclassification. Whenever the response rate is extremely low, we are likely to attach more importance to identifying a responder than to identifying a nonresponder. In direct-response advertising (whether by traditional mail, email, web, or mobile advertising), we may encounter only one or two responders for every hundred records—the value of finding such a customer far outweighs the costs of reaching him or her. In trying to identify fraudulent transactions, or customers unlikely to repay debt, the costs of failing to find the fraud or the nonpaying customer are likely to exceed the cost of more detailed review of a legitimate transaction or customer.

If the costs of failing to locate responders are comparable to the costs of misidentifying responders as nonresponders, our models would usually achieve highest overall accuracy if they identified everyone as a nonresponder (or almost everyone, if it is easy to identify a few responders without catching many nonresponders). In such a case, the misclassification rate is very low—equal to the rate of responders—but the model is of no value.

More generally, we want to train our model with the asymmetric costs in mind so that the algorithm will catch the more valuable responders, probably at the cost of "catching" and misclassifying more nonresponders as responders than would be the case if we assume equal costs. This subject is discussed in detail in Chapter 5.

Preprocessing and Cleaning the Data

Types of Variables   There are several ways of classifying variables. Variables can be numerical or text (character/string). They can be continuous (able to assume any real numerical value, usually in a given range), integer (taking only integer values), or categorical (assuming one of a limited number of values). Categorical variables can be either coded as numerical $(1, 2, 3)$ or text (payments current, payments not current, bankrupt). Categorical variables can also be unordered (called *nominal variables*) with categories such as North America, Europe, and Asia; or they can be ordered (called *ordinal variables*) with categories such as high value, low value, and nil value.

Continuous variables can be handled by most machine learning routines. In Analytic Solver Data Mining (ASDM), all supervised routines take continuous predictor variables, with the exception of the naive Bayes classifier, which deals exclusively with categorical predictor variables. Machine learning grew out of problems with categorical outcomes; the roots of statistics lie in the analysis of continuous variables. Sometimes, it is desirable to convert continuous variables to categorical variables. This is done most typically in the case of outcome variables, where the numerical variable is mapped to a decision (e.g., credit scores above a certain level mean "grant credit," a medical test result above a certain level means "start treatment"). ASDM has a facility for this type of conversion.

Handling Categorical Variables   Categorical variables can also be handled by most machine learning routines, but often require special handling. If the categorical variable is ordered (age group, degree of creditworthiness, etc.), we can sometimes code the categories numerically (1, 2, 3,. . .) and treat the variable as if it were a continuous variable. The smaller the number of categories, and the less they represent equal increments of value, the more problematic this approach becomes, but it often works well enough.

Nominal categorical variables, however, often cannot be used as is. In many cases, they must be decomposed into a series of binary variables called *dummy variables*. For example, a single categorical variable that can have possible values of "student," "unemployed," "employed," or "retired" would be split into four separate dummy variables:

Student: Yes/No
Unemployed: Yes/No
Employed: Yes/No
Retired: Yes/No

In some algorithms (e.g., regression models), only three of the dummy variables should be used; if the values of three are known, the fourth is also known. For example, given that these four values are the only possible ones, we can know that if a person is neither student, unemployed, nor employed, he or she must be retired. In fact, due to this redundant information, linear regression and logistic regression algorithms will fail if you use all four variables. ASDM has a utility to convert categorical variables to binary dummies. Yet, in other algorithms (e.g., trees, k-nearest neighbors), we must include all four dummy variables. This is called *one-hot encoding*.

Variable Selection   More is not necessarily better when it comes to selecting variables for a model. Other things being equal, parsimony, or compactness, is a desirable feature in a model. For one thing, the more variables we include, the greater the number of records we will need to assess relationships among the variables. Fifteen records may suffice to give us a rough idea of the relationship between Y and a single predictor variable X. If we now want information about the relationship between Y and 15 predictor variables $X_1, \ldots, X_{15}$, 15 records will not be enough (each estimated relationship would have an average of only one record's worth of information, making the estimate very unreliable). In addition, models based on many variables are often less robust, as they require the collection of more data in the future, are subject to more data quality and availability issues, and require more data cleaning and preprocessing.

How Many Variables and How Much Data?   Statisticians give us procedures to learn with some precision how many records we would need to achieve a given degree of reliability with a given dataset and a given model. These are called "power calculations" and are intended to assure that an average population effect will be estimated with sufficient precision from a sample. Predictive analytics needs are usually different because the focus is not on identifying an average effect but rather on predicting individual records. This purpose typically requires larger samples than those used for statistical inference. A good rule of thumb is to have 10 records for every predictor variable. Another, used by Delmaster and Hancock (2001, p. 68) for classification procedures, is to have at least $6 \times m \times p$ records, where m is the number of outcome classes and p is the number of variables.

In general, compactness or parsimony is a desirable feature in a machine learning model. Even when we start with a small number of variables, we often end up with many more after creating new variables (e.g., converting a categorical variable into a set of dummy variables). Data visualization and dimension reduction methods help reduce the number of variables so that redundancies are avoided.

Even when we have an ample supply of data, there are good reasons to pay close attention to the variables that are included in a model. Someone with domain knowledge (i.e., knowledge of the business process and the data) should be consulted, as knowledge of what the variables represent is typically critical for building a good model and avoiding errors and legal violations.

For example, suppose we're trying to predict the total purchase amount spent by customers, and we have a few predictor columns that are coded $X_1, X_2, X_3, \ldots$, where we don't know what those codes mean. We might find that X_1 is an excellent predictor of the total amount spent. However, if we discover that X_1 is the amount spent on shipping, calculated as a percentage of the purchase amount, then obviously a model that uses shipping amount cannot be used to predict purchase amount, since the shipping amount is not known until the transaction is completed. Another example is if we are trying to predict loan default at the time a customer applies for a loan. If our dataset includes only information on approved loan applications, we will not have information about what distinguishes defaulters from nondefaulters among denied applicants. A model based on approved loans alone can therefore not be used to predict defaulting behavior at the time of loan application but rather only once a loan is approved. Finally, in certain applications (e.g., credit scoring), variables such as gender and race are legally prohibited.

Outliers   The more data we are dealing with, the greater the chance of encountering erroneous values resulting from measurement error, data-entry error, or the like. If the erroneous value is in the same range as the rest of the data, it may be harmless. If it is well outside the range of the rest of the data (e.g., a misplaced decimal), it may have a substantial effect on some of the machine learning procedures we plan to use.

Values that lie far away from the bulk of the data are called *outliers*. The term *far away* is deliberately left vague because what is or is not called an outlier is basically an arbitrary decision. Analysts use rules of thumb such as "anything over 3 standard deviations away from the mean is an outlier," but no statistical rule can tell us whether such an outlier is the result of an error. In this statistical sense, an outlier is not necessarily an invalid data point; it is just a distant one.

The purpose of identifying outliers is usually to call attention to values that need further review. We might come up with an explanation looking at the data—in the case of a misplaced decimal, this is likely. We might have no explanation but know that the value is wrong—a temperature of 178 °F for a sick person. We might conclude that the value is within the realm of possibility and leave it alone. Or, it might be that the outliers are what we are looking for—unusual financial transactions or travel patterns. All these are judgments best made by someone with *domain knowledge*, knowledge of the particular application being considered: direct mail, mortgage finance, and so on, as opposed to technical knowledge of statistical or machine learning procedures. Statistical procedures can do little beyond identifying the record as something that needs review.

If manual review is feasible, some outliers may be identified and corrected. In any case, if the number of records with outliers is very small, they might be treated as missing data. How do we inspect for outliers? One technique in Excel is to sort the records by the first column, then review the data for very large or very small values in that column. Then repeat for each successive column. Another option is to examine the minimum and maximum values of each column using Excel's min and max functions. For a more automated approach that considers each record as a unit, clustering techniques could be used to identify clusters of one or a few records that are distant from others. Those records could then be examined.

Missing Values   Typically, some records will contain missing values. If the number of records with missing values is small, those records might be omitted. However, if we have a large number of variables, even a small proportion of missing values can affect a lot of records. Even with only 30 variables, if only 5% of the values are missing (spread randomly and independently among records and variables), almost 80% of the records would have to be omitted from the analysis. (The chance that a given record would escape having a missing value is $0.95^{30} = 0.215$.)

An alternative to omitting records with missing values is to replace the missing value with an imputed value, based on the other values for that variable across all records. For example, if among 30 variables, household income is missing for a particular record, we might substitute the mean household income across all records. Doing so does not, of course, add any information about how household income affects the outcome variable. It merely allows us to proceed with the analysis and not lose the information contained in this record for the other 29 variables. Note that using such a technique will understate the variability in a dataset. However, we can assess variability and the performance of our machine learning technique using the validation data, and therefore this need not present a major problem. ASDM offers the ability to replace missing values using fairly simple substitutes (e.g., mean, median). More sophisticated procedures do exist—for example, using linear regression, based on other variables, to fill in the missing values. These methods have been elaborated mainly for analysis of medical and scientific studies, where each patient or subject record comes at great expense. In machine learning, where data are typically plentiful, simpler methods usually suffice.

Some datasets contain variables that have a very large number of missing values. In other words, a measurement is missing for a large number of records. In that case, dropping records with missing values will lead to a large loss of data. Imputing the missing values might also be useless, as the imputations are based on a small number of existing records. An alternative is to examine the importance of the predictor. If it is not very crucial, it can be dropped. If it is important, perhaps a proxy variable with fewer missing values can be used instead. When such a predictor is deemed central, the best solution is to invest in obtaining the missing data.

Significant time may be required to deal with missing data, as not all situations are susceptible to automated solutions. In a messy dataset, for example, a "0" might mean two things: (1) the value is missing, or (2) the value is actually zero. In the credit industry, a "0" in the "past due" variable might mean a customer who is fully paid up, or a customer with no credit history at all—two very different situations. Human judgment may be required for individual cases or to determine a special rule to deal with the situation.

Normalizing (Standardizing) and Rescaling Data   Some algorithms require that the data be normalized before the algorithm can be implemented effectively. To normalize a variable, we subtract the mean from each value and then divide by the standard deviation. This operation is also sometimes called *standardizing*. In effect, we are expressing each value as the "number of standard deviations away from the mean," also called a *z-score*.

Normalizing is one way to bring all variables to the same scale. Another popular approach is rescaling each variable to a [0,1] scale. This is done by subtracting the minimum value and then dividing by the range. Subtracting the minimum shifts the variable origin to zero. Dividing by the range shrinks or expands the data to the range [0,1].

To consider why normalizing or scaling to [0,1] might be necessary, consider the case of clustering. Clustering typically involves calculating a distance measure that reflects how far each record is from a cluster center or from other records. With multiple variables, different units will be used: days, dollars, counts, and so on. If the dollars are in the thousands and everything else is in the tens, the dollar variable will come to dominate the distance measure. Moreover, changing units from, say, days to hours or months could alter the outcome completely.

Machine learning software, including ASDM, typically has an option to normalize the data in those algorithms where it may be required. It is an option rather than an automatic feature of such algorithms because there are situations where we want each variable to contribute to the distance measure in proportion to its original scale.

2.5 PREDICTIVE POWER AND OVERFITTING

In supervised learning, a key question presents itself: How well will our prediction or classification model perform when we apply it to new data? We are particularly interested in comparing the performance of different models so that we can choose the model that we think will do the best when it is implemented in practice. A key concept is to make sure that our chosen model generalizes beyond the dataset that we have at hand. To assure generalization, we use the concept of *data partitioning* and try to avoid *overfitting*. These two important concepts are described next.

Creation and Use of Data Partitions

At first glance, we might think it is best to choose the model that did the best job of classifying or predicting the outcome variable of interest with the data at hand. However, when we use the same data both to develop the model and to assess its performance, we introduce an "optimism" bias. This is because when we choose the model that works best with the data, this model's superior performance comes from two sources:

- A superior model
- Chance aspects of the data that happen to match the chosen model better than they match other models.

The latter is a particularly serious problem with techniques (e.g., trees and neural nets) that do not impose linear or other structure on the data, and thus end up overfitting it.

To address the overfitting problem, we simply divide (partition) our data and develop our model using only one of the partitions. After we have a model, we try it out on another partition and see how it performs, which we can measure in several ways. In a classification model, we can count the proportion of held-back records that were misclassified. In a prediction model, we can measure the residuals (prediction errors) between the predicted values and the actual values. This evaluation approach in effect mimics the deployment scenario, where our model is applied to data that it hasn't "seen."

We typically deal with two or three partitions: a training set, a validation set, and sometimes an additional test set. Partitioning the data into training, validation, and test sets is done either randomly according to predetermined proportions or by specifying which records go into which partition according to some relevant variable (e.g., in time series forecasting, the data are partitioned according to their chronological order). In most cases, the partitioning should be done randomly to minimize the chance of getting a biased partition. It is also possible (although cumbersome) to divide the data into more than three partitions by successive partitioning (e.g., divide the initial data into three partitions, then take one of those partitions and partition it further).

Training Partition   The training partition, typically the largest partition, contains the data used to build the various models we are examining. The same training partition is generally used to develop multiple models.

Validation Partition   The validation partition is used to assess the predictive performance of each model so that you can compare models and choose the best one. In some algorithms (e.g., classification and regression trees, k-nearest-neighbors), the validation partition may be used in an automated fashion to tune parameters and improve the model.

Test Partition   The test partition (sometimes called the *holdout* or *evaluation partition*) is used to assess the performance of the chosen model with new data.

Why have both a validation and a test partition? When we use the validation data to assess multiple models and then choose the model that performs best with the validation data, we again encounter another (lesser) facet of the overfitting problem—chance aspects of the validation data that happen to match the chosen model better than they match other models. In other words, by using the validation data to choose one of several models, the performance of the chosen model on the validation data will be overly optimistic.

The random features of the validation data that enhance the apparent performance of the chosen model will probably not be present in new data to which the model is applied. Therefore, we may have overestimated the accuracy of our model. The more models we test, the more likely it is that one of them will be particularly effective in modeling the noise in the validation data. Applying the model to the test data, which it has not seen before, will provide an unbiased estimate of how well the model will perform with new data. Figure 2.2 shows the three data partitions and their use in the machine learning process. When we are concerned mainly with finding the best model and less with exactly how well it will do, we might use only training and validation partitions.

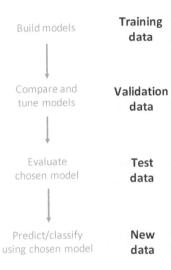

FIGURE 2.2   THREE DATA PARTITIONS AND THEIR ROLE IN THE MACHINE LEARNING PROCESS

Note that with some algorithms, such as nearest–neighbor algorithms, records in the validation and test partitions, and in new data, are compared to records in the training data to find the nearest neighbor(s). As k-nearest-neighbors is implemented in ASDM, and as discussed in this book, the use of two partitions is an essential part of the classification or prediction process, not merely a way to improve or assess it. Nonetheless, we can still interpret the error in the validation data in the same way that we would interpret error from any other model.

ASDM has a facility for partitioning a dataset randomly or according to a user-specified variable. For user-specified partitioning, create a new variable that contains the value "t" (training), "v" (validation), or "s" (test), according to the designation of that record. Partitioning is done either through the Partition menu or directly from within the menus of the supervised algorithms ("partition-on-the-fly"). For more details see www.solver.com/partition-data.

Overfitting

The more variables we include in a model, the greater the risk of overfitting the particular data used for modeling. What is overfitting?

In Table 2.1, we show hypothetical data about advertising expenditures in one time period and sales in a subsequent time period. A scatter plot of the data is shown in Figure 2.3. We could connect up these points with a smooth but complicated function, one that interpolates all these data points perfectly and leaves no error (residuals). This can be seen in Figure 2.4. However, we

TABLE 2.1	HYPOTHETICAL DATA ON ADVERTISING EXPENDITURES AND SUBSEQUENT SALES
Advertising	**Sales**
239	514
364	789
602	550
644	1386
770	1394
789	1440
911	1354

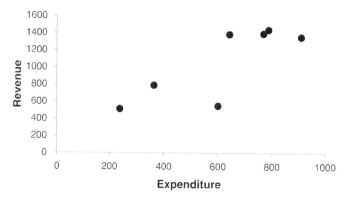

FIGURE 2.3   SCATTER PLOT FOR ADVERTISING AND SALES DATA

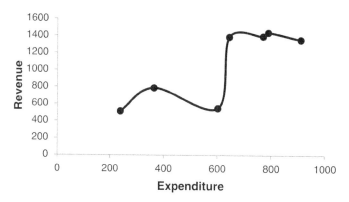

FIGURE 2.4   OVERFITTING: THIS FUNCTION FITS THE DATA WITH NO ERROR

can see that such a curve is unlikely to be accurate, or even useful, in predicting future sales on the basis of advertising expenditures. For instance, it is hard to believe that increasing expenditures from $400 to $500 will actually decrease revenue.

A basic purpose of building a model is to represent relationships among variables in such a way that this representation will do a good job of predicting future outcome values on the basis of future predictor values. Of course, we want the model to do a good job of describing the data we have, but we are more interested in its performance with future data.

In the example above, a simple straight line might do a better job than the complex function in terms of predicting future sales on the basis of advertising. Instead, we devised a complex function that fit the data perfectly, and in doing so, we overreached. We ended up modeling some variation in the data that is nothing more than chance variation. We mistreated the noise in the data as if it were a signal.

Similarly, we can add predictors to a model to sharpen its performance with the data at hand. Consider a database of 100 individuals, 50 of whom have contributed to a charitable cause. Information about income, family size, and zip code might do a fair job of predicting whether or not someone is a contributor. If we keep adding additional predictors, we can improve the performance of the model with the data at hand and reduce the misclassification error to a negligible level. However, this low error rate is misleading because it probably includes spurious effects that are specific to the 100 individuals but not beyond that sample.

For example, one of the variables might be height. We have no basis in theory to suppose that tall people might contribute more or less to charity, but if there are several tall people in our sample and they just happened to contribute heavily to charity, our model might include a term for height—the taller you are, the more you will contribute. Of course, when the model is applied to additional data, it is likely that this will not turn out to be a good predictor.

If the dataset is not much larger than the number of predictor variables, it is very likely that a spurious relationship like this will creep into the model. Continuing with our charity example, with a small sample just a few of whom are tall, whatever the contribution level of tall people may be, the algorithm is tempted to attribute it to their being tall. If the dataset is very large relative to the number of predictors, this is less likely to occur. In such a case, each predictor must help predict the outcome for a large number of cases, so the job it does is much less dependent on just a few cases that might be flukes.

Somewhat surprisingly, even if we know for a fact that a higher degree curve is the appropriate model, if the model-fitting dataset is not large enough, a lower degree function (i.e., not as likely to fit the noise) is likely to perform better. Overfitting can also result from the application of many different models, from which the best performing model is selected.

2.6 BUILDING A PREDICTIVE MODEL WITH ASDM

Let us go through the steps typical to many machine learning tasks using a familiar procedure: multiple linear regression. This will help you understand the overall process before we begin tackling new algorithms. We illustrate the procedure using ASDM.

Predicting Home Values in the West Roxbury Neighborhood

The Internet has revolutionized the real estate industry. Realtors now list houses and their prices on the web, and estimates of house and condominium prices have become widely available, even for units not on the market. In 2014, Zillow (www.zillow.com), a popular online real estate information site,[1] purchased its major rival, Trulia. By 2015 Zillow had become the dominant platform for checking house prices and, as such, the dominant online advertising venue for realtors. By 2021, another competitor, Redfin, had eclipsed Zillow in market capitalization, largely via its strategy of employing its own agents directly on a salaried basis. What used to be a comfortable 6% commission structure for independent realtors, affording them a handsome surplus (and an oversupply of realtors), was being rapidly eroded by an increasing need to pay for advertising on Zillow and by competition from Redfin. (This, in fact, was the original key to Zillow's business model—redirecting the 6% commission away from realtors and to itself.)

Zillow gets much of the data for its "Zestimates" of home values directly from publicly available city housing data, used to estimate property values for tax assessment. A competitor seeking to get into the market would likely take the same approach. So might realtors seeking to develop an alternative to Zillow.

A simple approach would be a naive, model-less method—just use the assessed values as determined by the city. Those values, however, do not necessarily include all properties, and they might not include changes warranted by remodeling, additions, and the like. Moreover, the assessment methods used by cities may not be transparent or always reflect true market values. However, the city property data can be used as a starting point to build a model, to which additional data (e.g., that collected by large realtors) can be added later.

Let's look at how Boston property assessment data, available from the city of Boston, might be used to predict home values. The data in *West Roxbury.xlsx*

---

[1]"Zestimates may not be as right as you'd like" *Washington Post* February 7, 2015, p. T10, by K. Harney.

includes information on single family owner-occupied homes in West Roxbury, a neighborhood in southwest Boston, in 2014. The data include values for various predictor variables and for an outcome—assessed home value ("total value"). This dataset has 14 variables and includes 5802 homes. A sample of the data[2] is shown in Table 2.2, and the "data dictionary" describing each variable[3] is in Table 2.3.

TABLE 2.2   FIRST 10 RECORDS IN THE WEST ROXBURY HOME VALUES DATASET

TOTAL VALUE	TAX	LOT SQ FT	YR BUILT	GROSS AREA	LIVING AREA	FLOORS	ROOMS	BED ROOMS	FULL BATH	HALF BATH	KIT CHEN	FIRE PLACE	REMODEL
344.2	4330	9965	1880	2436	1352	2	6	3	1	1	1	0	None
412.6	5190	6590	1945	3108	1976	2	10	4	2	1	1	0	Recent
330.1	4152	7500	1890	2294	1371	2	8	4	1	1	1	0	None
498.6	6272	13773	1957	5032	2608	1	9	5	1	1	1	1	None
331.5	4170	5000	1910	2370	1438	2	7	3	2	0	1	0	None
337.4	4244	5142	1950	2124	1060	1	6	3	1	0	1	1	Old
359.4	4521	5000	1954	3220	1916	2	7	3	1	1	1	0	None
320.4	4030	10000	1950	2208	1200	1	6	3	1	0	1	0	None
333.5	4195	6835	1958	2582	1092	1	5	3	1	0	1	1	Recent
409.4	5150	5093	1900	4818	2992	2	8	4	2	0	1	0	None

TABLE 2.3   DESCRIPTION OF VARIABLES IN WEST ROXBURY (BOSTON) HOME VALUE DATASET

TOTAL VALUE	Total assessed value for property, in thousands of USD
TAX	Tax bill amount based on total assessed value multiplied by the tax rate, in USD
LOT SQ FT	Total lot size of parcel in square feet
YR BUILT	Year property was built
GROSS AREA	Gross floor area
LIVING AREA	Total living area for residential properties (ft[2])
FLOORS	Number of floors
ROOMS	Total number of rooms
BEDROOMS	Total number of bedrooms
FULL BATH	Total number of full baths
HALF BATH	Total number of half baths
KITCHEN	Total number of kitchens
FIREPLACE	Total number of fireplaces
REMODEL	When house was remodeled (Recent/Old/None)

[2]The data are a slightly cleaned version of the Property Assessment FY2014 data at https://data.boston.gov/dataset/property-assessment (accessed December 2017).
[3]The full data dictionary provided by the City of Boston is available at https://data.boston.gov/dataset/property-assessment; we have modified a few variable names.

As we saw earlier, below the header row, each row in the data represents a home. For example, the first home was assessed at a total value of $344.2 thousand (TOTAL VALUE). Its tax bill was $4330. It has a lot size of 9965 square feet (ft^2), was built in year 1880, has two floors, six rooms, and so on.

Modeling Process

We now describe in detail the various model stages using the West Roxbury home values example.

1. *Determine the purpose*: Let's assume that the purpose of our machine learning project is to predict the value of homes in West Roxbury.

2. *Obtain the data*: We will use the 2014 West Roxbury housing data. The dataset in question is small enough that we do not need to sample from it—we can use it in its entirety.

3. *Explore, clean, and preprocess the data*: Let's look first at the description of the variables, also known as the "data dictionary," to be sure that we understand them all. These descriptions are available on the "description" worksheet in the Excel file and in Table 2.3. The variable names and descriptions in this dataset all seem fairly straightforward, but this is not always the case. Often variable names are cryptic and their descriptions are unclear or missing.

It is useful to pause and think about what the variables mean and whether they should be included in the model. Consider the variable TAX. At first glance, we consider that the tax on a home is usually a function of its assessed value, so there is some circularity in the model—we want to predict a home's value using TAX as a predictor, yet TAX itself is determined by a home's value. TAX might be a very good predictor of home value in a numerical sense, but would it be useful if we wanted to apply our model to homes whose assessed value might not be known? For this reason, we will exclude TAX from the analysis.

It is also useful to check for outliers that might be errors. For example, suppose that the column FLOORS (number of floors) looked like the one in Table 2.4, after sorting the data in descending order based on floors. We can tell right away that the 15 is in error—it is unlikely that a home has 15 floors. All other values are between 1 and 2. Probably, the decimal was misplaced and the value should be 1.5.

Last, we create dummy variables for categorical variables. Here, we have one categorical variable: REMODEL, which has three categories.

4. *Reduce the data dimension*: Our dataset has been prepared for presentation with fairly low dimension—it has only 14 variables, and the single categorical variable considered has only three categories (and hence adds two

TABLE 2.4   OUTLIER IN WEST ROXBURY DATA

Floors	Rooms
15	8
2	10
1.5	6
1	6

or three dummy variables). If we had many more variables, at this stage we might want to apply a variable reduction technique such as condensing multiple categories into a smaller number, or applying principal component analysis to consolidate multiple similar numerical variables (e.g., LIVING AREA, ROOMS, BEDROOMS, BATH, HALF BATH) into a smaller number of variables.

5. *Determine the machine learning task*: The specific task is to predict the value of TOTAL VALUE using the predictor variables. This is a supervised prediction task. For simplicity, we excluded several additional variables present in the original dataset, which have many categories (BLDG TYPE, ROOF TYPE, and EXT FIN). We therefore use all the numerical variables (except TAX) and the dummies created for the remaining categorical variables.

6. *Partition the data (for supervised tasks)*: In ASDM, select *Partition* from the *Data Mining* menu, and the dialog box shown in Figure 2.5 appears. Here we specify the data range to be partitioned and the variables to be included in the partitioned dataset. The partitioning can be handled in one of two ways:

   a. Using a partition variable: the dataset can have a partition variable that governs the division into training and validation partitions ("t" = training, "v" = validation).

   b. The partitioning can be done randomly. If the partitioning is done randomly, we have the option of specifying a seed for randomization (which has the advantage of letting us duplicate the same random partition later, should we need to). In this example, a seed of 12345 is used.

In this case, we divide the data into two partitions: training and validation. The training partition is used to build the model, and the validation partition is used to see how well the model does when applied to new data. We need to specify the percent of the data used in each partition. *Note*: Although not used in our example, a test partition might also be used.

FIGURE 2.5   PARTITIONING THE DATA. ASDM'S DEFAULT PARTITIONS THE DATA INTO 60% TRAINING DATA, 40% VALIDATION DATA, AND 0% TEST DATA. HERE A PARTITION OF 50% TRAINING AND 50% VALIDATION IS USED

7. *Choose the technique.* In this case, it is multiple linear regression. Having divided the data into training and validation partitions, we can use ASDM to build a multiple linear regression model with the training data. We want to predict the value of a house in West Roxbury on the basis of all the other predictors (except TAX).

8. *Use the algorithm to perform the task.* In ASDM, we select *Linear Regression* from the *Predict* menu. This includes three dialog boxes. The first dialog box ("Data" tab), shown in Figure 2.6, is where the predictor and output variables are specified. The variable TOTAL VALUE is selected as the Output Variable. All the other variables, except TAX and one of the REMODEL dummy variables, are selected as predictor variables (Selected Variables). The second dialog box ("Parameters" tab) provides further options that we describe in Chapter 6. For now, we use the default parameter setting. The third dialog box ("Scoring" tab), shown in Figure 2.7,

FIGURE 2.6   USING ASDM FOR MULTIPLE LINEAR REGRESSION: DATA TAB

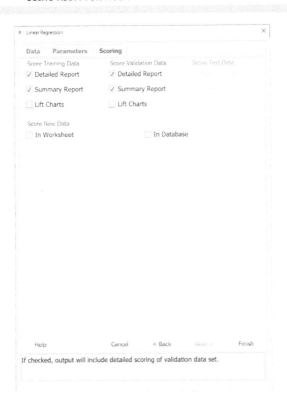

FIGURE 2.7   SPECIFYING THE OUTPUT: SCORING TAB

is where we can select what output to generate. We ask ASDM to show us the fitted values on the training data as well as the predicted values (scores) on the validation data. ASDM produces a standard regression output, but for now we defer that as well as the more advanced options displayed above (see Chapter 6 or the user documentation for ASDM for more information.) Rather, we review the predictions themselves. Figure 2.8 shows the predicted values for the first few records in the training data along with the actual values and the residuals (prediction errors). Note that the predicted values would often be called the *fitted values*, since they are for the records to which the model was fit. The results for the validation data are shown in Figure 2.9. The prediction errors for the training and validation data are compared in Figure 2.10.

Training: Prediction Details

Record ID	TOTAL VALUE	Prediction : TOTAL VALUE	Residual	TAX	LOT SQFT	YR BUILT	GROSS AREA	LIVING AREA	FLOORS	ROOMS	BEDROO MS	FULL BATH	HALF BATH	KITCHEN	FIREPLACE	REMODEL _None	REMODEL _Old
Record 1	344.2	378.2729	-34.073	4330	9965	1880	2436	1352	2	6	3	1	1	1	0	1	0
Record 5	331.5	342.9992	-11.499	4170	5000	1910	2370	1438	2	7	3	2	0	1	0	1	0
Record 8	320.4	316.3789	4.02106	4030	10000	1950	2208	1200	1	6	3	1	0	1	0	1	0
Record 11	313	362.3197	-49.32	3937	5000	1960	2624	1485	1.5	6	3	2	0	1	1	1	0
Record 12	344.5	384.3895	-39.89	4333	6768	1958	2844	1460	1.5	6	3	2	0	1	1	1	0
Record 15	326.2	347.9685	-21.769	4103	5000	1954	2536	1272	1.5	6	3	1	1	1	1	1	0
Record 16	298.2	272.2333	25.9667	3751	5000	1940	2129	864	1	7	3	2	0	1	0	1	0
Record 18	344.9	361.2712	-16.371	4338	10000	1950	2099	1445	1	7	3	1	1	1	1	1	0
Record 20	348	378.3477	-30.348	4377	9001	1875	2840	1632	2	7	3	1	0	1	0	1	0
Record 21	317.5	276.3738	41.1262	3994	4450	1920	1400	1232	2	7	3	1	0	1	0	1	0

FIGURE 2.8   PREDICTIONS FOR A SAMPLE OF TRAINING DATA

Validation: Prediction Details

Record ID	TOTAL VALUE	Prediction : TOTAL VALUE	Residual	TAX	LOT SQFT	YR BUILT	GROSS AREA	LIVING AREA	FLOORS	ROOMS	BEDROO MS	FULL BATH	HALF BATH	KITCHEN	FIREPLACE	REMODEL _None	REMODEL _Old
Record 4950	390.3	385.435	4.86498	5311	8350	1954	2666	1841	1	5	3	1	0	1	0	1	0
Record 5624	409.5	395.9625	13.5375	4909	5500	1930	2986	1710	2	7	3	1	1	1	0	1	0
Record 4159	321	319.6694	1.3306	5151	8114	1958	2705	1479	1	6	3	1	1	1	1	0	0
Record 4002	365.4	411.0741	-45.674	4038	4794	1954	2361	1261	1.5	6	2	1	1	1	0	1	0
Record 2523	593.5	634.523	-41.023	4596	5107	1960	2642	1634	2	7	3	1	1	1	2	1	0
Record 3439	384.4	441.9512	-57.551	7466	8580	1905	6075	3382	2	10	5	2	1	1	1	1	0
Record 1265	355	391.4235	-36.424	4835	7950	1954	4012	1975	1.5	9	4	1	1	1	0	0	1
Record 5599	345.4	319.2621	26.1379	4465	9331	1950	2522	1428	1.5	6	2	1	1	1	1	1	0
Record 5141	476.3	433.9011	42.3989	4345	6000	1954	2302	1103	1	5	2	1	1	1	1	1	0
Record 3255	302.7	310.1917	-7.4917	5991	5500	1925	2936	1836	2	8	4	1	1	1	1	0	0

FIGURE 2.9   PREDICTIONS FOR A SAMPLE OF VALIDATION DATA

Prediction error can be measured in several ways. Four measures produced by ASDM are shown in Figure 2.10: The *SSE (sum of squared errors)* adds up the squared errors, so whether an error is positive or negative, it contributes just the same. However, this sum does not yield information about the size of the typical error.

Training: Prediction Summary

Metric	Value
SSE	4854024.9804
MSE	1673.2247
RMSE	40.9051
MAD	31.2171
R2	0.8248

Validation: Prediction Summary

Metric	Value
SSE	5927610.0549
MSE	2043.2989
RMSE	45.2029
MAD	33.6150
R2	0.7979

FIGURE 2.10   ERROR RATES FOR TRAINING DATA (LEFT) AND VALIDATION DATA (RIGHT). ERROR FIGURES ARE IN THOUSANDS OF $

The *MSE (mean squared error)* is the average of the squared errors. MSE is always non-negative and is used mainly for comparing models.

The *RMSE (root-mean-squared error)* is perhaps the most useful term of all. It takes the square root of the MSE, so it gives an idea of the typical error (whether positive or negative) in the same scale as that used for the original outcome variable. As we might expect, the RMSE for the validation data (45.2 thousand dollars), which the model is seeing for the first time in making these predictions, is larger than for the training data (40.9 thousand dollars), which were used in training the model.

The *MAD (mean absolute deviation)* is the average of the absolute values of the errors. Similar to RMSE, lower values of MAD are better.

R2 (R^2 or R-squared value) measures the strength-of-fit in a regression model, based on the training data. It is not typically useful for evaluating predictive performance.

9. *Interpret the results.* At this stage, we would typically try other prediction algorithms (e.g., regression trees) and see how they do error-wise. We might also try different "settings" on the various models (e.g., we could use the *best subsets* option in multiple linear regression to choose a reduced set of variables that might perform better with the validation data). After choosing the best model—typically, the model with the lowest error on the validation data while also recognizing that "simpler is better"—we use that model to predict the output variable in fresh test data. These steps are covered in more detail in the analysis of cases.

10. *Deploy the model.* After the best model is chosen, it is applied to new data to predict TOTAL VALUE for homes where this value is unknown. This was, of course, the original purpose. Predicting the output value for new records is called *scoring*. For predictive tasks, scoring produces predicted numerical values. For classification tasks, scoring produces classes and/or propensities. In ASDM, we can score new records using one of the models we developed. To do that, we must first create a worksheet or file with the records to be predicted. For these records, we must include all the

predictor values. Figure 2.11 shows an example of a worksheet with three homes to be scored using our linear regression model. Note that all the required predictor columns are present, and the output column is absent.

	A	B	C	D	E	F	G	H	I	J	K	L	M	N	O
		LOT	YR	GROSS	LIVING			BEDR	FULL	HALF	KITC	FIREP	REMODEL	REMODEL	REMODEL
1	TAX	SQFT	BUILT	AREA	AREA	FLOORS	ROOMS	OOMS	BATH	BATH	HEN	LACE	_None	_Old	_Recent
2	3850	6877	1963	2240	1808	1	6	3	1	1	1	0	1	0	0
3	5386	5965	1963	2998	1637	1.5	8	3	3	0	1	1	0	1	0
4	4608	5662	1961	2805	1750	2	7	4	2	0	1	1	0	0	1

FIGURE 2.11   WORKSHEET WITH THREE RECORDS TO BE SCORED

Figure 2.12 shows the Score dialog box. We chose "match by name" to match the predictor columns in our model with the new records' worksheet. The result is shown in Figure 2.13, where the predictions are in the second column.

FIGURE 2.12   SCORE DIALOG BOX. NEW RECORDS COLUMN NAMES ARE MATCHED WITH PREDICTOR COLUMN NAMES IN MODEL

Note: In ASDM, scoring new data can also be done directly from a specific prediction or classification[4] method dialog box ("Scoring," typically in the last step). In our example, scoring can be done in step 3 in the multiple linear regression dialog box, as shown in Figure 2.7.

---

[4]*Note*: In some versions of ASDM, propensities for new records are produced only if "Scoring" is selected in the classification method dialog. They are not available in the option to score stored models.

Scoring

Record ID	Prediction: TOTAL VALUE	TAX	LOT SQFT	YR BUILT	GROSS AREA	LIVING AREA	FLOORS	ROOMS	BEDROOMS	FULL BATH	HALF BATH	KITCHEN	FIREPLACE	REMODEL None	REMODEL Old
Record 1	337.77376	3850	6877	1963	2240	1808	1	6	3	1	1	1	0	1	0
Record 2	412.7901	5386	5965	1963	2998	1637	1.5	8	3	3	0	1	1	0	1
Record 3	433.85814	4608	5662	1961	2805	1750	2	7	4	2	0	1	1	0	0

FIGURE 2.13   THREE RECORDS SCORED USING LINEAR REGRESSION MODEL

Machine Learning Workflow

The entire set of operations that we performed on the West Roxbury dataset, using ASDM, can be combined into a *workflow*, making it easy to visually view the process as well as to re-run it.

The workflow is shown in Figure 2.14. We can see the operations from opening the file, to creating dummy variables, then partitioning the dataset, running a linear regression model, and finally, scoring new data. See the box below on how to create and run workflows in ASDM.

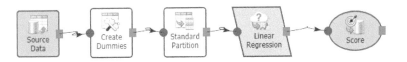

FIGURE 2.14   WORKFLOW FOR WEST ROXBURY ANALYSIS

CREATING AND USING WORKFLOWS IN ASDM

A complete analysis, such as the one illustrated in this section, comprises many operations. Repeating the analysis requires re-running each operation in order to regenerate the model output and to use the trained model to "score" new data. This can be time consuming. ASDM (since version V2018) includes a capability called *Workflow*. The workflow combines a set of operations into a pipeline, which is represented by a diagram. Creating a workflow can be done in one of two ways:

1. Using the Workflow tab in the Task Pane (see Figure 2.15), "drag and drop" icons onto a "canvas" to create a workflow diagram.

2. Turn on a workflow recorder, carry out the modeling steps by choosing menu options and dialog selections, and the workflow diagram will be created automatically. Specifically, first click on the red circle *Start recording* button, then perform all the needed analysis steps using the Data Mining menu, and finally click the *Stop Recording* button (two red bars). This will result in an all-inclusive machine learning workflow (as shown in Figure 2.16) for the model we fitted in this chapter.

Once the diagram or pipeline is created, you can "run" it by clicking on the *Execute Workflow* (green triangle) button. This will cause the operations in the workflow to be executed one after the other.

To switch between a vertical and horizontal workflow diagram, click the blue arrow icons (called Dock). Dock to the top creates a horizontal diagram (see Figure 2.14).

Workflows can be used to re-run an analysis and reproduce its results. They can also be used to communicate your work with others. The workflows for the chapter examples are included in the Excel files posted on www.dataminingbook.com.

FIGURE 2.15   WORKFLOW TAB IN THE TASK PANE (IN DATA MINING MENU)

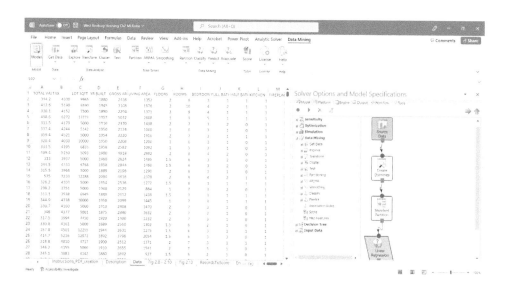

FIGURE 2.16   ALL-INCLUSIVE WORKFLOW FOR THE MULTIPLE LINEAR REGRESSION MODEL ON THE WEST ROXBURY DATA (VERTICAL DIAGRAM)

2.7 Using Excel for Machine Learning

An important aspect of this modeling process is that the heavy-duty analysis does not necessarily require a huge number of records. The dataset to be analyzed might have millions of records, or be part of a regular ongoing flow, but in applying multiple linear regression or applying a classification tree, the use of a sample of 20,000 is likely to yield as accurate an answer as that obtained when using the entire dataset. The principle involved is the same as the principle behind polling: If sampled judiciously, 2000 voters can give an estimate of the entire population's opinion within one or two percentage points. (See "How Many Variables and How Much Data" in Section 2.4 for further discussion.)

Therefore, in most cases, the number of records required in each partition (training, validation, and test) can be accommodated within the rows allowed by Excel. Of course, we need to get those records into Excel, and for this purpose the standard version of ASDM provides an interface for random sampling of records from an external database.

Similarly, we may need to apply the results of our analysis to a large database, and for this purpose the standard version of ASDM has a facility for storing models and scoring them to an external database. For example, ASDM would write an additional column (variable) to the database consisting of the predicted purchase amount for each record.

ASDM has a facility for drawing a sample from an external database. The sample can be drawn at random or it can be stratified. It also has a facility to score data in the external database using the model that was obtained from the training data.

2.8 Automating Machine Learning Solutions[5]

Automating machine learning solutions is often termed "machine learning operations" ("MLOps"), or "AI engineering." In most supervised machine learning applications, the goal is not a static, one-time analysis of a particular dataset. Rather, we want to develop a model that can be used on an ongoing basis to predict or classify new records. Our initial analysis will be in prototype mode, while we explore and define the problem and test different models. We will follow all the steps outlined earlier in this chapter.

---

[5] This section copyright 2021 Peter Bruce, Galit Shmueli, and Victor Diloreto; used by permission.

At the end of that process, we will typically want our chosen model to be deployed in automated fashion. For example, the US Internal Revenue Service (IRS) receives several hundred million tax returns per year—it does not want to have to pull each tax return out into an Excel sheet or other environment separate from its main database to determine the predicted probability that the return is fraudulent. Rather, it would prefer that determination be made as part of the normal tax filing environment and process. Music streaming services, such as Pandora or Spotify, need to determine "recommendations" for next songs quickly for each of millions of users; there is no time to extract the data for manual analysis.

In practice, this is done by building the chosen algorithm into the computational setting in which the rest of the process lies. A tax return is entered directly into the IRS system by a tax preparer, a predictive algorithm is immediately applied to the new data in the IRS system, and a predicted classification is decided by the algorithm. Business rules would then determine what happens with that classification. In the IRS case, the rule might be "if no predicted fraud, continue routine processing; if fraud is predicted, alert an examiner for possible audit."

This flow of the tax return from data entry, into the IRS system, through a predictive algorithm, then back out to a human user is an example of a "data pipeline." The different components of the system communicate with one another via application programming interfaces (APIs) that establish locally valid rules for transmitting data and associated communications. An API for a machine learning algorithm would establish the required elements for a predictive algorithm to work—the exact predictor variables, their order, data formats, and so on. It would also establish the requirements for communicating the results of the algorithm. Algorithms to be used in an automated data pipeline will need to be compliant with the rules of the APIs where they operate.

Finally, once the computational environment is set and functioning, the machine learning work is not done. The environment in which a model operates is typically dynamic, and predictive models often have a short shelf life—one leading consultant finds they rarely continue to function effectively for more than a year. So, even in a fully deployed state, models must be periodically checked and re-evaluated. Once performance flags, it is time to return to prototype mode and see if a new model can be developed.

As you can imagine, these computational environments are complex, and, as of 2022, large companies are only beginning to construct them. They are often driven to do so by the force of circumstance. In the following, we describe two examples of such environments.

Predicting Power Generator Failure[6]

Sira-Kvina, a major hydro-electric power company that supplies 7% of Norway's power, found that generator failures were taking a long time to diagnose, leading to lengthy off-line periods and loss of revenue and customer dissatisfaction. The company was using an engineering checklist approach: imagine a more complex version of the troubleshooting guide that comes with a fancy appliance, or the advice you encounter when trying to fix a software problem. Such an approach, however, could not begin to make use of all the data that comes in from hundreds of sensors producing tens of thousands of readings per day. A team from Elder Research investigated one particularly lengthy and costly outage and, after much data wrangling, visualization, and analysis, identified a set of separate events which, when they happened together, caused the failure. Moreover, generator failures were often preceded by a set of defined temperature spikes in one specific sensor (you can read a summary of the analysis at www.statistics.com/sira-kvina-hydro-power-the-case-of-the-faulty-generator). But an after-the-fact detective hunt is inherently unsatisfactory, since the generator down-time has already occurred. What is really needed is *proactive preventive maintenance*, triggered by advance warnings that are predictive of failure. Elder built such a system for Sira Kvina. Machine learning models that predict generator failure are the key analytical component, but they are embedded in a system that must also handle, in addition to training and fitting a model, the following tasks:

- collecting and ingesting data from sensors
- transforming data (especially aggregating and disaggregating granular time series data)
- passing alerts from models to humans and other elements of the system
- providing visualization tools for analysts
- applying case management of anomalies
- adding manual labels applied by analysts, to facilitate further training.

Dozens of tools are involved in this structure. Figure 2.17 illustrates how different layers of tools contribute to this process.

The "Infrastructure" base layer provides base computing capability, memory, and networking, either on-premises or in the cloud. The next layer up supports basic services for the layers above it. "Security" provides user admin capabilities, permission levels, and networking and access rules. "Monitoring"

---

[6]Thanks to Victor Diloreto, Chief Technical Officer of Elder Research, Inc., who wrote portions of this segment.

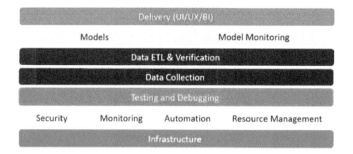

FIGURE 2.17   LAYERS OF TOOLS SUPPORTING MACHINE LEARNING AUTOMATION

ingests logs, implements needed thresholds, and issues alerts. "Automation" has a more limited meaning than the overall topic of this section: it refers to bringing up, configuring, and tearing down tools and infrastructure as needed. "Resource management" provides the oversight of the various resources used throughout the stack. This area is closely coupled to monitoring: understanding what resources could be coming close to exhaustion is important for maintenance purposes.

"Testing/debugging" is self-explanatory, while the "data collection" layer refers primarily to the data store (data warehouse, data lake, or data lake house). In the Sira-Kvina case, there is a raw immutable data store (IDS) where all source data is collected, plus an analytic base table (ABT) that holds derivatives of the main data store needed for analysis. The "data ETL" (Extract, Transform, Load) layer provides the tools to create these derivatives. The verification step within this layer checks that the transformations, aggregations, or any formula used to take a raw piece of data and convert it to something else is doing the job we think it's supposed to do. This verification function is wired into the monitoring capability of the system, which flags any issue with an alert to maintainers of the system. The modeling layer contains the model(s) that make predictions (i.e., the primary focus of this book), and is accompanied by the model-monitoring section, which checks that the model is performing to expectations. Tools in the latter are tied into the lower-level infrastructure monitoring to generate alerts when a model is missing on expectations. Finally, the "delivery" layer is the user window into the system, and can represent simple things like a spreadsheet or a text file, or be as elaborate as an enterprise-wide tool like Tableau or Power BI.

From the above, you can see that Sira-Kvina's predictive models occupy only a small part of the data pipeline through which sensor data could flow and, when needed, trigger alerts to operators about system components that need attention. For a more far-reaching structure, consider Uber.

Uber's Michelangelo

Uber, which provides ride-sharing, meal delivery services, and more, uses real-time predictive models for several purposes including:

- matching the optimal driver for a customer ride request
- predicting customer pickup time
- predicting ride duration
- estimating pricing (including which peak pricing tier applies)
- predicting Uber Eats delivery time.

To integrate model-building with deployment, Uber built its own machine learning (ML) structure (MLOps) called Michelangelo. Prior to Michelangelo, in Uber's words, "the impact of ML at Uber was limited to what a few data scientists and engineers could build in a short time frame with mostly open source tools. Specifically, there were no systems in place to build reliable, uniform, and reproducible pipelines for creating and managing training and prediction data at scale."

Uber is a company essentially built on data science; at more traditional companies, the model deployment challenge is exacerbated by the fact that data science and data engineering are often considered separate jobs and disciplines. One major retailer described the problem as follows: "Our highly trained data scientists would build great models, give them to the engineers, who would say 'thank you very much, now we will need to build it again from scratch.'"

Uber's Michelangelo is a development and deployment environment that Uber's data scientists use for a variety of models. It provides integration with the company's data stores and standard tools to build pipelines to ingest data. It has tools to split data into training and validation partitions, and to ensure that new data to be predicted follows the same format.

Some of Uber's goals (e.g., predicting the restaurant prep time component of Uber Eats delivery time) are not extremely time-sensitive, and batch processing can be used. Others (e.g., finding a driver) require nearly instantaneous action ("low-latency" response). Michelangelo supports both batch processing and real-time low-latency processing (Uber calls it "online"). Uber is constantly adding huge amounts of granular customer and driver data to its data store, so Michelangelo must have sufficient compute, data storage, and data flow capacity to scale efficiently. It also provides a facility to standardize feature definition and storage, so that data can be shared easily across users. It provides visualization and exploration tools for the prototyping and prep phases. Finally, it collects and makes available (via APIs and via a web user interface) standard information about each model[7]:

- Who trained the model

- Start and end times of the training job

- Full model configuration (features used, hyper-parameter values, etc.)

- Reference to training and test datasets

- Distribution and relative importance of each feature

- Model accuracy metrics

- Standard charts and graphs for each model type (e.g., ROC curve, PR curve, and confusion matrix for a binary classifier)

- Full learned parameters of the model

- Summary statistics for model visualization.

Finally, to ensure that model performance does not degrade over time, Michelangelo has facilities for periodically storing a sample of predictions, comparing predictions to outcomes, and sending signals to operators when the margin exceeds a certain standard.

A variety of tools, both proprietary and open source, can be used to build the MLOps pipeline. In the Sira-Kvina case, the infrastructure layer was built in the cloud using Amazon Web Services Cloud Development Kit (AWS CDK). AWS's Simple Notification Service (SNS) was used to transmit verification and monitoring messages between layers. Uber built Michelangelo with open source tools such as the Cassandra distributed database system and Kafka brokers to stream verification and monitoring messages.

In this book, our focus will be on the prototyping phase—all the steps that go into properly defining the model and developing and selecting a model. You should be aware, though, that most of the actual work of implementing a machine learning solution lies in the automated deployment phase. Much of this work is not in the analytic domain; rather, it lies in the domains of databases and computer engineering, to assure that detailed nuts and bolts of an automated dataflow all work properly. Nonetheless, some familiarity with the requirements and components of automated pipelines will benefit the data scientist, as it will facilitate communication with the engineers who must ultimately deploy their work.

---

[7]This list is from the Uber Engineering blog at https://eng.uber.com/michelangelo-machine-learning-platform; see also the discussion of "Model Cards" in Chapter 22.

2.9 ETHICAL PRACTICE IN MACHINE LEARNING

Prior to the advent of internet-connected devices, the biggest source of big data was public interaction on the internet. Social media users, as well as shoppers and searchers on the internet, have made an implicit deal with the big companies that provide these services: users can take advantage of powerful search, shopping and social interaction tools for free, and, in return, the companies get access to user data. Since the first edition of this book was published in 2007, ethical issues in machine learning and data science have received increasing attention, and new rules and laws have emerged. As a business analytics professional or data scientist, you must be aware of the rules and follow them, but you must also think about the implications and use of your work once it goes beyond the prototyping phase. It is now common for businesses, governments, and other organizations to require the explicit incorporation of ethical principles and audits into machine learning and AI applications. Chapter 22, Responsible Data Science, covers this topic in more detail.

**MACHINE LEARNING SOFTWARE TOOLS:
THE STATE OF THE MARKET**

by Herb Edelstein

Over time, three things are steadily increasing: the amount of data available for analysis, the power of the computing environment, and the number of organizations taking advantage of the first two changes for a widening variety of analytical and predictive goals. Software products for machine learning must deliver more comprehensive coverage than ever before. The term "data science" has become ubiquitous and covers the spectrum of tasks required for business analytics, starting with data engineering (including data gathering, building databases, and making the data suitable for analytics) and machine learning. Machine learning starts with describing and understanding the data, often utilizing advanced visualization techniques followed by sophisticated model building. After the models are constructed, they must be efficiently deployed so an organization can meet its goals. At the same time, the amount of data collected today presents a great opportunity to tease out subtle relationships that allow precise predictions while unfortunately making it easy to find spurious relationships or statistically significant results that have no practical value. The range of users that must be supported has also increased. Software must support people with diverse backgrounds, ranging from extensive education in machine learning, statistics, and programming to professionals performing such tasks as sales and marketing, risk analysis, fraud detection, reliability prediction, and engineering and scientific analysis. One of the biggest contributors to the hardware environment for machine learning is the spread of high powered GPUs (Graphic Processing Units). While originally intended for accelerating 3-D graphics, meeting the computational requirements for fast

3-D graphics also significantly accelerates machine learning. The algorithms used by the major cloud vendors all take advantage of GPUs. However, not all GPUs have the same interface and therefore not all stand-alone software will necessarily take advantage of the GPUs on your computer. Machine learning has also improved model building. As you read this book, you will see that the various algorithms have a plethora of tuning options to help you build the best model. While many experienced model builders can do a good job of manual tuning, it is impossible to try all the combinations of parameters that control the learning process (called hyperparameters) by hand, so an increasing number of products offer the ability to automatically tune the hyperparameters. The more hyperparameters, the larger the number of combinations to be searched. Autotuning can be particularly useful in building the neural networks used for deep learning.

R and Python

One of the most common open source statistical analysis and machine learning software languages is R. R is the successor to a Bell Labs program called S, which was commercialized as S+. Widely used in the academic community, R has become one of the most popular machine learning tools. New algorithms are frequently available first in R. R contains an enormous collection of machine learning algorithms contained in what are known as "packages," along with an abundance of statistical algorithms, data management tools, and visualization tools. Over 10,000 packages are in the CRAN (Comprehensive R Archive Network) library, and there are numerous packages outside of CRAN. This large number provides a great deal of choice. There are multiple packages that will perform essentially the same task, allowing the user to choose the one they think is most appropriate. However, there is a downside to all these options in that there is no uniformity in the R community. For example, in addition to the base R graphing tools, there are the packages Lattice, ggplot2, Plotly, and others. Because it is essentially a special purpose programming language, R has enormous flexibility but a steeper learning curve than many of the Graphical User Interface (GUI)-based tools. The most common tool used with R is RStudio, an interactive development environment that facilitates the use of R. RStudio has also created a collection of packages called the "tidyverse" which are designed to enhance the ability of R to manipulate and graph data. These have become widely used in the R community. In particular, R has excelled in creating publication quality visualizations using the ggplot2 package (part of the tidyverse) which is based on Leland Wilkinson's groundbreaking book *The Grammar of Graphics*. Some GUIs for R try to improve its usability. R Commander is the oldest of these and like R is extensible with add-on packages. Its creator views it as a gateway to writing R code for more complex analyses. BlueSky is a more recent interface that not only is more comprehensive than R Commander but allows the user to create their own dialogs to add R functionality.

Python is a widely used general programming language (developed in the 1980s by Guido van Rossum and named after the British comedy group Monty Python) that has overtaken R as the most popular machine learning package. This is due in part to its speed advantage over R, its data-wrangling capabilities, and its better functionality as a programming language. Furthermore, there is an interface to R that allows you to access R functionality should you need to. Pandas is an open-source Python library that provides extensive data-wrangling capabilities. Scikit-Learn is another open-source Python library that provides a very comprehensive suite of tools for machine learning that is widely used in the Python community. Python is more often used for deep neural networks than R. While R is still dominating in academia, Python appears to be dominating in commercial applications.

Stand-Alone Machine Learning Software

Many stand-alone software packages have appeared that are intended to simplify the process of creating machine learning models. The number of machine learning packages has grown considerably in response to the increasing demand. IBM offers two machine learning platforms: Watson and SPSS Modeler. Watson is cloud based and offers the same ability to utilize GPUs as the other major cloud providers. SPSS Modeler is aimed at local implementation. However, Watson Studio includes Modeler which can run under Studio. In addition to running on IBM's cloud servers, Watson is also available to run on local computers. SAS is the largest company specializing in statistical software. Recognizing the growing importance of machine learning, SAS added Enterprise Miner, a workflow drag-and-drop software, in 1999 to address this need. More recently, SAS created Viya Machine Learning. SAS Enterprise Miner has multiple client interfaces, whereas Viya's interface is a unified HTML5 interface. While both Enterprise Miner and Viya can operate in the cloud, Viya has a wider range of interfaces to the major cloud providers. It is aimed more directly at the data science and machine learning communities. SAS's JMP Pro has a comprehensive set of machine learning tools. It is widely used in the science and engineering world, but also competes in commercial and government settings. It has a unique GUI that is centered on what you are trying to accomplish. For example, to analyze data you go to the Analyze menu, choose Predictive Modeling, and then select a modeling method (which JMP calls a platform). JMP has its own scripting language, JSL, for tasks that are more complicated than can be accomplished through the GUI, but it also interfaces with R and Python.

Analytic Solver Data Mining (ASDM) is an add-in for Microsoft Excel that provides access to a suite of machine learning tools as well as data engineering capabilities without the need for programming. It is widely used in MBA programs because of its accessibility to students, but it is also used in industry, especially with its cloud interface to Microsoft's Azure. The original version (XLMiner) was developed by one of the authors of this book (Patel). It provides not only traditional machine learning tools such as tree-based learning and neural nets, but also a variety of ensemble methods which have become central to accurate prediction. Additionally, ASDM provides text mining capabilities.

Drag-and-Drop Workflow Interfaces

Since machine learning solutions are typically deployed in workflow pipelines (data ingestion > model fitting > model assessment > data scoring), some software use a drag-and-drop icon and arrows interface, where icons represent different stages of the process, and arrows connect different stages. While there are a variety of such software, we'll mention a few: IBM Modeler is based on the

SPSS Clementine program, which had one of the first workflow-based interfaces. This style of interface links the data engineering, exploration, machine learning, model evaluation, and deployment steps together. Modeler has a wide range of statistical and machine learning algorithms, and provides interfaces to Watson, Python, and R for additional functionality.

RapidMiner Studio was originally developed in Germany in 2001 (the original name was YALE), and has grown into a widely used platform for machine learning. It has a workflow drag-and-drop interface that supports data import, data cleansing, graphics, a large variety of machine learning tools, and model evaluation. One of the most difficult problems in building good models is feature selection. RapidMiner provides a number of tools including genetic algorithms for feature selection. Its Turbo Prep and Auto Model interfaces offer support for data preparation tasks and auto-tuning hyperparameters for standard machine learning algorithms, respectively. RapidMiner also has integration with R and Python to extend its capabilities. Orange is a visual interface for Python and Scikit-Learn using wrappers designed to make analysis easier. Developed at the University of Ljubljana in Slovenia, Orange is open-source software that uses a workflow interface to provide a greatly improved way to use Python for analysis.

Cloud Computing

Cloud computing vendors are actively promoting their services for machine learning. These products are oriented more toward application developers than machine learning prototypers and business analysts. A big part of the attraction of machine learning in the cloud is the ability to store and manage enormous amounts of data without requiring the expense and complexity of building an in-house capability. This can also enable a more rapid implementation of large distributed multi-user applications. Many of the non-cloud-based machine learning vendors provide interfaces to cloud storage to enable their tools to work with mammoth amounts of data. For example, RapidMiner offers a product Rapid-Miner AI Hub (formerly RapidMiner Server) that leverages the standard cloud computing platforms (Amazon AWS, Google Cloud, MS Azure) for automation and deployment of machine learning models. Amazon has several machine learning services. SageMaker is a machine learning platform that provides developers with functionality including acquiring and wrangling data, building models based on its large collection of algorithms, and deploying the resulting models. Models can be used with data stored in Amazon Web Services (AWS) or exported for use in local environments. There is also an automatic machine learning process that will choose the appropriate algorithm and create the model. AWS also has what it calls Deep Learning AMI's (Amazon Machine Images) that are preconfigured virtual machines with deep learning frameworks such as TensorFlow.

Google is very active in cloud analytics with its Vertex AI. The user can either custom train models or use Vertex AI's AutoML which will automatically build models based on your selected targets. Unfortunately, this is not a transparent process, and there is a limitation in the size of the data—100 GB or 100 million rows of tabular data. Models such as TensorFlow deep learning models can be exported for use in local environments. Microsoft is an active player in cloud analytics with its Azure Machine Learning. Azure ML also supports a workflow interface making it more accessible to the nonprogrammer data scientist.

Along with Amazon and Google, Azure Machine Learning also supports an automated machine learning mode. ASDM's cloud version is based on Microsoft Azure. Machine learning plays a central role in enabling many organizations to optimize everything from manufacturing and production to marketing and sales. New storage options and analytical tools promise even greater capabilities. The key is to select technology that's appropriate for an organization's unique goals and constraints. As always, human judgment is the most important component of a machine learning solution. The focus of *Machine Learning for Business Analytics* is on a comprehensive understanding of the different techniques and algorithms used in machine learning, and less on the data management requirements of real-time deployment of machine learning models.

***

Herb Edelstein is president of Two Crows Consulting (www.twocrows.com), a leading data mining consulting firm near Washington, DC. He is an internationally recognized expert in data mining and data warehousing, a widely published author on these topics, and a popular speaker.
©2022 Herb Edelstein.

PROBLEMS

2.1 Assuming that machine learning techniques are to be used in the following cases, identify whether the task required is supervised or unsupervised learning.

a. Deciding whether to issue a loan to an applicant based on demographic and financial data (with reference to a database of similar data on prior customers).

b. In an online bookstore, making recommendations to customers concerning additional items to buy based on the buying patterns in prior transactions.

c. Identifying a network data packet as dangerous (virus, hacker attack) based on comparison to other packets whose threat status is known.

d. Identifying segments of similar customers.

e. Predicting whether a company will go bankrupt based on comparing its financial data to those of similar bankrupt and nonbankrupt firms.

f. Estimating the repair time required for an aircraft based on a trouble ticket.

g. Automated sorting of mail by zip code scanning.

h. Printing of custom discount coupons at the conclusion of a grocery store checkout based on what you just bought and what others have bought previously.

2.2 Describe the difference in roles assumed by the validation partition and the test partition.

2.3 Consider the sample from a database of credit applicants in Table 2.5. Comment on the likelihood that it was sampled randomly, and whether it is likely to be a useful sample.

TABLE 2.5   SAMPLE FROM A DATABASE OF CREDIT APPLICATIONS

OBS	CHECK ACCT	DURATION	HISTORY	NEW CAR	USED CAR	FURNITURE	RADIO TV	EDUC	RETRAIN	AMOUNT	SAVE ACCT	RESPONSE
1	0	6	4	0	0	0	1	0	0	1169	4	1
8	1	36	2	0	1	0	0	0	0	6948	0	1
16	0	24	2	0	0	0	1	0	0	1282	1	0
24	1	12	4	0	1	0	0	0	0	1804	1	1
32	0	24	2	0	0	1	0	0	0	4020	0	1
40	1	9	2	0	0	0	1	0	0	458	0	1
48	0	6	2	0	1	0	0	0	0	1352	2	1
56	3	6	1	1	0	0	0	0	0	783	4	1
64	1	48	0	0	0	0	0	0	1	14421	0	0
72	3	7	4	0	0	0	1	0	0	730	4	1
80	1	30	2	0	0	1	0	0	0	3832	0	1
88	1	36	2	0	0	0	0	1	0	12612	1	0
96	1	54	0	0	0	0	0	0	1	15945	0	0
104	1	9	4	0	0	1	0	0	0	1919	0	1
112	2	15	2	0	0	0	0	1	0	392	0	1

2.4 Consider the sample from a bank database shown in Table 2.6; it was selected randomly from a larger database to be the training set. *Personal Loan* indicates whether a solicitation for a personal loan was accepted and is the response variable. A campaign is planned for a similar solicitation in the future, and the bank is looking for a model that will identify likely responders. Examine the data carefully and indicate what your next step would be.

TABLE 2.6   SAMPLE FROM A BANK DATABASE

OBS	AGE	EXPERIENCE	INCOME	ZIP CODE	FAMILY	CC AVG	EDUC	MORTGAGE	PERSONAL LOAN	SECURITIES ACCT
1	25	1	49	91107	4	1.6	1	0	0	1
4	35	9	100	94112	1	2.7	2	0	0	0
5	35	8	45	91330	4	1	2	0	0	0
9	35	10	81	90089	3	0.6	2	104	0	0
10	34	9	180	93023	1	8.9	3	0	1	0
12	29	5	45	90277	3	0.1	2	0	0	0
17	38	14	130	95010	4	4.7	3	134	1	0
18	42	18	81	94305	4	2.4	1	0	0	0
21	56	31	25	94015	4	0.9	2	111	0	0
26	43	19	29	94305	3	0.5	1	97	0	0
29	56	30	48	94539	1	2.2	3	0	0	0
30	38	13	119	94104	1	3.3	2	0	1	0
35	31	5	50	94035	4	1.8	3	0	0	0
36	48	24	81	92647	3	0.7	1	0	0	0
37	59	35	121	94720	1	2.9	1	0	0	0
38	51	25	71	95814	1	1.4	3	198	0	0
39	42	18	141	94114	3	5	3	0	1	1
41	57	32	84	92672	3	1.6	3	0	0	1

2.5 Using the concept of overfitting, explain why when a model is fit to training data, zero error with those data is not necessarily good.

2.6 In fitting a model to classify prospects as purchasers or nonpurchasers, a certain company drew the training data from internal data that include demographic and purchase information. Future data to be classified will be lists purchased from other sources, with demographic (but not purchase) data included. It was found that "refund issued" was a useful predictor in the training data. Why is this not an appropriate variable to include in the model?

2.7 A dataset has 1000 records and 50 variables with 5% of the values missing, spread randomly throughout the records and variables. An analyst decides to remove records with missing values. About how many records would you expect to be removed?

2.8 Normalize the data in Table 2.7, showing calculations.

TABLE 2.7

Age	Income ($)
25	49,000
56	156,000
65	99,000
32	192,000
41	39,000
49	57,000

2.9 The distance between two records can be measured in several ways. Consider Euclidean distance, measured as the square root of the sum of the squared differences.

For the first two records in Table 2.7, it is

$$\sqrt{(25-56)^2 + (49,000 - 156,000)^2}.$$

Can normalizing the data change which two records are farthest from each other in terms of Euclidean distance?

2.10 Two models are applied to a dataset that has been partitioned. Model A is considerably more accurate than model B on the training data, but slightly less accurate than model B on the validation data. Which model are you more likely to consider for final deployment?

2.11 The dataset ToyotaCorolla.xlsx contains data on used cars for sale during the late summer of 2004 in the Netherlands. It has 1436 records containing details on 38 attributes, including Price, Age, Kilometers, HP, and other specifications.

    We plan to analyze the data using various machine learning techniques described in future chapters. Prepare the data for use as follows:

a. The dataset has two categorical attributes, *Fuel Type* and *Color*. Describe how you would convert these to binary variables. Confirm this using ASDM's utility to transform categorical data into dummies. What would you do with the variable *Model*?

b. Prepare the dataset (as factored into dummies) for machine learning techniques of supervised learning by creating partitions using ASDM's data partitioning utility. Select variables and use default values for the random seed and partitioning percentages for training (50%), validation (30%), and test (20%) sets. Describe the roles that these partitions will play in modeling.

2.12 (For class or group discussion:) Sort the West Roxbury data by YR BUILT and report any anomalies. Discuss the implications for the analysis done in this chapter and possible steps to take.

## PART II

Data Exploration and
Dimension Reduction

## CHAPTER 3

Data Visualization

In this chapter, we describe a set of plots that can be used to explore the multi-dimensional nature of a dataset. We present basic plots (bar charts, line charts, and scatter plots), distribution plots (boxplots and histograms), and different enhancements that expand the capabilities of these plots to let the user visualize more information. We focus on how the different visualizations and operations can support machine learning tasks, from supervised tasks (prediction, classification, and time series forecasting) to unsupervised tasks, and provide a few guidelines on specific visualizations to use with each machine learning task. We also describe the advantages of interactive visualization over static plots. The chapter concludes with a presentation of specialized plots suitable for data with special structure (hierarchical, network, and geographical).

3.1 USES OF DATA VISUALIZATION[1]

The popular saying "a picture is worth a thousand words" refers to the ability to condense diffused verbal information into a compact and quickly understood graphical image. In the case of numbers, data visualization and numerical summarization provide us with both a powerful tool to explore data and an effective way to present results.

Where do visualization techniques fit into the machine learning process, as described so far? They are primarily used in the preprocessing portion of the machine learning process. Visualization supports data cleaning by finding incorrect values (e.g., patients whose age is 999 or -1), missing values, duplicate rows, columns with all the same value, and the like. Visualization techniques are

---

[1]This and subsequent sections in this chapter copyright ©2019 Datastats, LLC and Galit Shmueli. Used by permission.

---

also useful for variable derivation and selection: they can help determine which variables to include in the analysis and which might be redundant. They can also help with determining appropriate bin sizes, should binning of numerical variables be needed (e.g., a numerical outcome variable might need to be converted to a binary variable, as was done in the Boston housing data, if a yes/no decision is required). They can also play a role in combining categories as part of the data reduction process. Finally, if the data have yet to be collected and collection is expensive (as with the Pandora project at its outset; see Chapter 7), visualization methods can help determine, using a sample, which variables and metrics are useful.

In this chapter, we focus on the use of graphical presentations for the purpose of *data exploration*, particularly with relation to predictive analytics. Although our focus is not on visualization for the purpose of data reporting, this chapter offers ideas as to the effectiveness of various graphical displays for the purpose of data presentation. These offer a wealth of useful presentations beyond tabular summaries and basic bar charts, which are currently the most popular form of data presentation in the business environment. For an excellent discussion of using plots to report business data, see Few (2012). In terms of reporting machine learning results graphically, we describe common graphical displays elsewhere in the book, some of which are technique specific [e.g., dendrograms for hierarchical clustering (Chapter 16), network charts for social network analysis (Chapter 20), and tree charts for classification and regression trees (Chapter 9)], while others are more general [e.g., receiver operating characteristic (ROC) curves and lift charts for classification (Chapter 5) and profile plots and heatmaps for clustering (Chapter 16)].

Note: The term "graph" has two meanings in statistics. It can refer, particularly in popular usage, to any of a number of figures to represent data (e.g., line chart, bar plot, and histogram). In a more technical use, it refers to the data structure and visualization in networks (see Chapter 20). Using the terms "chart" or "plot" for the visualizations we explore in this chapter avoids this confusion.

Data exploration is a mandatory initial step whether or not more formal analysis follows. Graphical exploration can support free-form exploration for the purpose of understanding the data structure, cleaning the data (e.g., identifying unexpected gaps or "illegal" values), identifying outliers, discovering initial patterns (e.g., correlations among variables and surprising clusters), and generating interesting questions. Graphical exploration can also be more focused, geared toward specific questions of interest. In the machine learning context, a combination is needed: free-form exploration performed with the purpose of supporting a specific goal.

Graphical exploration can range from generating very basic plots to using operations such as filtering and zooming interactively to explore a set of interconnected visualizations that include advanced features such as color and multiple panels. This chapter is not meant to be an exhaustive guidebook on visualization techniques, but instead to discuss main principles and features that support data exploration in a machine learning context. We start by describing varying levels of sophistication in terms of visualization, and show the advantages of different features and operations. Our discussion is from the perspective of how visualization supports the subsequent machine learning goal. In particular, we distinguish between supervised and unsupervised learning; within supervised learning, we also further distinguish between classification (categorical Y) and prediction (numerical Y).

3.2 DATA EXAMPLES

To illustrate data visualization, we use two datasets that also appear in other chapters in the book. This allows the reader to compare some of the basic Excel plots used in other chapters to the improved plots, and easily see the merit of advanced visualization.

Example 1: Boston Housing Data

The Boston housing data contain information on census tracts in Boston[2] for which several measurements are taken (e.g., crime rate, pupil/teacher ratio). It has 14 variables. A description of each variable is given in Table 3.1 and a sample of the first nine records is shown in Table 3.2. In addition to the original

TABLE 3.1   DESCRIPTION OF VARIABLES IN BOSTON HOUSING DATASET

CRIM	Crime rate
ZN	Percentage of residential land zoned for lots over 25,000 ft^2
INDUS	Percentage of land occupied by nonretail business
CHAS	Does tract bound Charles River (= 1 if tract bounds river, = 0 otherwise)
NOX	Nitric oxide concentration (parts per 10 million)
RM	Average number of rooms per dwelling
AGE	Percentage of owner-occupied units built prior to 1940
DIS	Weighted distances to five Boston employment centers
RAD	Index of accessibility to radial highways
TAX	Full-value property tax rate per $10,000
PTRATIO	Pupil-to-teacher ratio by town
LSTAT	Percentage of lower status of the population
MEDV	Median value of owner-occupied homes in $1000s
CAT.MEDV	Is median value of owner-occupied homes in tract above $30,000 (CAT.MEDV = 1) or not (CAT.MEDV = 0)

---

[2]The Boston Housing dataset was originally published by Harrison and Rubinfeld in "Hedonic prices and the demand for clean air." *Journal of Environmental Economics and Management*, vol. 5, pp. 81–102, 1978. A census tract includes 1200–8000 homes.

TABLE 3.2   FIRST NINE RECORDS IN THE BOSTON HOUSING DATA

CRIM	ZN	INDUS	CHAS	NOX	RM	AGE	DIS	RAD	TAX	PTRATIO	LSTAT	MEDV	CAT.MEDV
0.00632	18.0	2.31	0	0.538	6.575	65.2	4.09	1	296	15.3	4.98	24.0	0
0.02731	0.0	7.07	0	0.469	6.421	78.9	4.9671	2	242	17.8	9.14	21.6	0
0.02729	0.0	7.07	0	0.469	7.185	61.1	4.9671	2	242	17.8	4.03	34.7	1
0.03237	0.0	2.18	0	0.458	6.998	45.8	6.0622	3	222	18.7	2.94	33.4	1
0.06905	0.0	2.18	0	0.458	7.147	54.2	6.0622	3	222	18.7	5.33	36.2	1
0.02985	0.0	2.18	0	0.458	6.43	58.7	6.0622	3	222	18.7	5.21	28.7	0
0.08829	12.5	7.87	0	0.524	6.012	66.6	5.5605	5	311	15.2	12.43	22.9	0
0.14455	12.5	7.87	0	0.524	6.172	96.1	5.9505	5	311	15.2	19.15	27.1	0
0.21124	12.5	7.87	0	0.524	5.631	100.0	6.0821	5	311	15.2	29.93	16.5	0

13 variables, the dataset contains the variable CAT.MEDV, which was created by categorizing median value (MEDV) into two categories, high and low.

We consider three possible tasks:

1. A supervised predictive task, where the outcome variable of interest is the median value of a home in the tract (MEDV).

2. A supervised classification task, where the outcome variable of interest is the binary variable CAT.MEDV that indicates whether the home value is above or below $30,000.

3. An unsupervised task, where the goal is to cluster census tracts.

(MEDV and CAT.MEDV are not used together in any of the three cases).

Example 2: Ridership on Amtrak Trains

Amtrak, a US railway company, routinely collects data on ridership. Here we focus on forecasting future ridership using the series of monthly ridership between January 1991 and March 2004. The data and their source are described in Chapter 17 and available in `Amtrak.xlsx`. Hence, our task here is (numerical) time series forecasting.

3.3   BASIC CHARTS: BAR CHARTS, LINE CHARTS, AND SCATTER PLOTS

The three most effective basic charts are bar charts, line charts, and scatter plots. These plots are easy to create in Microsoft Excel and are the most commonly used today in the business world, in both data exploration and presentation (unfortunately, pie charts are also popular, although usually ineffective visualizations). Basic charts support data exploration by displaying one or two columns of data (variables) at a time. This is useful in the early stages of getting familiar with the data structure, the amount and types of variables, the volume and type of missing values, and so on.

The nature of the machine learning task and domain knowledge about the data will affect the use of basic plots in terms of the amount of time and effort allocated to different variables. In supervised learning, there will be more focus on the outcome variable. In scatter plots, the outcome variable is typically associated with the y-axis. In unsupervised learning (for the purpose of data reduction or clustering), basic charts that convey relationships (e.g., scatter plots) are preferred.

The top left panel in Figure 3.1 displays a line chart for the time series of monthly railway passengers on Amtrak. Line graphs are used primarily for showing time series. The choice of time frame to plot, as well as the temporal scale, should depend on the horizon of the forecasting task and on the nature of the data.

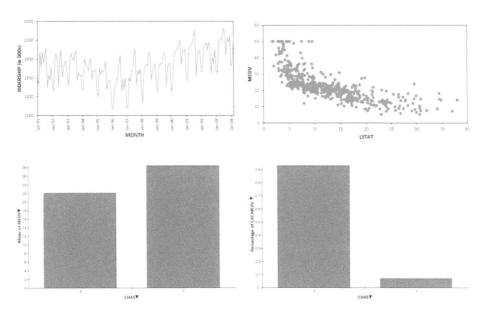

FIGURE 3.1   BASIC PLOTS: LINE CHART (TOP LEFT), SCATTER PLOT (TOP RIGHT), PRODUCED IN EXCEL, BAR CHART FOR NUMERICAL VARIABLE (BOTTOM LEFT), AND BAR CHART FOR CATEGORICAL VARIABLE (BOTTOM RIGHT), PRODUCED IN ASDM

Bar charts are useful for comparing a single statistic (e.g., average, count, percentage) across groups. The height of the bar (or length, in a horizontal display) represents the value of the statistic, and different bars correspond to different groups. Two examples are shown in the bottom panels in Figure 3.1. The left panel shows a bar chart for a numerical variable (MEDV) and the right panel shows a bar chart for a categorical variable (CAT.MEDV). In each, separate bars are used to denote homes in Boston that are near the Charles River vs. those that are not (thereby comparing the two categories of CHAS). The chart with the numerical output MEDV (bottom left) uses the average MEDV on the y-axis. This supports the predictive task: the numerical outcome is on the y-axis and the x-axis is used for a potential categorical predictor.[3] (Note that the x-axis on a bar chart must be used only for categorical variables because the order of bars in a bar chart should be interchangeable.) For the classification task, CAT.MEDV is on the y-axis (bottom right), but its aggregation is a percentage (the alternative would be a count). This plot shows us that the vast majority (over 90%) of the tracts do not border the Charles river (CHAS = 0). Note that the labeling of the y-axis can be confusing in this case: the value of CAT.MEDV plays no role and the y-axis is simply a percentage of all records.

The top right panel in Figure 3.1 displays a scatter plot of MEDV vs. LSTAT. This is an important plot in the prediction task. Note that the output MEDV is again on the y-axis (and LSTAT on the x-axis is a potential predictor). Because both variables in a basic scatter plot must be numerical, it cannot be used to display the relation between CAT.MEDV and potential predictors for the classification task (but we can enhance it to do so; see Section 3.4). For unsupervised learning, this particular scatter plot helps us study the association between two numerical variables in terms of information overlap as well as identifying clusters of observations.

All three basic plots highlight global information such as the overall level of ridership or MEDV, as well as changes over time (line chart), differences between subgroups (bar chart), and relationships between numerical variables (scatter plot).

Distribution Plots: Boxplots and Histograms

Before moving on to more sophisticated visualizations that enable multidimensional investigation, we note two important plots that are usually not considered "basic plots" but are very useful in statistical and data mining contexts. The *boxplot* and the *histogram* are two plots that display the entire distribution of a numerical variable. Although averages are very popular and useful summary statistics, there is usually much to be gained by looking at additional statistics such as the median and standard deviation of a variable, and even more so by examining the entire distribution. Whereas bar charts can only use a single aggregation, boxplots and histograms display the entire distribution of a numerical variable. Boxplots are also effective for comparing subgroups by generating side-by-side boxplots, or for looking at distributions over time by creating a series of boxplots.

---

[3]We refer here to a bar chart with vertical bars. The same principles apply if using a bar chart with horizontal lines, except that the x-axis is now associated with the numerical variable and the y-axis with the categorical variable.

Distribution plots are useful in supervised learning for determining potential machine learning methods and variable transformations. For example, skewed numerical variables might warrant transformation (e.g., moving to a logarithmic scale) if used in methods that assume normality (e.g., linear regression, discriminant analysis).

A histogram represents the frequencies of all x values with a series of vertical connected bars. For example, in the left panel of Figure 3.2, there are about 20 tracts where the MEDV is between \$5000 and \$10,000.

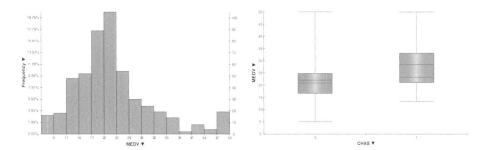

FIGURE 3.2   DISTRIBUTION CHARTS FOR NUMERICAL VARIABLE MEDV. LEFT: HISTOGRAM, RIGHT: BOXPLOT. CHARTS PRODUCED IN ASDM

A boxplot represents the variable being plotted on the y-axis (although the plot can potentially be turned in a 90° angle, so that the boxes are parallel to the x-axis). In the right panel of Figure 3.2, there are two boxplots (called a side-by-side boxplot). The box encloses 50% of the data—for example, in the right-hand box, half of the tracts have MEDVs between approximately \$20,000 and \$33,000. The horizontal line inside the box represents the median (50th percentile). The top and bottom of the box represent the 75th and 25th percentiles, respectively. Lines extending above and below the box cover the rest of the data range; outliers may be depicted as points or circles. Sometimes the average is marked by a + sign or a dashed line, as in the right panel of Figure 3.2. Comparing the average and the median helps in assessing how skewed the data are. Boxplots are often arranged in a series with a different plot for each of the various values of a second variable, shown on the x-axis.

Because histograms and boxplots are geared toward numerical variables, their basic form is useful for prediction tasks. Boxplots can also support unsupervised learning by displaying relationships between a numerical variable (y-axis) and a categorical variable (x-axis). For example, the histogram of MEDV in the left panel in Figure 3.2 reveals a skewed distribution. Transforming the output variable to log(MEDV) would likely improve results of a linear regression predictor. Compare the side-by-side boxplot in Figure 3.2 to the bottom-left bar chart in Figure 3.1 that only displays the average values. We see that not only is the average MEDV for river-bounding tracts (CHAS = 1) higher than the non–river-bounding tracts (CHAS = 0), the entire distribution is higher (median, quartiles, and minimum). We can also see that all river-bounding tracts have MEDV above $10,000, unlike non–river-bounding tracts. This information is useful for identifying the potential importance of this predictor (CHAS), and for choosing machine learning methods that can capture the nonoverlapping area between the two distributions (e.g., trees).

Boxplots and histograms applied to numerical variables can also provide directions for deriving new variables; for example, they can indicate how to bin a numerical variable (e.g., binning a numerical outcome in order to use a naive Bayes classifier, or in the Boston Housing example, choosing the cutoff to convert MEDV to CAT.MEDV).

Finally, side-by-side boxplots are useful in classification tasks for evaluating the potential of numerical predictors. This is done by using the x-axis for the categorical outcome and the y-axis for a numerical predictor. An example is shown in Figure 3.3, where we can see the effects of four numerical predictors on CAT.MEDV. The pairs that are most separated (e.g., PTRATIO and INDUS) indicate potentially useful predictors.

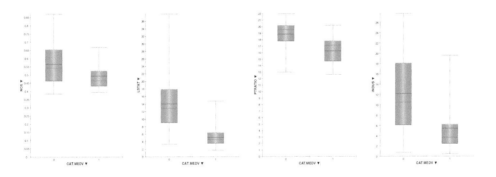

FIGURE 3.3   SIDE-BY-SIDE BOXPLOTS FOR EXPLORING THE CAT.MEDV OUTPUT VARIABLE BY DIFFERENT NUMERICAL PREDICTORS. IN A SIDE-BY-SIDE BOXPLOT, ONE AXIS IS USED FOR A CATEGORICAL VARIABLE, AND THE OTHER FOR A NUMERICAL VARIABLE. PLOTTING A CATEGORICAL OUTCOME VARIABLE AND A NUMERICAL PREDICTOR COMPARES THE PREDICTOR'S DISTRIBUTION ACROSS THE OUTCOME CATEGORIES. PLOTTING A NUMERICAL OUTCOME VARIABLE AND A CATEGORICAL PREDICTOR DISPLAYS THE DISTRIBUTION OF THE OUTCOME VARIABLE ACROSS DIFFERENT LEVELS OF THE PREDICTOR. CHARTS PRODUCED IN ASDM

Histograms and boxplots (also called Box and Whisker plots) are readily available in Microsoft Excel (*Insert > Charts*). In ASDM, they can be generated through the *Data Mining > Explore > Chart Wizard* (desktop version) or *Data Mining > Analysis > Charts* (cloud version) menu. ASDM allows up to 12 categories for side-by-side boxplots.

The main weakness of basic plots, and distribution plots in their basic form (that is, using position in relation to the axes to encode values), is that they can only display two variables and therefore cannot reveal high-dimensional information. Each of the basic plots has two dimensions, where each dimension is dedicated to a single variable. In machine learning, the data are usually multivariate by nature, and the analytics are designed to capture and measure multivariate information. Visual exploration should therefore also incorporate this important aspect. In the next section, we describe how to extend basic charts (and distribution plots) to multidimensional data visualization by adding features, employing manipulations, and incorporating interactivity. We then present several specialized plots geared toward displaying special data structures (Section 3.5).

Heatmaps: Visualizing Correlations and Missing Values

A *heatmap* is a graphical display of numerical data where color is used to denote values. In a machine learning context, heatmaps are especially useful for two purposes: for visualizing correlation tables and for visualizing missing values in the data. In both cases, the information is conveyed in a two-dimensional table. A correlation table for p variables has p rows and p columns. A data table contains p columns (variables) and n rows (observations). If the number of rows is huge, then a subset can be used. In both cases, it is much easier and faster to scan the color-coding rather than the values. Note that heatmaps are useful when examining a large number of values, but they are not a replacement for more precise graphical displays, such as bar charts, because color differences cannot be perceived accurately.

An example of a correlation table heatmap is shown in Figure 3.4, displaying all the pairwise correlations between 13 variables (MEDV and 12 predictors). Brighter shades correspond to stronger (positive or negative) correlation, making it is easy to quickly spot the high and low correlations. Adding color—here green and red—can be used to distinguish positive and negative values. This heatmap was produced using Excel's *Conditional Formatting*.

In a missing-value heatmap, rows correspond to records and columns to variables. We use a binary coding of the original dataset where 1 denotes a

	CRIM	ZN	INDUS	CHAS	NOX	RM	AGE	DIS	RAD	TAX	PTRATIO	LSTAT	MEDV
CRIM	1												
ZN	-0.20047	1											
INDUS	0.406583	-0.53383	1										
CHAS	-0.05589	-0.0427	0.062938	1									
NOX	0.420972	-0.5166	0.763651	0.091203	1								
RM	-0.21925	0.311991	-0.39168	0.091251	-0.30219	1							
AGE	0.352734	-0.56954	0.644779	0.086518	0.73147	-0.24026	1						
DIS	-0.37967	0.664408	-0.70803	-0.09918	-0.76923	0.205246	-0.74788	1					
RAD	0.625505	-0.31195	0.595129	-0.00737	0.611441	-0.20985	0.456022	-0.49459	1				
TAX	0.582764	-0.31456	0.72076	-0.03559	0.668023	-0.29205	0.506456	-0.53443	0.910228	1			
PTRATIO	0.289946	-0.39168	0.383248	-0.12152	0.188933	-0.3555	0.261515	-0.23247	0.464741	0.460853	1		
LSTAT	0.455621	-0.41299	0.6038	-0.05393	0.590879	-0.61381	0.602339	-0.497	0.488676	0.543993	0.374044	1	
MEDV	-0.3883	0.360445	-0.48373	0.17526	-0.42732	0.69536	-0.37695	0.249929	-0.38163	-0.46854	-0.50779	-0.73766	1

FIGURE 3.4   HEATMAP OF A CORRELATION TABLE. BRIGHT-GREEN DENOTES STRONG POSITIVE CORRELATION AND BRIGHT-RED DENOTES STRONG NEGATIVE CORRELATION. CHART PRODUCED IN EXCEL

missing value and 0 otherwise. This new binary table is then colored such that only missing-value cells (with value 1) are colored. Figure 3.5 shows an example of a missing-value heatmap for a dataset on motor vehicle collisions. The missing-data heatmap helps visualize the level and amount of "missingness" in the dataset. Some patterns of "missingness" easily emerge: variables that are missing for nearly all observations, as well as clusters of rows that are missing many values. Variables with little missingness are also visible. This information can then be used for determining how to handle the missingness (e.g., dropping some variables, dropping some records, imputing, or via other techniques).

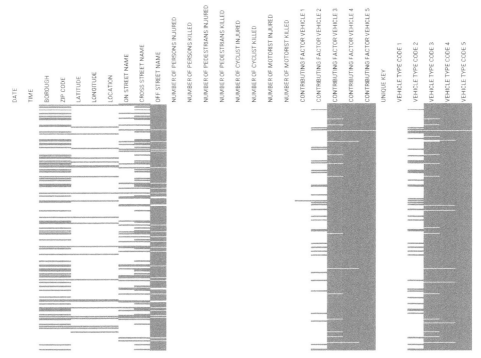

FIGURE 3.5   HEATMAP OF MISSING VALUES IN A DATASET ON MOTOR VEHICLE COLLISIONS. EACH ROW IS ONE RECORD. GRAY DENOTES MISSING VALUES. CHART PRODUCED IN EXCEL

3.4 MULTIDIMENSIONAL VISUALIZATION

Basic plots can convey richer information with features such as color, size, and multiple panels, and by enabling operations such as rescaling, aggregation, and interaction. These additions allow us to look at more than one or two variables at a time. The beauty of these additions is their effectiveness in displaying complex information in an easily understandable way. Effective features are based on understanding how visual perception works (see Few, 2009, for a discussion).

The purpose is to make the information more understandable, not just represent the data in higher dimensions (e.g., as three-dimensional plots that are usually ineffective visualizations).

Adding Variables: Color, Size, Shape, Multiple Panels, and Animation

In order to include more variables in a plot, we must consider the type of variable to include. To represent additional categorical information, the best way is to use hue, shape, or multiple panels. For additional numerical information, we can use color intensity or size. Temporal information can be added via animation.

Incorporating additional categorical and/or numerical variables into the basic (and distribution) plots means that we can now use all of them for both prediction and classification tasks! For example, we mentioned earlier that a basic scatter plot cannot be used for studying the relationship between a categorical outcome and predictors (in the context of classification). However, a very effective plot for classification is a scatter plot of two numerical predictors color-coded by the categorical outcome variable. An example is shown in the left panel of Figure 3.6, with color denoting CAT.MEDV; blue color denotes CAT.MEDV = 1 and orange for CAT.MEDV = 0.

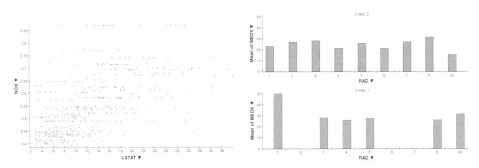

FIGURE 3.6   ADDING CATEGORICAL VARIABLES BY COLOR-CODING AND MULTIPLE PANELS. LEFT: SCATTER PLOT OF TWO NUMERICAL PREDICTORS, COLOR-CODED BY THE CATEGORICAL OUTCOME CAT.MEDV. RIGHT: BAR CHART OF MEDV BY TWO CATEGORICAL PREDICTORS (CHAS AND RAD), USING MULTIPLE PANELS FOR CHAS. CHARTS PRODUCED IN ASDM

In the context of prediction, color-coding supports the exploration of the conditional relationship between the numerical outcome (on the y-axis) and a numerical predictor. Color-coded scatter plots then help assess the need for creating interaction terms (e.g., is the relationship between MEDV and LSTAT different for tracts near the river compared to tracts away from the river?).

Color can also be used to include further categorical variables into a bar chart, as long as the number of categories is small. When the number of categories is large, a better alternative is to use multiple panels. Creating multiple panels (also called "trellising") is done by splitting the observations according to a categorical variable, and creating a separate plot (of the same type) for each category. An example is shown in the right-hand panel of Figure 3.6, where a bar chart of average MEDV by RAD is broken down into two panels by CHAS. We see that the average MEDV for different highway accessibility levels (RAD) behaves differently for tracts near the river (lower panel) compared to tracts away from the river (upper panel). This is especially salient for RAD = 1. We also see that there are no near-river tracts in RAD levels 2, 6, and 7. Such information might lead us to create an interaction term between RAD and CHAS, and to consider condensing some of the bins in RAD. All these explorations are useful for prediction and classification.

A special plot that uses scatter plots with multiple panels is the *scatter plot matrix*. In it, all pairwise scatter plots are shown in a single display. The panels in a matrix scatter plot are organized in a special way, such that each column corresponds to a variable and each row corresponds to a variable, thereby the intersections create all the possible pairwise scatter plots. The scatter plot matrix plot is useful in unsupervised learning for studying the associations between numerical variables, detecting outliers, and identifying clusters. For supervised learning, it can be used for examining pairwise relationships (and their nature) between predictors to support variable transformations and variable selection (see Correlation Analysis in Chapter 4). For prediction, it can also be used to depict the relationship of the outcome with the numerical predictors.

An example of a scatter plot matrix is shown in Figure 3.7, with MEDV and three predictors. Variable name indicates the *y*-axis variable. For example, the plots in the bottom row all have MEDV on the *y*-axis (which allows studying the individual outcome–predictor relations). We can see different types of relationships from the different shapes (e.g., an exponential relationship between MEDV and LSTAT and a highly skewed relationship between CRIM and INDUS), which can indicate needed transformations. Along the diagonal, where just a single variable is involved, that variable's frequency distribution is shown. Note that the plots above and to the right of the diagonal are mirror images of those below and to the left, but with the two axes flipped.

Once hue is used, further categorical variables can be added via shape and multiple panels. However, one must proceed cautiously in adding multiple variables, as the display can become overcluttered and then visual perception is lost.

Adding a numerical variable via size is useful especially in scatter plots (thereby creating "bubble plots") because, in a scatter plot, points represent individual observations. In plots that aggregate across observations (e.g., boxplots, histograms, bar charts), size and hue are not normally incorporated.

Finally, adding a temporal dimension to a plot to show how the information changes over time can be achieved via animation. A famous example is Rosling's animated scatter plots showing how world demographics changed over the

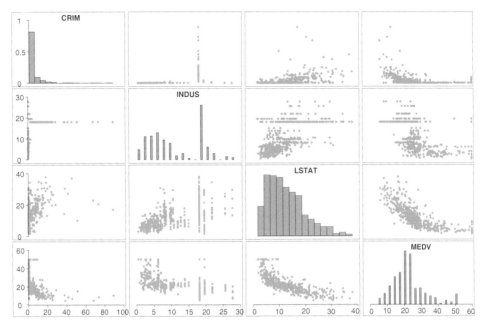

FIGURE 3.7 SCATTER PLOT MATRIX FOR MEDV AND THREE NUMERICAL PREDICTORS. CHART PRODUCED IN ASDM

years (www.gapminder.org). However, while animations of this type work for "statistical storytelling," they are not very effective for data exploration.

Manipulations: Rescaling, Aggregation and Hierarchies, Zooming, Filtering

Most of the time spent in machine learning projects is spent in data preprocessing. Typically, considerable effort is expended in getting all the data in a format that can actually be used in the machine learning software. Additional time is spent processing the data in ways that improve the performance of the machine learning procedures. This preprocessing step includes variable transformation and derivation of new variables to help models perform more effectively. Transformations include changing the numeric scale of a variable, binning numerical variables, condensing categories in categorical variables, and so on. The following manipulations support the preprocessing step as well as the choice of adequate machine learning methods. They do so by revealing patterns and their nature.

Rescaling Changing the scale in a display can enhance the plot and illuminate relationships. For example, in Figure 3.8 we see the effect of changing both axes of the scatter plot and the y-axis of a boxplot to logarithmic (log) scale. Whereas the original plots (left) are hard to understand, the patterns become visible in log scale (right). In the scatter plots, the nature of the relationship

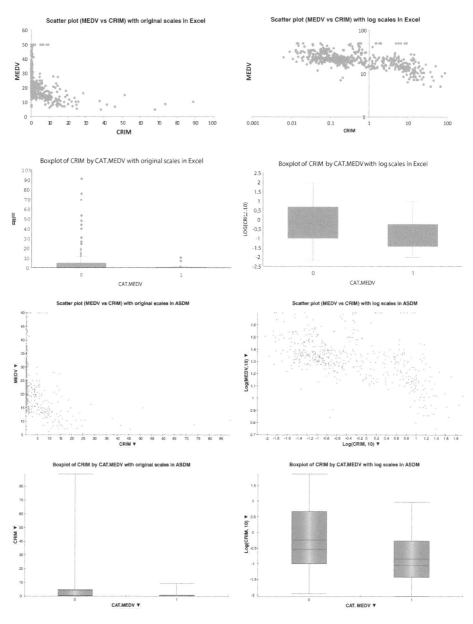

FIGURE 3.8   RESCALING CAN ENHANCE PLOTS AND REVEAL PATTERNS. LEFT: ORIGINAL SCALE. RIGHT: LOGARITHMIC SCALE

between MEDV and CRIM is hard to determine in the original scale because too many of the points are "crowded" near the y-axis. The rescaling removes this crowding and allows a better view of the linear relationship between the two log-scaled variables (indicating a log–log relationship). In the boxplot displays, the crowding toward the x-axis in the original units does not allow us to compare the two box sizes, their locations, lower outliers, and most of the distribution information. Rescaling removes the "crowding to the x-axis" effect, thereby allowing a comparison of the two boxplots.

Note: Creating the scatterplot in Excel with/out the logarithmic scale is easily done by selecting "Logarithmic scale." Unfortunately, this option is not available in ASDM charts or in Excel's boxplots. However, there is an alternative: creating log-transformed variables and then plotting those. In the right column of Figure 3.8, the re-scaled Excel boxplot (second row) and re-scaled ASDM scatter plot and boxplot (two bottom rows) are plotted using log-transformed variables.

Aggregation and Hierarchies   Another useful manipulation of scaling is changing the level of aggregation. For a temporal scale, we can aggregate by different granularity (e.g., monthly, daily, hourly) or even by a "seasonal" factor of interest such as month-of-year or day-of-week. A popular aggregation for time series is a moving average, where the average of neighboring values within a given window size is plotted. Moving average plots enhance global trend visualization (see Chapter 16).

Nontemporal variables can be aggregated if some meaningful hierarchy exists: geographical (tracts within a zip code in the Boston Housing example), organizational (people within departments within business units), and so on. Figure 3.9 illustrates two types of aggregation for the railway ridership time series. The original monthly series is shown in the top left panel. Seasonal aggregation (by month-of-year) is shown in the top-right panel, where it is easy

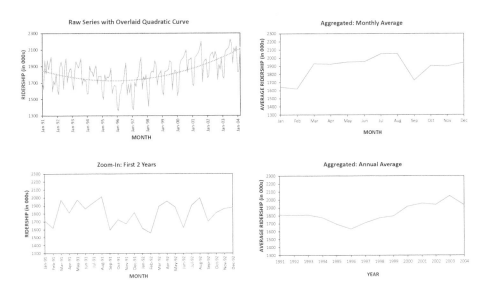

FIGURE 3.9   TIME SERIES LINE GRAPHS USING DIFFERENT AGGREGATIONS (RIGHT PANELS), ADDING CURVES (TOP LEFT PANEL), AND ZOOMING IN (BOTTOM LEFT PANEL). CHARTS PRODUCED IN EXCEL

to see the peak in ridership in July–August and the dip in January–February. The bottom right panel shows temporal aggregation, where the series is now displayed in yearly aggregates. This plot reveals the global long-term trend in ridership and the generally increasing trend from 1996 on.

Examining different scales, aggregations, or hierarchies supports both supervised and unsupervised tasks in that it can reveal patterns and relationships at various levels, and can suggest new sets of variables with which to work.

Zooming and Panning   The ability to zoom in and out of certain areas of the data on a plot is important for revealing patterns and outliers. We are often interested in more detail on areas of dense information or of special interest. Panning refers to the operation of moving the zoom window to other areas (popular in mapping applications such as Google Maps). An example of zooming is shown in the bottom left panel of Figure 3.9, where the ridership series is zoomed in to the first two years of the series.

Zooming and panning support supervised and unsupervised methods by detecting areas of different behavior, which may lead to creating new interaction terms, new variables, or even separate models for data subsets. In addition, zooming and panning can help choose between methods that assume global behavior (e.g., regression models) and data-driven methods (e.g., exponential smoothing forecasters and k-nearest-neighbors classifiers), and indicate the level of global/local behavior (as manifested by parameters such as k in k-nearest-neighbors, the size of a tree, or the smoothing parameters in exponential smoothing).

Filtering   Filtering means removing some of the observations from the plot. The purpose of filtering is to focus the attention on certain data while eliminating "noise" created by other data. Filtering supports supervised and unsupervised learning in a similar way to zooming and panning: it assists in identifying different or unusual local behavior.

Reference: Trend Line and Labels

Trend lines and in-plot labels also help to detect patterns and outliers. Trend lines serve as a reference and allow us to more easily assess the shape of a pattern. Although linearity is easy to visually perceive, more elaborate relationships such as exponential and polynomial trends are harder to assess by eye. Trend lines are useful in line graphs as well as in scatter plots. An example is shown in the top left panel of Figure 3.9, where a polynomial curve is overlaid on the original line graph (see also Chapter 17).

In displays that are not overcrowded, the use of in-plot labels can be useful for better exploration of outliers and clusters. An example is shown in Figure 3.10.

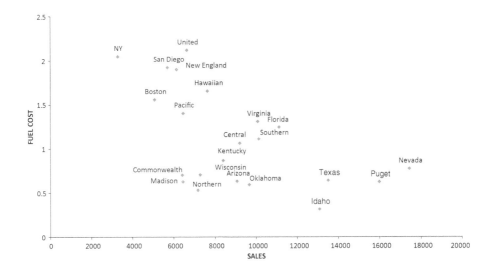

FIGURE 3.10   SCATTER PLOT WITH LABELED POINTS (CREATED IN EXCEL USING XY CHART LABELER ADD-ON HTTP://WWW.APPSPRO.COM/UTILITIES/CHARTLABELER.HTM)

The figure shows different utilities on a scatter plot that compares fuel cost with total sales. We might be interested in clustering the data, and using clustering algorithms to identify clusters of utilities that differ markedly with respect to fuel cost and sales. The scatter plot with the labels helps visualize clusters and their members: for example, Nevada and Puget are part of a clear cluster with low fuel costs and high sales. For more on clustering and on this example, see Chapter 16.

Scaling up to Large Datasets

When the number of observations (rows) is large, plots that display each individual observation (e.g., scatter plots) can become ineffective. Aside from using aggregated charts such as boxplots, some alternatives are:

1. Sampling—drawing a random sample and using it for plotting (ASDM has a sampling utility).

2. Reducing marker size.

3. Using more transparent marker colors and removing fill.

4. Breaking down the data into subsets (e.g., by creating multiple panels).

5. Using aggregation (e.g., bubble plots where size corresponds to number of observations in a certain range).

6. Using jittering (slightly moving each marker by adding a small amount of noise).

An example of the advantage of plotting a sample over the large dataset is shown in Chapter 12 (Figure 12.2), comparing a scatter plot of a large dataset to that of a sample. Figure 3.11 illustrates an improved plot of the full dataset obtained by using smaller markers, more transparent colors, and jittering to uncover overlaid points. We can see that larger areas of the plot are dominated by the light blue class, the dark blue class is mainly on the right, while there is a lot of overlap in the high-income area.

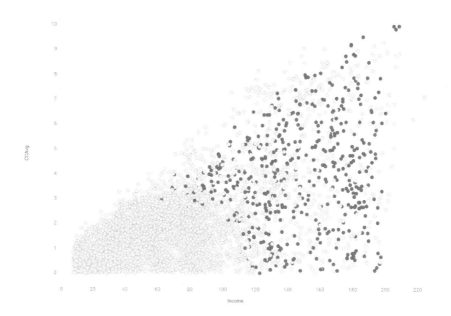

FIGURE 3.11   SCATTER PLOT OF LARGE DATASET WITH REDUCED MARKER SIZE, JITTERING, AND MORE TRANSPARENT COLORING. PRODUCED USING SPOTFIRE

Multivariate Plot: Parallel Coordinates Plot

Another approach toward presenting multidimensional information in a two-dimensional plot is via specialized plots such as the *parallel coordinates plot*. In this plot, a vertical axis is drawn for each variable. Then each observation is represented by drawing a line that connects its values on the different axes, thereby creating a "multivariate profile." An example is shown in Figure 3.12 for the Boston Housing data. In this display, separate panels are used for the two values of CAT.MEDV, in order to compare the profiles of tracts in the two classes (for a classification task). We see that the more expensive tracts (bottom panel) consistently have low CRIM, low LSAT, and high RM compared to cheaper tracts (top panel), which are more mixed on CRIM, and LSAT, and have a medium

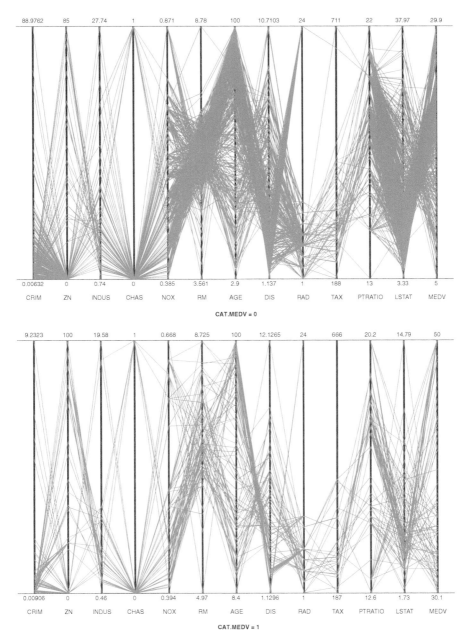

FIGURE 3.12   PARALLEL COORDINATES PLOT FOR BOSTON HOUSING DATA. EACH OF THE
VARIABLES (SHOWN ON THE HORIZONTAL AXIS) IS SCALED TO 0–100%.
PANELS ARE USED TO DISTINGUISH CAT.MEDV (TOP PANEL = HOMES BELOW
$30,000). PRODUCED USING ASDM

level of RM. This observation gives indication of useful predictors and suggests possible binning for some numerical predictors.

Parallel coordinates plots are also useful in unsupervised tasks. They can reveal clusters, outliers, and information overlap across variables. A useful manipulation is to re-order the columns to better reveal observation clusterings. Parallel coordinates plots are available in ASDM.

Interactive Visualization

Similar to the interactive nature of the machine learning process, interactivity is key to enhancing our ability to gain information from graphical visualization. In the words of Stephen Few (2021), an expert in data visualization,

> We can only learn so much when staring at a static visualization such as a printed graph…. If we can't interact with the data …, we hit the wall.

By interactive visualization, we mean an interface that supports the following principles:

1. Making changes to a chart is *easy, rapid, and reversible*.
2. Multiple concurrent charts and tables can be easily combined and displayed on a single screen.
3. A set of visualizations can be linked, so that operations in one display are reflected in the other displays.

Let us consider a few examples where we contrast a static plot generator (e.g., Excel) with an interactive visualization interface.

Histogram Re-binning   Consider the situation where we need to bin a numerical variable, and plan to use a histogram for that process. A static histogram would require re-plotting for each new binning choice If the user generates multiple plots, then the screen becomes cluttered. If the same plot is recreated, then it is hard to compare different binning choices. In contrast, an interactive visualization would provide an easy way to change bin width interactively (e.g., see the slider below the histogram in Figure 3.13), and then the histogram would automatically and rapidly replot as the user changes the bin width.

Aggregation and Zooming   Consider a time series forecasting task, given a long series of data. Temporal aggregation at multiple levels is needed for determining short- and long-term patterns. Zooming and panning are used to identify unusual periods. A static plotting software requires the user to create new data columns for each temporal aggregation (e.g., aggregate daily data to obtain weekly aggregates). Zooming and panning in Excel requires manually changing the min and max values on the axis scale of interest (thereby losing the ability to quickly move between different areas without creating multiple charts). An interactive visualization tool would provide immediate temporal hierarchies which the user can easily switch between. Zooming would be enabled as a slider

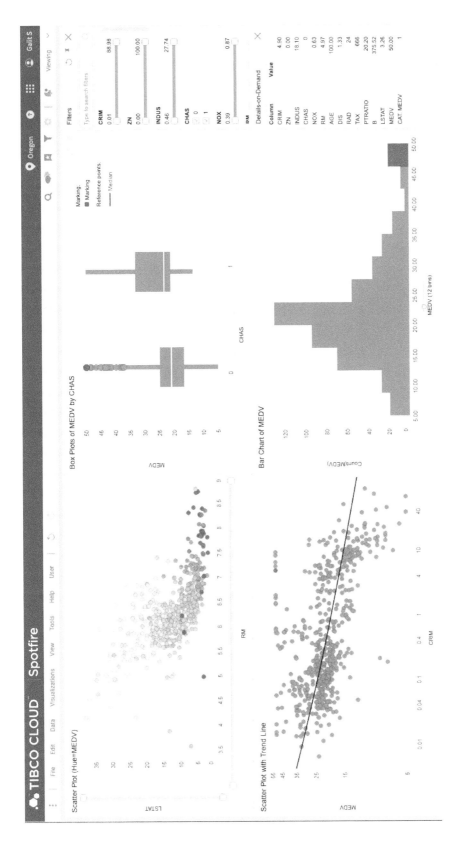

FIGURE 3.13   MULTIPLE INTER-LINKED PLOTS IN A SINGLE VIEW (USING SPOTFIRE). NOTE THE MARKED OBSERVATION IN THE TOP LEFT PANEL, WHICH IS ALSO HIGHLIGHTED IN ALL OTHER PLOTS. PRODUCED IN SPOTFIRE

near the axis (e.g., see the sliders on the top left panel in Figure 3.13), thereby allowing direct manipulation and rapid reaction.

Combining Multiple Linked Plots That Fit in a Single Screen   To support a classification task, multiple visualizations are created of the outcome variable vs. potential categorical and numerical predictors. These can include side-by-side boxplots, color-coded scatter plots, multipanel bar charts, and so on. The user wants to detect possible multidimensional relationships (and identify possible outliers) by selecting a certain subset of the data (e.g., a single category of some variable) and locating the observations on the other plots. In a static interface, the user would have to manually organize the plots of interest and re-size them in order to fit within a single screen. A static interface would usually not support inter-plot linkage, and even if it did, the entire set of plots would have to be re-generated each time that a selection is made. In contrast, an interactive visualization would provide an easy way to automatically organize and re-size the set of plots to fit within a screen. Linking the set of plots would be easy, and in response to the users' selection on one plot, the appropriate selection would be automatically highlighted in the other plots (e.g., see Figure 3.13).

Interactive Visualization Software   In earlier sections, we used plots to illustrate the advantages of visualizations, because "a picture is worth a thousand words." The advantages of an interactive visualization are even harder to convey in words. As Ben Shneiderman, a well-known researcher in information visualization and interfaces, puts it:

> A picture is worth a thousand words. An interface is worth a thousand pictures.

Some added features such as color, shape, and size are often available in software that produce static plots, while others (multiple panels, hierarchies, labels) are only available in more advanced visualization tools. Even when a feature is available (e.g., color), the ease of applying it to a plot can widely vary. For example, incorporating color into an Excel scatter plot is a daunting task.[4] Plot manipulation possibilities (e.g., zooming, filtering, and aggregation) and ease of implementation are also quite limited in standard "static plot" software.

Although we do not intend to provide a market survey of interactive visualization tools, we mention a few prominent packages. Spotfire (http://spotfire.tibco.com) and Tableau (https://www.tableau.com/) are two designated data visualization tools (some of the plots in this chapter were created using Spotfire). They both provide a high level of interactivity, can support large data sets, and produce high-quality plots that are also easy to export. JMP by SAS (www.jmp.com) is a "statistical discovery" software that also has strong interactive visualization capabilities. All three offer free trial versions.

---

[4]see www.bzst.com/2009/08/creating-color-coded-scatterplots-in.html

Programming environments like R and Python, which have become popular for statistical analysis, machine learning, and presentation graphics, can produce excellent static plots but are less suitable for interactive visualization, where a sophisticated and highly engineered user interface is required.

3.5 SPECIALIZED VISUALIZATIONS

In this section, we mention a few specialized visualizations that are able to capture data structures beyond the standard time series and cross-sectional structures—special types of relationships that are usually hard to capture with ordinary plots. In particular, we address hierarchical data, network data, and geographical data—three types of data that are becoming more available.

Visualizing Networked Data

Network analysis techniques were spawned by the explosion of social and product network data. Examples of social networks are networks of sellers and buyers on eBay and networks of Facebook users. An example of a product network is the network of products on Amazon (linked through the recommendation system). Network data visualization is available in various network-specialized software, and also in general-purpose software.

A network diagram consists of actors and relations between them. "Nodes" are the actors (e.g., people in a social network or products in a product network) and represented by circles. "Edges" are the relations between nodes, and are represented by lines connecting nodes. For example, in a social network such as Facebook, we can construct a list of users (nodes) and all the pairwise relations (edges) between users who are "Friends." Alternatively, we can define edges as a posting that one user posts on another user's Facebook page. In this setup, we might have more than a single edge between two nodes. Networks can also have nodes of multiple types. A common structure is networks with two types of nodes. An example of a two-type node network is shown in Figure 3.14, where we see a set of transactions between a network of sellers and buyers on the online auction site www.eBay.com (the data are for auctions selling Swarovski beads and took place during a period of several months; from Jank and Yahav, 2010). The circles with numerical labels represent sellers and the unlabeled circles represent buyers. Color is added by the software, but does not have meaning in this case. Each panel shows a single seller (the label is the seller's ID), with one or more buyers. We can see that this marketplace is dominated by three or four high-volume sellers. We can also see that many buyers interact with a single seller. The market structures for many individual products can be reviewed quickly in this way. Network providers can use the information, for example, to identify possible partnerships to explore with sellers.

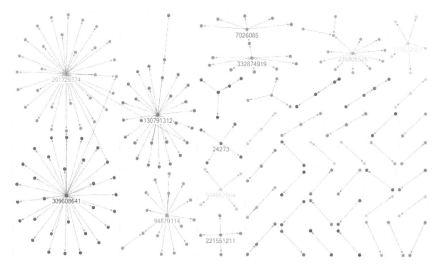

FIGURE 3.14   NETWORK GRAPH OF TRANSACTIONS BETWEEN EBAY SELLERS AND BUYERS OF SWAROVSKI BEADS. EACH PANEL SHOWS A SINGLE SELLER (THE LABEL IS THE SELLER'S ID), WITH ONE OR MORE BUYERS. PRODUCED USING NODEXL

Figure 3.14 was produced using NodeXL (www.smrfoundation.org/ nodexl), which is an Excel-based tool. The plot's appearance can be customized, and various interactive features are available such as zooming, scaling, and panning the plot, dynamically filtering nodes and edges, altering the plot's layout, finding clusters of related nodes, and calculating network metrics (see Chapter 20 for details and examples).

Network plots can be potentially useful in the context of association rules (see Chapter 15). For example, consider mining a dataset of consumers' grocery purchases to learn which items are purchased together ("what goes with what"). A network can be constructed with items as nodes and edges connecting items that were purchased together. After a set of rules is generated by the machine learning algorithm (which often contains an excessive number of rules, many of which are unimportant), the network plot can help visualize different rules for the purpose of choosing the interesting ones. For example, a popular "beer and diapers" combination would appear in the network plot as a pair of nodes with very high connectivity. An item that is almost always purchased regardless of other items (e.g., milk) would appear as a very large node with high connectivity to all other nodes.

Visualizing Hierarchical Data: Treemaps

We discussed hierarchical data and the exploration of data at different hierarchy levels in the context of plot manipulations. *Treemaps* are useful visualizations specialized for exploring large data sets that are hierarchically structured (tree-structured). They allow exploration of various dimensions of the data while maintaining the hierarchical nature of the data. An example is shown in Figure 3.15, which displays a large set of auctions from eBay.com,[5] hierarchically ordered by item category, sub-category, and brand. The levels in the hierarchy of the treemap are visualized as rectangles containing sub-rectangles. Categorical variables can be included in the display by using hue. Numerical variables can be included via rectangle size and color intensity (ordering of the rectangles is sometimes used to reinforce size). In the example in Figure 3.15 size is used to represent the average closing price (which reflects item value), and color intensity represents the percentage of sellers with negative feedback (a negative seller feedback indicates buyer dissatisfaction in past transactions and often indicative of fraudulent seller behavior). Consider the task of classifying ongoing auctions in terms of a fraudulent outcome. From the treemap, we see that the highest proportion of sellers with negative ratings (black) is concentrated in expensive item auctions (Rolex and Cartier wristwatches).

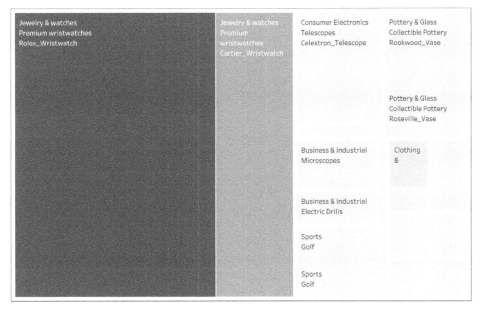

FIGURE 3.15   TREEMAP SHOWING NEARLY 11,000 EBAY AUCTIONS, ORGANIZED BY ITEM CATEGORY, SUBCATEGORY, AND BRAND. RECTANGLE SIZE REPRESENTS AVERAGE CLOSING PRICE (REFLECTING ITEM VALUE). SHADE REPRESENTS % OF SELLERS WITH NEGATIVE FEEDBACK (DARKER = HIGHER %). PRODUCED IN TABLEAU PUBLIC

Excel's treemap displays categories by color and proximity, but is limited to a single hierarchy level. ASDM currently does not offer treemaps. Ideally, treemaps should be explored interactively, zooming to different levels of the

[5]We thank Sharad Borle for sharing this dataset.

hierarchy. One example of an interactive online application of treemaps is currently available at www.drasticdata.nl. One of their examples displays player-level data from the 2014 World Cup, aggregated to team level. The user can choose to explore players and team data.

Visualizing Geographical Data: Map Charts

Many datasets used for machine learning now include geographical information. Zip codes are one example of a categorical variable with many categories, where it is not straightforward to create meaningful variables for analysis. Plotting the data on a geographic map can often reveal patterns that are harder to identify otherwise. A map chart uses a geographical map as its background, and then color, hue, and other features are used to include categorical or numerical variables. Besides specialized mapping software, maps are now becoming part of general-purpose software, and Google Maps provides APIs (application programming interfaces) that allow organizations to overlay their data on a Google map. While Google Maps is readily available, the resulting map charts (e.g., Figure 3.16) are somewhat inferior in terms of effectiveness compared to map charts in dedicated interactive visualization software.

FIGURE 3.16   MAP CHART OF STUDENTS' (ORANGE PINS) AND INSTRUCTORS' (BLUE PINS) LOCATIONS ON A GOOGLE MAP. SOURCE: FROM HTTP//STATISTICS.COM

Figure 3.17 shows two world map charts, created in Excel, comparing countries' "well-being" (according to a 2006 Gallup survey) in the top map, to gross domestic product (GDP) in the bottom map.[6] Darker shade means higher value

---

[6]Data from Veenhoven, R., World Database of Happiness, Erasmus University Rotterdam. Available at http://worlddatabaseofhappiness.eur.nl

FIGURE 3.17   WORLD MAPS COMPARING "WELL-BEING" (TOP) TO GDP (BOTTOM). SHADING BY
COUNTRY'S AVERAGE "GLOBAL WELL-BEING" SCORE (TOP) OR GDP (BOTTOM).
DARKER CORRESPONDS TO HIGHER SCORE OR LEVEL. DATA FROM VEENHOVEN'S
WORLD DATABASE OF HAPPINESS. PRODUCED USING EXCEL

(white areas are missing data). The latest versions of Excel 365 and the latest
updates for Excel 2016 provide a built-in feature to insert a map chart powered by Bing. To use the Map Charts feature in the Excel workbook, go to
Insert > Charts > Maps. You can use region, country, state, and city names
and corresponding numerical indicators. Since Excel uses Geonames for recognizing the area, these names should be spelled exactly as they are spelled
on http://www.geonames.org/. One issue to note when using this feature is
that your data is shared with Bing, which might be a concern for confidential
data.

3.6 SUMMARY: MAJOR VISUALIZATIONS AND OPERATIONS, BY MACHINE LEARNING GOAL

Prediction

- Plot outcome on the y-axis of boxplots, bar charts, scatter plots.
- Study relation of outcome to categorical predictors via side-by-side box-plots, bar charts, and multiple panels.
- Study relation of outcome to numerical predictors via scatter plots.
- Use distribution plots (boxplot, histogram) for determining needed transformations of the outcome variable (and/or numerical predictors).
- Examine scatter plots with added color/panels/size to determine the need for interaction terms.
- Use various aggregation levels and zooming to determine areas of the data with different behavior, and to evaluate the level of global vs. local patterns.

Classification

- Study relation of outcome to categorical predictors using bar charts with the outcome on the y-axis.
- Study relation of outcome to pairs of numerical predictors via color-coded scatter plots (color denotes the outcome).
- Study relation of outcome to numerical predictors via side-by-side box-plots: plot boxplots of a numerical variable by outcome. Create similar displays for each numerical predictor. The most separable boxes indicate potentially useful predictors.
- Use color to represent the outcome variable on a parallel coordinates plot.
- Use distribution plots (boxplot, histogram) for determining needed transformations of numerical predictor variables.
- Examine scatter plots with added color/panels/size to determine the need for interaction terms.
- Use various aggregation levels and zooming to determine areas of the data with different behavior, and to evaluate the level of global vs. local patterns.

Time Series Forecasting

- Create line charts at different temporal aggregations to determine types of patterns.
- Use zooming and panning to examine various shorter periods of the series to determine areas of the data with different behavior.

- Use various aggregation levels to identify global and local patterns.
- Identify missing values in the series (that will require handling).
- Overlay trend lines of different types to determine adequate modeling choices.

Unsupervised Learning

- Create scatter plot matrices to identify pairwise relationships and clustering of observations.
- Use heatmaps to examine the correlation table.
- Use various aggregation levels and zooming to determine areas of the data with different behavior.
- Generate a parallel coordinate plot to identify clusters of observations.

PROBLEMS

3.1 **Shipments of Household Appliances: Line Charts.** The file ApplianceShipments.xlsx contains the series of quarterly shipments (in millions of dollars) of US household appliances between 1985 and 1989.

    a. Create a well-formatted time plot of the data using Excel.

    b. Does there appear to be a quarterly pattern? For a closer view of the patterns, zoom in to the range of 3500–5000 on the y-axis.

    c. Using Excel, create one chart with four separate lines, one line for each of Q1, Q2, Q3, and Q4. In Excel this can be achieved by sorting the data by Q1, Q2, Q3, Q4 (alphabetical sorting will work), and then plotting them as separate series on the line graph. Zoom in to the range of 3500–5000 on the y-axis. Does there appear to be a difference between quarters?

    d. Using Excel, create a line graph of the series at a yearly aggregated level (i.e., the total shipments in each year).

    e. Re-create the plots above using an interactive visualization tool. Be sure to enter the quarter information in a format that is recognized by the software as a date.

    f. Compare the two processes of generating the line graphs in terms of effort as well as the quality of the resulting plots. What are the advantages of each?

3.2 **Sales of Riding Mowers: Scatter Plots.** A company that manufactures riding mowers wants to identify the best sales prospects for an intensive sales campaign. In particular, the manufacturer is interested in classifying households as prospective owners or nonowners on the basis of Income (in $1000s) and Lot Size (in 1000 ft^2). The marketing expert looked at a random sample of 24 households, given in the file RidingMowers.xlsx.

    a. Using Excel, create a scatter plot of Lot Size vs. Income, color coded by the outcome variable owner/nonowner. Make sure to obtain a well-formatted plot (remove excessive background and gridlines; create legible labels and a legend, etc.). *Hint:* First sort the data by the outcome variable, and then plot the data for each category as separate series.

    b. Create the same plot, this time using ASDM or an interactive visualization tool.

    c. Compare the two processes of generating the plot in terms of effort as well as the quality of the resulting plots. What are the advantages of each? Explain.

3.3 **Laptop Sales at a London Computer Chain: Bar Charts and Boxplots.** The file LaptopSalesJanuary2008.xlsx contains data for all sales of laptops at a computer chain in London in January 2008. This is a subset of the full dataset that includes data for the entire year.

    a. Create a bar chart, showing the average retail price by store. Which store has the highest average? Which has the lowest?

    b. To better compare retail prices across stores, create side-by-side boxplots of retail price by store. Now compare the prices in the two stores from (a). Does there seem to be a difference between their price distributions?

3.4 **Laptop Sales at a London Computer Chain: Interactive Visualization.** The next exercises are designed for using an interactive visualization tool. The file Laptop-Sales.txt is a comma-separated file with nearly 300,000 rows. ENBIS (the European Network for Business and Industrial Statistics) provided these data as part of a contest organized in the fall of 2009.

Scenario: Imagine that you are a new analyst for a company called Acell (a company selling laptops). You have been provided with data about products and sales. You need to help the company with their business goal of planning a product strategy and pricing policies that will maximize Acell's projected revenues in 2009. Using an interactive visualization tool, answer the following questions.

a. **Price Questions:**

   i. At what price are the laptops actually selling?

   ii. Does price change with time? (*Hint:* Make sure that the date column is recognized as such. The software should then enable different temporal aggregation choices, e.g., plotting the data by weekly or monthly aggregates, or even by day of week.)

   iii. Are prices consistent across retail outlets?

   iv. How does price change with configuration?

b. **Location Questions:**

   i. Where are the stores and customers located?

   ii. Which stores are selling the most?

   iii. How far would customers travel to buy a laptop?

   ○ *Hint 1:* You should be able to aggregate the data; for example, plot the sum or average of the prices.

   ○ *Hint 2:* Use the coordinated highlighting between multiple visualizations in the same page; for example, select a store in one view to see the matching customers in another visualization.

   ○ *Hint 3:* Explore the use of filters to see differences. Make sure to filter in the zoomed-out view; for example, try to use a "store location" slider as an alternative way to dynamically compare store locations. It might be more useful to spot outlier patterns if there were 50 store locations to compare.

   iv. Try an alternative way of looking at how far customers traveled. Do this by creating a new data column that computes the distance between customer and store.

c. **Revenue Questions:**

   i. How does the sales volume in each store relate to Acell's revenues?

   ii. How does this relationship depend on the configuration?

d. **Configuration Questions:**

   i. What are the details of each configuration? How does this relate to price?

   ii. Do all stores sell all configurations?

## CHAPTER 4

Dimension Reduction

In this chapter, we describe the important step of dimension reduction. The dimension of a dataset, which is the number of variables, must be reduced for the machine learning algorithms to operate efficiently. This process is part of the pilot/prototype phase of machine learning and is done before deploying a model. We present and discuss several dimension reduction approaches: (1) incorporating domain knowledge to remove or combine categories, (2) using data summaries to detect information overlap between variables (and remove or combine redundant variables or categories), (3) using data conversion techniques such as converting categorical variables into numerical variables, and (4) employing automated reduction techniques such as principal component analysis (PCA), where a new set of variables (which are weighted averages of the original variables) is created. These new variables are uncorrelated, and a small subset of them usually contains most of their combined information. Hence, we can reduce dimension by using only a subset of the new variables. Finally, we mention supervised learning methods such as regression models and classification and regression trees, which can be used for removing redundant variables and for combining "similar" categories of categorical variables.

4.1 INTRODUCTION

In machine learning, one often encounters situations where there are a large number of variables in the database. Even when the initial number of variables is small, this set quickly expands in the data preparation step, where new derived variables are created (e.g., dummies for categorical variables and new forms of existing variables). In such situations, it is likely that subsets of variables are highly correlated with each other. Including highly correlated variables

Machine Learning for Business Analytics: Concepts, Techniques, and Applications with Analytic Solver® Data Mining, Fourth Edition. Galit Shmueli, Peter C. Bruce, Kuber R. Deokar, and Nitin R. Patel
© 2023 John Wiley & Sons, Inc. Published 2023 by John Wiley & Sons, Inc.

in a classification or prediction model, or including variables that are unrelated to the outcome of interest, can lead to overfitting, and accuracy and reliability can suffer. A large number of variables also pose computational problems for some supervised as well as unsupervised algorithms (aside from questions of correlation). In model deployment, superfluous variables can increase costs due to the collection and processing of these variables.

4.2 CURSE OF DIMENSIONALITY

The *dimensionality* of a model is the number of predictors or input variables used by the model. The *curse of dimensionality* is the affliction caused by adding variables to multivariate data models. As variables are added, the data space becomes increasingly sparse, and classification and prediction models fail because the available data are insufficient to provide a useful model across so many variables. An important consideration is the fact that the difficulties posed by adding a variable increase exponentially with the addition of each variable. One way to think of this intuitively is to consider the location of an object on a chessboard. It has two dimensions and 64 squares or choices. If you expand the chessboard to a cube, you increase the dimensions by 50%—from two dimensions to three dimensions. However, the location options increase by 800%, to 512 ($8 \times 8 \times 8$). In statistical distance terms, the proliferation of variables means that nothing is close to anything else anymore—too much noise has been added and patterns and structure are no longer discernible. The problem is particularly acute in Big Data applications, including genomics, for example, where an analysis might have to deal with values for thousands of different genes. One of the key steps in machine learning, therefore, is finding ways to reduce dimensionality with minimal sacrifice of accuracy. In the artificial intelligence literature, dimension reduction is often referred to as *factor selection*, *feature selection*, or *feature extraction*.

4.3 PRACTICAL CONSIDERATIONS

Although machine learning prefers automated methods over domain knowledge, it is important at the first step of data exploration to make sure that the variables measured are reasonable for the task at hand. The integration of expert knowledge through a discussion with the data provider (or user) will probably lead to better results. Practical considerations include: Which variables are most important for the task at hand, and which are most likely to be useless? Which variables are likely to contain much error? Which variables will be available for measurement (and what will it cost to measure them) in the future if the analysis is repeated? Which variables can actually be measured before the outcome occurs? For example, if we want to predict the closing price of an ongoing online auction, we cannot use the number of bids as a predictor because this will not be known until the auction closes.

Example 1: House Prices in Boston

We return to the Boston housing example introduced in Chapter 3. For each neighborhood, a number of variables are given, such as the crime rate, the student/teacher ratio, and the median value of a housing unit in the neighborhood. A description of all 14 variables is given in Table 4.1. The first nine records of the data are shown in Table 4.2. The first row represents the first neighborhood, which had an average per capita crime rate of 0.006, 18% of the residential land zoned for lots over 25,000 ft^2, 2.31% of the land devoted to nonretail business, no border on the Charles River, and so on.

TABLE 4.1   **DESCRIPTION OF VARIABLES IN THE BOSTON HOUSING DATASET**

CRIM	Crime rate
ZN	Percentage of residential land zoned for lots over 25,000 ft^2
INDUS	Percentage of land occupied by nonretail business
CHAS	Does tract bound Charles River (=1 if tract bounds river, =0 otherwise)
NOX	Nitric oxide concentration (parts per 10 million)
RM	Average number of rooms per dwelling
AGE	Percentage of owner-occupied units built prior to 1940
DIS	Weighted distances to five Boston employment centers
RAD	Index of accessibility to radial highways
TAX	Full-value property tax rate per $10,000
PTRATIO	Pupil-to-teacher ratio by town
LSTAT	Percentage of lower status of the population
MEDV	Median value of owner-occupied homes in $1000s
CAT.MEDV	Is median value of owner-occupied homes in tract above $30,000 (CAT.MEDV = 1) or not (CAT.MEDV = 0)

TABLE 4.2   **FIRST NINE RECORDS IN THE BOSTON HOUSING DATA**

CRIM	ZN	INDUS	CHAS	NOX	RM	AGE	DIS	RAD	TAX	PTRATIO	LSTAT	MEDV	CAT.MEDV
0.00632	18.0	2.31	0	0.538	6.575	65.2	4.09	1	296	15.3	4.98	24.0	0
0.02731	0.0	7.07	0	0.469	6.421	78.9	4.9671	2	242	17.8	9.14	21.6	0
0.02729	0.0	7.07	0	0.469	7.185	61.1	4.9671	2	242	17.8	4.03	34.7	1
0.03237	0.0	2.18	0	0.458	6.998	45.8	6.0622	3	222	18.7	2.94	33.4	1
0.06905	0.0	2.18	0	0.458	7.147	54.2	6.0622	3	222	18.7	5.33	36.2	1
0.02985	0.0	2.18	0	0.458	6.43	58.7	6.0622	3	222	18.7	5.21	28.7	0
0.08829	12.5	7.87	0	0.524	6.012	66.6	5.5605	5	311	15.2	12.43	22.9	0
0.14455	12.5	7.87	0	0.524	6.172	96.1	5.9505	5	311	15.2	19.15	27.1	0
0.21124	12.5	7.87	0	0.524	5.631	100.0	6.0821	5	311	15.2	29.93	16.5	0

4.4 DATA SUMMARIES

As we have seen in the chapter on data visualization, an important initial step of data exploration is getting familiar with the data and their characteristics through summaries and graphs. The importance of this step cannot be overstated. The better you understand the data, the better will be the results from the modeling or mining process.

Numerical summaries and graphs of the data are very helpful for data reduction. The information that they convey can assist in combining categories of a categorical variable, in choosing variables to remove, in assessing the level of information overlap between variables, and more. Before discussing such strategies for reducing the dimension of a data set, let us consider useful summaries and tools.

Summary Statistics

Excel has several functions and facilities that assist in summarizing data. The functions *average, stdev, min, max, median,* and *count* are very helpful for learning about the characteristics of each variable. First, they give us information about the scale and type of values that the variable takes. The min and max functions can be used to detect extreme values that might be errors. The average and median give a sense of the central values of that variable, and a large deviation between the two also indicates skew. The standard deviation gives a sense of how dispersed the data are (relative to the mean). Other functions, such as *countblank,* which gives the number of empty cells, can alert us about missing values. It is also possible to use Excel's *Descriptive Statistics* facility in the *Data > Data Analysis* menu. This will generate a set of 13 summary statistics for each of the variables.

Figure 4.1 shows six summary statistics for the Boston housing example. We immediately see that the different variables have very different ranges of values. We will soon see how variation in scale across variables can distort analyses if

	Average	Median	Min	Max	Std	Count	Countblank
CRIM	3.61	0.26	0.01	88.98	8.60	506	0
ZN	11.36	0.00	0.00	100.00	23.32	506	0
INDUS	11.14	9.69	0.46	27.74	6.86	506	0
CHAS	0.07	0.00	0.00	1.00	0.25	506	0
NOX	0.55	0.54	0.39	0.87	0.12	506	0
RM	6.28	6.21	3.56	8.78	0.70	506	0
AGE	68.57	77.50	2.90	100.00	28.15	506	0
DIS	3.80	3.21	1.13	12.13	2.11	506	0
RAD	9.55	5.00	1.00	24.00	8.71	506	0
TAX	408.24	330.00	187.00	711.00	168.54	506	0
PTRATIO	18.46	19.05	12.60	22.00	2.16	506	0
LSTAT	12.65	11.36	1.73	37.97	7.14	506	0
MEDV	22.53	21.20	5.00	50.00	9.20	506	0

FIGURE 4.1 SUMMARY STATISTICS FOR THE BOSTON HOUSING DATA

not treated properly. Another observation that can be made is that the average of the first variable, CRIM (as well as several others), is much larger than the median, indicating right skew. None of the variables have empty cells. There also do not appear to be indications of extreme values that might result from typing errors. Next, we summarize relationships between two or more variables. For numerical variables, we can compute pairwise correlations (using the Excel function *correl*). We can also obtain a complete matrix of correlations between each pair of variables in the data using Excel's *Correlation* facility in the *Data >
Data Analysis* menu.

Figure 4.2 shows the correlation matrix for a subset of the Boston housing variables. We see that most correlations are low and that many are negative. Recall also the visual display of a correlation matrix via a heatmap (see Figure 3.4 in Chapter 3 for the heatmap corresponding to this correlation table). We will return to the importance of the correlation matrix soon, in the context of correlation analysis.

	CRIM	ZN	INDUS	CHAS	NOX	RM	AGE	DIS	RAD	TAX	PTRATIO	LSTAT	MEDV
CRIM	1.00												
ZN	-0.20	1.00											
INDUS	0.41	-0.53	1.00										
CHAS	-0.06	-0.04	0.06	1.00									
NOX	0.42	-0.52	0.76	0.09	1.00								
RM	-0.22	0.31	-0.39	0.09	-0.30	1.00							
AGE	0.35	-0.57	0.64	0.09	0.73	-0.24	1.00						
DIS	-0.38	0.66	-0.71	-0.10	-0.77	0.21	-0.75	1.00					
RAD	0.63	-0.31	0.60	-0.01	0.61	-0.21	0.46	-0.49	1.00				
TAX	0.58	-0.31	0.72	-0.04	0.67	-0.29	0.51	-0.53	0.91	1.00			
PTRATIO	0.29	-0.39	0.38	-0.12	0.19	-0.36	0.26	-0.23	0.46	0.46	1.00		
LSTAT	0.46	-0.41	0.60	-0.05	0.59	-0.61	0.60	-0.50	0.49	0.54	0.37	1.00	
MEDV	-0.39	0.36	-0.48	0.18	-0.43	0.70	-0.38	0.25	-0.38	-0.47	-0.51	-0.74	1.00

FIGURE 4.2   CORRELATION TABLE FOR BOSTON HOUSING DATA, GENERATED USING EXCEL'S DATA ANALYSIS MENU

Pivot Tables

Another very useful tool is Excel's *pivot tables*, available from the *Insert* menu. These are interactive tables that can combine information from multiple variables and compute a range of summary statistics (count, average, percentage, etc.). A simple example is the average MEDV for neighborhoods that bound the Charles River vs. those that do not (the variable CHAS is chosen as the column area). First, we get a count of neighborhoods bordering the river. This is shown in the top panel of Figure 4.3. The Excel pivot table was obtained by selecting CHAS as a "row labels" field and MEDV as a "values" field (using the "count" summary). It appears that the majority of neighborhoods (471 of 506) do not bound the river. By double-clicking on a certain cell, the complete data for records in that cell are shown on a new worksheet. For instance, double-clicking on the cell containing 471 will display the complete records of neighborhoods that do not bound the river. Pivot tables can be used for multiple variables. For categorical variables, we obtain a breakdown of the records by the combination of categories. For instance, the bottom panel of Figure 4.3 shows the average MEDV by CHAS (row) and RM (column). Note that the numerical variable RM (the average number of rooms per dwelling in the neighborhood) is grouped into bins of 3–4, 5–6, and so on. Excel's bin notation means that the lower number is included, and all values up to but not including the higher number. So 3–4 includes only three rooms and not four. Note also the empty cells, denoting that there are no neighborhoods in the dataset with those combinations (e.g., bounding the river and having on average three rooms). There are many more possibilities and options for using Excel's pivot tables. We leave it to the reader to explore these using Excel's documentation.

CHAS	Count of MEDV
0	471
1	35
Grand Total	506

Average of MEDV	CHAS		
RM	0	1	Grand Total
3-4	25.3		25.3
4-5	16.023077		16.02307692
5-6	17.133333	22.21818182	17.48734177
6-7	21.76917	25.91875	22.01598513
7-8	35.964444	44.06666667	36.91764706
8-9	45.7	35.95	44.2
Grand Total	22.093843	28.44	22.53280632

FIGURE 4.3   PIVOT TABLES FOR THE BOSTON HOUSING DATA

In classification tasks, where the goal is to find predictor variables that do a good job of distinguishing between two classes, a good exploratory step is to produce summaries for each class. This can assist in detecting useful predictors that display some separation between the two classes. Data summaries are useful for almost any machine learning task and are therefore an important preliminary step for cleaning and understanding the data before carrying out further analyses.

4.5 CORRELATION ANALYSIS

In datasets with a large number of variables (which are likely to serve as predictors), there is usually much overlap in the information covered by the set of variables. One simple way to find redundancies is to look at a correlation matrix.

This shows all the pairwise correlations between variables. Pairs that have a very strong (positive or negative) correlation contain a lot of overlap in information and are good candidates for data reduction by removing one of the variables. Removing variables that are strongly correlated to others is useful for avoiding multicollinearity problems that can arise in various models. (*Multicollinearity* is the presence of two or more predictors sharing the same linear relationship with the outcome variable.)

Correlation analysis is also a good method for detecting duplications of variables in the data. Sometimes the same variable appears accidentally more than once in the dataset (under a different name) because the dataset was merged from multiple sources, the same phenomenon is measured in different units, and so on. Using correlation table heatmaps, as shown in Chapter 3, can make the task of identifying strong correlations easier.

4.6 REDUCING THE NUMBER OF CATEGORIES IN CATEGORICAL VARIABLES

When a categorical variable has many categories, and this variable is destined to be a predictor, many machine learning methods will require converting it into many dummy variables. In particular, a variable with m categories will be transformed into either m or $m - 1$ dummy variables (depending on the method). This means that even if we have very few original categorical variables, they can greatly inflate the dimension of the dataset. One way to handle this is to reduce the number of categories by combining close or similar categories. Combining categories requires incorporating expert knowledge and common sense. Pivot tables are useful for this task. With pivot tables, we can examine the sizes of the various categories and how the response behaves at each category. Generally, categories that contain very few observations are good candidates for combining with other categories. Use only the categories that are most relevant to the analysis, and label the rest as "other." In classification tasks (with a categorical output), a pivot table broken down by the output classes can help identify categories that do not separate the classes. Those categories too are candidates for inclusion in the "other" category.

An example is shown in Figure 4.4, where the distribution of output variable CAT.MEDV is broken down by ZN (treated here as a categorical variable). We can see that the distribution of CAT.MEDV is identical for ZN = 17.5, 90, 95, and 100 (where all neighborhoods have CAT.MEDV = 1). These four categories can then be combined into a single category. Similarly categories ZN = 12.5, 25, 28, 30, and 70 can be combined. Further combination is also possible based on similar bars.

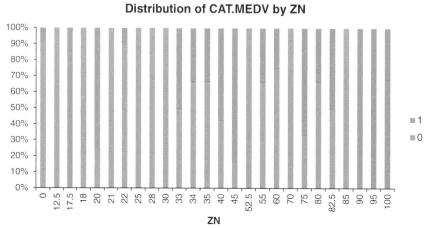

FIGURE 4.4   DISTRIBUTION OF CAT.MEDV (BLUE DENOTES CAT.MEDV = 0) BY ZN. SIMILAR BARS INDICATE LOW SEPARATION BETWEEN CLASSES, AND CAN BE COMBINED

In a time series context where we might have a categorical variable denoting season (e.g., month or hour of day) that will serve as a predictor, reducing categories can be done by examining the time series plot and identifying similar periods. For example, the time plot in Figure 4.5 shows the quarterly revenues of Toys "R" Us between 1992 and 1995. Only quarter 4 periods appear different, and therefore we can combine quarters 1–3 into a single category.

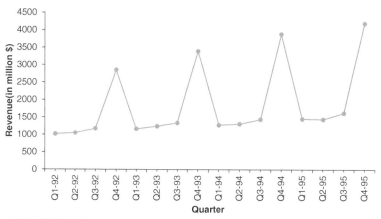

FIGURE 4.5   QUARTERLY REVENUES OF TOYS "R" US, 1992–1995

4.7 CONVERTING A CATEGORICAL VARIABLE TO A NUMERICAL VARIABLE

Sometimes the categories in a categorical variable represent intervals. Common examples are age group or income bracket. If the interval values are known (e.g., category 2 is the age interval 20–30), we can replace the categorical value

("2" in the example) with the mid-interval value (here "25"). The result will be a numerical variable that no longer requires multiple dummy variables.

4.8 PRINCIPAL COMPONENT ANALYSIS

Principal component analysis (PCA) is a useful method for dimension reduction, especially when the number of variables is large. PCA is especially valuable when we have subsets of measurements that are measured on the same scale and are highly correlated. In that case it provides a few variables (often as few as three) that are weighted linear combinations of the original variables, and that retain the majority of the information of the full original set. PCA is intended for use with quantitative variables. For categorical variables, other methods, such as correspondence analysis, are more suitable.

Example 2: Breakfast Cereals

Data were collected on the nutritional information and consumer rating of 77 breakfast cereals.[1] The consumer rating is a rating of cereal "healthiness" for consumer information (not a rating by consumers). For each cereal the data include 13 numerical variables, and we are interested in reducing this dimension. For each cereal the information is based on a bowl of cereal rather than a serving size, since most people simply fill a cereal bowl (resulting in constant volume, but not weight). A snapshot of these data is given in Table 4.3, and the description of the different variables is given in Table 4.4.

We focus first on two variables: *calories* and *consumer rating*. These are given in Table 4.5. The average calories across the 77 cereals is 106.88 with standard deviation 19.48. The average consumer rating is 42.67 with standard deviation 14.05.

The two variables are strongly correlated with a negative correlation of −0.69. Roughly speaking, 69% of the total variation in both variables is actually "co-variation," or variation in one variable that is duplicated by similar variation in the other variable. Can we use this fact to reduce the number of variables, while making maximum use of their unique contributions to the overall variation? Since there is redundancy in the information that the two variables contain, it might be possible to reduce the two variables to a single variable without losing too much information. The idea in PCA is to find a linear combination of the two variables that contains most, even if not all, of the information, so that this new variable can replace the two original variables. Information here is in the sense of variability: What can explain the most variability *among* the 77 cereals? The total variability here is the sum of the variances[2] of the two variables,

---

[1] The data are available at https://dasl.datadescription.com/datafile/cereals/
[2] The variance is the squared standard deviation.

TABLE 4.3   SAMPLE FROM THE 77 BREAKFAST CEREALS DATASET

Cereal name	mfr	Type	Calories	Protein	Fat	Sodium	Fiber	Carbo	Sugars	Potass	Vitamins
100% Bran	N	C	70	4	1	130	10	5	6	280	25
100% Natural Bran	Q	C	120	3	5	15	2	8	8	135	0
All-Bran	K	C	70	4	1	260	9	7	5	320	25
All-Bran with Extra Fiber	K	C	50	4	0	140	14	8	0	330	25
Almond Delight	R	C	110	2	2	200	1	14	8		25
Apple Cinnamon Cheerios	G	C	110	2	2	180	1.5	10.5	10	70	25
Apple Jacks	K	C	110	2	0	125	1	11	14	30	25
Basic 4	G	C	130	3	2	210	2	18	8	100	25
Bran Chex	R	C	90	2	1	200	4	15	6	125	25
Bran Flakes	P	C	90	3	0	210	5	13	5	190	25
Cap'n'Crunch	Q	C	120	1	2	220	0	12	12	35	25
Cheerios	G	C	110	6	2	290	2	17	1	105	25
Cinnamon Toast Crunch	G	C	120	1	3	210	0	13	9	45	25
Clusters	G	C	110	3	2	140	2	13	7	105	25
Cocoa Puffs	G	C	110	1	1	180	0	12	13	55	25
Corn Chex	R	C	110	2	0	280	0	22	3	25	25
Corn Flakes	K	C	100	2	0	290	1	21	2	35	25
Corn Pops	K	C	110	1	0	90	1	13	12	20	25
Count Chocula	G	C	110	1	1	180	0	12	13	65	25
Cracklin' Oat Bran	K	C	110	3	3	140	4	10	7	160	25

TABLE 4.4   DESCRIPTION OF THE VARIABLES IN THE BREAKFAST CEREAL DATASET

Variable	Description
mfr	Manufacturer of cereal (American Home Food Products, General Mills, Kellogg, etc.)
type	Cold or hot
calories	Calories per serving
protein	Grams of protein
fat	Grams of fat
sodium	Milligrams of sodium
fiber	Grams of dietary fiber
carbo	Grams of complex carbohydrates
sugars	Grams of sugars
potass	Milligrams of potassium
vitamins	Vitamins and minerals: 0, 25, or 100, indicating the typical percentage of FDA recommended
shelf	Display shelf (1, 2, or 3, counting from the floor)
weight	Weight in ounces of one serving
cups	Number of cups in one serving
rating	Rating of the cereal calculated by Consumer Reports

which in this case is $19.48^2 + 14.05^2 = 576.87$. This means that *calories* accounts for $66\% = 19.48^2/567.87$ of the total variability, and *rating* for the remaining 34%. If we drop one of the variables for the sake of dimension reduction, we lose at least 34% of the total variability. Can we redistribute the total variability between two new variables in a more polarized way? If so, it might be possible to keep only the one new variable that (hopefully) accounts for a large portion of the total variation.

TABLE 4.5   CEREAL CALORIES AND RATINGS

Cereal	Calories	Rating	Cereal	Calories	Rating
100% Bran	70	68.40297	Just Right Fruit & Nut	140	36.471512
100% Natural Bran	120	33.98368	Kix	110	39.241114
All-Bran	70	59.42551	Life	100	45.328074
All-Bran with Extra Fiber	50	93.70491	Lucky Charms	110	26.734515
Almond Delight	110	34.38484	Maypo	100	54.850917
Apple Cinnamon Cheerios	110	29.50954	Muesli Raisins, Dates & Almonds	150	37.136863
Apple Jacks	110	33.17409	Muesli Raisins, Peaches & Pecans	150	34.139765
Basic 4	130	37.03856	Mueslix Crispy Blend	160	30.313351
Bran Chex	90	49.12025	Multi-Grain Cheerios	100	40.105965
Bran Flakes	90	53.31381	Nut&Honey Crunch	120	29.924285
Cap'n'Crunch	120	18.04285	Nutri-Grain Almond-Raisin	140	40.69232
Cheerios	110	50.765	Nutri-grain Wheat	90	59.642837
Cinnamon Toast Crunch	120	19.82357	Oatmeal Raisin Crisp	130	30.450843
Clusters	110	40.40021	Post Nat. Raisin Bran	120	37.840594
Cocoa Puffs	110	22.73645	Product 19	100	41.50354
Corn Chex	110	41.44502	Puffed Rice	50	60.756112
Corn Flakes	100	45.86332	Puffed Wheat	50	63.005645
Corn Pops	110	35.78279	Quaker Oat Squares	100	49.511874
Count Chocula	110	22.39651	Quaker Oatmeal	100	50.828392
Cracklin' Oat Bran	110	40.44877	Raisin Bran	120	39.259197
Cream of Wheat (Quick)	100	64.53382	Raisin Nut Bran	100	39.7034
Crispix	110	46.89564	Raisin Squares	90	55.333142
Crispy Wheat & Raisins	100	36.1762	Rice Chex	110	41.998933
Double Chex	100	44.33086	Rice Krispies	110	40.560159
Froot Loops	110	32.20758	Shredded Wheat	80	68.235885
Frosted Flakes	110	31.43597	Shredded Wheat 'n'Bran	90	74.472949
Frosted Mini-Wheats	100	58.34514	Shredded Wheat spoon size	90	72.801787
Fruit & Fibre Dates, Walnuts & Oats	120	40.91705	Smacks	110	31.230054
Fruitful Bran	120	41.01549	Special K	110	53.131324
Fruity Pebbles	110	28.02577	Strawberry Fruit Wheats	90	59.363993
Golden Crisp	100	35.25244	Total Corn Flakes	110	38.839746
Golden Grahams	110	23.80404	Total Raisin Bran	140	28.592785
Grape Nuts Flakes	100	52.0769	Total Whole Grain	100	46.658844
Grape-Nuts	110	53.37101	Triples	110	39.106174
Great Grains Pecan	120	45.81172	Trix	110	27.753301
Honey Graham Ohs	120	21.87129	Wheat Chex	100	49.787445
Honey Nut Cheerios	110	31.07222	Wheaties	100	51.592193
Honey-comb	110	28.74241	Wheaties Honey Gold	110	36.187559
Just Right Crunchy Nuggets	110	36.52368			

Figure 4.6 shows a scatter plot of *rating* vs. *calories*. The line z_1 is the direction in which the variability of the points is largest. It is the line that captures the most variation in the data if we decide to reduce the dimensionality of the data from two to one. Among all possible lines, it is the line for which, if we project the points in the dataset orthogonally to get a set of 77 (one-dimensional) values, the variance of the z_1 values will be maximal. This is called the *first principal component*. It is also the line that minimizes the sum-of-squared perpendicular distances from the line. The z_2-axis is chosen to be perpendicular to the z_1-axis. In the case of two variables, there is only one line that is perpendicular to z_1, and it has the second largest variability, but its information is uncorrelated with z_1. This is called the *second principal component*. In general, when we have more than two variables, once we find the direction z_1 with the largest variability, we search among all the orthogonal directions to z_1 for the one with the next-highest variability. That is z_2. The idea is then to find the coordinates of these lines and to see how they redistribute the variability.

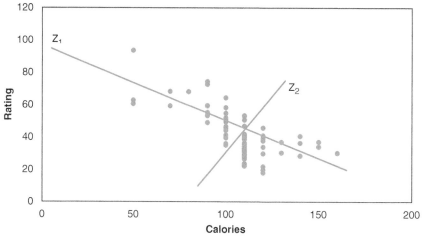

FIGURE 4.6   SCATTER PLOT OF *RATING* VS. *CALORIES* FOR 77 BREAKFAST CEREALS, WITH THE TWO PRINCIPAL COMPONENT DIRECTIONS

Figure 4.7 shows the ASDM output from running PCA on these two variables. The principal components table gives the weights that are used to project the original points onto the two new directions. The weights for z_1 are given by $(-0.847, 0.532)$, and for z_2 they are given by $(-0.532, -0.847)$. Figure 4.7 gives the reallocated variance: z_1 accounts for 86% of the total variability and z_2 for the remaining 14%. Therefore, if we drop z_2, we still maintain 86% of the total variability. The weights are used to compute principal component scores, which are the projected values of *calories* and *rating* onto the new axes (after subtracting the means). Figure 4.8 shows the scores for the two dimensions. The first column is the projection onto z_1 using the weights $(-0.847, 0.532)$. The second column is the projection onto z_2 using the weights $(-0.532, -0.847)$. For example,

Principal Components

Feature\Component	Component 1	Component 2
calories	-0.847053	-0.531508
rating	0.531508	-0.847053

Explained Variance

Component	Eigenvalue	Variance, %	Cumulative Variance, %
Component 1	498.02448	86.319135	86.319135
Component 2	78.932739	13.680865	100

FIGURE 4.7   OUTPUT FROM PRINCIPAL COMPONENT ANALYSIS OF *CALORIES* AND *RATING*

Record ID	Name	Comp1	Comp2
Record 1	100%_Bran	44.92152782	-2.197183255
Record 2	100%_Natural_Bran	-15.72526488	0.38241646
Record 3	All-Bran	40.14993478	5.407212287
Record 4	All-Bran_with_Extra_Fiber	75.31077196	-12.99912556
Record 5	Almond_Delight	-7.041508307	5.35768573
Record 6	Apple_Cinnamon_Cheerios	-9.632768681	9.487327272
Record 7	Apple_Jacks	-7.685030678	6.383254888
Record 8	Basic_4	-22.57210599	-7.520309459
Record 9	Bran_Chex	17.7315447	3.506158625
Record 10	Bran_Flakes	19.96045398	-0.046010981
Record 11	Cap'n'Crunch	-24.19793712	13.88515035
Record 12	Cheerios	1.664670134	-8.51718247
Record 13	Cinnamon_Toast_Crunch	-23.25146973	12.37678357
Record 14	Clusters	-3.844295711	0.262349852
Record 15	Cocoa_Puffs	-13.23272058	15.22450099
Record 16	Corn_Chex	-3.288970658	-0.622660945
Record 17	Corn_Flakes	7.529927143	0.949875047

FIGURE 4.8   PRINCIPAL SCORES FROM PRINCIPAL COMPONENT ANALYSIS OF *CALORIES* AND *RATING* FOR THE FIRST 17 CEREALS

the first score for the 100% Bran cereal (with 70 calories and a rating of 68.4) is $(-0.847)(70 - 106.88) + (0.532)(68.4 - 42.67) = 44.92$.

Note that the means of the new variables z_1 and z_2 are zero, since we've subtracted the mean of each variable. The sum of the variances $\text{var}(z_1) + \text{var}(z_2)$ is equal to the sum of the variances of the original variables, var*(calories)* + var*(rating)*. Furthermore the variances of z_1 and z_2 are 498 and 79, respectively, so the first principal component, z_1, accounts for 86% of the total variance. Since it captures most of the variability in the data, it seems reasonable to use one variable, the first principal score, to represent the two variables in the original data. Next, we generalize these ideas to more than two variables.

Principal Components

Let us formalize the procedure described above so that it can easily be generalized to $p > 2$ variables. Denote by $X_1, X_2, \ldots, X_p$ the original p variables. In PCA we are looking for a set of new variables $Z_1, Z_2, \ldots, Z_p$ that are weighted averages of the original variables (after subtracting their mean):

$$Z_i = a_{i,1}(X_1 - \bar{X}_1) + a_{i,2}(X_2 - \bar{X}_2) + \cdots + a_{i,p}(X_p - \bar{X}_p), \quad i = 1, \ldots, p,$$

$$(4.1)$$

where each pair of Z's has correlation $= 0$. We then order the resulting Z's by their variance, with Z_1 having the largest variance and Z_p having the smallest variance. The software computes the weights $a_{i,j}$, which are then used in computing the principal component scores.

A further advantage of the principal components compared to the original data is that they are uncorrelated (correlation coefficient $= 0$). If we construct regression models using these principal components as independent variables, we will not encounter problems of multicollinearity.

Let us return to the breakfast cereal dataset with all 15 variables, and apply PCA to the 13 numerical variables. The resulting output is shown in Figure 4.9. For simplicity, we removed three cereals that contained missing values.

Principal Components

Feature\Component	Component 1	Component 2	Component 3	Component 4	Component 5	Component 6	Component 7
calories	-0.078	0.009	0.629	0.601	0.455	-0.119	0.094
protein	0.001	-0.009	0.001	-0.003	0.056	-0.113	0.258
fat	0.000	-0.003	0.016	0.025	-0.016	0.132	0.373
sodium	-0.980	-0.141	-0.136	0.001	0.014	-0.023	0.005
fiber	0.005	-0.031	-0.018	-0.020	0.014	-0.263	0.043
carbo	-0.017	0.017	0.017	-0.026	0.349	0.538	-0.672
sugars	-0.003	0.000	0.098	0.115	-0.299	-0.648	-0.567
potass	0.135	-0.987	0.037	0.042	-0.047	0.050	-0.018
vitamins	-0.094	-0.017	0.692	-0.714	-0.037	-0.016	0.012
shelf	0.002	-0.004	0.012	-0.006	-0.008	0.060	0.092
weight	-0.001	-0.001	0.004	0.003	0.003	-0.009	-0.024
cups	-0.001	0.002	0.001	-0.001	0.002	0.010	-0.020
rating	0.075	-0.072	-0.308	-0.335	0.758	-0.413	0.018

Component 8	Component 9	Component 10	Component 11	Component 12	Component 13
0.026	-0.009	0.065	-0.009	-0.004	-0.042
-0.655	0.202	-0.256	0.045	0.005	0.616
0.118	-0.124	-0.841	0.062	0.009	-0.318
-0.001	0.004	-0.001	0.000	0.000	-0.010
0.659	-0.227	-0.144	-0.021	-0.001	0.648
-0.006	0.025	-0.300	0.042	-0.014	0.206
-0.103	0.117	-0.320	0.028	-0.019	-0.136
-0.015	-0.001	0.006	0.000	-0.001	-0.006
-0.004	-0.012	0.001	0.002	-0.001	-0.010
0.328	0.935	-0.046	-0.068	0.010	0.000
0.003	-0.002	0.006	0.093	0.995	0.000
-0.062	-0.054	-0.080	-0.989	0.092	0.000
-0.012	0.036	-0.023	-0.003	-0.003	-0.188

Explained Variance

Component	Eigenvalue	Variance, %	Cumulative Variance, %
Component 1	7016.42	53.95	53.95
Component 2	5028.83	38.67	92.62
Component 3	512.74	3.94	96.56
Component 4	367.93	2.83	99.39
Component 5	70.95	0.55	99.93
Component 6	4.38	0.03	99.97
Component 7	2.89	0.02	99.99
Component 8	0.61	0.00	100.00
Component 9	0.43	0.00	100.00
Component 10	0.14	0.00	100.00
Component 11	0.03	0.00	100.00
Component 12	0.00	0.00	100.00
Component 13	0.00	0.00	100.00

FIGURE 4.9   PCA OUTPUT USING ALL 13 NUMERICAL VARIABLES IN THE BREAKFAST CEREALS DATASET

Note that the first three components account for more than 96% of the total variation associated with all 13 of the original variables. This suggests that we can capture most of the variability in the data with less than 25% of the number of original dimensions in the data. In fact, the first two principal components alone capture 92.6% of the total variation. However, these results are influenced by the scales of the variables, as we describe next.

Normalizing the Data

A further use of PCA is to understand the structure of the data. This is done by examining the weights to see how the original variables contribute to the different principal components. In our example, it is clear that the first principal component is dominated by the sodium content of the cereal: it has the highest (in this case, positive) weight. This means that the first principal component is in fact measuring how much sodium is in the cereal. Similarly, the second principal component seems to be measuring the amount of potassium. Since both variables are measured in milligrams, whereas the other nutrients are measured in grams, the scale is obviously leading to this result. The variances of potassium and sodium are much larger than the variances of the other variables, and thus the total variance is dominated by these two variances. A solution is to normalize the data before performing the PCA. Normalization (or standardization) means replacing each original variable by a standardized version of the variable that has unit variance. This is easily accomplished by dividing each variable by its standard deviation. The effect of this normalization (standardization) is to give all variables equal importance in terms of the variability.

When should we normalize the data like this? It depends on the nature of the data. When the units of measurement are common for the variables (e.g., dollars), and when their scale reflects their importance (sales of jet fuel, sales of heating oil, etc.), it is probably best not to normalize (i.e., not to rescale the data so that they have unit variance). If the variables are measured in different units so that it is unclear how to compare the variability of different variables (e.g., dollars for some, parts per million for others) or if for variables measured in the same units, scale does not reflect importance (earnings per share, gross revenues), it is generally advisable to normalize. In this way, the changes in units of measurement do not change the principal components' weights. In the rare situations where we can give relative weights to variables, we multiply the normalized variables by these weights before doing the PCA.

PCA ON NORMALIZED DATA IN ASDM

In ASDM, applying PCA to normalized variables can be achieved in two ways:

1. Normalize the variables before applying PCA, and then apply PCA to the normalized variables. In this case, choose Method *Use Covariance Matrix*.

2. Apply PCA to the original un-normalized variables, and choose Method *Use Correlation Matrix (Use Standardized Variables)*. This will automatically normalize the variables (dividing each by its standard deviation).

Note: ASDM's default is *Use Correlation Matrix (Use Standardized Variables)*, which means that PCA will automatically normalize the variables unless otherwise specified by the user.

Returning to the breakfast cereal data, we normalize the 13 variables due to the different scales of the variables and then perform PCA (or equivalently, we use PCA applied to the correlation matrix—see box). The output is shown in Figure 4.10. Now we find that we need seven principal components to account

Principal Components

Feature\Component	Component 1	Component 2	Component 3	Component 4	Component 5	Component 6	Component 7
calories	-0.300	0.393	0.115	-0.204	0.204	-0.256	0.026
protein	0.307	0.165	0.277	-0.301	0.320	0.121	-0.283
fat	-0.040	0.346	-0.205	-0.187	0.587	0.348	0.051
sodium	-0.183	0.137	0.389	-0.120	-0.338	0.664	0.284
fiber	0.453	0.180	0.070	-0.039	-0.255	0.064	-0.112
carbo	-0.192	-0.149	0.562	-0.088	0.183	-0.326	0.260
sugars	-0.228	0.351	-0.355	0.023	-0.315	-0.152	-0.228
potass	0.402	0.301	0.068	-0.091	-0.148	0.025	-0.149
vitamins	-0.116	0.173	0.388	0.604	-0.049	0.129	-0.294
shelf	0.171	0.265	-0.002	0.639	0.329	-0.052	0.175
weight	-0.050	0.450	0.247	-0.153	-0.221	-0.399	-0.014
cups	-0.295	-0.212	0.140	-0.047	0.121	0.099	-0.749
rating	0.438	-0.252	0.182	-0.038	0.058	-0.186	-0.063

	Component 8	Component 9	Component 10	Component 11	Component 12	Component 13
	0.002	-0.030	0.500	-0.214	0.492	-0.234
	0.427	-0.535	-0.022	0.032	-0.100	0.186
	-0.063	0.460	-0.145	-0.067	-0.291	-0.090
	-0.177	-0.215	-0.001	-0.087	-0.054	-0.239
	-0.216	0.244	0.295	-0.531	-0.059	0.442
	-0.167	0.117	0.241	0.179	-0.476	0.225
	0.063	-0.225	0.252	-0.003	-0.614	-0.167
	-0.262	0.167	0.177	0.729	0.121	-0.128
	0.457	0.346	0.052	0.019	0.000	-0.060
	-0.414	-0.416	-0.046	-0.059	-0.017	0.000
	-0.075	0.065	-0.692	-0.113	0.031	0.000
	-0.499	-0.050	-0.077	-0.055	0.032	0.000
	-0.015	0.063	0.012	-0.276	-0.189	-0.743

Explained Variance

Component	Eigenvalue	Variance, %	Cumulative Variance, %
Component 1	3.634	27.95	27.95
Component 2	3.148	24.22	52.17
Component 3	1.909	14.69	66.85
Component 4	1.019	7.84	74.70
Component 5	0.989	7.61	82.31
Component 6	0.722	5.55	87.86
Component 7	0.672	5.17	93.03
Component 8	0.416	3.20	96.23
Component 9	0.316	2.43	98.66
Component 10	0.092	0.71	99.36
Component 11	0.063	0.49	99.85
Component 12	0.019	0.15	100.00
Component 13	0.000	0.00	100.00

FIGURE 4.10   PCA OUTPUT USING ALL *NORMALIZED* 13 NUMERICAL VARIABLES IN THE BREAKFAST CEREALS DATASET

for more than 90% of the total variability. The first two principal components account for only 52% of the total variability, and thus reducing the number of variables to two would mean losing a lot of information. Examining the weights, we see that the first principal component measures the balance between two quantities: (1) calories and cups (large negative weights) vs. (2) protein, fiber, potassium, and consumer rating (large positive weights). High scores on principal component 1 mean that the cereal is low in calories and the amount per bowl, and high in protein and potassium. Unsurprisingly, this type of cereal is associated with a low consumer rating. The second principal component is most affected by the weight of a serving, and the third principal component by the carbohydrate content. We can continue labeling the next principal components in a similar fashion to learn about the structure of the data.

When the data can be reduced to two dimensions, a useful plot is a scatter plot of the first vs. second principal scores with labels for the observations (if the dataset is not too large). To illustrate this, Figure 4.11 displays the first two principal component scores for the breakfast cereals. We can see that as we move from right (bran cereals) to left, the cereals are less "healthy" in the sense of high calories, low protein and fiber, and so on. Also, moving from bottom to top, we get heavier cereals (moving from puffed rice to raisin bran). These plots are especially useful if interesting clusterings of observations can be found. For instance, we see here that children's cereals are close together on the middle-right part of the plot.

The machine learning workflow for the PCA procedures for the outputs shown in Figure 4.9 and Figure 4.10 is shown in Figure 4.12. The left branch corresponds to Figure 4.9, which is a PCA output using all 13 numerical variables in the breakfast cereals dataset, whereas the right branch corresponds to Figure 4.10 which is a PCA output using all *normalized* 13 numerical variables in the breakfast cereals dataset.

Using Principal Components for Classification and Prediction

When the goal of the data reduction is to have a smaller set of variables that will serve as predictors, we can proceed as following: Apply PCA to the predictors using the training data. Use the output to determine the number of principal components to be retained. The predictors in the model now use the (reduced number of) principal scores columns. For the validation set, we can use the weights computed from the training data to obtain a set of principal scores by applying the weights to the variables in the validation set. These new variables are then treated as the predictors.

One disadvantage of using a subset of principal components as predictors in a supervised task is that we might lose predictive information that is nonlinear (e.g., a quadratic effect of a predictor on the outcome or an interaction between

FIGURE 4.11   SCATTER PLOT OF THE SECOND VS. FIRST PRINCIPAL COMPONENTS SCORES FOR THE NORMALIZED BREAKFAST CEREAL OUTPUT

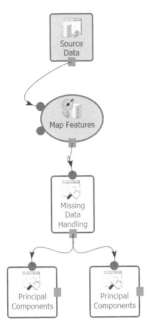

FIGURE 4.12   MACHINE LEARNING WORKFLOW FOR PCA ON CEREALS DATASET

predictors). This is because PCA produces linear transformations, thereby capturing linear relationships between the original variables.

4.9 DIMENSION REDUCTION USING REGRESSION MODELS

In this chapter, we discussed methods for reducing the number of columns using summary statistics, plots, and PCA. All these are considered exploratory methods. Some of them completely ignore the output variable (e.g., PCA), and in other methods we informally try to incorporate the relationship between the predictors and the output variable (e.g., combining similar categories, in terms of their behavior with y). Another approach to reducing the number of predictors, which directly considers the predictive or classification task, is by fitting a regression model. For prediction, a linear regression model is used (see Chapter 6) and for classification, a logistic regression model (see Chapter 10). In both cases, we can employ subset selection procedures that algorithmically choose a subset of variables among the larger set (see details in the relevant chapters).

Fitted regression models can also be used to further combine similar categories: categories that have coefficients that are not statistically significant (i.e., have a high p-value) can be combined with the reference category because their distinction from the reference category appears to have no significant effect on the output variable. Moreover, categories that have similar coefficient values (and the same sign) can often be combined because their effect on the output variable is similar. See the example in Chapter 10 on predicting delayed flights for an illustration of how regression models can be used for dimension reduction.

4.10 DIMENSION REDUCTION USING CLASSIFICATION AND REGRESSION TREES

Another method for reducing the number of columns and for combining categories of a categorical variable is by applying classification and regression trees (see Chapter 9). Classification trees are used for classification tasks and regression trees for prediction tasks. In both cases, the algorithm creates binary splits on the predictors that best classify/predict the outcome (e.g., above/below age 30). Although we defer the detailed discussion to Chapter 9, we note here that the resulting tree diagram can be used for determining the important predictors. Predictors (numerical or categorical) that do not appear in the tree can be removed. Similarly, categories that do not appear in the tree can be combined.

PROBLEMS

4.1   **Breakfast Cereals.** Use the data for the breakfast cereals example in Section 4.8 to explore and summarize the data as follows. (Note that a few records contain missing values; since there are just a few, a simple solution is to remove them first. You can use the "Missing Data Handling" utility in ASDM.)

   a. Which variables are quantitative/numerical? Which are ordinal? Which are nominal?

   b. Create a table with the average, median, min, max, and standard deviation for each of the quantitative variables. This can be done through Excel's functions or Excel's *Data → Data Analysis → Descriptive Statistics* menu.

   c. Use ASDM to plot a histogram for each of the quantitative variables. Based on the histograms and summary statistics, answer the following questions:

      i. Which variables have the largest variability?

      ii. Which variables seem skewed?

      iii. Are there any values that seem extreme?

   d. Use ASDM to plot a side-by-side boxplot comparing the calories in hot vs. cold cereals. What does this plot show us?

   e. Use ASDM to plot a side-by-side boxplot of consumer rating as a function of the shelf height. If we were to predict consumer rating from shelf height, does it appear that we need to keep all three categories of shelf height?

   f. Compute the correlation table for the quantitative variables (use Excel's *Data → Data Analysis → Correlation* menu). In addition, use ASDM to generate a matrix plot for these variables.

      i. Which pair of variables is most strongly correlated?

      ii. How can we reduce the number of variables based on these correlations?

      iii. How would the correlations change if we normalized the data first?

   g. Consider the first column on the left in Figure 4.9. Describe briefly what this column represents.

4.2   **University Rankings.** The dataset on American college and university rankings (available from www.dataminingbook.com) contains information on 1302 American colleges and universities offering an undergraduate program. For each university, there are 17 measurements that include continuous measurements (e.g., tuition and graduation rate) and categorical measurements (e.g., location by state and whether it is a private or a public school).

   a. Remove all categorical variables. Then remove all records with missing numerical measurements from the dataset (by creating a new worksheet).

   b. Conduct a principal component analysis on the cleaned data and comment on the results. Should the data be normalized? Discuss what characterizes the components you consider key.

4.3   **Sales of Toyota Corolla Cars.** The file `ToyotaCorolla.xlsx` contains data on used cars (Toyota Corollas) on sale during late summer of 2004 in The Netherlands. It has 1436 records containing details on 38 attributes, including *Price, Age, Kilometers, HP*, and other specifications. The goal will be to predict the price of a used Toyota Corolla based on its specifications.

a. Identify the categorical variables.

b. Explain the relationship between a categorical variable and the series of binary dummy variables derived from it.

c. How many dummy binary variables are required to capture the information in a categorical variable with N categories?

d. Using ASDM's data utilities, convert the categorical variables in this dataset into dummy binaries, and explain in words, for one record, the values in the derived binary dummies.

e. Use Excel's correlation command (*Data → Data Analysis → Correlation* menu) to produce a correlation matrix and ASDM's matrix plot to obtain a matrix of all scatter plots. Comment on the relationships among variables.

4.4 **Chemical Features of Wine.** Figure 4.13 shows the PCA output on data (nonnormalized) in which the variables represent chemical characteristics of wine, and each case is a different wine.

a. The data are in the file `Wine.xlsx`. Consider the column *Variance, %* in the Explained Variance table. Explain why component 1's variance is so much greater than that of any other column.

b. Comment on the use of normalization (standardization) in part (a).

Principal Components

Feature\Component	Component 1	Component 2	Component 3	Component 4	Component 5	Component 6
Alcohol	0.002	-0.001	-0.017	0.141	-0.020	0.194
Malic_Acid	-0.001	-0.002	-0.122	0.160	0.613	0.742
Ash	0.000	-0.005	-0.052	-0.010	-0.020	0.042
Ash_Alcalinity	-0.005	-0.026	-0.939	-0.331	-0.064	-0.024
Magnesium	0.018	-0.999	0.030	-0.005	0.006	-0.002
Total_Phenols	0.001	-0.001	0.040	-0.075	-0.315	0.279
Flavanoids	0.002	0.000	0.085	-0.169	-0.525	0.434
Nonflavanoid_Phenols	0.000	0.001	-0.014	0.011	0.030	-0.022
Proanthocyanins	0.001	-0.005	0.025	-0.050	-0.251	0.242
Color_Intensity	0.002	-0.015	-0.291	0.879	-0.332	0.003
Hue	0.000	0.001	0.026	-0.060	-0.052	-0.024
OD280_OD315	0.001	0.003	0.070	-0.178	-0.261	0.289
Proline	1.000	0.018	-0.005	-0.003	0.002	-0.001

Explained Variance

Component	Eigenvalue	Variance, %	Cumulative Variance, %
Component 1	99201.790	99.809	99.809
Component 2	172.535	0.174	99.983
Component 3	9.438	0.009	99.992
Component 4	4.991	0.005	99.997
Component 5	1.229	0.001	99.998
Component 6	0.841	0.001	99.999

FIGURE 4.13   **PRINCIPAL COMPONENTS OF NONNORMALIZED WINE DATA**

## PART III

Performance Evaluation

## CHAPTER 5

Evaluating Predictive Performance

In this chapter, we discuss how the predictive performance of machine learning methods can be assessed. We point out the danger of overfitting to the training data, and the need to test model performance on data that were not used in the training step. We discuss popular performance metrics. For prediction, metrics include average error, mean absolute percentage error (MAPE), and root-mean-squared error (RMSE) (based on the validation data). For classification tasks, metrics based on the classification matrix include overall accuracy, specificity, and sensitivity and metrics that account for misclassification costs. We also show the relation between the choice of cutoff value and classification performance, and present the receiver operating characteristic (ROC) curve, which is a popular chart for assessing method performance at different cutoff values. When the goal is to accurately classify the most interesting or important cases, called *ranking*, rather than accurately classify the entire sample (e.g., the 10% of customers most likely to respond to an offer, or the 5% of claims most likely to be fraudulent), lift charts are used to assess performance. We also discuss the need for oversampling rare classes and how to adjust performance metrics for the oversampling. Finally, we mention the usefulness of comparing metrics based on the validation data to those based on the training data for the purpose of detecting overfitting. While some differences are expected, extreme differences can be indicative of overfitting.

5.1 INTRODUCTION

In supervised learning, we are interested in predicting the outcome variable for new records. There are three main types of outcomes of interest:

Machine Learning for Business Analytics: Concepts, Techniques, and Applications with Analytic Solver® Data Mining,
Fourth Edition. Galit Shmueli, Peter C. Bruce, Kuber R. Deokar, and Nitin R. Patel.
© 2023 John Wiley & Sons, Inc. Published 2023 by John Wiley & Sons, Inc.

Predicted numerical value: when the outcome variable is numerical (e.g., house price).

Predicted class membership: when the outcome variable is categorical (e.g., buyer/nonbuyer).

Propensity: the probability of class membership, when the outcome variable is categorical (e.g., the propensity to default).

Prediction methods are used for generating numerical predictions, while classification methods ("classifiers") are used for generating propensities, and using a cutoff value on the propensities, we can generate predicted class memberships.

A subtle distinction to keep in mind is the two distinct predictive uses of classifiers: one use, *classification*, is aimed at predicting class membership for new records. The other, *ranking*, is detecting among a set of new records the ones most likely to belong to a class of interest.

Let's now examine the approach for judging the usefulness of a prediction method used for generating numerical predictions (Section 5.2), a classifier used for classification (Section 5.3), and a classifier used for ranking (Section 5.4). In Section 5.5, we'll look at evaluating performance under the scenario of oversampling.

5.2 EVALUATING PREDICTIVE PERFORMANCE

First, let us emphasize that predictive accuracy is not the same as goodness-of-fit. Classical statistical measures of performance are aimed at finding a model that fits well to the data on which the model was trained. In machine learning, we are interested in models that have high predictive accuracy when applied to *new* records. Measures such as R^2 and standard error of estimate are common metrics in classical regression modeling, and residual analysis is used to gauge goodness-of-fit in that situation. However, these measures do not tell us much about the ability of the model to predict new cases.

For assessing prediction performance, several measures are used. In all cases the measures are based on the validation set, which serves as a more objective ground than the training set to assess predictive accuracy. This is because records in the validation set are more similar to the future records to be predicted, in the sense that they are not used to select predictors or to estimate the model coefficients. Models are trained on the training data, applied to the validation data, and measures of accuracy then use the prediction errors on that validation set.

Naive Benchmark: The Average

The benchmark criterion in prediction is using the average outcome (thereby ignoring all predictor information). In other words, the prediction for a new record is simply the average outcome of the records in the training set ($\bar{y}$). A good predictive model should outperform the benchmark criterion in terms of predictive accuracy.

Prediction Accuracy Measures

The prediction error for record i is defined as the difference between its actual y value and its predicted y value: $e_i = y_i - \hat{y}_i$. A few popular numerical measures of predictive accuracy are:

- *MAE* or *MAD* (mean absolute error/deviation) = $\frac{1}{n} \sum_{i=1}^{n} |e_i|$. This gives the magnitude of the average absolute error.

- *Average error* = $\frac{1}{n} \sum_{i=1}^{n} e_i$. This measure is similar to MAD except that it retains the sign of the errors, so that negative errors cancel out positive errors of the same magnitude. It therefore gives an indication of whether the predictions are on average over- or underpredicting the response.

- *MAPE* (mean absolute percentage error) = $100\% \times \frac{1}{n} \sum_{i=1}^{n} |e_i/y_i|$. This measure gives a percentage score of how predictions deviate (on average) from the actual values.

- *RMSE* (root-mean-squared error) = $\sqrt{\frac{1}{n} \sum_{i=1}^{n} e_i^2}$. This is similar to the standard error of estimate in linear regression, except that it is computed on the validation data rather than on the training data. It has the same units as the variable predicted.

- Total *SSE* (total sum of squared errors) = $\sum_{i=1}^{n} e_i^2$.

Such measures can be used to compare models and to assess their degree of prediction accuracy. Note that all these measures are influenced by outliers. To check outlier influence, we can compute median-based measures (and compare to the mean-based measures) or simply plot a histogram or boxplot of the errors. Plotting the prediction errors' distribution is in fact very useful and can highlight more information than the metrics alone.

To illustrate the use of predictive accuracy measures and charts of prediction error distribution, consider the error metrics and charts shown in Figures 5.1 and 5.2. These are the result of fitting a certain predictive model to prices of used Toyota Corolla cars. The training set includes 600 cars and the validation set includes 400 cars. The prediction errors for the validation set are summarized in the right table in Figure 5.1. The histogram and boxplot in Figure 5.2

Training: Prediction Summary

Metric	Value
SSE	1060787797.9
MSE	1767979.6632
RMSE	1329.6539637
MAD	987.00345401
R2	0.8737257485

Validation: Prediction Summary

Metric	Value
SSE	799341491.7
MSE	1998353.729
RMSE	1413.631398
MAD	1109.211492
R2	0.858243580

FIGURE 5.1   PREDICTION ERROR METRICS FROM A MODEL FOR TOYOTA CAR PRICES. TRAINING (LEFT) AND VALIDATION (RIGHT)

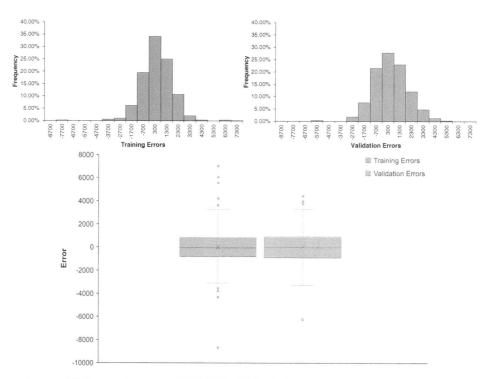

FIGURE 5.2   HISTOGRAMS AND BOXPLOTS OF TOYOTA PRICE PREDICTION ERRORS FOR TRAINING AND VALIDATION SETS. GRAPHS PRODUCED IN EXCEL

corresponding to the validation set show a small number of outliers (all under-predictions), with most errors in the [−1000,1000] range.

Comparing Training and Validation Performance

Residuals that are based on the training set tell us about model fit, whereas those that are based on the validation set (called "prediction errors") measure the model's ability to predict new data (predictive performance). We expect training errors to be smaller than the validation errors (because the model was fitted using the training set), and the more complex the model, the greater is the likelihood that it will *overfit* the training data (indicated by a greater difference between the training and validation errors). In an extreme case of overfitting, the training errors would be zero (perfect fit of the model to the training data), and the validation errors would be nonzero and nonnegligible. For this reason, it is important to compare the error plots and metrics (RMSE, MAD, etc.) of the training and validation sets. Figure 5.1 illustrates this comparison: the RMSE and MAD for the training set are slightly lower than those for the validation set, as expected, but are not drastically different from the validation metrics.

The charts reveal more than the metrics alone: looking at the charts in Figure 5.2 shows that the discrepancies are also due to some outliers, and especially the large negative training error. Last, the validation errors have slightly more high positive errors (underpredictions) than the training errors, as reflected by the medians and outliers.

Lift Chart

In some applications the goal is to search, among a set of new records, for a subset of records that gives the highest cumulative predicted values. In such cases, a graphical way to assess predictive performance is through a *lift chart*. This compares the model's predictive performance to a baseline model that has no predictors. A lift chart for a continuous response is relevant only when we are searching for a set of records that gives the highest cumulative predicted values. It is not relevant, if we are interested in predicting the outcome for each new record.

To illustrate this type of goal, consider a car rental firm that renews its fleet regularly so that customers drive late-model cars. This entails disposing of a large quantity of used vehicles on a continuing basis. Since the firm is not primarily in the used car sales business, it tries to dispose of as much of its fleet as possible through volume sales to used car dealers. However, it is profitable to sell a limited number of cars through its own channels. Its volume deals with the used car dealers allow it flexibility to pick and choose which cars to sell in this fashion, so it would like to have a model for selecting cars for resale through its own channels. Since all cars were purchased some time ago and the deals with the used car dealers are for fixed prices (specifying a given number of cars of a certain make and model class), the cars' costs are now irrelevant and the dealer is interested only in maximizing revenue. This is done by selecting for its own resale the cars likely to generate the most revenue. The lift chart in this case gives the predicted lift for revenue.

The lift chart is based on ordering the set of records of interest (typically, validation data) by their predicted value, from high to low. Then, we accumulate the actual values and plot their cumulative value on the y-axis as a function of the number of records accumulated (the x-axis value). This curve is compared to assigning a naive prediction ($\bar{y}$) to each record and accumulating these average values, which results in a diagonal line. The farther away the lift curve is from the diagonal benchmark line, the better the model is doing in separating records with high-value outcomes from those with low-value outcomes. The same information can be presented in a decile lift chart, where the ordered records are grouped into 10 deciles, and for each decile the chart presents the ratio of model lift to naive benchmark lift.

Figure 5.3 shows a lift chart and decile lift chart based on fitting a linear regression model to the Toyota data.[1] The charts are based on the validation data of 400 cars. It can be seen that the model's predictive performance in terms of lift is better than the baseline model, since its lift curve is higher than that of the baseline model. The lift and decile charts in Figure 5.3 would be useful in the following scenario: Choosing the top 10% of the cars that gave the highest predicted sales, for example, we would gain 1.7 times the amount of revenue, compared to choosing 10% of the cars at random. This can be seen from the decile chart (Figure 5.3). This number can also be computed from the lift chart by comparing the sales for 40 random cars (the value of the baseline curve at $x = 40$), which is \$473,797 (= the sum of the actual sales for the 400 validation set cars divided by 10) with the actual sales of the 40 cars that have the highest predicted values (the value of the lift curve at $x = 40$), which is \$814,750. The ratio between these numbers is 1.7.

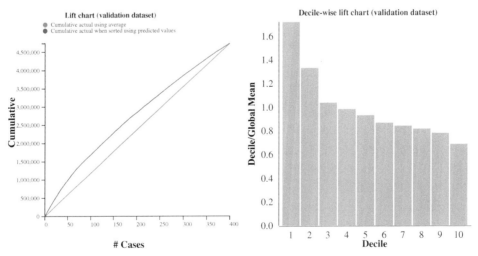

FIGURE 5.3   LIFT CHART (LEFT) AND DECILE LIFT CHART (RIGHT) FOR CONTINUOUS RESPONSE (SALES OF TOYOTA CARS)

[1] Figure 5.3 (left) is actually a *cumulative gains chart*, but since ASDM refers to such a chart as *lift chart*, we will use the term "lift chart" in this book.

5.3 JUDGING CLASSIFIER PERFORMANCE

The need for performance measures arises from the wide choice of classifiers and predictive methods. Not only do we have several different methods, but even within a single method there are usually many options that can lead to completely different results. A simple example is the choice of predictors used within a particular predictive algorithm. Before we study these various algorithms in detail and face decisions on how to set these options, we need to know how we will measure success.

A natural criterion for judging the performance of a classifier is the probability of making a *misclassification error*. Misclassification means that the observation belongs to one class, but the model classifies it as a member of a different class. A classifier that makes no errors would be perfect, but we do not expect to be able to construct such classifiers in the real world due to "noise" and not having all the information needed to classify cases precisely. Is there a minimal probability of misclassification that we should require of a classifier?

Benchmark: The Naive Rule

A very simple rule for classifying a record into one of m classes, ignoring all predictor information $(x_1, x_2, \ldots, x_p)$ that we may have, is to classify the record as a member of the majority class. In other words, "classify as belonging to the most prevalent class." The *naive rule* is used mainly as a baseline or benchmark for evaluating the performance of more complicated classifiers. Clearly, a classifier that uses external predictor information (on top of the class membership allocation) should outperform the naive rule. There are various performance measures based on the naive rule that measure how much better than the naive rule a certain classifier performs.

Similar to using the sample mean ($\bar{y}$) as the naive benchmark in the numerical outcome case, the naive rule for classification relies solely on the y information and excludes any additional predictor information.

Class Separation

If the classes are well separated by the predictor information, even a small dataset will suffice in finding a good classifier, whereas if the classes are not separated at all by the predictors, even a very large dataset will not help. Figure 5.4 illustrates this for a two-class case. The top panel includes a small dataset ($n = 24$ observations) where two predictors (income and lot size) are used for separating owners from nonowners (we thank Dean Wichern for this example, described in Johnson and Wichern (2002)). Here the predictor information seems useful in that it separates the two classes (owners/nonowners). The bottom panel shows a much larger dataset ($n = 5000$ observations) where the two predictors (income and

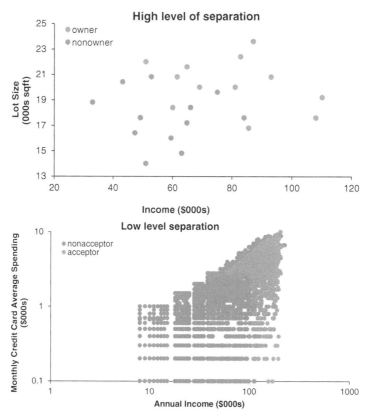

FIGURE 5.4   HIGH (TOP) AND LOW (BOTTOM) LEVELS OF SEPARATION BETWEEN TWO CLASSES, USING TWO PREDICTORS

average credit card spending) do not separate the two classes well in most of the higher ranges; nonacceptors are present throughout these ranges, though the acceptor marker color tends to dominate.

The Classification (Confusion) Matrix

In practice, most accuracy measures are derived from the *classification matrix*, also called the *confusion matrix*. This matrix summarizes the correct and incorrect classifications that a classifier produced for a certain dataset. Rows and columns of the classification matrix correspond to the true and predicted classes, respectively. Figure 5.5 shows an example of a classification (confusion) matrix for a two-class (0/1) problem resulting from applying a certain classifier to 3000 observations. The two diagonal cells (upper left, lower right) give the number of correct classifications, where the predicted class coincides with the actual class of the observation. The off-diagonal cells give counts of misclassification. The bottom left cell gives the number of class 1 members that were misclassified as 0's (in this example, there were 85 such misclassifications). Similarly, the

Confusion Matrix		
Actual\Predicted	0	1
0	2689	25
1	85	201

FIGURE 5.5   CLASSIFICATION MATRIX BASED ON 3000 OBSERVATIONS AND TWO CLASSES

upper right cell gives the number of class 0 members that were misclassified as 1's (25 such observations).

The classification matrix gives estimates of the true classification and misclassification rates. Of course, these are estimates and they may be incorrect, but if we have a large enough dataset and neither class is very rare, our estimates will be reliable. Sometimes we may be able to use public data such as US Census data to estimate these proportions. However, in most business settings, we will not know them.

Using the Validation Data

To obtain an honest estimate of future classification error, we use the classification matrix that is computed from the *validation data*. In other words, we first partition the data into training and validation sets by random selection of cases. We then construct a classifier using the training data and apply it to the validation data. This will yield the predicted classifications for observations in the validation set (see Figure 2.2 in Chapter 2). We next summarize these classifications in a classification matrix. Although we can summarize our results in a classification matrix for training data as well, the resulting classification matrix is not useful for getting an honest estimate of the misclassification rate for new data due to the danger of overfitting.

In addition to examining the validation data classification matrix to assess the classification performance on new data, we compare the training data classification matrix to the validation data classification matrix, in order to detect overfitting: although we expect somewhat inferior results on the validation data, a large discrepancy in training and validation performance might be indicative of overfitting.

Accuracy Measures

Different accuracy measures can be derived from the classification matrix. Consider a two-class case with classes C_0 and C_1 (e.g., non-buyer/buyer). The schematic classification matrix in Table 5.1 uses the notation $n_{i,j}$ to denote the number of cases that are class C_i members and were classified as C_j members. Of course, if $i \neq j$, these are counts of misclassifications. The total number of observations is $n = n_{0,0} + n_{0,1} + n_{1,0} + n_{1,1}$.

TABLE 5.1   CLASSIFICATION MATRIX: MEANING OF EACH CELL

| Actual class | Predicted class | |
	C_0	C_1
C_0	$n_{0,0}$ = number of C_0 cases classified correctly	$n_{0,1}$ = number of C_0 cases classified incorrectly as C_1
C_1	$n_{1,0}$ = number of C_1 cases classified incorrectly as C_0	$n_{1,1}$ = number of C_1 cases classified correctly

A main accuracy measure is the *estimated misclassification rate*, also called the *overall error rate*. It is given by

$$\text{err} = \frac{n_{1,0} + n_{0,1}}{n},$$

where n is the total number of cases in the validation dataset. In the example in Figure 5.5, we get err $= (85+25)/3000 = 3.67\%$.

We can measure accuracy by looking at the correct classifications—the full half of the cup—instead of the misclassifications. The *overall accuracy* of a classifier is estimated by

$$\text{accuracy} = 1 - \text{err} = \frac{n_{1,1} + n_{0,0}}{n}.$$

In the example, we have $(201 + 2689)/3000 = 96.33\%$.

Propensities and Cutoff for Classification

The first step in most classification algorithms is to estimate the probability that a case belongs to each of the classes. These probabilities are also called *propensities*. Propensities are typically used either as an interim step for generating predicted class membership (classification), or for rank-ordering the records by their probability of belonging to a class of interest. Let us consider their first use in this section. The second use is discussed in Section 5.4.

If overall classification accuracy (involving all the classes) is of interest, the case can be assigned to the class with the highest probability. In many contexts, a single class is of special interest, which is also called the positive class. So we will focus on the positive class and compare the propensity of belonging to that class to a *cutoff value* set by the analyst. This approach can be used with two classes or more than two classes, though it may make sense in such cases to consolidate classes so that you end up with two: the class of interest and all other classes. If the probability of belonging to the class of interest is above the cutoff, the case is assigned to that class.

CUTOFF VALUES FOR TRIAGE

In some cases it is useful to have two cutoffs, and allow a "cannot say" option for the classifier. In a two-class situation, this means that for a case, we can make one of three predictions: The case belongs to C_1, or the case belongs to C_0, or we cannot make a prediction because there is not enough information to pick C_1 or C_0 confidently. Cases that the classifier cannot classify are subjected to closer scrutiny either by using expert judgment or by enriching the set of predictor variables by gathering additional information that is perhaps more difficult or expensive to obtain. An example is classification of documents found during legal discovery (reciprocal forced document disclosure in a legal proceeding). Under traditional human-review systems, qualified legal personnel are needed to review what might be tens of thousands of documents to determine their relevance to a case. Using a classifier and a triage outcome, documents could be sorted into clearly relevant, clearly not relevant, and the gray area documents requiring human review. This substantially reduces the costs of discovery.

The default cutoff value in two-class classifiers is 0.5. Thus, if the probability of a record being a class C_1 member is greater than 0.5, that record is classified as a C_1. Any record with an estimated probability of less than 0.5 would be classified as a C_0. It is possible, however, to use a cutoff that is either higher or lower than 0.5. A cutoff greater than 0.5 will end up classifying fewer records as C_1's, whereas a cutoff less than 0.5 will end up classifying more records as C_1. Typically, the misclassification rate will rise in either case.

Consider the data in Table 5.2, showing the actual class for 24 records, sorted by the probability that the record is an "owner" (as estimated by a machine learning algorithm). If we adopt the standard 0.5 as the cutoff, our misclassification rate is 3/24, whereas if we instead adopt a cutoff of 0.25, we classify more records

TABLE 5.2   24 RECORDS WITH THEIR ACTUAL CLASS AND THE PROBABILITY (PROPENSITY) OF THEM BEING CLASS "OWNER" MEMBERS, AS ESTIMATED BY A CLASSIFIER

Actual class	Probability of class "Owner"	Actual class	Probability of class "Owner"
Owner	0.9959	Owner	0.5055
Owner	0.9875	Nonowner	0.4713
Owner	0.9844	Nonowner	0.3371
Owner	0.9804	Owner	0.2179
Owner	0.9481	Nonowner	0.1992
Owner	0.8892	Nonowner	0.1494
Owner	0.8476	Nonowner	0.0479
Nonowner	0.7628	Nonowner	0.0383
Owner	0.7069	Nonowner	0.0248
Owner	0.6807	Nonowner	0.0218
Owner	0.6563	Nonowner	0.0161
Nonowner	0.6224	Nonowner	0.0031

as owners and the misclassification rate goes up (comprising more nonowners misclassified as owners) to 5/24. Conversely, if we adopt a cutoff of 0.75, we classify fewer records as owners. The misclassification rate goes up (comprising more owners misclassified as nonowners) to 6/24. All this can be seen in the classification tables in Figure 5.6.

Cutoff Prob.Val for Success = 0.5

Confusion Matrix

Actual\Predicted	nonowner	owner
nonowner	10	2
owner	1	11

Cutoff Prob.Val for Success = 0.25

Confusion Matrix

Actual\Predicted	nonowner	owner
nonowner	8	4
owner	1	11

Cutoff Prob.Val for Success = 0.75

Confusion Matrix

Actual\Predicted	nonowner	owner
nonowner	11	1
owner	5	7

FIGURE 5.6   CLASSIFICATION MATRICES BASED ON CUTOFFS OF 0.5, 0.25, AND 0.75

To see the entire range of cutoff values and how the accuracy or misclassification rates change as a function of the cutoff, we can use an interactive confusion matrix and one-variable tables in Excel (see the accompanying box), and then plot the performance measure of interest vs. the cutoff. The results for the data above are shown in Figure 5.7. We can see that the accuracy level is pretty stable around 0.8 for cutoff values between 0.2 and 0.8.

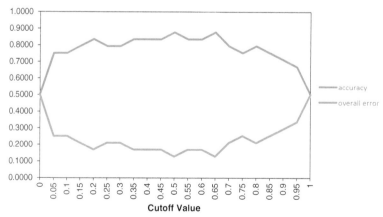

FIGURE 5.7   PLOTTING RESULTS FROM THE ONE-WAY TABLE: ACCURACY AND OVERALL ERROR AS A FUNCTION OF THE CUTOFF VALUE

Why would we want to use cutoff values different from 0.5 if they increase the misclassification rate? The answer is that it might be more important to classify owners properly than nonowners, and we would tolerate a greater misclassification of the latter. Or the reverse might be true; in other words, the costs of misclassification might be asymmetric. We can adjust the cutoff value in such a case to classify more records as the high-value class, that is, accept more misclassifications where the misclassification cost is low. Keep in mind that we are doing so after the machine learning model has already been selected—we are not changing that model. It is also possible to incorporate costs into the picture before deriving the model. These subjects are discussed in greater detail below.

STUDYING THE EFFECT OF THE CUTOFF VALUE: INTERACTIVE CONFUSION MATRIX AND ONE-VARIABLE TABLES IN EXCEL

An interactive confusion matrix is one that gets updated as the cutoff value is changed. It is useful for studying the effect of the cutoff value on counts of correct and incorrect classifications.

Excel's one-variable data tables are very useful for studying how the cutoff affects different performance measures. They will change the cutoff values to values in a user-specified column and calculate different functions based on the corresponding confusion matrix. Before creating the one-way table, we must create an interactive confusion matrix that updates as a function of the cutoff value.

Creating an interactive confusion matrix:

We create the confusion matrix from the actual values, predicted scores, and cutoff value. Suppose the predicted probabilities are in column A2:A25, the actual classes in B2:B25, and the cutoff value in cell E1 (see Figure 5.8).

1. Create a 2×2 table with *actual class* in rows and *predicted class* in columns.

2. Use Excel's =COUNTIFS formula to populate the four cells. For example, in the cell where actual and predicted class are both 1, use =COUNTIFS(A2:A25, ">"E1,B2:B25,"=1"). Use a similar function for the other three cells
   (see Figure 5.8 and example sheet at www.dataminingbook.com).

Creating a one-variable data table (see Figure 5.8):

1. Create column names for each of the measures you wish to compute. (We created "accuracy" and "overall error" in E9 and F9) The leftmost column should be titled "cutoff" (D9).

2. In the row below, add formulas, using references to the relevant confusion matrix cells. [The formula in E10 is $= (E5 + F6)/(E5 + F5 + E6 + F6)$.]

3. In the leftmost column, list the cutoff values that you want to evaluate. (We chose $0, 0.05, \ldots, 1$ in D11 to D31.)

4. Select the range excluding the first row (D10:F31). In Excel 2010 and up go to *Data > Whatif Analysis > Data Table*

5. In "column input cell," select the cell that changes (here, the cell with the cutoff value, E1). Click OK.

6. The table will now be automatically completed.

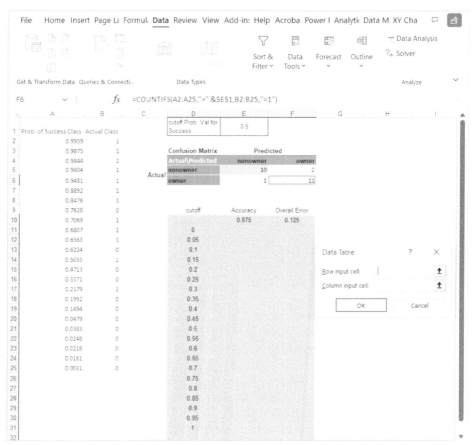

FIGURE 5.8   CREATING ONE-VARIABLE TABLES IN EXCEL. ACCURACY AND OVERALL ERROR ARE COMPUTED FOR DIFFERENT VALUES OF THE CUTOFF

Performance in Unequal Importance of Classes

Suppose that it is more important to predict membership correctly in class C_1 than in class C_0. An example is predicting the financial status (bankrupt/solvent) of firms. It may be more important to predict correctly a firm that is going bankrupt than to predict correctly a firm that is going to remain solvent. The classifier is essentially used as a system for detecting or signaling bankruptcy. In such a case, the overall accuracy is not a good measure for evaluating the classifier. Suppose that the important (positive) class is C_1. The following pair of accuracy measures are the most popular:

The **sensitivity** of a classifier is its ability to correctly detect all the important class members. This is measured by $n_{1,1}/(n_{1,1} + n_{1,0})$, the percentage of C_1 (positive) members that are correctly classified. Sensitivity is also called the True Positive Rate (TPR).

The **specificity** of a classifier is its ability to rule out C_0 (negative class) members correctly. This is measured by $n_{0,0}/(n_{0,1} + n_{0,0})$, the percentage of C_0 (negative) members that are correctly classified. Specificity is also called the True Negative Rate (TNR).

It can be useful to plot these measures vs. the cutoff value (using one-variable tables in Excel, as described above) in order to find a cutoff value that balances these measures.

ROC Curve   A more popular method for plotting the two measures is through *ROC* (Receiver Operating Characteristic) *curves*. The ROC curve plots the pairs {sensitivity, 1-specificity} as the cutoff value increases from 0 and 1. Better performance is reflected by curves that are closer to the top left corner. The comparison curve is the diagonal, which reflects the average performance of a guessing classifier that has no information about the predictors or outcome variable. This guessing classifier guesses that a proportion α of the records is 1's and therefore assigns each record an equal probability $P(Y = 1) = \alpha$. In this case, on average, a proportion α of the 1's will be correctly classified (Sensitivity = α), and a proportion α of the 0's will be correctly classified (1-Specificity = α). As we increase the cutoff value α from 0 to 1, we get the diagonal line Sensitivity = 1-Specificity. Note that the naive rule is one point on this diagonal line, where α = proportion of actual 1's.

A common metric to summarize an ROC curve is "area under the curve (AUC)," which ranges from 1 (perfect discrimination between classes) to 0.5 (no better than random guessing). AUC is commonly used to compare algorithms, especially when there are many algorithms under consideration. It has the advantage of simplicity and can be compared across datasets with different positive class rates. However, the AUC has several critical deficiencies arising from the fact that it considers all misclassifications (negatives as positives and positives as negatives) as being of equal value. For example, some areas of the ROC curve are irrelevant (e.g., if extremely low sensitivity is unacceptable). Second, when ROC curves of different algorithms cross, AUC comparisons can be misleading: a larger AUC value might correspond to poorer performance over almost the entire range of threshold values (Hand, 2009). For further issues see Lobo et al. (2008). We therefore advocate not using AUC as a single performance metric for selecting an algorithm.

The ROC curve for our 24-case example above is shown in Figure 5.9.

Precision and Recall   Sensitivity is also called *recall*. In addition to sensitivity and specificity, there is another performance measure called *precision* that is often considered in tandem with *recall* (sensitivity): The **precision** of a classifier is

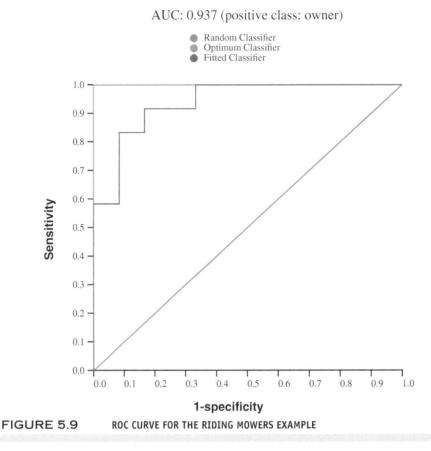

AUC: 0.937 (positive class: owner)

FIGURE 5.9   ROC CURVE FOR THE RIDING MOWERS EXAMPLE

its ability to correctly detect only the important (positive) class members. This is measured by $n_{1,1}/(n_{1,1} + n_{0,1})$, the percentage of correctly classified positive (C_1) members among all those classified as positive.

For a two-class classifier, there tends to be a tradeoff between precision and recall. While precision is a measure of *exactness* (what percentage of members classified as C_1 actually belong to C_1), recall is a measure of *completeness* (what percentage of C_1 members are classified as such). Depending on the business context, precision may be more important than recall, and vice versa. For example, for credit card fraud detection (positive class = fraudulent), we would want recall close to 1 since we want to find *all* transactions that are truly fraudulent, and we can accept low precision (mistakenly classifying non-fraudulent transactions as fraudulent) if the cost of such misclassification is not too high. The threshold value can be selected based on whether precision or recall is a more important consideration.

A metric called *F1-score* is used to combine precision and recall values into a single measure, giving them equal weights. The F1-score is given by

$$F1 = \frac{2 \times \text{precision} \times \text{recall}}{(\text{precision} + \text{recall})}.$$

Precision-Recall Curve   Similar to ROC curves that plot sensitivity vs. specificity, one can plot precision vs. recall for different cutoff values. (ASDM does not create such plots, but they can be created using Excel's one-variable table.)

COMPUTING RATES: FROM WHOSE POINT OF VIEW?

Sensitivity and specificity measure the performance of a classifier from the point of view of the "classifying agency" (e.g., a company classifying customers or a hospital classifying patients). They answer the question "how well does the classifier segregate the important class members?" It is also possible to measure accuracy from the perspective of the entity that is being predicted (e.g., the customer or the patient), who asks "what is my chance of belonging to the important class?" The terms "false discovery rate" and "false omission rate" are measures of performance from the perspective of the individual entity. If C_1 is the important (positive) class, then they are defined as

The false discovery rate (FDR) is the proportion of C_1 predictions that are wrong, equal to $n_{0,1}/(n_{1,1} + n_{0,1})$. Note that this is a ratio within the column of C_1 predictions (i.e., it uses only records that were classified as C_1).

The false omission rate (FOR) is the proportion of C_0 predictions that are wrong, equal to $n_{1,0}/(n_{1,0} + n_{0,0})$. Note that this is a ratio within the column of C_0 predictions (that is, it uses only records that were classified as C_0).

Asymmetric Misclassification Costs

Implicit in our discussion of the lift curve, which measures how effective we are in identifying the members of one particular class, is the assumption that the error of misclassifying a case belonging to one class is more serious than for the other class. For example, misclassifying a household as unlikely to respond to a sales offer when it belongs to the class that would respond incurs a greater cost (the opportunity cost of the forgone sale) than the converse error. In the former case, you are missing out on a sale worth perhaps tens or hundreds of dollars. In the latter, you are incurring the costs of mailing a letter to someone who will not purchase. In such a scenario, using the misclassification rate as a criterion can be misleading.

Note that we are assuming that the cost (or benefit) of making correct classifications is zero. At first glance, this may seem incomplete. After all, the benefit (negative cost) of classifying a buyer correctly as a buyer would seem substantial. And in other circumstances (e.g., scoring our classification algorithm to fresh data to implement our decisions), it will be appropriate to consider the actual net dollar impact of each possible classification (or misclassification). Here, however, we are attempting to assess the value of a classifier in terms of classification error, so it greatly simplifies matters if we can capture all cost/benefit information in the misclassification cells. So, instead of recording the benefit of classifying a respondent household correctly, we record the cost of failing to classify it as a respondent household. It amounts to the same thing and our goal becomes the minimization of costs, whether the costs are actual costs or missed benefits (opportunity costs).

Consider the situation where the sales offer is mailed to a random sample of people for the purpose of constructing a good classifier. Suppose that the offer is accepted by 1% of those households. For these data, if a classifier simply classifies every household as a nonresponder, it will have an error rate of only 1%, but it will be useless in practice. A classifier that misclassifies 2% of buying households as nonbuyers and 20% of the nonbuyers as buyers would have a higher error rate but would be better if the profit from a sale is substantially higher than the cost of sending out an offer. In these situations, if we have estimates of the cost of both types of misclassification, we can use the classification matrix to compute the expected cost of misclassification for each case in the validation data. This enables us to compare different classifiers using overall expected costs (or profits) as the criterion.

Suppose that we are considering sending an offer to 1000 more people, 1% of whom respond (1), on average. Naively classifying everyone as a 0 has an error rate of only 1%. Using a machine learning process, suppose that we can produce these classifications:

	Predict class 0	Predict class 1
Actual 0	970	20
Actual 1	2	8

These classifications have an error rate of $100 \times (20 + 2)/1000 = 2.2\%$—higher than the naive rate.

Now suppose that the profit from a 1 is $10 and the cost of sending the offer is $1. Classifying everyone as a 0 still has a misclassification rate of only 1% but yields a profit of $0. Using the machine learning process, despite the higher misclassification rate, yields a profit of $60.

The matrix of profit is as follows (nothing is sent to the predicted 0's, so there are no costs or sales in that column):

Profit	Predict class 0	Predict class 1
Actual 0	0	−$20
Actual 1	0	$80

Looked at purely in terms of costs, when everyone is classified as a 0, there are no costs of sending the offer; the only costs are the opportunity costs of failing to make sales to the 10 1's = $100. The cost (actual costs of sending the offer plus the opportunity costs of missed sales) of using the machine learning process to select people to send the offer to is only $48, as follows:

Costs	Predict class 0	Predict class 1
Actual 0	0	$20
Actual 1	$20	$8

However, this does not improve the actual classifications. A better method is to change the classification rules (and hence the misclassification rates), as discussed in the preceding section, to reflect the asymmetric costs.

A popular performance measure that includes costs is the *average misclassification cost*, which measures the average cost of misclassification per classified observation. Denote by q_1 the cost of misclassifying a class C_1 observation (as belonging to class C_0) and by q_0 the cost of misclassifying a class C_0 observation (as belonging to class C_1). The average misclassification cost is

$$\frac{q_1 n_{1,0} + q_0 n_{0,1}}{n}.$$

Thus we are looking for a classifier that minimizes this quantity. This can be computed, for instance, for different cutoff values.

It turns out that the optimal parameters are affected by the misclassification costs only through the ratio of these costs. This can be seen if we write the foregoing measure slightly differently:

$$\frac{q_1 n_{1,0} + q_0 n_{0,1}}{n} = \frac{n_{1,0}}{n_{1,1} + n_{1,0}} \frac{n_{1,1} + n_{1,0}}{n} q_1 + \frac{n_{0,1}}{n_{0,1} + n_{0,0}} \frac{n_{0,1} + n_{0,0}}{n} q_0.$$

Minimizing this expression is equivalent to minimizing the same expression divided by a constant. If we divide by q_1, it can be seen clearly that the minimization depends only on q_0/q_1 and not on their individual values. This is very practical, since in many cases it is difficult to assess the costs associated with misclassifying a C_1 member and a C_0 member, but estimating the ratio is easier.

This expression is a reasonable estimate of future misclassification cost if the proportions of classes C_1 and C_0 in the sample data are similar to the proportions of classes C_1 and C_0 that are expected in the future. If, instead of a random sample, we draw a sample such that one class is oversampled (as described in the next section), then the sample proportions of C_1's and C_0's will be distorted compared to the future or population. We can then correct the average misclassification cost measure for the distorted sample proportions by incorporating estimates of the true proportions (from external data or domain knowledge), denoted by $p(C_1)$ and $p(C_0)$, into the formula

$$\frac{n_{1,0}}{n_{1,1}+n_{1,0}}p(C_1)\,q_1 + \frac{n_{0,1}}{n_{0,1}+n_{0,0}}p(C_0)\,q_0.$$

Using the same logic as above, it can be shown that optimizing this quantity depends on the costs only through their ratio (q_0/q_1) and on the prior probabilities only through their ratio $[p(C_0)/p(C_1)]$. This is why software packages that incorporate costs and prior probabilities might prompt the user for ratios rather than actual costs and probabilities.

Generalization to More Than Two Classes

All the comments made above about two-class classifiers extend readily to classification into more than two classes. Let us suppose that we have m classes $C_1, C_2, \ldots, C_m$. The classification matrix has m rows and m columns. The misclassification cost associated with the diagonal cells is, of course, always zero. Incorporating prior probabilities of the various classes (where now we have m such numbers) is still done in the same manner. However, evaluating misclassification costs becomes much more complicated: For an m-class case we have $m(m-1)$ types of misclassifications. Constructing a matrix of misclassification costs thus becomes prohibitively complicated.

5.4 Judging Ranking Performance

We now turn to the predictive goal of detecting, among a set of new records, the ones most likely to belong to a class of interest. Recall that this differs from the goal of predicting class membership for each new record.

Lift Charts for Binary Outcome

We already introduced lift charts in the context of a numerical outcome (Section 5.2). We now describe lift charts, also called *lift curves*, *gains curves*, or *gains charts*, for a binary outcome. This is a more common usage than for predicted continuous outcomes. The lift curve helps us determine how effectively we can "skim the cream" by selecting a relatively small number of cases and getting a relatively large portion of the responders. The input required to construct a lift curve is a validation dataset that has been "scored" by appending to each case the propensity that it will belong to a given class.

Let's continue with the case in which a particular class is relatively rare and of much more interest than the other class: tax cheats, debt defaulters, or responders to a mailing. We would like our classification model to sift through the records and sort them according to which ones are most likely to be tax cheats, responders to the mailing, and so on. We can then make more informed decisions. For example, we can decide how many and which tax returns to examine if looking for tax cheats. The model will give us an estimate of the extent to which we will encounter more and more noncheaters as we proceed through the sorted data starting with the records most likely to be tax cheats. Or we can use the sorted data to decide to which potential customers a limited-budget mailing should be targeted. In other words, we are describing the case where our goal is to obtain a rank ordering among the records according to their class membership propensities.

Sorting by Propensity   To construct a lift chart, we sort the set of records by propensity, in descending order. This is the propensity to belong to the important (positive) class, say C_1. Then in each row we compute the cumulative number of C_1 members (Actual Class = C_1). For example, Table 5.3 shows the 24 records ordered in descending class "1" propensity. The rightmost

TABLE 5.3	RECORDS SORTED (HIGH TO LOW) BY PROPENSITY OF OWNERSHIP, FOR THE RIDING MOWERS EXAMPLE		
Obs	Predicted probability of 1	Actual class	Cumulative actual class
1	0.995976750	1	1
2	0.987533203	1	2
3	0.984456467	1	3
4	0.980439689	1	4
5	0.948110866	1	5
6	0.889297671	1	6
7	0.847632493	1	7
8	0.762807097	0	7
9	0.706992840	1	8
10	0.680755073	1	9
11	0.656344803	1	10
12	0.622420495	0	10
13	0.505507885	1	11
14	0.471341530	0	11
15	0.337118228	0	11
16	0.217968446	1	12
17	0.199241067	0	12
18	0.149483096	0	12
19	0.047962735	0	12
20	0.038341510	0	12
21	0.024851077	0	12
22	0.021806086	0	12
23	0.016129950	0	12
24	0.003559993	0	12

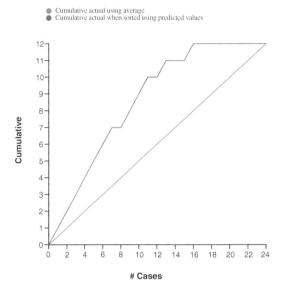

FIGURE 5.10   LIFT CHART FOR THE RIDING MOWERS EXAMPLE

column accumulates the number of actual 1's. The lift chart (Figure 5.10) then plots this cumulative column against the number of records.

Interpreting the Lift Chart   What is considered good or bad performance? The ideal ranking performance would place all the 1's at the beginning (the actual 1's would have the highest propensities and be at the top of the table) and all the 0's at the end. A lift chart corresponding to this ideal case would be a diagonal line with slope 1 that turns into a horizontal line (once all the 1's were accumulated). In the example, the lift curve for the best possible classifier—a classifier that makes no errors—would overlap the existing curve at the start, continue with a slope of 1 until it reaches all the 12 1's, then continue horizontally to the right.

In contrast, a useless model would be one that randomly assigns propensities (shuffling the 1's and 0's randomly in the Actual Class column). Such behavior would increase the cumulative number of 1's, on average, by $\frac{\#1's}{n}$ in each row. And in fact, this is the diagonal line joining the points $(0, 0)$ to $(24, 12)$ seen in Figure 5.10. This serves as a reference line. For any given number of cases (the x-axis value), it represents the expected number of 1 classifications if we did not have a model but simply selected cases at random. It provides a benchmark against which we can evaluate the ranking performance of the model. In this example, although our model is not perfect, it seems to perform much better than the random benchmark.

How do we read a lift chart? For a given number of cases (x-axis), the lift curve value on the y-axis tells us how much better we are doing compared to random assignment. For example, looking at Figure 5.10, if we use our model to choose the top 10 records, the lift curve tells us that we would be right for about nine of them. If we simply select 10 cases at random, we expect to be right for $10 \times 12/24 = 5$ cases. The model gives us a "lift" in detecting class 1 members of $9/5 = 1.8$. The lift will vary with the number of cases we choose to act on. A good classifier will give us a high lift when we act on only a few cases. As we include more cases, the lift will decrease.

Decile Lift Charts

The information from the lift chart can be portrayed as a *decile chart*, as shown in Figure 5.11, which is widely used in direct marketing predictive modeling. The decile chart aggregates all the lift information into 10 buckets. The bars show, on the y-axis, the factor by which our model outperforms a random assignment of 0's and 1's, taking one decile at a time. Reading the first bar on the left, we see that taking the 10% of the records that are ranked by the model as "the most probable 1's" (having the highest propensities) yields twice as many 1's as would a random selection of 10% of the records. In this example, the decile chart indicates that we can even use the model to select the top 30% records with the highest propensities and still perform twice as well as random.

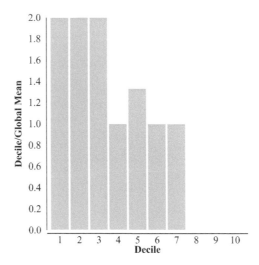

FIGURE 5.11   DECILE LIFT CHART

ASDM automatically creates lift (and decile) charts from probabilities (propensities) predicted by classifiers for both training and validation data. Of course, the lift curve based on the validation data is a better estimator of performance for new cases.

Beyond Two Classes

A lift chart cannot be used with a multiclass classifier unless a single "important class" is defined and the classifications are reduced to "important" and "unimportant" classes (or equivalently, *positive* and *negative* classes).

Lift Charts Incorporating Costs and Benefits

When the benefits and costs of correct and incorrect classification are known or can be estimated, the lift chart is still a useful presentation and decision tool. As before, we need a classifier that assigns to each record a propensity that it belongs to a particular class. The procedure is then as follows:

1. Sort the records in descending order of predicted probability of success (where *success* = belonging to the class of interest).

2. For each record, record the cost (benefit) associated with the actual outcome.

3. For the highest propensity (i.e., first) record, its x-axis value is 1 and its y-axis value is its cost or benefit (computed in step 2) on the lift curve.

4. For the next record, again calculate the cost (benefit) associated with the actual outcome. Add this to the cost (benefit) for the previous record. This sum is the y-axis coordinate of the second point on the lift curve. Its x-axis value is 2.

5. Repeat step 4 until all records have been examined. Connect all the points, and this is the lift curve.

6. The reference line is a straight line from the origin to the point y = total net benefit and $x = n$ (n = number of records).

Note: It is entirely possible for a reference line that incorporates costs and benefits to have a negative slope if the net value for the entire dataset is negative. For example, if the cost of mailing to a person is $0.65, the value of a responder is $25, and the overall response rate is 2%, the expected net value of mailing to a list of 10,000 is $(0.02 \times \$25 \times 10{,}000)(\$0.65 \times 10{,}000) = \$5000 - \$6500 = -\$1500$. Hence the y-value at the far right of the lift curve ($x = 10{.}000$) is -1500, and the slope of the reference line from the origin will be negative. The optimal point will be where the lift curve is at a maximum (i.e., mailing to about 3000 people) in Figure 5.12.

Lift as Function of Cutoff

We could also plot the lift as a function of the cutoff value. The only difference is the scale on the x-axis. When the goal is to select the top records based on a certain budget, the lift vs. number of records is preferable. In contrast, when the

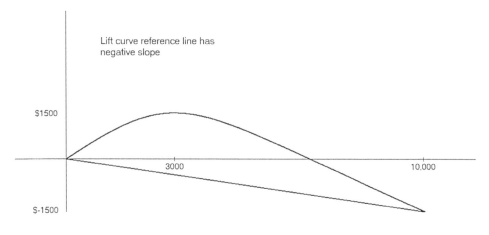

FIGURE 5.12   LIFT CURVE INCORPORATING COSTS

goal is to find a cutoff that distinguishes well between the two classes, the lift vs. cutoff value is more useful.

5.5 OVERSAMPLING

As we saw briefly in Chapter 2, when classes are present in very unequal proportions, simple random sampling may produce too few of the rare class to yield useful information about what distinguishes them from the dominant class. In such cases stratified sampling is often used to oversample the cases from the rarer class and improve the performance of classifiers. It is often the case that the rarer events are the more interesting or important ones: responders to a mailing, those who commit fraud, defaulters on debt, and the like. This same stratified sampling procedure is sometimes called *weighted sampling* or *undersampling*, the latter referring to the fact that the more plentiful class is undersampled, relative to the rare class. We will stick to the term *oversampling*.

> In all discussions of *oversampling*, we assume the common situation in which there are two classes, one of much greater interest than the other. Data with more than two classes do not lend themselves to this procedure.

Consider the data in Figure 5.13, where × represents nonresponders, and ○, responders. The two axes correspond to two predictors. The dashed vertical line does the best job of classification under the assumption of equal costs: It results in just one misclassification (one ○ is misclassified as an ×). If we incorporate more realistic misclassification costs—let's say that failing to catch a ○ is five times as costly as failing to catch an ×—the costs of misclassification jump to 5. In such

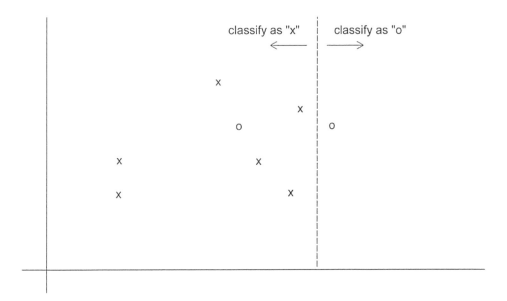

FIGURE 5.13 CLASSIFICATION ASSUMING EQUAL COSTS OF MISCLASSIFICATION

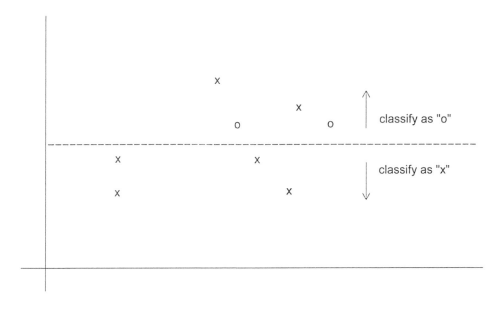

FIGURE 5.14 CLASSIFICATION ASSUMING UNEQUAL COSTS OF MISCLASSIFICATION

a case, a horizontal line as shown in Figure 5.14 does a better job: It results in misclassification costs of just 2.

Oversampling is one way of incorporating these costs into the training process. In Figure 5.15, we can see that classification algorithms would auto- matically determine the appropriate classification line if four additional o's were

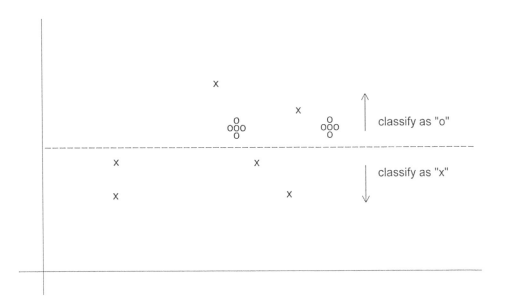

FIGURE 5.15   CLASSIFICATION USING OVERSAMPLING TO ACCOUNT FOR UNEQUAL COSTS

present at each existing ○. We can achieve appropriate results either by taking five times as many ○'s as we would get from simple random sampling (by sampling with replacement if necessary) or by replicating the existing ○'s fourfold.

Oversampling without replacement in accord with the ratio of costs (the first option above) is the optimal solution, but that may not always be practical. There may not be an adequate number of responders to assure that there will be enough of them to fit a model if they constitute only a small proportion of the total. Also, it is often the case that our interest in discovering responders is known to be much greater than our interest in discovering nonresponders, but the exact ratio of costs is difficult to determine. When faced with very low response rates in a classification problem, practitioners often sample equal numbers of responders and nonresponders as a relatively effective and convenient approach. Whatever approach is used, when it comes time to assess and predict model performance, we will need to adjust for the oversampling in one of two ways:

1. Score the model to a validation set that has been selected without over-sampling (i.e., via simple random sampling).

2. Score the model to an oversampled validation set, and reweight the results to remove the effects of oversampling.

The first method is more straightforward and easier to implement. We describe how to oversample and how to evaluate performance for each of the two methods.

> When classifying data with very low response rates, practitioners typically:
> - Train models on data that are 50% responder, 50% nonresponder.
> - Validate the models with an unweighted (simple random) sample from the original data.

Oversampling the Training Set

How is weighted sampling done? When responders are sufficiently scarce that you will want to use all of them, one common procedure is as follows:

1. First, the response and nonresponse data are separated into two distinct sets, or *strata*.

2. Records are then randomly selected for the training set from each stratum. Typically, one might select half the (scarce) responders for the training set, then an equal number of nonresponders.

3. The remaining responders are put in the validation set.

4. Nonresponders are randomly selected for the validation set in sufficient numbers to maintain the original ratio of responders to nonresponders.

5. If a test set is required, it can be taken randomly from the validation set.

Note: ASDM has a utility for this purpose.

Evaluating Model Performance Using a Non-oversampled Validation Set

Although the oversampled data can be used to train models, they are often not suitable for evaluating model performance because the number of responders will (of course) be exaggerated. The most straightforward way of gaining an unbiased estimate of model performance is to apply the model to regular data (i.e., data not oversampled). In short: Train the model on oversampled data, but validate it with regular data.

Evaluating Model Performance If Only Oversampled Validation Set Exists

In some cases, very low response rates may make it more practical to use over-sampled data not only for the training data but also for the validation data. This might happen, for example, if an analyst is given a dataset for exploration and prototyping that is already oversampled to boost the proportion with the rare response of interest (perhaps because it is more convenient to transfer and work with a smaller dataset). In such cases, it is still possible to assess how well the model will do with real data, but this requires the oversampled validation set to be reweighted, in order to restore the class of observations that were underrepresented in the sampling process. This adjustment should be made to the classification matrix and to the lift chart in order to derive good accuracy measures. These adjustments are described next.

I. Adjusting the Confusion Matrix for Oversampling   Suppose that the response rate in the data as a whole is 2%, and that the data were oversampled, yielding a sample in which the response rate is 25 times higher (50% responders). The relationship is as follows:

Responders: 2% of the whole data; 50% of the sample

Nonresponders: 98% of the whole data, 50% of the sample

Each responder in the whole data is worth 25 responders in the sample (50/2). Each nonresponder in the whole data is worth 0.5102 nonresponders in the sample (50/98). We call these values *oversampling weights*.

Assume that the validation confusion matrix looks like this:

CONFUSION MATRIX, OVERSAMPLED DATA (VALIDATION)

	Predicted 0	Predicted 1	Total
Actual 0	390	110	500
Actual 1	80	420	500
Total	470	530	1000

At this point the misclassification rate appears to be $(80 + 110)/1000 = 19\%$, and the model ends up classifying 53% of the records as 1's. However, this reflects the performance on a sample where 50% are responders.

To estimate predictive performance when this model is used to score the original population (with 2% responders), we need to undo the effects of the oversampling. The actual number of responders must be divided by 25, and the actual number of nonresponders divided by 0.5102.

The revised confusion matrix is as follows:

CONFUSION MATRIX, REWEIGHTED

	Predicted 0	Predicted 1	Total
Actual 0	$390/0.5102 = 764.4$	$110/0.5102 = 215.6$	980
Actual 1	$80/25 = 3.2$	$420/25 = 16.8$	20
Total			1000

The adjusted misclassification rate is $(3.2 + 215.6)/1000 = 21.9\%$. The model ends up classifying $(215.6 + 16.8)/1000 = 23.24\%$ of the records as 1's, when we assume 2% responders.

II. Adjusting the Lift Curve for Oversampling   The lift curve is likely to be a more useful measure in low-response situations, where our interest lies not so much in classifying all the records correctly as in finding a model that guides us toward those records most likely to contain the response of interest (under the assumption that scarce resources preclude examining or contacting all the records). Typically, our interest in such a case is in maximizing value or minimizing cost, so we will show the adjustment process incorporating the benefit/cost element. The following procedure can be used (and easily implemented in Excel):

1. Sort the validation records in order of the predicted probability of success (where success = belonging to the class of interest).

2. For each record, record the cost (benefit) associated with the actual outcome.

3. Divide that value by the oversampling rate. For example, if responders are overweighted by a factor of 25, divide by 25.

4. For the highest probability (i.e., first) record, the value above is the y-coordinate of the first point on the lift chart. The x-coordinate is index number 1.

5. For the next record, again calculate the adjusted value associated with the actual outcome. Add this to the adjusted cost (benefit) for the previous record. This sum is the y-coordinate of the second point on the lift curve. The x-coordinate is index number 2.

6. Repeat step 5 until all records have been examined. Connect all the points, and this is the lift curve.

7. The reference line is a straight line from the origin to the point y = total net benefit and $x = n$ (n = number of records).

PROBLEMS

5.1 A machine learning routine has been applied to a transaction dataset and has classified 88 records as fraudulent (30 correctly so) and 952 as nonfraudulent (920 correctly so). Construct the confusion matrix and calculate the error rate.

5.2 Suppose that this routine has an adjustable cutoff value mechanism by which you can alter the proportion of records classified as fraudulent. Describe how moving the cutoff up or down would affect the following:

  a. The classification error rate for records that are truly fraudulent.

  b. The classification error rate for records that are truly nonfraudulent.

5.3 Consider Figure 5.16, the decile-wise lift chart for the transaction data model, applied to new data.

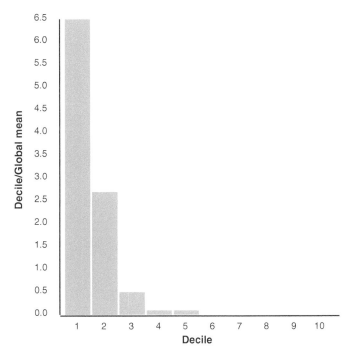

FIGURE 5.16   DECILE-WISE LIFT CHART FOR TRANSACTION DATA

  a. Interpret the meaning of the first and second bars from the left.

  b. Explain how you might use this information in practice.

  c. Another analyst comments that you could improve the accuracy of the model by classifying everything as nonfraudulent. If you do that, what is the error rate?

  d. Comment on the usefulness, in this situation, of these two metrics of model performance (error rate and lift).

5.4 FiscalNote is a startup founded by a Washington, DC entrepreneur and funded by a Singapore sovereign wealth fund, the Winklevoss twins of Facebook fame, and others. It uses machine learning techniques to predict for its clients whether legislation in the

US Congress and in US state legislatures will pass. The company reports 94% accuracy. (*Washington Post*, November 21, 2014, "Capital Business")

Considering just bills introduced in the US Congress, do a bit of Internet research to learn about numbers of bills introduced and passage rates. Identify the possible types of misclassifications, and comment on the use of overall accuracy as a metric. Include a discussion of other possible metrics and the potential role of propensities.

5.5 A large number of insurance records are to be examined to develop a model for predicting fraudulent claims. Of the claims in the historical database, 1% were judged to be fraudulent. A sample is taken to develop a model, and oversampling is used to provide a balanced sample in light of the very low response rate. When applied to this sample ($n = 800$), the model ends up correctly classifying 310 frauds and 270 nonfrauds. It missed 90 frauds, and classified 130 records incorrectly as frauds when they were not.

a. Produce the classification matrix for the sample as it stands.

b. Find the adjusted misclassification rate (adjusting for the oversampling).

c. What percentage of new records would you expect to be classified as fraudulent?

5.6 A firm that sells software services has been piloting a new product and has records of 500 customers who have either bought the services or decided not to. The target value is the estimated profit from each sale (excluding sales costs). The global mean is $2128. However, the cost of the sales effort is not cheap—the company figures it comes to $2500 for each of the 500 customers (whether or not they buy). The firm developed a predictive model to identify the top spenders in the future. The decile chart is shown in Figure 5.17.

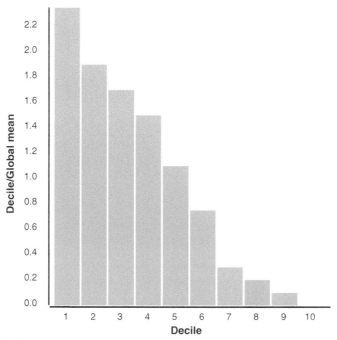

FIGURE 5.17   DECILE-WISE LIFT CHART FOR SOFTWARE SERVICES PRODUCT PROFIT

a. If the company begins working with a new set of 1000 leads to sell the same services, similar to the 500 in the pilot study, without any use of predictive modeling to target sales efforts, what is the estimated profit?

b. If the firm wants the average profit on each sale to at least double the sales effort cost, and applies an appropriate cutoff with this predictive model to a new set of 1000 leads, how far down the new list of 1000 should it proceed (how many deciles)?

c. Still considering the new list of 1000 leads, if the company applies this predictive model with a lower cutoff of $2500, how far should it proceed down the ranked leads, in terms of deciles?

d. Why use this two-stage process for predicting profit—why not simply develop a model for predicting profit for the 1000 new leads?

5.7   Table 5.4 shows a small set of predictive model validation results for a classification model, with both actual values and propensities.

a. Calculate error rates, sensitivity, and specificity using cutoffs of 0.25, 0.5, and 0.75.

b. Using a cutoff of 0.5, create a decile lift chart. First, create a table where column 1 is the decile and column 2 is the lift ratio for each decile. Then, use a bar chart to plot the decile lift chart using the two columns of the table.

TABLE 5.4   **PROPENSITIES AND ACTUAL CLASS MEMBERSHIP FOR VALIDATION DATA**

Propensity	Actual
0.03	0
0.52	0
0.38	0
0.82	1
0.33	0
0.42	0
0.55	1
0.59	0
0.09	0
0.21	0
0.43	0
0.04	0
0.08	0
0.13	0
0.01	0
0.79	1
0.42	0
0.29	0
0.08	0
0.02	0

Prediction and Classification Methods

## CHAPTER 6

Multiple Linear Regression

In this chapter, we introduce linear regression models for the purpose of prediction. We discuss the differences between fitting and using regression models for the purpose of inference (as in classical statistics) and for prediction. A predictive goal calls for evaluating model performance on a validation set and for using predictive metrics. We then raise the challenges of using many predictors and describe variable selection algorithms that are often implemented in linear regression procedures.

6.1 INTRODUCTION

The most popular model for making predictions is the *multiple linear regression model* encountered in most introductory statistics courses and textbooks. This model is used to fit a relationship between a quantitative *dependent variable* Y (also called the *outcome, target,* or *response variable*) and a set of *predictors* $X_1, X_2, \ldots, X_p$ (also referred to as *independent variables, input variables, regressors,* or *covariates*). The assumption is that the following function approximates the relationship between the input and outcome variables:

$$Y = \beta_0 + \beta_1 x_1 + \beta_2 x_2 + \cdots + \beta_p x_p + \varepsilon, \qquad (6.1)$$

where $\beta_0, \ldots, \beta_p$ are *coefficients* and ε is the *noise* or *unexplained* part. Data are then used to estimate the coefficients and to quantify the noise. In predictive modeling, the data are also used to evaluate model performance.

Regression modeling means not only estimating the coefficients but also choosing which input variables to include and in what form. For example, a numerical input can be included as-is, or in logarithmic form ($\log X$), or in a

Machine Learning for Business Analytics: Concepts, Techniques, and Applications with Analytic Solver® Data Mining, Fourth Edition. Galit Shmueli, Peter C. Bruce, Kuber R. Deokar, and Nitin R. Patel.

binned form (e.g., age group). Choosing the right form depends on domain knowledge, data availability, and needed predictive power.

Multiple linear regression is applicable to numerous predictive modeling situations. Examples are predicting customer activity on credit cards from their demographics and historical activity patterns, predicting the time to failure of equipment based on utilization and environment conditions, predicting expenditures on vacation travel based on historical frequent flyer data, predicting staffing requirements at help desks based on historical data and product and sales information, predicting sales from cross selling of products from historical information, and predicting the impact of discounts on sales in retail outlets.

6.2 EXPLANATORY VS. PREDICTIVE MODELING

Before introducing the use of linear regression for prediction, we must clarify an important distinction that often escapes those with earlier familiarity with linear regression from courses in statistics. In particular, the two popular but different objectives behind fitting a regression model are:

1. Explaining or quantifying the average effect of inputs on an output (explanatory or descriptive task, respectively).

2. Predicting the outcome value for new records, given their input values (predictive task).

The classical statistical approach is focused on the first objective. In that scenario, the data are treated as a random sample from a larger population of interest. The regression model estimated from this sample is an attempt to capture the *average* relationship in the larger population. This model is then used in decision making to generate statements such as "a unit increase in service speed (X_1) is associated with an average increase of five points in customer satisfaction (Y), all other factors $(X_2, X_3, \ldots, X_p)$ being equal." If X_1 is known to *cause* Y, then such a statement indicates actionable policy changes—this is called explanatory modeling. When the causal structure is unknown, then this model quantifies the degree of *association* between the inputs and output, and the approach is called descriptive modeling.

In predictive analytics, however, the focus is typically on the second goal: predicting new individual observations. Here we are not interested in the coefficients themselves, nor in the "average record," but rather in the predictions that this model can generate for new records. In this scenario, the model is used for micro-decision-making at the record level. In our previous example, we would use the regression model to predict customer satisfaction for each new customer of interest.

Both explanatory and predictive modeling involve using a dataset to fit a model (i.e., to estimate coefficients), checking model validity, assessing its performance, and comparing to other models. However, the modeling steps and performance assessment differ in the two cases, usually leading to different final models. Therefore, the choice of model is closely tied to whether the goal is explanatory or predictive.

In explanatory and descriptive modeling, where the focus is on modeling the average record, we try to fit the best model to the data in an attempt to learn about the underlying relationship in the population. In contrast, in predictive modeling (machine learning), the goal is to find a regression model that best predicts new individual records. A regression model that fits the existing data too well is not likely to perform well with new data. Hence, we look for a model that has the highest predictive power by evaluating it on a holdout set and using predictive metrics (see Chapter 5).

Let us summarize the main differences in using a linear regression in the two scenarios:

1. A good explanatory model is one that fits the data closely, whereas a good predictive model is one that predicts new cases accurately. Choices of input variables and their form can therefore differ.

2. In explanatory models, the entire dataset is used for estimating the best-fit model, to maximize the amount of information that we have about the hypothesized relationship in the population. When the goal is to predict outcomes of new individual cases, the data are typically split into a training set and a validation set. The training set is used to estimate the model, and the validation or *holdout set* is used to assess this model's predictive performance on new, unobserved data.[1]

3. Performance measures for explanatory models measure how close the data fit the model (how well the model approximates the data) and how strong the average relationship is, whereas in predictive models performance is measured by predictive accuracy (how well the model predicts new individual cases).

4. In explanatory models the focus is on the coefficients (β), whereas in predictive models the focus is on the predictions ($\hat{y}$).

For these reasons, it is extremely important to know the goal of the analysis before beginning the modeling process. A good predictive model can have a

---

[1]When we are comparing different model options (e.g., different predictors) or multiple models, the data should be partitioned into three sets: training, validation, and test. The validation set is used for selecting the model with the best performance, while the test set is used to assess the performance of the "best model" on new, unobserved data before model deployment.

looser fit to the data on which it is based, and a good explanatory model can have low prediction accuracy. In the remainder of this chapter, we focus on predictive models because these are more popular in machine learning and because most statistics textbooks focus on explanatory modeling.

6.3 ESTIMATING THE REGRESSION EQUATION AND PREDICTION

Once we determine the input variables to include and their form, we estimate the coefficients of the regression formula from the data using a method called *ordinary least squares* (OLS). This method finds values $\hat{\beta}_0, \hat{\beta}_1, \hat{\beta}_2, \ldots, \hat{\beta}_p$ that minimize the sum of squared deviations between the actual values (Y) and their predicted values based on that model $(\hat{Y})$.

To predict the value of the output variable for a record with input values $x_1, x_2, \ldots, x_p$, we use the equation

$$\hat{Y} = \hat{\beta}_0 + \hat{\beta}_1 x_1 + \hat{\beta}_2 x_2 + \cdots + \hat{\beta}_p x_p. \tag{6.2}$$

Predictions based on this equation are the best predictions possible in the sense that they will be unbiased (equal to the true values on average) and will have the smallest average squared error compared to any unbiased estimates *if* we make the following assumptions:

1. The noise ε (or equivalently, Y) follows a normal distribution.
2. The choice of variables and their form is correct (*linearity*).
3. The cases are independent of each other.
4. The variability in Y values for a given set of predictors is the same regardless of the values of the predictors (*homoskedasticity*).

An important and interesting fact for the predictive goal is that *even if we drop the first assumption and allow the noise to follow an arbitrary distribution, these estimates are very good for prediction,* in the sense that among all linear models, as defined by equation (6.1), the model using the least squares estimates, $\hat{\beta}_0, \hat{\beta}_1, \hat{\beta}_2, \ldots, \hat{\beta}_p$, will have the smallest average squared errors. The assumption of a normal distribution is required in explanatory modeling, where it is used for constructing confidence intervals and statistical tests for the model parameters.

Even if the other assumptions are violated, it is still possible that the resulting predictions are sufficiently accurate and precise for the purpose they are intended for. The key is to evaluate predictive performance of the model, which is the main priority. Satisfying assumptions is of secondary interest and residual analysis can give clues to potential improved models to examine.

Example: Predicting the Price of Used Toyota Corolla Cars

A large Toyota car dealership offers purchasers of new Toyota cars the option to buy their used car as part of a trade-in. In particular, a new promotion promises to pay high prices for used Toyota Corolla cars for purchasers of a new car. The dealer then sells the used cars for a small profit. To ensure a reasonable profit, the dealer needs to be able to predict the price that the dealership will get for the used cars. For that reason, data were collected on all previous sales of used Toyota Corollas at the dealership. The data include the sales price and other information on the car, such as its age, mileage, fuel type, and engine size. A description of each of these variables is given in Table 6.1. A sample of this dataset is shown in Table 6.2.

TABLE 6.1   VARIABLES IN THE TOYOTA COROLLA EXAMPLE

Variable	Description
Price	Offer price in Euros
Age	Age in months as of August 2004
Kilometers	Accumulated kilometers on odometer
Fuel Type	Fuel type (*Petrol, Diesel, CNG*)
HP	Horsepower
Metallic	Metallic color? (Yes = 1, No = 0)
Automatic	Automatic (Yes = 1, No = 0)
CC	Cylinder volume in cubic centimeters
Doors	Number of doors
QuartTax	Quarterly road tax in Euros
Weight	Weight in kilograms

The total number of records in the dataset is 1436 cars (we use the first 1000 cars from the dataset `ToyotoCorolla.xlsx` for analysis). After creating dummy variables for the categorical predictor *Fuel Type*[2] and partitioning the data into training (60%) and validation (40%) sets, we fit a multiple linear regression model between price (the output variable) and the other variables (as predictors) using only the training set. Figure 6.1 shows the estimated coefficients, as computed by ASDM.

Notice that the Fuel Type predictor has three categories (*Petrol, Diesel,* and *CNG*). We therefore have two dummy variables in the model: Petrol (0/1) and Diesel (0/1); the third, CNG (0/1), is redundant given the information on the first two dummies. Inclusion of this redundant variable will cause typical

---

[2]In ASDM, it is possible to avoid the step of creating dummy variables by directly including categorical predictors in the Categorical Variables field in the Linear Regression menu. However, due to a pre-processing step performed by the software, sometimes the resulting estimated model excludes an intercept. Both approaches (dummy creation or direct inclusion of categorical predictors) will lead to the same predictions, and therefore the user can choose either approach in a prediction scenario.

TABLE 6.2   PRICES AND ATTRIBUTES FOR USED TOYOTA COROLLA CARS (SELECTED ROWS
                 AND COLUMNS ONLY)

Price	Age	Kilometers	Fuel type	HP	Metallic	Auto-matic	CC	Doors	Quart Tax	Weight
13,500	23	46,986	Diesel	90	1	0	2000	3	210	1165
13,750	23	72,937	Diesel	90	1	0	2000	3	210	1165
13,950	24	41,711	Diesel	90	1	0	2000	3	210	1165
14,950	26	48,000	Diesel	90	0	0	2000	3	210	1165
13,750	30	38,500	Diesel	90	0	0	2000	3	210	1170
12,950	32	61,000	Diesel	90	0	0	2000	3	210	1170
16,900	27	94,612	Diesel	90	1	0	2000	3	210	1245
18,600	30	75,889	Diesel	90	1	0	2000	3	210	1245
21,500	27	19,700	Petrol	192	0	0	1800	3	100	1185
12,950	23	71,138	Diesel	69	0	0	1900	3	185	1105
20,950	25	31,461	Petrol	192	0	0	1800	3	100	1185
19,950	22	43,610	Petrol	192	0	0	1800	3	100	1185
19,600	25	32,189	Petrol	192	0	0	1800	3	100	1185
21,500	31	23,000	Petrol	192	1	0	1800	3	100	1185
22,500	32	34,131	Petrol	192	1	0	1800	3	100	1185
22,000	28	18,739	Petrol	192	0	0	1800	3	100	1185
22,750	30	34,000	Petrol	192	1	0	1800	3	100	1185
17,950	24	21,716	Petrol	110	1	0	1600	3	85	1105
16,750	24	25,563	Petrol	110	0	0	1600	3	19	1065
16,950	30	64,359	Petrol	110	1	0	1600	3	85	1105
15,950	30	67,660	Petrol	110	1	0	1600	3	85	1105
16,950	29	43,905	Petrol	110	0	1	1600	3	100	1170
15,950	28	56,349	Petrol	110	1	0	1600	3	85	1120
16,950	28	32,220	Petrol	110	1	0	1600	3	85	1120
16,250	29	25,813	Petrol	110	1	0	1600	3	85	1120
15,950	25	28,450	Petrol	110	1	0	1600	3	85	1120
17,495	27	34,545	Petrol	110	1	0	1600	3	85	1120
15,750	29	41,415	Petrol	110	1	0	1600	3	85	1120
11,950	39	98,823	CNG	110	1	0	1600	5	197	1119

Coefficients

Predictor	Estimate	Confidence Interval: Lower	Confidence Interval: Upper	Standard Error	T-Statistic	P-Value
Intercept	-3092.3662	-6251.7994	67.0670	1608.6673	-1.9223	0.0550
Age_08_04	-132.6615	-141.8995	-123.4236	4.7036	-28.2041	0.0000
KM	-0.0212	-0.0256	-0.0168	0.0022	-9.4588	0.0000
HP	42.0362	32.7017	51.3708	4.7528	8.8445	0.0000
Met_Color	165.2588	-75.0337	405.5514	122.3481	1.3507	0.1773
Automatic	454.3259	-44.8779	953.5298	254.1763	1.7874	0.0744
CC	0.0037	-0.1815	0.1888	0.0943	0.0389	0.9690
Doors	-129.4727	-249.6833	-9.2621	61.2068	-2.1153	0.0348
Quarterly_Tax	15.3352	10.1466	20.5237	2.6418	5.8048	0.0000
Weight	13.9023	10.8882	16.9163	1.5347	9.0589	0.0000
Fuel_Type_Diesel	1389.9271	466.3193	2313.5350	470.2672	2.9556	0.0032
Fuel_Type_Petrol	2515.8331	1568.7759	3462.8902	482.2067	5.2173	0.0000

FIGURE 6.1   ESTIMATED COEFFICIENTS FOR REGRESSION MODEL OF PRICE VS. CAR
                  ATTRIBUTES

regression software to fail due to a *multicollinearity* error since the redundant variable will be a perfect linear combination of the other two (see Section 4.5).

The regression coefficients are then used to predict prices of individual used Toyota Corolla cars based on their age, mileage, and so on. Figure 6.2 shows a sample of predicted prices for 20 cars in the validation set, using the estimated model. It gives the predictions and their errors (relative to the actual prices) for these 20 cars, as well as overall measures of predictive accuracy. Note that RMSE is $1413 and the average error is $35 (calculated by taking a simple average of the residuals on the validation data). A histogram of the residuals (Figure 6.3) shows that most of the errors are in the range ±$1500. This error magnitude can be meaningful relative to the car price and therefore should be taken into account when considering the profit. Another observation of interest is the large positive residuals (underpredictions), which may or may not be a concern, depending on the application. Measures such as the RMSE, MAD, average error, and error percentiles are used to assess the predictive performance of a model and to compare models. We discuss such measures in the next section. This example also illustrates the point about the relaxation of the normality assumption. A histogram or probability plot of prices shows a right-skewed distribution. In a descriptive/explanatory modeling case where the goal is to obtain a good fit to the data, the output variable would be transformed (e.g., by taking a logarithm)

(a) Validation: Prediction Details

Record ID	Price	Prediction: Price	Residual
Record 774	10950	9282.1065	1667.8935
Record 104	18500	18694.6944	-194.6944
Record 903	9950	7633.4346	2316.5654
Record 660	10500	8810.3560	1689.6440
Record 575	9980	11185.8312	-1205.8312
Record 163	19600	19019.6580	580.3420
Record 411	7900	10398.2070	-2498.2070
Record 694	9900	7141.5331	2758.4669
Record 460	10990	10661.7933	328.2067
Record 795	11950	10415.4776	1534.5224
Record 290	12950	13190.5301	-240.5301
Record 207	12500	12703.5841	-203.5841
Record 328	12950	14729.9383	-1779.9383
Record 350	12750	14864.5311	-2114.5311
Record 971	9950	8457.1722	1492.8278
Record 470	11250	11464.4207	-214.4207
Record 869	9950	9166.8561	783.1439
Record 964	9950	10535.0076	-585.0076
Record 966	9900	9854.2586	45.7414
Record 667	9500	8320.2497	1179.7503

(b) Validation: Prediction Summary

Metric	Value
SSE	799341491.6681
MSE	1998353.7292
RMSE	1413.6314
MAD	1109.2115
R2	0.8582

FIGURE 6.2   (a) PREDICTED PRICES (AND ERRORS) FOR 20 CARS IN VALIDATION SET, AND (b) SUMMARY PREDICTIVE MEASURES FOR VALIDATION SET

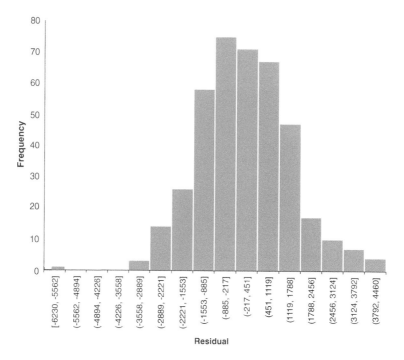

FIGURE 6.3   HISTOGRAM OF RESIDUALS (BASED ON VALIDATION SET). PRODUCED IN EXCEL

to achieve a more "normal" variable. Although the fit of such a model to the training data is expected to be better, it may or may not necessarily improve predictive performance. In this example the RMSE in a model of log(price) is $1285.88, compared to $1413.63 in the original model for price.

6.4 VARIABLE SELECTION IN LINEAR REGRESSION

Reducing the Number of Predictors

A frequent problem in machine learning is that of using a regression equation to predict the value of a dependent variable when we have many variables available to choose as predictors in our model. Given the high speed of modern algorithms for multiple linear regression calculations, it is tempting in such a situation to take a kitchen-sink approach: Why bother to select a subset? Just use all the variables in the model.

Another consideration favoring the inclusions of numerous variables is the hope that a previously hidden relationship will emerge. For example, a company found that customers who had purchased anti-scuff protectors for chair and table legs had lower credit risks. However, there are several reasons for exercising caution before throwing all possible variables into a model.

- It may be expensive or not feasible to collect a full complement of predictors for future predictions.

- We may be able to measure fewer predictors more accurately (e.g., in surveys).

- The more predictors there are, the higher the chance of missing values in the data. If we delete or impute cases with missing values, multiple predictors will lead to a higher rate of case deletion or imputation.

- *Parsimony* is an important property of good models. We obtain more insight into the influence of predictors in models with few parameters.

- Estimates of regression coefficients are likely to be unstable, due to *multicollinearity* in models with many variables. (Multicollinearity is the presence of two or more predictors sharing the same linear relationship with the outcome variable.) Regression coefficients are more stable for parsimonious models. One very rough rule of thumb is to have a number of cases n larger than $5(p + 2)$, where p is the number of predictors.

- It can be shown that using predictors that are uncorrelated with the dependent variable increases the variance of predictions.

- It can be shown that dropping predictors that are actually correlated with the dependent variable can increase the average error (bias) of predictions.

The last two points mean that there is a trade-off between too few and too many predictors. In general, accepting some bias can reduce the variance in predictions. This *bias–variance trade-off* is particularly important for large numbers of predictors, since in that case it is very likely that there are variables in the model that have small coefficients relative to the standard deviation of the noise and also exhibit at least moderate correlation with other variables. Dropping such variables will improve the predictions, as it reduces the prediction variance. This type of bias–variance trade-off is a basic aspect of most machine learning procedures for prediction and classification. In light of this, methods for reducing the number of predictors p to a smaller set are often used.

How to Reduce the Number of Predictors

The first step in trying to reduce the number of predictors should always be to use domain knowledge. It is important to understand what the various predictors are measuring and why they are relevant for predicting the response. With this knowledge, the set of predictors should be reduced to a sensible set that reflects the problem at hand. Some practical reasons for predictor elimination are the expense of collecting this information in the future, inaccuracy, high correlation with another predictor, many missing values, or simply irrelevance. Also helpful in examining potential predictors are summary statistics and graphs, such as frequency and correlation tables, predictor-specific summary statistics and plots, and missing value counts.

The next step makes use of computational power and statistical significance. In general, there are two types of methods for reducing the number of predictors in a model. The first is an *exhaustive search* for the "best" subset of predictors by fitting regression models with all the possible combinations of predictors. The second is to search through a partial set of models. We describe these two approaches next. In any case, using computational variable selection methods involves comparing many models and choosing the best one. In such cases, it is advisable to have a test set in addition to the training and validation sets. The validation set is used to compare the models and select the best one. The holdout set is then used to evaluate the predictive performance of this selected model.

Exhaustive Search (Best Subset)   The idea here is to evaluate all subsets. Since the number of subsets for even moderate values of p is very large, after the algorithm creates the subsets and runs all the models, we need some way to examine the most promising subsets and to select from them. Criteria for evaluating and comparing models are based on metrics computed from the training data. One popular criterion is the *adjusted R^2*, which is defined as

$$R^2_{\text{adj}} = 1 - \frac{n-1}{n-p-1}(1 - R^2),$$

where R^2 is the proportion of explained variability in the model (in a model with a single predictor, this is the squared correlation). Like R^2, higher values of adjusted R^2 indicate better fit. Unlike R^2, which does not account for the number of predictors used, adjusted R^2 uses a penalty on the number of predictors. This avoids the artificial increase in R^2 that can result from simply increasing the number of predictors but not the amount of information. It can be shown that using R^2_{adj} to choose a subset is equivalent to choosing the subset that minimizes the training RMSE.

Another criterion that is often used for subset selection is known as *Mallow's C_p* (see formula below). This criterion assumes that the full model (with all predictors) is unbiased, although it may have predictors that, if dropped, would reduce prediction variability. With this assumption we can show that if a subset model is unbiased, the average C_p value equals the number of parameters $p + 1$ (= number of predictors + 1), the size of the subset. So a reasonable approach to identifying subset models with small bias is to examine those with values of C_p that are near $p + 1$. C_p is also an estimate of the error[3] for predictions at the x-values observed in the training set. Thus, good models are those that have values of C_p near $p + 1$ and that have small p (i.e., are of small size). C_p is computed from the formula

$$C_p = \frac{\text{SSE}}{\hat{\sigma}^2_{\text{full}}} + 2(p+1) - n, \tag{6.3}$$

---

[3]In particular, it is the sum of the MSE standardized by dividing by σ^2.

where $\hat{\sigma}^2_{\text{full}}$ is the estimated value of σ^2 in the full model that includes all predictors. It is important to remember that the usefulness of this approach depends heavily on the reliability of the estimate of σ^2 for the full model. This requires that the training set contain a large number of observations relative to the number of predictors. Finally, a useful point to note is that for a fixed size of subset, R^2, R^2_{adj}, and C_p all select the same subset. There is in fact no difference among them in the order of merit that they ascribe to subsets of a fixed size. This is good to know if comparing models with the same number of predictors, but often we want to compare models with different numbers of predictors.

Figure 6.4 gives the results of applying an exhaustive search ("best subsets" in ASDM) on the Toyota Corolla price data (with the 11 predictors). It reports the best model with a single predictor, two predictors, and so on. It can be seen that the R^2_{adj} increases until six predictors are used (#coefficients = 7) and then stabilizes. The C_p indicates that a model with 9–11 predictors is good. The dominant predictor in all models is the age of the car, with horsepower and mileage playing important roles as well.

Feature Selection

Best Subsets

Subset ID	Intercept	Age_08_04	KM	HP	Met_Color	Automatic	CC	Doors	Quarterly_Tax	Weight	Fuel_Type_Diesel	Fuel_Type_Petrol
Subset 1	1	0	0	0	0	0	0	0	0	0	0	0
Subset 2	1	1	0	0	0	0	0	0	0	0	0	0
Subset 3	1	1	0	1	0	0	0	0	0	0	0	0
Subset 4	1	1	1	0	0	0	0	0	0	1	0	0
Subset 5	1	1	1	1	0	0	0	0	0	1	0	0
Subset 6	1	1	1	1	0	0	0	0	1	1	0	0
Subset 7	1	1	1	1	0	0	0	0	1	1	0	1
Subset 8	1	1	1	1	0	0	0	0	1	1	1	1
Subset 9	1	1	1	1	0	0	0	1	1	1	1	1
Subset 10	1	1	1	1	0	1	0	1	1	1	1	1
Subset 11	1	1	1	1	1	1	0	1	1	1	1	1
Subset 12	1	1	1	1	1	1	1	1	1	1	1	1

Best Subsets Details

Subset ID	#Coefficients	RSS	Mallows's Cp	R2	Adjusted R2	Probability
Subset 1	1	8400665894	4058.5313	0.0000	0.0000	0.0000
Subset 2	2	2052522022	541.7233	0.7557	0.7553	0.0000
Subset 3	3	1694127987	345.0636	0.7983	0.7977	0.0000
Subset 4	4	1348575230	155.5220	0.8395	0.8387	0.0000
Subset 5	5	1153590564	49.4410	0.8627	0.8618	0.0000
Subset 6	6	1125330324	35.7762	0.8660	0.8649	0.0000
Subset 7	7	1092561716	19.6124	0.8699	0.8686	0.0038
Subset 8	8	1077566856	13.3007	0.8717	0.8702	0.0553
Subset 9	9	1069490729	10.8241	0.8727	0.8710	0.1864
Subset 10	10	1064093126	9.8322	0.8733	0.8714	0.4007
Subset 11	11	1060790523	10.0015	0.8737	0.8716	0.9690
Subset 12	12	1060787798	12.0000	0.8737	0.8714	N/A

FIGURE 6.4   EXHAUSTIVE SEARCH RESULT FOR REDUCING PREDICTORS IN TOYOTA COROLLA PRICE EXAMPLE

Popular Subset Selection Algorithms   The second method of finding the best subset of predictors relies on a partial, iterative search through the space of all possible regression models. The end product is one best subset of predictors (although there do exist variations of these methods that identify several close-to-best choices for different sizes of predictor subsets). This approach is computationally cheaper, but it has the potential of missing "good" combinations of predictors. None of the methods guarantee that they yield the best subset for any criterion, such as adjusted R^2. They are reasonable methods for situations with large numbers of predictors, but for moderate numbers of predictors, the exhaustive search is preferable.

Three popular iterative search algorithms are *forward selection*, *backward elimination*, and *stepwise regression*. In *forward selection*, we start with no predictors and then add predictors one by one. Each predictor added is the one (among all predictors) that has the largest contribution to R^2 on top of the predictors that are already in it. The algorithm stops when the contribution of additional predictors is not statistically significant. The main disadvantage of this method is that the algorithm will miss pairs or groups of predictors that perform very well together but perform poorly as single predictors. This is similar to interviewing job candidates for a team project one by one, thereby missing groups of candidates who perform superiorly together, but poorly on their own.

In *backward elimination*, we start with all predictors and then at each step eliminate the least useful predictor (according to statistical significance). The algorithm stops when all the remaining predictors have significant contributions. The weakness of this algorithm is that computing the initial model with all predictors can be time consuming and unstable. *Stepwise regression* is like forward selection except that at each step we consider dropping predictors that are not statistically significant, as in backward elimination.

Note: In ASDM, unlike other popular software packages (SAS, Minitab, etc.), these three algorithms, like exhaustive search, yield a table of multiple models rather than a single model. This allows the user to decide on the subset size after reviewing all possible sizes based on criteria such as R^2_{adj} and C_p.

For the Toyota Corolla price example, forward selection yields exactly the same results as those found in an exhaustive search for models with up to 10 predictors (compare Figures 6.4 and 6.5). Forward stops at 10 predictors, because no other predictors at this point exceed the needed threshold to enter. Notice that this is not always the case.

Backward elimination starts with the full model and then drops predictors one by one, first dropping CC then Met_Color (see Figure 6.6). The R^2_{adj} and C_p measures indicate exactly the same subsets as those suggested by the exhaustive search. In other words, it correctly identifies CC and Met_Color as the least useful predictors.

The results for stepwise selection can be seen in Figure 6.7. In this case, it chooses the same subsets as forward selection.

This example shows that the search algorithms yield fairly good solutions, but we need to carefully determine the number of predictors to retain. It also shows

Feature Selection

Best Subsets

Subset ID	Intercept	Age_08_04	KM	HP	Met_Color	Automatic	CC	Doors	Quarterly_Tax	Weight	Fuel_Type_Diesel	Fuel_Type_Petrol
Subset 1	1	0	0	0	0	0	0	0	0	0	0	0
Subset 2	1	1	0	0	0	0	0	0	0	0	0	0
Subset 3	1	1	0	1	0	0	0	0	0	0	0	0
Subset 4	1	1	0	1	0	0	0	0	0	1	0	0
Subset 5	1	1	1	1	0	0	0	0	0	1	0	0
Subset 6	1	1	1	1	0	0	0	0	1	1	0	0
Subset 7	1	1	1	1	0	0	0	0	1	1	0	1
Subset 8	1	1	1	1	0	0	0	0	1	1	1	1
Subset 9	1	1	1	1	0	0	0	1	1	1	1	1

Best Subsets Details

Subset ID	#Coefficients	RSS	Mallows's Cp	R2	Adjusted R2	Probability
Subset 1	1	8400665894	4058.5313	0.0000	0.0000	0.0000
Subset 2	2	2052522022	541.7233	0.7557	0.7553	0.0000
Subset 3	3	1694127987	345.0636	0.7983	0.7977	0.0000
Subset 4	4	1374080258	169.6596	0.8364	0.8356	0.0000
Subset 5	5	1153590564	49.4410	0.8627	0.8618	0.0000
Subset 6	6	1125330324	35.7762	0.8660	0.8649	0.0000
Subset 7	7	1092561716	19.6124	0.8699	0.8686	0.0038
Subset 8	8	1077566856	13.3007	0.8717	0.8702	0.0553
Subset 9	9	1069490729	10.8241	0.8727	0.8710	0.1864

FIGURE 6.5   FORWARD SELECTION RESULT FOR REDUCING PREDICTORS IN TOYOTA COROLLA PRICE EXAMPLE

Feature Selection

Best Subsets

Subset ID	Intercept	Age_08_04	KM	HP	Met_Color	Automatic	CC	Doors	Quarterly_Tax	Weight	Fuel_Type_Diesel	Fuel_Type_Petrol
Subset 1	1	1	1	1	1	1	1	1	1	1	1	1
Subset 2	1	1	1	1	1	1	0	1	1	1	1	1
Subset 3	1	1	1	1	0	1	0	1	1	1	1	1

Best Subsets Details

Subset ID	#Coefficients	RSS	Mallows's Cp	R2	Adjusted R2	Probability
Subset 1	12	1060787798	12.0000	0.8737	0.8714	N/A
Subset 2	11	1060790523	10.0015	0.8737	0.8716	0.9690
Subset 3	10	1064093126	9.8322	0.8733	0.8714	0.4007

FIGURE 6.6   BACKWARD ELIMINATION RESULT FOR REDUCING PREDICTORS IN TOYOTA COROLLA PRICE EXAMPLE

the merits of running a few searches and using the combined results to determine the subset to choose. There is a popular (but false) notion that stepwise regression is superior to backward elimination and forward selection because of its ability to add and to drop predictors.

Additional ways to reduce the dimension of the data are by using principal components (Chapter 4) and regression trees (Chapter 9).

The machine learning workflow for the multiple linear regression model and four variable selection methods (exhaustive search, forward selection, backward elimination, and stepwise regression) that we used in this chapter are shown in Figure 6.8. This all-inclusive workflow can be used to run and reproduce the results (see Chapter 2 on how to create and run workflows in ASDM).

Feature Selection

Best Subsets

Subset ID	Intercept	Age_08_04	KM	HP	Met_Color	Automatic	CC	Doors	Quarterly_Tax	Weight	Fuel_Type_Diesel	Fuel_Type_Petrol
Subset 1	1	0	0	0	0	0	0	0	0	0	0	0
Subset 2	1	1	0	0	0	0	0	0	0	0	0	0
Subset 3	1	1	0	1	0	0	0	0	0	0	0	0
Subset 4	1	1	0	1	0	0	0	0	0	1	0	0
Subset 5	1	1	1	1	0	0	0	0	0	1	0	0
Subset 6	1	1	1	1	0	0	0	0	1	1	0	0
Subset 7	1	1	1	1	0	0	0	0	1	1	0	1
Subset 8	1	1	1	1	0	0	0	0	1	1	1	1
Subset 9	1	1	1	1	0	0	0	1	1	1	1	1

Best Subsets Details

Subset ID	#Coefficients	RSS	Mallows's Cp	R2	Adjusted R2	Probability
Subset 1	1	8400665894	4058.5313	0.0000	0.0000	0.0000
Subset 2	2	2052522022	541.7233	0.7557	0.7553	0.0000
Subset 3	3	1694127987	345.0636	0.7983	0.7977	0.0000
Subset 4	4	1374080258	169.6596	0.8364	0.8356	0.0000
Subset 5	5	1153590564	49.4410	0.8627	0.8618	0.0000
Subset 6	6	1125330324	35.7762	0.8660	0.8649	0.0000
Subset 7	7	1092561716	19.6124	0.8699	0.8686	0.0038
Subset 8	8	1077566856	13.3007	0.8717	0.8702	0.0553
Subset 9	9	1069490729	10.8241	0.8727	0.8710	0.1864

FIGURE 6.7   STEPWISE REGRESSION RESULT FOR REDUCING PREDICTORS IN TOYOTA COROLLA PRICE EXAMPLE

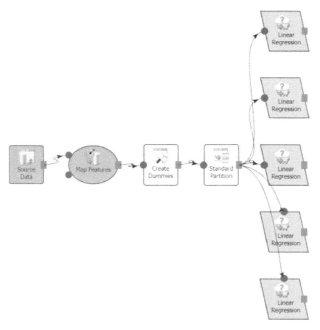

FIGURE 6.8   WORKFLOW FOR LINEAR REGRESSION MODEL AND FOUR VARIABLE SELECTION METHODS (EXHAUSTIVE SEARCH, FORWARD SELECTION, BACKWARD ELIMINATION, AND STEPWISE REGRESSION)

PROBLEMS

6.1 **Predicting Boston Housing Prices.** The file BostonHousing.xlsx contains information collected by the US Bureau of the Census concerning housing in the area of Boston, Massachusetts. The dataset includes information on 506 census housing tracts in the Boston area. The goal is to predict the median house price in new tracts based on information such as crime rate, pollution, and number of rooms. The dataset contains 12 predictors, and the response is the median house price (MEDV). Table 6.3 describes each of the predictors and the outcome variable.

TABLE 6.3   DESCRIPTION OF VARIABLES FOR BOSTON HOUSING EXAMPLE

CRIM	Per capita crime rate by town
ZN	Proportion of residential land zoned for lots over 25,000 ft^2
INDUS	Proportion of nonretail business acres per town
CHAS	Charles River dummy variable (= 1 if tract bounds river; = 0 otherwise)
NOX	Nitric oxide concentration (parts per 10 million)
RM	Average number of rooms per dwelling
AGE	Proportion of owner-occupied units built prior to 1940
DIS	Weighted distances to five Boston employment centers
RAD	Index of accessibility to radial highways
TAX	Full-value property-tax rate per $10,000
PTRATIO	Pupil/teacher ratio by town
LSTAT	% Lower status of the population
MEDV	Median value of owner-occupied homes in $1000s

a. Why should the data be partitioned into training and validation sets? What will the training set be used for? What will the validation set be used for?

b. Partition the data into training/validation/test with proportions 60 : 25 : 15. Fit a multiple linear regression model to the median house price (MEDV) as a function of CRIM, CHAS, and RM. Write the equation for predicting the median house price from the predictors in the model.

c. Using the estimated regression model, what median house price is predicted for a tract in the Boston area that does not bound the Charles River, has a crime rate of 0.1, and where the average number of rooms per house is 6?

d. Reduce the number of predictors:

i. Which predictors are likely to be measuring the same thing among the 13 predictors? Discuss the relationships among INDUS, NOX, and TAX.

ii. Compute the correlation table for the 12 numerical predictors and search for highly correlated pairs. These have potential redundancy and can cause multicollinearity. Choose which ones to remove based on this table.

iii. Use an exhaustive search to reduce the remaining predictors as follows: First, choose the top three models. Then run each of these models separately on the training set, and compare their predictive accuracy for the validation set. Compare RMSE and MAD, as well as lift charts. Finally, describe the best model.

iv. Evaluate the performance of the best model on the test data. Report the test RMSE and MAD.

6.2 **Predicting Software Reselling Profits.** Tayko Software is a software catalog firm that sells games and educational software. It started out as a software manufacturer and then added third-party titles to its offerings. It recently revised its collection of items in a new catalog, which it mailed out to its customers. This mailing yielded 1000 purchases. Based on these data, Tayko wants to devise a model for predicting the spending amount that a purchasing customer will yield. The file `Tayko.xlsx` contains information on 1000 purchases. Table 6.4 describes the variables to be used in the problem (the Excel file contains additional variables).

TABLE 6.4   DESCRIPTION OF VARIABLES FOR TAYKO SOFTWARE EXAMPLE

FREQ	Number of transactions in the preceding year
LAST_UPDATE	Number of days since last update to customer record
WEB	Whether customer purchased by Web order at least once
GENDER	Male or female
ADDRESS_RES	Whether it is a residential address
ADDRESS_US	Whether it is a U.S. address
SPENDING (response)	Amount spent by customer in test mailing (in dollars)

a. Explore the spending amount by creating a pivot table for the categorical variables and computing the average and standard deviation of spending in each category.

b. Explore the relationship between spending and each of the two continuous predictors by creating two scatterplots (SPENDING vs. FREQ, and SPENDING vs. LAST_UPDATE). Does there seem to be a linear relationship?

c. To fit a predictive model for SPENDING:

   i. Partition the 1000 records into training and validation sets.

   ii. Run a multiple linear regression model for SPENDING vs. all six predictors. Give the estimated predictive equation.

   iii. Based on this model, what type of purchaser is most likely to spend a large amount of money?

   iv. If we used backward elimination to reduce the number of predictors, which predictor would be dropped first from the model?

   v. Show how the prediction and the prediction error are computed for the first purchase in the validation set.

   vi. Evaluate the predictive accuracy of the model by examining its performance on the validation set.

   vii. Create a histogram of the model residuals. Do they appear to follow a normal distribution? How does this affect the predictive performance of the model?

6.3 **Predicting Airfare on New Routes.** The following problem takes place in the United States in the late 1990s, when many major US cities were facing issues with airport congestion, partly as a result of the 1978 deregulation of airlines. Both fares and routes were freed from regulation, and low-fare carriers such as Southwest began competing on existing routes and starting nonstop service on routes that previously lacked it. Building completely new airports is generally not feasible, but sometimes decommissioned military bases or smaller municipal airports can be reconfigured as regional or larger commercial airports. There are numerous players and interests involved in the issue (airlines, city, state and federal authorities, civic groups, the military, airport operators), and an aviation consulting firm is seeking advisory contracts with these players. The firm needs predictive models to support its consulting service. One thing the firm might want to be able to predict is fares, in the event a new airport is brought into service. The firm starts with the file `Airfares.xlsx`, which contains real data that were collected between Q3-1996 and Q2-97. The variables in these data are listed in Table 6.5, and are believed to be important in predicting FARE. Some airport-to-airport data are available, but most data are at the city-to-city level. One question that will be of interest in the analysis is the effect that the presence or absence of Southwest (SW) has on FARE.

TABLE 6.5   DESCRIPTION OF VARIABLES FOR AIRFARE EXAMPLE

S_CODE	Starting airport's code
S_CITY	Starting city
E_CODE	Ending airport's code
E_CITY	Ending city
COUPON	Average number of coupons (a one-coupon flight is a nonstop flight, a two-coupon flight is a one-stop flight, etc.) for that route
NEW	Number of new carriers entering that route between Q3-96 and Q2-97
VACATION	Whether (Yes) or not (No) a vacation route
SW	Whether (Yes) or not (No) Southwest Airlines serves that route
HI	Herfindahl index: measure of market concentration
S_INCOME	Starting city's average personal income
E_INCOME	Ending city's average personal income
S_POP	Starting city's population
E_POP	Ending city's population
SLOT	Whether or not either endpoint airport is slot controlled (this is a measure of airport congestion)
GATE	Whether or not either endpoint airport has gate constraints (this is another measure of airport congestion)
DISTANCE	Distance between two endpoint airports in miles
PAX	Number of passengers on that route during period of data collection
FARE	Average fare on that route

a. Explore the numerical predictors and response (FARE) by creating a correlation table and examining some scatterplots between FARE and those predictors. What seems to be the best single predictor of FARE?

b. Explore the categorical predictors (excluding the first four) by computing the percentage of flights in each category. Create a pivot table with the average fare in each category. Which categorical predictor seems best for predicting FARE?

c. Find a model for predicting the average fare on a new route:

  i. Convert categorical variables into dummy variables. Then partition the data into training and validation sets. The model will be fit to the training data and evaluated on the validation set.

  ii. Use stepwise regression to reduce the number of predictors. You can ignore the first four predictors (S_CODE, S_CITY, E_CODE, E_CITY). Report the estimated model selected.

  iii. Repeat (ii) using exhaustive search instead of stepwise regression. Compare the resulting best model to the one you obtained in (ii) in terms of the predictors that are in the model.

  iv. Compare the predictive accuracy of both models (ii) and (iii) using measures such as RMSE and MAD and lift charts.

   v. Using model (iii), predict the average fare on a route with the following characteristics: COUPON = 1.202, NEW = 3, VACATION = No, SW = No, HI = 4442.141, S_INCOME = $28,760, E_INCOME = $27,664, S_POP = 4,557,004, E_POP = 3,195,503, SLOT = Free, GATE = Free, PAX = 12,782, DISTANCE = 1976 miles.

   vi. Using model (iii), predict the reduction in average fare on the route in (v) if Southwest decides to cover this route.

   vii. In reality, which of the factors will not be available for predicting the average fare from a new airport (i.e., before flights start operating on those routes)? Which ones can be estimated? How?

   viii. Select a model that includes only factors that are available before flights begin to operate on the new route. Use an exhaustive search to find such a model.

   ix. Use the model in (viii) to predict the average fare on a route with characteristics COUPON = 1.202, NEW = 3, VACATION = No, SW = No, HI = 4442.141, S_INCOME = $28,760, E_INCOME = $27,664, S_ POP = 4,557,004, E_POP = 3,195,503, SLOT = Free, GATE = Free, PAX = 12,782, DISTANCE = 1976 miles.

   x. Compare the predictive accuracy of this model with model (iii). Is this model good enough, or is it worthwhile re-evaluating the model once flights begin on the new route?

  d. In competitive industries, a new entrant with a novel business plan can have a disruptive effect on existing firms. If a new entrant's business model is sustainable, other players are forced to respond by changing their business practices. If the goal of the analysis was to evaluate the effect of Southwest Airlines' presence on the airline industry rather than predicting fares on new routes, how would the analysis be different? Describe technical and conceptual aspects.

6.4 **Predicting Prices of Used Cars.** The file `ToyotaCorolla.xlsx` contains data on used cars (Toyota Corolla) on sale during late summer of 2004 in the Netherlands. It has 1436 records containing details on 38 attributes, including Price, Age, Kilometers, HP, and other specifications. The goal is to predict the price of a used Toyota Corolla based on its specifications. (The example in Section 6.3 is a subset of this dataset.)

- Create dummy variables for the categorical predictors Fuel_Type and Color. Split the data into training (50%), validation (30%), and test (20%) datasets.

- Run a multiple linear regression with the output variable Price and input variables Age_08_04, KM, Fuel_Type, HP, Automatic, Doors, Quarterly_Tax, Mfr_Guarantee, Guarantee_Period, Airco, Automatic_Airco, CD_Player, Powered_Windows, Sport_Model, and Tow_Bar.

  a. What appear to be the three or four most important car specifications for predicting the car's price?

  b. Using metrics you consider useful, assess the performance of the model in predicting prices.

k-Nearest-Neighbors (k-NN)

In this chapter, we describe the k-nearest-neighbors algorithm that can be used for classification (of a categorical outcome) or prediction (of a numerical outcome). To classify or predict a new record, the method relies on finding "similar" records in the training data. These "neighbors" are then used to derive a classification or prediction for the new record by voting (for classification) or averaging (for prediction). We explain how similarity is determined, how the number of neighbors is chosen, and how a classification or prediction is computed. k-NN is a highly automated data-driven method. We discuss the advantages and weaknesses of the k-NN method in terms of performance and practical considerations such as computational time.

7.1 THE k-NN CLASSIFIER (CATEGORICAL OUTCOME)

The idea in k-nearest-neighbors methods is to identify k records in the training dataset that are similar to a new record that we wish to classify. We then use these similar (neighboring) records to classify the new record into a class, assigning the new record to the predominant class among these neighbors. Denote by $(x_1, x_2, \ldots, x_p)$ the values of the predictors for this new record. We look for records in our training data that are similar or "near" the record to be classified in the predictor space (i.e., records that have values close to $x_1, x_2, \ldots, x_p$). Then, based on the classes to which those proximate records belong, we assign a class to the record that we want to classify.

Machine Learning for Business Analytics: Concepts, Techniques, and Applications with Analytic Solver® Data Mining, Fourth Edition. Galit Shmueli, Peter C. Bruce, Kuber R. Deokar, and Nitin R. Patel

Determining Neighbors

The k-nearest-neighbors algorithm is a classification method that does not make assumptions about the form of the relationship between the class member-ship (Y) and the predictors $X_1, X_2, \ldots, X_p$. This is a nonparametric method because it does not involve estimation of parameters in an assumed function form, such as the linear form assumed in linear regression (Chapter 6). Instead, this method draws information from similarities between the predictor values of the records in the dataset.

A central question is how to measure the distance between records based on their predictor values. The most popular measure of distance is the Euclidean distance. The Euclidean distance between two records $(x_1, x_2, \ldots, x_p)$ and $(u_1, u_2, \ldots, u_p)$ is

$$\sqrt{(x_1 - u_1)^2 + (x_2 - u_2)^2 + \cdots + (x_p - u_p)^2}. \tag{7.1}$$

You will find a host of other distance metrics in Chapters 12 and 16 for both numerical and categorical variables. However, the k-NN algorithm relies on many distance computations (between each record to be predicted and every record in the training set), and therefore the Euclidean distance, which is com-putationally cheap, is the most popular in k-NN.

To equalize the scales that the various predictors may have, note that in most cases, predictors should first be re-scaled (e.g., standardized or normalized) before computing a Euclidean distance.

Classification Rule

After computing the distances between the record to be classified and existing records, we need a rule to assign a class to the record to be classified, based on the classes of its neighbors. The simplest case is $k = 1$, where we look for the record that is closest (the nearest neighbor) and classify the new record as belonging to the same class as its closest neighbor. It is a remarkable fact that this simple, intuitive idea of using a single nearest neighbor to classify records can be very powerful when we have a large number of records in our training set. In turns out that the misclassification error of the 1-nearest-neighbor scheme has a misclassification rate that is no more than twice the error when we know exactly the probability density functions for each class.

The idea of the **1-nearest-neighbor** can be extended to $k > 1$ neighbors as follows:

1. Find the nearest k neighbors to the record to be classified.
2. Use a majority decision rule to classify the record, where the record is classified as a member of the majority class of the k neighbors.

Example: Riding Mowers

A riding-mower manufacturer would like to find a way of classifying families in a city into those likely to purchase a riding mower and those not likely to buy one. A pilot random sample is undertaken of 12 owners and 12 nonowners in the city. The data are shown in Table 7.1. We first partition the data into training data (18 households) and validation data (6 households). Obviously, this dataset is too small for partitioning, which can result in unstable results, but we will continue with this partitioning for illustration purposes. A scatter plot of the training data is shown in Figure 7.1.

TABLE 7.1	LOT SIZE, INCOME, AND OWNERSHIP OF A RIDING MOWER FOR 24 HOUSEHOLDS		
Household number	Income ($000s)	Lot size (000s ft^2)	Ownership of riding mower
1	60.0	18.4	Owner
2	85.5	16.8	Owner
3	64.8	21.6	Owner
4	61.5	20.8	Owner
5	87.0	23.6	Owner
6	110.1	19.2	Owner
7	108.0	17.6	Owner
8	82.8	22.4	Owner
9	69.0	20.0	Owner
10	93.0	20.8	Owner
11	51.0	22.0	Owner
12	81.0	20.0	Owner
13	75.0	19.6	Non-owner
14	52.8	20.8	Non-owner
15	64.8	17.2	Non-owner
16	43.2	20.4	Non-owner
17	84.0	17.6	Non-owner
18	49.2	17.6	Non-owner
19	59.4	16.0	Non-owner
20	66.0	18.4	Non-owner
21	47.4	16.4	Non-owner
22	33.0	18.8	Non-owner
23	51.0	14.0	Non-owner
24	63.0	14.8	Non-owner

Now consider a new household with $60,000 income and lot size 20,000 ft^2 (also shown in Figure 7.1). Among the households in the training set, the one closest to the new household (in Euclidean distance after normalizing income and lot size) is household 4, with $61,500 income and lot size 20,800 ft^2. If we use a 1-NN classifier, we would classify the new household as an owner, like household 4. If we use $k = 3$, the three nearest households are 4, 9, and 14. The first two are owners of riding mowers, and the last is a nonowner. The majority vote is therefore *owner*, and the new household would be classified as an owner.

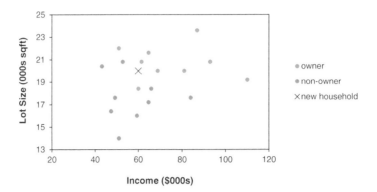

FIGURE 7.1   SCATTERPLOT OF *LOT SIZE* VS. *INCOME* FOR THE 18 HOUSEHOLDS IN THE TRAINING SET AND THE NEW HOUSEHOLD TO BE CLASSIFIED

Choosing k

The advantage of choosing $k > 1$ is that higher values of k provide smoothing that reduces the risk of overfitting due to noise in the training data. Generally speaking, if k is too low, we may be fitting to the noise in the data. However, if k is too high, we will miss out on the method's ability to capture the local structure in the data, one of its main advantages. In the extreme, $k = n =$ the number of records in the training dataset. In that case we simply assign all records to the majority class in the training data, regardless of the values of $(x_1, x_2, \ldots, x_p)$, which coincides with the naive rule! This is clearly a case of oversmoothing in the absence of useful information in the predictors about the class membership. In other words, we want to balance between overfitting to the predictor information and ignoring this information completely. A balanced choice depends greatly on the nature of the data. The more complex and irregular the structure of the data, the lower is the optimum value of k. Typically, values of k fall in the range 1–20. Often an odd number is chosen, to avoid ties. *Note:* In the ASDM Education version, the maximum allowed value of k (number of neighbors) is 10.

So how is k chosen? Answer: We choose the k that has the best classification performance. We use the training data to classify the records in the validation data, then compute error rates for various choices of k. For our example, if, on the one hand, we choose $k = 1$, we will classify in a way that is very sensitive to the local characteristics of the training data. If, on the other hand, we choose a large value of k, such as $k = 18$, we will simply predict the most frequent class in the dataset in all cases. This is a very stable prediction, but it completely ignores the information in the predictors. To find a balance, we examine the misclassification rate (of the validation set) that results for different choices of k between 1 and 10. This is shown in Figure 7.2. The note shown in Figure 7.2

Search Log

K	% Misclassification
1	33.3333
2	33.3333
3	33.3333
4	33.3333
5	33.3333
6	33.3333
7	33.3333
8	16.6667
9	16.6667
10	16.6667

Note: Scoring will be done using K=8

FIGURE 7.2   MISCLASSIFICATION RATE OF VALIDATION SET FOR VARIOUS CHOICES OF k

beneath the table tells us which k was best in terms of minimum misclassification. As indicated by ASDM, we would choose $k = 8$, which is the smallest k that minimizes the misclassification rate in the validation set.[1] Note, however, that now the validation set is used as an addition to the training set and does not reflect a holdout set as before. Ideally, we would want a third test set to evaluate the performance of the method on data that it did not see.

Once k is chosen, the algorithm uses it to generate classifications of new records. An example is shown in Figure 7.3, where eight neighbors are used to classify the new household.

New: Classification Details

Record ID	Prediction: Ownership	PostProb: non-owner	PostProb: owner
Record 1	owner	0.375	0.625

FIGURE 7.3   CLASSIFYING A NEW HOUSEHOLD USING THE "BEST k"= 8

Setting the Cutoff Value

k-NN uses a majority decision rule to classify a new record, where the record is classified as a member of the majority class of the k neighbors. The definition of "majority" is directly linked to the notion of a cutoff value applied to the class membership probabilities. Let us consider a binary outcome case. For a new record, the proportion of class 1 members among its neighbors is an estimate of its propensity (probability) of belonging to class 1. In the riding mowers

---

[1]Partitioning such a small dataset is unwise in practice, as results will heavily rely on the particular partition. For instance, if you use a different partitioning, you might obtain a different "optimal" k. The validation set in this example includes households 2, 7, 8, 13, 22, and 24.

example with $k = 3$, we found that the three nearest neighbors to the new household (with income = \$60,000 and lot size = 20,000 ft^2) are households 4, 9, and 14. Since 4 and 9 are owners and 14 is a nonowner, we can estimate for the new household a probability of 2/3 of being an owner (and 1/3 for being a nonowner). Using a simple majority rule is equivalent to setting the cutoff value to 0.5. Another example can be seen in Figure 7.3, where $k = 8$ was used to classify the new household. The "Prob for Owner" of 0.625 was obtained because five of the eight neighbors were owners. Using a cutoff of 0.5 leads to a classification of "owner" for the new household.

As mentioned in Chapter 5, changing the cutoff value affects the classification matrix (i.e., the error rates). Hence, in some cases, we might want to choose a cutoff other than the default 0.5 for the purpose of maximizing accuracy or for incorporating misclassification costs. In ASDM, once a model has been run, the cutoff cannot be changed directly (it requires rerunning the k-NN menu with a new choice of cutoff). To explore the effect of different cutoff values on some error metric, use the Classification Details table to manually create a confusion matrix with the individual records' predicted probabilities for some cutoff value, and then use Excel's one-variable tables to modify the cutoff value, as explained in Chapter 5 (e.g., Figure 5.8).

k-NN with More Than Two Classes

The k-NN classifier can easily be applied to an outcome with m classes, where $m > 2$. The "majority rule" means that a new record is classified as a member of the majority class of its k neighbors. An alternative, when there is a specific class that we are interested in identifying (and are willing to "overidentify" records as belonging to this class), is to calculate the proportion of the k neighbors that belong to this class of interest, use that as an estimate of the probability (propensity) that the new record belongs to that class, and then refer to a user-specified cutoff value to decide whether to assign the new record to that class. For more on the use of cutoff value in classification where there is a single class of interest, see Chapter 5.

Converting Categorical Variables to Binary Dummies

It usually does not make sense to calculate Euclidean distance between two non-numeric categories (e.g., cookbooks and maps in a bookstore). Therefore, before k-NN can be applied, categorical variables must be converted to binary dummies. In contrast to the situation with statistical models such as regression, all m binaries should be created and used with k-NN. While mathematically this is redundant, since $m - 1$ dummies contain the same information as m dummies, this redundant information does not create the multicollinearity problems that it does for linear models. Moreover, in k-NN, the use of $m - 1$ dummies can yield different classifications than the use of m dummies, and lead to an imbalance in the contribution of the different categories to the model.

7.2 k-NN FOR A NUMERICAL RESPONSE

The idea of k-NN can readily be extended to predicting a continuous value (as is our aim with multiple linear regression models). The first step of determining neighbors by computing distances remains unchanged. The second step, where a majority vote of the neighbors is used to determine class, is modified such that we take the average response value of the k-nearest-neighbors to determine the prediction. Often this average is a weighted average, with the weight decreasing with increasing distance from the point at which the prediction is required.

Another modification is in the error metric used for determining the "best k." Rather than the overall error rate used in classification, RMS error (or another prediction error metric) is used in prediction (see Chapter 5).

7.3 MACHINE LEARNING WORKFLOW

The machine learning workflow for the k-NN model that we used in this chapter is shown in Figure 7.4. Note that the workflow contains the components *Rescale Continuous Data* and *Score*. These two steps are completed on the fly while fitting the k-NN model: Rescaling of numeric predictors is done by clicking the *Rescale Data* button on the *Parameters* screen (normalization is chosen here); Scoring a new tract is done by clicking *In Worksheet* (under *Score New Data*) and then *Match by Name*.

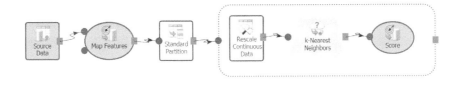

FIGURE 7.4   **ALL-INCLUSIVE WORKFLOW FOR k-NN MODEL**

7.4 ADVANTAGES AND SHORTCOMINGS OF k-NN ALGORITHMS

The main advantage of k-NN methods is their simplicity and lack of parametric assumptions. In the presence of a large enough training set, these methods perform surprisingly well, especially when each class is characterized by multiple combinations of predictor values. For instance, in real-estate databases there are likely to be multiple combinations of {home type, number of rooms, neighborhood, asking price, etc.} that characterize homes that sell quickly vs. those that remain for a long period on the market.

There are three difficulties with the practical exploitation of the power of the *k*-NN approach. First, although no time is required to estimate parameters from the training data (as would be the case for parametric models such as regression), the time to find the nearest neighbors in a large training set can be prohibitive. A number of ideas have been implemented to overcome this difficulty. The main ideas are:

- Reduce the time taken to compute distances by working in a reduced dimension using dimension reduction techniques such as principal component analysis (Chapter 4).

- Use sophisticated data structures such as search trees to speed up identification of the nearest neighbor. This approach often settles for an "almost nearest" neighbor to improve speed. An example is using *bucketing*, where the records are grouped into buckets so that records within each bucket are close to each other. For a to-be-predicted record, buckets are ordered by their distance to the record. Starting from the nearest bucket, the distance to each of the records within the bucket is measured. The algorithm stops when the distance to a bucket is larger than the distance to the closest record thus far.

Second, the number of records required in the training set to qualify as large increases exponentially with the number of predictors p. This is because the expected distance to the nearest neighbor goes up dramatically with p unless the size of the training set increases exponentially with p. This phenomenon is known as the *curse of dimensionality*, a fundamental issue pertinent to all classification, prediction, and clustering techniques. This is why we often seek to reduce the number of predictors through methods such as selecting subsets of the predictors for our model or by combining them using methods such as principal component analysis, singular value decomposition, and factor analysis (see Chapter 4).

Third, *k*-NN is a "lazy learner": the time-consuming computation is deferred to the time of prediction. For every record to be predicted, we compute its distances from the entire set of training records only at the time of prediction. This behavior prohibits using this algorithm for real-time prediction of a large number of records simultaneously.

PANDORA

Pandora is an Internet music radio service that allows users to build customized "stations" that play music similar to a song or artist that they have specified. When it started, Pandora used a k-NN style clustering/classification process called the Music Genome Project to locate new songs or artists that are close to the user-specified song or artist.

Pandora was the brainchild of Tim Westergren, who worked as a musician and a nanny when he graduated from Stanford in the 1980s. Together with Nolan Gasser, who was studying medieval music, he developed a "matching engine" by entering data about a song's characteristics into a spreadsheet. The first result was surprising—a Beatles song matched to a Bee Gees song, but they built a company around the concept. The early days were hard—Westergren racked up over $300,000 in personal debt, maxed out 11 credit cards, and ended up in the hospital once due to stress-induced heart palpitations. A venture capitalist finally invested funds in 2004 to rescue the firm, and it eventually went public.

In simplified terms, the process works roughly as follows for songs:

1. Pandora established hundreds of variables on which a song can be measured on a scale from 0 to 5. Four such variables from the beginning of the list are:

- Acid Rock Qualities
- Accordion Playing
- Acousti-Lectric Sonority
- Acousti-Synthetic Sonority.

2. Pandora pays musicians to analyze tens of thousands of songs, and rate each song on each of these attributes. Each song will then be represented by a row vector of values between 0 and 5, for example, for Led Zeppelin's *Kashmir*:

    Kashmir 4 0 3 3 ... (high on acid rock attributes, no accordion, etc.)

   This step represents a significant investment, and lies at the heart of Pandora's value because these variables have been tested and selected because they accurately reflect the essence of a song, and provide a basis for defining highly individualized preferences.

3. The online user specifies a song that s/he likes (the song must be in Pandora's database).

4. Pandora then calculates the statistical distance[1] between the user's song and the songs in its database. It selects a song that is close to the user-specified song and plays it.

5. The user then has the option of saying "I like this song," "I don't like this song," or saying nothing.

6. If "like" is chosen, the original song plus the new song are merged into a 2-song cluster[2] that is represented by a single vector comprising means of the variables in the original two song vectors.

7. If "dislike" is chosen, the vector of the song that is not liked is stored for future reference. (If the user does not express an opinion about the song, in our simplified example here, the new song is not used for further comparisons.)

8. Pandora looks in its database for a new song, one whose statistical distance is close to the "like" song cluster,[3] and not too close to the "dislike" song. Depending on the user's reaction, this new song might be added to the "like" cluster or "dislike" cluster.

Over time, Pandora develops the ability to deliver songs that match a particular taste of a particular user. A single user might build up multiple stations around different song clusters. Clearly, this is a less limiting approach than selecting music in terms of which "genre" it belongs to.

While the process described above is a bit more complex than the basic "classification of new data" process described in this chapter, the fundamental process—classifying a record according to its proximity to other records—is the same at its core. Note the role of domain knowledge in this machine learning process—the variables have been tested and selected by the project leaders, and the measurements have been made by human experts. In another sense, this human role represented the Achilles heel of Pandora – it was costly, and constituted a bottleneck obstructing the flow of new songs into the system.

Music streaming services later came to omit this step of pre-labeling songs, and to rely on machine learning algorithms that get input only from users. Collaborative filtering, for example, recommends songs that are liked by other people who share your tastes (i.e., like the same songs); see Chapter 15 for more on collaborative filtering. Deep learning networks (which were not practically available at Pandora's inception) can take the sound waves in songs and derive features from them, in the same way that these networks derive features from images. These derived features can then be used to predict user choices. See Chapter 11 for more on neural networks.

Pandora was a pioneer in licensed music streaming, but was later eclipsed by Spotify and Apple Music, which offered features that Pandora's "customized radio station" model did not, such as the ability to play a specific song on demand, and the ability to download music.

Further reading: See www.pandora.com, Wikipedia's article on the Music Genome Project, and Joyce John's article "Pandora and the music genome project." *Scientific Computing*, vol. 23, number 10: 14, pp. 40–41, September 2006.

---

[1] See Section 12.5 in Chapter 12 for an explanation of statistical distance.

[2] See Chapter 16 for more on clusters.

[3] See Case 23.6 "Segmenting Consumers of Bath Soap" for an exercise involving the identification of clusters, which are then used for classification purposes.

PROBLEMS

7.1   Calculating Distance with Categorical Predictors. This exercise with a tiny dataset illustrates the calculation of Euclidean distance and the creation of binary dummies. The online education company Statistics.com segments its customers and prospects into three main categories: IT professionals (IT), statisticians (Stat), and other (Other). It also tracks, for each customer, the number of years since first contact (years). Consider the following customers; information about whether they have taken a course or not (the outcome to be predicted) is included:

Customer 1: Stat, 1 year, did not take course
Customer 2: Other, 1.1 year, took course

    a. Consider now the following new prospect:

        Prospect 1: IT, 1 year

    Using the information above on the two customers and one prospect, create one dataset for all three with the categorical predictor variable transformed into two binaries, and a similar dataset with the categorical predictor variable transformed into three binaries.

    b. For each derived dataset, calculate the Euclidean distance between the prospect and each of the other two customers. (*Note:* While it is typical to normalize data for k-NN, this is not an iron-clad rule and you may proceed here without normalization.)

    c. Using k-NN with $k = 1$, classify the prospect as taking or not taking a course using each of the two derived datasets. Does it make a difference whether you use two or three dummies?

7.2   Personal Loan Acceptance. Universal Bank is a relatively young bank growing rapidly in terms of overall customer acquisition. The majority of these customers are liability customers (depositors) with varying sizes of relationship with the bank. The customer base of asset customers (borrowers) is quite small, and the bank is interested in expanding this base rapidly to bring in more loan business. In particular, it wants to explore ways of converting its liability customers to personal loan customers (while retaining them as depositors).

    A campaign that the bank ran last year for liability customers showed a healthy conversion rate of over 9% success. This has encouraged the retail marketing department to devise smarter campaigns with better target marketing. The goal is to use k-NN to predict whether a new customer will accept a loan offer.
This will serve as the basis for the design of a new campaign.

    The file `UniversalBank.xlsx` contains data on 5000 customers. The data include customer demographic information (age, income, etc.), the customer's relationship with the bank (mortgage, securities account, etc.), and the customer response to the last personal loan campaign (*Personal Loan*). Among these 5000 customers, only 480 (= 9.6%) accepted the personal loan that was offered to them in the earlier campaign.

    Transform categorical predictors with more than two categories into dummy variables, then, partition the data into training (60%) and validation (40%) sets.

    a. Consider the following customer:

        Age = 40, Experience = 10, Income = 84, Family = 2, CCAvg = 2, Education_1 = 0, Education_2 = 1, Education_3 = 0, Mortgage = 0, Securities Account = 0, CD Account = 0, Online = 1, and Credit Card = 1. Perform a k-NN classification with all predictors except ID and ZIP code using $k = 1$. Specify the *success* class as 1 (loan acceptance), and use the default cutoff value of 0.5. How would this customer be classified?

b. What is a choice of k that balances between overfitting and ignoring the predictor information?

c. Show the classification matrix for the validation data that results from using the best k.

d. Consider the following customer: Age = 40, Experience = 10, Income = 84, Family = 2, CCAvg = 2, Education_1 = 0, Education_2 = 1, Education_3 = 0, Mortgage = 0, Securities Account = 0, CD Account = 0, Online = 1, and Credit Card = 1. Classify the customer using the best k.

e. Repartition the data, this time into training, validation, and test sets (50% : 30% : 20%). Apply the k-NN method with the k chosen above. Compare the classification matrix of the test set with that of the training and validation sets. Comment on the differences and their reason.

7.3 **Predicting Housing Median Prices.** The file `BostonHousing.xlsx` contains information on over 500 census tracts in Boston, where for each tract multiple variables are recorded. The last column (CAT.MEDV) was derived from MEDV, such that it obtains the value 1 if MEDV > 30 and 0 otherwise. Consider the goal of predicting the median value (MEDV) of a tract, given the information in the first 12 columns.

Partition the data into training (60%) and validation (40%) sets.

a. Perform a k-NN prediction with all 12 predictors (ignore the CAT.MEDV column), trying values of k from 1 to 5. Make sure to normalize the data (click *Parameters > Rescale Data > Normalization*). What is the best k chosen? What does it mean?

b. Predict the MEDV for a tract with the following information, using the best k:

CRIM	ZN	INDUS	CHAS	NO	RM	AGE	DI	RAD	TAX	PTRATIO	LSTAT
0.2	0	7	0	0.538	6	62	4.7	4	307	21	10

(In a new worksheet, create an identical table with these column names and values, and then in "Score New Data" choose "In Worksheet.")

c. Why is the error of the training data zero?

d. Why is the validation data error overly optimistic compared to the error rate when applying this k-NN predictor to new data?

e. If the purpose is to predict MEDV for several thousands of new tracts, what would be the disadvantage of using k-NN prediction? List the operations that the algorithm goes through in order to produce each prediction.

## CHAPTER 8

The Naive Bayes Classifier

In this chapter, we introduce the naive Bayes classifier, which can be applied to data with categorical predictors. We review the concept of conditional probabilities, then present the complete, or exact, Bayesian classifier. We next see how it is impractical in most cases, and learn how to modify it and use instead the "naive Bayes" classifier, which is more generally applicable.

8.1 INTRODUCTION

The naive Bayes method (and, indeed, an entire branch of statistics) is named after the Reverend Thomas Bayes (1702–1761). To understand the naive Bayes classifier, we first look at the complete, or exact, Bayesian classifier. The basic principle is simple. For each record to be classified:

1. Find all the other records with the same predictor profile (i.e., where the predictor values are the same).
2. Determine what classes the records belong to and which class is most prevalent.
3. Assign that class to the new record.

Alternatively (or in addition), it may be desirable to tweak the method so that it answers the question: "What is the propensity of belonging to the class of interest?" instead of "Which class is the most probable?" Obtaining class probabilities allows using a sliding cutoff to classify a record as belonging to class C_i, even if C_i is not the most probable class for that record. This approach is useful when there is a specific class of interest that we are interested in identifying, and we are willing to "overidentify" records as belonging to this class.

Machine Learning for Business Analytics: Concepts, Techniques, and Applications with Analytic Solver® Data Mining,
Fourth Edition. Galit Shmueli, Peter C. Bruce, Kuber R. Deokar, and Nitin R. Patel.
© 2023 John Wiley & Sons, Inc. Published 2023 by John Wiley & Sons, Inc.

(See Chapter 5 for more details on the use of cutoffs for classification and on asymmetric misclassification costs.)

Cutoff Probability Method

1. Establish a cutoff probability for the class of interest above which we consider that a record belongs to that class.
2. Find all the training records with the same predictor profile as the new record (i.e., where the predictor values are the same).
3. Determine the probability that those records belong to the class of interest.
4. If that probability is above the cutoff probability, assign the new record to the class of interest.

Conditional Probability

Both procedures incorporate the concept of *conditional probability*, or the probability of event A given that event B has occurred [denoted $P(A|B)$]. In this case, we will be looking at the probability of the record belonging to class C_i given that its predictor values are $x_1, x_2, \ldots, x_p$. In general, for a response with m classes $C_1, C_2, \ldots, C_m$, and the predictor values $x_1, x_2, \ldots, x_p$, we want to compute

$$P(C_i|x_1, \ldots, x_p). \tag{8.1}$$

To classify a record, we compute its probability of belonging to each of the classes in this way, then classify the record to the class that has the highest probability or use the cutoff probability to decide whether it should be assigned to the class of interest.

From this definition, we see that the Bayesian classifier works only with categorical predictors. If we use a set of numerical predictors, then it is highly unlikely that multiple records will have identical values on these numerical predictors. Therefore, numerical predictors must be binned and converted to categorical predictors. *The Bayesian classifier is the only classification or prediction method presented in this book that is especially suited for categorical predictor variables.*

Example 1: Predicting Fraudulent Financial Reporting

An accounting firm has many large companies as customers. Each customer submits an annual financial report to the firm, which is then audited by the accounting firm. For simplicity, we will designate the outcome of the audit as "fraudulent" or "truthful," referring to the accounting firm's assessment of the customer's financial report. The accounting firm has a strong incentive to be accurate in identifying fraudulent reports—if it passes a fraudulent report as truthful, it would be in legal trouble.

The accounting firm notes that, in addition to all the financial records, it has information on whether or not the customer has had prior legal trouble (criminal or civil charges of any nature filed against it). This information has not been used in previous audits, but the accounting firm is wondering whether it could be used in the future to identify reports that merit more intensive review. Specifically, it wants to know whether having had prior legal trouble is predictive of fraudulent reporting.

In this case, each customer is a record, and the response of interest, $Y = $ {fraudulent, truthful}, has two classes into which a company can be classified: $C_1 = $ fraudulent and $C_2 = $ truthful. The predictor variable—"prior legal trouble"—has two values: 0 (no prior legal trouble) and 1 (prior legal trouble).

The accounting firm has data on 1500 companies that it has investigated in the past. For each company, it has information on whether the financial report was judged fraudulent or truthful and whether the company had prior legal trouble. The data were partitioned into a training set (1000 firms) and a validation set (500 firms), and the counts in the training set are shown in Table 8.1.

TABLE 8.1   PIVOT TABLE FOR FINANCIAL REPORTING EXAMPLE

	Prior legal ($X = 1$)	No prior legal ($X = 0$)	Total
Fraudulent (C_1)	50	50	100
Truthful (C_2)	180	720	900
Total	230	770	1000

8.2 APPLYING THE FULL (EXACT) BAYESIAN CLASSIFIER

Now consider the financial report from a new company, which we wish to classify as either fraudulent or truthful by using these data. To do this, we compute the probabilities, as above, of belonging to each of the two classes.

If the new company had prior legal trouble, the probability of belonging to the fraudulent class would be P(fraudulent|prior legal) = 50/230 (there were 230 companies with prior legal trouble in the training set, and 50 of them had fraudulent financial reports). The probability of belonging to the other class, "truthful," is, of course, the remainder = 180/230.

Using the "Assign to the Most Probable Class" Method

If a company had prior legal trouble, we assign it to the "truthful" class. Similar calculations for the case of no prior legal trouble are left as an exercise to the reader. In this example, using the rule "assign to the most probable class," all records are assigned to the "truthful" class. This is the same result as the naive rule of "assign all records to the majority class."

Using the Cutoff Probability Method

In this example, we are more interested in identifying the fraudulent reports—those are the ones that can land the auditor in jail. We recognize that, in order to identify the fraudulent reports, some truthful reports will be misidentified as fraudulent, and the overall classification accuracy may decline. Our approach is therefore to establish a cutoff value for the probability of being fraudulent, and classify all records above that value as fraudulent. The Bayesian formula for the calculation of this probability that a record belongs to class C_i is as follows:

$$P(C_i|x_1,\ldots,x_p) = \frac{P(x_1,\ldots,x_p|C_i)P(C_i)}{P(x_1,\ldots,x_p|C_1)P(C_1) + \cdots + P(x_1,\ldots,x_p|C_m)P(C_m)}.$$

(8.2)

In this example (where frauds are rarer), if the cutoff were established at 0.20, we would classify a prior legal trouble record as fraudulent because $P(\text{fraudulent}|\text{prior legal}) = 50/230 = 0.22$. The user can treat this cutoff as a "slider" to be adjusted to optimize performance, like other parameters in any classification model.

Practical Difficulty with the Complete (Exact) Bayes Procedure

The approach outlined above amounts to finding all the records in the sample that are exactly like the new record to be classified in the sense that all the predictor values are all identical. This was easy in the small example presented above, where there was just one predictor.

When the number of predictors gets larger (even to a modest number like 20), many of the records to be classified will be without exact matches. This can be understood in the context of a model to predict voting on the basis of demographic variables. Even a sizable sample may not contain even a single match for a new record who is a male Hispanic with high income from the US Midwest who voted in the last election, did not vote in the prior election, has three daughters and one son, and is divorced. And this is just eight variables, a small number for most machine learning exercises. The addition of just a single new variable with five equally frequent categories reduces the probability of a match by a factor of 5.

8.3 Solution: Naive Bayes

In the naive Bayes solution, we no longer restrict the probability calculation to those records that match the record to be classified. Instead, we use the entire dataset.

Returning to our original basic classification procedure outlined at the beginning of the chapter, we recall that this procedure for classifying a new record was:

1. Find all the other records with the same predictor profile (i.e., where the predictor values are the same).

2. Determine what classes the records belong to and which class is most prevalent.

3. Assign that class to the new record.

The naive Bayes modification (for the basic classification procedure) is as follows:

1. For class C_1, estimate the individual conditional probabilities for each predictor $P(x_j|C_1)$—these are the probabilities that the predictor value in the record to be classified occurs in class C_1. For example, for X_1 this probability is estimated by the proportion of x_1 values among the C_1 records in the training set.

2. Multiply these probabilities by each other, then by the proportion of records belonging to class C_1.

3. Repeat steps 1 and 2 for all the classes.

4. Estimate a probability for class C_i by taking the value calculated in step 2 for class C_i and dividing it by the sum of such values for all classes.

5. Assign the record to the class with the highest probability for this set of predictor values.

The preceding steps lead to the naive Bayes formula for calculating the probability that a record with a given set of predictor values $x_1, \ldots, x_p$ belongs to class C_1 among m classes. The formula can be written as follows:

$$P_{\text{nb}}(C_1|x_1, \ldots x_p) = \frac{P(C_1)[P(x_1|C_1)P(x_2|C_1)\cdots P(x_p|C_1)]}{P(C_1)[P(x_1|C_1)P(x_2|C_1)\cdots P(x_p|C_1)] + \cdots + P(C_m)[P(x_1|C_m)P(x_2|C_m)\cdots P(x_p|C_m)]}.$$

$$(8.3)$$

This is a somewhat formidable formula; see Example 2 for a simpler numerical version. Note that all the needed quantities can be obtained from pivot tables of Y vs. each of the categorical predictors.

The Naive Bayes Assumption of Conditional Independence   In probability terms, we have made a simplifying assumption that the exact *conditional probability* of seeing a record with predictor profile $x_1, x_2, \ldots, x_p$ within a certain class, $P(x_1, x_2, \ldots, x_p | C_i)$, is well approximated by the product of the individual conditional probabilities $P(x_1 | C_i) \times P(x_2 | C_i) \times \cdots \times P(x_p | C_i)$. These two quantities are identical when the predictors are independent within each class.

For example, suppose that "lost money last year" is an additional variable in the accounting fraud example. The simplifying assumption we make with naive Bayes is that, within a given class, we no longer need to look for the records characterized both by "prior legal trouble" and "lost money last year." Rather, assuming that the two are independent, we can simply multiply the probability of "prior legal trouble" by the probability of "lost money last year." Of course, complete independence is unlikely in practice, where some correlation between predictors is expected.

In practice, despite the assumption violation, the procedure works quite well—primarily because what is usually needed is not a propensity for each record that is accurate in absolute terms but just a reasonably accurate *rank ordering* of propensities. Even when the assumption is violated, the rank ordering of the records' propensities is typically preserved.

Note that if all we are interested in is a rank ordering, and the denominator remains the same for all classes, it is sufficient to concentrate only on the numerator. The disadvantage of this approach is that the probability values it yields (the propensities), while ordered correctly, are not on the same scale as the exact values that the user would anticipate.

Using the Cutoff Probability Method   The procedure above is for the basic case where we seek maximum classification accuracy for all classes. In the case of the *relatively rare class of special interest*, the procedure is:

1. Establish a cutoff probability for the class of interest above which we consider that a record belongs to that class.
2. For the class of interest, compute the probability that each individual predictor value in the record to be classified occurs in the training data.
3. Multiply these probabilities times each other, then times the proportion of records belonging to the class of interest.
4. Estimate the probability for the class of interest by taking the value calculated in step 3 for the class of interest and dividing it by the sum of the similar values for all classes.

5. If this value falls above the cutoff, assign the new record to the class of interest; otherwise not.

6. Adjust the cutoff value as needed, as a parameter of the model.

Example 2: Predicting Fraudulent Financial Reports, Two Predictors

Let us expand the financial reports example to two predictors, and, using a small subset of data, compare the complete (exact) Bayes calculations to the naive Bayes calculations.

Consider the 10 customers of the accounting firm listed in Table 8.2. For each customer, we have information on whether it had prior legal trouble, whether it is a small or large company, and whether the financial report was found to be fraudulent or truthful. Using this information, we will calculate the conditional probability of fraud, given each of the four possible combinations {yes, small}, {yes, large}, {no, small}, {no, large}.

TABLE 8.2   INFORMATION ON 10 COMPANIES

Company	Prior legal trouble	Company size	Status
1	Yes	Small	Truthful
2	No	Small	Truthful
3	No	Large	Truthful
4	No	Large	Truthful
5	No	Small	Truthful
6	No	Small	Truthful
7	Yes	Small	Fraudulent
8	Yes	Large	Fraudulent
9	No	Large	Fraudulent
10	Yes	Large	Fraudulent

Complete (Exact) Bayes Calculations: The probabilities are computed as

$$P(\text{fraudulent}|\text{PriorLegal} = \text{yes}, \text{Size} = \text{small}) = 1/2 = 0.5$$

$$P(\text{fraudulent}|\text{PriorLegal} = \text{yes}, \text{Size} = \text{large}) = 2/2 = 1$$

$$P(\text{fraudulent}|\text{PriorLegal} = \text{no}, \text{Size} = \text{small}) = 0/3 = 0$$

$$P(\text{fraudulent}|\text{PriorLegal} = \text{no}, \text{Size} = \text{large}) = 1/3 = 0.33$$

Naive Bayes Calculations: Now we compute the naive Bayes probabilities. For the conditional probability of fraudulent behaviors given {PriorLegal = yes, Size = small}, the numerator is a multiplication of the proportion of {PriorLegal = yes} instances among the fraudulent companies, times the proportion of {Size = small} instances among the fraudulent companies, times the proportion of fraudulent companies: $(3/4)(1/4)(4/10) = 0.075$. To get the actual probabilities, we must also compute the numerator for the conditional probability of truthful behaviors given {PriorLegal = yes, Size = small}: $(1/6)(4/6)(6/10) = 0.067$. The denominator is then the sum of these two conditional probabilities $(0.075 + 0.067 = 0.14)$. The conditional probability of fraudulent behaviors given {PriorLegal = yes, Size = small} is therefore $0.075/0.14 = 0.53$. In a similar fashion, we compute all four conditional probabilities:

$$P_{nb}(\text{fraudulent}|\text{PriorLegal} = \text{yes}, \text{Size} = \text{small})$$
$$= \frac{(3/4)(1/4)(4/10)}{(3/4)(1/4)(4/10) + (1/6)(4/6)(6/10)}$$
$$= 0.53$$
$$P_{nb}(\text{fraudulent}|\text{PriorLegal} = \text{yes}, \text{Size} = \text{large}) = 0.87$$
$$P_{nb}(\text{fraudulent}|\text{PriorLegal} = \text{no}, \text{Size} = \text{small}) = 0.07$$
$$P_{nb}(\text{fraudulent}|\text{PriorLegal} = \text{no}, \text{Size} = \text{large}) = 0.31$$

Note how close these naive Bayes probabilities are to the exact Bayes probabilities. Although they are not equal, both would lead to exactly the same classification for a cutoff of 0.5 (and many other values). It is often the case that the rank ordering of probabilities is even closer to the exact Bayes method than the probabilities themselves, and for classification purposes it is the rank orderings that matter.

We now consider a larger numerical example, where information on flights is used to predict flight delays.

Example 3: Predicting Delayed Flights

Predicting flight delays can be useful to a variety of organizations: airport authorities, airlines, and aviation authorities. At times, joint task forces have been formed to address the problem. If such an organization were to provide ongoing real-time assistance with flight delays, it would benefit from some advance notice about flights that are likely to be delayed.

In this simplified illustration, we look at six predictors (see Table 8.3). The outcome of interest is whether or not the flight is delayed (*delayed* here means

TABLE 8.3   DESCRIPTION OF VARIABLES FOR FLIGHT DELAYS EXAMPLE

Day of week (DAY_WEEK)	Coded as: 1 = Monday, 2 = Tuesday,..., 7 = Sunday
Sch. dep. time (CRS_DEP_TIME)	Broken down into 18 intervals between 6:00 AM and 10:00 PM
Origin (ORIGIN)	Three airport codes: DCA (Reagan National), IAD (Dulles), BWI (Baltimore–Washington Int'l)
Destination (DEST)	Three airport codes: JFK (Kennedy), LGA (LaGuardia), EWR (Newark)
Carrier (CARRIER)	Eight airline codes: CO (Continental), DH (Atlantic Coast), DL (Delta), MQ (American Eagle), OH (Comair), RU (Continental Express), UA (United), and US (USAirways)
Weather	Coded as 1 if there was a weather-related delay

arrived more than 15 minutes late). Our data consist of all flights from the Washington, DC area into the New York City area during January 2004. A record is a particular flight. The percentage of delayed flights among these 2201 flights is 19.5%. The data were obtained from the Bureau of Transportation Statistics (available on the Web at www.transtats.bts.gov). The goal is to accurately predict whether or not a new flight (not in this dataset) will be delayed. The outcome variable is whether the flight was delayed, and thus it has two classes (1 = delayed and 0 = on-time). In addition, information is collected on the predictors listed in Table 8.3.

The data were first partitioned into training (60%) and validation (40%) sets, and then a naive Bayes classifier was applied to the training set.

The top table in Figure 8.1 shows the ratios of delayed flights and on-time flights in the training set (called prior class probabilities). The bottom table shows the conditional probabilities for each class, as a function of the predictor values. Note that the conditional probabilities in the output can be computed simply by using pivot tables in Excel, looking at the percentage of records in a cell relative to the entire class. This is illustrated in Table 8.4, which displays the percent of delayed (or on-time) flights by destination airport as a percentage of the total delayed (or on-time) flights.

Note that in this example there are no predictor values that were not represented in the training data except for on-time flights (Class = 0) when the weather was bad (Weather = 1). When the weather was bad, all flights in the training set were delayed.

To classify a new flight, we compute the probability that it will be delayed and the probability that it will be on-time. Recall that since both will have the same denominator, we can just compare the numerators. Each numerator is computed by multiplying all the conditional probabilities of the relevant predictor values and, finally, multiplying by the proportion of that class (in this case $\hat{P}(\text{delayed}) = 0.19$). For example, to classify a Delta flight from DCA to LGA between 10 and 11 AM on a Sunday with good weather, we compute the numerators:

$$\hat{P}(\text{delayed} \,|\, \text{CARRIER} = \text{DL}, \text{DAY\_WEEK} = 7, \text{BinnedTime} = 1000 - 1059,$$
$$\text{DEST} = \text{LGA}, \text{ORIGIN} = \text{DCA}, \text{Weather} = 0)$$
$$\propto (0.11)(0.18)(0.027)(0.43)(0.53)(0.92)(0.19) = 0.000021.$$
$$\hat{P}(\text{ontime} \,|\, \text{CARRIER} = \text{DL}, \text{DAY\_WEEK} = 7, \text{BinnedTime} = 1000 - 1059,$$
$$\text{DEST} = \text{LGA}, \text{ORIGIN} = \text{DCA}, \text{Weather} = 0)$$
$$\propto (0.19)(0.11)(0.04)(0.53)(0.65)(1)(0.81) = 0.00023.$$

The symbol $\propto$ means "is proportional to," reflecting the fact that this calculation deals only with the numerator in the naive Bayes formula (8.3).

Prior Probability

Class	Probability
0	0.8138
1	0.1862

Prior Conditional Probability: Training

Input Variables	Value	Class Probabilities	
		P(Class=1)	P(Class=0)
CARRIER	CO	0.0787	0.0434
	DH	0.2992	0.2281
	DL	0.1142	0.1921
	MQ	0.1811	0.1154
	OH	0.0157	0.0166
	RU	0.2087	0.1837
	UA	0.0157	0.0157
	US	0.0866	0.2050
DEST	EWR	0.3815	0.2950
	JFK	0.1847	0.1716
	LGA	0.4337	0.5334
ORIGIN	BWI	0.0884	0.0659
	DCA	0.5261	0.6456
	IAD	0.3855	0.2885
Weather	0	0.9194	0.9991
	1	0.0806	0.0009
DAY_WEEK	1	0.1818	0.1220
	2	0.1344	0.1294
	3	0.1225	0.1571
	4	0.1502	0.1710
	5	0.1581	0.1885
	6	0.0711	0.1322
	7	0.1818	0.0998
BinnedTime	0600-0659	0.0534	0.0605
	0700-0759	0.0611	0.0642
	0800-0859	0.0458	0.0724
	0900-0959	0.0305	0.0541
	1000-1059	0.0267	0.0422
	1100-1159	0.0229	0.0376
	1200-1259	0.0611	0.0687
	1300-1359	0.0496	0.0880
	1400-1459	0.1603	0.0990
	1500-1559	0.0954	0.0568
	1600-1659	0.0687	0.0843
	1700-1759	0.1069	0.0944
	1800-1859	0.0344	0.0412
	1900-1959	0.0763	0.0458
	2000-2059	0.0229	0.0266
	2100-2159	0.0840	0.0642

FIGURE 8.1   OUTPUT FROM NAIVE BAYES CLASSIFIER APPLIED TO FLIGHT DELAYS (TRAINING) DATA

TABLE 8.4   PIVOT TABLE OF DELAYED AND ON-TIME
FLIGHTS BY DESTINATION AIRPORT (ROWS)

	Delayed %	On-time %	Total %
EWR	38.67	28.36	30.36
JFK	18.75	17.65	17.87
LGA	42.58	53.99	51.78
Total	100.00	100.00	100.00

It is therefore more likely that the flight will be on-time. Note that a record with such a combination of predictor values does not exist in the training set, and therefore we use the naive Bayes rather than the exact Bayes. To compute the actual probability, we divide each of the numerators by their sum:

$$\hat{P}(\text{delayed}|\text{CARRIER} = \text{DL}, \text{DAY\_WEEK} = 7, \text{BinnedTime} = 1000 - 1059,$$
$$\text{DEST} = \text{LGA}, \text{ORIGIN} = \text{DCA}, \text{Weather} = 0)$$
$$= \frac{0.000021}{0.000021 + 0.00023} = 0.08.$$

$$\hat{P}(\text{ontime}|\text{CARRIER} = \text{DL}, \text{DAY\_WEEK} = 7, \text{BinnedTime} = 1000 - 1059,$$
$$\text{DEST} = \text{LGA}, \text{ORIGIN} = \text{DCA}, \text{Weather} = 0)$$
$$= \frac{0.00023}{0.000021 + 0.00023} = 0.92.$$

Of course, we rely on software to compute these probabilities for any records of interest (in the training set, the validation set, or for scoring new data). Figure 8.2 shows the estimated probabilities and classifications for a sample of flights in the validation set.

Validation: Classification Details

Record ID	Flight Status	Prediction: Flight Status	PostProb: ontime	PostProb: delayed	CARRIER	DEST	ORIGIN	Weather	DAY_WEEK	BinnedTime
Record 208	delayed	ontime	0.6963016	0.3036984	DH	JFK	IAD	0	5	2100-2159
Record 1637	ontime	ontime	0.9060763	0.0939237	MQ	LGA	DCA	0	5	0900-0959
Record 1823	delayed	delayed	0.0485636	0.9514364	DL	LGA	DCA	1	1	1500-1559
Record 694	ontime	ontime	0.6730403	0.3269597	DH	LGA	IAD	0	7	1200-1259
Record 1789	ontime	ontime	0.5038822	0.4961178	DH	EWR	IAD	0	7	1700-1759
Record 1733	ontime	ontime	0.8668717	0.1331283	RU	EWR	DCA	0	6	1700-1759
Record 460	ontime	ontime	0.7524875	0.2475125	DH	EWR	IAD	0	3	0600-0659
Record 2015	delayed	ontime	0.7005268	0.2994732	MQ	JFK	DCA	0	4	1500-1559
Record 795	ontime	ontime	0.8444293	0.1555707	MQ	LGA	DCA	0	1	0900-0959
Record 290	delayed	ontime	0.5538404	0.4461596	DH	EWR	IAD	0	1	1700-1759
Record 1897	delayed	ontime	0.6642563	0.3357437	MQ	JFK	DCA	0	2	1500-1559
Record 1307	ontime	ontime	0.9228228	0.0771772	US	LGA	DCA	0	1	0700-0759
Record 2020	ontime	ontime	0.9020462	0.0979538	MQ	LGA	DCA	0	4	0900-0959
Record 207	ontime	ontime	0.9153121	0.0846879	US	LGA	DCA	0	7	2000-2059
Record 328	ontime	ontime	0.87757	0.12243	DL	LGA	DCA	0	2	1400-1459
Record 2187	ontime	ontime	0.7981969	0.2018031	RU	EWR	BWI	0	6	1700-1759
Record 350	ontime	ontime	0.9449274	0.0550726	US	LGA	DCA	0	2	0700-0759
Record 1194	ontime	ontime	0.7981969	0.2018031	RU	EWR	BWI	0	6	1700-1759
Record 971	ontime	ontime	0.8982743	0.1017257	UA	LGA	IAD	0	3	0800-0859
Record 1974	ontime	ontime	0.672338	0.327662	DH	EWR	IAD	0	3	2100-2159

FIGURE 8.2   ESTIMATED PROBABILITIES OF ON-TIME AND DELAYED ARRIVAL FOR A SAMPLE
OF FLIGHTS IN THE VALIDATION SET

Finally, to evaluate the performance of the naive Bayes classifier for our data, we use the classification matrix, lift charts, and all the measures that were described in Chapter 5. For our example, the classification matrices for the training and validation sets are shown in Figure 8.3. We see that the overall error level is around 17% for both the training and validation data. In comparison, a naive rule that would classify all 880 flights in the validation set as on-time would have missed the 172 delayed flights, resulting in a 20% error level. In other words,

Training: Classification Summary

Confusion Matrix

Actual\Predicted	delayed	ontime
delayed	33	213
ontime	8	1067

Error Report

Class	# Cases	# Errors	% Error
delayed	246	213	86.59
ontime	1075	8	0.74
Overall	1321	221	16.73

Validation: Classification Summary

Confusion Matrix

Actual\Predicted	delayed	ontime
delayed	20	162
ontime	10	688

Error Report

Class	# Cases	# Errors	% Error
delayed	182	162	89.011
ontime	698	10	1.43266
Overall	880	172	19.5455

FIGURE 8.3   CLASSIFICATION MATRICES FOR FLIGHT DELAYS USING A NAIVE BAYES CLASSIFIER

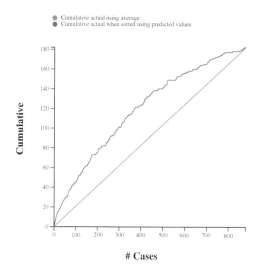

FIGURE 8.4   LIFT CHART (VALIDATION DATA) OF NAIVE BAYES CLASSIFIER APPLIED TO FLIGHT DELAY DATA ("SUCCESS" CLASS IS DELAYED)

the naive rule is only slightly less accurate. However, examining the lift chart (Figure 8.4) shows the strength of the naive Bayes in capturing the delayed flights well.

The machine learning workflow for the naive Bayes model that we used in this chapter is shown in Figure 8.5.

FIGURE 8.5   **ALL-INCLUSIVE WORKFLOW FOR NAIVE BAYES MODEL**

8.4 ADVANTAGES AND SHORTCOMINGS OF THE NAIVE BAYES CLASSIFIER

The naive Bayes classifier's beauty is in its simplicity, computational efficiency, good classification performance, and ability to handle categorical variables directly. In fact, it often outperforms more sophisticated classifiers even when the underlying assumption of independent predictors is far from true. This advantage is especially pronounced when the number of predictors is very large.

Three main issues should be kept in mind, however. First, the naive Bayes classifier requires a very large number of records to obtain good results. Second, where a predictor category is not present in the training data, naive Bayes assumes that a new record with that category of the predictor has zero probability. This can be a problem if this rare predictor value is important. For example, assume that the target variable is *bought high-value life insurance* and a predictor category is *owns yacht*. If the training data have no records with *owns yacht* = 1, for any new records where *owns yacht* = 1, naive Bayes will assign a probability of 0 to the target variable *bought high-value life insurance*. With no training records with *owns yacht* = 1, of course, no machine learning technique will be able to incorporate this potentially important variable into the classification model—it will be ignored. With naive Bayes, however, the absence of this predictor actively "outvotes" any other information in the record to assign a 0 to the target value (when, in this case, it has a relatively good chance of being a 1). The presence of a large training set (and judicious binning of continuous variables, if required) helps mitigate this effect.

Finally, good performance is obtained when the goal is *classification* or *ranking* of records according to their probability of belonging to a certain class. However, when the goal is actually to *estimate* the probability of class membership (propensity), this method provides very biased results. For this reason, the naive Bayes method is rarely used in credit scoring (Larsen, 2005).

SPAM FILTERING

Filtering spam in email has long been a widely familiar application of machine learning. Spam filtering, which is based in large part on natural language vocabulary, is a natural fit for a naive Bayesian classifier, which uses exclusively categorical variables. Most spam filters are based on this method, which works as follows:

1. Humans review a large number of emails, classify them as "spam" or "not spam," from these select an equal (also large) number of spam emails and nonspam emails. This is the training data.

2. These emails will contain thousands of words; for each word compute the frequency with which it occurs in the spam dataset, and the frequency with which it occurs in the nonspam dataset. Convert these frequencies into estimated probabilities (i.e., if the word "free" occurs in 500 out of 1000 spam emails, and only 100 out of 1000 nonspam emails, the probability that a spam email will contain the word "free" is 0.5, and the probability that a nonspam email will contain the word "free" is 0.1).

3. If the only word in a new message that needs to be classified as spam or not spam is "free," we would classify the message as spam, since the Bayesian posterior probability is $0.5/(0.5 + 01)$ or 5/6 that, given the appearance of "free," the message is spam.

4. Of course, we will have many more words to consider. For each such word, the probabilities described in step 2 are calculated, and multiplied together, and formula (8.3) is applied to determine the naive Bayes probability of belonging to the classes. In the simple version, class membership (spam or not spam) is determined by the higher probability.

5. In a more flexible interpretation, the ratio between the "spam" and "not spam" probabilities is treated as a score for which the operator can establish (and change) a cutoff threshold—anything above that level is classified as spam.

6. Users have the option of building a personalized training database by classifying incoming messages as spam or not spam, and adding them to the training database. One person's spam may be another person's substance.

It is clear that, even with the "naive" simplification, this is an enormous computational burden. Spam filters now typically operate at two levels—at servers (intercepting some spam that never makes it to your computer) and on individual computers (where you have the option of reviewing it). Spammers have also found ways to "poison" the vocabulary-based Bayesian approach, by including sequences of randomly selected irrelevant words. Since these words are randomly selected, they are unlikely to be systematically more prevalent in spam than in nonspam, and they dilute the effect of key spam terms such as "Viagra" and "free." For this reason, sophisticated spam classifiers also include variables based on elements other than vocabulary, such as the number of links in the message, the vocabulary in the subject line, determination of whether the "From:" email address is the real originator (anti-spoofing), use of HTML and images, and origination at a dynamic or static IP address (the latter are more expensive and cannot be set up quickly).

PROBLEMS

8.1 **Personal Loan Acceptance.** The file `UniversalBank.xlsx` contains data on 5000 customers of Universal Bank. The data include customer demographic information (age, income, etc.), the customer's relationship with the bank (mortgage, securities account, etc.), and the customer response to the last personal loan campaign (Personal Loan). Among these 5000 customers, only 480 (= 9.6%) accepted the personal loan that was offered to them in the earlier campaign. In this exercise we focus on two predictors: Online (whether or not the customer is an active user of online banking services) and Credit Card (abbreviated CC below) (does the customer hold a credit card issued by the bank), and the outcome Personal Loan (abbreviated Loan below).

    Partition the data into training (60%) and validation (40%) sets.

a. Create a pivot table for the training data with Online as a column variable, CC as a row variable, and Loan as a secondary row variable. The values inside the cells should convey the count (how many records are in that cell).

b. Consider the task of classifying a customer who owns a bank credit card and is actively using online banking services. Looking at the pivot table, what is the probability that this customer will accept the loan offer? [This is the probability of loan acceptance (Loan = 1) conditional on having a bank credit card (CC = 1) and being an active user of online banking services (Online = 1)].

c. Create two separate pivot tables for the training data. One will have Loan (rows) as a function of Online (columns) and the other will have Loan (rows) as a function of CC.

d. Compute the following quantities [$P(A|B)$ means "the probability of A given B"]:

    i. $P(CC = 1|Loan = 1)$ (the proportion of credit card holders among the loan acceptors)

    ii. $P(Online = 1|Loan = 1)$

    iii. $P(Loan = 1)$ (the proportion of loan acceptors)

    iv. $P(CC = 1|Loan = 0)$

    v. $P(Online = 1|Loan = 0)$

    vi. $P(Loan = 0)$

e. Use the quantities computed above to compute the naive Bayes probability $P(Loan = 1|CC = 1, Online = 1)$.

f. Compare this value with the one obtained from the crossed pivot table in (b). Which is a more accurate estimate?

g. In ASDM, run naive Bayes on the data. Examine the "Detailed report on training data," and find the entry that corresponds to $P(Loan = 1|CC = 1, Online = 1)$. Compare this to the number you obtained in (e).

8.2 **Automobile Accidents.** The file `Accidents.xlsx` contains information on 42,183 actual automobile accidents in 2001 in the United States that involved one of three levels of injury: NO INJURY, INJURY, or FATALITY. For each accident, additional information is recorded, such as day of week, weather conditions, and road type. A firm might be interested in developing a system for quickly classifying the severity of an accident based on initial reports and associated data in the system (some of which rely on GPS-assisted reporting).

Our goal here is to predict whether an accident just reported will involve an injury (MAX_SEV_IR = 1 or 2) or will not (MAX_SEV_IR = 0). For this purpose, create a dummy variable called INJURY that takes the value "yes" if MAX_SEV_IR = 1 or 2, and otherwise "no."

a. Using the information in this dataset, if an accident has just been reported and no further information is available, what should the prediction be? (INJURY = Yes or No?) Why?

b. Select the first 12 records in the dataset and look only at the response (INJURY) and the two predictors WEATHER_R and TRAF_CON_R.

   i. Create a pivot table that examines INJURY as a function of the two predictors for these 12 records. Use all three variables in the pivot table as rows/columns, and use counts for the cells.

   ii. Compute the exact Bayes conditional probabilities of an injury (INJURY = Yes) given the six possible combinations of the predictors.

   iii. Classify the 12 accidents using these probabilities and a cutoff of 0.5.

   iv. Compute manually the naive Bayes conditional probability of an injury given WEATHER_R = 1 and TRAF_CON_R = 1.

   v. Run a naive Bayes classifier on the 12 records and two predictors using ASDM. Check *detailed report* to obtain probabilities and classifications for all 12 records. Compare this to the exact Bayes classification. Are the resulting classifications equivalent? Is the ranking (= ordering) of observations equivalent?

c. Let us now return to the entire dataset. Partition the data into training/validation sets (use ASDM's "automatic" option for partitioning percentages).

   i. Assuming that no information or initial reports about the accident itself are available at the time of prediction (only location characteristics, weather conditions, etc.), which predictors can we include in the analysis? (Use the Data_Codes sheet.)

   ii. Run a naive Bayes classifier on the complete training set with the relevant predictors (and INJURY as the response). Note that all predictors are categorical. Show the classification matrix.

   iii. What is the overall error for the validation set?

   iv. What is the percent improvement relative to the naive rule (using the validation set)?

   v. Examine the conditional probabilities output. Why do we get a probability of zero for $P(\text{INJURY} = \text{No}|\text{SPD\_LIM} = 5)$?

## CHAPTER 9

Classification and Regression Trees

This chapter describes a flexible data-driven method that can be used for both classification (called *classification tree*) and prediction (called *regression tree*). Among the data-driven methods, trees are the most transparent and easy to interpret. Trees are based on separating observations into subgroups by creating splits on predictors. These splits create logical rules that are transparent and easily understandable, such as "IF Age < 55 AND Education > 12 THEN class $= 1$." The resulting subgroups should be more homogeneous in terms of the outcome variable, thereby creating useful prediction or classification rules. We discuss the two key ideas underlying trees: *recursive partitioning* (for constructing the tree) and *pruning* (for cutting the tree back). In the context of tree construction, we also describe a few metrics of homogeneity that are popular in tree algorithms, for determining the homogeneity of the resulting subgroups of observations. We explain that pruning is a useful strategy for avoiding overfitting and show how it is done. We also describe alternative strategies for avoiding overfitting. As with other data-driven methods, trees require large amounts of data. However, once constructed, they are computationally cheap to deploy even on large samples. They also have other advantages such as being highly automated, robust to outliers, and able to handle missing values. In addition to prediction and classification, we describe how trees can be used for dimension reduction. Finally, we introduce *random forests* and *boosted trees*, which combine results from multiple trees to improve predictive power.

9.1 INTRODUCTION

If one had to choose a classification technique that performs well across a wide range of situations without requiring much effort from the analyst while being

Machine Learning for Business Analytics: Concepts, Techniques, and Applications with Analytic Solver® Data Mining,
Fourth Edition. Galit Shmueli, Peter C. Bruce, Kuber R. Deokar, and Nitin R. Patel
© 2023 John Wiley & Sons, Inc. Published 2023 by John Wiley & Sons, Inc.

readily understandable by the consumer of the analysis, a strong contender would be the tree methodology developed by Breiman et al. (1984). Trees can be used for both classification and prediction. We discuss the classification procedure first, and then in later sections we show how the procedure can be extended to prediction of a numerical outcome. The program that Breiman et al. created to implement these procedures was called CART (Classification And Regression Trees). A related procedure is called C4.5.

What is a classification tree? Figure 9.1 shows a tree for classifying bank customers who receive a loan offer as either acceptors or nonacceptors, based on information such as their income, education level, and average credit card expenditure.

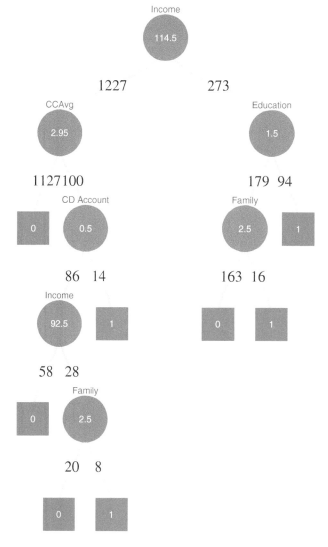

FIGURE 9.1   EXAMPLE OF A TREE FOR CLASSIFYING BANK CUSTOMERS AS LOAN ACCEPTORS OR NONACCEPTORS

Tree Structure

We have two types of nodes in a tree: decision (= splitting) nodes and terminal nodes. Nodes that have successors are called *decision nodes* because if we were to use a tree to classify a new record for which we knew only the predictor values, we would "drop" the record down the tree so that at each decision node, the appropriate branch is taken until we get to a node that has no successors. Such nodes are called the *terminal nodes* (or *leaves* of the tree) and represent the partitioning of the data by predictors.

The type of trees grown by ASDM always creates binary splits at each decision node. Therefore the number of terminal nodes is exactly one more than the number of decision nodes. ASDM's trees use circles for decision nodes and squares for terminal nodes (see Figure 9.1). Above each decision node appears the name of the predictor chosen for splitting. The splitting value appears inside the circle. Of the two child nodes connected below a decision node, the left node is for records that meet the splitting condition "< splitting value," while the right box is for records that meet the complementary condition ("≥ splitting value"). Numerical values on the fork from a decision node refer to the number of records in each of its child nodes.

Decision Rules

One of the reasons that tree classifiers are very popular is that they provide easily understandable classification rules (at least if the trees are not too large). Consider the tree in the example. The square *terminal nodes* are marked with 0 or 1, corresponding to a nonacceptor (0) or acceptor (1). The values in the circle nodes give the splitting value on a predictor. This tree can easily be translated into a set of rules for classifying a bank customer. For example, the bottom left rectangle node under the "Family" circle in this tree gives us the following rule:

$$\text{IF}(Income \geq 114.5) \text{ AND } (Education < 1.5) \text{ AND } (Family < 2.5),$$
$$\text{THEN } Class = 0 \text{ (nonacceptor)}.$$

Classifying a New Observation

To classify a new observation, it is "dropped" down the tree. When it has dropped all the way down to a terminal node, we can assign its class simply by taking a "vote" (or average, if the outcome is numerical) of all the training data that belonged to the terminal node when the tree was grown. The class with the highest vote is assigned to the new observation. For instance, a new observation reaching the rightmost terminal node in Figure 9.1, which has a majority of observations that belong to the acceptor class, would be classified as "acceptor." Alternatively, we can convert the number of acceptor records in the node to a proportion (propensity) and then compare the proportion to a user-specified cutoff value. In a binary classification situation where the success class is relatively rare and of particular interest, we can also establish a lower cutoff to better capture those rare successes (at the cost of lumping in more failures as successes). With a lower cutoff, the votes for the success class only need attain that lower cutoff level for the entire terminal node to be classified as a success. The cutoff therefore determines the proportion of votes needed for determining the terminal node class. See Chapter 5 for further discussion of the use of a cutoff value in classification, for cases where a single class is of interest.

In the following, we show how trees are constructed and evaluated.

9.2 CLASSIFICATION TREES

Two key ideas underlie classification trees. The first is the idea of *recursive partitioning* of the space of the predictor variables. The second is the idea of *pruning* using validation data. In the next few sections we describe recursive partitioning and in subsequent sections explain the pruning methodology.

Recursive Partitioning

Let us denote the outcome (response) variable by Y and the input (predictor) variables by $X_1, X_2, X_3, \ldots, X_p$. In classification, the outcome variable will be a categorical variable. Recursive partitioning divides up the p-dimensional space of the X variables into non-overlapping multidimensional rectangles. The X variables here are considered to be continuous, binary, or ordinal. This division is accomplished recursively (i.e., operating on the results of prior divisions). First, one of the predictor variables is selected, say X_i, and a value of X_i, say s_i, is chosen to split the p-dimensional space into two parts: one part that contains all the points with $X_i < s_i$ and the other with all the points with $X_i \geq s_i$. Then one of these two parts is divided in a similar manner by again choosing a predictor variable (it could be X_i or another variable) and a split value for that variable. This results in three (multidimensional) rectangular regions. This process is continued so that we get smaller and smaller rectangular regions. The idea is to divide the entire X-space up into rectangles such that each rectangle is as homogeneous or "pure" as possible. By *pure*, we mean containing records that belong to just one class. (Of course, this is not always possible, as there may be records that belong to different classes but have exactly the same values for every one of the predictor variables.)

Let us illustrate recursive partitioning with an example.

Example 1: Riding Mowers

We again use the riding-mower example presented in Chapter 3. A riding-mower manufacturer would like to find a way of classifying families in a city into those likely to purchase a riding mower and those not likely to buy one. A pilot random sample of 12 owners and 12 nonowners in the city is undertaken. The data are shown and plotted in Table 9.1 and Figure 9.2.

TABLE 9.1   LOT SIZE, INCOME, AND OWNERSHIP OF A RIDING MOWER FOR 24 HOUSEHOLDS

Household number	Income ($000s)	Lot size (000s ft²)	Ownership of riding mower
1	60.0	18.4	Owner
2	85.5	16.8	Owner
3	64.8	21.6	Owner
4	61.5	20.8	Owner
5	87.0	23.6	Owner
6	110.1	19.2	Owner
7	108.0	17.6	Owner
8	82.8	22.4	Owner
9	69.0	20.0	Owner
10	93.0	20.8	Owner
11	51.0	22.0	Owner
12	81.0	20.0	Owner
13	75.0	19.6	Nonowner
14	52.8	20.8	Nonowner
15	64.8	17.2	Nonowner
16	43.2	20.4	Nonowner
17	84.0	17.6	Nonowner
18	49.2	17.6	Nonowner
19	59.4	16.0	Nonowner
20	66.0	18.4	Nonowner
21	47.4	16.4	Nonowner
22	33.0	18.8	Nonowner
23	51.0	14.0	Nonowner
24	63.0	14.8	Nonowner

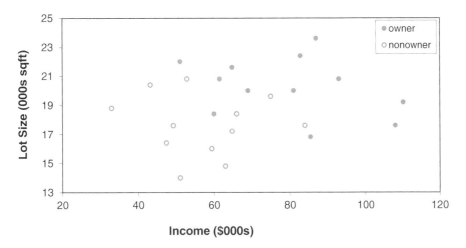

FIGURE 9.2   SCATTER PLOT OF LOT SIZE VS. INCOME FOR 24 OWNERS AND NONOWNERS OF RIDING MOWERS

If we apply the classification tree procedure to these data, the procedure will choose *Income* for the first split with a splitting value of 59.7. The (X_1, X_2)-space is now divided into two rectangles, one with Income < 59.7 and the other with Income ≥ 59.7. This is illustrated in Figure 9.3.

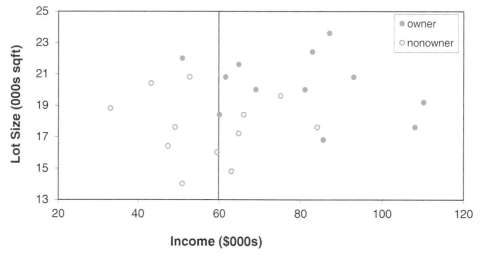

FIGURE 9.3   SPLITTING THE 24 OBSERVATIONS BY INCOME VALUE OF 59.7

Notice how the split has created two rectangles, each of which is much more homogeneous than the rectangle before the split. The left rectangle contains points that are mostly nonowners (seven nonowners and one owner) and the right rectangle contains mostly owners (eleven owners and five nonowners).

How was this particular split selected? The algorithm examined each predictor variable (in this case, Income and Lot Size) and all possible split values for each variable to find the best split. What are the possible split values for a variable? They are simply the midpoints between pairs of consecutive values for the variable. The possible split points for Income are $\{38.1, 45.3, 50.1, \ldots, 109.5\}$ and those for Lot Size are $\{14.4, 15.4, 16.2, \ldots, 23\}$. These split points are ranked according to how much they reduce impurity (heterogeneity) in the resulting rectangle. A pure rectangle is one that is composed of a single class (e.g., owners). The reduction in impurity is defined as overall impurity before the split minus the sum of the impurities for the two rectangles that result from a split.

Categorical Predictors   The previous description used numerical predictors; however, categorical predictors can also be used in the recursive partitioning context. To handle categorical predictors, the split choices for a categorical predictor are all ways in which the set of categories can be divided into two subsets. For example, a categorical variable with four categories, say $\{a, b, c, d\}$, can be split in seven ways into two subsets: $\{a\}$ and $\{b, c, d\}$; $\{b\}$ and $\{a, c, d\}$; $\{c\}$ and $\{a, b, d\}$; $\{d\}$ and $\{a, b, c\}$; $\{a, b\}$ and $\{c, d\}$; $\{a, c\}$ and $\{b, d\}$; and finally $\{a, d\}$ and $\{b, c\}$. When the number of categories is large, the number of splits becomes very large. ASDM supports only binary categorical variables (coded as 0/1). As with k-nearest neighbors, a predictor with m categories ($m > 2$) should be factored into m dummies (not $m - 1$).

Normalization   Whether predictors are numerical or categorical, it does not make any difference if they are standardized (normalized) or not.

Measures of Impurity

There are a number of ways to measure impurity. The two most popular measures are the *Gini measure* and an *entropy measure*. We describe both next. Denote the m classes of the response variable by $k = 1, 2, \ldots, m$.

The Gini impurity measure for a rectangle A is defined by

$$I(A) = 1 - \sum_{k=1}^{m} p_k^2,$$

where p_k is the proportion of observations in rectangle A that belong to class k. This measure takes values between 0 (when all the observations belong to the same class) and $(m - 1)/m$ (when all m classes are equally represented). Figure 9.4 shows the values of the Gini measure for a two-class case as a function of p_k. It can be seen that the impurity measure is at its peak when $p_k = 0.5$ (that is, when the rectangle contains 50% of each of the two classes).

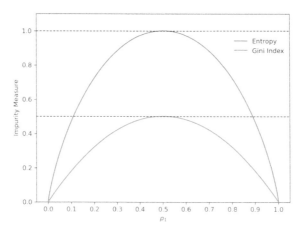

FIGURE 9.4   VALUES OF THE GINI AND ENTROPY MEASURES FOR A TWO-CLASS CASE AS A FUNCTION OF THE PROPORTION OF OBSERVATIONS IN CLASS 1 (p_1)

A second impurity measure is the entropy measure. The entropy for a rect-angle A is defined by

$$\text{entropy}(A) = -\sum_{k=1}^{m} p_k \log_2(p_k)$$

[to compute $\log_2(x)$ in Excel, use the function $= log(x, 2)$]. This measure ranges between 0 (most pure, all observations belong to the same class) and $\log_2(m)$ (when all m classes are represented equally). In the two-class case, the entropy measure is maximized (like the Gini measure) at $p_k = 0.5$.

Let us compute the impurity in the riding-mower example before and after the first split (using Income with the value of 59.7). The unsplit dataset contains 12 owners and 12 nonowners. This is a two-class case with an equal number of observations from each class. Both impurity measures are therefore at their maximum value: Gini = 0.5 and entropy = $\log_2(2) = 1$. After the split, the left rectangle contains seven nonowners and one nonowner. The impurity measures for this rectangle are

Gini_left = $1 - (7/8)^2 - (1/8)^2 = 0.219$.

entropy_left = $-(7/8) \log_2(7/8) - (1/8) \log_2(1/8) = 0.544$.

The right rectangle contains 11 owners and 5 nonowners. The impurity mea-sures of the right rectangle are therefore

Gini_right = $1 - (11/16)^2 - (5/16)^2 = 0.430$.

entropy_right = $-(11/16) \log_2(11/16) - (5/16) \log_2(5/16) = 0.896$.

The combined impurity of the two rectangles that were created by the split is a weighted average of the two impurity measures, weighted by the number of observations in each:

Gini = $(8/24)(0.219) + (16/24)(0.430) = 0.359$.

entropy = $(8/24)(0.544) + (16/24)(0.896) = 0.779$.

Thus the Gini impurity index decreased from 0.5 before the split to 0.359 after the split. Similarly, the entropy impurity measure decreased from 1 before the split to 0.779 after the split.

By comparing the reduction in impurity across all possible splits in all possible predictors, the next split is chosen. If we continue splitting the mower data, the next split is on the Lot Size variable at the value 21.4. Figure 9.5 shows that once again the tree procedure has astutely chosen to split a rectangle to increase the purity of the resulting rectangles. The lower left rectangle, which contains data points with Income < 59.7 and Lot Size < 21.4, has all points that are nonowners, whereas the upper-left rectangle, which contains data points with Income < 59.7 and Lot Size ≥ 21.4, consists exclusively of a single owner. In other words, the two left rectangles are now "pure." We can see how the

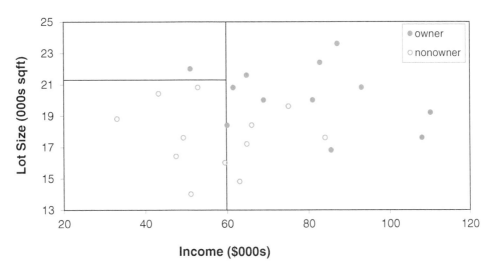

FIGURE 9.5   SPLITTING THE 24 OBSERVATIONS FIRST BY INCOME VALUE OF 59.7 AND THEN BY LOT SIZE VALUE OF 21.4

recursive partitioning is refining the set of constituent rectangles to become purer as the algorithm proceeds.

The final stage of the recursive partitioning is shown in Figure 9.6. Notice that each rectangle is now pure: it contains records from just one of the two classes.

The reason the method is called a *classification tree algorithm* is that each split can be depicted as a split of a node into two successor nodes. The first split

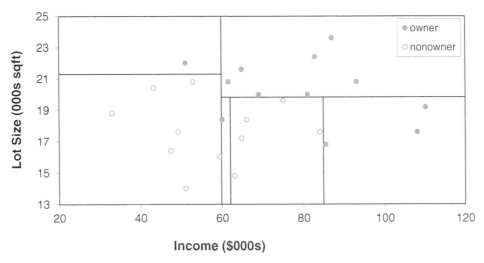

FIGURE 9.6   FINAL STAGE OF RECURSIVE PARTITIONING; EACH RECTANGLE CONSISTING OF A SINGLE CLASS (OWNERS OR NONOWNERS)

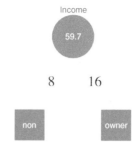

FIGURE 9.7   TREE REPRESENTATION OF FIRST SPLIT (CORRESPONDS TO FIGURE 9.3)

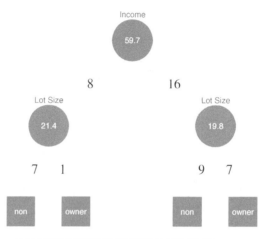

FIGURE 9.8   TREE REPRESENTATION OF FIRST THREE SPLITS

is shown as a branching of the root node of a tree in Figure 9.7. The tree representing the first three splits is shown in Figure 9.8. The full-grown tree is shown in Figure 9.9.

9.3 EVALUATING THE PERFORMANCE OF A CLASSIFICATION TREE

We have seen with previous methods that the modeling job is not completed by fitting a model to training data; we need out-of-sample data to assess and tune the model. This is particularly true with classification and regression trees, for two reasons:

- Tree structure can be quite unstable, shifting substantially depending on the sample chosen.

- A fully-fit tree will invariably lead to overfitting.

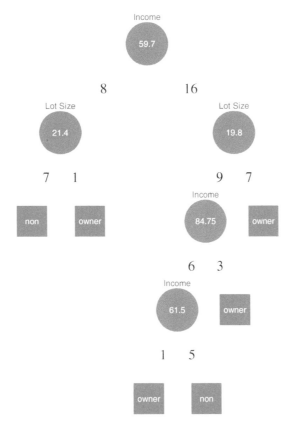

FIGURE 9.9   TREE REPRESENTATION AFTER ALL SPLITS (CORRESPONDS TO FIGURE 9.6). THIS IS THE FULL-GROWN TREE

To visualize the first challenge, potential instability, imagine that we partition the data randomly into two samples, A and B, and we build a tree with each. If there are several predictors of roughly equal predictive power, you can see that it would be easy for samples A and B to select different predictors for the top level split, just based on which records ended up in which sample. And a different split at the top level would likely cascade down and yield completely different sets of rules. So we should view the results of a single tree with some caution.

To illustrate the second challenge, overfitting, let's examine another example.

Example 2: Acceptance of Personal Loan

Universal Bank is a relatively young bank that is growing rapidly in terms of overall customer acquisition. The majority of these customers are liability customers with varying sizes of relationship with the bank. The customer base of asset customers is quite small, and the bank is interested in growing this base rapidly to bring in more loan business. In particular, it wants to explore ways of converting its liability (deposit) customers to personal loan customers.

TABLE 9.2   SAMPLE OF DATA FOR 20 CUSTOMERS OF UNIVERSAL BANK

ID	Age	Professional Experience	Income	Family Size	CC Avg	Education	Mortgage	Personal Loan	Securities Account	CD Account	Online Banking	Credit Card
1	25	1	49	4	1.60	UG	0	No	Yes	No	No	No
2	45	19	34	3	1.50	UG	0	No	Yes	No	No	No
3	39	15	11	1	1.00	UG	0	No	No	No	No	No
4	35	9	100	1	2.70	Grad	0	No	No	No	No	No
5	35	8	45	4	1.00	Grad	0	No	No	No	No	Yes
6	37	13	29	4	0.40	Grad	155	No	No	No	Yes	No
7	53	27	72	2	1.50	Grad	0	No	No	No	Yes	No
8	50	24	22	1	0.30	Prof	0	No	No	No	No	Yes
9	35	10	81	3	0.60	Grad	104	No	No	No	Yes	No
10	34	9	180	1	8.90	Prof	0	Yes	No	No	No	No
11	65	39	105	4	2.40	Prof	0	No	No	No	Yes	No
12	29	5	45	3	0.10	Grad	0	No	No	No	No	No
13	48	23	114	2	3.80	Prof	0	No	Yes	No	Yes	No
14	59	32	40	4	2.50	Grad	0	No	No	No	No	No
15	67	41	112	1	2.00	UG	0	No	Yes	No	Yes	No
16	60	30	22	1	1.50	Prof	0	No	No	No	No	Yes
17	38	14	130	4	4.70	Prof	134	Yes	No	No	Yes	No
18	42	18	81	4	2.40	UG	0	No	No	No	No	No
19	46	21	193	2	8.10	Prof	0	Yes	No	No	No	No
20	55	28	21	1	0.50	Grad	0	No	Yes	No	No	Yes

A campaign the bank ran for liability customers showed a healthy conversion rate of over 9% successes. This has encouraged the retail marketing department to devise smarter campaigns with better target marketing. The goal of our analysis is to model the previous campaign's customer behavior to find what combination of factors make a customer more likely to accept a personal loan. This will serve as the basis for the design of a new campaign.

The bank's dataset includes data on 5000 customers. The data include customer demographic information (age, income, etc.), customer response to the last personal loan campaign (*Personal Loan*), and the customer's relationship with the bank (mortgage, securities account, etc.). Among these 5000 customers, only 480 (= 9.6%) accepted the personal loan that was offered to them in the earlier campaign. Table 9.2 contains a sample of the bank's customer database for 20 customers, to illustrate the structure of the data.

After randomly partitioning the data into training (2500 observations), validation (1500 observations), and test (1000 observations) sets, we use the training data to construct a full-grown tree.[1] The first four levels of the tree are shown in Figure 9.10.

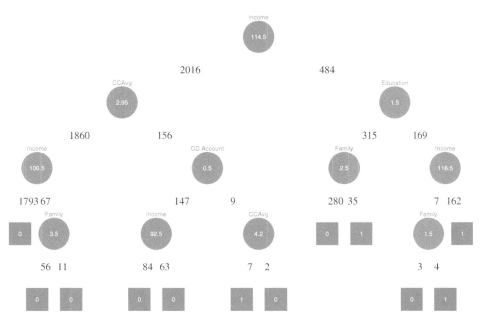

FIGURE 9.10   FIRST FOUR LEVELS OF THE FULL-GROWN TREE FOR THE LOAN ACCEPTANCE DATA USING THE TRAINING SET (2500 OBSERVATIONS). NOTE: THE ASDM EDUCATION EDITION LIMITS MAXIMUM NUMBER OF LEVELS IN TREE DRAWING TO SEVEN. YOU CAN COLLAPSE DECISION NODE(S) BY CLICKING ON A NODE. CLICK AGAIN TO EXPAND THE NODE

---

[1]In ASDM, we set the maximum number of tree levels to 100 and the minimum number of records in a terminal node to 1.

Even with just four levels, it is difficult to see the complete picture. A look at the top tree node or the first row of the table reveals that the first predictor that is chosen to split the data is *Income*, with a value of 114.5 ($000s).

Since the full-grown tree leads to completely pure terminal leaves, it is 100% accurate in classifying the training data. This can be seen in Figure 9.11. In contrast, the confusion matrices for the validation and test data[2] (which were not used to construct the full-grown tree) show lower classification accuracy. The main reason is that the full-grown tree overfits the training data (to complete

Training: Classification Summary

Confusion Matrix

Actual\Predicted	0	1
0	2255	0
1	0	245

Error Report

Class	# Cases	# Errors	% Error
0	2255	0	0
1	245	0	0
Overall	2500	0	0

Validation: Classification Summary

Confusion Matrix

Actual\Predicted	0	1
0	1353	9
1	10	128

Error Report

Class	# Cases	# Errors	% Error
0	1362	9	0.66
1	138	10	7.25
Overall	1500	19	1.27

Testing: Classification Summary

Confusion Matrix

Actual\Predicted	0	1
0	897	6
1	11	86

Error Report

Class	# Cases	# Errors	% Error
0	903	6	0.66
1	97	11	11.34
Overall	1000	17	1.70

FIGURE 9.11   LOAN ACCEPTANCE DATA: CLASSIFICATION MATRIX AND ERROR RATES FOR THE TRAINING, VALIDATION, AND TEST DATA USING THE FULL TREE

---

[2]The confusion matrices for the validation and test sets were obtained manually: For each set, we first scored the data using the Score function. We then used Excel's Pivot Table to get a confusion matrix.

accuracy!). This motivates the next section, where we describe ways to avoid overfitting either by stopping the growth of the tree before it is fully grown or by pruning the full-grown tree.

9.4 AVOIDING OVERFITTING

As the last example illustrated, using a full-grown tree (based on the training data) leads to complete overfitting of the data. As discussed in Chapter 5, overfitting will lead to poor performance on new data. If we look at the overall error at the various levels of the tree, it is expected to decrease as the number of levels grows until the point of overfitting. Of course, for the training data the overall error decreases more and more until it is zero (or close to zero[3]) at the maximum level of the tree. However, for new data, the overall error is expected to decrease until the point where the tree fully models the relationship between class and the predictors. After that, the tree starts to model the noise in the training set, and we expect the overall error for the validation set to start increasing. This is depicted in Figure 9.12. One intuitive reason for the overfitting at the deep levels of the tree is that these splits are based on very small numbers of observations. In such cases, class difference is likely to be attributed to noise rather than predictor information.

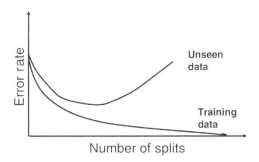

FIGURE 9.12   ERROR RATE AS A FUNCTION OF THE NUMBER OF SPLITS FOR TRAINING VS. VALIDATION DATA: OVERFITTING

Two ways to try and avoid exceeding this level, thereby limiting overfitting, are by setting rules to stop tree growth, or alternatively, by pruning the full-grown tree back to a level where it does not overfit. These solutions are discussed next.

Stopping Tree Growth: CHAID

One can think of different criteria for stopping the tree growth before it starts overfitting the data. Examples are tree depth (i.e., number of splits), minimum

---

[3]Non-zero terminal nodes can result if the training data contains records that have identical values for all predictors, but have different classes.

number of records in a terminal node, and minimum reduction in impurity. The problem is that it is not simple to determine what is a good stopping point using such rules.

Previous methods developed were based on the idea of recursive partitioning, using rules to prevent the tree from growing excessively and overfitting the training data. One popular method called *CHAID* (chi-squared automatic interaction detection) is a recursive partitioning method that predates classification and regression tree (CART) procedures by several years and is widely used in database marketing applications to this day. It uses a well-known statistical test (the chi-square test for independence) to assess whether splitting a node improves the purity by a statistically significant amount. In particular, at each node we split on the predictor that has the strongest association with the response variable. The strength of association is measured by the p-value of a chi-squared test of independence. If for the best predictor the test does not show a significant improvement, the split is not carried out, and the tree is terminated. This method is more suitable for categorical predictors, but it can be adapted to continuous predictors by binning the continuous values into categorical bins.

Pruning the Tree

An alternative solution that has proved to be more successful than stopping tree growth is pruning the full-grown tree. This is the basis of methods such as CART (developed by Breiman et al., implemented in multiple machine learning software packages such as SAS Enterprise Miner, CART, MARS, and in ASDM) and C4.5 (developed by Quinlan and implemented in packages such as IBM SPSS Modeler, Weka, and RapidMiner). In C4.5, the training data are used both for growing and pruning the tree. In CART, the innovation is to use the validation data to prune back the tree that is grown from training data. CART and CART-like procedures use validation data to prune back the tree that has deliberately been overgrown using the training data. This approach is also used by ASDM.

The idea behind pruning is to recognize that a very large tree is likely to be overfitting the training data, and that the weakest branches, which hardly reduce the error rate, should be removed. In the mower example, the last few splits resulted in rectangles with very few points (four rectangles in the full tree had just one point). We can see intuitively that these last splits are likely just capturing noise in the training set rather than reflecting patterns that would occur in future data, such as the validation data. Pruning consists of successively selecting a decision node and re-designating it as a terminal node [lopping off the branches extending beyond that decision node (its *subtree*) and thereby reducing the size of the tree]. The pruning process trades off misclassification error in the validation dataset against the number of decision nodes in the pruned tree to arrive at a tree that captures the patterns—but not the noise—in the training data. Returning to Figure 9.12, we would like to find the point where the curve for the unseen data begins to increase.

To find the degree of pruning that captures the patterns but not the noise, the CART algorithm uses a criterion called the *cost complexity* of a tree to generate a sequence of trees that are successively smaller to the point of having a tree with just the root node. (What is the classification rule for a tree with just one node?) This means that the first step is to find the best subtree of each size $(1, 2, 3, \ldots)$. Then we choose among these trees the tree that minimizes the misclassification error rate of the validation set. This is called the *minimum error tree*. Let us look at this process in a little more detail next.

Constructing the best tree of each size is based on the CC criterion, which is equal to the misclassification error of a tree (based on the training data) plus a penalty factor for the size of the tree. For a tree T that has $L(T)$ terminal nodes, the cost complexity can be written as

$$CC(T) = \text{err}(T) + \alpha L(T),$$

where $\text{err}(T)$ is the fraction of training data observations that are misclassified by tree T and α is a penalty factor for tree size. When $\alpha = 0$, there is no penalty for having too many nodes in a tree, and the best tree using the cost complexity criterion is the full-grown unpruned tree. When we increase α to a very large value the penalty cost component swamps the misclassification error component of the cost complexity criterion function, and the best tree is simply the tree with the fewest terminal nodes: namely the tree with simply one node. The idea is therefore to start with the full-grown tree and then increase the penalty factor α gradually until the cost complexity of the full tree exceeds that of a subtree. Then the same procedure is repeated using the subtree. Continuing in this manner, we generate a succession of trees with a diminishing number of nodes all the way to a trivial tree consisting of just one terminal node.

From this sequence of trees, it seems natural to choose the one that gave the lowest misclassification error on the validation dataset. We call this the *minimum error tree*. To illustrate this, Figure 9.13 shows the error rate for both the training and validation data as a function of the tree size. It can be seen that the training set error steadily decreases as the tree grows, with a noticeable drop in error rate between two and three nodes. The validation set error rate, however, reaches a minimum at seven nodes and then either remains the same or starts to increase as the tree grows. At this point, the tree is pruned, and we obtain the *minimum error tree*.

A further enhancement is to incorporate the sampling error that might cause this minimum to vary if we had a different sample. The enhancement uses the estimated standard error of the error rate to prune the tree even further;

# Decision Nodes	Training Error Rate	Validation Error Rate	
49	0.00%	1.27%	
48	0.04%	1.33%	
47	0.08%	1.33%	
46	0.12%	1.33%	
45	0.12%	1.33%	
44	0.12%	1.33%	
43	0.12%	1.33%	
42	0.16%	1.33%	
41	0.20%	1.33%	
40	0.24%	1.33%	
39	0.24%	1.33%	
38	0.28%	1.33%	
37	0.32%	1.33%	
36	0.32%	1.33%	
35	0.36%	1.33%	
34	0.36%	1.33%	
33	0.36%	1.33%	
32	0.36%	1.33%	
31	0.40%	1.33%	
30	0.44%	1.33%	
29	0.44%	1.33%	
28	0.48%	1.33%	
27	0.52%	1.40%	
26	0.52%	1.40%	
25	0.60%	1.40%	
24	0.64%	1.40%	
23	0.68%	1.40%	
22	0.84%	1.40%	
21	0.92%	1.40%	
20	0.92%	1.40%	
19	0.96%	1.40%	
18	1.04%	1.40%	
17	1.08%	1.13%	
16	1.08%	1.13%	
15	1.12%	1.13%	
14	1.36%	1.13%	
13	1.40%	1.13%	
12	1.48%	1.13%	
11	1.48%	1.13%	
10	1.52%	1.13%	
9	1.60%	1.13%	<-- Best-Pruned and Min. Error Tree
8	1.60%	2.00%	
7	1.60%	2.00%	
6	1.60%	2.00%	
5	3.00%	2.00%	
4	3.20%	2.00%	
3	3.20%	2.00%	
2	9.80%	3.07%	
1	9.80%	9.20%	
0	9.80%	9.20%	

FIGURE 9.13   ERROR RATE AS A FUNCTION OF THE NUMBER OF SPLITS FOR TRAINING VS. VALIDATION DATA FOR THE LOAN EXAMPLE

we add one standard error to the minimum validation error. If the minimum validation error is e and the validation set has n records, then the standard error is $\sqrt{e(1-e)/n}$.

The *best-pruned tree* is the smallest tree in the pruning sequence with error within one standard error of the minimum error tree. The best-pruned tree for the loan acceptance example is shown in Figure 9.14. In this case, it coincides

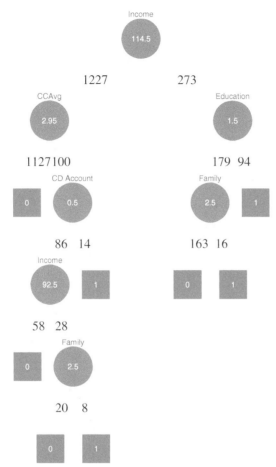

FIGURE 9.14   BEST-PRUNED TREE OBTAINED BY FITTING A FULL TREE TO THE TRAINING DATA, PRUNING IT USING THE VALIDATION DATA, AND CHOOSING THE SMALLEST TREE WITHIN ONE STANDARD ERROR OF THE MINIMUM ERROR TREE

with the minimum error tree. It is obtained by adding one standard error[4] (0.27327%) to the validation error of the minimum error tree (1.13%). The smallest tree with validation error below the total of 1.3866% is the best-pruned tree. In this example, the best-pruned tree coincides with the minimum error tree (see Figure 9.13).

Returning to the loan acceptance example, we expect that the classification accuracy of the validation set using the pruned tree would be higher than using the full-grown tree (compare Figure 9.11 with Figure 9.15). However, the performance of the pruned tree on the validation data is not fully reflective of the performance on completely new data, since the validation data were actually

---

[4]*Note*: The version of ASDM that produced this figure expresses error as a percent, but standard error as a proportion, so a conversion of one of them is required for comparability.

Training: Classification Summary

Confusion Matrix

Actual\Predicted	0	1
0	2255	0
1	0	245

Error Report

Class	# Cases	# Errors	% Error
0	2255	0	0
1	245	0	0
Overall	2500	0	0

Validation: Classification Summary

Confusion Matrix

Actual\Predicted	0	1
0	1358	4
1	13	125

Error Report

Class	# Cases	# Errors	% Error
0	1362	4	0.29
1	138	13	9.42
Overall	1500	17	1.13

Testing: Classification Summary

Confusion Matrix

Actual\Predicted	0	1
0	899	4
1	15	82

Error Report

Class	# Cases	# Errors	% Error
0	903	4	0.44
1	97	15	15.46
Overall	1000	19	1.90

FIGURE 9.15   LOAN ACCEPTANCE DATA: CONFUSION MATRIX AND ERROR RATES FOR THE TRAINING, VALIDATION, AND TEST DATA BASED ON THE PRUNED TREE

used for the pruning. This is a situation where it is particularly useful to evaluate the performance of the chosen model—whatever it may be—on a third set of data: the test set, which has not been used at all. In our example, the pruned tree applied to the test data yields an overall error rate of 1.9% (compared to 1.13% for the validation data). This is a highly accurate model, yielding only 19 errors in the test set, and thus small differences in error rates between test and validation data are in the range of chance fluctuation. With much larger datasets and less accurate classifiers, the typical tendency will be for the test data to show higher error rates than the validation data, since the latter are in effect part of the model-building process.

9.5 CLASSIFICATION RULES FROM TREES

As described in Section 9.1, classification trees provide easily understandable *classification rules* (if the trees are not too large). Each terminal node is equivalent to a classification rule. Returning to the example, the third-from right terminal node in the best-pruned tree (Figure 9.14) gives us the rule

$$\text{IF } (Income \geq 114.5) \text{ AND } (Education < 1.5) \text{ AND } (Family < 2.5),$$
$$\text{THEN } Class = 0.$$

However, in many cases the number of rules can be reduced by removing redundancies. For example, consider the rule from the fourth-from-left terminal node in Figure 9.10:

$$\text{IF } (\textit{Income} < 114.5) \text{ AND } (\textit{CCAvg} \geq 2.95)$$
$$\text{AND } (\textit{CD Account} < 0.5) \text{ AND } (\textit{Income} < 92.5),$$
$$\text{THEN } \textit{Class} = 0.$$

This rule can be simplified to

$$\text{IF } (\textit{Income} < 92.5) \text{ AND } (\textit{CCAvg} \geq 2.95) \text{ AND } (\textit{CD Account} < 0.5),$$
$$\text{THEN } \textit{Class} = 0.$$

This transparency in the process and understandability of the algorithm that leads to classifying a record as belonging to a certain class is very advantageous in settings where the final classification is not solely of interest. Berry and Linoff (2000) give the example of health insurance underwriting, where the insurer is required to show that coverage denial is not based on discrimination. By showing rules that led to denial (e.g., income < $20K AND low credit history), the company can avoid law suits. Compared to the output of other classifiers, such as discriminant functions, tree-based classification rules are easily explained to managers and operating staff. Their logic is certainly far more transparent than that of weights in neural networks!

9.6 CLASSIFICATION TREES FOR MORE THAN TWO CLASSES

Classification trees can be used with an outcome that has more than two classes. In terms of measuring impurity, the two measures that were presented earlier (the Gini impurity index and the entropy measure) were defined for m classes and hence can be used for any number of classes. The tree itself would have the same structure, except that its terminal nodes would take one of the m-class labels.

9.7 REGRESSION TREES

The tree method can also be used for numerical response variables. Regression trees for prediction operate in much the same fashion as classification trees. The output variable, Y, is a numerical variable in this case, but both the principle and the procedure are the same: Many splits are attempted, and for each, we measure "impurity" in each branch of the resulting tree. The tree procedure then selects the split that minimizes the sum of such measures. To illustrate a regression tree, consider the example of predicting prices of Toyota Corolla automobiles (from Chapter 5). The dataset includes information on 1436 sold Toyota Corolla cars. (We use the first 1000 cars from the dataset `ToyotoCorolla.xlsx`.) The goal is to find a predictive model of price as a function of 10 predictors (mileage, horsepower, number of doors, etc.). A regression tree for these data was built using a training set of 600. The best-pruned tree is shown in Figure 9.16.

We see that from the 12 input variables (including dummies), only six predictors show up as useful for predicting price: the age of the car, its weight, mileage, quarterly tax, horsepower, and CC. Three details differ between regression trees and classification trees: prediction, impurity measures, and evaluating performance. We describe these next.

Prediction

Predicting the value of the response Y for an observation is performed in a fashion similar to the classification case: The predictor information is used for "dropping" the observation down the tree until reaching a terminal node. For instance, to predict the price of a Toyota Corolla with Age = 60, Mileage = 160,000, Horse_Power = 100, Weight = 1200, Quarterly_Tax = 50, and CC = 1000, we drop it down the tree and reach the node that has the value \$7823.53. This is the price prediction for this car according to the tree. In classification trees the value of the terminal node (which is one of the categories) is determined by the "voting" of the training observations that were in that terminal node. In regression trees, the value of the terminal node is determined by the average output value of the training observations in that terminal node. In the example above, the value \$7823.53 is the average of the 11 cars in the training set that fall in the category of Age $\geq$ 56.5 AND Mileage $\geq$ 128,400.

Measuring Impurity

We described two types of impurity measures for nodes in classification trees: the Gini measure and the entropy-based measure. In both cases the index is a function of the ratio between the categories of the observations in that node. In regression trees, a typical impurity measure is the sum of the squared deviations from the mean of the terminal node. This is equivalent to the squared errors, since the mean of the terminal node is exactly the prediction. In the example above, the impurity of the node with the value \$7823.53 is computed by subtracting 7823.53 from the price of each of the 11 cars in the training set that fell in that terminal node and then squaring these deviations and summing them up. The lowest impurity possible is zero, when all values in the node are equal.

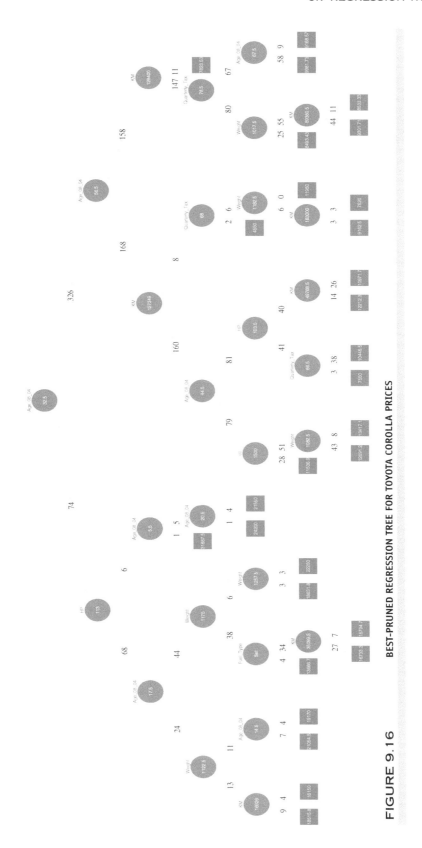

FIGURE 9.16   BEST-PRUNED REGRESSION TREE FOR TOYOTA COROLLA PRICES

Evaluating Performance

As stated above, predictions are obtained by averaging the values of the responses in the nodes. We therefore have the usual definition of predictions and errors. The predictive performance of regression trees can be measured in the same way that other predictive methods are evaluated, using summary measures such as RMSE and charts such as lift charts.

9.8 ADVANTAGES AND WEAKNESSES OF SINGLE TREES

Tree methods are good off-the-shelf classifiers and predictors. They are also useful for variable selection, with the most important predictors usually showing up at the top of the tree. Trees require relatively little effort from users in the following senses: First, there is no need for transformation of variables (any monotone transformation of the variables will give the same trees). Second, variable subset selection is automatic because it is part of the split selection. In the loan example, note that the best-pruned tree has automatically selected just three variables (Income, Education, and Family) out of the set of 14 variables available.

Trees are also intrinsically robust to outliers, since the choice of a split depends on the *ordering* of observation values and not on the absolute *magnitudes* of these values. However, they are sensitive to changes in the data, and even a slight change can cause very different splits!

Unlike models that assume a particular relationship between the response and predictors (e.g., a linear relationship such as in linear regression and linear discriminant analysis), classification and regression trees are nonlinear and nonparametric. This allows for a wide range of relationships between the predictors and the response. However, this can also be a weakness: because the splits are done on single predictors rather than on combinations of predictors, the tree is likely to miss relationships between predictors, in particular linear structures like those in linear or logistic regression models. Classification trees are useful classifiers in cases where horizontal and vertical splitting of the predictor space adequately divides the classes. But consider, for instance, a dataset with two predictors and two classes, where separation between the two classes is obviously achieved by using a diagonal line (as shown in Figure 9.17). In such cases, a classification tree is expected to have lower performance than methods such as discriminant analysis. One way to improve performance is to create new predictors that are derived from existing predictors, which can capture hypothesized relationships between predictors (similar to interactions in regression models).

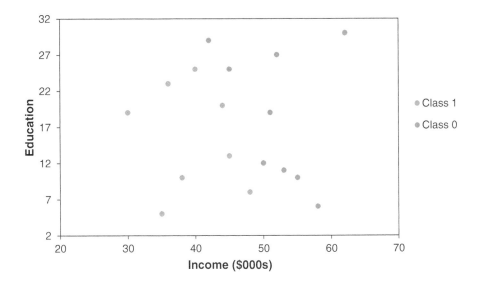

FIGURE 9.17   SCATTER PLOT DESCRIBING A TWO-PREDICTOR CASE WITH TWO CLASSES.
THE BEST SEPARATION IS ACHIEVED WITH A DIAGONAL LINE, WHICH
CLASSIFICATION TREES CANNOT DO. CHART PRODUCED IN EXCEL

Another performance issue with classification trees is that they require a large dataset in order to construct a good classifier. From a computational point of view, trees can be relatively expensive to grow because of the multiple sorting involved in computing all possible splits on every variable. Pruning the data using the validation set adds further computation time.

Although trees are useful for variable selection, one challenge is that they "favor" predictors with many potential split points. This includes categorical predictors with many categories and numerical predictors with many different values. Such predictors have a higher chance of appearing in a tree. One simplistic solution is to combine multiple categories into a smaller set and bin numerical predictors with many values. Alternatively, there are special algorithms that avoid this problem by using a two-step process: the first step chooses a predictor (e.g., via a statistical test) and the second step selects the splitting point on the chosen predictor. Examples include *conditional inference trees* (see Hothorn et al., 2006) and in QUEST classification trees (see Loh and Shih, 1997).

An appealing feature of trees is that they handle missing data without having to impute values or delete observations with missing values. Finally, a very important practical advantage of trees is the transparent rules that they generate. Such transparency is often useful in managerial applications.

9.9 IMPROVING PREDICTION: RANDOM FORESTS AND BOOSTED TREES

To address the shortcomings of a single tree—especially poor predictive power—researchers developed several extensions to trees that combine results from multiple trees. These are examples of *ensembles* (see Chapter 13). Two popular multi-tree approaches are *random forests* and *boosted trees*.

Breiman and Cutler introduced *random forests*.[5] Random forests are a special case of *bagging*, a method for improving predictive power by combining multiple classifiers or prediction algorithms. See Chapter 13 for further details on bagging.

Random Forests

The basic idea in random forests is to:

1. Draw multiple random samples, with replacement, from the data (this sampling approach is called the *bootstrap*).
2. Fit a classification (or regression) tree to each sample (and thus obtain a "forest").
3. Combine the predictions/classifications from the individual trees to obtain improved predictions. Use voting for classification and averaging for prediction.

To run a random forest in ASDM, choose "Random Trees" in Classify > Ensemble or in Predict > Ensemble.

Unlike a single tree, results from a random forest cannot be displayed in a tree-like diagram, thereby losing the interpretability that a single tree provides. However, random forests can produce *variable importance scores*, which measure the relative contribution of the different predictors. The importance score for a particular predictor X is obtained by computing the decrease in node impurities (using, e.g., the Gini value for classification trees or RMSE for regression trees) from splitting on X in each tree, and then taking an average across all the trees in the forest. The predictor with the highest average reduction in Gini or MSE has the highest predictor importance score.

Boosted Trees

The second type of multi-tree improvement is *boosted trees*. Here a sequence of trees is fitted, so that each tree concentrates on misclassified records from the previous tree.[6] The general steps are:

---

[5] For further details on random forests, see www.stat.berkeley.edu/users/breiman/RandomForests/cc_home.htm

[6] In "boosted trees" algorithms, predictors are randomly drawn for each tree; in contrast, in random forests, the number of predictors is fixed.

1. Fit a single tree.

2. Draw a sample that gives higher selection probabilities to misclassified records.

3. Fit a tree to the new sample.

4. Repeat steps 2 and 3 multiple times.

5. Use weighted voting to classify records, where heavier weight is given to later trees.

Figure 9.18 shows the result of running a boosted tree on the loan acceptance example that we saw earlier. In ASDM, we choose "Boosting" in Classify > Ensemble (a similar option is available for predicting a numerical outcome in the Predict > Ensemble), and set the number of trees (called "weak learners") to 10. We can see that compared to the performance of the single best-pruned tree (Figure 9.15), the boosted tree has better performance on the validation and test sets in terms of lower overall error rate and especially in terms of correct

Training: Classification Summary

Confusion Matrix

Actual\Predicted	0	1
0	2255	0
1	0	245

Error Report

Class	# Cases	# Errors	% Error
0	2255	0	0
1	245	0	0
Overall	2500	0	0

Validation: Classification Summary

Confusion Matrix

Actual\Predicted	0	1
0	1358	4
1	19	119

Error Report

Class	# Cases	# Errors	% Error
0	1362	4	0.29
1	138	19	13.77
Overall	1500	23	1.53

Testing: Classification Summary

Confusion Matrix

Actual\Predicted	0	1
0	899	4
1	10	87

Error Report

Class	# Cases	# Errors	% Error
0	903	4	0.44
1	97	10	10.31
Overall	1000	14	1.40

FIGURE 9.18   LOAN ACCEPTANCE DATA: CONFUSION MATRIX AND ERROR RATES FOR THE TRAINING, VALIDATION, AND TEST DATA BASED ON BOOSTED TREE

classification of 1s—the rare class of special interest. Where does boosting's special talent for finding 1s come from? When one class is dominant (0s constitute over 90% of the data here), basic classifiers are tempted to classify cases as belonging to the dominant class, and the 1s in this case constitute most of the misclassifications with the single best-pruned tree. The boosting algorithm concentrates on the misclassifications (which are mostly 1s), so it is naturally going to do well in reducing the misclassification of 1s (from 15 in the single tree to 12 in the boosted tree, in the test sets).

The machine learning workflow for the personal loan example is shown in Figure 9.19. The left branch corresponds to Figure 9.10, which is a full-grown tree. The middle branch corresponds to the best-pruned tree in Figure 9.16. The right branch corresponds to the boosted tree shown in Figure 9.18.

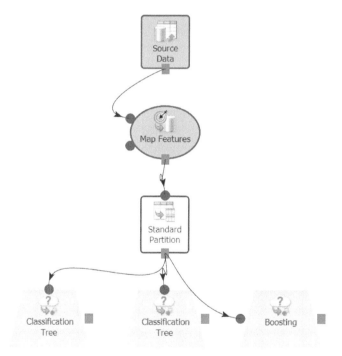

FIGURE 9.19   THE MACHINE LEARNING WORKFLOW FOR THE PERSONAL LOAN EXAMPLE

PROBLEMS

9.1 **Competitive Auctions on eBay.com.** The file eBayAuctions.xlsx contains information on 1972 auctions that transacted on eBay.com during May–June 2004. The goal is to use these data to build a model that will classify auctions as competitive or noncompetitive. A *competitive auction* is defined as an auction with at least two bids placed on the item auctioned. The data include variables that describe the item (auction category), the seller (his/her eBay rating), and the auction terms that the seller selected (auction duration, opening price, currency, day-of-week of auction close). In addition, we have the price at which the auction closed. The task is to predict whether or not the auction will be competitive.

Data Preprocessing. Create dummy variables for the categorical predictors. These include *Category* (18 categories), *Currency* (USD, GBP, euro), *EndDay* (Monday–Sunday), and *Duration* (1, 3, 5, 7, or 10 days). Split the data into training and validation datasets using a 60:40% ratio.

a. Fit a classification tree using all predictors, using the best-pruned tree. To avoid overfitting, set the minimum number of records in a terminal node to 50. Also set the maximum number of levels to be displayed at seven (the maximum allowed in ASDM). Write down the results in terms of rules. (*Note*: If you had to slightly reduce the number of predictors due to software limitations, or for clarity of presentation, which would be a good variable to choose?)

b. Is this model practical for predicting the outcome of a new auction?

c. Describe the interesting and uninteresting information that these rules provide.

d. Fit another classification tree (using the best-pruned tree, with a minimum number of records per terminal node = 50 and maximum allowed number of displayed levels), this time only with predictors that can be used for predicting the outcome of a new auction. Describe the resulting tree in terms of rules. Make sure to report the smallest set of rules required for classification.

e. Plot the resulting tree on a scatter plot: Use the two axes for the two best (quantitative) predictors. Each auction will appear as a point, with coordinates corresponding to its values on those two predictors. Use different colors or symbols to separate competitive and noncompetitive auctions. Draw lines (you can sketch these by hand or use Excel) at the values that create splits. Does this splitting seem reasonable with respect to the meaning of the two predictors? Does it seem to do a good job of separating the two classes?

f. Examine the lift chart and the classification table for the tree. What can you say about the predictive performance of this model?

g. Based on this last tree, what can you conclude from these data about the chances of an auction obtaining at least two bids and its relationship to the auction settings set by the seller (duration, opening price, ending day, currency)? What would you recommend for a seller as the strategy that will most likely lead to a competitive auction?

9.2 **Predicting Delayed Flights.** The file FlightDelays.xlsx contains information on all commercial flights departing the Washington, DC, area and arriving at New York during January 2004. For each flight, there is information on the departure and arrival airports, the distance of the route, the scheduled time and date of the flight, and so on. The variable that we are trying to predict is whether or not a flight is delayed. A delay is defined as an arrival that is at least 15 minutes later than scheduled.

Data Preprocessing. Create dummies for day of week, carrier, departure airport, and arrival airport. This will give you 17 dummies. Bin the scheduled departure time into eight bins (in ASDM use *Transform → Bin Continuous Data* and select equal interval). After binning CRS_DEP_TIME into the eight bins, this new variable should be broken down into dummies (because the effect will not be linear, due to the morning and afternoon rush hours). This will avoid treating the departure time as a continuous predictor, since it is reasonable that delays are related to rush-hour times. Partition the data into training and validation sets.

a. Fit a classification tree to the flight delay variable using all the relevant predictors. Do not include DEP_TIME (actual departure time) in the model because it is unknown at the time of prediction (unless we are generating our predictions of delays after the plane takes off, which is unlikely). In the third step of the Classification Tree menu, choose "Maximum # levels to be displayed = 6." Use the best-pruned tree, setting the minimum number of observations in the final nodes to 1. Express the resulting tree as a set of rules.

b. If you needed to fly between DCA and EWR on a Monday at 7 AM, would you be able to use this tree? What other information would you need? Is it available in practice? What information is redundant?

c. Fit another tree, this time excluding the Weather predictor. (Why?) Select the option of seeing both the full tree and the best-pruned tree. You will find that the best-pruned tree contains a single terminal node.

    i. How is this tree used for classification? (What is the rule for classifying?)

    ii. To what is this rule equivalent?

    iii. Examine the full tree. What are the top three predictors according to this tree?

    iv. Why, technically, does the pruned tree result in a tree with a single node?

    v. What is the disadvantage of using the top levels of the full tree as opposed to the best-pruned tree?

    vi. Compare this general result to that from logistic regression in the example in Chapter 10. What are possible reasons for the classification tree's failure to find a good predictive model?

9.3   **Predicting Prices of Used Cars (Regression Trees).**
The file `ToyotaCorolla.xlsx` contains the data on used cars (Toyota Corolla) on sale during late summer of 2004 in the Netherlands. It has 1436 records containing details on 38 attributes, including Price, Age, Kilometers, HP, and other specifications. The goal is to predict the price of a used Toyota Corolla based on its specifications. (The example in Section 9.7 is a subset of this dataset.)

- Create dummy variables for the categorical predictors (Fuel Type and Color).
- Split the data into training (50%), validation (30%), and test (20%) datasets.
- Run a regression tree (RT) using the Prediction menu in ASDM with the output variable Price and input variables Age_08_04, KM, Fuel_Type, HP, Automatic, Doors, Quarterly_Tax, Mfg_Guarantee, Guarantee_Period, Airco, Automatic_Airco, CD_Player, Powered_Windows, Sport_Model, and Tow_Bar. Set the parameters for the tree so as to produce as deep a tree as possible and obtain scores from this deep tree.

a. Which appear to be the three or four most important car specifications for predicting the car's price?

i. Compare the prediction errors of the training, validation, and test sets by examining their RMSE and by plotting the three boxplots. What is happening with the training set predictions? How does the predictive performance of the test set compare to the other two? Why does this occur?

ii. How might we achieve better validation predictive performance at the expense of training performance?

iii. Create a best-pruned tree using the same data partitioning. Compared to the deeper tree, what is the predictive performance on the validation set? and on the training set?

b. Let us see the effect of turning the price variable into a categorical variable. First, create a new variable that categorizes price into 20 bins. Use *Transform → Bin continuous data* to categorize Price into 20 bins of equal counts (leave all other options at their default). Next, repartition the data keeping Binned_Price instead of Price. Run a classification tree (CT) using the *Classification* menu of ASDM with the same set of input variables as in the RT, and with Binned_Price as the output variable. Set the parameters for the tree so as to produce as deep a tree as possible and obtain scores from this deep tree.

i. Compare the tree generated by the CT with the one generated by the RT. Are they different? (Look at structure, the top predictors, size of tree, etc.) Why?

ii. Predict the price, using the RT and the CT, of a used Toyota Corolla with the specifications listed in Table 9.3.

TABLE 9.3   **SPECIFICATIONS FOR A PARTICULAR TOYOTA COROLLA**

Variable	Value
Age_-08_-04	77
KM	117000
Fuel_Type	Petrol
HP	110
Automatic	No
Doors	5
Quarterly_Tax	100
Mfg_Guarantee	No
Guarantee_Period	3
Airco	Yes
Automatic_Airco	No
CD_Player	No
Powered_Windows	No
Sport_Model	No
Tow_Bar	Yes

iii. Compare the predictions in terms of the predictors that were used, the magnitude of the difference between the two predictions, and the advantages and disadvantages of the two methods.

## CHAPTER 10

Logistic Regression

In this chapter, we describe the highly popular and powerful classification method called logistic regression. Like linear regression, it relies on a specific model relating the predictors with the outcome. The user must specify the predictors to include as well as their form (e.g., including any interaction terms). This means that even small datasets can be used for building logistic regression classifiers, and that once the model is estimated, it is computationally fast and cheap to classify even large samples of new observations. We describe the logistic regression model formulation and its estimation from data. We also explain the concepts of "logit," "odds," and "probability" of an event that arise in the logistic model context and the relations among the three. We discuss variable importance and coefficient interpretation, as well as variable selection for dimension reduction. We describe extensions to multiclass models in the Appendix at the end of this chapter.

10.1 INTRODUCTION

Logistic regression extends the ideas of linear regression to the situation where the outcome variable Y is categorical. We can think of a categorical variable as dividing the observations into classes. For example, if Y denotes a recommendation on holding/selling/buying a stock, we have a categorical variable with three categories. We then consider each of the stocks in the dataset (the observations) as belonging to one of three classes: the *hold* class, the *sell* class, and the *buy* class. Logistic regression can be used for classifying a new observation, where its class is unknown, into one of the classes, based on the values of its predictor variables (called *classification*). It can also be used in data where the class is known, to find factors distinguishing between observations in different classes in terms of their

Machine Learning for Business Analytics: Concepts, Techniques, and Applications with Analytic Solver® Data Mining, Fourth Edition. Galit Shmueli, Peter C. Bruce, Kuber R. Deokar, and Nitin R. Patel
© 2023 John Wiley & Sons, Inc. Published 2023 by John Wiley & Sons, Inc.

predictor variables, or "predictor profile" (called *profiling*). Logistic regression is used in applications such as:

1. Classifying customers as returning or nonreturning (classification).
2. Finding factors that differentiate between male and female top executives (profiling).
3. Predicting the approval or disapproval of a loan based on information such as credit scores (classification).

The logistic regression model is used in a variety of fields: whenever a structured model is needed to explain or predict categorical (in particular, binary) outcomes. One such application is in describing choice behavior in econometrics.

In this chapter, we focus on the use of logistic regression for classification. We deal only with a binary outcome variable having two possible classes. In the Appendix, we show how the results can be extended to the case where Y assumes more than two possible outcomes. Popular examples of binary response outcomes are success/failure, yes/no, buy/don't buy, default/don't default, and survive/die. For convenience, we often code the values of a binary response Y as 0 and 1.

Note that in some cases we may choose to convert a continuous outcome variable or an outcome variable with multiple classes into a binary outcome variable for purposes of simplification, reflecting the fact that decision-making may be binary (approve the loan/don't approve, make an offer/don't make an offer). As with multiple linear regression, the predictor variables $X_1, X_2, \ldots, X_k$ may be categorical variables, continuous variables, or a mixture of these two types. While in multiple linear regression the aim is to predict the value of the continuous Y for a new observation, in logistic regression the goal is to predict which class a new observation will belong to, or simply to *classify* the observation into one of the classes. In the stock example, we would want to classify a new stock into one of the three recommendation classes: sell, hold, or buy. Or, we might want to compute for a new observation its *propensity* (= the probability) to belong to each class, and then possibly rank a set of new observations from highest to lowest propensity in order to act on those with the highest propensity.

Potentially, one could use linear regression for classification, by training a linear regression on a 0/1 outcome (called a *Linear Probability Model*). The model is then used to generate numerical predictions which are converted into binary classifications using a threshold. However, linear probability models, despite their name, do not produce proper predicted probabilities. The numerical predictions they produce are useful for comparison to the classification threshold, but are otherwise meaningless.

In logistic regression we take two steps: the first step yields estimates of the *propensities* or *probabilities* of belonging to each class. In the binary case we get an estimate of $p = P(Y = 1)$, the probability of belonging to class 1 (which also tells us the probability of belonging to class 0). In the next step, we use a cutoff value on these probabilities in order to classify each case into one of the classes. For example, in a binary case, a cutoff of 0.5 means that cases with an estimated probability of $P(Y = 1) \geq 0.5$ are classified as belonging to class 1, whereas cases with $P(Y = 1) < 0.5$ are classified as belonging to class 0. This cutoff does not need to be set at 0.5. When the event in question is a low-probability, but notable or important event (e.g., 1 = fraudulent transaction), a lower cutoff may be used to classify more cases as belonging to class 1.

10.2 THE LOGISTIC REGRESSION MODEL

The idea behind logistic regression is straightforward: instead of using Y as the outcome variable, we use a function of it, which is called the *logit*. The logit, it turns out, can be modeled as a linear function of the predictors. Once the logit has been predicted, it can be mapped back to a probability.

To understand the logit, we take several intermediate steps: First, we look at $p = P(Y = 1)$, the probability of belonging to class 1 (as opposed to class 0). In contrast to Y, the class label, which only takes the values 0 and 1, p can take any value in the interval $[0, 1]$. However, if we express p as a linear function of the q predictors[1] in the form

$$p = \beta_0 + \beta_1 x_1 + \beta_2 x_2 + \cdots + \beta_q x_q, \tag{10.1}$$

it is not guaranteed that the right-hand side will lead to values within the interval $[0, 1]$. The solution is to use a nonlinear function of the predictors in the form

$$p = \frac{1}{1 + e^{-(\beta_0 + \beta_1 x_1 + \beta_2 x_2 + \cdots + \beta_q x_q)}}. \tag{10.2}$$

This is called the *logistic response function*. For any values of $x_1, \ldots, x_q$, the right-hand side will always lead to values in the interval $[0, 1]$. Next, we look at a different measure of belonging to a certain class, known as *odds*. The odds of belonging to class 1 ($Y = 1$) is defined as *the ratio of the probability of belonging to class 1 to the probability of belonging to class 0*:

$$\text{Odds}(Y = 1) = \frac{p}{1 - p}. \tag{10.3}$$

This metric is very popular in horse races, sports, gambling, epidemiology, and many other areas. Instead of talking about the *probability* of winning or contacting

---

[1]Unlike elsewhere in the book, where p denotes the number of predictors, in this chapter we indicate predictors by q, to avoid confusion with the probability p.

a disease, people talk about the *odds* of winning or contacting a disease. How are these two different? If, for example, the probability of winning is 0.5, the odds of winning are $0.5/0.5 = 1$. We can also perform the reverse calculation: Given the odds of an event, we can compute its probability by manipulating equation (10.3):

$$p = \frac{\text{Odds}}{1 + \text{Odds}}. \qquad (10.4)$$

Substituting (10.2) into (10.4), we can write the relationship between the odds and the predictors as

$$\text{Odds}(Y = 1) = e^{\beta_0 + \beta_1 x_1 + \beta_2 x_2 + \cdots + \beta_q x_q}. \qquad (10.5)$$

This last equation describes a multiplicative (proportional) relationship between the predictors and the odds. Such a relationship is interpretable in terms of percentages: for example, a unit increase in predictor x_j is associated with an average increase of $e^{\beta_j} \times 100\%$ in the odds (holding all other predictors constant).

Now, if we take a natural logarithm[2] on both sides, we get the standard formulation of a logistic model:

$$\log(\text{odds}) = \beta_0 + \beta_1 x_1 + \beta_2 x_2 + \cdots + \beta_q x_q. \qquad (10.6)$$

The log(odds), called the *logit*, takes values from $-\infty$ (very low odds) to ∞ (very high odds).[3] A logit of 0 corresponds to even odds of 1 (probability = 0.5). Thus, our final formulation of the relation between the response and the predictors uses the logit as the outcome variable and models it as a *linear function* of the q predictors.

To see the relation between the probability, odds, and logit of belonging to class 1, look at Figure 10.1, which shows the odds (top) and logit (bottom) as a function of p. Notice that the odds can take any nonnegative value and that the logit can take any real value. Let us examine some data to illustrate the use of logistic regression.

Example: Acceptance of Personal Loan

Recall the example described in Chapter 9 of acceptance of a personal loan by Universal Bank. The bank's dataset includes data on 5000 customers. The data include customer demographic information (*Age, Income*, etc.), customer response to the last personal loan campaign (*Personal Loan*), and the customer's relationship with the bank (mortgage, securities account, etc.). Among these 5000 customers, only 480 (= 9.6%) accepted the personal loan that was offered to them in a previous campaign. The goal is to build a model that identifies customers who are most likely to accept the loan offer in future mailings.

---

[2]The natural logarithm function is typically denoted ln() or log(). In this book, we use log().
[3]We use the terms *odds* and *odds(Y = 1)* interchangeably.

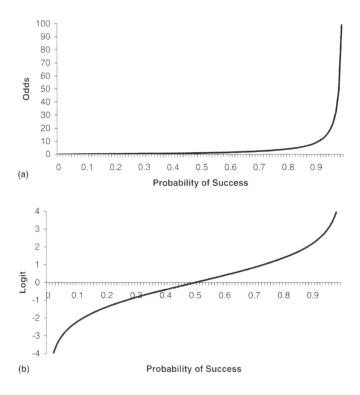

FIGURE 10.1   (a) ODDS AND (b) LOGIT AS A FUNCTION OF p

Model with a Single Predictor

Consider first a simple logistic regression model with just one predictor. This is conceptually analogous to the simple linear regression model in which we fit a straight line to relate the outcome, Y, to a single predictor, X.

Let us construct a simple logistic regression model for classification of customers using the single predictor *Income*. The equation relating the outcome variable to the predictor in terms of probabilities is

$$P(\text{Personal Loan} = \textit{Yes}|\text{Income} = x) = \frac{1}{1 + e^{-(\beta_0 + \beta_1 x)}},$$

or equivalently, in terms of odds,

$$\text{Odds}(\text{Personal Loan} = \textit{Yes}) = e^{\beta_0 + \beta_1 x}. \tag{10.7}$$

Assume the estimated coefficients for the model are $\hat{\beta}_0 = -6.1531$ and $\hat{\beta}_1 = 0.0378$. So the fitted model is

$$P(\text{Personal Loan} = \textit{Yes}|\text{Income} = x) = \frac{1}{1 + e^{6.1531 - 0.0378x}}. \tag{10.8}$$

Although logistic regression can be used for prediction in the sense that we predict the *probability* of a categorical outcome, it is most often used for classification. To see the difference between the two, consider predicting the probability of a customer accepting the loan offer as opposed to classifying the customer as an acceptor/nonacceptor. From Figure 10.2 it can be seen that the loan acceptance probabilities that are produced by the logistic regression model (the S-shaped curve in Figure 10.2) can yield values between 0 and 1. To end up with classifications into either 1 or 0 (e.g., a customer either accepts the loan offer or not), we need a threshold, or cutoff value (see section on "Propensities and Cutoff for Classification" in Chapter 5). This is true in the case of multiple predictor variables as well.

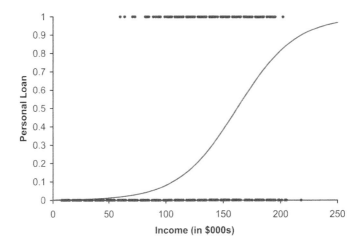

FIGURE 10.2   PLOT OF DATA POINTS (PERSONAL LOAN AS A FUNCTION OF INCOME) AND THE FITTED LOGISTIC CURVE

In the Universal Bank example, in order to classify a new customer as an acceptor/nonacceptor of the loan offer, we use the information on his/her income by plugging it into the fitted equation in (10.8). This yields an estimated probability of accepting the loan offer. We then compare it to the cutoff value. The customer is classified as an acceptor if the probability of his/her accepting the offer is above the cutoff.[4]

Estimating the Logistic Model from Data: Computing Parameter Estimates

In logistic regression, the relation between Y and the β parameters is nonlinear. For this reason, the β parameters are not estimated using the method of least squares (as in multiple linear regression). Instead, a method called *maximum likelihood* is used. The idea, in brief, is to find the estimates that maximize

---

[4]Here we compared the probability to a cutoff c. If we prefer to look at *odds* of accepting rather than the probability, an equivalent method is to use the equation in (10.7) and compare the odds to $c/(1-c)$. If the odds are higher than this number, the customer is classified as an acceptor. If the odds are lower, we classify the customer as a nonacceptor.

the chance of obtaining the data that we have. This requires iterations using a computer program.[5]

Algorithms to compute the coefficient estimates are less robust than algorithms for linear regression. Computed estimates are generally reliable for well-behaved datasets where the number of observations with outcome variable values of both 0 and 1 is large; their ratio is "not too close" to either 0 or 1; and when the number of coefficients in the logistic regression model is small relative to the sample size (e.g., no more than 10%). As with linear regression, collinearity (strong correlation among the predictors) can lead to computational difficulties. Computationally intensive algorithms have been developed recently that circumvent some of these difficulties. For technical details on the maximum likelihood estimation in logistic regression, see Hosmer and Lemeshow (2000).

To illustrate a typical output from such a procedure, look at the output in Figure 10.3 for the logistic model fitted to a training set of 3000 Universal Bank customers. The outcome variable is *Personal Loan*, with Yes defined as the *success* (this is equivalent to setting the outcome variable to 1 for an acceptor and 0 for a nonacceptor). Here we use all 12 predictors, but note that for each categorical predictor with m categories we use only $m - 1$ dummies.

Coefficients

Predictor	Estimate	Confidence Interval: Lower	Confidence Interval: Upper	Odds	Standard Error	Chi2 - Statistic	P-Value
Intercept	-6.2628	-10.6025	-1.9231	0.0019	2.2142	8.0004	0.0047
Age	-0.0184	-0.1790	0.1423	0.9818	0.0820	0.0501	0.8229
Experience	0.0169	-0.1424	0.1763	1.0171	0.0813	0.0433	0.8352
Income	0.0605	0.0531	0.0679	1.0624	0.0038	253.4398	0.0000
Family	0.5699	0.3833	0.7566	1.7681	0.0952	35.8121	0.0000
CCAvg	0.1491	0.0383	0.2599	1.1608	0.0565	6.9560	0.0084
Mortgage	-0.0001	-0.0016	0.0015	0.9999	0.0008	0.0104	0.9189
Education_1	-4.1723	-4.8522	-3.4925	0.0154	0.3469	144.6835	0.0000
Education_2	-0.1879	-0.6607	0.2849	0.8287	0.2412	0.6068	0.4360
Education_3	0.0000	0.0000	0.0000	1.0000	0.0000	N/A	N/A
Securities Account_0	0.7483	0.0170	1.4796	2.1133	0.3731	4.0216	0.0449
Securities Account_1	0.0000	0.0000	0.0000	1.0000	0.0000	N/A	N/A
CD Account_0	-3.5957	-4.4631	-2.7283	0.0274	0.4426	66.0148	0.0000
CD Account_1	0.0000	0.0000	0.0000	1.0000	0.0000	N/A	N/A
Online_0	0.0000	0.0000	0.0000	1.0000	0.0000	N/A	N/A
Online_1	-0.5993	-1.0143	-0.1844	0.5492	0.2117	8.0152	0.0046
CreditCard_0	0.7854	0.2711	1.2998	2.1933	0.2624	8.9583	0.0028
CreditCard_1	0.0000	0.0000	0.0000	1.0000	0.0000	N/A	N/A

FIGURE 10.3   LOGISTIC REGRESSION COEFFICIENT TABLE FOR PERSONAL LOAN ACCEPTANCE AS A FUNCTION OF 12 PREDICTORS

---

[5]The method of maximum likelihood ensures good asymptotic (large sample) properties for the estimates. Under very general conditions, maximum likelihood estimators are: (1) *consistent*—the probability of the estimator differing from the true value approaches zero with increasing sample size; (2) *asymptotically efficient*—the variance is the smallest possible among consistent estimators; and (3) *asymptotically normally distributed*—this allows us to compute confidence intervals and perform statistical tests in a manner analogous to the analysis of multiple linear regression models, provided that the sample size is *large*.

Data Preprocessing Using categorical predictors in ASDM's logistic regression can be done in one of two ways. One option is to create the dummy variables using the Create Dummies (*Data Mining > Transform > Transform Categorical Data > Create Dummies*) option (before data partitioning) and then select the subset of dummies in the Logistic Regression menu. The other option is to directly select the categorical predictors in the Logistic Regression menu, in which case ASDM will set one of the dummies for each categorical predictor as a reference category. Below we explain the first approach, where dummy variables are created manually, so the concept is clear. We will then use the second approach to generate the output.

We start by creating dummy variables for each of the categorical predictors. Except for Education, which has three categories, the remaining four categorical variables have two categories. We therefore need $6 = 2 + 1 + 1 + 1 + 1$ dummy variables to describe these five categorical predictors. We use the following coding:

$$\text{Education\_1} = \begin{cases} 1 & \text{if education is } \textit{Undergrad} \text{ level} \\ 0 & \text{otherwise} \end{cases}$$

$$\text{Education\_2} = \begin{cases} 1 & \text{if education is at } \textit{Graduate} \text{ level} \\ 0 & \text{otherwise} \end{cases}$$

$$\text{Securities\_1} = \begin{cases} 1 & \text{if customer has securities account in bank} \\ 0 & \text{otherwise} \end{cases}$$

$$\text{CD\_1} = \begin{cases} 1 & \text{if customer has CD account in bank} \\ 0 & \text{otherwise} \end{cases}$$

$$\text{Online\_1} = \begin{cases} 1 & \text{if customer uses online banking} \\ 0 & \text{otherwise} \end{cases}$$

$$\text{CreditCard\_1} = \begin{cases} 1 & \text{if customer holds Universal Bank credit card} \\ 0 & \text{otherwise} \end{cases}$$

Next, we partition the data randomly into training (60%) and validation (40%) sets. We use the training set to fit a model and the validation set to assess the model's performance.

Figure 10.3 shows the estimated coefficients from directly selecting the categorical predictors in ASDM's logistic regression menu. The lines in red show the reference categories chosen by the software (*Education_3, Securities Account_1, CD Account_1, Online_0, CreditCard_1*). These are the dummies that are omitted from the regression equation. Note that these are slightly different from the reference categories that we omitted in the manual example above.

Ignoring p-values for the coefficients, a model based on all 12 predictors would have the estimated logistic equation

$$
\begin{aligned}
\text{Logit(Personal Loan} = \textit{Yes}) = \ & -6.263 - 0.018\,\textit{Age} + 0.017\,\textit{Experience} \\
& + 0.061\,\textit{Income} + 0.570\,\textit{Family} + 0.149\,\textit{CCAvg} \\
& - 0.000\,\textit{Mortgage} - 4.172\,\textit{Education\_1} \\
& - 0.189\,\textit{Education\_2} \\
& - 0.748\,\textit{Securities Account\_0} - 3.596\,\textit{CD Account\_0} \\
& - 0.599\,\textit{Online\_1} + 0.785\,\textit{CreditCard\_0}. \qquad (10.9)
\end{aligned}
$$

The negative coefficients for the dummy variables *CD Account_0, Education_1*, and *Education_2* mean that not holding a CD account and having undergraduate or graduate education are associated with lower probabilities of accepting the loan offer. In contrast, the positive coefficients of *Securities Account_0, Online_1* and *CreditCard_0* indicate that not having a securities account, using online banking, and not owning a Universal Bank credit card are associated with higher acceptance rates. For the continuous predictors, positive coefficients indicate that a higher value on that predictor is associated with a higher probability of accepting the loan offer (e.g., income: higher income customers tend more to accept the offer). Similarly, negative coefficients indicate that a higher value on that predictor is associated with a lower probability of accepting the loan offer (e.g., *Age*: older customers are less likely to accept the offer).

If we want to talk about the *odds* of offer acceptance, we can use the column entitled "odds" to obtain the equation:

$$
\begin{aligned}
\text{Odds(Personal Loan} = \textit{Yes}) = \ & e^{-6.263}(0.982)^{\textit{Age}}\,(1.017)^{\textit{Experience}}\,(1.062)^{\textit{Income}} \\
& \times (1.768)^{\textit{Family}}\,(1.161)^{\textit{CCAvg}}\,(1)^{\textit{Mortgage}} \\
& \times (0.015)^{\textit{Education\_1}}\,(0.829)^{\textit{Education\_2}} \\
& \times (2.113)^{\textit{Securities Account\_0}} \\
& \times (0.027)^{\textit{CD Account\_0}}\,(0.549)^{\textit{Online\_1}}(2.193)^{\textit{CreditCard\_0}}.
\end{aligned}
$$

$$(10.10)$$

Notice how positive coefficients in the logit model translate into coefficients larger than 1 in the odds model, and negative coefficients in the logit translate into coefficients smaller than 1 in the odds.

A third option is to look directly at an equation for the probability of acceptance, using equation (10.2). This is the probability (the *propensity*) of accepting the offer for a customer with given values of the 12 predictors.[6]

---

[6]If all q predictors are categorical, each having m_q categories, we need not compute probabilities/odds for each of the n observations. The number of different probabilities/odds is exactly $m_1 \times m_2 \times \cdots \times m_q$.

Interpreting Results in Terms of Odds (for a Profiling Goal)

Logistic models, when they are appropriate for the data, can give useful information about the roles played by different predictor variables. Say we want to know how increasing family income by one unit will affect the probability of loan acceptance. This can be found straightforwardly if we consider not probabilities, but odds.

Recall that the odds are given by

$$\text{Odds} = e^{\beta_0 + \beta_1 x_1 + \beta_2 x_2 + \cdots + \beta_k x_q}.$$

At first let us return to the single predictor example, where we model a customer's acceptance of a personal loan offer as a function of his/her income:

$$\text{Odds}(\text{Personal Loan} = \text{Yes}) = e^{\beta_0 + \beta_1 \cdot \text{Income}}.$$

We can think of the model as a multiplicative model of odds. The odds that a customer with income zero will accept the loan is estimated by $e^{-6.153 + (0.0378)(0)} = 0.002$. These are the *base-case odds*. In this example, it is obviously economically meaningless to talk about a zero income; the value zero and the corresponding base-case odds could be meaningful, however, in the context of other predictors. The odds of accepting the loan with an income of \$100K will increase by a multiplicative factor of $e^{(0.0378)(100)} = 43.6$ over the base case, so the odds that such a customer will accept the offer are $e^{-6.153 + (0.0378)(100)} = 0.093$.

To generalize this to the multiple-predictor case, consider the 12 predictors in the personal loan offer example. The odds of a customer accepting the offer as a function of the 12 predictors are given in (10.10).

Suppose that the value of Income, or in general x_1, is increased by one unit from x_1 to $x_1 + 1$, while the other predictors (denoted $x_2, \ldots, x_{12}$) are held at their current value. We get the odds ratio

$$\frac{\text{Odds}(x_1 + 1, x_2, \ldots, x_{12})}{\text{Odds}(x_1, \ldots x_{12})} = \frac{e^{\beta_0 + \beta_1(x_1 + 1) + \beta_2 x_2 + \cdots + \beta_{12} x_{12}}}{e^{\beta_0 + \beta_1 x_1 + \beta_2 x_2 + \cdots + \beta_{12} x_{12}}} = e^{\beta_1}.$$

This tells us that a single unit increase in x_1, holding $x_2, \ldots, x_{12}$ constant, is associated with an increase in the odds that a customer accepts the offer by a factor of e^{β_1}. In other words, e^{β_1} is the multiplicative factor by which the odds (of belonging to class 1) increase when the value of x_1 is increased by 1 unit, *holding all other predictors constant*. If $\beta_1 < 0$, an increase in x_1 is associated with a decrease in the odds of belonging to class 1, whereas a positive value of β_1 is associated with an increase in the odds.

When a predictor is a dummy variable, the interpretation is technically the same but has a different practical meaning. For instance, the coefficient for *CreditCard_0* was estimated from the data to be 0.785. Recall that the reference group is customers holding a Universal Bank credit card. We interpret this coefficient as follows: the odds that a customer who does not hold a Universal Bank credit card will accept the offer are more than double ($e^{0.785} = 2.193$) relative to a customer who has a credit card, holding all other factors constant. This means that customers who do not hold Universal Bank credit cards are more likely to accept the offer than customers who do have a credit card (holding all other variables constant).

The advantage of reporting results in odds as opposed to probabilities is that statements such as those above are true for any value of x_1. Unless x_1 is a dummy variable, we cannot apply such statements about the effect of increasing x_1 by a single unit to probabilities. This is because the result depends on the actual value of x_1. So, if we increase x_1 from, say, 3 to 4, the effect on p, the probability of belonging to class 1, will be different than if we increase x_1 from 30 to 31. In short, the change in the probability, p, for a unit increase in a particular predictor variable, while holding all other predictors constant, is not a constant—it depends on the specific values of the predictor variables. We therefore talk about probabilities only in the context of specific observations.

Evaluating Classification Performance

The general measures of performance that were described in Chapter 5 are used to assess how well the logistic model does. Recall that there are several performance measures, the most popular being those based on the classification matrix (accuracy alone or combined with costs) and the lift chart. As in other classification methods, the goal is to find a model that accurately classifies observations to their class, using only the predictor information. A variant of this goal is to find a model that does a superior job of identifying the members of a particular class of interest (which might come at some cost to overall accuracy). Since the training data are used for selecting the model, we expect the model to perform quite well for those data, and therefore prefer to test its performance on the validation set. Recall that the data in the validation set were not involved in the model building, and thus we can use them to test the model's ability to classify data that it has not "seen" before.

To obtain the classification matrix from a logistic regression analysis, we use the estimated equation to predict the probability of class membership (the *propensities*) for each observation in the validation set and use the cutoff value to decide on the class assignment of these observations. We then compare these classifications to the actual class memberships of these observations. In the Universal Bank, case we use the estimated model in equation (10.9) to predict the probability of offer acceptance in a validation set that contains 2000 customers (these data were not used in the modeling step). Technically, this is done by predicting the logit using the estimated model in equation (10.9) and then obtaining the probabilities p through the relation $p = e^{\text{logit}}/(1 + e^{\text{logit}})$. We next compare these probabilities to our chosen cutoff value in order to classify each of the 2000 validation observations as acceptors or nonacceptors. ASDM created the validation classification matrix automatically, and it is possible to obtain the detailed probabilities and classification for each observation. For example, Figure 10.4 shows a partial ASDM output of scoring the validation set. We see that the first four customers have a probability of accepting the offer that is lower than the cutoff of 0.5, and therefore they are classified as nonacceptors (0). The fifth customer's probability of acceptance is estimated by the model to exceed 0.5, and he or she is therefore classified as an acceptor (1), which in fact is a misclassification (ASDM uses red to indicates a misclassified record).

Record ID	Personal Loan	Prediction: Personal Loan	PostProb: 1	PostProb: 0	Age	Experience	Income	Family	CCAvg
Record 2474	0	0	0.0003	0.9997	57	32	39	4	0.9
Record 4642	0	0	0.0000	1.0000	36	11	31	4	1.7
Record 2411	0	0	0.0231	0.9769	29	4	130	2	6.7
Record 1733	0	0	0.0253	0.9747	25	0	88	2	1.8
Record 2465	0	1	0.6638	0.3362	35	10	200	2	3

FIGURE 10.4   SCORING THE VALIDATION DATA: ASDM'S OUTPUT FOR FIVE CUSTOMERS OF UNIVERSAL BANK (BASED ON 12 PREDICTORS)

Another useful tool for assessing model classification performance is the lift (gains) chart (see Chapter 5). Figure 10.5 (top) illustrates the lift chart obtained

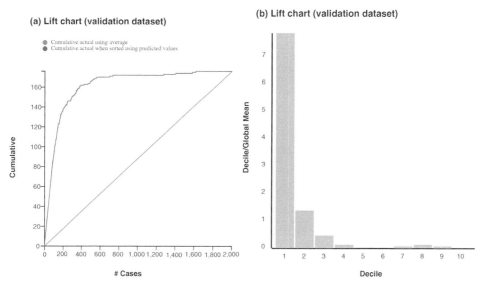

FIGURE 10.5   (a) LIFT AND (b) DECILE CHARTS OF VALIDATION DATA FOR UNIVERSAL BANK LOAN OFFER: COMPARING LOGISTIC MODEL RANKING WITH RANDOM RANKING

for the personal loan offer model using the validation set. The "lift" over the base curve indicates for a given number of cases (read on the x-axis), the additional responders that you can identify by using the model. The same information is portrayed in in Figure 10.5 (bottom): Taking the 10% of the records that are ranked by the model as "most probable 1's" yields 7.84 times as many 1's as would simply selecting 10% of the records at random.

Variable Selection

The next step includes searching for alternative models. As with multiple linear regression, each categorical variable must be turned into dummy variables, resulting in additional columns. In addition, we can build more complex models that reflect interactions among predictors by including new variables that are derived from the predictors. For example, if we hypothesize that there is an interactive effect between income and family size, we should add an interaction term of the form Income × Family. The choice among the set of alternative models is guided primarily by performance on the validation data. For models that perform roughly equally well, simpler models are generally preferred over more complex models. Note also that performance on validation data may be overly optimistic when it comes to predicting performance on data that have not been exposed to the model at all. This is because when the validation data are used to select a final model, we are selecting based on how well the model performs with those data and therefore may be incorporating some of the random idiosyncrasies of those data into the judgment about the best model. The model still may be the best among those considered, but it will probably not do as well with the unseen data. Therefore, it is useful to evaluate the chosen model on a new test set to get a sense of how well it will perform on new data. In addition, one must consider practical issues such as costs of collecting variables, error-proneness, and model complexity in the selection of the final model.

As in linear regression, in logistic regression we can use automated variable selection heuristics such as stepwise selection, forward selection, and backward elimination (see Section 6.4 in Chapter 6). If the dataset is not too large, we can even try an exhaustive search (Best Subset in ASDM) over all possible models.

Workflow

The machine learning workflow for the example used in this section is shown in Figure 10.6. The upper branch generates the model with the single predictor *Income*. The lower branch generates the 12-predictor model in Figure 10.3.

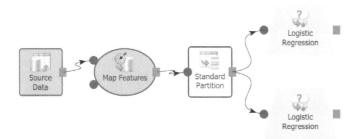

FIGURE 10.6   THE MACHINE LEARNING WORKFLOW FOR THE SINGLE PREDICTOR AND 12-PREDICTOR LOGISTIC REGRESSION MODELS FOR THE PERSONAL LOAN EXAMPLE

10.3 EXAMPLE OF COMPLETE ANALYSIS: PREDICTING DELAYED FLIGHTS

Predicting flight delays would be useful to a variety of organizations: airport authorities, airlines, aviation authorities. At times, joint task forces have been formed to address the problem. Such an organization, if it were to provide ongoing real-time assistance with flight delays, would benefit from some advance notice about flights that are likely to be delayed.

In this simplified illustration, we look at six predictors (see Table 10.1). The outcome of interest is whether the flight is delayed or not (*delayed* means more than 15 minutes late). Our data consist of all flights from the Washington, DC area into the New York City area during January 2004. The percent of delayed flights among these 2201 flights is 19.5%. The data were obtained from the Bureau of Transportation Statistics website (www.transtats.bts.gov).

TABLE 10.1   DESCRIPTION OF PREDICTORS FOR FLIGHT DELAYS EXAMPLE

Day of week (DOW)	Coded as: 1 = Monday, 2 = Tuesday,..., 7 = Sunday
Departure time (DEP_TIME_BLK)	Broken down into 18 intervals between 6 AM and 10 PM
Origin	Three airport codes: DCA (Reagan National), IAD (Dulles), BWI (Baltimore–Washington Int'l)
Destination	Three airport codes: JFK (Kennedy), LGA (LaGuardia), EWR (Newark)
Carrier	Eight airline codes: CO (Continental), DH (Atlantic Coast), DL (Delta), MQ (American Eagle), OH (Comair), RU (Continental Express), UA (United), and US (USAirways)
Weather	Coded as 1 if there was a weather-related delay

The goal is to predict accurately whether or not a new flight, not in this dataset, will be delayed. Our outcome variable is a binary variable called *Delayed*, coded as 1 for a delayed flight and 0 otherwise.

Other information that is available on the website, such as distance and arrival time, is irrelevant because we are looking at a certain route (distance, flight time, etc., should be approximately equal). A sample of the data for 20 flights is shown in Table 10.2.

TABLE 10.2   SAMPLE OF 20 FLIGHTS

Delayed	Carrier	Day of week	Departure time	Destination	Origin	Weather
0	DL	2	728	LGA	DCA	0
1	US	3	1600	LGA	DCA	0
0	DH	5	1242	EWR	IAD	0
0	US	2	2057	LGA	DCA	0
0	DH	3	1603	JFK	IAD	0
0	CO	6	1252	EWR	DCA	0
0	RU	6	1728	EWR	DCA	0
0	DL	5	1031	LGA	DCA	0
0	RU	6	1722	EWR	IAD	0
1	US	1	627	LGA	DCA	0
1	DH	2	1756	JFK	IAD	0
0	MQ	6	1529	JFK	DCA	0
0	US	6	1259	LGA	DCA	0
0	DL	2	1329	LGA	DCA	0
0	RU	2	1453	EWR	BWI	0
0	RU	5	1356	EWR	DCA	0
1	DH	7	2244	LGA	IAD	0
0	US	7	1053	LGA	DCA	0
0	US	2	1057	LGA	DCA	0
0	US	4	632	LGA	DCA	0

Data Visualization

Figures 10.7 and 10.8 show visualizations of the relationships between flight delays and different predictors or combinations of predictors. From Figure 10.7, we see that Sundays and Mondays saw the largest proportion of delays. Delay rates also seem to differ by carrier, by time of day, as well as by origin and destination airports. For Weather, we see a strong distinction between delays when Weather = 1 (in that case there is always a delay) and Weather = 0. The heatmap in Figure 10.8 reveals some specific combinations with high rates of delays, such as Sunday flights by carrier RU, departing from BWI, or Sunday flights by MQ departing from DCA. We can also see combinations with very low delay rates.

Our main goal is to find a model that can obtain accurate classifications of new flights based on their predictor information. An alternative goal is finding a certain percentage of flights that are most/least likely to get delayed (*ranking*). And a third different goal is profiling flights: finding out which factors are associated with a delay (not only in this sample but in the entire population of flights

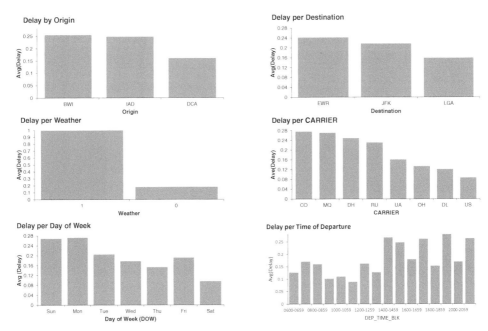

FIGURE 10.7   PROPORTION OF DELAYED FLIGHTS BY EACH OF THE FIVE PREDICTORS. TIME OF DAY IS DIVIDED INTO HOURLY BINS

	Origin, CARRIER										
% Delays by	BWI		DCA						IAD		
DOW	OH	RU	CO	DH	DL	MQ	RU	US	DH	RU	UA
Mon	0.25	0.38	0.43	0.33	0.13	0.34	0.23	0.15	0.40	0.33	0.25
Tue	0.00	0.38	0.43	0.33	0.16	0.24	0.16	0.02	0.30	0.29	0.25
Wed	0.00	0.27	0.33	0.00	0.11	0.22	0.17	0.15	0.20	0.21	0.00
Thu	0.20	0.16	0.18	0.20	0.14	0.16	0.18	0.14	0.16	0.13	0.20
Fri	0.20	0.35	0.17	0.00	0.07	0.34	0.19	0.06	0.21	0.38	0.40
Sat	0.00	0.05	0.00	0.25	0.14	0.12	0.00	0.00	0.17	0.07	0.00
Sun	0.25	0.53	0.27	0.25	0.12	0.48	0.36	0.06	0.35	0.31	0.00

Day of Week(FL_Date)

FIGURE 10.8   PERCENT OF DELAYED FLIGHTS (DARKER = HIGHER % DELAYS) BY DAY OF WEEK, ORIGIN, AND CARRIER. THE FIRST TWO COLUMNS ARE BWI DEPARTURES, THE NEXT 5 DCA, AND THE LAST 3 IAD

on this route), and for those factors we would like to quantify these effects. A logistic regression model can be used for all these goals, albeit in different ways.

Data Preprocessing

We partition the data into training set (60%) and validation set (40%). We use the training set to fit a model and the validation set to assess the model's performance.

Model Fitting and Estimation

The estimated model with the six categorical predictors is given in Figure 10.9. Notice how negative coefficients in the logit model (the "Estimate" column) translate into odds coefficients lower than 1, and positive logit coefficients translate into odds coefficients larger than 1. (Recall that red lines indicate the reference categories for each of the categorical predictors, as selected by the software.)

Coefficients

Predictor	Estimate	Confidence Interval: Lower	Confidence Interval: Upper	Odds	Standard Error	Chi2 - Statistic	P-Value
Intercept	-3.2708	-4.9866	-1.5551	0.0380	0.8754	13.9607	0.0002
CARRIER_CO	2.0078	0.2095	3.8061	7.4470	0.9175	4.7886	0.0286
CARRIER_DH	1.1444	-0.4111	2.6999	3.1405	0.7936	2.0791	0.1493
CARRIER_DL	0.6100	-1.0196	2.2395	1.8404	0.8314	0.5383	0.4632
CARRIER_MQ	1.6345	0.0384	3.2305	5.1268	0.8143	4.0285	0.0447
CARRIER_OH	0.0000	0.0000	0.0000	1.0000	0.0000	N/A	N/A
CARRIER_RU	1.0926	-0.4570	2.6422	2.9819	0.7906	1.9097	0.1670
CARRIER_UA	0.0123	-2.6779	2.7025	1.0124	1.3726	0.0001	0.9928
CARRIER_US	0.3061	-1.3465	1.9587	1.3581	0.8432	0.1318	0.7166
DEP_TIME_BLK_0600-0659	0.1405	-1.0274	1.3083	1.1508	0.5959	0.0556	0.8136
DEP_TIME_BLK_0700-0759	0.0157	-1.1673	1.1988	1.0158	0.6036	0.0007	0.9792
DEP_TIME_BLK_0800-0859	-0.3877	-1.6769	0.9014	0.6786	0.6577	0.3475	0.5555
DEP_TIME_BLK_0900-0959	-0.3200	-1.6164	0.9763	0.7261	0.6614	0.2341	0.6285
DEP_TIME_BLK_1000-1059	-0.4209	-1.8059	0.9642	0.6565	0.7067	0.3547	0.5515
DEP_TIME_BLK_1100-1159	0.0000	0.0000	0.0000	1.0000	0.0000	N/A	N/A
DEP_TIME_BLK_1200-1259	0.0602	-1.1249	1.2453	1.0621	0.6046	0.0099	0.9207
DEP_TIME_BLK_1300-1359	-0.4559	-1.6330	0.7213	0.6339	0.6006	0.5761	0.4478
DEP_TIME_BLK_1400-1459	0.9400	-0.1358	2.0158	2.5599	0.5489	2.9327	0.0868
DEP_TIME_BLK_1500-1559	0.8219	-0.2756	1.9194	2.2749	0.5599	2.1546	0.1421
DEP_TIME_BLK_1600-1659	0.2684	-0.8772	1.4141	1.3079	0.5845	0.2109	0.6461
DEP_TIME_BLK_1700-1759	0.2194	-0.8707	1.3095	1.2454	0.5562	0.1556	0.6932
DEP_TIME_BLK_1800-1859	0.3141	-0.9676	1.5958	1.3691	0.6539	0.2307	0.6310
DEP_TIME_BLK_1900-1959	0.7938	-0.3483	1.9360	2.2118	0.5827	1.8556	0.1731
DEP_TIME_BLK_2000-2059	0.7107	-0.6738	2.0952	2.0355	0.7064	1.0123	0.3143
DEP_TIME_BLK_2100-2159	0.4870	-0.6610	1.6351	1.6275	0.5857	0.6914	0.4057
Destination_EWR	0.2178	-0.4349	0.8705	1.2433	0.3330	0.4278	0.5131
Destination_JFK	0.0000	0.0000	0.0000	1.0000	0.0000	N/A	N/A
Destination_LGA	0.3645	-0.1408	0.8698	1.4398	0.2578	1.9987	0.1574
DOW_Fri	0.4103	-0.2196	1.0401	1.5072	0.3214	1.6300	0.2017
DOW_Mon	0.9146	0.2739	1.5554	2.4959	0.3269	7.8277	0.0051
DOW_Sat	0.0000	0.0000	0.0000	1.0000	0.0000	N/A	N/A
DOW_Sun	1.1953	0.5588	1.8319	3.3047	0.3248	13.5478	0.0002
DOW_Thu	0.4296	-0.2045	1.0638	1.5367	0.3236	1.7632	0.1842
DOW_Tue	0.3880	-0.2987	1.0747	1.4740	0.3504	1.2262	0.2682
DOW_Wed	0.3469	-0.3104	1.0042	1.4147	0.3354	1.0699	0.3010
Origin_BWI	0.0000	0.0000	0.0000	1.0000	0.0000	N/A	N/A
Origin_DCA	-0.5998	-1.4586	0.2590	0.5489	0.4382	1.8736	0.1711
Origin_IAD	-0.1028	-0.9405	0.7349	0.9023	0.4274	0.0578	0.8099
Weather_0	0.0000	0.0000	0.0000	1.0000	0.0000	N/A	N/A
Weather_1	8.7271	-7.2498	24.7040	6167.9140	8.1516	1.1462	0.2844

FIGURE 10.9   ESTIMATED LOGISTIC REGRESSION MODEL FOR DELAYED FLIGHTS (BASED ON THE TRAINING SET)

Model Interpretation

The coefficient for arrival airport LGA (*Destination_LGA*) is estimated as 0.36. Recall that the reference category is JFK. We interpret this coefficient as follows: $e^{0.36} = 1.44$ are the odds of a flight arriving at LGA being delayed relative to a flight to JFK being delayed (= the base-case odds), holding all other factors constant. This means that, all else constant, flights to LGA are more likely to be delayed than those to JFK. For departure airports (where BWI is the reference category), coefficients for both DCA and IAD are negative, indicating that BWI has the highest odds of delay, while DCA has the largest negative coefficient, and thereby the lowest odds of delay (holding everything else constant). For carriers (OH is the reference category), coefficients for all carrier dummies are positive, indicating that OH has the lowest odds of delay, while CO has the largest positive coefficient, indicating the highest odds of delay (holding everything else constant). For day of week, relative to Saturday (*DOW_Sat*), which is the reference category, all days have positive coefficients, with Sunday having the largest coefficient, and thereby the highest odds of delay (holding everything else constant). Also, the odds of delays appear to change over the course of the day, with the most noticeable difference from the reference category of 11:00–11:59 AM being the later afternoon hours of 14:00–15:59 and evening hours of 19:00–20:59. Finally, *Weather_1* has the largest coefficient, indicating a large gap between flights with Weather = 0 and Weather = 1. Note that we have considered above only coefficient magnitude and not statistical significance. Since our eventual goal is prediction, we will rely instead on predictive performance.

Model Performance

How should we measure the performance of models? One possible measure is "percent of flights correctly classified." Accurate classification can be obtained from the classification matrix for the validation data. The classification matrix gives a sense of the classification accuracy and what type of misclassification is more frequent. From the classification matrix and error rates in Figure 10.10, it can be seen that the model more accurately classifies nondelayed flights and is less accurate in classifying flights that were delayed. (*Note*: The same pattern appears in the classification matrix for the training data, so it is not surprising to see it emerge for new data.) If there is an asymmetric cost structure so that one type of misclassification is more costly than the other, the cutoff value can be selected to minimize the cost. Of course, this tweaking should be carried out on the training data and assessed only using the validation data.

In most conceivable situations, the purpose of the model would be to identify those flights most likely to be delayed so that resources can be directed toward either reducing the delay or mitigating its effects. Air traffic controllers might

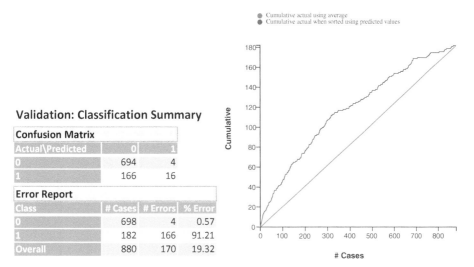

● Cumulative actual using average
● Cumulative actual when sorted using predicted values

Validation: Classification Summary

Confusion Matrix

Actual\Predicted	0	1
0	694	4
1	166	16

Error Report

Class	# Cases	# Errors	% Error
0	698	4	0.57
1	182	166	91.21
Overall	880	170	19.32

FIGURE 10.10   CLASSIFICATION MATRIX AND ERROR RATES, AND LIFT CHART FOR THE FLIGHT DELAY VALIDATION DATA

work to open up additional air routes or allocate more controllers to a specific area for a short time. Airlines might bring on personnel to rebook passengers and to activate standby flight crews and aircraft. Hotels might allocate space for stranded travelers. In all cases, the resources available are going to be limited and might vary over time and from organization to organization. In this situation, the most useful model would provide an ordering of flights by their probability of delay, letting the model users decide how far down that list to go in taking action. Therefore, model lift is a useful measure of performance—as you move down that list of flights, ordered by their delay probability, how much better does the model do in predicting delay than would a naive model which is simply the average delay rate for all flights? From the lift curve for the validation data (Figure 10.10) we see that our model is superior to the baseline (simple random selection of flights).

Variable Selection

From the data exploration charts (Figures 10.7 and 10.8) and from the coefficient table for the flights delay model, it appears that several of the variables might be dropped or coded differently. Additionally, we look at the number of flights in different categories to identify categories with very few or no flights—such categories are candidates for removal or merger (see Table 10.3).

First, we find that most carriers depart from a single airport (DCA). For those that depart from all three airports, the delay rates are similar regardless of airport. We therefore drop the departure airport distinction by excluding Origin dummies and find that the model performance and fit is not harmed. We also drop the destination airport for a practical reason: not all carriers fly

TABLE 10.3		NUMBER OF FLIGHTS BY CARRIER AND ORIGIN		
	BWI	DCA	IAD	Total
CO		94		94
DH		27	524	551
DL		388		388
MQ		295		295
OH	30			30
RU	115	162	131	408
UA			31	31
US		404		404
Total	145	1370	686	2201

to all airports. Our model would then be invalid for prediction in nonexistent combinations of carrier and destination airport. We also try grouping carriers, day of week, and hour of day into fewer categories that are more distinguishable with respect to delays (this can be done using ASDM's Reduce Categories utility; see Figure 10.11). For example, Sundays and Mondays seem to have a similar rate

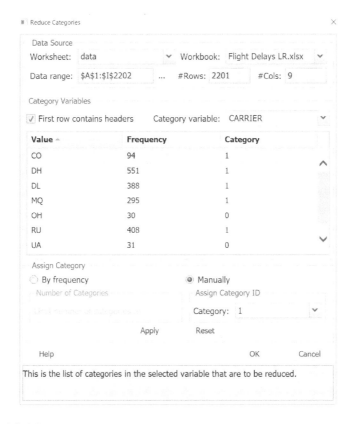

FIGURE 10.11   ASDM'S REDUCE CATEGORIES UTILITY (*TRANSFORM > TRANSFORM CATEGORICAL DATA*). HERE WE USE IT MANUALLY TO CREATE TWO CATEGORIES OF CARRIERS FROM THE ORIGINAL EIGHT CATEGORIES

of delays, which differs from the lower rate on Tuesday to Saturday. We therefore group the days of week into Sunday + Monday and Other, resulting in a single dummy variable. For hour of day, we can reduce the categories to three groups: "before 2 PM", "2–4 PM and 7–9 PM" and "Other." Also, carriers CO, DH, MQ, and RU have a similar rate of delays, which differs from the lower rate of delays for DL, OH, US, and UA. We therefore reduce the eight carriers into a two-category predictor (see Figure 10.11).

Figure 10.12 displays the estimated model, with its validation classification matrix and error rates, as well as the lift chart. It can be seen that this model competes well with the larger model in terms of classification accuracy and lift, while using much less information.

Coefficients

Predictor	Estimate	Confidence Interval: Lower	Confidence Interval: Upper	Odds	Standard Error	Chi2 - Statistic	P-Value
Intercept	-0.8180	-1.1161	-0.5199	0.4413	0.1521	28.9170	0.0000
Reduced_CARRIER_0	-1.0357	-1.3796	-0.6917	0.3550	0.1755	34.8345	0.0000
Reduced_CARRIER_1	0.0000	0.0000	0.0000	1.0000	0.0000	N/A	N/A
Reduced_DEP_TIME_BLK_0	-1.0194	-1.3777	-0.6612	0.3608	0.1828	31.1028	0.0000
Reduced_DEP_TIME_BLK_1	0.0000	0.0000	0.0000	1.0000	0.0000	N/A	N/A
Reduced_DEP_TIME_BLK_2	-0.6346	-1.0089	-0.2602	0.5302	0.1910	11.0393	0.0009
Reduced_DOW_0	0.0000	0.0000	0.0000	1.0000	0.0000	N/A	N/A
Reduced_DOW_1	0.6871	0.3697	1.0045	1.9879	0.1620	17.9986	0.0000
Weather_0	0.0000	0.0000	0.0000	1.0000	0.0000	N/A	N/A
Weather_1	8.7693	-7.2104	24.7491	6433.9489	8.1531	1.1569	0.2821

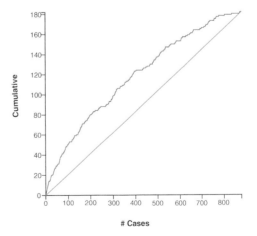

Lift chart (validation dataset

● Cumulative actual using average
● Cumulative actual when sorted using predicted values

Validation: Classification Summary

Confusion Matrix

Actual\Predicted	0	1
0	698	0
1	169	13

Error Report

Class	# Cases	# Errors	% Error
0	698	0	0.00
1	182	169	92.86
Overall	880	169	19.20

FIGURE 10.12   OUTPUT FOR LOGISTIC REGRESSION WITH FEWER PREDICTORS. *REDUCED_CARRIER_0* IS A DUMMY WITH "1" FOR DL, OH, US, AND AU. *REDUCED_DEP_TIME_BLK_0* IS A DUMMY FOR "BEFORE 2 PM", *REDUCED_TIME_BLK_2* IS A DUMMY FOR "OTHER TIME", AND *REDUCED_DOW_1* IS A DUMMY FOR SUNDAY/MONDAY

We therefore conclude with a six-predictor model that requires only knowledge of the carrier, the day of week, the hour of the day, and whether the day had inclement weather. However, this weather variable refers to actual weather at flight time, not a forecast, and is not known in advance! If the aim is to predict in advance whether a particular flight will be delayed, a model without *Weather* must be used. In contrast, if the goal is profiling delayed vs. nondelayed flights, we can keep *Weather* in the model to allow evaluating the impact of the other factors while holding weather constant [i.e., (approximately) comparing days with inclement weather to days without inclement weather].

To conclude, based on the model built from the January 2004 data, the highest chance of a nondelayed flight from DC to New York is on Tuesday to Saturday between 2 and 4 PM, on Delta, Comair, United, or USAirways. And, clearly, good weather is advantageous!

Workflow

The machine learning workflow for the delayed flights example is shown in Figure 10.13. It generates the logistic model with 33 predictors (Figure 10.9).

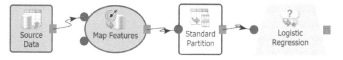

FIGURE 10.13   THE MACHINE LEARNING WORKFLOW FOR THE LOGISTIC REGRESSION MODEL IN DELAYED FLIGHTS EXAMPLE WITH 33 PREDICTORS

10.4 APPENDIX: LOGISTIC REGRESSION FOR MORE THAN TWO CLASSES

The logistic model for a binary response can be extended for more than two classes. Suppose that there are m classes. Using a logistic regression model, for each observation we would have m probabilities of belonging to each of the m classes. Since the m probabilities must add up to 1, we need estimate only $m-1$ probabilities.

Ordinal Classes   Ordinal classes are classes that have a meaningful order. For example, in stock recommendations, the three classes *buy*, *hold*, and *sell* can be treated as ordered. As a simple rule, if classes can be numbered in a meaningful way, we consider them ordinal. When the number of classes is large (typically, more than five), we can treat the outcome variable as continuous and perform multiple linear regression. When $m = 2$, the logistic model described above is used. We therefore need an extension of the logistic regression for a small number of ordinal classes ($3 \leq m \leq 5$). There are several ways to extend the binary-class case. Here we describe the *proportional odds* or *cumulative logit method*. For other methods, see Hosmer and Lemeshow (2000).

For simplicity of interpretation and computation, we look at *cumulative* probabilities of class membership. For example, in the stock recommendations, we have $m = 3$ classes. Let us denote them by 1 = *buy*, 2 = *hold*, and 3 = *sell*. The probabilities that are estimated by the model are $P(Y \leq 1)$, (the probability of a *buy* recommendation) and $P(Y \leq 2)$ (the probability of a *buy* or *hold* recommendation). The three noncumulative probabilities of class membership can easily be recovered from the two cumulative probabilities:

$$P(Y = 1) = P(Y \leq 1),$$
$$P(Y = 2) = P(Y \leq 2) - P(Y \leq 1),$$
$$P(Y = 3) = 1 - P(Y \leq 2).$$

Next, we want to model each logit as a function of the predictors. Corresponding to each of the $m - 1$ cumulative probabilities is a logit. In our example, we would have

$$\text{logit(buy)} = \log\frac{P(Y \leq 1)}{1 - P(Y \leq 1)},$$
$$\text{logit (buy or hold)} = \log\frac{P(Y \leq 2)}{1 - P(Y \leq 2)}.$$

Each of the logits is then modeled as a linear function of the predictors (as in the two-class case). If in the stock recommendations we have a single predictor x, we have two equations:

$$\text{logit(buy)} = \alpha_0 + \beta_1 x,$$
$$\text{logit(buy or hold)} = \beta_0 + \beta_1 x.$$

This means that both lines have the same slope (β_1) but different intercepts. Once the coefficients $\alpha_0, \beta_0, \beta_1$ are estimated, we can compute the class membership probabilities by rewriting the logit equations in terms of probabilities. For the three-class case, for example, we would have

$$P(Y = 1) = P(Y \leq 1) = \frac{1}{1 + e^{-(a_0 + b_1 x)}},$$
$$P(Y = 2) = P(Y \leq 2) - P(Y \leq 1) = \frac{1}{1 + e^{-(b_0 + b_1 x)}} - \frac{1}{1 + e^{-(a_0 + b_1 x)}},$$
$$P(Y = 3) = 1 - P(Y \leq 2) = 1 - \frac{1}{1 + e^{-(b_0 + b_1 x)}},$$

where a_0, b_0, and b_1 are the estimates obtained from the training set.

For each observation, we now have the estimated probabilities that it belongs to each of the classes. In our example, each stock would have three probabilities: for a *buy* recommendation, a *hold* recommendation, and a *sell* recommendation. The last step is to classify the observation into one of the classes. This is done by assigning it to the class with the highest membership probability. So, if a stock had estimated probabilities $P(Y = 1) = 0.2$, $P(Y = 2) = 0.3$, and $P(Y = 3) = 0.5$, we would classify it as getting a *sell* recommendation.

This procedure is currently not implemented in ASDM. Other non–Excel-based packages that do have such an implementation are Minitab and SAS.

Nominal Classes   When the classes cannot be ordered and are simply different from one another, we are in the case of nominal classes. An example is the choice between several brands of cereal. A simple way to verify that the classes are nominal is when it makes sense to tag them as $A, B, C, \ldots$, and the assignment of letters to classes does not matter. For simplicity, let us assume that there are $m = 3$ brands of cereal that consumers can choose from (assuming that each consumer chooses one). Then, we estimate the probabilities $P(Y = A)$, $P(Y = B)$, and $P(Y = C)$. As before, if we know two of the probabilities, the third probability is determined. We therefore use one of the classes as the reference class. Let us use C as the reference brand.

The goal, once again, is to model the class membership as a function of predictors. So in the cereals example we might want to predict which cereal will be chosen if we know the cereal's price, x.

Next, we form $m - 1$ pseudologit equations that are linear in the predictors. In our example, we would have

$$\text{logit}(A) = \log \frac{P(Y = A)}{P(Y = C)} = \alpha_0 + \alpha_1 x,$$

$$\text{logit}(B) = \log \frac{P(Y = B)}{P(Y = C)} = \beta_0 + \beta_1 x.$$

Once the four coefficients are estimated from the training set, we can estimate the class membership probabilities[7]

$$P(Y = A) = \frac{e^{a_0 + a_1 x}}{1 + e^{a_0 + a_1 x} + e^{b_0 + b_1 x}},$$

$$P(Y = B) = \frac{e^{b_0 + b_1 x}}{1 + e^{a_0 + a_1 x} + e^{b_0 + b_1 x}},$$

$$P(Y = C) = 1 - P(Y = A) - P(Y = B),$$

where a_0, a_1, b_0, and b_1 are the coefficient estimates obtained from the training set. Finally, an observation is assigned to the class that has the highest probability.

---

[7]From the two logit equations we see that $P(Y = A) = P(Y = C)e^{\alpha_0 + \alpha_1 x}$ and $P(Y = B) = P(Y = C)e^{\beta_0 + \beta_1 x}$. Since $P(Y = A) + P(Y = B) + P(Y = C) = 1$, we get $P(Y = C) = 1 - P(Y = C)e^{\alpha_0 + \alpha_1 x} - P(Y = C)e^{\beta_0 + \beta_1 x} = \frac{1}{e^{-(\alpha_0 + \alpha_1 x + \beta_0 + \beta_1 x)}}$. By plugging this form into the two equations above it, we also obtain the membership probabilities in classes A and B.

PROBLEMS

10.1 Financial Condition of Banks. The file `Banks.xlsx` includes data on a sample of 20 banks. The "Financial Condition" column records the judgment of an expert on the financial condition of each bank. This outcome variable takes one of two possible values—*weak* or *strong*—according to the financial condition of the bank. The predictors are two ratios used in the financial analysis of banks: TotLns&Lses/Assets is the ratio of total loans and leases to total assets and TotExp/Assets is the ratio of total expenses to total assets. The target is to use the two ratios for classifying the financial condition of a new bank.

Run a logistic regression (on the entire dataset) that models the status of a bank as a function of the two financial measures provided. Specify the *success* class as *weak* (this is similar to creating a dummy that is 1 for financially weak banks and 0 otherwise), and use the default cutoff value of 0.5.

   a. Write the estimated equation that associates the financial condition of a bank with its two predictors in three formats:

      i. The logit as a function of the predictors.

      ii. The odds as a function of the predictors.

      iii. The probability as a function of the predictors.

   b. Consider a new bank whose total loans and leases/assets ratio = 0.6 and total expenses/assets ratio = 0.11. From your logistic regression model, estimate the following four quantities for this bank (use Excel to do all the intermediate calculations; show your final answers to four decimal places): the logit, the odds, the probability of being financially weak, and the classification of the bank (use cutoff = 0.5).

   c. The cutoff value of 0.5 is used in conjunction with the probability of being financially weak. Compute the threshold that should be used if we want to make a classification based on the odds of being financially weak and the threshold for the corresponding logit.

   d. Interpret the estimated coefficient for the total loans and leases to total assets ratio (TotLns&Lses/Assets) in terms of the odds of being financially weak.

   e. When a bank that is in poor financial condition is misclassified as financially strong, the misclassification cost is much higher than when a financially strong bank is misclassified as weak. To minimize the expected cost of misclassification, should the cutoff value for classification (which is currently at 0.5) be increased or decreased?

10.2 Identifying Good System Administrators. A management consultant is studying the roles played by experience and training in a system administrator's ability to complete a set of tasks in a specified amount of time. In particular, she is interested in discriminating between administrators who are able to complete given tasks within a specified time and those who are not. Data are collected on the performance of 75 randomly selected administrators. They are stored in the file `SystemAdministrators.xlsx`. The variable Experience measures months of full-time system administrator experience, while Training measures the number of relevant training credits. The outcome variable Completed is either Yes or No, according to whether or not the administrator completed the tasks.

a. Create a scatterplot of *Experience* vs. *Training* using color or symbol to differentiate programmers who complete the task from those who did not complete it. Which predictor(s) appear(s) potentially useful for classifying task completion?

b. Run a logistic regression model with both predictors using the entire dataset as training data. Among those who complete the task, what is the percentage of programmers who are incorrectly classified as failing to complete the task?

c. To decrease the percentage in part (b), should the cutoff probability be increased or decreased?

d. How much experience must be accumulated by a programmer with four years of training before his or her estimated probability of completing the task exceeds 0.5?

10.3 **Sales of Riding Mowers.** A company that manufactures riding mowers wants to identify the best sales prospects for an intensive sales campaign. In particular, the manufacturer is interested in classifying households as prospective owners or nonowners on the basis of Income (in $1000s) and Lot Size (in 1000 ft^2). The marketing expert looked at a random sample of 24 households, given in the file `RidingMowers.xlsx`. Use all the data to fit a logistic regression of ownership on the two predictors.

a. What percentage of households in the study were owners of a riding mower?

b. Create a scatterplot of Income vs. Lot Size using color or symbol to differentiate owners from nonowners. From the scatterplot, which class seems to have the higher average income, owners or nonowners?

c. Among nonowners, what is the percentage of households classified correctly?

d. To increase the percentage of correctly classified nonowners, should the cutoff probability be increased or decreased?

e. What are the odds that a household with a $60K income and a lot size of 20,000 ft^2 is an owner?

f. What is the classification of a household with a $60K income and a lot size of 20,000 ft^2? Use cutoff = 0.5.

g. What is the minimum income that a household with 16,000 ft^2 lot size should have before it is classified as an owner?

10.4 **Competitive Auctions on eBay.com.** The file `eBayAuctions.xlsx` contains information on 1972 auctions transacted on eBay.com during May–June 2004. The goal is to use these data to build a model that will distinguish competitive auctions from noncompetitive ones. A competitive auction is defined as an auction with at least two bids placed on the item being auctioned. The data include variables that describe the item (auction category), the seller (his or her eBay rating), and the auction terms that the seller selected (auction duration, opening price, currency, day of week of auction close). In addition, we have the price at which the auction closed. The goal is to predict whether or not the auction will be competitive.

Data Preprocessing. Split the data into training (60%) and validation (40%) datasets.

a. Create pivot tables for the average of the binary outcome variable (Competitive?) as a function of the various categorical variables. Use the information in the tables to reduce the number of dummies that will be used in the model. For example, categories that appear most similar with respect to the distribution of competitive auctions could be combined.

b. Run a logistic model with all predictors with a cutoff of 0.5.

c. If we want to predict at the start of an auction whether it will be competitive, we cannot use the information on the closing price. Run a logistic model with all predictors as above, excluding price. How does this model compare to the full model with respect to accurate prediction?

d. Interpret the meaning of the coefficient for closing price. Does closing price have a practical significance? Is it statistically significant for predicting competitiveness of auctions? (Use a 10% significance level.)

e. Use stepwise selection and an exhaustive search (Best Subsets in ASDM) to find the model with the best fit to the training data. Which predictors are used?

f. Use stepwise selection and an exhaustive search (Best Subsets in ASDM) to find the model with the lowest predictive error rate (use the validation data). Which predictors are used?

g. What is the danger of using the best-predictive model that you found?

h. Explain why the best-fitting model and the best-predictive models are the same or different.

i. If the major objective is accurate classification, what cutoff value should be used?

j. Based on these data, what auction settings set by the seller (duration, opening price, ending day, currency) would you recommend as being most likely to lead to a competitive auction?

## CHAPTER 11

Neural Nets

In this chapter, we describe neural networks, a flexible (albeit blackbox) data-driven method that can be used for classification, prediction, and feature extraction, and is the basis for deep learning—a powerful technique that lies behind many artificial intelligence applications like image and voice recognition. We discuss the concepts of "nodes" and "layers" (input layers, output layers, and hidden layers) and how they connect to form the structure of a network. We then explain how a neural network is fitted to data using a numerical example. Because overfitting is a major danger with neural nets, we present a strategy for avoiding it. We describe the different parameters that a user must specify and explain the effect of each on the process. Finally, we move from a detailed description of a basic neural net to a more general discussion of the deeper and more complex neural nets that power deep learning.

11.1 INTRODUCTION

Neural networks, also called *artificial neural networks*, are models for classification and prediction. The neural network is based on a model of biological activity in the brain, where neurons are interconnected and learn from experience. Neural networks mimic the way that human experts learn. The learning and memory properties of neural networks resemble the properties of human learning and memory, and they also have a capacity to generalize from particulars.

Neural nets began to be applied successfully in the late 1990s in areas such as bankruptcy trading and detecting fraud in credit card and monetary transactions. They really took off in the early 2000s with the development of more complex networks and the growing power of computers. Often called "deep learning," these complex networks have been primarily responsible for a powerful revolution in machine learning. Indeed, much of what the public thinks of

Machine Learning for Business Analytics: Concepts, Techniques, and Applications with Analytic Solver® Data Mining,
Fourth Edition. Galit Shmueli, Peter C. Bruce, Kuber R. Deokar, and Nitin R. Patel.
© 2023 John Wiley & Sons, Inc. Published 2023 by John Wiley & Sons, Inc.

as "artificial intelligence" has at its heart deep (multilayer) neural networks. Text classification and image recognition are perhaps the most ubiquitous examples, but what has captured the public imagination the most is the promise of self-driving cars. It might surprise many machine learning practitioners today to learn that an application of neural nets from the 1980s was ALVINN, an autonomous vehicle driving application for normal speeds on highways. Using as input a 30×32 grid of pixel intensities from a fixed camera on the vehicle, the classifier provides the direction of steering. The outcome is a categorical one with 30 classes, such as *sharp left*, *straight ahead*, and *bear right*.

The main strength of neural networks is their high predictive performance. Their structure supports capturing very complex relationships between predictors and a response, which is often not possible with other predictive models.

11.2 CONCEPT AND STRUCTURE OF A NEURAL NETWORK

The idea behind neural networks is to combine the input information in a very flexible way that captures complicated relationships among these variables and between them and the response variable. For instance, recall that in linear regression models the form of the relationship between the response and the predictors is specified directly by the user (see Chapter 6). In many cases, the exact form of the relationship is very complicated or is generally unknown. In linear regression modeling we might try different transformations of the predictors, interactions between predictors, and so on, but the specified form of the relationship remains linear. In comparison, in neural networks, the user is not required to specify the correct form. The network tries instead to learn about such relationships from the data. In fact linear regression and logistic regression can be thought of as special cases of very simple neural networks that have only input and output layers and no hidden layers.

Although researchers have studied numerous different neural network architectures, the most successful applications in machine learning of neural networks have been *multilayer feedforward networks*. These are networks in which there is an *input layer* consisting of nodes (sometimes called *neurons*) that simply accept the input values, and successive layers of nodes that receive input from the previous layers. The outputs of nodes in each layer are inputs to nodes in the next layer. The last layer is called the *output layer*. Layers between the input and output layers are known as *hidden layers*. A feedforward network is a fully connected network with a one-way flow and no cycles. Figure 11.1 shows a diagram for this architecture, with two hidden layers and one node in the output layer representing the target value to be predicted. In a classification problem with m classes, there would be m output nodes (or $m - 1$ output nodes, depending on the software).

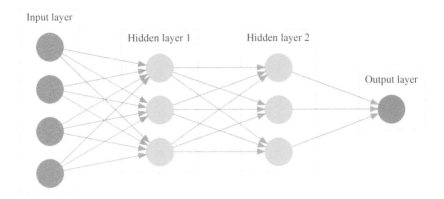

FIGURE 11.1   MULTILAYER FEEDFORWARD NEURAL NETWORK

11.3 FITTING A NETWORK TO DATA

To illustrate how a neural network is fitted to data, we start with a very small illustrative example. Although the method is by no means operational in such a small example, it is useful for explaining the main steps and operations, for showing how computations are done and for integrating all the different aspects of neural network data fitting. We will later discuss a more realistic setting.

Example 1: Tiny Dataset

Consider the following very small dataset. Table 11.1 includes information on a tasting score for a certain processed cheese. The two predictors are scores for fat and salt, indicating the relative presence of fat and salt in the particular cheese sample (where 0 is the minimum amount possible in the manufacturing process, and 1 the maximum). The output variable is the cheese sample's consumer taste preference, where *like* or *dislike* indicates whether or not the consumer likes the cheese.

TABLE 11.1   TINY EXAMPLE ON TASTING SCORES FOR SIX CONSUMERS AND TWO PREDICTORS

Consumer	Fat score	Salt score	Acceptance
1	0.2	0.9	like
2	0.1	0.1	dislike
3	0.2	0.4	dislike
4	0.2	0.5	dislike
5	0.4	0.5	like
6	0.3	0.8	like

Figure 11.2 describes an example of a typical neural net that could be used for predicting cheese preference (*like/dislike*) by new consumers, based on these data. We numbered the nodes in the example from N1 to N7. Nodes N1 and N2 belong to the input layer, nodes N3–N5 belong to the hidden layer, and nodes N6 and N7 belong to the output layer. The values on the connecting arrows are called *weights*, and the weight on the arrow from node i to node j is denoted by $w_{i,j}$. Additional weights θ_j (also called the *bias* of a node) serve as an intercept for the output from node j. These are all explained in further detail below.

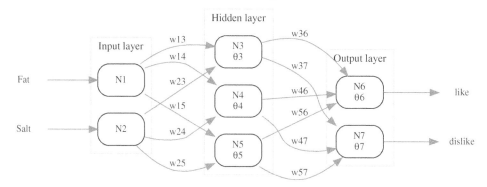

FIGURE 11.2   **NEURAL NETWORK FOR THE TINY EXAMPLE. RECTANGLES REPRESENT NODES ("NEURONS"), w_{ij} ON ARROWS ARE WEIGHTS, AND θ_j INSIDE NODES ARE BIAS VALUES**

Computing Output of Nodes

We discuss the input and output of the nodes separately for each of the three types of layers (input, hidden, and output). The main difference is the function used to map from the input to the output of the node.

Input nodes take as input the values of the predictors. Their output is the same as the input. If we have p predictors, the input layer will usually include p nodes. In our example there are two predictors, and therefore the input layer (shown in Figure 11.2) includes two nodes, each feeding into each node of the hidden layer. Consider the first observation: the input into the input layer is Fat $= 0.2$ and Salt $= 0.9$, and the output of this layer is also $x_1 = 0.2$ and $x_2 = 0.9$.

Hidden layer nodes take as input the output values from the input layer. The hidden layer in this example consists of three nodes, each receiving input from all the input nodes. To compute the output of a hidden layer node, we compute a weighted sum of the inputs and apply a certain function to it. More formally, for a set of input values $x_1, x_2, \ldots, x_p$, we compute the output of node j by taking the weighted sum[1] $\theta_j + \sum_{i=1}^{p} w_{ij}x_i$, where $\theta_j, w_{1,j}, \ldots, w_{p,j}$ are weights

---

[1] Other options exist for combining inputs, such as taking the maximum or minimum of the weighted inputs rather than their sum, but they are much less popular.

that are initially set randomly and then adjusted as the network "learns." Note that θ_j, also called the *bias* of node j, is a constant that controls the level of contribution of node j.

In the next step, we take a function g of this sum. The function g, also called a *transfer function* or *activation function*, is some monotone function, and examples are a linear function $[g(s) = bs]$, an exponential function $[g(s) = \exp(bs)]$, and a logistic/sigmoidal function $[g(s) = 1/1 + e^{-s}]$. This last function is by far the most popular one in neural networks. Its practical value arises from the fact that it has a squashing effect on very small or very large values but is almost linear in the range where the value of the function is between 0.1 and 0.9. Another common activation function is the *ReLU* (rectified linear unit) activation function. This function is identical to the linear function but set to zero for $s < 0$.

If we use a logistic activation function, we can write the output of node j in the hidden layer as

$$\text{Output}_j = g\left(\theta_j + \sum_{i=1}^{p} w_{ij} x_i\right) = \frac{1}{1 + e^{-(\theta_j + \sum_{i=1}^{p} w_{ij} x_i)}}. \tag{11.1}$$

Initializing the Weights The values of θ_j and w_{ij} are initialized to small, usually random, numbers around zero. Such values represent a state of no knowledge by the network, similar to a model with no predictors. The initial weights are used in the first round of training.

Returning to our example, suppose that the initial bias and weights for node N3 are $\theta_3 = -0.3$, $w_{1,3} = 0.05$, and $w_{2,3} = 0.01$ (as shown in Figure 11.3). Using the logistic function, we can compute the output of node N3 in the hidden layer (using the first record) as

$$\text{Output}_{\text{N3}} = \frac{1}{1 + e^{-[-0.300 + (0.050)(0.20) + (0.010)(0.90)]}} = 0.430.$$

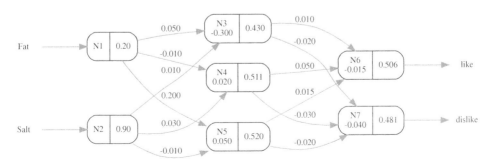

FIGURE 11.3   COMPUTING NODE OUTPUTS (VALUES ARE ON RIGHT SIDE WITHIN EACH NODE) USING THE FIRST RECORD IN THE TINY EXAMPLE AND A LOGISTIC FUNCTION

Figure 11.3 shows the initial weights, bias, inputs, and outputs for the first record in our tiny example. If there is more than one hidden layer, the same calculation applies, except that the input values for the second, third, and further hidden layers would be the output of the preceding hidden layer. This means that the number of input values into a certain node is equal to the number of nodes in the preceding layer. (If there was an additional hidden layer in our example, its nodes would receive input from the three nodes in the first hidden layer.)

Finally, the output layer obtains input values from the (last) hidden layer. It applies the same function as above to create the output. In other words, it takes a weighted sum of its input values and then applies the function g. In our example, output node N6 and N7 receive input from the three hidden layer nodes. We can compute the output of these nodes by

$$\text{Output}_{N6} = \frac{1}{1 + e^{-[-0.015 + (0.010)(0.430) + (0.050)(0.511) + (0.015)(0.520)]}} = 0.506.$$

$$\text{Output}_{N7} = \frac{1}{1 + e^{-[-0.040 + (-0.020)(0.430) + (-0.030)(0.511) + (-0.020)(0.520)]}} = 0.481.$$

These two numbers are *almost* the propensities $P(Y = like \,|\, \text{Fat} = 0.2, \text{Salt} = 0.9)$ and $P(Y = dislike \,|\, \text{Fat} = 0.2, \text{Salt} = 0.9)$. The last step involves normalizing these two values so that they add up to 1 (this operation is called *softmax*). In other words,

$$P(Y = like) = \text{Output}_{N6}/(\text{Output}_{N6} + \text{Output}_{N7}) = 0.506/(0.481 + 0.506) = 0.49.$$
$$P(Y = dislike) = 1 - P(Y = like) = 0.481/(0.481 + 0.506) = 0.51.$$

For classification, we use a cutoff value (for a binary outcome) on the propensity. Using a cutoff of 0.5, we would classify this record as *like*. For applications with more than two classes, we choose the output node with the largest value.

Relation to Linear and Logistic Regression   Consider a neural network with a single output node and no hidden layers. For a dataset with p predictors, the output node receives $x_1, x_2, \ldots, x_p$, takes a weighted sum of these, and applies the g function. The output of the neural network is therefore $g\left(\theta + \sum_{i=1}^{p} w_i x_i\right)$.

First, consider a numerical output variable Y. If g is the identity function $[g(s) = s]$, the output is simply

$$\hat{y} = \theta + \sum_{i=1}^{p} w_i x_i.$$

This is exactly equivalent to the formulation of a multiple linear regression! This means that a neural network with no hidden layers, a single output node, and an identity function g searches only for linear relationships between the response and the predictors.

Now consider a binary output variable Y. If g is the logistic function, the output is simply

$$\hat{P}(Y = 1) = \frac{1}{1 + e^{-\left(\theta + \sum_{i=1}^{p} w_i x_i\right)}},$$

which is equivalent to the logistic regression formulation!

In both cases, although the formulation is equivalent to the linear and logistic regression models, the resulting estimates for the weights (*coefficients* in linear and logistic regression) can differ because the estimation method is different. The neural net estimation method is different from *least squares*, the method used to calculate coefficients in linear regression, and the *maximum likelihood* method used in logistic regression. We explain below the method by which the neural network learns.

Preprocessing the Data

When using a logistic activation function (called "Sigmoid" in ASDM), neural networks perform best when the predictors are on a scale of [0,1] (called *normalization* in ASDM) or have a mean of zero and standard deviation of 1 (or *standardization* in ASDM). For this reason, all variables should be scaled either to a [0,1] interval or to z-scores before entering them into the network.

For a numerical variable X that takes values in the range $[a, b]$ where $a < b$, we normalize the measurements by subtracting a and dividing by $b - a$. The normalized measurement is then

$$X_{\text{norm}} = \frac{X - a}{b - a}.$$

Note that if $[a, b]$ is within the [0,1] interval, the original scale will be stretched. If a and b are unknown, we can estimate them from the minimal and maximal values of X in the data. Even if new data exceed this range by a small amount, yielding normalized values slightly lower than 0 or larger than 1, will not affect the results much.

For binary variables, no adjustment is needed other than creating dummy variables. For categorical variables with m categories, if they are ordinal in nature, a choice of m fractions in [0,1] should reflect their perceived ordering. For example, if four ordinal categories are equally distant from each other, we can map them to [0, 0.25, 0.5, 1]. If the categories are nominal, transforming into $m - 1$ dummies is a good solution.

Another operation that improves the performance of the network is to transform highly skewed predictors. In business applications, there tend to be many highly right-skewed variables (such as income). Taking a log transform of a

right-skewed variable (before converting to a [0,1] scale or a z-score) will usually spread out the values more symmetrically.

Another common activation function is the hyperbolic tangent (tanh).
When using this function, it is usually better to scale predictors to a $[-1,1]$
scale (called *Adjusted Normalization* in ASDM).

Training the Model

Training the model means estimating θ_j and w_{ij} (bias and weights) that lead to
the best predictive results. The process that we described earlier (Section 11.1)
for computing the neural network output for an observation is repeated for all
the observations in the training set. For each observation the model produces a
prediction that is then compared with the actual response value. Their difference
is the error for the output node. However, unlike least squares or maximum
likelihood, where a global function of the errors (e.g., sum of squared errors) is
used for estimating the coefficients, in neural networks, the estimation process
uses the errors iteratively to update the estimated parameters (bias and weights).

In particular, the error for the output node is distributed across all the hidden
nodes that led to it so that each node is assigned "responsibility" for part of the
error. Each of these node-specific errors is then used for updating the weights
and bias values.

Back Propagation of Error   The most popular method for using model
errors to update weights ("learning") is an algorithm called *back propagation*. As
the name implies, errors are computed from the last layer (the output layer) back
to the hidden layers.

Let us denote by $\hat{y}_k$ the output from output node k. y_k is 1 or 0 depending
on whether the actual class of the observation coincides with node k's label or
not (for example, in Figure 11.3, for a person with output class 'like' we have
$y_6 = 1$ and $y_7 = 0$). The error associated with output node k is computed by

$$\text{err}_k = \hat{y}_k(1 - \hat{y}_k)(y_k - \hat{y}_k).$$

Notice that this is similar to the ordinary definition of an error $(y_k - \hat{y}_k)$ multiplied by a correction factor. The weights are then updated as follows:

$$\begin{aligned}
\theta_j^{\text{new}} &= \theta_j^{\text{old}} + l \times \text{err}_j, \\
w_{i,j}^{\text{new}} &= w_{i,j}^{\text{old}} + l \times \text{err}_j,
\end{aligned} \tag{11.2}$$

where l is a *learning rate* or *weight decay* parameter, a constant ranging typically
between 0 and 1, which controls the amount of change in weights from one
iteration to the next.

In our example, the error associated with output node N6 for the first observation is $(0.506)(1 - 0.506)(1 - 0.506) = 0.123$. For output node N7, the
error is $0.481(1 - 0.481)(0 - 0.481) = -0.120$. These errors are then used to

compute the errors associated with the hidden layer nodes, and those weights are updated accordingly using a formula similar to (11.2).

Two methods for updating the weights are case updating and batch updating. In *case updating*, the weights are updated after each observation is run through the network (called a *trial*). For example, if we used case updating in the tiny example, with a learning rate of 0.5, the weights θ_6, $w_{3,6}$, $w_{4,6}$, and $w_{5,6}$ would first be updated after running observation 1 as follows:

$$
\begin{aligned}
\theta_6 &= -0.015 + (0.5)(0.123) = 0.047, \\
w_{3,6} &= 0.01 + (0.5)(0.123) = 0.072, \\
w_{4,6} &= 0.05 + (0.5)(0.123) = 0.112, \\
w_{5,6} &= 0.015 + (0.5)(0.123) = 0.077.
\end{aligned}
$$

Similarly, we obtain updated weights $\theta_7 = 0.025$, $w_{3,7} = 0.045$, $w_{4,7} = 0.035$, and $w_{5,7} = 0.045$. These new weights are next updated after the second observation is run through the network, the third, and so on, until all observations are used. This is called one *epoch*, *sweep*, or *iteration* through the data. Typically, there are many epochs.

In *batch updating*, the entire training set is run through the network before each updating of weights takes place. In that case, the error err_k in the updating equation is the sum of the errors from all observations. In practice, case updating tends to yield more accurate results than batch updating but requires a longer runtime. This is a serious consideration, since even in batch updating hundreds or even thousands of sweeps through the training data are executed.

When does the updating stop? The most common conditions are one of the following:

1. When the new weights are only incrementally different from those of the preceding iteration

2. When the misclassification rate reaches a required threshold

3. When the limit on the number of runs is reached

To run a neural net in ASDM, choose the *Neural Network* option in either the *Prediction* or *Classification* menu, depending on whether your response variable is numerical or categorical. The software guide describes various options. Notice, however, the following considerations:

- When using the logistic ("Sigmoid") activation function, use either normalization or standardization. *Normalization* scales predictors into the range [0,1], while *Standardization* scales predictors to have a mean of 0 and a standard deviation of 1 (by subtracting the mean and dividing by the standard deviation).

- When using the Hyperbolic Tangent (tanh) activation function, it is better to use *Adjusted Normalization* to scale the predictors to [−1,1].

- ASDM employs case updating. The user can specify the number of epochs.

Let us examine the output from running a neural network on the tiny data. Following Figures 11.2 and 11.3, we used a single hidden layer with three nodes (with no rescaling—for simplicity we assume the two predictors have already been scaled). The weights and classification matrix are shown in Figure 11.4. We can see that the network misclassifies all three *dislike* observations and correctly classifies the three *like* observations. Notice how close all probabilities are to 0.5 (in the bottom-most table), indicating that a small change in the cutoff value would result in different classifications. For instance, using a cutoff of 0.55 can lead to perfect classification performance. This unstable result is not surprising, since the number of observations is too small for estimating the 17 weights. However, for purposes of illustration, we discuss below the remainder of the output.

Training: Classification Summary

Confusion Matrix

Actual\Predicted	dislike	like
dislike	0	3
like	0	3

Error Report

Class	# Cases	# Errors	% Error
dislike	3	3	100
like	3	0	0
Overall	6	3	50

Neuron Weights

Neuron Weights: Input Layer - Hidden Layer 1

Neurons	Fat Score	Salt Score	Bias
Neuron 1	-0.1481	0.4482	-0.0453
Neuron 2	-1.6424	0.6433	-0.0109
Neuron 3	0.6660	0.6384	-0.1405

Neuron Weights: Hidden Layer 1 - Output Layer

Neurons	Neuron 1	Neuron 2	Neuron 3	Bias
dislike	0.0098	0.4935	-1.2197	0.2905
like	0.3641	0.3741	0.3356	-0.3520

Training: Classification Details

Record ID	Acceptance	Prediction: Acceptance	PostProb: dislike	PostProb: like
Record 1	like	like	0.4403	0.5597
Record 2	dislike	like	0.4695	0.5305
Record 3	dislike	like	0.4557	0.5443
Record 4	dislike	like	0.4525	0.5475
Record 5	like	like	0.4442	0.5558
Record 6	like	like	0.4392	0.5608

FIGURE 11.4   OUTPUT FOR NEURAL NETWORK WITH A SINGLE HIDDEN LAYER WITH THREE NODES FOR THE TINY DATA EXAMPLE

The final network weights are shown in two tables in the ASDM output. Figure 11.5 shows these weights in a format similar to that of our previous diagrams.

The first table in the Neuron Weights shows the bias and the weights that connect the input layer and the hidden layer. The *bias nodes* are what we called θ_3, θ_4, and θ_5. The weights in this table are used to compute the output of the hidden layer nodes. They were computed iteratively after choosing a random initial set of weights (like the set we chose in Figure 11.3). We use the weights in the way we described earlier to compute the hidden layer's output. For instance,

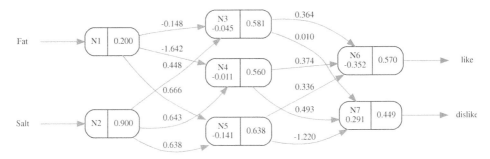

FIGURE 11.5   NEURAL NETWORK FOR THE TINY EXAMPLE WITH FINAL WEIGHTS FROM ASDM
OUTPUT

for the first observation, the output of our previous node N3 (denoted *Neuron 1* in ASDM) is

$$\text{Output}_{N3} = \frac{1}{1 + e^{-[-0.045 + (-0.148)(0.2) + (0.448)(0.9)]}} = 0.581.$$

Similarly, we can compute the output from the two other hidden nodes for the same observation and get $\text{Output}_{N4} = 0.560$ for (ASDM *Neuron 2*) and $\text{Output}_{N5} = 0.638$ (ASDM *Neuron 3*).

The second table gives the weights connecting the hidden and output layer nodes. To compute the output for the *like* output node (N6) for the first record, we use the outputs from the hidden layer that we computed above and get

$$\text{Output}_{N6} = \frac{1}{1 + e^{-[-0.352 + (0.364)(0.581) + (0.374)(0.560) + (0.336)(0.638)]}} = 0.5703.$$

Similarly, we can compute the output for the *dislike* output node, obtaining the value $\text{Output}_{N7} = 0.4487$. Last, we can compute the probability (= propensity) of *like* as 0.5703/(0.5703+0.4487) = 0.5597. This is the probability shown in the bottom-most table in Figure 11.4 (for observation 1), which gives the neural network's predicted probabilities and the classifications based on these values. The probabilities for the other five observations are computed equivalently, replacing the input value in the computation of the hidden layer outputs and then plugging these outputs into the computation for the output layer.

11.4   REQUIRED USER INPUT FOR TRAINING A NETWORK

One of the time-consuming and complex aspects of training a model using back propagation is that we first need to decide on a network architecture. This means specifying the number of hidden layers and the number of nodes in each layer. The usual procedure is to make intelligent guesses using past experience and to do several trial-and-error runs on different architectures. Algorithms exist that grow the number of nodes selectively during training or trim them in a manner analogous to what is done in classification and regression trees (see Chapter 9). Research continues on such methods. As of now, no automatic method seems clearly superior to the trial-and-error approach. A few general guidelines for choosing an architecture follow:

Number of hidden layers: The most popular choice for the number of hidden layers is one. A single hidden layer is usually sufficient to capture even very complex relationships between the predictors.

Size of hidden layer: The number of nodes in the hidden layer also determines the level of complexity of the relationship between the predictors that the network captures. The trade-off is between under- and overfitting. On the one hand, using too few nodes might not be sufficient to capture complex relationships (recall the special cases of a linear relationship such as in linear and logistic regression, in the extreme case of zero nodes or no hidden layer). On the other hand, too many nodes might lead to overfitting. A rule of thumb is to start with p (number of predictors) nodes and gradually decrease or increase while checking for overfitting.

Number of output nodes: For a binary response, a single node is sufficient and a cutoff is used for classification. For a categorical response with $m > 2$ classes, the number of nodes should equal the number of classes. Finally, for a numerical response, typically a single output node is used unless we are interested in predicting more than one function.

In addition to the choice of architecture, the user should pay attention to the *choice of predictors*. Since neural networks are highly dependent on the quality of their input, the choice of predictors should be done carefully, using domain knowledge, variable selection, and dimension reduction techniques before using the network. We return to this point in the discussion of advantages and weaknesses below.

Other parameters that the user can control are the *learning rate, weight decay*, and the *momentum*. These paramters can be found in ASDM's Parameters tab within the Neural Networks menu, under *Optimization*. The *learning rate* parameter is the multiplying factor for the error correction during backpropagation; it is roughly equivalent to the learning rate for the neural network. A low value produces slow but steady learning, while a high value produces rapid but erratic learning. Values for the step size typically range from 0.1 to 0.9.

The *weight decay* parameter is used primarily to avoid overfitting, by down-weighting new information. This helps to tone down the effect of outliers on the weights and avoids getting stuck in local optima. This parameter typically takes a value in the range [0,1]. Berry and Linoff (2000) suggest starting with a large value (moving away from the random initial weights, thereby "learning quickly" from the data) and then slowly decreasing it as the iterations progress and the weights are more reliable. Han and Kamber (2001) suggest the more concrete rule of thumb of setting *weight decay* = 1/(current number of iterations). This means that at the start, *weight decay* = 1, during the second iteration it is 0.5, and then it keeps decaying toward zero. In ASDM, the default *weight decay* is 0, which means that the weights do not decay at all.

The third parameter, called *momentum*, is used to "keep the ball rolling" (hence the term *momentum*) in the convergence of the weights to the optimum. The idea is to keep the weights changing in the same direction as they did in the preceding iteration. This helps avoid getting stuck in a local optimum. High values of momentum mean that the network will be "reluctant" to learn from data that want to change the direction of the weights, especially when we consider case updating. In general, values in the range 0–2 are used.

Example 2: Classifying Accident Severity

Let's apply the network training process to some real data: US automobile accidents that have been classified by their level of severity as *no injury*, *injury*, or *fatality*. A firm might be interested in developing a system for quickly classifying the severity of an accident, based on initial reports and associated data in the system (some of which rely on GPS-assisted reporting). Such a system could be used to assign emergency response team priorities. Table 11.2 shows a small extract (10 records, four predictor variables) from a US government database.

TABLE 11.2   SUBSET FROM THE ACCIDENTS DATA, FOR A HIGH-FATALITY REGION

Obs.	ALCHL_I	PROFIL_I_R	SUR_COND	VEH_INVL	MAX_SEV_IR
1	1	1	1	1	1
2	2	1	1	1	0
3	2	1	1	1	1
4	1	1	1	1	0
5	2	1	1	1	2
6	2	0	1	1	1
7	2	0	1	3	1
8	2	0	1	4	1
9	2	0	1	2	0
10	2	0	1	2	0

The explanation of the four predictor variables and response is given in Table 11.3. For the analysis, we convert ALCHL_I to a 0/1 dummy variable (1 = presence of alcohol) and create four dummies for SUR_COND.[2] This gives us a total of seven predictors.

---

[2] We could also include the dummy for SUR_COND_9 ("unknown"), and use all five dummies.

TABLE 11.3   DESCRIPTION OF VARIABLES FOR AUTOMOBILE ACCIDENT EXAMPLE

ALCHL_I	Presence (1) or absence (2) of alcohol
PROFIL_I_R	Profile of the roadway: level (1), other (0)
SUR_COND	Surface condition of the road: dry (1), wet (2), snow/slush (3), ice (4), unknown (9)
VEH_INVL	Number of vehicles involved
MAX_SEV_IR	Presence of injuries/fatalities: no injuries (0), injury (1), fatality (2)

With the exception of alcohol involvement and a few other variables in the larger database, most of the variables are ones that we might reasonably expect to be available at the time of the initial accident report, before accident details and severity have been determined by first responders. A machine learning model that could predict accident severity on the basis of these initial reports would have value in allocating first responder resources.

To use a neural net architecture for this classification problem, we use seven nodes (neurons) in the input layer, one for each of the seven predictors, and three neurons (one for each class) in the output layer. We use a single hidden layer and experiment with the number of nodes. If we increase the number of nodes from four to eight and examine the resulting confusion matrices, we find that four nodes gives a good balance between improving the predictive performance on the training set without deteriorating the performance on the validation set. (Networks with more than five nodes in the hidden layer performed as well as the five-node network but add undesirable complexity.) Some software allow exploring multiple architectures in an automated way. ASDM's Automatic Network can be used to compare multiple architectures—it tries networks with different numbers of hidden layers and different numbers of nodes in the hidden layer(s).

Note that there are a total of four connections from each node in the input layer to each node in the hidden layer, and a total of $7 \times 4 = 28$ connections between the input layer and the hidden layer. In addition, there is a total of three connections from each node in the hidden layer to each node in the output layer, a total of $4 \times 3 = 12$ connections between the hidden layer and the output layer.

We train the network on the training partition of 600 records. Each iteration in the neural network process consists of a presentation to the input layer of the predictors in a case, followed by successive computations of the outputs of the hidden layer nodes and the output layer nodes using the appropriate weights. The output values of the output layer nodes are used to compute the error. The backward propagation algorithm completes one iteration, using the error to adjust the weights of all the connections in the network. Since the training data has 600 cases, one sweep through the data, termed an *epoch*, consists of 600 iterations. We trained the network using 300 epochs, which yields a total of 180,000 iterations. Other settings used are rescaling using *Standardization* and *learning rate* set to 0.90. Recall that in ASDM *Normalization* refers to rescaling the values into a range of [0,1] and *Standardization* means rescaling the data to have a mean of 0 and a standard deviation of 1 (unit variance). Standardization works slightly better in this case. The resulting classification results, error rates, and weights following the last epoch of training the neural net on these data are shown in Figure 11.6. The machine learning workflow for generating this output is shown in Figure 11.7. The last icon in the flow, Manual Network, reflects that we have determined the network settings manually, as described above. ASDM also has an option to auto-optimize these settings.

Training: Classification Summary

Confusion Matrix

Actual\Predicted	0	1	2
0	321	0	0
1	0	171	11
2	33	44	20

Error Report

Class	# Cases	# Errors	% Error
0	321	0	0.00
1	182	11	6.04
2	97	77	79.38
Overall	600	88	14.67

Validation: Classification Summary

Confusion Matrix

Actual\Predicted	0	1	2
0	229	0	1
1	0	117	0
2	22	18	12

Error Report

Class	# Cases	# Errors	% Error
0	230	1	0.43
1	117	0	0.00
2	52	40	76.92
Overall	399	41	10.28

Neuron Weights

Neuron Weights: Input Layer - Hidden Layer 1

Neurons	PROFIL_I_R	VEH_INVL	ALCHL_I_1	SUR_COND_1	SUR_COND_2	SUR_COND_3	SUR_COND_4	Bias
Neuron 1	1.1268	0.3635	-1.2854	-0.8341	1.3043	0.4696	0.4602	-1.0074
Neuron 2	1.9468	1.1856	0.9056	-1.1392	0.5250	0.0884	0.2085	0.6149
Neuron 3	-1.7333	-0.4233	-0.0701	0.9740	-0.4563	-0.1883	-0.4239	-0.0390
Neuron 4	-2.5314	-2.0375	-0.5652	1.0249	-0.9970	-0.3109	-0.5585	-0.8641

Neuron Weights: Hidden Layer 1 - Output Layer

Neurons	Neuron 1	Neuron 2	Neuron 3	Neuron 4	Bias
0	-2.0982	-2.9767	0.8139	3.9689	-1.0241
1	2.4101	1.2102	-2.7523	-3.0077	-1.3246
2	-2.5306	1.3792	-0.1719	-1.7960	-0.6368

FIGURE 11.6   ASDM OUTPUT FOR NEURAL NETWORK FOR ACCIDENTS DATA, WITH FOUR NODES IN THE HIDDEN LAYER. RESULTS AFTER 300 EPOCHS

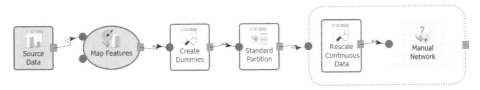

FIGURE 11.7   THE MACHINE LEARNING WORKFLOW FOR THE NEURAL NETS MODELS IN ACCIDENTS DATA EXAMPLE

Note that had we stopped after only one pass of the data (600 iterations), the error would have been much worse, and none of the fatal accidents (coded as 2) would have been spotted, as can be seen in Figure 11.8. Our results can depend on how we set the different parameters, and the major danger is overfitting. We discuss this issue in the next section.

Training: Classification Summary			
Confusion Matrix			
Actual\Predicted	0	1	2
0	0	321	0
1	1	181	0
2	0	97	0

Error Report			
Class	# Cases	# Errors	% Error
0	321	321	100.00
1	182	1	0.55
2	97	97	100.00
Overall	600	419	69.83

Validation: Classification Summary			
Confusion Matrix			
Actual\Predicted	0	1	2
0	0	230	0
1	2	115	0
2	1	51	0

Error Report			
Class	# Cases	# Errors	% Error
0	230	230	100
1	117	2	1.7094
2	52	52	100
Overall	399	284	71.178

Neuron Weights

Neuron Weights: Input Layer - Hidden Layer 1								
Neurons	PROFIL_I_R	VEH_INVL	ALCHL_I_1	SUR_COND_1	SUR_COND_2	SUR_COND_3	SUR_COND_4	Bias
Neuron 1	-0.0687	0.2440	-0.8752	0.3336	0.3653	0.3235	-0.1961	-0.0096
Neuron 2	0.4027	-0.1252	0.5660	-0.3273	-0.2308	0.0628	-0.0607	-0.0283
Neuron 3	-0.3493	-0.1053	-0.4309	0.4146	-0.0474	-0.2413	0.0672	0.0071
Neuron 4	0.1185	-0.3562	0.1002	0.0491	-0.3350	-0.1403	0.2417	-0.0033

Neuron Weights: Hidden Layer 1 - Output Layer					
Neurons	Neuron 1	Neuron 2	Neuron 3	Neuron 4	Bias
0	-0.0826	0.3120	-1.1130	0.4861	0.0356
1	0.4085	0.3719	-0.3451	0.4571	-0.1220
2	-0.2302	0.6923	-0.4923	-0.3624	-0.1133

FIGURE 11.8   ASDM OUTPUT FOR NEURAL NETWORK FOR ACCIDENTS DATA, WITH FOUR NODES IN THE HIDDEN LAYER. RESULTS AFTER ONLY ONE EPOCH

11.5 MODEL VALIDATION AND USE

Avoiding Overfitting

A weakness of the neural network is that it can easily overfit the data, causing the error rate on validation data (and most important, on new data) to be too large. It is therefore important to limit the number of training epochs and not to overtrain on the data. As in classification and regression trees, overfitting can be detected by examining the performance on the validation set and seeing when it starts deteriorating, while the training set performance is still improving. This approach is used in some algorithms to limit the number of training epochs: the error rate on the validation dataset is computed periodically while the network is being trained. In ASDM's Stopping Rules dialog box, the user can choose to use the validation data for estimating the error after each epoch. The validation error typically decreases in the early epochs of the training, but after a while, it begins to increase. The point of minimum validation error is a good indicator of the best number of epochs for training, and the weights at that stage are likely to provide the best error rate in new data.

Using the Output for Prediction and Classification

When the neural network is used for predicting a numerical response, the resulting output after applying the various activation function(s) at the hidden and output layers needs to be scaled back to the original units of that response. If "rescale data" was chosen during the model fitting process, ASDM will perform this scaling back automatically, resulting in predicted values on the original scale.

For a binary response, although we typically use a cutoff of 0.5 with other classifiers, in neural networks there is a tendency for values to cluster around 0.5 (from above and below), as seen in the tiny data example. An alternative is to use the validation set to determine a cutoff that produces reasonable predictive performance.

For multi-class classification, where we have a categorical outcome with m classes, we saw that the neural net produces m output nodes, one for each class. How do we translate these m outputs into a classification rule? Usually the output node with the largest value determines the net's classification.

Exploring the Relationship Between Predictors and Outcome

Neural networks are known to be "blackboxes" in the sense that their output does not shed light on the patterns in the data that it models (like our brains). In fact, that is one of the biggest criticisms of the method. However, in some cases, it is possible to learn more about the relationships that the network captures by conducting a sensitivity analysis on the validation set. This is done by setting all predictor values to their mean and obtaining the network's prediction. Then, the process is repeated by setting each predictor sequentially to its minimum, and then maximum, value. By comparing the predictions from different levels of the predictors, we can get a sense of which predictors affect predictions more and in what way.

11.6 DEEP LEARNING[3]

Neural nets had their greatest impact in the period from 2006 onward, with a paper published by AI researcher Geoffrey Hinton, and the rapidly growing popularity of what came to be called *deep learning*. Deep learning involves complex networks with many layers, incorporating processes for dimension reduction and feature discovery.

The data we have dealt with so far in this book are structured data, typically from organizational databases. The predictor variables, or features, that we think

---

[3]This section copyright ©2019 Datastats, LLC, Galit Shmueli, and Peter Gedeck. Used by permission.

might be meaningful in predicting an outcome of interest already exist in our data. In predicting possible bank failure, for example, we would guess that certain financial ratios (return on assets, return on equity, etc.) might have predictive value. In predicting insurance fraud, we might guess that policy age would be predictive. We are not limited, of course, to variables that we know are predictive; sometimes a useful predictor emerges in an unexpected way.

With tasks like voice and image recognition, structured high-level predictor information like this is not available. All we have are individual "low-level" sound wave frequency and amplitude or pixel values indicating intensity and color. You'd like to be able to tell the computer "just look for two eyes" and then provide further detail on how an eye appears—a small solid circle (pupil), surrounded by a ring (iris), surrounded by a white area. But, again, all the computer has are columns of (low-level) pixel values—you'd need to do a lot of extra work to define all the different (higher-level) pixel patterns that correspond to eyes. That's where deep learning comes in—it can "learn" how to identify these higher level features by itself.

Deep learning is a rapidly growing and evolving field, with many aspects that distinguish it from simpler predictive models. A full examination of the field of deep learning is beyond the scope of this book, but let us consider one key innovation in the area of algorithmic design that is associated with deep learning and extends the ability of simple neural networks to perform the tasks of supervised and unsupervised learning that we have been discussing. This innovation is "convolution." Convolutional neural networks are used in many different applications and fields and have enabled major advances in voice recognition and the extraction of meaning from text via natural language processing. The basic idea of convolution is illustrated well in the context of image recognition.

Convolutional Neural Networks (CNNs)

In a standard neural network, each predictor gets its own weight at each layer of the network. A convolution, by contrast, selects a subset of predictors (pixels) and applies the same operation to the entire subset. It is this grouping that fosters the automated discovery of features. Recall that the data in image recognition tasks consist of a large number of pixel values, which, in a black and white image, range from 0 (black) to 255 (white). Since we are interested in detecting the black lines and shadings, we will reverse this to 255 for black and 0 for white.

Consider the line drawing in Figure 11.9, from a 1893 Funk and Wagnalls publication. Before the computer can begin to identify complex features like eyes, ears, noses, heads, it needs to master very simple features like lines and borders. For example, the line of the man's chin (Figure 11.10). In a typical convolution, the algorithm considers a small area at a time, say, 3 pixels × 3 pixels. Figure 11.11 illustrates such a case. The line at the chin might look like the Figure 11.11(a); the matrix in Figure 11.11(b) might be our pixel values. In its first convolution operation, the network could apply a filter operation by multiplying the pixel values by a 3×3 matrix of values that happens to be good at identifying vertical lines, such as the matrix in Figure 11.11(c). The sum of the individual cell multiplications is $(0 + 0 + 0 + 200 + 225 + 225 + 0 + 0 + 0) = 650$. This is a relatively high value, compared to what another arrangement of the filter matrix might produce, because both the image section

FIGURE 11.9   LINE DRAWING, FROM A 1893 FUNK AND WAGNALLS PUBLICATION

FIGURE 11.10   FOCUSING ON THE LINE OF THE MAN'S CHIN

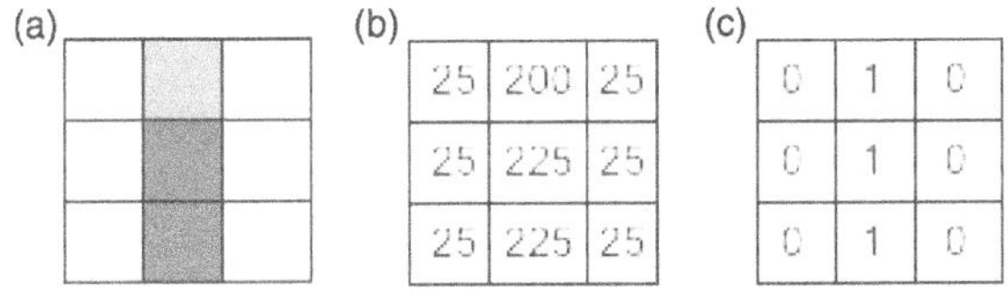

(a)			(b)			(c)		
			25	200	25	0	1	0
			25	225	25	0	1	0
			25	225	25	0	1	0

FIGURE 11.11 3×3 PIXEL REPRESENTATION OF LINE ON MAN'S CHIN USING SHADING (a) AND VALUES (b). THE FILTER (c) IDENTIFIES VERTICAL LINES

and the filter have high values in the center column and low values elsewhere. (A little experimentation with other 3×3 arrangements of three 1's and six 0's will reveal why this particular matrix is good at identifying vertical lines.) So, for this initial filter action, we can say that the filter has detected a vertical line, and thus we can consolidate the initial nine values of the image section into a single value (say, a value between 0 and 1 to indicate the absence or presence of a vertical line).

Local Feature Map

The "vertical line detector" filter moves across and down the original image matrix, recalculating and producing a single output each time. We end up with a smaller matrix; how much smaller depends on whether the filter moves one pixel at a time, two, or more. While the original image values were simply individual pixel values, the new, smaller matrix is a map of features, answering the question, "is there a vertical line in this section?"

The fact that the frame for the convolution is relatively small means that the overall operation can identify features that are local in character. We could imagine other local filters to discover horizontal lines, diagonal lines, curves, boundaries, etc. Further layers of different convolutional operations, taking these local feature maps as inputs, can then successively build up higher level features (corners, rectangles, circles, etc.).

A Hierarchy of Features

The first feature map is of vertical lines; we could repeat the process to identify horizontal lines and diagonal lines. We could also imagine filters to identify boundaries between light and dark areas. Then, having produced a set of initial low-level feature maps, the process could repeat, except this time working with these feature maps instead of the original pixel values. This iterative process continues, building up multidimensional matrix maps, or tensors, of higher and higher level features. As the process proceeds, the matrix representation of higher level features becomes somewhat abstract, so it is not necessarily possible to peer into a deep network and identify, for example, an eye.

In this process, the information is progressively compressed (simplified) as the higher level features emerge, as illustrated in Figure 11.12.

The Learning Process

How does the net know which convolutional operations to do? Put simply, it retains the ones that lead to successful classifications. In a basic neural net, the individual weights are what get adjusted in the iterative learning process. In a convolutional network, the net also learns which convolutions to do.

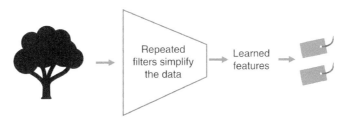

FIGURE 11.12   CONVOLUTION NETWORK PROCESS, SUPERVISED LEARNING: THE REPEATED FILTERING IN THE NETWORK CONVOLUTION PROCESS PRODUCES HIGH-LEVEL FEATURES THAT FACILITATE THE APPLICATION OF CLASS LABELS, WHICH ARE COMPARED TO ACTUAL CLASSES TO TRAIN THE NETWORK

In a supervised learning setting, the network keeps building up features up to the highest level, which might be the goal of the learning task. Consider the task of deciding whether an image contains a face. You have a training set of labeled images with faces, and images without faces. The training process yields convolutions that identify hierarchies of features (e.g., edges > circles > eyes) that lead to success in the classification process. Other hierarchies that the net might conceivably encounter (e.g., edges > rectangles > houses) get dropped because they do not contribute to success in the identification of faces. Sometimes it is the case that the output of a single neuron in the network is an effective classifier, an indication that this neuron codes for the feature you are focusing on.

Unsupervised Learning

The most magical-seeming accomplishment of deep learning is its ability to identify features and, hence, objects in an unsupervised setting. Famous examples include identifying images with faces and identifying dogs and cats in images (see, e.g., Le et al., 2012). How is this done?

One method is to use a so-called autoencoder network. These networks are trained to reproduce the input that is fed into them, by first creating a lower-dimensional representation of the data and then using the created representation to reproduce the original data. The network is trained to retain the features that facilitate accurate reproduction of the input.

Viewed in the context of our image example, autoencoders have the high-level architecture shown in Figure 11.13.

Up to the learned features point (the bottleneck in the image), the network is similar to the supervised network. Once it has developed the learned features, which are a low-dimensional representation of the data, it expands those features into an image by a reverse process. The output image is compared to the input image, and if they are not similar, the network keeps working (using the same backpropagation method we discussed earlier). Once the network reliably produces output images that are similar to the inputs, the process stops.

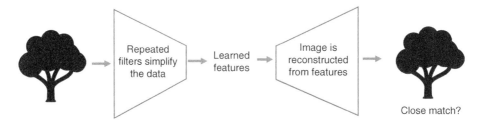

FIGURE 11.13   AUTOENCODER NETWORK PROCESS: THE REPEATED FILTERING IN THE NETWORK CONVOLUTION PROCESS PRODUCES HIGH-LEVEL FEATURES THAT ARE THEN USED TO RECONSTRUCT THE IMAGE. THE RECONSTRUCTED IMAGE IS COMPARED TO THE ORIGINAL; NETWORK ARCHITECTURES THAT PRODUCE CLOSE MATCHES ARE SAVED AS THE NETWORK IS "TRAINED" WITHOUT BENEFIT OF LABELED DATA

This internal representation at the bottleneck now has useful information about the general domain (here, images) on which the network was trained. It turns out that the learned features (outputs of neurons at the bottleneck) that emerge in this process are often useful. Since the features can be considered a low-dimensional representation of the original data (similar in spirit to principal components in PCA—see Chapter 4), they can be used, for example, for building a supervised predictive model or for unsupervised clustering.

Conclusion

The key to convolutional networks' success is their ability to build, through iteration, multidimensional feature maps of great complexity (requiring substantial computing power and capacity), leading to the development of learned features that form a lower-dimensional representation of the data. You can see that different convolutional architectures (e.g., types of filtering operations) would be suitable for different tasks. The AI community shares pre-trained networks that allow analysts to short-circuit the lengthy and complex training process that is required, as well as datasets that allow training and benchmarking to certain tasks (e.g., datasets of generic images in many different classes, images specifically of faces, satellite imagery, text data, voice data, etc.).

Finally, you may have heard of other types of deep learning. At the time of writing, Recurrent Neural Networks (RNN) are very popular. They are usually implemented with either Long Short-Term Memory (LSTM) or Gated Recurrent Unit (GRU) building blocks. These networks are especially useful for data that are sequential in nature or have temporal behavior, such as time series, music, text, and speech (where the order of words in a sentence matters), and user or robot behavior (e.g., clickstream data, where the order of a user's actions can be important). These networks' memory help them capture such sequences. In deciding whether to use such methods in a given business analytics application, a key consideration is their performance relative to other methods and their required resources (in terms of data and computing).

11.7 ADVANTAGES AND WEAKNESSES OF NEURAL NETWORKS

The most prominent advantage of neural networks is their good predictive performance. They are known to have high tolerance to noisy data and the ability to capture highly complicated relationships between the predictors and a response. Their weakest point is in providing insight into the structure of the relationship, hence their blackbox reputation.

Several considerations and dangers should be kept in mind when using neural networks. First, although they are capable of generalizing from a set of examples, extrapolation is still a serious danger. If the network sees only cases in a certain range, its predictions outside this range may be completely invalid.

Second, the extreme flexibility of the neural network relies on having sufficient data for training purposes. A related issue is that in classification problems, the network requires sufficient records of the minority class in order to learn it. This is achieved by oversampling, as explained in Chapter 2.

Finally, a practical consideration that can determine the usefulness of a neural network is the timeliness of computation. Neural networks are relatively heavy on computation time, requiring a longer runtime than other classifiers. This runtime grows greatly when the number of predictors is increased (as there will be many more weights to compute). In applications where real-time or near-real-time prediction is required, runtime should be measured to make sure that it does not cause unacceptable delay in the decision making.

PROBLEMS

11.1 **Credit Card Use.** Consider the following hypothetical bank data on consumers' use of credit card credit facilities in Table 11.4. Create a small worksheet in Excel to illustrate one pass through a simple neural network.

TABLE 11.4   DATA FOR CREDIT CARD EXAMPLE AND VARIABLE
DESCRIPTIONS[a]

Years	Salary	Used credit
4	43	0
18	65	1
1	53	0
3	95	0
15	88	1
6	112	1

[a] Years = Number of years that a customer has been with the bank;
Salary = customer's salary (in thousands of dollars);
Used credit 1 = customer has left an unpaid credit card balance at the end of at least one month in the prior year and 0 = balance was paid off at the end of each month.

11.2 **Neural Net Evolution.** A neural net typically starts out with random coefficients; hence it produces essentially random predictions when presented with its first case. What is the key ingredient by which the net evolves to produce a more accurate prediction?

11.3 **Car Sales.** Consider again the data on used cars (`ToyotaCorolla.xlsx`) with 1436 records and details on 38 attributes, including Price, Age, KM, HP, and other specifications. The goal is to predict the price of a used Toyota Corolla based on its specifications.

- Use ASDM's neural network routine to fit a model. Use the default values for the neural net parameters, select a Sigmoid activation function for the hidden layers, Linear activation function for the output layer, and select appropriate scaling options. Error tolerance may need to be set to 0.

- Record the RMSE for the training data and the validation data.

- Repeat the process, changing the number of epochs (and only this) to 30, 300, 3000, and 10,000.

  a. What happens to the RMS error for the training data as the number of epochs increases?

  b. What happens to the RMS error for the validation data?

  c. Comment on the appropriate number of epochs for the model.

11.4 **Direct Mailing to Airline Customers.** East-West Airlines has entered into a partnership with the wireless phone company Telcon to sell the latter's service via direct mail. The file `EastWestAirlinesNN.xlsx` contains a subset of a data sample of who has already received a test offer. About 13% accepted.

You are asked to develop a model to classify East-West customers as to whether they purchased a wireless phone service contract (target variable Phone_Sale), a model that can be used to classify additional customers.

Using ASDM, run a manual neural net model on these data with one hidden layer and 25 hidden neurons. Select the sigmoid activation function and appropriate scaling options. In Training Pentameters, set *Learning Rate* = 0.01 and *Error Tolerance* = 0. And for Stopping Rules, set the number of epochs at 100. Request lift charts and decile-wise lift charts for both the training and validation data.

a. Interpret the meaning (in business terms) of the left-most bar of the validation decile-wise lift chart (the bar chart).

b. Comment on the difference between the training and validation lift curves.

c. Run a second neural net model on the data, this time with no hidden layers. (Keep all other settings identical to the previous model.) Look at the lift curves. Comment now on the difference between this model and the model you ran earlier, and how overfitting might have affected results.

d. What sort of information, if any, is provided about the effects of the various variables?

## CHAPTER 12

Discriminant Analysis

In this chapter we describe the method of discriminant analysis, which is a model-based approach to classification. We discuss the main principle, where classification is based on the distance of an observation from each of the class averages. We explain the underlying measure of "statistical distance," which takes into account the correlation between predictors. The output of a discriminant analysis procedure generates estimated "classification functions," which are then used to produce classification scores that can be translated into classifications or propensities (probabilities of class membership). One can also directly integrate misclassification costs into the discriminant analysis setup, and we explain how this is achieved. Finally, we discuss the underlying model assumptions, the practical robustness to some, and the advantages of discriminant analysis when the assumptions are reasonably met (e.g., the sufficiency of a small training sample).

12.1 INTRODUCTION

Discriminant analysis is a classification method. Like logistic regression, it is a classical statistical technique that can be used for classification and profiling. It uses sets of measurements on different classes of items to classify new items into one of those classes (*classification*). Common uses of the method have been in classifying organisms into species and subspecies; classifying applications for loans, credit cards, and insurance into low- and high-risk categories; classifying customers of new products into early adopters, early majority, late majority, and laggards; classifying bonds into bond-rating categories; classifying skulls of human fossils; research studies involving disputed authorship; decision on college admission; medical studies involving alcoholics and nonalcoholics; and

Machine Learning for Business Analytics: Concepts, Techniques, and Applications with Analytic Solver® Data Mining,
Fourth Edition. Galit Shmueli, Peter C. Bruce, Kuber R. Deokar, and Nitin R. Patel
© 2023 John Wiley & Sons, Inc. Published 2023 by John Wiley & Sons, Inc.

methods to identify human fingerprints. Discriminant analysis can also be used to highlight the characteristics that distinguish the classes (*profiling*).

We return to two examples that were described in earlier chapters, the riding-mowers and personal loan acceptance examples. In each of these, the response has two classes. We close with a third example involving more than two classes.

Example 1: Riding Mowers

We return to the example from Chapter 7, where a riding-mower manufacturer would like to find a way of classifying families in a city into those likely to purchase a riding mower and those not likely to purchase one. A pilot random sample of 12 owners and 12 nonowners in the city is undertaken. The data are given in Chapter 7 (Table 7.1), and a scatter plot is shown in Figure 12.1. We can think of a linear classification rule as a line that separates the two-dimensional region into two parts, with most of the owners in one half-plane and most nonowners in the complementary half-plane. A good classification rule would separate the data so that the fewest points are misclassified: The line shown in Figure 12.1 seems to do a good job in discriminating between the two classes as it makes four misclassifications out of 24 points. Can we do better?

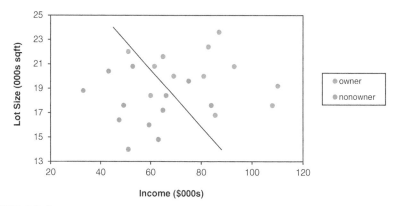

FIGURE 12.1   SCATTER PLOT OF LOT SIZE VS. INCOME FOR 24 OWNERS AND NONOWNERS OF RIDING MOWERS. THE (AD HOC) LINE TRIES TO SEPARATE OWNERS FROM NONOWNERS

Example 2: Personal Loan Acceptance

The riding-mowers example is a classic example and is useful in describing the concept and goal of discriminant analysis. However, in today's business applications, the number of observations is much larger, and the separation of observations into classes is much less distinct. To illustrate this, we return to the Universal Bank example described in Chapter 9, where the bank's goal is to identify new customers most likely to accept a personal loan. For simplicity, we will consider only two predictor variables: the customer's annual income (Income, in $000s), and the average monthly credit card spending (CCAvg, in $000s). The first part of Figure 12.2 shows the acceptance of a personal loan by a subset of 200 customers from the bank's database as a function of Income and CCAvg. We use a logarithmic scale on both axes to enhance visibility because there are many points condensed in the low-income, low-CC spending area. Even for this small subset, the separation is not clear. The second figure shows all 5000 customers and the added complexity of dealing with large numbers of observations.

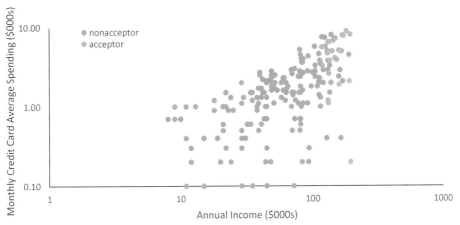

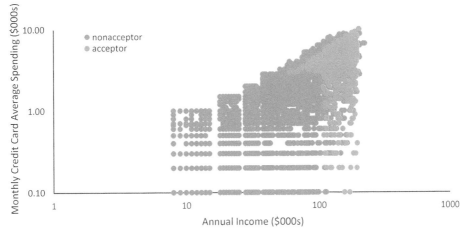

FIGURE 12.2 PERSONAL LOAN ACCEPTANCE AS A FUNCTION OF INCOME AND CREDIT CARD SPENDING FOR 5000 CUSTOMERS OF THE UNIVERSAL BANK (IN LOG SCALE). CREATED IN EXCEL

12.2 DISTANCE OF AN OBSERVATION FROM A CLASS

Finding the best separation between observations involves measuring their distance from their class. The general idea is to classify an observation to the class to which it is closest. Suppose that we are required to classify a new customer of Universal Bank as being an acceptor or a nonacceptor of their personal loan offer, based on an income of x. From the bank's database, we find that the average income for loan acceptors was \$144.75K and for nonacceptors \$66.24K. We can use *Income* as a predictor of loan acceptance via a simple *Euclidean distance rule*: If x is closer to the average income of the acceptor class than to the average income of the nonacceptor class, classify the customer as an acceptor; otherwise, classify the customer as a nonacceptor. In other words, if $|x - 144.75| < |x - 66.24|$, then classification = acceptor; otherwise, nonacceptor. Moving from a single predictor variable (income) to two or more predictor variables, the equivalent of the mean of a class is the *centroid* of a class. This is simply the vector of means $\overline{\mathbf{x}} = [\overline{x}_1, \ldots, \overline{x}_p]$. The Euclidean distance between an observation with p measurements $\mathbf{x} = [x_1, \ldots, x_p]$ and the centroid $\overline{\mathbf{x}}$ is defined as the root of the sum of the squared differences between the individual values and the means:

$$D_{\text{Euclidean}}(\mathbf{x}, \overline{\mathbf{x}}) = \sqrt{(x_1 - \overline{x}_1)^2 + \cdots + (x_p - \overline{x}_p)^2}. \qquad (12.1)$$

Using the Euclidean distance has three drawbacks. First, the distance depends on the units we choose to measure the predictor variables. We will get different answers if we decide to measure income in dollars, for instance, rather than in thousands of dollars.

Second, Euclidean distance does not take into account the variability of the variables. For example, if we compare the variability in income in the two classes, we find that for acceptors the standard deviation is lower than for nonacceptors (\$31.6K vs. \$40.6K). The income of a new customer might be closer to the acceptors' average income in dollars, but because of the large variability in income for nonacceptors, this customer is just as likely to be a nonacceptor. We therefore want the distance measure to take into account the variance of the different variables and measure a distance in standard deviations rather than in the original units. This is equivalent to z-scores.

Third, Euclidean distance ignores the correlation between the variables. This is often a very important consideration, especially when we are using many predictor variables to separate classes. In this case, there will often be variables that alone are useful discriminators between classes but in the presence of other predictor variables are practically redundant, as they capture the same effects as the other variables.

A solution to these drawbacks is to use a measure called *statistical distance* (or *Mahalanobis distance*). Let us denote by S the covariance matrix between the p variables. The definition of a statistical distance is

$$D_{\text{Statistical}}(\mathbf{x}, \overline{\mathbf{x}}) = \sqrt{[\mathbf{x} - \overline{\mathbf{x}}]' S^{-1} [\mathbf{x} - \overline{\mathbf{x}}]}$$

$$= \sqrt{[(x_1 - \overline{x}_1), (x_2 - \overline{x}_2), \ldots, (x_p - \overline{x}_p)] S^{-1} \begin{bmatrix} x_1 - \overline{x}_1 \\ x_2 - \overline{x}_2 \\ \vdots \\ x_p - \overline{x}_p \end{bmatrix}}.$$

$$(12.2)$$

(the notation $'$, which represents *transpose operation*, simply turns the column vector into a row vector). S^{-1} is the inverse matrix of S, which is the p-dimension extension to division. When there is a single predictor ($p = 1$), this reduces to a z-score, since we subtract the mean and divide by the standard deviation. The statistical distance takes into account not only the predictor averages but also the spread of the predictor values and the correlations between the different predictors. To compute a statistical distance between an observation and a class, we first compute the predictor averages (the centroid) and the covariances between each pair of predictors. These are then used to construct the distances. The method of discriminant analysis uses statistical distance as the basis for finding a separating line (or, if there are more than two variables, a separating hyperplane) that is equally distant from the different class means.[1] The method is based on measuring the statistical distances of an observation to each of the classes and allocating it to the closest class. The measuring is done through *classification functions*, which are explained next.

12.3 FISHER'S LINEAR CLASSIFICATION FUNCTIONS

Linear classification functions were proposed in 1936 by the noted statistician R. A. Fisher as the basis for improved separation of observations into classes. The idea is to find linear functions of the measurements that maximize the ratio of between-class variability to within-class variability. In other words, we would obtain classes that are very homogeneous and that differ the most from each other. For each observation, these functions are used to compute scores that measure the proximity of that observation to each of the classes. An observation

---

[1]An alternative approach finds a separating line or hyperplane that is "best" at separating the different clouds of points. In the case of two classes, the two methods coincide.

is classified as belonging to the class for which it has the highest classification score (equivalent to the smallest statistical distance).

USING CLASSIFICATION FUNCTION SCORES TO CLASSIFY RECORDS

For each observation, we calculate the value of the classification function (one for each class); whichever class's function has the highest value (= score) is the class assigned to that observation.

The classification functions are estimated using software. For example, Figure 12.3 shows the output for the riding-mowers data in the case of two predictors. Note that the number of classification functions is equal to the number of classes (here two: owner/nonowner).

Linear Discriminant Functions

Variable	non-owner	owner
Intercepts	-51.4214500	-73.1602116
Income	0.3293554	0.4295857
Lot Size	4.6815655	5.4667502

FIGURE 12.3   DISCRIMINANT ANALYSIS OUTPUT FOR RIDING-MOWER DATA, DISPLAYING THE ESTIMATED CLASSIFICATION FUNCTIONS (CALLED "LINEAR DISCRIMINANT FUNCTIONS" IN ASDM)

To classify a family into the class of owners or nonowners, we use the functions above to compute the family's classification scores: a family is classified into the class of *owners* if the owner function score is higher than the nonowner function score, and into *nonowners* if the reverse is the case. These functions are specified in a way that can be generalized easily to more than two classes. The values given for the functions are simply the weights to be associated with each variable in the linear function in a manner analogous to multiple linear regression. For instance, the first household has an income of $60K and a lot size of 18.4K ft^2. Their *owner* score is therefore $-73.16 + (0.43)(60) + (5.47)(18.4) = 53.2$, and their *nonowner* score is $-51.42 + (0.33)(60) + (4.68)(18.4) = 54.48$. Since the second score is higher, the household is (mis)classified by the model as a nonowner. The scores for all 24 households are given in Figure 12.4.

An alternative way for classifying an observation into one of the classes is to compute the probability of belonging to each of the classes and assigning the observation to the most likely class. If we have two classes, we need only compute a single probability for each observation (e.g., of belonging to *owners*). Using a cutoff of 0.5 is equivalent to assigning the observation to the class with the highest classification score. The advantage of this approach is that we obtain propensities,

Record ID	Ownership	Prediction: Ownership	Classification Scores	
			Owners	Nonowners
Record 1	owner	non-owner	53.2031351	54.4806799
Record 2	owner	owner	55.4107705	55.3887380
Record 3	owner	owner	72.7587472	71.0425955
Record 4	owner	owner	66.9677142	66.2104702
Record 5	owner	owner	93.2290505	87.7174166
Record 6	owner	owner	79.0987795	74.7266383
Record 7	owner	owner	69.4498492	66.5444871
Record 8	owner	owner	84.8646902	80.7162453
Record 9	owner	owner	65.8162069	64.9353834
Record 10	owner	owner	80.4996642	76.5851656
Record 11	owner	owner	69.0171645	68.3701170
Record 12	owner	owner	70.9712354	68.8876483
Record 13	non-owner	owner	66.2070211	65.0388896
Record 14	non-owner	non-owner	63.2303185	63.3450782
Record 15	non-owner	non-owner	48.7050463	50.4437073
Record 16	non-owner	non-owner	56.9195956	58.3106400
Record 17	non-owner	owner	59.1397921	58.6399573
Record 18	non-owner	non-owner	44.1902093	47.1783891
Record 19	non-owner	non-owner	39.8251832	43.0473094
Record 20	non-owner	non-owner	55.7806494	56.4568124
Record 21	non-owner	non-owner	36.8568547	40.9676707
Record 22	non-owner	non-owner	43.7910210	47.4607101
Record 23	non-owner	non-owner	25.2831628	30.9175930
Record 24	non-owner	non-owner	34.8115915	38.6151103

FIGURE 12.4   CLASSIFICATION SCORES FOR RIDING-MOWER DATA. THESE SCORES WERE COMPUTED MANUALLY

which can be used for goals such as ranking: we sort the observations in order of descending probabilities and generate lift curves.

Let us assume that there are m classes. To compute the probability of belonging to a certain class k, for a certain observation i, we need to compute all the classification scores $c_1(i), c_2(i), \ldots, c_m(i)$ and combine them using the following formula:

$$P[\text{observation } i(\text{with measurements } x_1, x_2, \ldots, x_p) \text{ belongs to class } k]$$
$$= \frac{e^{c_k(i)}}{e^{c_1(i)} + e^{c_2(i)} + \cdots + e^{c_m(i)}}.$$

In ASDM, these probabilities are computed automatically (see Figure 12.5).

We now have three misclassifications, compared to four in our original (ad hoc) classification. This can be seen in Figure 12.6, which includes the line resulting from the discriminant model.[2]

Finally, the machine learning workflow of applying discriminant analysis to the riding mowers dataset is shown in Figure 12.7.

---

[2]The slope of the line is given by $-a_1/a_2$ and the intercept is $a_1/a_2 \, \overline{x}_1 + \overline{x}_2$, where a_i is the difference between the ith classification function coefficients of owners and nonowners (e.g., here $a_{\text{income}} = 0.43 - 0.33$).

Training: Classification Details

Record ID	Ownership	Prediction: Ownership	PostProb: non-owner	PostProb: owner	Income	Lot Size
Record 1	owner	non-owner	0.7820316	0.2179684	60	18.4
Record 2	owner	owner	0.4944921	0.5055079	85.5	16.8
Record 3	owner	owner	0.1523675	0.8476325	64.8	21.6
Record 4	owner	owner	0.3192449	0.6807551	61.5	20.8
Record 5	owner	owner	0.0040232	0.9959768	87	23.6
Record 6	owner	owner	0.0124668	0.9875332	110.1	19.2
Record 7	owner	owner	0.0518891	0.9481109	108	17.6
Record 8	owner	owner	0.0155435	0.9844565	82.8	22.4
Record 9	owner	owner	0.2930072	0.7069928	69	20
Record 10	owner	owner	0.0195603	0.9804397	93	20.8
Record 11	owner	owner	0.3436552	0.6563448	51	22
Record 12	owner	owner	0.1107023	0.8892977	81	20
Record 13	non-owner	owner	0.2371929	0.7628071	75	19.6
Record 14	non-owner	non-owner	0.5286585	0.4713415	52.8	20.8
Record 15	non-owner	non-owner	0.8505169	0.1494831	64.8	17.2
Record 16	non-owner	non-owner	0.8007589	0.1992411	43.2	20.4
Record 17	non-owner	owner	0.3775795	0.6224205	84	17.6
Record 18	non-owner	non-owner	0.9520373	0.0479627	49.2	17.6
Record 19	non-owner	non-owner	0.9616585	0.0383415	59.4	16
Record 20	non-owner	non-owner	0.6628818	0.3371182	66	18.4
Record 21	non-owner	non-owner	0.9838700	0.0161300	47.4	16.4
Record 22	non-owner	non-owner	0.9751489	0.0248511	33	18.8
Record 23	non-owner	non-owner	0.9964400	0.0035600	51	14
Record 24	non-owner	non-owner	0.9781939	0.0218061	63	14.8

FIGURE 12.5   DISCRIMINANT ANALYSIS OUTPUT FOR RIDING-MOWER DATA, DISPLAYING THE PROPENSITIES (ESTIMATED PROBABILITY) OF OWNERSHIP FOR EACH FAMILY

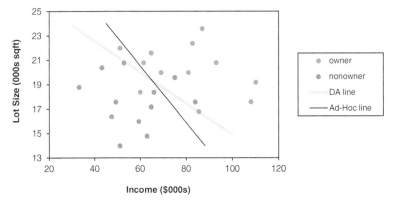

FIGURE 12.6   CLASS SEPARATION OBTAINED FROM THE DISCRIMINANT MODEL (COMPARED TO AD HOC LINE FROM FIGURE 12.1)

FIGURE 12.7   THE MACHINE LEARNING WORKFLOW OF DISCRIMINANT ANALYSIS FOR THE RIDING MOWERS EXAMPLE

12.4 CLASSIFICATION PERFORMANCE OF DISCRIMINANT ANALYSIS

The discriminant analysis method relies on two main assumptions to arrive at classification scores. The first assumption is that the measurements in all classes come from a multivariate normal distribution. When this assumption is reasonably met, discriminant analysis has been proved to be a more powerful tool than other classification methods, such as logistic regression. In fact Efron (1975) showed that discriminant analysis is 30% more efficient than logistic regression if the data are multivariate normal, in the sense that we require 30% fewer observations to arrive at the same results. Moreover, in practice, it has been shown that this method is relatively robust to departures from normality in the sense that predictors can be nonnormal and even dummy variables. This is true as long as the smallest class is sufficiently large (approximately more than 20 observations). This method is also known to be sensitive to outliers in both the univariate space of single predictors and in the multivariate space. Exploratory analysis should therefore be used to locate extreme cases and determine whether they can be eliminated.

The second assumption behind discriminant analysis is that the correlation structure between the different predictors within a class is the same across classes. This can be roughly checked by computing the correlation matrix between the predictors for each class and comparing matrices. If the correlations differ substantially across classes, the classifier will tend to classify cases into the class with the largest variability. When the correlation structure differs significantly and the dataset is very large, an alternative is to use quadratic discriminant analysis.[3]

Notwithstanding the caveats embodied in these statistical assumptions, recall that in a predictive modeling environment, the ultimate test is whether the model works effectively. A reasonable approach is to conduct some exploratory analysis with respect to normality and correlation, train and evaluate a model, and then, depending on classification accuracy and what you learned from the initial exploration, circle back and explore further whether outliers should be examined or choice of variables revisited.

With respect to the evaluation of classification accuracy, we once again use the general measures of performance that were described in Chapter 5 (judging the performance of a classifier), with the principal ones based on the confusion matrix (accuracy alone or combined with costs) for classification and the lift chart for ranking. The same argument for using the validation set for evaluating performance still holds. For example, in the riding-mowers example, families 1, 13, and 17 are misclassified. This means that the model yields an error rate of 12.5% for these data. However, this rate is a biased estimate—it is overly optimistic, since we have used the same data for fitting the classification functions and for estimating the error. Therefore, as with all other models, we test performance on a validation set that includes data that were not involved in estimating the classification functions.

To obtain the confusion matrix from a discriminant analysis, we either use the classification scores directly or the propensities (probabilities of class membership) that are computed from the classification scores. In both cases, we decide on the class assignment of each observation based on the highest score or probability. We then compare these classifications to the actual class memberships of these observations. This yields the confusion matrix.

12.5 PRIOR PROBABILITIES

So far we have assumed that our objective is to minimize the classification error. The method presented above assumes that the chances of encountering an observation from either class are the same. If the probability of encountering an observation for classification in the future is not equal for the different classes, we should modify our functions to reduce our expected (long-run average) error rate. The modification is done as follows: Let p_j denote the prior or future probability of membership in class j (in the two-class case we have p_1 and

---

[3]In practice, quadratic discriminant analysis has not been found useful except when the difference in the correlation matrices is large and the number of observations available for training and testing is large. The reason is that the quadratic model requires estimating many more parameters that are all subject to error [for c classes and p variables, the total number of parameters to be estimated for all the different correlation matrices is $cp(p + 1)/2$].

$p_2 = 1 - p_1$). We modify the classification function for each class by adding $\log(p_j)$.[4] To illustrate this, suppose that the percentage of riding-mower owners in the population is 15%, compared to 50% in the sample. This means that the model should classify fewer households as owners. To account for this distortion, adjust the constants in the classification functions from Figure 12.3 and obtain the adjusted constants $-73.16 + \log(0.15) = -75.06$ for owners and $-51.42 + \log(0.85) = -51.58$ for nonowners. To see how this can affect classifications, consider family 13, which was misclassified as an owner in the case involving equal probability of class membership. When we account for the lower probability of owning a mower in the population, family 13 is classified properly as a nonowner (its owner classification score is below the nonowner score).

12.6 UNEQUAL MISCLASSIFICATION COSTS

A second practical modification is needed when misclassification costs are not symmetrical. If the cost of misclassifying a class 1 item is very different from the cost of misclassifying a class 2 item, we may want to minimize the expected cost of misclassification rather than the simple error rate (which does not account for unequal misclassification costs). In the two-class case, it is easy to manipulate the classification functions to account for differing misclassification costs (in addition to prior probabilities). We denote by q_1 the cost of misclassifying a class 1 member (into class 2). Similarly, q_2 denotes the cost of misclassifying a class 2 member (into class 1). These costs are integrated into the constants of the classification functions by adding $\log(q_1)$ to the constant for class 1 and $\log(q_2)$ to the constant of class 2. To incorporate both prior probabilities and misclassification costs, add $\log(p_1 q_1)$ to the constant of class 1 and $\log(p_2 q_2)$ to that of class 2.

In practice, it is not always simple to come up with misclassification costs q_1 and q_2 for each class. It is usually much easier to estimate the ratio of costs q_2/q_1 (e.g., the cost of misclassifying a credit defaulter is 10 times more expensive than that of misclassifying a nondefaulter). Luckily, the relationship between the classification functions depends only on this ratio. Therefore, we can set $q_1 = 1$ and $q_2 = ratio$ and simply add $\log(q_2/q_1)$ to the constant for class 2.

12.7 CLASSIFYING MORE THAN TWO CLASSES

Example 3: Medical Dispatch to Accident Scenes

Ideally, every automobile accident call to the emergency number 911 results in the immediate dispatch of an ambulance to the accident scene. However, in

---

[4]ASDM by default sets the prior class probabilities as the ratios in the dataset. This is based on the assumption that a random sample will yield a reasonable estimate of membership probabilities.

some cases, the dispatch might be delayed (e.g., at peak accident hours or in some resource-strapped towns or shifts). In such cases, the 911 dispatchers must make decisions about which units to send based on sketchy information. It is useful to augment the limited information provided in the initial call with additional information in order to classify the accident as minor injury, serious injury, or death. For this purpose, we can use data that were collected on automobile accidents in the United States in 2001 that involved some type of injury. For each accident, additional information is recorded, such as day of week, weather conditions, and road type. Table 12.1 shows a small sample of observations with 11 measurements of interest.

TABLE 12.1   SAMPLE OF 20 AUTOMOBILE ACCIDENTS FROM THE 2001 DEPARTMENT OF TRANSPORTATION DATABASE

Accident #	RushH our	WRK_ ZONE	WKDY	INT_ HWY	LGTCON	LEVEL	SPD_ LIM	SUR_ COND	TRAF_ WAY	WEATHER	MAX_SEV
1	1	0	1	1	dark_light	1	70	ice	one_way	adverse	no-injury
2	1	0	1	0	dark_light	0	70	ice	divided	adverse	no-injury
3	1	0	1	0	dark_light	0	65	ice	divided	adverse	non-fatal
4	1	0	1	0	dark_light	0	55	ice	two_way	not_adverse	non-fatal
5	1	0	0	0	dark_light	0	35	snow	one_way	adverse	no-injury
6	1	0	1	0	dark_light	1	35	wet	divided	adverse	no-injury
7	0	0	1	1	dark_light	1	70	wet	divided	adverse	non-fatal
8	0	0	1	0	dark_light	1	35	wet	two_way	adverse	no-injury
9	1	0	1	0	dark_light	0	25	wet	one_way	adverse	non-fatal
10	1	0	1	0	dark_light	0	35	wet	divided	adverse	non-fatal
11	1	0	1	0	dark_light	0	30	wet	divided	adverse	non-fatal
12	1	0	1	0	dark_light	0	60	wet	divided	not_adverse	no-injury
13	1	0	1	0	dark_light	0	40	wet	two_way	not_adverse	no-injury
14	0	0	1	0	day	1	65	dry	two_way	not_adverse	fatal
15	1	0	0	0	day	0	55	dry	two_way	not_adverse	fatal
16	1	0	1	0	day	0	55	dry	two_way	not_adverse	non-fatal
17	1	0	0	0	day	0	55	dry	two_way	not_adverse	non-fatal
18	0	0	1	0	dark	0	55	ice	two_way	not_adverse	no-injury
19	0	0	0	0	dark	0	50	ice	two_way	adverse	no-injury
20	0	0	0	0	dark	1	55	snow	divided	adverse	no-injury

Each accident is classified as one of three injury types (no-injury, nonfatal, or fatal), and has 10 more measurements (extracted from a larger set of measurements)

The goal is to see how well the predictors can be used to classify injury type correctly. To evaluate this, a sample of 1000 observations was drawn and partitioned into training and validation sets, and a discriminant analysis was performed on the training data, using a subset of all the predictors, after multi-category predictors were factored into dummies (see the machine learning workflow in Figure 12.8). The output structure is very similar to that for the two-class case. The only difference is that each observation now has three classification functions (one for each injury type), and the confusion and error matrices are 3×3 to account for all the combinations of correct and incorrect classifications (see Figure 12.9). The rule for classification is still to classify an observation to the class that has the highest corresponding classification score. The classification

FIGURE 12.8   MACHINE LEARNING WORKFLOW OF DISCRIMINANT ANALYSIS FOR THE AUTOMOBILE ACCIDENTS EXAMPLE

(a) Linear Discriminant Functions

Variable	fatal	no-injury	non-fatal
Intercepts	-23.71082	-23.87583	-23.24921
RushHour	0.40034	1.12972	1.19965
WRK_ZONE	1.12540	1.95130	2.55758
WKDY	4.78784	6.22550	6.08453
INT_HWY	-1.75163	-2.10510	-1.82977
LEVEL	0.02803	0.05363	0.35492
SPD_LIM	0.42261	0.43620	0.42318
LGTCON_day	2.99691	3.37616	3.38139
SUR_COND_dry	13.75896	16.10672	16.21842
TRAF_WAY_two_way	7.10198	7.14246	6.97902
WEATHER_adverse	12.72825	16.35121	16.02538

(b) Training: Classification Summary

Confusion Matrix

Actual\Predicted	fatal	no-injury	non-fatal
fatal	0	2	3
no-injury	0	134	155
non-fatal	0	97	209

Error Report

Class	# Cases	# Errors	% Error
fatal	5	5	100
no-injury	289	155	53.633
non-fatal	306	97	31.699
Overall	600	257	42.833

FIGURE 12.9   ASDM'S DISCRIMINANT ANALYSIS OUTPUT FOR THE THREE-CLASS INJURY EXAMPLE: (a) CLASSIFICATION FUNCTIONS AND (b) CONFUSION MATRIX FOR TRAINING SET

scores are computed, as before, using the classification function coefficients. This can be seen in Figure 12.9. For instance, the *no-injury* classification score for the first accident in the training set is $-23.88 + (1.13)(1) + (1.95)(0) + \cdots + (16.35)(1) = 28.58$. The *nonfatal* score is similarly computed as 27.97, and the

Record ID	MAX_SEV	Prediction: MAX_SEV	Score for fatal	Score for non-fatal	Score for no-injury	PostProb: fatal	PostProb: injury	PostProb: non-fatal	RushHour	WRK_ZONE	WKDY	INT_HWY	LGTCON_day	LEVEL	SPD_LIM	SUR_COND_dry	TRAF_two_way	WEATHER_adverse
Record 1	no-injury	no-injury	202.66	234.4927	235.3513	0.001016252	0.525684271	0.473299476	1	0	1	1	1	1	70	0	0	1
Record 5	no-injury	no-injury	94.3095	111.7706	112.3246	0.004894987	0.518674049	0.476430964	1	0	0	0	0	0	35	0	0	1
Record 8	no-injury	no-injury	106.222	124.445	124.6117	0.002341368	0.538157679	0.459500953	0	0	1	0	0	1	35	0	1	1
Record 11	no-injury	non-fatal	84.1128	101.1153	101.5021	0.001293997	0.539421794	0.459284209	1	0	1	1	0	0	30	0	0	1
Record 12	no-injury	no-injury	161.292	186.0488	186.9186	0.032162039	0.538268812	0.429569149	1	0	0	0	0	0	60	0	0	0
Record 15	non-fatal	non-fatal	107.653	125.3303	126.0044	0.00309561	0.412235299	0.58466909	1	0	1	0	0	1	35	1	1	0
Record 16	no-injury	non-fatal	137.622	159.0919	159.8183	0.002911111	0.444107248	0.552981641	0	0	0	0	0	0	45	1	1	0
Record 18	no-injury	non-fatal	157.914	182.0399	183.2006	0.008251756	0.457123035	0.534625209	0	0	1	0	0	0	55	1	1	0
Record 20	non-fatal	non-fatal	187.883	215.8015	217.0145	0.007714622	0.489588933	0.502696444	0	0	0	1	0	0	65	1	0	0
Record 21	non-fatal	non-fatal	115.113	134.6324	135.5091	0.003461538	0.461834891	0.534703571	1	0	1	0	0	0	40	1	1	0
Record 22	no-injury	non-fatal	100.128	117.7516	118.6022	0.003575501	0.445696804	0.550727695	1	0	1	1	0	0	35	1	0	0
Record 23	non-fatal	non-fatal	130.097	151.5132	152.4161	0.003347677	0.478053347	0.518598976	1	0	0	0	0	0	45	1	1	0
Record 24	non-fatal	non-fatal	155.278	179.0493	180.1455	0.012128171	0.47118458	0.516687249	1	0	1	0	0	0	55	1	0	0
Record 25	non-fatal	non-fatal	72.4731	84.90701	85.68271	0.015399047	0.41436037	0.570240583	1	0	0	0	0	0	25	1	0	0
Record 26	non-fatal	non-fatal	132.411	152.4302	153.3106	0.013555377	0.478692174	0.507752449	0	0	0	0	0	1	45	1	1	0
Record 28	no-injury	no-injury	106.83	123.7644	124.3815	0.008010606	0.501395527	0.490593867	0	0	1	0	0	0	35	1	1	1
Record 29	non-fatal	non-fatal	92.2455	108.0133	108.6742	0.003874617	0.469889128	0.526236255	1	0	1	0	0	0	30	1	1	0
Record 32	no-injury	non-fatal	77.2609	91.13251	91.76724	0.004004269	0.453706248	0.542289483	1	0	0	0	0	0	25	1	1	0
Record 33	no-injury	no-injury	167.168	192.4172	193.209	0.003234932	0.551070541	0.445694527	1	0	1	0	0	0	55	1	1	0
Record 35	no-injury	non-fatal	99.1196	117.3026	117.6326	0.002253968	0.497517581	0.500228451	0	0	1	0	0	1	35	0	0	1

FIGURE 12.10   CLASSIFICATION SCORES, MEMBERSHIP PROBABILITIES, AND CLASSIFICATIONS FOR THE THREE-CLASS INJURY TRAINING DATASET

fatal score as 21.89. Since the *no-injury* score is highest, this accident is (correctly) classified as having no injuries.

We can also compute for each accident the propensities (estimated probabilities) of belonging to each of the three classes using the same relationship between classification scores and probabilities as in the two-class case. For instance, the probability of the accident above involving nonfatal injuries is estimated by the model as

$$\frac{e^{27.97}}{e^{28.58} + e^{27.97} + e^{21.89}} = 0.35. \tag{12.3}$$

The probabilities of an accident involving no injuries or fatal injuries are computed in a similar manner. For the first accident in the training set, the highest probability is that of involving no injuries, and therefore it is classified as a *no-injury* accident (see Figure 12.10). In general, membership probabilities can be obtained directly from ASDM for the training set, the validation set, and new observations.

12.8 ADVANTAGES AND WEAKNESSES

Discriminant analysis is typically considered more of a statistical classification method than a machine learning method. This is reflected in its absence or short mention in many machine learning resources. However, it is very popular in social sciences and has shown good performance. The use and performance of discriminant analysis are similar to those of multiple linear regression. The two methods therefore share several advantages and weaknesses.

Like linear regression, discriminant analysis searches for the optimal weighting of predictors. In linear regression, weighting is with relation to the numerical response, whereas in discriminant analysis it is with relation to separating the classes. Both use least squares for estimation and the resulting estimates are robust to local optima.

In both methods, an underlying assumption is normality. In discriminant analysis, we assume that the predictors are approximately from a multivariate normal distribution. Although this assumption is violated in many practical situations (e.g., with commonly used binary predictors), the method is surprisingly robust. According to Hastie et al. (2001), the reason may be that data can usually support only simple separation boundaries, such as linear boundaries. However, for continuous variables that are found to be very skewed (as can be seen through a histogram), transformations such as the log transform can improve performance. In addition, the method's sensitivity to outliers commands exploring the data for extreme values and removing those observations from the analysis.

An advantage of discriminant analysis as a classifier is that it provides estimates of single-predictor contributions (it is like logistic regression in this respect).[5] This is useful for obtaining a ranking of predictor importance and for variable selection.

Finally, the method is computationally simple, parsimonious, and especially useful for small datasets. With its parametric form, discriminant analysis makes the most out of the data and is therefore especially useful with small samples (as explained in Section 12.4).

---

[5]Comparing predictor contribution requires normalizing all the predictors before running discriminant analysis. Then each coefficient is compared across the two classification functions: coefficients with large differences indicate a predictor with high separation power.

PROBLEMS

12.1 **Personal Loan Acceptance.** Universal Bank is a relatively young bank growing rapidly in terms of overall customer acquisition. The majority of these customers are liability customers with varying sizes of relationship with the bank. The customer base of asset customers is quite small, and the bank is interested in expanding this base rapidly to bring in more loan business. In particular, it wants to explore ways of converting its liability customers to personal loan customers.

A campaign the bank ran for liability customers last year showed a healthy conversion rate of over 9% successes. This has encouraged the retail marketing department to devise smarter campaigns with better target marketing. The goal of our analysis is to model the previous campaign's customer behavior to analyze what combination of factors make a customer more likely to accept a personal loan. This will serve as the basis for the design of a new campaign.

The file `UniversalBank.xlsx` contains data on 5000 customers. The data include customer demographic information (e.g., age, income), the customer's relationship with the bank (e.g., mortgage, securities account), and the customer response to the last personal loan campaign (Personal Loan). Among these 5000 customers, only 480 (= 9.6%) accepted the personal loan that was offered to them in the previous campaign.

Partition the data (60% training and 40% validation) and then perform a discriminant analysis that models Personal Loan as a function of the remaining predictors (excluding zip code). Remember to turn categorical predictors with more than two categories into dummy variables first. Specify the success class as 1 (loan acceptance), and use the default cutoff value of 0.5.

a. Compute summary statistics for the predictors separately for loan acceptors and nonacceptors. For continuous predictors, compute the mean and standard deviation. For categorical predictors, compute the percentages. Are there predictors where the two classes differ substantially?

b. Examine the model performance on the validation set.

   i. What is the misclassification rate?

   ii. Is one type of misclassification more likely than the other?

   iii. Select three customers who were misclassified as acceptors and three who were misclassified as nonacceptors. The goal is to determine why they are misclassified. First, examine their probability of being classified as acceptors: is it close to the threshold of 0.5? If not, compare their predictor values to the summary statistics of the two classes to determine why they were misclassified.

c. As in many marketing campaigns, it is more important to identify customers who will accept the offer rather than customers who will not accept it. Therefore, a good model should be especially accurate at detecting acceptors. Examine the lift chart and decile chart for the validation set and interpret them in light of this ranking goal.

d. Compare the results from the discriminant analysis with those from a logistic regression (both with cutoff 0.5 and the same predictors). Examine the confusion matrices, the lift charts, and the decile charts. Which method performs better on your validation set in detecting the acceptors?

e. The bank is planning to continue its campaign by sending its offer to 1000 additional customers. Suppose that the cost of sending the offer is $1 and the profit from an accepted offer is $50. What is the expected profitability of this campaign?

f. The cost of misclassifying a loan acceptor customer as a nonacceptor is much higher than the opposite misclassification cost. To minimize the expected cost of misclassification, should the cutoff value for classification (which is currently at 0.5) be increased or decreased?

12.2 Identifying Good System Administrators. A management consultant is studying the roles played by experience and training in a system administrator's ability to complete a set of tasks in a specified amount of time. In particular, she is interested in discriminating between administrators who are able to complete given tasks within a specified time and those who are not. Data are collected on the performance of 75 randomly selected administrators. They are stored in the file SystemAdministrators.xlsx.

Using these data, the consultant performs a discriminant analysis. The variable Experience measures months of full-time system administrator experience, while Training measures number of relevant training credits. The dependent variable Completed is either *Yes* or *No*, according to whether or not the administrator completed the tasks.

a. Create a scatter plot of Experience vs. Training using color or symbol to differentiate administrators who completed the tasks from those who did not complete them. See if you can identify a line that separates the two classes with minimum misclassification.

b. Run a discriminant analysis with both predictors using the entire dataset as training data. Among those who completed the tasks, what is the percentage of administrators who are classified incorrectly as failing to complete the tasks?

c. Compute the two classification scores for an administrator with four months of experience and six credits of training. Based on these, how would you classify this administrator?

d. How much experience must be accumulated by an administrator with four training credits before his or her estimated probability of completing the tasks exceeds 0.5?

e. Compare the classification accuracy of this model to that resulting from a logistic regression with cutoff 0.5.

12.3 Detecting Spam Email (from the UCI Machine Learning Repository). A team at Hewlett-Packard collected data on a large number of email messages from their postmaster and personal email for the purpose of finding a classifier that can separate email messages that are spam vs. nonspam (a.k.a. "ham"). The spam concept is diverse: it includes advertisements for products or websites, "make money fast" schemes, chain letters, pornography, and so on. The definition used here is "unsolicited commercial email." The file Spambase.xlsx contains information on 4601 email messages, among which 1813 are tagged "spam." The predictors include 57 attributes, most of them are the average number of times a certain word (e.g., mail, George) or symbol (e.g., #, !) appears in the email. A few predictors are related to the number and length of capitalized words.

a. To reduce the number of predictors to a manageable size, examine how each predictor differs between the spam and nonspam emails by comparing the spam-class average and nonspam-class average. Which are the 11 predictors that appear to vary the most between spam and nonspam emails? From these 11, which words or signs occur more often in spam?

b. Partition the data into training and validation sets; then perform a discriminant analysis on the training data using only the 11 predictors.

c. If we are interested mainly in detecting spam messages, is this model useful? Use the confusion matrix, lift chart, and decile chart for the validation set for the evaluation.

d. In the sample, almost 40% of the email messages were tagged as spam. However, suppose that the actual proportion of spam messages in these email accounts is 10%. Compute the constants of the classification functions to account for this information.

e. A spam filter that is based on your model is used, so that only messages that are classified as nonspam are delivered, while messages that are classified as spam are quarantined. In this case, misclassifying a nonspam email (as spam) has much heftier results. Suppose that the cost of quarantining a nonspam email is 20 times that of not detecting a spam message. Compute the constants of the classification functions to account for these costs (assume that the proportion of spam is reflected correctly by the sample proportion).

## CHAPTER 13

Generating, Comparing, and Combining Multiple Models

The previous chapters in this part of the book introduced different supervised methods for prediction and classification. Earlier, in Chapter 5, we learned about evaluating predictive performance, which can be used to compare several models and choose the best one. In this chapter, we look at collections of supervised models. First, we look at an approach for handling multiple models called *ensembles*, which combines multiple supervised models into a "super-model." Instead of choosing a single predictive model, we can combine several models to achieve improved predictive accuracy. We explain the underlying logic of why ensembles can improve predictive accuracy and introduce popular approaches for combining models, including simple averaging, bagging, and boosting. Secondly, we introduce the idea of *automated machine learning*, or *AutoML*, which allows us to automatically train many supervised models and see their resulting performance. While in previous chapters we have shown how to manually tune parameters for each supervised method, AutoML automates the full pipeline from data loading to generating a rank-ordered list of candidate models with automatic parameter tuning. We illustrate this process and its results using the *Find Best Model* option within ASDM's Classify and Predict menus and highlight some of its key features.

Machine Learning for Business Analytics: Concepts, Techniques, and Applications with Analytic Solver® Data Mining, Fourth Edition. Galit Shmueli, Peter C. Bruce, Kuber R. Deokar, and Nitin R. Patel
© 2023 John Wiley & Sons, Inc. Published 2023 by John Wiley & Sons, Inc.

13.1 ENSEMBLES[1]

Ensembles played a major role in the million-dollar Netflix Prize contest that started in 2006. At the time, Netflix, the largest DVD rental service in the United States, wanted to improve their movie recommendation system (from www.netflixprize.com):

> Netflix is all about connecting people to the movies they love. To help customers find those movies, we've developed our world-class movie recommendation system: Cinematch[SM]…And while Cinematch is doing pretty well, it can always be made better.

In a bold move, the company decided to share a large amount of data on movie ratings by their users, and set up a contest, open to the public, aimed at improving their recommendation system:

> We provide you with a lot of anonymous rating data, and a prediction accuracy bar that is 10% better than what Cinematch can do on the same training data set.

During the contest, an active leader-board showed the results of the competing teams. An interesting behavior started appearing: Different teams joined forces to create combined, or *ensemble* predictions, which proved more accurate than the individual predictions. The winning team, called "BellKor's Pragmatic Chaos" combined results from the "BellKor" and "Big Chaos" teams alongside additional members. In a 2010 article in *Chance* magazine, the Netflix Prize winners described the power of their ensemble approach:

> An early lesson of the competition was the value of combining sets of predictions from multiple models or algorithms. If two prediction sets achieved similar RMSEs, it was quicker and more effective to simply average the two sets than to try to develop a new model that incorporated the best of each method. Even if the RMSE for one set was much worse than the other, there was almost certainly a linear combination that improved on the better set.

Why Ensembles Can Improve Predictive Power

The principle of combining methods is popular for reducing risk. For example, in finance, portfolios are created for reducing investment risk. The return from a portfolio is typically less risky, because the variation is smaller than each of the individual components.

THE WISDOM OF CROWDS

In his book *The Wisdom of Crowds*, James Surowiecki recounts how Francis Galton, a prominent statistician from the 19th century, watched a contest at a county fair in England. The contest's objective was to guess the weight of an ox. Individual contest entries were highly variable, but the mean of all the estimates was surprisingly accurate—within 1% of the true weight of the ox. On balance, the errors from multiple guesses tended to cancel one another out. You can think of the output of a predictive model as a more informed version of these guesses. Averaging together multiple guesses will yield a more precise answer than the vast majority of the individual guesses. Note that in Galton's story, there were a few (lucky) individuals who scored better than the average. An ensemble estimate will not always be more accurate than all the individual estimates in all cases, but it will be more accurate most of the time.

In predictive modeling, "risk" is equivalent to variation in prediction error. The more our prediction errors vary, the more volatile our predictive model. Consider predictions from two different models for a set of n records. $e_{1,i}$ is the prediction error for the ith record by method 1 and $e_{2,i}$ is the prediction error for the same record by method 2.

Suppose that each model produces prediction errors that are, on average, zero (for some records the model over-predicts and for some it under-predicts, but on average the error is zero):

$$E(e_{1,i}) = E(e_{2,i}) = 0.$$

If, for each record, we take an average of the two predictions: $\overline{y}_i = \frac{\hat{y}_{1,i} + \hat{y}_{2,i}}{2}$, then the expected mean error will also be zero:

$$
\begin{aligned}
E\left(y_i - \overline{y}_i\right) &= E\left(y_i - \frac{\hat{y}_{1,i} + \hat{y}_{2,i}}{2}\right) \quad\quad\quad\quad (13.1)\\
&= E\left(\frac{y_i - \hat{y}_{1,i}}{2} + \frac{y_i - \hat{y}_{2,i}}{2}\right) = E\left(\frac{e_{1,i} + e_{2,i}}{2}\right) = 0.
\end{aligned}
$$

This means that the ensemble has the same mean error as the individual models. Now let us examine the variance of the ensemble's prediction errors:

$$\mathrm{Var}\left(\frac{e_{1,i} + e_{2,i}}{2}\right) = \frac{1}{4}\left(\mathrm{Var}(e_{1,i}) + \mathrm{Var}(e_{2,i})\right) + \frac{1}{4} \times 2\mathrm{Cov}\left(e_{1,i}, e_{2,i}\right). \quad (13.2)$$

This variance can be lower than each of the individual variances $\mathrm{Var}(e_{1,i})$ and $\mathrm{Var}(e_{2,i})$ under some circumstances. A key component is the covariance (or equivalently, correlation) between the two prediction errors. The case of no correlation leaves us with a quantity that can be smaller than each of the individual variances. The variance of the average prediction error will be even smaller when the two prediction errors are negatively correlated.

In summary, using an average of two predictions can potentially lead to smaller error variance and therefore better predictive power. These results generalize to more than two methods; you can combine results from multiple prediction methods or classifiers.

Simple Averaging or Voting

The simplest approach for creating an ensemble is to combine the predictions, classifications, or propensities from multiple models. For example, we might have a linear regression model, a regression tree, and a k-NN algorithm. We use each of the three methods to score, say, a test set. We then combine the three sets of results.

The three models can also be variations that use the same algorithm. For example, we might have three linear regression models, each using a different set of predictors.

Combining Predictions   In prediction tasks, where the outcome variable is numerical, we can combine the predictions from the different methods simply by taking an average. In the above example, for each record in the test set, we have three predictions (one from each model). The ensemble prediction is then the average of the three values.

One alternative to a simple average is taking the median prediction, which would be less affected by extreme predictions. Another possibility is computing a weighted average, where weights are proportional to a quantity of interest. For instance, weights can be proportional to the accuracy of the model, or if different data sources are used, the weights can be proportional to the quality of the data.

Ensembles for prediction are useful not only in cross-sectional prediction, but also in time series forecasting (see Chapters 17–19). In forecasting, the same approach of combining future forecasts from multiple methods can lead to more precise predictions. One example is the weather forecasting application mobile app Dark Sky (formerly Forecast.io, www.darksky.net/app), which described their algorithm as follows:

> Forecast.io is backed by a wide range of data sources, which are aggregated
> together statistically to provide the most accurate forecast possible for a given
> location.

Combining Classifications   In the case of classification, combining the results from multiple classifiers can be done using "voting": For each record, we have multiple classifications. A simple rule would be to choose the most popular class among these classifications. For example, we might use a classification tree, a naive Bayes classifier, and discriminant analysis for classifying a binary outcome. For each record, we then generate three predicted classes. Simple voting would choose the most common class among the three.

As in prediction, we can assign heavier weights to scores from some models, based on considerations such as model accuracy or data quality. This would be done by setting a "majority rule" that is different from 50%.

Combining Propensities   Similar to predictions, propensities can be combined by taking a simple (or weighted) average. Recall that some algorithms, such as naive Bayes (see Chapter 8), produce biased propensities and should therefore not be simply averaged with propensities from other methods.

Bagging

Another form of ensembles is based on averaging across multiple random data samples. *Bagging*, short for "bootstrap aggregating," comprises two steps:

1. Generate multiple random samples (by sampling with replacement from the original data)—this method is called "bootstrap sampling."
2. Running an algorithm on each sample and producing scores.

Bagging improves the performance stability of a model and helps avoid overfitting by separately modeling different data samples and then combining the results. It is therefore especially useful for algorithms such as trees and neural networks.

Boosting

Boosting is a slightly different approach to creating ensembles that sequentially builds better models by leveraging the prediction errors from the previous model. Here the goal is to directly improve areas in the data where our model makes errors, by forcing the model to pay more attention to those records. The steps in boosting are:

1. Fit a model to the data.
2. Draw a sample from the data so that misclassified records (or records with large prediction errors) have higher probabilities of selection.
3. Fit the model to the new sample.
4. Repeat Steps 2–3 multiple times.

Bagging and Boosting in ASDM

Bagging and boosting can be applied to any supervised machine learning method. ASDM's *Ensemble—Bagging* and *Ensemble—Boosting* menus provide ensembles based on a tree, linear and logistic regression, k-NN, naive Bayes, discriminant analysis, and a neural network. The user selects the algorithm (called "Weak Learner") and the number of random samples (for bagging) or repetitions (for boosting) (see Figure 13.1).

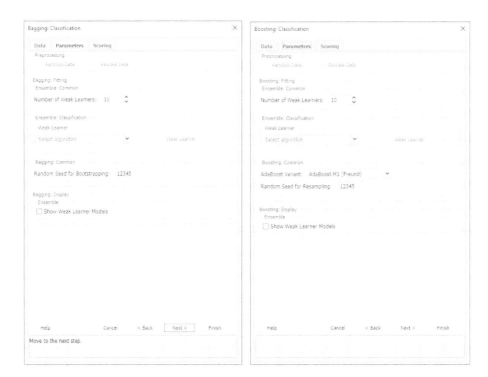

FIGURE 13.1   ASDM'S BAGGING (LEFT) AND BOOSTING (RIGHT)) DIALOG BOXES, WHERE THE USER SELECTS THE ALGORITHM (WEAK LEARNER) AND THE NUMBER OF WEAK LEARNERS

In practice, however, most applications are for trees, where bagging and boosting have proved extremely effective. In Chapter 9, we described random forests, an ensemble based on bagged trees, and boosted trees, in which the model focuses on misclassified records. In ASDM, both the *Ensemble—Bagging* and *Ensemble—Random Forest* procedures can be used to generate bagged trees, while *Ensemble—Boosting* can be used to generate boosted trees. We illustrate these three tree ensemble options by applying them to the personal loan data. Figure 13.2 compares the ROC curves of a single tree with the three tree ensembles (bagged trees, random forest, and boosted trees), each applied to the personal loan validation dataset. We see that, for these data, the bagged and boosted trees show a slight improvement over the single tree in certain parts of the ROC curve.

Advantages and Weaknesses of Ensembles

Combining scores from multiple models is aimed at generating more precise predictions (lowering the prediction error variance). The ensemble approach is most useful when the combined models generate prediction errors that are negatively associated, but it can also be useful when the correlation is low. Ensembles can use simple averaging, weighted averaging, voting, medians, etc. Models can

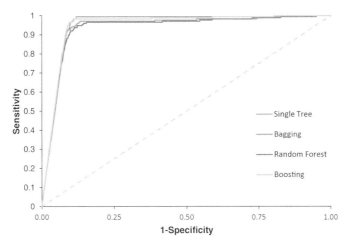

FIGURE 13.2   EXAMPLE OF THREE TREE ENSEMBLES (VS. SINGLE TREE) FOR THE PERSONAL
LOAN DATA (VALIDATION SET): ROC CURVES FOR SINGLE TREE, BAGGED TREES,
RANDOM FOREST, AND BOOSTED TREES

be based on the same algorithm or on different algorithms, using the same sample or different samples. Ensembles have become a major strategy for participants in machine learning contests (e.g., Kaggle), where the goal is to optimize some predictive measure. In that sense, ensembles also provide an operational way to obtain solutions with high predictive power in a fast way, by engaging multiple teams of "data crunchers" working in parallel and combining their results.

Ensembles that are based on different data samples help avoid overfitting. However, remember that you can also overfit the data with an ensemble if you tweak it (e.g., choosing the "best" weights when using a weighted average).

The major disadvantage of an ensemble is the resources that it requires: computationally, as well as in terms of software availability and the analyst's skill and time investment. Ensembles that combine results from different algorithms require developing each of the models and evaluating them. Boosting-type ensembles and bagging-type ensembles do not require such effort, but they do have a computational cost (although boosting can be parallelized easily). Ensembles that rely on multiple data sources require collecting and maintaining multiple data sources. And finally, ensembles are "blackbox" methods, in that the relationship between the predictors and the outcome variable usually becomes nontransparent.

13.2 AUTOMATED MACHINE LEARNING (AUTOML)

Machine learning platforms have now started incorporating features for automating the machine learning workflow from data loading to generating a rank-ordered list of candidate models with automatic parameter tuning. This is called *automated machine learning* or *AutoML*. As we have seen in previous chapters, ASDM provides a consistent interface to a large variety of machine learning models, and it is straightforward to train a variety of models and rank them based on their performance. ASDM's *Find Best Model* option within each of the *Classify* and *Predict* menus provides a complete *AutoML* implementation.

The steps in this example follow the general machine learning steps shown earlier in Figure 2.1 and are discussed next in the context of the personal loan example.

AutoML: Explore and Clean Data

Once the data relevant to the business purpose is imported and loaded, machine learning platforms vary in terms of the integration of data preparation steps as part of the AutoML process. Most platforms support some elementary tasks related to data transformation and feature selection; however, since these steps rightly require domain knowledge application, they are handled separately or in a semi-automatic manner. In ASDM, the *Data Analysis* menu can be used for data exploration and transformation.

AutoML: Determine Machine Learning Task

ASDM's *Find Best Model* supports classification (including binary and multi-class classification) and prediction of a numerical outcome. The specific task is selected based on the type of the outcome variable. In the personal loan dataset, the outcome variable *Personal Loan* is a categorical (here binary) variable. We therefore use *Find Best Model* within the *Classify* menu.

If one class has many more records than the other, we call the dataset *imbalanced*. For imbalanced datasets, we can use *Partition with Oversampling* in ASDM to oversample the minority class and thus obtain a balanced representation of both classes in the partitioned data. In the personal loan case, 90% of the records belong to the *No* class, and only 10% belong to the *Yes* class. We could potentially build models with and without balancing during training.

AutoML: Choose Features and Machine Learning Methods

At this step, we select the features to be used as predictors in the supervised model. ASDM has *Feature Selection* capability (under the *Explore* menu) which can used for selecting appropriate predictors. As is the case when fitting individual models, the decision should be guided by considerations of data quality and regulatory/ethical requirements (in some applications some variables are forbidden, such as using gender in loan applications in the USA). We also select the machine learning algorithms we'd like to run. Considerations include potential run time (for example, some algorithms might take much longer to train, and/or to score), and the suitability of the algorithm to the type and size of our data and our goal. For example, k-nearest neighbors requires a large training sample; simple classification and regression trees are not stable and can result in different trees for slightly different data; linear and logistic regression without regularization have trouble with highly correlated predictors.

Figure 13.3 shows the different machine learning algorithms available under the *Find Best Model* option for applying AutoML in ASDM.

FIGURE 13.3   ASDM'S FIND BEST MODEL (AUTOML) OPTIONS FOR CLASSIFICATION TASK

ASDM's *Find Best Model* model-building phase explores regression models (linear or logistic), k-nearest neighbors, classification or regression trees (called decision tree), neural networks, discriminant analysis (for classification), bagging, boosting, and random forest (called Random Trees).

To illustrate this procedure, we use the personal loan data and fit a (single) tree, k-NN, a neural network, logistic regression, bagging, boosting, and random forest, keeping their default parameters, except for tree, where we select pruning (the default is no pruning). We partition the data (50% training, 30% validation, and 20% test) using the random seed 12345.

AutoML: Evaluate Model Performance

The result of *Find Best Model* shows the performance of each trained model on the training and on the validation sets. Figure 13.4 shows the training and validation performance output obtained using *Find Best Model* on the personal loan example. The best performing model, marked in red, is the decision tree. This model performed best in terms of validation accuracy. Bagging and boosting performed almost as well.

Model Performance: Training

Metric	Accuracy (#correct)	Accuracy (%correct)	Specificity	Sensitivity	Precision	F1 score
Logistic Regression	2378	95.1200	0.9849	0.6408	0.8220	0.7202
Decision Tree	2472	98.8800	0.9982	0.9020	0.9822	0.9404
Nearest Neighbors	2500	100.0000	1.0000	1.0000	1.0000	1.0000
Neural Network	2255	90.2000	1.0000	0.0000	N/A	N/A
Bagging	2499	99.9600	1.0000	0.9959	1.0000	0.9980
Boosting	2500	100.0000	1.0000	1.0000	1.0000	1.0000
Random Trees	2488	99.5200	1.0000	0.9510	1.0000	0.9749

Model Performance: Validation

Metric	Accuracy (#correct)	Accuracy (%correct)	Specificity	Sensitivity	Precision	F1 score
Logistic Regression	1422	94.8000	0.9787	0.6449	0.7542	0.6953
Decision Tree	1483	98.8667	0.9971	0.9058	0.9690	0.9363
Nearest Neighbors	1360	90.6667	0.9501	0.4783	0.4925	0.4853
Neural Network	1362	90.8000	1.0000	0.0000	N/A	N/A
Bagging	1480	98.6667	0.9963	0.8913	0.9609	0.9248
Boosting	1480	98.6667	0.9978	0.8768	0.9758	0.9237
Random Trees	1476	98.4000	0.9985	0.8406	0.9831	0.9063

FIGURE 13.4   OUTPUT FROM ASDM'S "FIND BEST MODEL" PROCEDURE APPLIED TO THE PERSONAL LOAN DATA. MODEL PERFORMANCE ON TRAINING DATA (TOP) AND VALIDATION DATA (BOTTOM)

Because we used the validation set to compare and select the best model, the validation performance is over-optimistic. We therefore need to evaluate performance on the test set to estimate potential performance at deployment. ASDM provides the top performer's performance on the test set, if the data were partitioned into training/validation/test. Figure 13.5 shows performance of the best model (tree) on the test loan acceptance data. We see that the tree performs well, but slightly worse than on the validation set, with 1.9% overall error (98.1 accuracy).

Testing: Classification Summary

Confusion Matrix

Actual\Predicted	0	1
0	899	4
1	15	82

Error Report

Class	# Cases	# Errors	% Error
0	903	4	0.44
1	97	15	15.46
Overall	1000	19	1.90

FIGURE 13.5   ACCURACY OF BEST MODEL MODEL ON TEST DATA (PERSONAL LOAN DATA)

AutoML: Model Deployment

In general, full deployment solutions usually require tailored solutions with engineering considerations (see Section 2.8 in Chapter 2). ASDM provides a facility for converting trained models to what is called a Rason cloud-based model (see https://rason.com), where it can be embedded in other processes. See https://youtu.be/kmVPp15u13oo for more detail.

The machine learning workflow applying ASDM's *Find Best Model* to the personal loan data is shown in Figure 13.6.

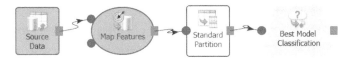

FIGURE 13.6   MACHINE LEARNING WORKFLOW APPLYING "FIND BEST MODEL" TO THE PERSONAL LOAN DATA

Advantages and Weaknesses of Automated Machine Learning

Automated machine learning functionality, such as ASDM's *Find Best Model*, can be a valuable tool for beginners and advanced data scientists. For beginners, it can provide a useful starting point for quickly experimenting with a dataset for a business problem by building predictive models that can then be used for further understanding and learning. For advanced users, it can save time in creating common machine learning workflows by relying on automated model selection and tuning for getting quick insights into a business problem before spending extensive efforts on fine-tuning models.

Automated machine learning has the additional advantage of providing transparency in modeling. By analyzing the final model resulting from the AutoML process, the data scientist can spend more efforts in data understanding, preparation, feature generation, and so on. Also, the data scientist can focus on further fine tuning the models of interest. For example, consider an AutoML implementation that optimizes a decision tree by only changing the *Limit Number of Levels* parameter. What would be the effect of changing other parameters such as *Limit Number of Records in Terminal Nodes*? While automated machine learning speeds up the general model tuning process by considering important model parameters, depending on the problem context or the nature of the data, the data scientist would need to consider further model tuning.

The major disadvantage of automated machine learning is its deceptive ability to hide attention to key business related details and questions. Since the AutoML process lends itself to importing and loading data and generating results fairly quickly, data scientists may not spend adequate time in understanding the nuances of data, exploring and preparing it for the modeling phase, which can lead to garbage-in, garbage-out outcomes, and thoughtless models.

13.3 SUMMARY

In practice, the methods discussed earlier in this book are often used not in isolation, but as building blocks in an analytic process whose goal is always to inform and provide insight.

In this chapter, we looked at two ways that multiple models are deployed, and at ways in which predicted values can be investigated. In ensembles, multiple models are weighted and combined to produce improved predictions. Through automated machine learning, the machine learning process of selecting, applying, and tuning different models for better model performance can be made more efficient, while focusing on evaluating the results and comparing the models.

PROBLEMS

13.1 **Acceptance of Consumer Loan.** Universal Bank has begun a program to encourage its existing customers to borrow via a consumer loan program. The bank has promoted the loan to 5000 customers, of whom 480 accepted the offer. The data are available in dataset *UniversalBank.xlsx*. The bank now wants to develop a model to predict which customers have the greatest probability of accepting the loan, to reduce promotion costs and send the offer only to a subset of its customers.

We will develop several models, then combine them in an ensemble. The models we will use are (1) logistic regression, (2) k-nearest neighbors with $k = 3$, and (3) classification trees. Preprocess the data as follows:

- Zip code can be ignored.

- Partition the data: 60% training, 40% validation.

   a. Fit models to the data for (1) logistic regression, (2) k-nearest neighbors with $k = 3$, and (3) classification trees. Use Personal Loan as the outcome variable. Report the validation confusion matrix for each of the three models.

   b. Create a data frame with the actual outcome, predicted outcome, and each of the three models. Report the first 10 rows of this data frame.

   c. Add two columns to this data frame for (1) a majority vote of predicted outcomes, and (2) the average of the predicted probabilities. Using the classifications generated by these two methods, derive a confusion matrix for each method and report the overall accuracy.

   d. Compare the error rates for the three individual methods and the two ensemble methods.

13.2 **eBay Auctions—Boosting and Bagging.** Using the eBay auction data (file *eBayAuctions.xlsx*) with variable Competitive as the outcome variable, partition the data into training (60%) and validation (40%).

   a. Run a classification tree, using *prune (using validation set)* and leaving other parameters at their default settings. Looking at the validation set, what is the overall accuracy? What is the lift on the first decile?

   b. Run a boosted tree with the same predictors set the Weak Learner parameter to Decision Tree and leaving other parameters at their default. For the validation set, what is the overall accuracy? What is the lift on the first decile?

   c. Run a bagged tree with the same predictors set Week Learner parameter to Decision Tree and leaving other parameters at their default. For the validation set, what is the overall accuracy? What is the lift on the first decile?

   d. Run a random forest. Compare the bagged tree to the random forest in terms of validation accuracy and lift on first decile. How are the two methods conceptually different?

13.3 **Predicting Delayed Flights (Boosting).** The dataset *FlightDelays.xlsx* contains information on all commercial flights departing the Washington, DC area and arriving at New York during January 2004. For each flight there is information on the departure and arrival airports, the distance of the route, the scheduled time and date of the flight, and so on. The variable that we are trying to predict is whether or not a flight is delayed. A delay is defined as an arrival that is at least 15 minutes later than scheduled.

Data Preprocessing. Transform variable day of week info a categorical variable. Bin the scheduled departure time into eight bins using Transform menu in ASDM. Partition the data into training (60%) and validation (40%).

Run a boosted classification tree for delay. Leave the default number of weak learners, and select resampling.

a. Compared with the single tree, how does the boosted tree behave in terms of overall accuracy?

b. Compared with the single tree, how does the boosted tree behave in terms of accuracy in identifying delayed flights?

c. Explain why this model might have the best performance over the other models you fit.

Intervention and User Feedback

## CHAPTER 14

Interventions: Experiments, Uplift Modeling, and Reinforcement Learning

In this chapter, we describe a third paradigm of machine learning, different from supervised and unsupervised learning, that deals with interventions and feedback. Data used in supervised and unsupervised learning are typically *observational data*, being passively collected about the entities of interest (customers, households, transactions, flights, etc.). In contrast, in this chapter we discuss *experimental* data, resulting from applying interventions to the entities of interest, and measuring the outcomes of those interventions. We start with the simplest form of intervention—the A/B test, which is a randomized experiment for testing the causal effect of a treatment or intervention on outcomes of interest. A/B tests are routinely used by internet platforms such as Google, Microsoft, and Uber for testing new features. We then describe *uplift modeling*, a method that combines A/B testing with supervised learning for providing customized targeting. Uplift modeling is commonly used in direct marketing and in political analytics. Finally, we describe *reinforcement learning*, a general machine learning methodology used in personalization, where the algorithm (or *agent*) learns the best treatment assignment policy by interacting with experimental units through dynamic treatment assignment, and gathering their feedback.

14.1 A/B TESTING

A/B testing is the marketing industry's term for a standard scientific experiment in which results can be tracked for each individual experiment. The idea is to test one treatment against another, or a treatment against a control. "Treatment"

Machine Learning for Business Analytics: Concepts, Techniques, and Applications with Analytic Solver® Data Mining, Fourth Edition. Galit Shmueli, Peter C. Bruce, Kuber R. Deokar, and Nitin R. Patel

is simply the term for the intervention you are testing: In a medical trial it is typically a drug, device, vaccine, or other therapy; in marketing it is typically an offering to a consumer—for example, an e-mail, online ad, push notification, or a webpage shown to a consumer. A display ad in a magazine would not generally qualify, unless it had a specific call to action that allowed the marketer to trace the action (e.g., purchase) to a given ad, plus the ability to split the magazine distribution randomly and provide a different offer to each segment of consumers.

A/B testing has become extremely popular online. Amazon, Microsoft, Facebook, Google, and similar companies conduct thousands to tens of thousands of A/B tests each year, on millions of users, testing user interface changes, enhancements to algorithms (search, ads, personalization, recommendation, etc.), changes to apps, content management system, and more.[1] A/B testing on an internet or mobile platform involves randomizing user traffic to one of two experiences (current version and new version), computing the difference in relevant outcome metrics between the two groups, and performing statistical tests to rule out differences that are likely due to noise.

In an A/B test, a "subject" can be an individual customer, a user, an online user session, or any unit of interest.

An important element of A/B testing is random allocation—the treatments are assigned or delivered to subjects randomly. That way, any difference between treatments A and B can be attributed to the treatment (unless it is due to chance). For this reason, A/B tests are extremely popular in online advertising, where it is relatively easy to randomly serve different ad designs or content ("treatments") to different users, and where user reactions are automatically recorded. A/B tests are also routinely used by internet platforms and website owners for evaluating new small intended improvements to the user interface design, such as changing the color of a submit button or adding a new navigation link. For example, Optimizely describes a case study showing how Electronic Arts, the maker of the popular SimCity franchise, created and tested several different versions of their pre-order webpage. They hypothesized that placing a call-to-action higher on the webpage by changing the way the promotional offer was displayed could drive more purchases and increase revenue generated from SimCity.com. Using A/B testing, they found that, contrary to their hypothesis, the version *without* a special promotion offer across the top of the page performed 43% better than the other variation.[2]

In an A/B test, only two measurements are needed for each subject: which treatment it received (A or B) and the outcome. For example, in an online advertising A/B test that compares a new ad design to an existing one, for each

---

[1]See *Trustworthy online controlled experiments: A practical guide to A/B testing* by Kohavi et al. (2020).
[2]https://www.optimizely.com/insights/blog/ea_simcity_optimizely_casestudy/

user we would record which ad they were served (*Treat*={old,new}) and what was the outcome, such as whether they clicked the ad or not (*Y*={click,no-click}). Table 14.1 shows a schematic sample of such data. In practice, we do not need to keep all individual outcome values for each subject (unless the results will be used beyond the A/B test, such as in uplift modeling). For a binary outcome (e.g., click/no-click), we only need the proportion of clicks in each treatment group. In the ad example that means the proportion of clicks among users who viewed the old ad ($\hat{p}_A$), and the proportion of clicks among users who viewed the new ad ($\hat{p}_B$). For a numerical outcome (e.g., engagement time), we need only the average and standard deviation of the outcome in each treatment group ($\overline{y}_A$, $\hat{\sigma}_A$ and $\overline{y}_B$, $\hat{\sigma}_B$).

TABLE 14.1   EXAMPLE OF RAW DATA RESULTING FROM A/B TEST

User ID	Treatment	Outcome
1234	A	Click
1235	A	No click
1236	B	No click
...	...	...

Example: Testing a New Feature in a Photo Sharing App

PhoToTo, a fictitious photo sharing app, is interested in testing a new feature that allows users to make uploaded photos disappear after 24 hours. Their goal is to gauge their customers' interest in this feature, with the purpose of increasing user activity and converting users from the free version to the advanced paid version. PhoToTo deploys an A/B test to 2000 of its users who use the free version: 1000 of these users are randomly assigned to an interface with the new feature, while the other 1000 remain with the existing functionality. The experiment is run for a week. For each of the 2000 users, two performance metrics are measured at the end of the experimental week: the total number of uploaded photos, and whether the user upgraded to the paid version of PhoToTo. The results of the experiment are shown in Table 14.2. We can see that the average number of photo uploads and the conversion to paid users are both higher in the treatment group where the new feature was introduced. But can we infer the difference

TABLE 14.2   RESULTS FROM A/B TEST AT PHOTOTO, EVALUATING THE EFFECT OF A NEW FEATURE

Metric	Existing interface (A)	New feature available (B)
Average number of photo uploads	50	60
Standard deviation of photo uploads	50	100
Proportion converting to paid users	0.02	0.04

Success is measured by the number of photo uploads and user conversion

between the two groups will generalize when deployed to the larger population of users, or is this a "fluke sample?"

The Statistical Test for Comparing Two Groups (*t*-test)

The A/B test is a statistical test comparing the average outcome of a treatment group to that of a control group (or, in general, of two groups A and B). Suppose group A receives the existing ad, and group B receives the new design. Suppose the outcome of interest is whether users click on the ad. What if 5% of users shown the new ad clicked, and 4% of those shown the existing ad clicked? In many cases, we would now be ready to go with the treatment that did best. This is especially so if we are starting fresh with two new treatments— say, sending our prospects email version A or B to promote a new product. Or testing a new web landing page with a blue banner at the top or an orange banner.

In other cases, there may be a substantial cost difference between the treatments, or we may be testing a new treatment against an existing "standard." In such a case, we may worry about fluke results in an A/B test, particularly if based on a small sample. If random chance produced a result in favor of the costlier or the new treatment, we might not want to switch away from the cheaper or the tried-and-true standard treatment. Doing so regularly would mean chasing after inconsequential results, and losing a firm base of information. In such a case, we can use a statistical test to determine how "unusual" our result is, compared to what chance might produce. If our result is very unusual (say, it might not occur more often than 5% of the time in a chance model), we would be prepared to abandon our existing standard in favor of the new treatment. If, on the other hand, our new treatment produced an outcome that occurs 35% of the time by chance anyway, we might stick with the standard treatment. In this way, we minimize our chance of being fooled by chance.

Such a statistical test is termed a *significance test*. The metric "percent of time a chance model produces an outcome at least as unusual as the experiment" is termed a *p-value*. We could calculate *p*-values by constituting a chance model and simulating results. For example, in a test of engagement times, we could put all the engagement times from both treatments into a hat, shuffle the hat, and then repeatedly draw out pairs of samples like the original samples. Do those pairs rarely yield a difference in mean engagement times across the two re-samples as great as we saw in our actual experiment? If so, we conclude that the difference we saw in the experiment was unlikely to happen by chance: it is "statistically significant." A formula-based equivalent of this procedure is the *t-test for independent samples* (see box), and is included in most statistical software and in some platforms for automating marketing experiments.

T-TEST FOR COMPARING TWO INDEPENDENT GROUPS

All basic statistics courses and textbooks cover the t-test for testing the difference between two group means (or proportions). Here is a quick reminder of the basics for the case relevant for A/B testing. For testing whether the difference between two group means (or proportions) is significantly in favor of group B (e.g., the new ad design) or not—that is, whether there's evidence the difference between the population means $\mu_B - \mu_A > 0$—we compute the t-statistic:

$$T = \frac{\overline{y}_B - \overline{y}_A}{\text{Standard Error}(\overline{y}_B - \overline{y}_A)}.$$

When the outcome metric of interest is binary (e.g., buy/not-buy), a similar formula is used, replacing averages ($\overline{y}$) with proportions ($\hat{p}$).

The denominator of the T-statistic (the standard error of the difference in means or proportions) has the following formulas.[3] For a numerical measure:

$$\text{Standard Error}(\overline{y}_B - \overline{y}_A) = \sqrt{s_A^2/n_A + s_B^2/n_B},$$

and for a binary measure:

$$\text{Standard Error}(\hat{p}_B - \hat{p}_A) = \sqrt{\frac{\hat{p}_A(1 - \hat{p}_A)}{n_A} + \frac{\hat{p}_B(1 - \hat{p}_B)}{n_B}}.$$

The statistical significance of the t-value (its p-value) is computed by software. Comparing the p-value to a user-determined threshold will then yield a result. For example, if the threshold is 5%, then a p-value below 5% will indicate the click-through rate on the new design is statistically higher than on the existing design. The results of such tests are subject to two potential errors: false discovery (called Type I error) and missed discovery (Type II error). The choice of threshold value is determined by the false discovery risk level we are prepared to take.

Critically, one must carefully consider the magnitude of the difference and its practical meaning. Especially since A/B tests are typically conducted on very large samples of users (tens and even hundreds of thousands of users). Statistical significance is strongly affected by the sample size: the larger the groups, the more likely even a very small difference that is practically meaningless will appear statistically significant. For example, with sufficiently large groups, a CTR of 5.000001% will appear significantly (statistically) higher than 5%.

Returning to our earlier example of the photo sharing app PhoToTo, we can compute the T-statistics for each of the two metrics of interest: the number of uploaded photos and the conversion rate to paid users:

$$T_{\text{photo uploads}} = \frac{60 - 50}{\sqrt{(50^2/1000 + 100^2/1000)}} = 2.828.$$

$$T_{\text{paid users}} = \frac{0.04 - 0.02}{\sqrt{(0.04)(0.96)/1000 + (0.02)(0.98)/1000}} = 2.626.$$

The corresponding two p-values are as follows: for the increase[4] in average photo uploads p-value $= 0.0024$ (in Excel =tdist(2.828,1998,1)); for the increase in paid users p-value $= 0.0044$ (in Excel =tdist(2.626,1998,1)). Both p-values are very small, thereby indicating that the effect of the new feature on number of uploads and conversion to paid users will generalize to the larger population of users. Note that with much smaller sample sizes, the same outcome values in Table 14.2 could yield statistical insignificance. For example, for $n_A = n_B = 100$, we get p-values of 0.186 and 0.204, respectively.

Multiple Treatment Groups: A/B/n tests

A/B testing can be extended from two groups (treatment and control, or two groups) to multiple groups. In A/B/n testing, we have n groups. For example, testing three new ad designs against an existing design would use an A/B/4 test. The procedure is very similar to A/B testing, with the difference being the replacement of the t-test with ANOVA (analysis of variance) for a numerical outcome, or a Chi-square test for comparing proportions. For more on these tests, consult a statistics textbook such as Anderson et al. (2021).

Multiple A/B Tests and the Danger of Multiple Testing

As we mentioned earlier, digital platforms and their business customers (e.g., advertisers and marketers) often perform routine and frequent A/B tests, resulting in thousands of tests. Large companies such as Microsoft have their internal experimentation infrastructure. But even small companies can perform such testing using services by third parties: Optimizely (https://www.optimizely.com/) is one commercial service that provides online tools for routine A/B testing for online advertisers.

When deploying many A/B tests, there is a high risk of false discoveries: mistakenly concluding that a treatment effect is real, where it is just due to chance. While each statistical t-test carries with it a small probability of false discovery, a combination of many A/B tests dramatically increases the overall false discovery probability. This phenomenon is known as *multiple testing*. Multiple testing can arise from testing multiple metrics (CTR, views, purchases, etc.), running the test for multiple use subgroups (countries, zip codes, device type, etc.), and from repeating the same A/B test many times. Kohavi et al. (2020) describe a case of multiple testing that arose in early versions of Optimizely, which allowed those running an A/B test to "peek" at the p-values before the experimental period has been completed. For example, if the A/B test was supposed to run for a week, the tester could peek at test results throughout the week. This peeking

---

[4]We use a *one-sided test*, because we are testing whether the average number of uploads *increases* with the new feature. When the direction of the effect is unknown, we'd use a two-sided test.

was effectively multiple testing, leading to false discoveries of apparent effects. The problem was later detected and eliminated.

Solutions to false discoveries due to multiple testing are based on adjusting the threshold on each p-value, or adjusting the p-values themselves, by considering the total number of tests.[5] However, beyond technical solutions, it is good practice to carefully consider which tests are essential, set the experimental period in advance, disallow "peeking," and select treatments that have reasonable justification (although sometimes new ideas are hard to justify but turn out to be successes).

14.2 UPLIFT (PERSUASION) MODELING

Long before the advent of the Internet, sending messages directly to individuals (i.e., direct mail) held a big share of the advertising market. Direct marketing affords the marketer the ability to invite and monitor direct responses from consumers. This, in turn, allows the marketer to learn whether the messaging is paying off. A message can be tested with a small section of a large list and, if it pays off, the message can be rolled out to the entire list. With predictive modeling, we have seen that the rollout can be targeted to that portion of the list that is most likely to respond or behave in a certain way. None of this was possible with traditional media advertising (television, radio, newspaper, magazine).

Direct response also made it possible to test one message against another and find out which does better.

An A/B test tells you which treatment does better on average, but says nothing about which treatment does better for which individual. A classic example is in political campaigns. Consider the following scenario: The campaign director for Smith, a Democratic Congressional candidate, would like to know which voters should be called to encourage to support Smith. Voters that tend to vote Democratic but are not activists might be more inclined to vote for Smith if they got a call. Active Democrats are probably already supportive of him, and therefore a call to them would be wasted. Calls to Republicans are not only wasteful, but they could be harmful.

Campaigns now maintain extensive data on voters to help guide decisions about outreach to individual voters. Prior to the 2008 Obama campaign, the practice was to make rule-based decisions based on expert political judgment. Since 2008, it has increasingly been recognized that, rather than relying on judgment or supposition to determine whether an individual should be called, it is best to use the data to develop a model that can predict whether a voter will respond positively to outreach.

---

[5]One common method is the "False Discovery Rate" (FDR), which is the expected number of false discoveries among all discoveries. Using the FDR entails sorting the p-values from low to high and assigning different thresholds.

Gathering the Data

US states maintain publicly available files of voters, as part of the transparent oversight process for elections. The voter file contains data such as name, address, and date of birth. Political parties have "poll-watchers" at elections to record who votes, so they have additional data on which elections voters voted in. Census data for neighborhoods can be appended, based on voter address. Finally, commercial demographic data can be purchased and matched to the voter data. Table 14.3 shows a small extract of data derived from the voter file for the US state of Delaware.[6] The actual data used in this problem are in the file *Voter-Persuasion.xlsx* and contain 10,000 records and many additional variables beyond those shown in Table 14.3.

TABLE 14.3   DATA ON VOTERS (SMALL SUBSET OF VARIABLES AND RECORDS) AND DATA DICTIONARY

Voter	Age	NH_White	Comm_PT	H_F1	Reg_Days	PR_Pelig	E_Elig	Political_C
1	28	70	0	0	3997	0	20	1
2	23	67	3	0	300	0	0	1
3	57	64	4	0	2967	0	0	0
4	70	53	2	1	16620	100	90	1
5	37	76	2	0	3786	0	20	0

Data Dictionary

Age	Voter age in years
NH_White	Neighborhood average of % non-Hispanic white in household
Comm_PT	Neighborhood % of workers who take public transit
H_F1	Single female household (1 = yes)
Reg_Days	Days since voter registered at current address
PR_Pelig	Voted in what % of non-presidential primaries
E_Pelig	Voted in what % of any primaries
Political_C	Is there a political contributor in the home? (1 = yes)

First, the campaign director conducts a survey of 10,000 voters to determine their inclination to vote Democratic. Then she conducts an experiment, randomly splitting the sample of 10,000 voters in half and mailing a message promoting Smith to half the list (treatment A), and nothing to the other half (treatment B). The control group that gets no message is essential, since other campaigns or news events might cause a shift in opinion. The goal is to measure the change in opinion after the message is sent out, relative to the no-message control group.

The next step is conducting a post-message survey of the same sample of 10,000 voters, to measure whether each voter's opinion of Smith has shifted in a positive direction. A binary variable, Moved_AD, will be added to the above

---

[6]Thanks to Ken Strasma, founder of the microtargeting firm HaystaqDNA and director of targeting for the 2004 Kerry campaign and the 2008 Obama campaign, for these data.

data, indicating whether opinion has moved in a Democratic direction (1) or not (0).

Table 14.4 summarizes the results of the survey, by comparing the movement in a Democratic direction for each of the treatments. Overall, the message (Message = 1) is modestly effective.

TABLE 14.4   RESULTS OF SENDING A PRO-DEMOCRATIC MESSAGE TO VOTERS

	#Voters	# Moved Dem.	% Moved Dem.
Message = 1 (message sent)	5000	2012	40.2
Message = 0 (no message sent)	5000	1722	34.4

Movement in a Democratic direction among those who got no message is 34.4%. This probably reflects the approach of the election, the heightening campaign activity, and the reduction in the "no opinion" category. It also illustrates the need for a control group. Among those who did get the message, the movement in a Democratic direction is 40.2%. So, overall, the lift from the message is 5.8%.

We can now append two variables to the voter data shown earlier in Table 14.3: *message* [whether they received the message (1) or not (0)] and *Moved_AD* [whether they moved in a Democratic direction (1) or not (0)]. The augmented data are shown in Table 14.5.

TABLE 14.5   OUTCOME VARIABLE (MOVED_AD) AND TREATMENT VARIABLE (MESSAGE) ADDED TO VOTER DATA

Voter	Age	NH_White	Comm_PT	H_F1	Reg_Days	PR_Pelig	E_Elig	Political_C	Message	Moved_AD
1	28	70	0	0	3997	0	20	1	0	1
2	23	67	3	0	300	0	0	1	1	1
3	57	64	4	0	2967	0	0	0	0	0
4	70	53	2	1	16620	100	90	1	0	0
5	37	76	2	0	3786	0	20	0	1	0

A Simple Model

We can develop a predictive model with Moved_AD as the outcome variable, and various predictor variables, *including the treatment Message*. Any classification method can be used; Table 14.6 shows the first few lines from the output of some predictive model used to predict Moved_AD.

However, our interest is not just how the message did overall, nor is it whether we can predict the probability that a voter's opinion will move in a favorable direction. Rather our goal is to predict how much (positive) impact the message will have on a specific voter. That way the campaign can direct its limited resources toward the voters who are the most persuadable—those for whom sending the message will have the greatest positive effect.

TABLE 14.6   CLASSIFICATIONS AND PROPENSITIES FROM PREDICTIVE MODEL (SMALL EXTRACT)

Voter	Message	Actual Moved_AD	Predicted Moved_AD	Predicted Prob.
1	0	1	1	0.5975
2	1	1	1	0.5005
3	0	0	0	0.2235
4	0	0	0	0.3052
5	1	0	0	0.4140

Modeling Individual Uplift

To answer the question about the message's impact on each voter, we need to model the effect of the message at the individual voter level. For each voter, uplift is defined as follows:

Uplift = increase in propensity of favorable opinion after receiving message

To build an uplift model, we follow the following steps to estimate the change in probability of "success" (propensity) that comes from receiving the treatment (the message):

1. Randomly split a data sample into treatment and control groups, conduct an A/B test, and record the outcome (in our example: Moved_AD).

2. Recombining the data sample, partition it into training and validation sets; build a predictive model with this outcome variable and include a predictor variable that denotes treatment status (in our example: Message). If logistic regression is used, additional interaction terms between treatment status and other predictors can be added as predictors to allow the treatment effect to vary across records (in data-driven methods such as trees and k-NN this happens automatically).

3. Score this predictive model to a partition of the data; you can use the validation partition. This will yield, for each validation record, its propensity of success given its treatment.

4. Reverse the value of the treatment variable and re-score the same model to that partition. This will yield for each validation record its propensity of success had it received the other treatment.

5. Uplift is estimated for each individual by $P(\text{Success}|\text{Treatment} = 1) - P(\text{Success}|\text{Treatment} = 0)$.

6. For new data where no experiment has been performed, simply add a synthetic predictor variable for treatment and assign first a "1," score the model, then a "0," and score the model again. Estimate uplift for the new record(s) as above.

Continuing with the small voter example, the results from Step 3 are shown in Table 14.7—the right column shows the propensities from the model. Next,

TABLE 14.7 CLASSIFICATIONS AND PROPENSITIES FROM PREDICTIVE MODEL (SMALL EXTRACT) WITH MESSAGE VALUES REVERSED

Voter	Message	Actual Moved_AD	Predicted Moved_AD	Predicted Prob.
1	1	1	1	0.6908
2	0	1	1	0.3996
3	1	0	0	0.3022
4	1	0	0	0.3980
5	0	0	0	0.3194

we re-train the predictive model, but with the values of the treatment variable Message reversed for each row. Table 14.7 shows the propensities with variable Message reversed (you can see the reversed values in column Message). Finally, in Step 5, we calculate the uplift for each voter.

Table 14.8 shows the uplift for each voter—the success (Moved_AD = 1) propensity given Message = 1 minus the success propensity given Message = 0.

TABLE 14.8 UPLIFT: CHANGE IN PROPENSITIES FROM SENDING MESSAGE VS. NOT SENDING MESSAGE

Voter	Prob. if Message = 1	Prob. if Message = 0	Uplift
1	0.6908	0.5975	0.0933
2	0.5005	0.3996	0.1009
3	0.3022	0.2235	0.0787
4	0.3980	0.3052	0.0928
5	0.4140	0.3194	0.0946

COMPUTING UPLIFT WITH ASDM AND EXCEL

The process that we showed manually can be done using a combination of ASDM and Excel:

1. After recombining the treatment and control groups into a worksheet, use ASDM's data partitioning to generate training and validation sets.

2. Using ASDM's Classify menu, train your selected classifier on the training data. Score the validation set. This will result in *P(success)* for each validation record.

3. Create a new worksheet, copying the original validation set. Now flip the values in the treatment column. This can be done by creating a new column that replaces the previous treatment column. For example, if the original treatment column had value 0 for control and 1 for treatment, these values should be flipped in the new column.

4. Use ASDM to score the validation set that you created in step 3. This will result for each record in *P(success)* that is based on the flipped treatment group.

5. Copy the pairs of scores for the validation set (from steps 2 and 4). Use Excel to compute the uplift: this is the difference $P(\text{Success}|\text{Treatment} = 1) - P(\text{Success}|\text{Treatment} = 0)$.

Using the Results of an Uplift Model

Once we have estimated the uplift for each individual, the results can be ordered by uplift. The message could then be sent to all those voters with a positive uplift, or, if resources are limited, only to a subset—those with the greatest uplift.

Uplift modeling is used mainly in marketing and, more recently, in political campaigns. It has two main purposes:

- To determine whether to send someone a persuasion message, or just leave them alone.
- When a message is definitely going to be sent, to determine which message, among several possibilities, to send.

Technically, this amounts to the same thing—"send no message" is simply another category of treatment, and an experiment can be constructed with multiple treatments, for example, no message, message A, and message B. However, practitioners tend to think of the two purposes as distinct and tend to focus on the first. Marketers want to avoid sending discount offers to customers who would make a purchase anyway, or renew a subscription anyway. Political campaigns, likewise, want to avoid calling voters who would vote for their candidate in any case. And both parties especially want to avoid sending messages or offers where the effect might be antagonistic—where the uplift is negative.

14.3 REINFORCEMENT LEARNING

A/B testing derives causal knowledge about an intervention of interest by actively assigning experimental units (customers, website users, etc.) to treatment/intervention groups, measuring the outcome(s) of interest, and drawing a conclusion about the effectiveness of the intervention. We can think of this process as "learning by interacting" with the experimental units. The notion of *learning by interaction* is what separates supervised and unsupervised learning methods from interventional methods such as A/B testing and reinforcement learning. For example, in recommendation algorithms such as collaborative filtering, we might generate a recommended item (or set of items) for a user. However, unless we actually display the recommendation to the user and measure the outcome, it is impossible to know what the user would have done given the recommendation.

We've seen that interventional methods such as uplift modeling are intended to answer the personalized "what if" question: what would be the user's outcome if s/he were served (or not) a certain recommendation or offer. We now turn to a family of methods called *reinforcement learning*, which are computational algorithms (or *agents*) that "learn by interacting" with experimental units, through dynamic treatment assignment. In both supervised learning and reinforcement learning, the goal is to "learn" a predictive model of the outcome Y as a function of predictors $X_1, X_2, \ldots$. But whereas in supervised learning we train the model on preexisting data, in reinforcement learning we start without data, and the algorithm decides which X (treatment) information to deploy that would generate outcome Y data most useful for learning the optimal treatment-outcome model. In the recommendation example above, a reinforcement learning approach would choose which items to recommend in order to collect user feedback useful for learning the optimal input-output model.

We describe two popular frameworks: multi-armed bandits and Markov Decision Processes (MDPs). In both cases, the challenge is identifying the best treatment assignment policy in the presence of a plethora of potential interventions (e.g., which news item to display on a user's social media feed; which song to recommend in a music streaming service; which of many coupons to offer a customer on an e-commerce website).

Note: Reinforcement learning is not available in ASDM.

Explore-Exploit: Multi-Armed Bandits

The name *multi-armed bandit* (MAB, or simply "bandit") derives from a gambler playing multiple slot machines, each with a different unknown payoff rate. The gambler's goal is to figure out which machine has the highest payoff rate.

In an A/B test, after learning which treatment did best, you deploy that treatment, and the other treatment(s) get left behind. A multi-armed bandit uses sequential assignment of experimental units to treatment groups, dynamically updating treatment assignments to new units as the experiment progresses. The idea is to increase the proportion of assignments to the treatment group that shows the best performance (the best slot machine). This is especially useful when there are multiple treatments (e.g., multiple ad designs). For example, if we initially display 10 new ad designs to mobile app users, each with equal probability, then if initial experimental results indicate the new ad #3 leads to the best outcomes, for the next set of users we might increase the probability of displaying ad #3 compared to all other designs. However, we do not increase this probability to 100% because there is still uncertainty regarding the superiority of this ad design—perhaps with more data a different ad design will turn out to be the best one. We therefore still want to continue testing the value of the other nine ad designs. A multi-armed bandit tries to achieve a dual goal: improving the outcome by increasing the chance of assignment to the "winning" treatment (called *Exploit*) while continuing to evaluate the potential of the "losing" treatment(s) (called *Explore*).

There are different multi-armed bandit parameters and implementations, which differ in terms of determining how and when to update the treatment assignment probabilities. For example, an *Epsilon First* strategy explores randomly for some period of time, then exploits the treatment with the highest estimated outcome (if one treatment is clearly better than the others, it assigns all new subjects to this treatment). Another approach, the *Epsilon-Greedy* approach, explores ϵ% of the time and exploits $1-\epsilon$% of the time. A variation of the

Epsilon-Greedy strategy adjusts the ϵ parameter over time, exploring sub-optimal treatments less frequently.

The multi-armed bandit scenario assumes the intervention effects remain constant from one assignment to the next. However, in some cases, the best intervention will depend on a changing context. For example, in music rec-ommendation, it is likely that song preference changes for the same user over different times of the day (waking up, while commuting to work, in the evening, etc.) or across devices (mobile phone, TV, etc.). In such cases, we'd want the algorithm to take into account the context. *Contextual multi-armed bandits*, also known as *contextual bandits*, do exactly this: they search for the best context-specific intervention, thereby combining trial-and-error treatment assignment search with estimating the association between treatment assignment and con-text variables.

MULTI-ARMED BANDIT: SIMPLE EXAMPLE

Let's consider the scenario of selecting the best online ad to display among 10 different designs, by running a 7-day experiment. Suppose that each day we have a large number of customers accessing the webpage where the ad will be displayed. A 10-armed bandit algorithm that uses an Epsilon-first strategy would take the following steps:

- **Day 1 initialization:** Each ad i has probability $p_i = 0.1$ to be displayed. In other words, each customer is randomly assigned to view one of the 10 ads.
- **Day 1 evaluation and update:** At the end of Day 1, compute the *reward* metric of interest r_i [e.g., click-through rate (CTR), average ad revenues per ad-view] resulting from each of the 10 ads.
- **Day 2 deployment:** All customers assigned to view the best performing Day 1 ad.
- **Day 2 evaluation and update:** At the end of Day 2, compute the average daily *reward* for the displayed ad.
- **Day 3, 5, 7 deployment:** Each customer is randomly assigned to view one of the 10 ads (as in Day 1).
- **Day 3, 5, 7 evaluation and update:** At the end of the day, compute the average daily *reward* for each of the 10 ads (accumulated across the days thus far).
- **Day 4, 6 deployment:** All customers assigned to view the best performing ad thus far.
- **Day 4, 6 evaluation and update:** At the end of the day, compute the average daily *reward* for each of the 10 ads (accumulated across the days thus far).
- **Day 7 experiment conclusion:** The ad with the highest average 7-day reward is selected and will be displayed in the future.

  Note that on odd days, where customers are randomized across all 10 ads, the scenario is similar to A/B/10 testing in terms of treatment assignment strategy. The difference is that we do not carry out a statistical test at the end of an odd day to conclude about the best ad. Instead, we accumulate the rewards since Day 1 and reach a conclusion only after the multi-day experiment is complete.

  The above example treats each day separately. An alternative is to consider batches of customers visiting the webpage (for example, replacing a day with 10,000 customer visits).

Markov Decision Process (MDP)

In contrast to A/B tests, in bandit algorithms the allocation of treatments to users is a multi-stage process, in which the allocation at one stage might depend on what happened in the previous stage. Bandit algorithms are actually a special case of a more general staged process, termed a Markov Decision Process (MDP).

MDPs can allow the algorithm to learn a longer-term relationship between interventions (treatments) and outcomes—for example, a movie recommendation might lead to higher long-term user satisfaction even if the user's immediate reaction is not the most profitable. Hence, MDPs are especially useful in digital environments where long-term goals, such as user satisfaction or brand recognition, are of interest.

A MDP represents the problem of learning the optimal intervention policy through *states* and *rewards*. Consider a music streaming service that provides a recommendation system to its users. Suppose the business goal is to increase overall user engagement with the service (by providing useful recommendations), where engagement is measured by the number of songs played by the user. The algorithm (agent) must discover which song recommendations (interventions) yield the best outcome overall by trying them and recording the user's reactions. To achieve this, we define for the agent an intermediate "reward" such as whether the recommended song was played for at least 30 seconds. The agent's objective is to maximize the total reward over the long run. With such a longer-term optimization, we might recommend an item with a low immediate reward (e.g., low-profit item), but that is likely to lead to profitable rewards in the future. Another advantage of the MDP formulation is that the reward can represent the business value of a particular recommendation, so that we might recommend high-profit items even if they have a low probability of purchase.

In addition to the rewards, the MDP records the *state* at each time of treatment assignment. The state includes all the information available to the algorithm about the user, the context, and the items. In the music streaming example, the state might be the user's profile (age, gender, etc.), behavior on the platform (app use frequency, songs played, sharing with friends, etc.), context (time of day, location, device, etc.), and song features (singer, genre, etc.).

The agent's actions (e.g., recommendation or ad displayed) might affect not only the reward but also the next state (e.g., the user's time on app, songs played), thereby affecting future rewards.[7] To capture this, the MDP has a *value function* (specified by the data scientist) that assigns to each state a value corresponding to the expected long-term overall rewards when starting from that state and using a specific treatment assignment policy.

---

[7]A multi-armed bandit is a simplified type of reinforcement learning where the assignment to intervention (action) affects only the immediate reward.

Figure 14.1 shows a schematic of an MDP, and how the agent interacts with the user by assigning an intervention (action) and recording the user's reaction (reward) and new state. The terms "agent" and "environment," sometimes called "controller" and "controlled system," reflect the origins of reinforcement learning in engineering applications (such as thermostats for regulating the temperature in a room) and more recently in games such as chess and Go where the algorithm searches for the best next move.

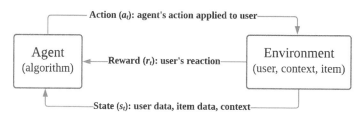

FIGURE 14.1   SCHEMATIC OF REINFORCEMENT LEARNING, WHERE THE SOFTWARE AGENT "LEARNS" THE HUMAN USER BY PROVIDING ACTIONS, RECORDING THE USER'S NEW STATE, AND RECEIVING A REWARD BASED ON THE USER'S REACTION

The term "Markov" in MDP implies that we think of rewards, states, and treatment assignments (actions) in discrete time (periods $t = 1, 2, 3, \ldots$), and that the sequence of rewards, states, and actions form a *Markov chain*—this is a sequence of possible events in which the probability of each event depends only on the state attained in the previous event. In other words, to determine its next action (a_{t+1}), the agent only uses information on the most recent state (s_t), reward (r_t), and action (a_t).

For an item recommendation scenario, a generic MDP strategy might look like this:

1. *Initialization:* Using a predictive model, predict what item user u will select next given their user data (state).[8] (This model is based on data without recommendations.)

2. *Action (a_t):* Recommend to user u an item based on the user's data, context, and the item's features (state s_{t_1}). (The item is the result of step 1 for the initial run, then of step 4 thereafter.)

3. *Reward (r_t):* Collect the user's feedback to the recommendation (e.g., purchase, clicks)

4. *Model update:* Using the pre-recommendation user/context/item data (state s_{t-1}), the recommendation (action a_t), and the user's feedback (reward r_t), the agent updates its predictive model linking the outcome

---

[8]This means estimating the initial *state transition function* that includes the probabilities of moving from each state to each of the other states.

(next step's state and reward) to the input (current step's state and action) $P(s_{t+1}, r_{t+1} | s_t, a_t)$. The agent then computes the value function (the expected long-term overall reward) to choose the next best action.

5. *Repeat* steps 2–4

There exist a variety of ways to implement MDPs and reinforcement learning algorithms in practice, as well variations and extensions, some including deep neural networks for the model updating step. The interested reader can learn more in the classic book *Reinforcement Learning* by Sutton and Barto (2018).

As a final note about reinforcement learning, it is important to realize that while in this AI technique the data scientist determines the rewards, value function, the set of states, and set of possible actions, this does not guarantee that the agent will arrive at an optimal solution. In his book *Human Compatible*, AI expert Stewart Russell describes how agents designed to achieve a human-designed goal ended up reaching the goal by unacceptable solutions: The ECHO smart home controller was designed to reduce energy consumption by learning from the household behavior. However, inhabitants at Washington State University "often had to sit in the dark if their visitors stayed later than the usual bedtime." The agent has not fully "understood" the human objective, because the goals and rules have not, and perhaps cannot, be fully specified. By contrast, in games like Go or chess, the ends are easy to define and the rules can be comprehensively specified. In such games, highly creative solutions may result. The solution path may seem outlandish to a human in its initial stages, but the agent does not care and has been able to determine that it will be ultimately successful.

Reinforcement learning algorithms were designed for tasks that are fully observable, involve short time horizons, and have a small number of states and simple, predictable rules. Stewart Russell (2019) concludes: "Relaxing any of these conditions means that the standard methods will fail."

14.4 Summary

In this chapter, we looked at the use of randomized experiments and user feedback for determining the best intervention. These methods differ from supervised learning and unsupervised learning and involve interaction with the units of interest (customers, website users, etc.). We described A/B testing, uplift modeling, and reinforcement learning.

A/B testing is used to test the effect of an intervention on an outcome of interest. This is done by randomly assigning units to an intervention group or a control (non-intervention) group and comparing the two groups' outcomes. A/B/n testing extends the idea to more than two groups.

In uplift modeling, the results of A/B testing are folded into the predictive modeling process as a predictor variable to guide choices not just about whether to send an offer or persuasion message, but also as to who to send it to.

Reinforcement learning uses computational algorithms for identifying best intervention assignments. This is especially useful when there are many possible interventions (such as in recommendation systems) and in environments that allow user-algorithm interaction. The algorithm learns the best intervention policy by trial-and-error, balancing between exploration (trying different treatment assignments) and exploitation (assigning the best-so-far treatment). Two popular reinforcement learning formulations are multi-armed bandits and Markov decision processes.

PROBLEMS

14.1 **Marketing Message—A/B Testing.** Which is a more effective marketing message—a plain text email, or an email with images and design elements? Statistics.com conducted an A/B test in June, 2012, sending an email to a list of potential customers that was randomly split into two groups. The measure of success was whether the email was opened by the receiver or not. For some reason, the email service used by Statistics.com did not produce an even split. The results for each of the 426 sent emails are in the file *email-A-B-test.xlsx*.

    a. Before conducting such a test, would you have an opinion as to which would do better: a message with or without images?

    b. What were the results in terms of open rates? Which message did better? (*Hint:* in Excel, you can use pivot tables to get this summary.)

    c. We would like to know whether this difference could be due to chance, and so will conduct a statistical test. Conduct a t-test to determine whether the difference is statistically significant and report the p-value.

    d. Summarize your conclusion from the A/B test.

14.2 **Hair Care Product—Uplift Modeling.** This problem uses the data set in *Hair-Care-Product.xlsx*, courtesy of SAS. In this hypothetical case, a promotion for a hair care product was sent to some members of a buyers' club. Purchases were then recorded for both the members who got the promotion and those who did not.

    a. What is the purchase propensity

      i. among those who received the promotion?

      ii. among those who did not receive the promotion?

    b. Partition the data into training (60%) and validation (40%) and fit a model of your choice, with *Purchase* as the target. Report the predicted class and propensities for the first 10 records in the validation set.

    c. Copy the validation data to a new worksheet and reverse the values of the *Promotion* variable (call it *Promotion-R* to avoid confusion). This means that for every record, if the original had *Promotion* = 1, the copy will have *Promotion-R* = 0, and vice versa.

    Score the model to the new copy of the validation data. In ASDM you can do this either with the Score function, or by re-running the model and selecting the copy as new data in the Score New Data area. You will need to match *Promotion* to *Promotion-R*. Report the predicted class and propensities for the first 10 records in the validation set.

    d. In a new worksheet, copy the purchase propensities from the original validation data alongside those from the reversed-promotion validation data. Subtract the purchase propensity when *Promotion* = 0 from the purchase propensity when *Promotion* = 1. This is the uplift. Report the uplift for the first 10 records in your validation set.

## PART VI

Mining Relationships Among Records

## CHAPTER 15

Association Rules and Collaborative Filtering

In this chapter, we describe the unsupervised learning methods of association rules (also called "affinity analysis" and "market basket analysis") and collaborative filtering. Both methods are popular in marketing for cross-selling products associated with an item that a consumer is considering.

In association rules, the goal is to identify item clusters in transaction-type databases. Association rule discovery in marketing is termed "market basket analysis" and is aimed at discovering which groups of products tend to be purchased together. These items can then be displayed together, offered in post-transaction coupons, or recommended in online shopping. We describe the two-stage process of rule generation and then assessment of rule strength to choose a subset. We look at the popular rule-generating Apriori algorithm and then criteria for judging the strength of rules.

In collaborative filtering, the goal is to provide personalized recommendations that leverage user-level information. User-based collaborative filtering starts with a user, then finds users who have purchased a similar set of items or ranked items in similar fashion, and makes a recommendation to the initial user based on what the similar users purchase or like. Item-based collaborative filtering starts with an item being considered by a user, then locates other items that tend to be co-purchased with that first item. We explain the technique and the requirements for applying it in practice.

15.1 ASSOCIATION RULES

Put simply, association rules, or *affinity analysis*, constitute a study of "what goes with what." This method is also called *market basket analysis* because it originated

Machine Learning for Business Analytics: Concepts, Techniques, and Applications with Analytic Solver® Data Mining, Fourth Edition. Galit Shmueli, Peter C. Bruce, Kuber R. Deokar, and Nitin R. Patel.
© 2023 John Wiley & Sons, Inc. Published 2023 by John Wiley & Sons, Inc.

with the study of customer transactions databases to determine dependencies between purchases of different items. Association rules are heavily used in retail for learning about items that are purchased together, but they are also useful in other fields. For example, a medical researcher might want to learn what symptoms appear together. In law, word combinations that appear too often might indicate plagiarism.

Discovering Association Rules in Transaction Databases

The availability of detailed information on customer transactions has led to the development of techniques that automatically look for associations between items that are stored in the database. An example is data collected using bar-code scanners in supermarkets. Such *market basket databases* consist of a large number of transaction records. Each record lists all items bought by a customer on a single-purchase transaction. Managers are interested to know if certain groups of items are consistently purchased together. They could use such information for making decisions on store layouts and item placement, for cross-selling, for promotions, for catalog design, and for identifying customer segments based on buying patterns. Association rules provide information of this type in the form of "if–then" statements. These rules are computed from the data; unlike the if–then rules of logic, association rules are probabilistic in nature.

Association rules are commonly encountered in online *recommendation systems* (or *recommender systems*), where customers examining an item or items for possible purchase are shown other items that are often purchased in conjunction with the first item(s). The display from Amazon.com's online shopping system illustrates the application of rules like this under "Frequently bought together." In the example shown in Figure 15.1, a user browsing a Samsung Galaxy S5 cell phone is shown a case and a screen protector that are often purchased along with this phone.

We introduce a simple artificial example and use it throughout the chapter to demonstrate the concepts, computations, and steps of association rules. We end by applying association rules to a more realistic example of book purchases.

Example 1: Synthetic Data on Purchases of Phone Faceplates

A store that sells accessories for cellular phones runs a promotion on faceplates. Customers who purchase multiple faceplates from a choice of six different colors get a discount. The store managers, who would like to know what colors of faceplates customers are likely to purchase together, collected the transaction database as shown in Table 15.1.

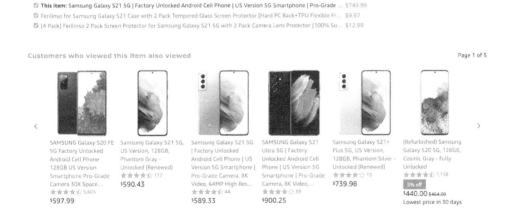

FIGURE 15.1   RECOMMENDATIONS UNDER "FREQUENTLY BOUGHT TOGETHER" ARE BASED ON ASSOCIATION RULES

Generating Candidate Rules

The idea behind association rules is to examine all possible rules between items in an if-then format, and select only those that are most likely to be indicators of true dependence. We use the term *antecedent* to describe the IF part and *consequent* to describe the THEN part. In association analysis, the antecedent and consequent are sets of items (called *itemsets*) that are disjoint (do not have any items in common). Note that itemsets are not records of what people buy; they are simply possible combinations of items, including single items.

TABLE 15.1   TRANSACTIONS FOR PURCHASES OF DIFFERENT-COLORED CELLULAR PHONE FACEPLATES

Transaction	Faceplate colors purchased			
1	red	white	green	
2	white	orange		
3	white	blue		
4	red	white	orange	
5	red	blue		
6	white	blue		
7	white	orange		
8	red	white	blue	green
9	red	white	blue	
10	yellow			

Returning to the phone faceplate purchase example, one example of a possible rule is "if red, then white," meaning that if a red faceplate is purchased, a white one is too. Here, the antecedent is *red* and the consequent is *white*. The antecedent and consequent each contain a single item in this case. Another possible rule is "if red and white, then green." Here the antecedent includes the itemset {*red, white*} and the consequent is {*green*}.

The first step in association rules is to generate all the rules that would be candidates for indicating associations between items. Ideally, we might want to look at all possible combinations of items in a database with p distinct items (in the phone faceplate example, $p = 6$). This means finding all combinations of single items, pairs of items, triplets of items, and so on, in the transactions database. However, generating all these combinations requires a long computation time that grows exponentially[1] in p. A practical solution is to consider only combinations that occur with higher frequency in the database. These are called *frequent itemsets*.

Determining what qualifies as a frequent itemset is related to the concept of *support*. The support of a rule is simply the number of transactions that include both the antecedent and consequent itemsets. It is called a support because it measures the degree to which the data "support" the validity of the rule. The support is sometimes expressed as a percentage of the total number of records in the database. For example, the support for the itemset {red, white} in the phone faceplate example is 4 ($100 \times \frac{4}{10} = 40\%$).

What constitutes a frequent itemset is therefore defined as an itemset that has a support that exceeds a selected minimum support, determined by the user.

---

[1]The number of rules that one can generate for p items is $3^p - 2^{p+1} + 1$. Computation time therefore grows by a factor for each additional item. For six items we have 602 rules, and for seven items the number of rules grows to 1932.

The Apriori Algorithm

Several algorithms have been proposed for generating frequent itemsets, but the classic algorithm is the *Apriori algorithm* of Agrawal et al. (1993). The key idea of the algorithm is to begin by generating frequent itemsets with just one item (one-item sets) and to recursively generate frequent itemsets with two items, then with three items, and so on, until we have generated frequent itemsets of all sizes.

It is easy to generate frequent one-itemsets. All we need to do is to count, for each item, how many transactions in the database include the item. These transaction counts are the supports for the one-itemsets. We drop one-itemsets that have support below the desired minimum support to create a list of the frequent one-itemsets.

To generate frequent two-itemsets, we use the frequent one-itemsets. The reasoning is that if a certain one-itemset did not exceed the minimum support, any larger size itemset that includes it will not exceed the minimum support. In general, generating k-itemsets uses the frequent $(k-1)$-itemsets that were generated in the preceding step. Each step requires a single run through the database, and therefore the Apriori algorithm is very fast even for a large number of unique items in a database.

Selecting Strong Rules

From the abundance of rules generated, the goal is to find only the rules that indicate a strong dependence between the antecedent and consequent itemsets. To measure the strength of association implied by a rule, we use the measures of *confidence* and *lift ratio*, as described below.

Support and Confidence   In addition to support, which we described earlier, there is another measure that expresses the degree of uncertainty about the if–then rule. This is known as the *confidence*[2] of the rule. This measure compares the co-occurrence of the antecedent and consequent itemsets in the database to the occurrence of the antecedent itemsets. Confidence is defined as the ratio of the number of transactions that include all antecedent and consequent itemsets (i.e., the support) to the number of transactions that include all the antecedent itemsets:

$$\text{Confidence} = \frac{\text{Number of transactions with both antecedent and consequent itemsets}}{\text{Number of transactions with antecedent itemset}}.$$

---

[2]The concept of confidence is different from and unrelated to the ideas of confidence intervals and confidence levels used in statistical inference.

For example, suppose that a supermarket database has 100,000 test point-of-sale transactions. Of these transactions, 2000 include both orange juice and (over-the-counter) flu medication, and 800 of these include soup purchases. The association rule "IF orange juice and flu medication are purchased, THEN soup is purchased on the same trip" has a support of 800 transactions (alternatively, $0.8\% = 800/100{,}000$) and a confidence of 40% ($= 800/2000$).

To see the relationship between support and confidence, let us think about what each is measuring (estimating). One way to think of support is that it is the (estimated) probability that a transaction selected randomly from the database will contain all items in the antecedent and the consequent:

$$P(\text{antecedent AND consequent}).$$

In comparison, the confidence is the (estimated) *conditional probability* that a transaction selected randomly will include all the items in the consequent *given* that the transaction includes all the items in the antecedent:

$$\frac{P(\text{antecedent AND consequent})}{P(\text{antecedent})} = P(\text{consequent} \mid \text{antecedent}).$$

A high value of confidence suggests a strong association rule (in which we are highly confident). However, this can be deceptive because if the antecedent and/or the consequent has a high level of support, we can have a high value for confidence even when the antecedent and consequent are independent! For example, if nearly all customers buy bananas and nearly all customers buy ice cream, the confidence level will be high regardless of whether there is an association between the items.

Lift Ratio   A better way to judge the strength of an association rule is to compare the confidence of the rule with a benchmark value, where we assume that the occurrence of the consequent itemset in a transaction is independent of the occurrence of the antecedent for each rule. In other words, if the antecedent and consequent itemsets are independent, what confidence values would we expect to see? Under independence, the support would be

$$P(\text{antecedent AND consequent}) = P(\text{antecedent}) \times P(\text{consequent}),$$

and the benchmark confidence would be

$$\frac{P(\text{antecedent}) \times P(\text{consequent})}{P(\text{antecedent})} = P(\text{consequent}).$$

The estimate of this benchmark from the data, called the *benchmark confidence value* for a rule, is computed by

$$\text{Benchmark confidence} = \frac{\text{Number of transactions with consequent itemset}}{\text{Number of transactions in database}}.$$

We compare the confidence to the benchmark confidence by looking at their ratio: this is called the *lift ratio* of a rule. The lift ratio is the confidence of the rule divided by the benchmark confidence, assuming independence of consequent from antecedent:

$$\text{Lift ratio} = \frac{\text{Confidence}}{\text{Benchmark confidence}}.$$

A lift ratio greater than 1.0 suggests that there is some usefulness to the rule. In other words, the level of association between the antecedent and consequent itemsets is higher than would be expected if they were independent. The larger the lift ratio, the greater is the strength of the association.

To illustrate the computation of support, confidence, and lift ratio for the cellular phone faceplate example, we introduce a presentation of the data better suited to this purpose.

Data Format

Transaction data are usually displayed in one of two formats: a list of items purchased (each row representing a transaction), or a binary matrix in which columns are items, rows again represent transactions, and each cell has either a 1 or a 0, indicating the presence or absence of an item in the transaction. For example, Table 15.1 displays the data for the cellular faceplate purchases in item list format. We translate these into a binary matrix format in Table 15.2.

TABLE 15.2   PHONE FACEPLATE DATA IN BINARY MATRIX FORMAT

Transaction	Red	White	Blue	Orange	Green	Yellow
1	1	1	0	0	1	0
2	0	1	0	1	0	0
3	0	1	1	0	0	0
4	1	1	0	1	0	0
5	1	0	1	0	0	0
6	0	1	1	0	0	0
7	1	0	1	0	0	0
8	1	1	1	0	1	0
9	1	1	1	0	0	0
10	0	0	0	0	0	1

Now suppose that we want association rules between items for this database that have a support count of at least 2 (equivalent to a percentage support of $2/10 = 20\%$): that is, rules based on items that were purchased together in at least 20% of the transactions. By enumeration, we can see that only the itemsets listed in Table 15.3 have a count of at least 2.

The first itemset {red} has a support of 6 because six of the transactions included a red faceplate. Similarly, the last itemset {red, white, green} has a support of 2 because only two transactions included red, white, and green faceplates.

TABLE 15.3   ITEMSETS WITH SUPPORT COUNT
OF AT LEAST TWO

Itemset	Support (Count)
{red}	6
{white}	7
{blue}	6
{orange}	2
{green}	2
{red, white}	4
{red, blue}	4
{red, green}	2
{white, blue}	4
{white, orange}	2
{white, green}	2
{red, white, blue}	2
{red, white, green}	2

In ASDM, the user can choose to input data using the *Associate > Association Rules* facility in either item-list format or binary matrix format.

The Process of Rule Selection

The process of selecting strong rules is based on generating all association rules that meet stipulated support and confidence requirements. This is done in two stages. The first stage, described earlier, consists of finding all "frequent" item-sets, those itemsets that have a requisite support. In the second stage we generate, from the frequent itemsets, association rules that meet a confidence requirement. The first step is aimed at removing item combinations that are rare in the database. The second stage then filters the remaining rules and selects only those with high confidence. For most association analysis data, the computational challenge is the first stage, as described in the discussion of the Apriori algorithm.

The computation of confidence in the second stage is simple. Since any subset (e.g., {red} in the phone faceplate example) must occur at least as frequently as the set it belongs to (e.g., {red, white}), each subset will also be in the list. It is then straightforward to compute the confidence as the ratio of the support for the itemset to the support for each subset of the itemset. We retain the corresponding association rule only if it exceeds the desired cutoff value for confidence. For example, from the itemset {red, white, green} in the phone faceplate purchases, we get the following association rules and confidence values:

Rule		Confidence	
Rule 1:	{red, white} $\Rightarrow$ {green}	$\dfrac{\text{support of \{red, white, green\}}}{\text{support of \{red, white\}}}$	= 2/4 = 50%
Rule 2:	{red, green} $\Rightarrow$ {white}	$\dfrac{\text{support of \{red, white, green\}}}{\text{support of \{red, green\}}}$	= 2/2 = 100%
Rule 3:	{white, green} $\Rightarrow$ {red}	$\dfrac{\text{support of \{red, white, green\}}}{\text{support of \{white, green\}}}$	= 2/2 = 100%
Rule 4:	{red} $\Rightarrow$ {white, green}	$\dfrac{\text{support of \{red, white, green\}}}{\text{support of \{red\}}}$	= 2/6 = 33%
Rule 5:	{white} $\Rightarrow$ {red, green}	$\dfrac{\text{support of \{red, white, green\}}}{\text{support of \{white\}}}$	= 2/7 = 29%
Rule 6:	{green} $\Rightarrow$ {red, white}	$\dfrac{\text{support of \{red, white, green\}}}{\text{support of \{green\}}}$	= 2/2 = 100%

If the desired minimum confidence is 70%, we would report only the second, third, and last rules.

We can generate association rules in ASDM by specifying the minimum support count (2) and minimum confidence level percentage (70%). Figure 15.2 shows the output. Note that here we consider all possible itemsets, not just {red, white, green} as above.

Summary

Metric	Value
# Transactions	10
# Items	6
# Rules	6

Rules

Rule ID	A-Support	C-Support	Support	Confidence	Lift-Ratio	Antecedent	Consequent
Rule 1	2	6	2	100	1.67	[Green]	[Red]
Rule 2	2	7	2	100	1.43	[Orange]	[White]
Rule 3	2	7	2	100	1.43	[Green]	[White]
Rule 4	2	4	2	100	2.50	[Green]	[Red,White]
Rule 5	2	7	2	100	1.43	[Red,Green]	[White]
Rule 6	2	6	2	100	1.67	[White,Green]	[Red]

FIGURE 15.2   ASSOCIATION RULES FOR PHONE FACEPLATE TRANSACTIONS: ASDM OUTPUT

The output includes information on the support of the antecedent, the support of the consequent, and the support of the combined set. It also gives the confidence of the rule (in %) and the lift ratio.

Interpreting the Results

We can translate each of the rules from Figure 15.2 into an understandable sentence that provides information about performance. For example, we can read the first rule as follows:

> If green is purchased, then with confidence 100% red will also be purchased.
> This rule has a lift ratio of 1.67.

In interpreting results, it is useful to look at the various measures. The support for the rule indicates its impact in terms of overall size: How many transactions are affected? If only a small number of transactions are affected, the rule may be of little use (unless the consequent is very valuable and/or the rule is very efficient in finding it).

The lift ratio indicates how efficient the rule is in finding consequents, compared to random selection. A very efficient rule is preferred to an inefficient rule, but we must still consider support: a very efficient rule that has very low support may not be as desirable as a less efficient rule with much greater support.

The confidence tells us at what rate consequents will be found, and it is useful in determining the business or operational usefulness of a rule. A rule with low confidence may find consequents at too low a rate to be worth the cost of (say) promoting the consequent in all the transactions that involve the antecedent.

The machine learning workflow for the phone faceplate example used in this chapter is shown in Figure 15.3.

FIGURE 15.3   MACHINE LEARNING WORKFLOW FOR THE PHONE FACEPLATE EXAMPLE

Rules and Chance

What about confidence in the nontechnical sense? How sure can we be that the rules we develop are meaningful? Considering the matter from a statistical perspective, we can ask: are we finding associations that are really just chance occurrences?

Let us examine the output from an application of this algorithm to a small database of 50 transactions, where each of the nine items is assigned randomly to each transaction. The data are shown in Table 15.4, and the association rules generated are shown in Figure 15.4. In looking at this figure, remember that A and C refer to itemsets, not records. ASDM's *Support* is the support of the union of itemsets A and C not of the union of records with those items.

In this example, the lift ratios highlight rule 2 as most interesting, as it suggests that purchase of item 4 is almost five times as likely when items 8 and 3 are purchased than if item 4 was not associated with the itemset {8, 3}. Yet we know there is no fundamental association underlying these data—they were generated randomly.

TABLE 15.4   FIFTY TRANSACTIONS OF RANDOMLY ASSIGNED ITEMS

Transaction	Items					Transaction	Items					Transaction	Items			
1	8					18	8					35	3	4	6	8
2	3	4	8			19						36	1	4	8	
3	8					20	9					37	4	7	8	
4	3	9				21	2	5	6	8		38	8	9		
5	9					22	4	6	9			39	4	5	7	9
6	1	8				23	4	9				40	2	8	9	
7	6	9				24	8	9				41	2	5	9	
8	3	5	7	9		25	6	8				42	1	2	7	9
9	8					26	1	6	8			43	5	8		
10						27	5	8				44	1	7	8	
11	1	7	9			28	4	8	9			45	8			
12	1	4	5	8	9	29	9					46	2	7	9	
13	5	7	9			30	8					47	4	6	9	
14	6	7	8			31	1	5	8			48	9			
15	3	7	9			32	3	6	9			49	9			
16	1	4	9			33	7	9				50	6	7	8	
17	6	7	8			34	7	8	9							

Summary

Metric	Value
# Transactions	50
# Items	9
# Rules	9

Rules

Rule ID	A-Support	C-Support	Support	Confidence	Lift-Ratio	Antecedent	Consequent
Rule 1	5	27	4	80	1.48	[2]	[9]
Rule 2	2	11	2	100	4.55	[8,3]	[4]
Rule 3	2	27	2	100	1.85	[3,4]	[8]
Rule 4	2	27	2	100	1.85	[1,5]	[8]
Rule 5	3	27	3	100	1.85	[6,7]	[8]
Rule 6	2	27	2	100	1.85	[3,7]	[9]
Rule 7	2	27	2	100	1.85	[4,5]	[9]
Rule 8	3	27	3	100	1.85	[5,7]	[9]
Rule 9	2	27	2	100	1.85	[7,2]	[9]

FIGURE 15.4   ASSOCIATION RULES OUTPUT FOR RANDOM DATA

Two principles can guide us in assessing rules for possible spuriousness due to chance effects:

1. The more records the rule is based on, the more solid is the conclusion.
2. The more distinct are the rules we consider seriously (perhaps consolidating multiple rules that deal with the same items), the more likely it is that at least some will be based on chance sampling results. For one person to toss a coin 10 times and get 10 heads would be quite surprising. If 1000 people toss a coin 10 times each, it would not be nearly so surprising to have one get 10 heads. Formal adjustment of "statistical significance" when multiple comparisons are made is a complex subject in its own right and beyond the scope of this book. A reasonable approach is to consider rules from the top down in terms of business or operational applicability, and not consider more than can reasonably be incorporated in a human decision-making process. This will impose a rough constraint on the dangers that arise from an automated review of hundreds or thousands of rules in search of "something interesting."

We now consider a more realistic example, using a larger database and real transactional data.

Example 2: Rules for Similar Book Purchases

The following example (drawn from the Charles Book Club case) examines associations among transactions involving various types of books. The database includes 2000 transactions, and there are 11 different types of books. The data, in binary matrix form, are shown in Table 15.5.

TABLE 15.5   SUBSET OF BOOK PURCHASE TRANSACTIONS IN BINARY MATRIX FORMAT

ChildBks	YouthBks	CookBks	DoItYBks	cefBks	ArtBks	GeogBks	ItalCook	ItalAtlas	ItalArt	Florence
0	1	0	1	0	0	1	0	0	0	0
1	0	0	0	0	0	0	0	0	0	0
0	0	0	0	0	0	0	0	0	0	0
1	1	1	0	1	0	1	0	0	0	0
0	0	1	0	0	0	1	0	0	0	0
1	0	0	0	0	1	0	0	0	0	1
0	1	0	0	0	0	0	0	0	0	0
0	1	0	0	1	0	0	0	0	0	0
1	0	0	1	0	0	0	0	0	0	0
1	1	1	0	0	0	1	0	0	0	0
0	0	0	0	0	0	0	0	0	0	0

For instance, the first transaction included *YouthBks* (youth books) *DoItYBks* (do-it-yourself books), and *GeogBks* (geography books). Figure 15.5 shows (part of) the rules generated by ASDM's *Association Rules* on these data. We specified

Summary

Metric	Value
# Transactions	2000
# Items	11
# Rules	49

Rules

Rule ID	A - Support	C - Support	Support	Confidence	Lift - Ratio	Antecedent	Consequent
Rule 13	227	862	227	100	2.32	[ItalCook]	[CookBks]
Rule 38	325	552	204	62.77	2.27	[ChildBks,ArtBks]	[GeogBks]
Rule 41	375	482	203	54.13	2.25	[CookBks,DoItYBks]	[ArtBks]
Rule 47	334	552	207	61.98	2.25	[CookBks,ArtBks]	[GeogBks]
Rule 48	385	482	207	53.77	2.23	[CookBks,GeogBks]	[ArtBks]
Rule 25	429	512	245	57.11	2.23	[RefBks]	[ChildBks,CookBks]
Rule 39	390	482	204	52.31	2.17	[ChildBks,GeogBks]	[ArtBks]
Rule 42	334	564	203	60.78	2.16	[CookBks,ArtBks]	[DoItYBks]
Rule 31	552	512	299	54.17	2.12	[GeogBks]	[ChildBks,CookBks]
Rule 32	512	552	299	58.40	2.12	[ChildBks,CookBks]	[GeogBks]
Rule 44	375	552	217	57.87	2.10	[CookBks,DoItYBks]	[GeogBks]
Rule 35	368	552	209	56.79	2.06	[ChildBks,DoItYBks]	[GeogBks]
Rule 28	482	512	253	52.49	2.05	[ArtBks]	[ChildBks,CookBks]
Rule 17	495	512	258	52.12	2.04	[YouthBks]	[ChildBks,CookBks]
Rule 19	512	495	258	50.39	2.04	[ChildBks,CookBks]	[YouthBks]
Rule 21	564	512	292	51.77	2.02	[DoItYBks]	[ChildBks,CookBks]
Rule 22	512	564	292	57.03	2.02	[ChildBks,CookBks]	[DoItYBks]
Rule 45	385	564	217	56.36	2.00	[CookBks,GeogBks]	[DoItYBks]
Rule 16	482	552	255	52.90	1.92	[ArtBks]	[GeogBks]
Rule 43	247	862	203	82.19	1.91	[DoItYBks,ArtBks]	[CookBks]
Rule 36	390	564	209	53.59	1.90	[ChildBks,GeogBks]	[DoItYBks]
Rule 46	265	862	217	81.89	1.90	[DoItYBks,GeogBks]	[CookBks]
Rule 27	305	846	245	80.33	1.90	[CookBks,RefBks]	[ChildBks]
Rule 40	255	846	204	80.00	1.89	[ArtBks,GeogBks]	[ChildBks]
Rule 49	255	862	207	81.18	1.88	[ArtBks,GeogBks]	[CookBks]
Rule 20	324	846	258	79.63	1.88	[YouthBks,CookBks]	[ChildBks]

FIGURE 15.5   ASSOCIATION RULES FOR BOOK PURCHASE TRANSACTIONS: ASDM OUTPUT

a minimal support of 200 transactions and a minimal confidence of 50%. This resulted in 49 rules (the 26 rules with the highest lift ratio are shown in Figure 15.5).

In reviewing these rules, we see that the the information can be compressed. First, rule 13 (top), which appears from the confidence level to be a very promising rule, is probably meaningless. It says: "If Italian cooking books have been purchased, then cookbooks are purchased." It seems likely that Italian cooking books are simply a subset of cookbooks. Rules 38, 39, and 40 involve the same trio of books with different antecedents and consequents. The same is true of the pair of rules 19 and 20 and the pair of rules 21 and 22. (Pairs and groups like this are easy to track down by looking for rows that share the same support.) This does not mean that the rules are not useful. On the contrary, it can reduce the number of itemsets to be considered for possible action from a business perspective.

FIGURE 15.6   THE MACHINE LEARNING WORKFLOW FOR THE BOOK PURCHASE EXAMPLE

The machine learning workflow for the book purchase example used in this chapter is shown in Figure 15.6.

15.2 COLLABORATIVE FILTERING[3]

Recommendation systems are a critically important part of websites that offer a large variety of products or services. Examples include Amazon.com, which offers millions of different products; Netflix has thousands of movies for rental; Google searches over huge numbers Internet radio websites such as Spotify and Pandora include a large variety of music albums by various artists; travel websites offer many destinations and hotels; social network websites have many groups. The recommender engine provides personalized recommendations to a user based on the user's information as well as on similar users' information. Information means behaviors indicative of preference, such as purchase, ratings, and clicking.

The value that recommendation systems provide to users helps online companies convert browsers into buyers, increases cross-selling, and builds loyalty.

Collaborative filtering is a popular technique used by such recommendation systems. The term *collaborative filtering* is based on the notions of identifying relevant items for a specific user from the very large set of items ("filtering") by considering preferences of many users ("collaboration").

The Fortune.com article "Amazon's Recommendation Secret" (June 30, 2012) describes the company's use of collaborative filtering not only for

---

[3]This section copyright © 2019 Datastats, LLC, Galit Shmueli, and Peter Bruce.

providing personalized product recommendations, but also for customizing the entire website interface for each user:

> At root, the retail giant's recommendation system is based on a number of simple elements: what a user has bought in the past, which items they have in their virtual shopping cart, items they've rated and liked, and what other customers have viewed and purchased. Amazon calls this homegrown math "item-to-item collaborative filtering," and it's used this algorithm to heavily customize the browsing experience for returning customers.

Data Type and Format

Collaborative filtering requires availability of all item-user information. Specifically, for each item-user combination, we should have some measure of the user's preference for that item. Preference can be a numerical rating or a binary behavior such as a purchase, a "like," or a click.

For n users $(u_1, u_2, \ldots, u_n)$ and p items $(i_1, i_2, \ldots, i_p)$, we can think of the data as an $n \times p$ matrix of n rows (users) by p columns (items). Each cell includes the rating or the binary event corresponding to the user's preference of the item (see the schematic in Table 15.6). Typically, not every user purchases or rates every item, and therefore a purchase matrix will have many zeros (it is sparse), and a rating matrix will have many missing values. Such missing values sometimes convey "uninterested" (as opposed to non-missing values that convey interest).

TABLE 15.6   SCHEMATIC OF MATRIX FORMAT WITH RATINGS DATA

User ID	Item ID			
	I_1	I_2	$\cdots$	I_p
U_1	$r_{1,1}$	$r_{1,2}$	$\cdots$	$r_{1,p}$
U_2	$r_{2,1}$	$r_{2,2}$	$\cdots$	$r_{2,p}$
$\vdots$				
U_n	$r_{n,1}$	$r_{n,2}$	$\cdots$	$r_{n,p}$

When both n and p are large, it is not practical to store the preferences data $(r_{u,i})$ in an $n \times p$ table. Instead, the data can be stored in many rows of triplets of the form $(U_u, I_i, r_{u,i})$, where each triplet contains the user ID, the item ID, and the preference information.

Example 3: Netflix Prize Contest

We have been considering both association rules and collaborative filtering as unsupervised techniques, but it is possible to judge how well they do by looking at holdout data to see what users purchase and how they rate items. The famous

Netflix contest, mentioned in Chapter 13, did just this and provides a useful example to illustrate collaborative filtering, though the extension into training and validation is beyond the scope of this book.

In 2006, Netflix, the largest movie rental service in North America, announced a one million USD contest (www.netflixprize.com) for the purpose of improving its recommendation system called *Cinematch*. Participants were provided with a number of datasets, one for each movie. Each dataset included all the customer ratings for that movie (and the timestamp). We can think of one large combined dataset of the form [customer ID, movie ID, rating, date] where each record includes the rating given by a certain customer to a certain movie on a certain date. Ratings were on a 1-5 star scale. Contestants were asked to develop a recommendation algorithm that would improve over the existing Netflix system. Table 15.7 shows a small sample from the contest data, organized in matrix format. Rows indicate customers and columns are different movies.

TABLE 15.7   SAMPLE OF RECORDS FROM THE NETFLIX PRIZE CONTEST, FOR A SUBSET OF 10 CUSTOMERS AND 9 MOVIES

Customer ID	Movie ID								
	1	5	8	17	18	28	30	44	48
30878	4	1			3	3	4	5	
124105	4								
822109	5								
823519	3		1	4		4	5		
885013	4	5							
893988	3						4	4	
1248029	3					2	4		3
1503895	4								
1842128	4						3		
2238063	3								

It is interesting to note that the winning team was able to improve their system by considering not just the ratings for a movie, but whether a movie was rated by a particular customer or not. In other words, the information on which movies a customer decided to rate turned out to be critically informative of customers' preferences, more than simply considering the 1-5 rating information:[4]

> Collaborative filtering methods address the sparse set of rating values. However, much accuracy is obtained by also looking at other features of the data. First is the information on which movies each user chose to rate, regardless of specific rating value ("the binary view"). This played a decisive role in our 2007 solution, and reflects the fact that the movies to be rated are selected deliberately by the user, and are not a random sample.

This is an example where converting the rating information into a binary matrix of rated/unrated proved to be useful.

---

[4]"The BellKor 2008 Solution to the Netflix Prize," Bell, R. M., Koren, Y., and Volinsky, C., http://citeseerx.ist.psu.edu/viewdoc/summary?doi=10.1.1.142.9009

User-Based Collaborative Filtering: "People Like You"

One approach to generating personalized recommendations for a user using collaborative filtering is based on finding users with similar preferences and recommending items that they liked but the user hasn't purchased. The algorithm has two steps:

1. Find users who are most similar to the user of interest (neighbors). This is done by comparing the preference of our user to the preferences of other users.

2. Considering only the items that the user has *not* yet purchased, recommend the ones that are most preferred by the user's neighbors.

This is the approach behind Amazon's "Customers Who Viewed This Item Also Viewed ..." (see Figure 15.1). It is also used in a Google search for generating the "Similar pages" link shown near each search result.

Step 1 requires choosing a distance (or proximity) metric to measure the distance between our user and the other users. Once the distances are computed, we can use a threshold on the distance or on the number of required neighbors to determine the nearest neighbors to be used in step 2. This approach is called "user-based top-N recommendation."

A nearest-neighbors approach measures the distance of our user to each of the other users in the database, similar to the k-nearest-neighbors algorithm (see Chapter 7). The Euclidean distance measure we discussed in that chapter does not perform as well for collaborative filtering as some other measures. A popular proximity measure between two users is the Pearson correlation between their ratings. We denote the ratings of items $I_1, \ldots, I_p$ by user U_1 as $r_{1,1}, r_{1,2}, \ldots, r_{1,p}$ and their average by $\bar{r}_1$. Similarly, the ratings by user U_2 are $r_{2,1}, r_{2,2}, \ldots, r_{2,p}$, with average $\bar{r}_2$. The correlation proximity between the two users is defined by

$$\mathrm{Corr}(U_1, U_2) = \frac{\sum (r_{1,i} - \bar{r}_1)(r_{2,i} - \bar{r}_2)}{\sqrt{\sum (r_{1,i} - \bar{r}_1)^2}\sqrt{\sum (r_{2,i} - \bar{r}_2)^2}}, \qquad (15.1)$$

where the summations are only over the items co-rated by both users.

To illustrate this, let us compute the correlation between customer 30878 and customer 823519 in the small Netflix sample in Table 15.7. We'll assume that the data shown in the table is the entire information. First, we compute the average rating by each of these users:

$$\begin{aligned} \bar{r}_{30878} &= (4 + 1 + 3 + 3 + 4 + 5)/6 = 3.333. \\ \bar{r}_{823519} &= (3 + 1 + 4 + 4 + 5)/5 = 3.4. \end{aligned}$$

Note that the average is computed over a different number of movies for each of these customers, because they each rated a different set of movies. The average for a customer is computed over *all* the movies that a customer rated. The calculations for the correlation involve the departures from the average, but *only for the items that they co-rated*. In this case the co-rated movie IDs are 1, 28, and 30:

$$\text{Corr}(U_{30878}, U_{823519})$$
$$= \frac{(4 - 3.333)(3 - 3.4) + (3 - 3.333)(4 - 3.4) + (4 - 3.333)(5 - 3.4)}{\sqrt{(4 - 3.333)^2 + (3 - 3.333)^2 + (4 - 3.333)^2}\sqrt{(3 - 3.4)^2 + (4 - 3.4)^2 + (5 - 3.4)^2}}$$
$$= 0.6/1.75 = 0.34.$$

The same approach can be used when the data are in the form of a binary matrix (e.g., purchased or didn't purchase.)

Another popular measure is a variant of the Pearson correlation called *cosine similarity*. It differs from the correlation formula by not subtracting the means. Subtracting the mean in the correlation formula adjusts for users' different overall approaches to rating-for example, a customer who always rates highly vs. one who tends to give low ratings.[5]

For example, the cosine similarity between the two Netflix customers is

$$\text{Cos Sim}(U_{30878}, U_{823519}) = \frac{4 \times 3 + 3 \times 4 + 4 \times 5}{\sqrt{4^2 + 3^2 + 4^2}\sqrt{3^2 + 4^2 + 5^2}}$$
$$= 44/45.277 = 0.972.$$

Note that when the data are in the form of a binary matrix, say, for purchase or no-purchase, the cosine similarity must be calculated over all items that either user has purchased; it cannot be limited to just the items that were co-purchased.

> Collaborative filtering suffers from what is called a *cold start*: it cannot be used as-is to create recommendations for new users or new items. For a user who rated a single item, the correlation coefficient between this and other users (in user-generated collaborative filtering) will have a denominator of zero and the cosine proximity will be 1 regardless of the rating. In a similar vein, users with just one item, and items with just one user, do not qualify as candidates for nearby neighbors.

For a user of interest, we compute his/her similarity to each of the users in our database using a correlation, cosine similarity, or another measure. Then, in step 2, we look only at the k-nearest users, and among all the other items that they rated/purchased, we choose the best one and recommend it to our user. What is the best one? For binary purchase data, it is the item most purchased.

---

[5]Correlation and cosine similarity are popular in collaborative filtering because they are computationally fast for high-dimensional sparse data, and they account both for the rating values and the number of rated items.

For rating data, it could be the highest rated, most rated, or a weighting of the two.

The nearest-neighbors approach can be computationally expensive when we have a large database of users. One solution is to use clustering methods (see Chapter 15) to group users into homogeneous clusters in terms of their preferences and then to measure the distance of our user to each of the clusters. This approach places the computational load on the clustering step that can take place earlier and offline; it is then cheaper (and faster) to compare our user to each of the clusters in realtime. The price of clustering is less accurate recommendations, because not all the members of the closest cluster are the most similar to our user.

> Collaborative filtering is not implemented in ASDM as well as in many other similar machine learning software packages because the algorithm typically operates directly on a large user database and provides real-time recommendations. Such an implementation is beyond the scope of machine learning software designed for model building and evaluation.

Item-Based Collaborative Filtering

When the number of users is much larger than the number of items, it is computationally cheaper (and faster) to find similar items rather than similar users. Specifically, when a user expresses interest in a particular item, the item–based collaborative filtering algorithm has two steps:

1. Find the items that were co-rated, or co-purchased, (by any user) with the item of interest.

2. Recommend the most popular or correlated item(s) among the similar items.

Similarity is now computed between items, instead of users. For example, in our small Netflix sample (Table 15.7), the correlation between movie 1 (with average $\bar{r}_1 = 3.7$) and movie 5 (with average $\bar{r}_5 = 3$) is

$$\text{Corr}(I_1, I_5) = \frac{(4 - 3.7)(1 - 3) + (4 - 3.7)(5 - 3)}{\sqrt{(4 - 3.7)^2 + (4 - 3.7)^2}\sqrt{(1 - 3)^2 + (5 - 3)^2}} = 0.$$

(15.2)

The zero correlation is due to the two opposite ratings of movie 5 by the users who also rated 1. One user rated it 5 stars and the other gave it a 1 star.

In like fashion, we can compute similarity between all the movies. This can be done offline. In realtime, for a user who rates a certain movie highly, we can look up the movie correlation table and recommend the movie with the highest positive correlation to the user's newly rated movie.

According to an industry report[6] by researchers who developed the Amazon item-to-item recommendation system,

> [The item-based] algorithm produces recommendations in real time, scales to massive data sets, and generates high quality recommendations.

The disadvantage of item-based recommendations is that there is less diversity between items (compared to users' taste), and therefore the recommendations are often obvious.

Advantages and Weaknesses of Collaborative Filtering

Collaborative filtering relies on the availability of subjective information regarding users' preferences. It provides useful recommendations, even for "long tail" items, if our database contains sufficient similar users (not necessarily many, but at least a few per user), so that each user can find others users with similar tastes. Similarly, the data should include sufficient per-item ratings or purchases. One limitation of collaborative filtering is therefore that it cannot generate recommendations for new users, nor for new items. There are various approaches for tackling this challenge.

User-based collaborative filtering looks for similarity in terms of highly rated or preferred items. However, it is blind to data on low-rated or unwanted items. We can therefore not expect to use it as-is for detecting unwanted items.

User-based collaborative filtering helps leverage similarities between people's tastes for providing personalized recommendations. However, when the number of users becomes very large, collaborative filtering becomes computationally difficult. Solutions include item-based algorithms, clustering of users, and dimension reduction. The most popular dimension reduction method used in such cases is *singular value decomposition*, a computationally superior form of principal component analysis (see Chapter 4).

Although the term "prediction" is often used to describe the output of collaborative filtering, this method is unsupervised by nature. It can be used to generate predicted ratings or purchase indication for a user, but usually we do not have the true outcome value in practice. Evaluating performance is therefore challenging and treats the user's actual behavior as if it were their response to the recommendation. One important way to improve recommendations generated by collaborative filtering is by getting actual user feedback. Once a recommendation is generated, the user can indicate whether the recommendation was adequate or not. For this reason, many recommender systems entice users to provide feedback on their recommendations. When user reactions are measured with respect to the presented recommendations, this is called *online learning*. This

---

[6]Linden, G., Smith, B., and York J., "Amazon.com Recommendations: Item-to-Item Collaborative Filtering", *IEEE Internet Computing*, vol. 7, no. 1, p. 76–80, 2003.

is in contrast to *offline learning*, where such "online" feedback information is not used. Lastly, using online learning, many companies now measure the direct impact of a recommender system in terms of a business-relevant metric, such as conversion rate. In Chapter 14 we describe approaches that obtain user feedback that are useful for evaluating recommender systems as well as other interventions.

Collaborative Filtering vs. Association Rules

While collaborative filtering and association rules are both unsupervised methods used for generating recommendations, they differ in several ways:

Frequent itemsets vs. personalized recommendations: Association rules look for frequent item combinations and will provide recommendations only for those items. In contrast, collaborative filtering provides personalized recommendations for every item, thereby catering to users with unusual taste. In this sense, collaborative filtering is useful for capturing the "long tail" of user preferences, while association rules look for the "head." This difference has implications for the data needed: association rules require data on a very large number of "baskets" (transactions) in order to find a sufficient number of baskets that contain certain combinations of items. In contrast, collaborative filtering does not require many "baskets," but it does require data on as many items as possible for many users. Also association rules operate at the basket level (our database can include multiple transactions for each user), while collaborative filtering operates at the user level.

Because association rules produce generic, impersonal rules (association-based recommendations such as Amazon's "Frequently Bought Together" display the same recommendations to all users searching for a specific item), they can be used for setting common strategies such as product placement in a store or sequencing of diagnostic tests in hospitals. In contrast, collaborative filtering generates user-specific recommendations (e.g., Amazon's "Customers Who Viewed This Item Also Viewed ...") and is therefore a tool designed for personalization.

Transactional data vs. user data: Association rules provide recommendations of items based on their co-purchase with other items in *many transactions/baskets*. In contrast, collaborative filtering provides recommendations of items based on their co-purchase or co-rating by even a small number of other *users*. Considering distinct baskets is useful when the same items are purchased over and over again (e.g., in grocery shopping). Considering distinct users is useful when each item is typically purchased/rated once (e.g., purchases of books, music, and movies).

Binary data and ratings data: Association rules treat items as binary data (1 = purchase, 0 = nonpurchase), whereas collaborative filtering can operate on either binary data or on numerical ratings.

Two or more items: In association rules, the antecedent and consequent can each include one or more items (e.g., IF milk THEN cookies and cornflakes). Hence, a recommendation might be a bundle of the item of interest with multiple items ("buy milk, cookies, and cornflakes and receive 10% discount"). In contrast, in collaborative filtering, similarity is measured between *pairs* of items or pairs of users. A recommendation will therefore be either for a single item (the most popular item purchased by people like you, which you haven't purchased), or for multiple single items that do not necessarily relate to each other (the top two most popular items purchased by people like you, which you haven't purchased).

These distinctions are sharper for purchases and recommendations of non-popular items, especially when comparing association rules to user-based collaborative filtering. When considering what to recommend to a user who purchased a popular item, then association rules and item-based collaborative filtering might yield the same recommendation for a single item. But a user-based recommendation will likely differ. Consider a customer who purchases milk every week as well as gluten-free products (which are rarely purchased by other customers). Suppose that using association rules on the transaction database we identify the rule "IF milk THEN cookies." Then the next time our customer purchases milk, s/he will receive a recommendation (e.g., a coupon) to purchase cookies, whether or not s/he purchased cookies, and regardless of his/her gluten-free item purchases. In item-based collaborative filtering, we would look at all items co-purchased with milk across all users and recommend the most popular item among them (which was not purchased by our customer). This might also lead to a recommendation of cookies, because this item was not purchased by our customer.[7] Now consider user-based collaborative filtering. User-based collaborative filtering searches for similar customers—those who purchased the same set of items—and then recommend the item most commonly purchased by these neighbors, which *was not purchased by our customer*. The user-based recommendation is therefore unlikely to recommend cookies and more likely to recommend popular gluten-free items that the customer has not purchased.

15.3 SUMMARY

Association rules (also called market basket analysis) and collaborative filtering are unsupervised methods for deducing associations between purchased items from databases of transactions. Association rules search for generic rules about

---

[7]If the rule is "IF milk, THEN cookies and cornflakes," then the association rules would recommend cookies and cornflakes to a milk purchaser, while item-based collaborative filtering would recommend the most popular single item purchased with milk.

items that are purchased together. The main advantage of this method is that it generates clear, simple rules of the form "IF X is purchased, THEN Y is also likely to be purchased." The method is very transparent and easy to understand.

The process of creating association rules is two-staged. First, a set of candidate rules based on frequent itemsets is generated (the Apriori algorithm being the most popular rule generating algorithm). Then from these candidate rules, the rules that indicate the strongest association between items are selected. We use the measures of support and confidence to evaluate the uncertainty in a rule. The user also specifies minimal support and confidence values to be used in the rule generation and selection process. A third measure, the lift ratio, compares the efficiency of the rule to detect a real association compared to a random combination.

One shortcoming of association rules is the profusion of rules that are generated. There is therefore a need for ways to reduce these to a small set of useful and strong rules. An important nonautomated method to condense the information involves examining the rules for uninformative and trivial rules as well as for rules that share the same support. Another issue that needs to be kept in mind is that rare combinations tend to be ignored because they do not meet the minimum support requirement. For this reason, it is better to have items that are approximately equally frequent in the data. This can be achieved by using higher-level hierarchies as the items. An example is to use types of books rather than titles of individual books in deriving association rules from a database of bookstore transactions.

Collaborative filtering is a popular technique used in online recommendation systems. It is based on the relationship between items formed by users who acted similarly on an item, such as purchasing or rating an item highly. User-based collaborative filtering operates on data on item-user combinations, calculates the similarities between users, and provides personalized recommendations to users. An important component for the success of collaborative filtering is that users provide feedback about the recommendations provided and have sufficient information on each item. One disadvantage of collaborative filtering methods is that they cannot generate recommendations for new users or new items. Also, with a huge number of users, user-based collaborative filtering becomes computationally challenging, and alternatives such as item-based methods or dimension reduction are popularly used.

PROBLEMS

15.1 Satellite Radio Customers. An analyst at a subscription-based satellite radio company has been given a sample of data from their customer database, with the goal of finding groups of customers who are associated with one another. The data consist of company data, together with purchased demographic data that are mapped to the company data (see Table 15.8). The analyst decides to apply association rules to learn more about the associations between customers. Comment on this approach.

TABLE 15.8   SAMPLE OF DATA ON SATELLITE RADIO CUSTOMERS

Row ID	zipconvert_2	zipconvert_3	zipconvert_4	zipconvert_5	homeowner dummy	NUMCHLD	INCOME	gender dummy	WEALTH
17	0	1	0	0	1	1	5	1	9
25	1	0	0	0	1	1	1	0	7
29	0	0	0	1	0	2	5	1	8
38	0	0	0	1	1	1	3	0	4
40	0	1	0	0	1	1	4	0	8
53	0	1	0	0	1	1	4	1	8
58	0	0	0	1	1	1	4	1	8
61	1	0	0	0	1	1	1	0	7
71	0	0	1	0	1	1	4	0	5
87	1	0	0	0	1	1	4	1	8
100	0	0	0	1	1	1	4	1	8
104	1	0	0	0	1	1	1	1	5
121	0	0	1	0	1	1	4	1	5
142	1	0	0	0	0	1	5	0	8

15.2 Identifying Course Combinations. The Institute for Statistics Education at Statistics.com offers online courses in statistics and analytics, and it is seeking information that will help in packaging and sequencing courses. Consider the data in the file `CourseTopics.xlsx`, the first few rows of which are shown in Table 15.9.

TABLE 15.9   DATA ON PURCHASES OF ONLINE STATISTICS COURSES

Intro	DataMining	Survey	CatData	Regression	Forecast	DOE	SW
1	1	0	0	0	0	0	0
0	0	1	0	0	0	0	0
0	1	0	1	1	0	0	1
1	0	0	0	0	0	0	0
1	1	0	0	0	0	0	0
0	1	0	0	0	0	0	0
1	0	0	0	0	0	0	0
0	0	0	1	0	1	1	1
1	0	0	0	0	0	0	0
0	0	0	1	0	0	0	0
1	0	0	0	0	0	0	0

These data are for purchases of online statistics courses at Statistics.com. Each row represents the courses attended by a single customer. The firm wishes to assess alternative sequencings and bundling of courses. Use association rules to analyze these data, and interpret several of the resulting rules.

15.3 **Cosmetics Purchases.** The data shown in Table 15.10 and the output in Figure 15.7 are based on a subset of a dataset on cosmetic purchases (`Cosmetics.xlsx`) at a large chain drugstore. The store wants to analyze associations among purchases of these items for purposes of point-of-sale display, guidance to sales personnel in promoting cross sales, and guidance for piloting an eventual time-of-purchase electronic recommender system to boost cross sales. Consider first only the data shown in Table 15.10, given in binary matrix form.

  a. Select several values in the matrix and explain their meaning.

  b. Consider the results of the association rules analysis shown in Figure 15.7.

   i. For the first row, explain the Confidence value and how it is calculated.

   ii. For the first row, explain the meaning of the values for support for A (column A-Support), support for C (column C-Support), and support for A and C (column Support) and how they are calculated.

   iii. For the first row, explain the Lift-Ratio value and how it is calculated.

   iv. For the first row, explain the rule that is represented there in words.

Now use the complete dataset on the cosmetics purchases (in the file `Cosmetics .xlsx`).

   v. Using ASDM, apply association rules to these data (use the default parameters).

   vi. Interpret the first three rules in the output in words.

   vii. Reviewing the first couple of dozen rules, comment on their redundancy and how you would assess their utility.

TABLE 15.10   EXCERPT FROM DATA ON COSMETICS PURCHASES IN BINARY MATRIX FORM

Trans. #	Bag	Blush	Nail Polish	Brushes	Concealer	Eyebrow Pencils	Bronzer
1	0	1	1	1	1	0	1
2	0	0	1	0	1	0	1
3	0	1	0	0	1	1	1
4	0	0	1	1	1	0	1
5	0	1	0	0	1	0	1
6	0	0	0	0	1	0	0
7	0	1	1	1	1	0	1
8	0	0	1	1	0	0	1
9	0	0	0	0	1	0	0
10	1	1	1	1	0	0	0
11	0	0	1	0	0	0	1
12	0	0	1	1	1	0	1

Rule ID	A-Support	C-Support	Support	Confidence	Lift-Ratio	Antecedent	Consequent
Rule 49	77	103	62	80.51948052	3.90871265	[Brushes,Concealer]	[Nail Polish,Bronzer]
Rule 48	103	77	62	60.19417476	3.90871265	[Nail Polish,Bronzer]	[Brushes,Concealer]
Rule 53	76	110	62	81.57894737	3.70813397	[Nail Polish,Concealer,Bronzer]	[Brushes]
Rule 45	110	76	62	56.36363636	3.70813397	[Brushes]	[Nail Polish,Concealer,Bronzer]
Rule 29	110	103	84	76.36363636	3.70697264	[Brushes]	[Nail Polish,Bronzer]
Rule 31	103	110	84	81.55339806	3.70697264	[Nail Polish,Bronzer]	[Brushes]
Rule 47	109	84	62	56.88073394	3.38575797	[Nail Polish,Concealer]	[Brushes,Bronzer]
Rule 50	84	109	62	73.80952381	3.38575797	[Brushes,Bronzer]	[Nail Polish,Concealer]
Rule 25	110	109	77	70	3.21100917	[Brushes]	[Nail Polish,Concealer]
Rule 27	109	110	77	70.64220183	3.21100917	[Nail Polish,Concealer]	[Brushes]
Rule 13	110	82	55	50	3.04878049	[Brushes]	[Blush,Nail Polish]
Rule 14	82	110	55	67.07317073	3.04878049	[Blush,Nail Polish]	[Brushes]

FIGURE 15.7   ASSOCIATION RULES FOR COSMETICS PURCHASES DATA

15.4 **Course Ratings.** The Institute for Statistics Education at Statistics.com asks students to rate a variety of aspects of a course as soon as the student completes it. The Institute is contemplating instituting a recommendation system that would provide students with recommendations for additional courses as soon as they submit their rating for a completed course. Consider the excerpt from student ratings of online statistics courses shown in Table 15.11, and the problem of what to recommend to student E.N.

TABLE 15.11 RATINGS OF ONLINE STATISTICS COURSES: 4 = BEST, 1 = WORST, BLANK = NOT TAKEN

	SQL	Spatial	PA 1	DM in R	Python	Forecast	R Prog	Hadoop	Regression
L N	4				3	2	4		2
M H	3	4			4				
J H	2	2							
E N	4			4			4		3
D U	4	4							
F L		4							
G L		4							
A H		3							
S A			4						
R W			2					4	
B A			4						
M G			4			4			
A F			4						
K G			3						
D S	4			2			4		

a. First consider a user-based collaborative filter. This requires computing correlations between all student pairs. For which students is it possible to compute correlations with E.N.? Compute them.

b. Based on the single nearest student to E.N., which single course should we recommend to E.N.? Explain why.

c. Replace the ratings with a binary matrix indicating whether or not a student took the course. Compute the cosine similarity of E.N. from each of the other students for which such a calculation is feasible.

d. Based on the cosine similarities of the nearest students to E.N., which course should be recommended to E.N.?

e. What is the conceptual difference between using the actual ratings as opposed to a binary matrix showing whether a student took each course or not? (*Hint*: How are the missing values in the matrix handled in each case?)

f. With large datasets, it is computationally difficult to compute user-based recommendations in real time, and an item-based approach is used instead. Returning to the rating data (not the binary matrix), let's now take that approach.

    i. If the goal is still to find a recommendation for E.N., for which course pairs is it possible and useful to calculate correlations?

    ii. Just looking at the data, and without yet calculating course pair correlations, which course would you recommend to E.N., relying on item-based filtering? Calculate two course pair correlations involving your guess and report the results.

## CHAPTER 16

Cluster Analysis

This chapter is about the popular unsupervised learning task of clustering, where the goal is to segment the data into a set of homogeneous clusters of observations for the purpose of generating insight. Separating a dataset into clusters of homogeneous records is also useful for improving performance of supervised methods, by modeling each cluster separately rather than the entire, heterogeneous dataset. Clustering is used in a vast variety of business applications, from customized marketing to industry analysis. We describe two popular clustering approaches: *hierarchical clustering* and *k-means clustering*. In hierarchical clustering, observations are sequentially grouped to create clusters, based on distances between observations and distances between clusters. We describe how the algorithm works in terms of the clustering process and mention several common distance metrics used. Hierarchical clustering also produces a useful graphical display of the clustering process and results, called a dendrogram. We present dendrograms and illustrate their usefulness. k-means clustering is widely used in large dataset applications. In k-means clustering, observations are allocated to one of a pre-specified set of clusters, according to their distance from each cluster. We describe the k-means clustering algorithm and its computational advantages. Finally, we present techniques that assist in generating insight from clustering results.

16.1 INTRODUCTION

Cluster analysis is used to form groups or clusters of similar observations based on several measurements made on these observations. The key idea is to characterize the clusters in ways that would be useful for the aims of the analysis. This idea has been applied in many areas, including astronomy, archaeology, medicine,

Machine Learning for Business Analytics: Concepts, Techniques, and Applications with Analytic Solver® Data Mining,
Fourth Edition. Galit Shmueli, Peter C. Bruce, Kuber R. Deokar, and Nitin R. Patel.
© 2023 John Wiley & Sons, Inc. Published 2023 by John Wiley & Sons, Inc.

chemistry, education, psychology, linguistics, and sociology. Biologists, for example, have made extensive use of classes and subclasses to organize species. A spectacular success of the clustering idea in chemistry was Mendeleev's periodic table of the elements.

One popular use of cluster analysis in marketing is for *market segmentation:* customers are segmented based on demographic and transaction history information, and a marketing strategy is tailored for each segment. In countries such as India, where customer diversity is extremely location-sensitive, chain stores often perform market segmentation at the store level, rather than chain-wide (called "micro segmentation"). Another use is for *market structure analysis:* identifying groups of similar products according to competitive measures of similarity. In marketing and political forecasting, clustering of neighborhoods using US postal zip codes has been used successfully to group neighborhoods by lifestyles. Claritas, a company that pioneered this approach, grouped neighborhoods into 40 clusters using various measures of consumer expenditure and demographics. Examining the clusters enabled Claritas to come up with evocative names, such as "Bohemian Mix," "Furs and Station Wagons," and "Money and Brains," for the groups that captured the dominant lifestyles. Knowledge of lifestyles can be used to estimate the potential demand for products (e.g., sports utility vehicles) and services (e.g., pleasure cruises). Similarly, sales organizations will derive customer segments and give them names—"personas"—to focus sales efforts.

In finance, cluster analysis can be used for creating *balanced portfolios*: given data on a variety of investment opportunities (e.g., stocks), one may find clusters based on financial performance variables such as return (daily, weekly, or monthly), volatility, beta, and other characteristics, such as industry and market capitalization. Selecting securities from different clusters can help create a balanced portfolio. Another application of cluster analysis in finance is for *industry analysis*: for a given industry, we are interested in finding groups of similar firms based on measures such as growth rate, profitability, market size, product range, and presence in various international markets. These groups can then be analyzed in order to understand industry structure and to determine, for instance, who is a competitor.

An interesting and unusual application of cluster analysis, described in Berry and Linoff (1997), is the design of a new set of sizes for army uniforms for women in the US Army. The study came up with a new clothing size system with only 20 sizes, where different sizes fit different body types. The 20 sizes are combinations of five measurements: chest, neck, and shoulder circumference, sleeve outseam, and neck-to-buttock length (for further details, see McCullugh et al., 1998). This example is important because it shows how a completely new insightful view can be gained by examining clusters of records.

Cluster analysis can be applied to huge amounts of data. For instance, Internet search engines use clustering techniques to cluster queries that users submit.

These can then be used for improving search algorithms. The objective of this chapter is to describe the key ideas underlying the most commonly used techniques for cluster analysis and to lay out their strengths and weaknesses.

Typically, the basic data used to form clusters are a table of measurements on several numerical variables, where each column represents a variable and a row represents an observation. Our goal is to form groups of records so that similar observations are in the same group. The number of clusters may be prespecified or determined from the data.

Example: Public Utilities

Table 16.1 gives corporate data on 22 public utilities in the United States (the variable definitions are given in the table footnote). We are interested in forming groups of similar utilities. The observations to be clustered are the utilities, and the clustering will be based on the eight measurements on each utility. An example where clustering would be useful is a study to predict the cost impact of deregulation. To do the requisite analysis, economists would need to build a detailed cost model of the various utilities. It would save a considerable amount

TABLE 16.1   DATA ON 22 PUBLIC UTILITIES[a]

Company	Fixed	RoR	Cost	Load	Demand	Sales	Nuclear	Fuel Cost
Arizona Public Service	1.06	9.2	151	54.4	1.6	9077	0.0	0.628
Boston Edison Co.	0.89	10.3	202	57.9	2.2	5088	25.3	1.555
Central Louisiana Co.	1.43	15.4	113	53.0	3.4	9212	0.0	1.058
Commonwealth Edison Co.	1.02	11.2	168	56.0	0.3	6423	34.3	0.700
Consolidated Edison Co. (NY)	1.49	8.8	192	51.2	1.0	3300	15.6	2.044
Florida Power & Light Co.	1.32	13.5	111	60.0	−2.2	11127	22.5	1.241
Hawaiian Electric Co.	1.22	12.2	175	67.6	2.2	7642	0.0	1.652
daho Power Co.	1.10	9.2	245	57.0	3.3	13082	0.0	0.309
Kentucky Utilities Co.	1.34	13.0	168	60.4	7.2	8406	0.0	0.862
Madison Gas & Electric Co.	1.12	12.4	197	53.0	2.7	6455	39.2	0.623
Nevada Power Co.	0.75	7.5	173	51.5	6.5	17441	0.0	0.768
New England Electric Co.	1.13	10.9	178	62.0	3.7	6154	0.0	1.897
Northern States Power Co.	1.15	12.7	199	53.7	6.4	7179	50.2	0.527
Oklahoma Gas & Electric Co.	1.09	12.0	96	49.8	1.4	9673	0.0	0.588
Pacific Gas & Electric Co.	0.96	7.6	164	62.2	−0.1	6468	0.9	1.400
Puget Sound Power & Light Co.	1.16	9.9	252	56.0	9.2	15991	0.0	0.620
San Diego Gas & Electric Co.	0.76	6.4	136	61.9	9.0	5714	8.3	1.920
The Southern Co.	1.05	12.6	150	56.7	2.7	10140	0.0	1.108
Texas Utilities Co.	1.16	11.7	104	54.0	−2.1	13507	0.0	0.636
Wisconsin Electric Power Co.	1.20	11.8	148	59.9	3.5	7287	41.1	0.702
United Illuminating Co.	1.04	8.6	204	61.0	3.5	6650	0.0	2.116
Virginia Electric & Power Co.	1.07	9.3	174	54.3	5.9	10093	26.6	1.306

[a] Fixed = fixed-charge covering ratio (income/debt); RoR = rate of return on capital; Cost = cost per kilowatt capacity in place; Load = annual load factor; Demand = peak kilowatthour demand growth from 1974 to 1975; Sales = sales (kilowatthour use per year); Nuclear = percent nuclear; Fuel Cost = total fuel costs (cents per kilowatthour).

of time and effort if we could cluster similar types of utilities and build detailed cost models for just one "typical" utility in each cluster and then scale up from these models to estimate results for all utilities.

For simplicity, let us consider only two of the measurements: *Sales* and *Fuel Cost*. Figure 16.1 shows a scatterplot of these two variables, with labels marking each company. At first glance, there appear to be two or three clusters of utilities: one with utilities that have high fuel costs, a second with utilities that have lower fuel costs and relatively low sales, and a third with utilities with low fuel costs but high sales. We can therefore think of cluster analysis as a more formal algorithm that measures the distance between records and, according to these distances (here, two-dimensional distances), forms clusters.

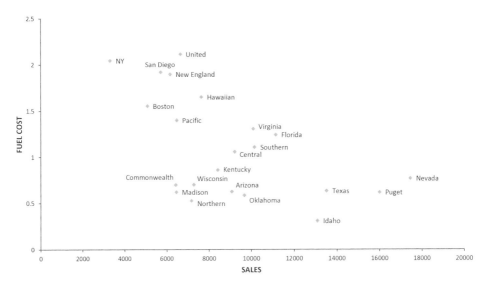

FIGURE 16.1   SCATTER PLOT OF FUEL COST VS. SALES FOR THE 22 UTILITIES. CREATED IN
EXCEL USING XY CHART LABELER ADD-ON
http://www.appspro.com/Utilities/ChartLabeler.htm

Two general types of clustering algorithms for a dataset of n observations are hierarchical and non-hierarchical clustering:

- **Hierarchical methods** can be either *agglomerative* or *divisive*. Agglomerative methods begin with n clusters and sequentially merge similar clusters until a single cluster is obtained. Divisive methods work in the opposite direction, starting with one cluster that includes all observations. Hierarchical methods are especially useful when the goal is to arrange the clusters into a natural hierarchy.

- **Non-hierarchical methods,** such as k-means. Using a prespecified number of clusters, the method assigns observations to each cluster. These methods are generally less computationally intensive and are therefore preferred with very large datasets.

We concentrate here on the two most popular methods: hierarchical agglomerative clustering and k-means clustering. In both cases, we need to define two types of distances: distance between two observations and distance between two clusters. In both cases, there is a variety of metrics that can be used.

16.2 MEASURING DISTANCE BETWEEN TWO OBSERVATIONS

We denote by d_{ij} a *distance metric*, or *dissimilarity measure*, between observations i and j. For observation i we have the vector of p measurements $(x_{i1}, x_{i2}, \ldots, x_{ip})$, while for observation j we have the vector of measurements $(x_{j1}, x_{j2}, \ldots, x_{jp})$. For example, we can write the measurement vector for Arizona Public Service as $[1.06, 9.2, 151, 54.4, 1.6, 9077, 0, 0.628]$.

Distances can be defined in multiple ways, but in general, the following properties are required:

Nonnegative: $d_{ij} \geq 0$

Self-proximity: $d_{ii} = 0$ (the distance from an observation to itself is zero)

Symmetry: $d_{ij} = d_{ji}$

Triangle inequality: $d_{ij} \leq d_{ik} + d_{kj}$ (the distance between any pair cannot exceed the sum of distances between the other two pairs)

Euclidean Distance

The most popular distance measure is the *Euclidean distance*, d_{ij}, which between two observations, i and j, is defined by

$$d_{ij} = \sqrt{(x_{i1} - x_{j1})^2 + (x_{i2} - x_{j2})^2 + \cdots + (x_{ip} - x_{jp})^2}.$$

For instance, the Euclidean distance between Arizona Public Service and Boston Edison Co. can be computed from the raw data by

$$
\begin{aligned}
d_{12} &= \sqrt{(1.06 - 0.89)^2 + (9.2 - 10.3)^2 + (151 - 202)^2 + \cdots + (0.628 - 1.555)^2} \\
&= 3989.408.
\end{aligned}
$$

Normalizing Numerical Variables

The measure computed above is highly influenced by the scale of each variable, so that variables with larger scales (e.g., Sales) have a much greater influence over the total distance. It is therefore customary to *normalize* continuous variables before computing the Euclidean distance. This converts all numerical variables to the same scale. Normalizing a variable means subtracting the average and dividing by the standard deviation (normalized values are also called *z-scores*). For instance, the average sales amount across the 22 utilities is 8914.045 and the standard deviation is 3549.984. The normalized sales for Arizona Public Service is therefore $(9077 - 8914.045)/3549.984 = 0.046$.

Returning to the simplified utilities data with only two measurements (Sales and Fuel Cost), we first normalize the measurements (see Table 16.2), and then compute the Euclidean distance between each pair. Table 16.3 gives these pairwise distances for the first five utilities. A similar table can be constructed for all 22 utilities.

TABLE 16.2   ORIGINAL AND NORMALIZED MEASUREMENTS FOR SALES AND FUEL COST

Company	Sales	Fuel Cost	NormSales	NormFuel
Arizona Public Service	9077	0.628	0.0459	−0.8537
Boston Edison Co.	5088	1.555	−1.0778	0.8133
Central Louisiana Co.	9212	1.058	0.0839	−0.0804
Commonwealth Edison Co.	6423	0.7	−0.7017	−0.7242
Consolidated Edison Co. (NY)	3300	2.044	−1.5814	1.6926
Florida Power & Light Co.	11127	1.241	0.6234	0.2486
Hawaiian Electric Co.	7642	1.652	−0.3583	0.9877
Idaho Power Co.	13082	0.309	1.1741	−1.4273
Kentucky Utilities Co.	8406	0.862	−0.1431	−0.4329
Madison Gas & Electric Co.	6455	0.623	−0.6927	−0.8627
Nevada Power Co.	17441	0.768	2.4020	−0.6019
New England Electric Co.	6154	1.897	−0.7775	1.4283
Northern States Power Co.	7179	0.527	−0.4887	−1.0353
Oklahoma Gas & Electric Co.	9673	0.588	0.2138	−0.9256
Pacific Gas & Electric Co.	6468	1.4	−0.6890	0.5346
Puget Sound Power & Light Co.	15991	0.62	1.9935	−0.8681
San Diego Gas & Electric Co.	5714	1.92	−0.9014	1.4697
The Southern Co.	10140	1.108	0.3453	0.0095
Texas Utilities Co.	13507	0.636	1.2938	−0.8393
Wisconsin Electric Power Co.	7287	0.702	−0.4583	−0.7206
United Illuminating Co.	6650	2.116	−0.6378	1.8221
Virginia Electric & Power Co.	10093	1.306	0.3321	0.3655
Mean	8914.05	1.10	0.00	0.00
Standard deviation	3549.98	0.56	1.00	1.00

TABLE 16.3   DISTANCE MATRIX BETWEEN PAIRS OF THE FIRST FIVE UTILITIES, USING EUCLIDEAN DISTANCE AND NORMALIZED VARIABLES

	Arizona	Boston	Central	Commonwealth	Consolidated
Arizona	0				
Boston	2.01	0			
Central	0.77	1.47	0		
Commonwealth	0.76	1.58	1.02	0	
Consolidated	3.02	1.01	2.43	2.57	0

Other Distance Measures for Numerical Data

It is important to note that the choice of the distance measure plays a major role in cluster analysis. The main guideline is domain dependent: What exactly is being measured? How are the different variables related? What scale should each variable be treated as (numerical, ordinal, or nominal)? Are there outliers? Finally, depending on the goal of the analysis, should the clusters be distinguished mostly by a small set of variables, or should they be separated by multiple variables that weight moderately?

Although Euclidean distance is the most widely used distance, it has three main features that need to be kept in mind. First, as mentioned earlier, it is highly scale dependent. Changing the units of one variable (e.g., from cents to dollars) can have a huge influence on the results. Normalizing is therefore a common solution. But unequal weighting should be considered if we want the clusters to depend more on certain variables and less on others. The second feature of Euclidean distance is that it completely ignores the relationship between the variables. Thus, if the variables are in fact strongly correlated, a different distance (e.g., the statistical distance, described below) is likely to be a better choice. Third, Euclidean distance is sensitive to outliers. If the data are believed to contain outliers and careful removal is not a choice, the use of more robust distances (e.g., the Manhattan distance described below) is preferred.

Additional popular distance metrics are often used (for reasons such as the ones above):

Correlation-based similarity: Sometimes it is more natural or convenient to work with a similarity measure between observations rather than distance, which measures dissimilarity. A popular similarity measure is the square of the Pearson correlation coefficient, r_{ij}^2, where the correlation coefficient is defined by

$$r_{ij} = \frac{\sum_{m=1}^{p}(x_{im} - \overline{x}_m)(x_{jm} - \overline{x}_m)}{\sqrt{\sum_{m=1}^{p}(x_{im} - \overline{x}_m)^2 \sum_{m=1}^{p}(x_{jm} - \overline{x}_m)^2}}. \tag{16.1}$$

Such measures can always be converted to distance measures. In the example above, we could define a distance measure $d_{ij} = 1 - r_{ij}^2$.

Statistical distance (also called Mahalanobis distance): This metric has an advantage over the other metrics mentioned in that it takes into account the correlation between variables. With this metric, variables that are highly correlated with other variables do not contribute as much as those that are uncorrelated or mildly correlated. The statistical distance between observations i and j is defined as

$$d_{i,j} = \sqrt{(\mathbf{x}_i - \mathbf{x}_j)' S^{-1}(\mathbf{x}_i - \mathbf{x}_j)},$$

where $\mathbf{x}_i$ and $\mathbf{x}_j$ are p-dimensional vectors of the variables' values for observations i and j, respectively, and S is the covariance matrix for these vectors. ($'$, a transpose operation, simply turns a column vector into a row vector). S^{-1} is the inverse matrix of S, which is the p-dimension extension to division. For further information on statistical distance, see Chapter 12.

Manhattan distance ("city block"): This distance looks at the absolute differences rather than squared differences and is defined by

$$d_{ij} = \sum_{m=1}^{p} | x_{im} - x_{jm} | .$$

Maximum coordinate distance: This distance looks only at the measurement on which observations i and j deviate most. It is defined by

$$d_{ij} = \max_{m=1,2,\dots,p} | x_{im} - x_{jm} | .$$

Distance Measures for Categorical Data

In the case of variables with binary values, it is more intuitively appealing to use similarity measures than distance measures. Suppose that we have binary values for all the p variables, and for observations i and j we have the following 2×2 table:

		Observation j		
		0	1	
Observation i	0	a	b	$a+b$
	1	c	d	$c+d$
		$a+c$	$b+d$	p

(16.2)

where a denotes the number of variables for which observations i and j each have value 0 for that variable (measurement absent), d is the number of variables for which the two observations each have a value 1 for that variable (measurement present), and so on. The most useful similarity measures in this situation are:

Matching coefficient: $(a + d)/p$.

Jaccard's coefficient: $d/(b + c + d)$. This coefficient ignores zero matches. This is desirable when we do not want to consider two people to be similar simply because a large number of characteristics are absent in both. For example, if *owns a Corvette* is one of the variables, a matching "yes" would be evidence of similarity, but a matching "no" tells us little about whether the two people are similar.

Distance Measures for Mixed Data

When the variables are mixed (some continuous and some binary), a similarity coefficient suggested by Gower is very useful. *Gower's similarity measure* is a weighted average of the distances computed for each variable, after scaling each variable to a [0,1] scale. It is defined as

$$s_{ij} = \frac{\sum_{m=1}^{p} w_{ijm} s_{ijm}}{\sum_{m=1}^{p} w_{ijm}},$$

where s_{ijm} is the similarity between observations i and j on variable m, and w_{ijm} is a binary weight given to the corresponding distance.

The similarity measures s_{ijm} and weights w_{ijm} are computed as follows:

1. For continuous variables, $s_{ijm} = 1 - \frac{|x_{im} - x_{jm}|}{\max(x_m) - \min(x_m)}$ and $w_{ijm} = 1$ unless the value for variable m is unknown for one or both of the observations, in which case $w_{ijm} = 0$.

2. For binary variables, $s_{ijm} = 1$ if $x_{im} = x_{jm} = 1$ and 0 otherwise. $w_{ijm} = 1$ unless $x_{im} = x_{jm} = 0$.

3. For nonbinary categorical variables, $s_{ijm} = 1$ if both observations are in the same category, and otherwise $s_{ijm} = 0$. As in continuous variables, $w_{ijm} = 1$ unless the category for variable m is unknown for one or both of the observations, in which case $w_{ijm} = 0$.

16.3 MEASURING DISTANCE BETWEEN TWO CLUSTERS

We define a cluster as a set of one or more observations. How do we measure distance between clusters? The idea is to extend measures of *distance between observations* into *distances between clusters*. Consider cluster A, which includes the m observations $A_1, A_2, \ldots, A_m$, and cluster B, which includes n observations $B_1, B_2, \ldots, B_n$. There are four widely used measures of distance between clusters: minimum distance, maximum distance, average distance, and centroid distance.

Minimum Distance

The distance between the pair of observations A_i and B_j that are closest:

$$\min(\text{distance}(A_i, B_j)), \quad i = 1, 2, \ldots, m; \ j = 1, 2, \ldots, n.$$

Maximum Distance

The distance between the pair of observations A_i and B_j that are farthest:

$$\max(\text{distance}(A_i, B_j)), \quad i = 1, 2, \ldots, m; \; j = 1, 2, \ldots, n.$$

Average Distance

The average distance of all possible distances between observations in one cluster and observations in the other cluster:

$$\text{Average}(\text{distance}(A_i, B_j)), \quad i = 1, 2, \ldots, m; \; j = 1, 2, \ldots, n.$$

Centroid Distance

The distance between the two cluster centroids. A *cluster centroid* is the vector of variable averages across all the observations in that cluster. For cluster A, this is the vector $\overline{x}_A = [(1/m \sum_{i=1}^{m} x_{1i}, \ldots, 1/m \sum_{i=1}^{m} x_{pi})]$. The centroid distance between clusters A and B is

$$\text{distance}(\overline{x}_A, \overline{x}_B).$$

Minimum distance, maximum distance, and centroid distance are illustrated visually for two dimensions using a map of Portugal and France in Figure 16.2.

As a numerical example, consider again the first two utilities (Arizona, Boston) as cluster A, and the next three utilities (Central, Commonwealth, Consolidated) as cluster B. Using the normalized scores in Table 16.2 and the distance matrix in Table 16.3, we can compute each of the distances described above. Using Euclidean distance for each distance calculation, we get:

- The closest pair is Arizona and Commonwealth, and therefore the minimum distance between clusters A and B is 0.76.

- The farthest pair is Arizona and Consolidated, and therefore the maximum distance between clusters A and B is 3.02.

- The average distance is $(0.77 + 0.76 + 3.02 + 1.47 + 1.58 + 1.01)/6 = 1.44$.

- The centroid of cluster A is

$$\left[\frac{0.0459 - 1.0778}{2}, \frac{-0.8537 + 0.8133}{2} \right] = [-0.516, -0.020],$$

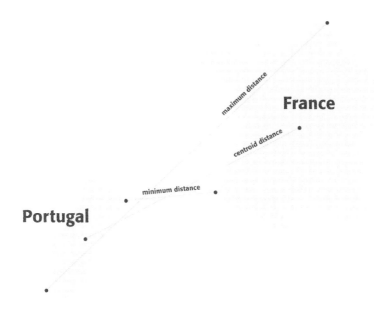

FIGURE 16.2   TWO-DIMENSIONAL REPRESENTATION OF SEVERAL DIFFERENT DISTANCE
MEASURES BETWEEN PORTUGAL AND FRANCE

and the centroid of cluster B is

$$\left[\frac{0.0839 - 0.7017 - 1.5814}{3}, \frac{-0.0804 - 0.7242 + 1.6926}{3}\right]$$
$$= [-0.733, 0.296].$$

The distance between the two centroids is then

$$\sqrt{(-0.516 + 0.733)^2 + (-0.020 - 0.296)^2} = 0.38.$$

In deciding among clustering methods, domain knowledge is key. If you have good reason to believe that the clusters might be chain- or sausage-like, minimum distance would be a good choice. This method does not require that cluster members all be close to one another, only that the new members being added be close to one of the existing members. An example of an application where this might be the case would be characteristics of crops planted in long rows, or disease outbreaks along navigable waterways that are the main areas of settlement in a region. Another example is laying and finding mines (land or marine). Minimum distance is also fairly robust to small deviations in the distances. However, adding or removing data can influence it greatly.

Maximum and average distance are better choices if you know that the clusters are more likely to be spherical (e.g., customers clustered on the basis of numerous variables). If you do not know the probable nature of the cluster, these are good default choices, since most clusters tend to be spherical in nature.

We now move to a more detailed description of the two major types of clustering algorithms: hierarchical (agglomerative) and non-hierarchical.

16.4 HIERARCHICAL (AGGLOMERATIVE) CLUSTERING

The idea behind hierarchical agglomerative clustering is to start with each cluster comprising exactly one observation and then progressively agglomerating (combining) the two nearest clusters until there is just one cluster left at the end, which consists of all the observations.

Returning to the small example of five utilities and two measures (Sales and Fuel Cost) and using the distance matrix (Table 16.3), the first step in the hierarchical clustering would join Arizona and Commonwealth, which are the closest (using normalized variables and Euclidean distance). Next we would recalculate a 4×4 distance matrix that would have the distances between these four clusters: {Arizona, Commonwealth}, {Boston}, {Central}, and {Consolidated}. At this point we use a measure of distance between clusters, such as the ones described in Section 16.3. Each of these distances (minimum, maximum, average, and centroid distance) can be implemented in the hierarchical scheme as described next.

HIERARCHICAL AGGLOMERATIVE CLUSTERING ALGORITHM:

1. Start with n clusters (each observation = cluster).
2. The two closest observations are merged into one cluster.
3. At every step, the two clusters with the smallest distance are merged. This means that either single observations are added to existing clusters or two existing clusters are combined.

Single Linkage

In *single linkage clustering*, the distance measure that we use is the minimum distance (the distance between the nearest pair of observations in the two clusters, one observation in each cluster). In our utilities example, we would compute the distances between each of {Boston}, {Central}, and {Consolidated} with {Arizona, Commonwealth} to create the 4×4 distance matrix shown in Table 16.4.

TABLE 16.4   DISTANCE MATRIX AFTER ARIZONA AND COMMONWEALTH CONSOLIDATION
CLUSTER TOGETHER, USING SINGLE LINKAGE

	Arizona–Commonwealth	Boston	Central	Consolidated
Arizona–Commonwealth	0			
Boston	min(2.01,1.58)	0		
Central	min(0.77,1.02)	1.47	0	
Consolidated	min(3.02,2.57)	1.01	2.43	0

The next step would consolidate {Central} with {Arizona, Commonwealth} because these two clusters are closest. The distance matrix will again be recomputed (this time it will be 3×3), and so on.

This method has a tendency to cluster together at an early stage observations that are distant from each other because of a chain of intermediate observations in the same cluster. Such clusters have elongated sausage-like shapes when visualized as objects in space.

Complete Linkage

In *complete linkage clustering*, the distance between two clusters is the maximum distance (between the farthest pair of observations). If we used complete linkage with the five-utilities example, the recomputed distance matrix would be equivalent to Table 16.4, except that the "min" function would be replaced with a "max."

This method tends to produce clusters at the early stages with observations that are within a narrow range of distances from each other. If we visualize them as objects in space, the observations in such clusters would have roughly spherical shapes.

Average Linkage (in ASDM: "Group Average Linkage")

Average linkage clustering is based on the average distance between clusters (between all possible pairs of observations). If we used average linkage with the five-utilities example, the recomputed distance matrix would be equivalent to Table 16.4, except that the "min" function would be replaced with "average." This method is also called *unweighted pair-group method using averages* (UPGMA).

Note that unlike average linkage, the results of the single and complete linkage methods depend only on the ordering of the inter-observation distances. Linear transformations of the distances (and other transformations that do not change the ordering) do not affect the results.

Centroid Linkage

Centroid linkage clustering is based on centroid distance, where clusters are represented by their mean values for each variable, which forms a vector of means. The distance between two clusters is the distance between these two vectors. In average linkage, each pairwise distance is calculated, and the average of all such distances is calculated. In contrast, in centroid distance clustering, just one distance is calculated: the distance between group means. This method is also called *unweighted pair-group method using centroids* (UPGMC).

Ward's Method

Ward's method is also agglomerative, in that it joins observations and clusters together progressively to produce larger and larger clusters, but operates slightly differently from the general approach described above. Ward's method considers the "loss of information" that occurs when observations are clustered together. When each cluster has one observation, there is no loss of information and all individual values remain available. When observations are joined together and represented in clusters, information about an individual observation is replaced by the information for the cluster to which it belongs. To measure loss of information, Ward's method employs a measure "error sum of squares" (ESS) that measures the difference between individual observations and a group mean.

This is easiest to see in univariate data. For example, consider the values (2, 6, 5, 6, 2, 2, 2, 2, 0, 0, 0) with a mean of 2.5. Their ESS is equal to

$$(2 - 2.5)^2 + (6 - 2.5)^2 + (5 - 2.5)^2 + \cdots + (0 - 2.5)^2 = 50.5.$$

The loss of information associated with grouping the values into a single group is therefore 50.5. Now group the observations into four groups: (0, 0, 0), (2, 2, 2, 2), (5), (6, 6). The loss of information is the sum of the ESS's for each group, which is 0 (each observation in each group is equal to the mean for that group, so the ESS for each group is 0). Thus clustering the 10 observations into 4 clusters results in no loss of information, and this would be the first step in Ward's method. In moving to a smaller number of clusters, Ward's method would choose the configuration that results in the smallest incremental loss of information.

Ward's method tends to result in convex clusters that are of roughly equal size, which can be an important consideration in some applications (e.g., in establishing meaningful customer segments).

Dendrograms: Displaying Clustering Process and Results

A *dendrogram* is a treelike diagram that summarizes the process of clustering. At the bottom are the individual observations (or clusters[1]). Similar observations are joined by lines whose vertical length reflects the distance between the observations. Figure 16.3 (top) shows the dendrogram that results from clustering all 22 utilities using the eight normalized variables, Euclidean distance, and single linkage. We set[2] cluster IDs listed along the x-axis. The Cluster Legend table in Figure 16.3 (bottom) maps each of the observation IDs to the cluster ID (called "sub-cluster") that it belongs to.

How were the 10 clusters obtained? Figure 16.4 shows the history of the cluster formation (Clustering Stages) and the final assignment of observations to the clusters (Cluster Labels) related to the dendrogram shown in Figure 16.3. Recall that initially, each individual observation is considered its own cluster (# clusters = # observations = 22). We see that in Stage 1, observations 12 and 21 had the smallest distance and were therefore joined into "sub-cluster 1" (we see the sub-cluster number in the Cluster Labels table). The remaining 19 clusters still each have one observation each. At stage 2, clusters 10 and 13 are found to have the smallest distance and are joined into "sub-cluster 10." This process continues until there is just one cluster. At various stages of the clustering process, there are different numbers of clusters. The dendrogram in Figure 16.3 displaying 10 sub-clusters on the x-axis is based on one of these stages.

By choosing a cutoff distance on the y-axis of the dendrogram, a set of clusters is created. Visually, this means drawing a horizontal line on a dendrogram. Observations/clusters with connections below the horizontal line (i.e., their distance is smaller than the cutoff distance) belong to the same cluster. For

---

[1] In ASDM, if the number of leaves is set to a number smaller than the number of observations, the bottom of the dendrogram displays clusters rather than individual observations.
[2] Currently the largest value allowed in the ASDM Education version is 10. *Maximum Number of Leaves*=10. The resulting dendrogram has 10

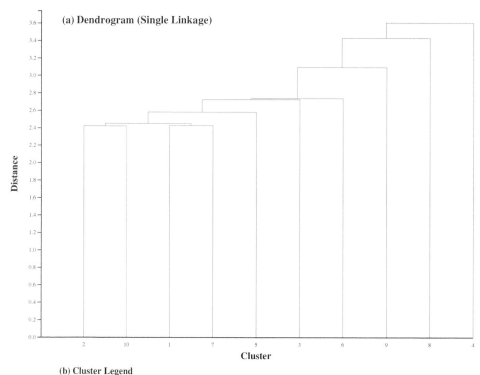

(a) Dendrogram (Single Linkage)

(b) Cluster Legend

Cluster Legend (Numbers show the record sequence relative to the original data)									
Sub-Cluster 1	Sub-Cluster 2	Sub-Cluster 3	Sub-Cluster 4	Sub-Cluster 5	Sub-Cluster 6	Sub-Cluster 7	Sub-Cluster 8	Sub-Cluster 9	Sub-Cluster 10
1	2	3	5	6	8	9	11	17	22
14	4				16				
18	7								
19	10								
	12								
	13								
	15								
	20								
	21								

FIGURE 16.3   (a) DENDROGRAM: SINGLE LINKAGE FOR ALL 22 UTILITIES, USING ALL 8 MEASUREMENTS. (b) LIST OF OBSERVATION IDS BELONGING TO EACH CLUSTER ("SUB-CLUSTER") ID

example, setting the cutoff distance to 2.7 in Figure 16.3 results in six clusters. The six clusters are (from right to left on the dendrogram):

Sub-cluster(s)	Observation(s)
4	5 (NY)
8	11 (Nevada)
9	17 (San Diego)
6	8 (Idaho), 16 (Puget)
3	3 (Central)
2, 10, 1, 7, 5	2,4,7,10,12,13,15,20,21,22,1,14,18,19,9,6

(a) Clustering Stages

Stage	Cluster 1	Cluster 2	Distance
Stage1	12	21	1.3841238
Stage2	10	13	1.4070319
Stage3	4	10	1.4914269
Stage4	7	12	1.6600468
Stage5	4	20	1.8164648
Stage6	14	19	1.8760515
Stage7	1	18	1.8772476
Stage8	7	15	2.0971503
Stage9	1	14	2.1134896
Stage10	2	4	2.1642126
Stage11	8	16	2.2014572
Stage12	2	7	2.3184513
Stage13	2	22	2.4219162
Stage14	1	9	2.428533
Stage15	1	2	2.4519353
Stage16	1	6	2.5812082
Stage17	1	3	2.723954
Stage18	1	8	2.7374066
Stage19	1	17	3.0950017
Stage20	1	11	3.4299621
Stage21	1	5	3.603863

(b) Cluster Labels

Record ID	Cluster	Sub-Cluster
Record 1	1	1
Record 2	1	2
Record 3	2	3
Record 4	1	2
Record 5	3	4
Record 6	1	5
Record 7	1	2
Record 8	4	6
Record 9	1	7
Record 10	1	2
Record 11	5	8
Record 12	1	2
Record 13	1	2
Record 14	1	1
Record 15	1	2
Record 16	4	6
Record 17	6	9
Record 18	1	1
Record 19	1	1
Record 20	1	2
Record 21	1	2
Record 22	1	10

FIGURE 16.4   (a) CLUSTERING STAGES: THE HISTORY OF THE CLUSTER FORMATION.
(b) CLUSTER LABELS: ASSIGNMENT OF CASES TO THE CLUSTERS

Note that if we wanted five clusters, they would be identical to the six above, with the exception that the first two clusters would be merged into one cluster. In general, all hierarchical methods have clusters that are nested within each other as we decrease the number of clusters. This is a valuable property for interpreting clusters and is essential in certain applications, such as taxonomy of varieties of living organisms.

The average linkage dendrogram (along with its cluster legend) is shown in Figure 16.5. Here too we set *Max Number of Leaves*=10, resulting in 10 clusters on the x-axis. If we want six clusters using average linkage, we can choose a cutoff distance of 3.5. The resulting six clusters would include the following observation IDs (from left to right in the dendrogram):
{3,9,1,14,18,19,6}; {2,4,10,13,20,22}; {7,12,15,21}; {17}; {5}; {8,16,11}.

Validating Clusters

One important goal of cluster analysis is to come up with *meaningful clusters*. Since there are many variations that can be chosen, it is important to make sure that the resulting clusters are valid, in the sense that they really generate some insight. To see whether the cluster analysis is useful, consider each of the following aspects:

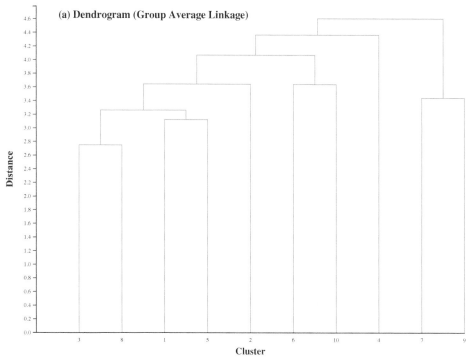

(a) Dendrogram (Group Average Linkage)

(b) Cluster Legend

Cluster Legend (Numbers show the record sequence relative to the original data)

Sub-Cluster 1	Sub-Cluster 2	Sub-Cluster 3	Sub-Cluster 4	Sub-Cluster 5	Sub-Cluster 6	Sub-Cluster 7	Sub-Cluster 8	Sub-Cluster 9	Sub-Cluster 10
1	2	3	5	6	7	8	9	11	17
14	4				12	16			
18	10				15				
19	13				21				
	20								
	22								

FIGURE 16.5   (a) DENDROGRAM: AVERAGE LINKAGE FOR ALL 22 UTILITIES, USING ALL 8 MEASUREMENTS. (b) CLUSTER ID AND THEIR OBSERVATIONS

1. *Cluster interpretability*: Is the interpretation of the resulting clusters reasonable? To interpret the clusters, explore the characteristics of each cluster by

   a. obtaining summary statistics (e.g., average, min, max) from each cluster on each variable that was used in the cluster analysis,

   b. examining the clusters for separation along some common feature (variable) that was not used in the cluster analysis, and

   c. labeling the clusters: based on the interpretation, trying to assign a name or label to each cluster.

2. *Cluster stability*: Do cluster assignments change significantly if some of the inputs are altered slightly? Another way to check stability is to partition the data and see how well clusters formed based on one part apply to the other part. To do this:

  a. Cluster partition A.

  b. Use the cluster centroids from A to assign each observation in partition B (each observation is assigned to the cluster with the closest centroid).

  c. Assess how consistent the cluster assignments are compared to the assignments based on all the data.

3. *Cluster separation*: Examine the ratio of between-cluster variation to within-cluster variation to see whether the separation is reasonable. There exist statistical tests for this task (an F-ratio), but their usefulness is somewhat controversial.

4. *Number of clusters*: The number of resulting clusters must be useful, given the purpose of the analysis. For example, suppose the goal of the clustering is to identify categories of customers and assign labels to them for market segmentation purposes. If the marketing department can only manage to sustain three different marketing presentations, it would probably not make sense to identify more than three clusters.

Returning to the utilities example, we notice that both methods (single and average linkage) identify {5} (NY) and {17} (San Diego) as singleton clusters. Also both dendrograms imply that a reasonable number of clusters in this dataset is four. One insight that can be derived from the average linkage clustering is that clusters tend to group geographically. The four non-singleton clusters form (approximately) a southern group, a northern group, an east/west seaboard group, and a west group.

We can further characterize each of the clusters by examining the summary statistics of their variables or visually looking at a heatmap of their individual variables. Figure 16.6 shows a heatmap of the four clusters and two singletons, highlighting the different profile that each cluster has in terms of the eight variables. We see, for instance, that cluster 2 is characterized by utilities with a high percent of nuclear power; cluster 1 is characterized by high fixed cost and RoR; cluster 4 has high fuel costs.

The machine learning workflow for the Single Linkage and Average Linkage clustering applied to the utilities data is shown in Figure 16.7.

Limitations of Hierarchical Clustering

Hierarchical clustering is very appealing in that it does not require specification of the number of clusters, and in that sense is purely data driven. The ability to represent the clustering process and results through dendrograms is also an

Company	Cluster ID	Sub-Cluster	Fixed	RoR	Cost	Load	Demand	Sales	Nuclear	Fuel_Cost
Arizona	1	1	1.06	9.2	151	54.4	1.6	9077	0	0.628
Central	1	3	1.43	15.4	113	53	3.4	9212	0	1.058
Florida	1	5	1.32	13.5	111	60	-2.2	11127	22.5	1.241
Kentucky	1	8	1.34	13	168	60.4	7.2	8406	0	0.862
Oklahoma	1	1	1.09	12	96	49.8	1.4	9673	0	0.588
Southern	1	1	1.05	12.6	150	56.7	2.7	10140	0	1.108
Texas	1	1	1.16	11.7	104	54	-2.1	13507	0	0.636
Boston	2	2	0.89	10.3	202	57.9	2.2	5088	25.3	1.555
Commonwealth	2	2	1.02	11.2	168	56	0.3	6423	34.3	0.7
Madison	2	2	1.12	12.4	197	53	2.7	6455	39.2	0.623
Northern	2	2	1.15	12.7	199	53.7	6.4	7179	50.2	0.527
Wisconsin	2	2	1.2	11.8	148	59.9	3.5	7287	41.1	0.702
Virginia	2	2	1.07	9.3	174	54.3	5.9	10093	26.6	1.306
NY	3	4	1.49	8.8	192	51.2	1	3300	15.6	2.044
Hawaiian	4	6	1.22	12.2	175	67.6	2.2	7642	0	1.652
New England	4	6	1.13	10.9	178	62	3.7	6154	0	1.897
Pacific	4	6	0.96	7.6	164	62.2	-0.1	6468	0.9	1.4
United	4	6	1.04	8.6	204	61	3.5	6650	0	2.116
Idaho	5	7	1.1	9.2	245	57	3.3	13082	0	0.309
Nevada	5	9	0.75	7.5	173	51.5	6.5	17441	0	0.768
Puget	5	7	1.16	9.9	252	56	9.2	15991	0	0.62
San Diego	6	10	0.76	6.4	136	61.9	9	5714	8.3	1.92

FIGURE 16.6   HEATMAP FOR THE 22 UTILITIES (IN ROWS). ROWS ARE SORTED BY THE SIX CLUSTERS FROM AVERAGE LINKAGE CLUSTERING. DARKER DENOTES HIGHER VALUES WITHIN A COLUMN

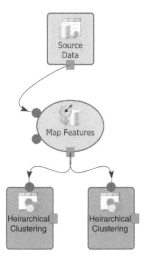

FIGURE 16.7   THE MACHINE LEARNING WORKFLOW FOR SINGLE LINKAGE (LEFT) AND AVERAGE LINKAGE (RIGHT) FOR ALL 22 UTILITIES, USING ALL 8 MEASUREMENTS

advantage of this method, as it is easier to understand and interpret. There are, however, a few limitations to consider:

1. Hierarchical clustering requires the computation and storage of a $n \times n$ distance matrix. For very large datasets, this can be expensive and slow.

2. The hierarchical algorithm makes only one pass through the data. This means that observations that are allocated incorrectly early in the process cannot be reallocated subsequently.

3. Hierarchical clustering also tends to have low stability. Reordering data or dropping a few observations can lead to a different solution.

4. With respect to the choice of distance between clusters, single and complete linkage are robust to changes in the distance metric (e.g., Euclidean, statistical distance) as long as the relative ordering is kept. In contrast, average linkage is more influenced by the choice of distance metric, and might lead to completely different clusters when the metric is changed.

5. Hierarchical clustering is sensitive to outliers.

16.5 NON-HIERARCHICAL CLUSTERING: THE k-MEANS ALGORITHM

A non-hierarchical approach to forming good clusters is to pre-specify a desired number of clusters, k, and assign each case to one of the k clusters so as to minimize a measure of dispersion within the clusters. In other words, the goal is to divide the sample into a predetermined number k of non-overlapping clusters so that clusters are as homogeneous as possible with respect to the variables used.

A common measure of within-cluster dispersion is the sum of distances (or sum of squared Euclidean distances) of observations from their cluster centroid. The problem can be set up as an optimization problem involving integer programming, but because solving integer programs with a large number of variables is time-consuming, clusters are often computed using a fast, heuristic method that produces good (although not necessarily optimal) solutions. The k-means algorithm is one such method.

The k-means algorithm starts with an initial partition of the observations into k clusters. Subsequent steps modify the partition to reduce the sum of the distances of each observation from its cluster centroid. The modification consists of allocating each observation to the nearest of the k centroids of the previous partition. This leads to a new partition for which the sum of distances is smaller than before. The means of the new clusters are computed and the improvement step is repeated until the improvement is very small.

---

k-MEANS CLUSTERING ALGORITHM:

1. Start with k initial clusters (user chooses k).

2. At every step, each observation is reassigned to the cluster with the "closest" centroid.

3. Recompute the centroids of clusters that lost or gained an observation, and repeat step 2.

4. Stop when moving any more observations between clusters increases cluster dispersion.

Returning to the example with the five utilities and two variables, let us assume that $k = 2$ and that the initial clusters are A = {Arizona, Boston} and B = {Central, Commonwealth, Consolidated}. The cluster centroids were computed in Section 16.4:

$$\bar{x}_A = [-0.516, -0.020] \text{ and } \bar{x}_B = [-0.733, 0.296].$$

The distance of each observation from each of these two centroids is shown in Table 16.5.

TABLE 16.5   DISTANCE OF EACH OBSERVATION FROM EACH CENTROID

	Distance from Centroid A	Distance from Centroid B
Arizona	1.0052	1.3887
Boston	1.0052	0.6216
Central	0.6029	0.8995
Commonwealth	0.7281	1.0207
Consolidated	2.0172	1.6341

We see that Boston is closer to cluster B, and that Central and Commonwealth are each closer to cluster A. We therefore move each of these observations to the other cluster and obtain A = {Arizona, Central, Commonwealth} and B = {Consolidated, Boston}. Recalculating the centroids gives

$$\bar{x}_A = [-0.191, -0.553] \text{ and } \bar{x}_B = [-1.33, 1.253].$$

The distance of each observation from each of the newly calculated centroids is given in Table 16.6. At this point, we stop because each observation is allocated to its closest cluster.

TABLE 16.6   DISTANCE OF EACH OBSERVATION FROM EACH NEWLY CALCULATED CENTROID

	Distance from Centroid A	Distance from Centroid B
Arizona	0.3827	2.5159
Boston	1.6289	0.5067
Central	0.5463	1.9432
Commonwealth	0.5391	2.0745
Consolidated	2.6412	0.5067

Initial Partition into k Clusters

The choice of the number of clusters can either be driven by external considerations (e.g., previous knowledge, practical constraints, etc.), or we can try a few different values for k and compare the resulting clusters. After choosing k, the n observations are partitioned into these initial clusters. If there is external reasoning that suggests a certain partitioning, this information should be used. Alternatively, if there exists external information on the centroids of the k-clusters, this can be used to initially allocate the observations.

In many cases, there is no information to be used for the initial partition. In these cases, the algorithm can be rerun with different randomly generated starting partitions to reduce chances of the heuristic producing a poor solution. The number of clusters in the data is generally not known, so it is a good idea to run the algorithm with different values for k that are near the number of clusters that one expects from the data to see how the sum of distances reduces with increasing values of k. Note that the clusters obtained using different values of k will not be nested (unlike those obtained by hierarchical methods).

The results of running the k-means algorithm for all 22 utilities and eight measurements with $k = 6$ are shown in Figure 16.8. As in the results from the hierarchical clustering, we see once again that observation {17} (San Diego) is a singleton cluster. Two more clusters (clusters 4 and 6) are nearly identical to those that emerged in the hierarchical clustering with average linkage. Cluster 3 has the largest within-cluster variability.

To characterize the resulting clusters, we examine the cluster centroids (numerically in Figure 16.9 or in the line chart ("profile plot") in Figure 16.10.) We see, for instance, that cluster 6 has the highest average Nuclear, a very high RoR, and a slow Demand growth. In contrast, cluster 4 has the highest Sales, with no Nuclear, a high Demand growth, and the highest average Cost.

Data Mining: K-Means Clustering - Predicted Clusters

Cluster Labels

Record ID	Cluster	Cluster 1	Cluster 2	Cluster 3	Cluster 4	Cluster 5	Cluster 6
Record 17	1	0	5.77458	4.15029	4.94622	3.10505	4.56809
Record 3	2	6.35655	1.89626	3.05473	5.09685	4.87548	3.64040
Record 6	2	6.09946	1.96562	3.03627	5.31665	4.09907	3.33991
Record 14	2	5.55800	1.64875	3.56882	4.26641	4.30507	3.08465
Record 19	2	6.08960	1.42217	3.65746	4.28835	4.36318	3.52430
Record 5	3	5.62859	4.43022	3.18561	5.55651	3.69180	3.87441
Record 7	3	4.57729	3.91717	1.89977	4.86112	2.72590	3.84065
Record 9	3	4.90104	3.19159	1.94984	3.80043	3.70788	2.98262
Record 12	3	3.49755	3.75219	1.17378	4.29731	1.62415	3.23251
Record 18	3	4.42613	1.92214	1.84793	3.28158	2.72219	2.34089
Record 8	4	5.42651	4.25808	3.55421	1.56017	3.67186	3.22996
Record 11	4	4.75139	4.94403	4.99643	2.17720	4.61541	4.35684
Record 16	4	5.55932	5.09275	4.17567	1.53596	4.68013	4.07580
Record 2	5	3.62359	4.18172	2.62281	4.16272	1.44777	2.30230
Record 15	5	3.39966	4.03561	2.67130	4.26211	1.33053	3.42161
Record 21	5	3.09500	4.58558	2.19796	4.12359	1.21521	3.65691
Record 1	6	4.39668	2.48085	2.62197	2.96724	2.76256	2.28346
Record 4	6	4.89368	3.05587	2.95976	4.18105	2.86391	1.18613
Record 10	6	5.48454	3.46543	3.22648	4.09549	3.61411	1.16536
Record 13	6	5.60658	4.24636	3.82850	4.29025	4.35422	1.84073
Record 20	6	4.86654	3.14161	2.77243	4.44009	3.42194	1.47053
Record 22	6	3.62806	3.49928	2.59366	2.87079	2.63544	1.70418

FIGURE 16.8   OUTPUT FOR k-MEANS CLUSTERING OF 22 UTILITIES INTO $k = 6$ CLUSTERS (SORTED BY CLUSTER ID; APPLIED TO NORMALIZED DATA)

Cluster Centers

Cluster	Fixed_charge	RoR	Cost	Load_factor	Demand_growth	Sales	Nuclear	Fuel_Cost
Cluster 1	1.49	8.80	192.00	51.20	1.00	3300.00	15.60	2.04
Cluster 2	1.17	12.00	132.50	54.70	2.13	9887.00	8.18	0.99
Cluster 3	0.83	8.35	169.00	59.90	5.60	5401.00	16.80	1.74
Cluster 4	1.04	9.58	193.50	54.63	4.23	15005.25	0.00	0.58
Cluster 5	1.05	10.14	182.20	58.84	2.02	6430.00	14.88	1.35
Cluster 6	1.23	12.43	172.50	60.40	4.83	7628.50	22.83	0.94

Inter-Cluster Distances

Cluster	Cluster 1	Cluster 2	Cluster 3	Cluster 4	Cluster 5	Cluster 6
Cluster 1	0.00	6587.27	2101.15	11705.26	3130.03	4328.56
Cluster 2	6587.27	0.00	4486.16	5118.62	3457.37	2258.91
Cluster 3	2101.15	4486.16	0.00	9604.30	1029.09	2227.51
Cluster 4	11705.26	5118.62	9604.30	0.00	8575.27	7376.82
Cluster 5	3130.03	3457.37	1029.09	8575.27	0.00	1198.57
Cluster 6	4328.56	2258.91	2227.51	7376.82	1198.57	0.00

Cluster Summary

Original coordinates

Cluster	Size	Average Distance
Cluster 1	1	0
Cluster 2	6	567.9887722
Cluster 3	2	314.8803742
Cluster 4	4	1712.053765
Cluster 5	5	121.2838939
Cluster 6	4	399.9029775
Total	22	595.0881737

Normalized coordinates

Cluster	Size	Average Distance
Cluster 1	1	0
Cluster 2	4	1.733201872
Cluster 3	5	2.011385986
Cluster 4	3	1.757778325
Cluster 5	3	1.331169075
Cluster 6	6	1.608397833
Total	22	1.632134846

FIGURE 16.9   CLUSTER CENTROIDS AND DISTANCES FOR k-MEANS WITH $k = 6$

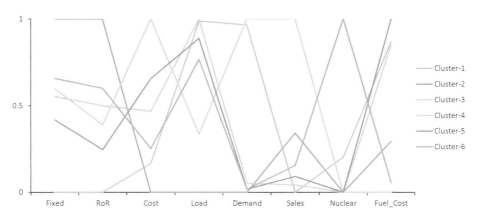

FIGURE 16.10   VISUAL PRESENTATION OF CLUSTER CENTROIDS (SCALED TO [0, 1] ON EACH MEASURE, FOR EASY COMPARISON). CREATED USING EXCEL'S *LINE CHART*

We can also inspect the information on the within-cluster dispersion. Examining the normalized results in the Cluster Summary, we see that cluster 3 has the largest within-cluster average distance, and it includes five records. In comparison, cluster 6, with six records, has a smaller within-cluster average distance. This means that cluster 6 is more homogeneous than cluster 3. Cluster 1 has just one record, so measuring its within-cluster dispersion is not meaningful.

When the number of clusters is not predetermined by domain requirements, we can use a graphical approach to evaluate different numbers of clusters. An "elbow chart" is a line chart depicting the decline in cluster heterogeneity as we add more clusters. Figure 16.11 shows the overall average within-cluster squared distance (normalized) for different choices of k. Moving from 3 to 4 tightens clusters considerably (reflected by the large reduction in within-cluster squared distance), and so does moving from 4 to 5. Adding more clusters beyond 5 brings less improvement to cluster homogeneity.

From the distances between clusters, we can learn about the separation of the different clusters. We can see that clusters 2 and 4 are the most distinctive, each being relatively distant from all the other clusters. We can also see that, perhaps, cluster 1, which has just one record, may belong with cluster 5, to which it is fairly close.

Finally, we can use the information on the distance between the final clusters to evaluate the cluster validity. The ratio of the sum of within-cluster squared distances to cluster means for a given k to the sum of squared distances to the

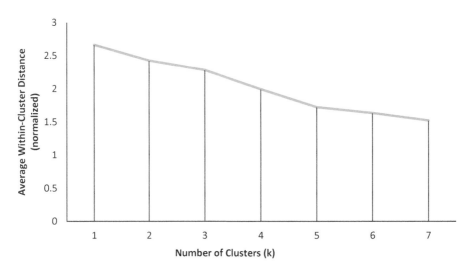

FIGURE 16.11   COMPARING DIFFERENT CHOICES OF *k* IN TERMS OF OVERALL AVERAGE WITHIN-CLUSTER DISTANCE. CREATED USING EXCEL'S *LINE CHART*

mean of all the records (in other words, $k = 1$) is a useful measure for the usefulness of the clustering. If the ratio is near 1.0, the clustering has not been very effective, whereas if it is small, we have well-separated groups.

The machine learning workflow for the k-means clustering on the utilities data is shown in Figure 16.12, for the normalized data (left-most branch) and non-normalized data (right-most branch), both with $k = 6$. The middle branches (left to right) correspond to running the k-means algorithms with $k = 1, 2, 3, 4, 5,$ and 7 (on normalized data), corresponding to the results shown in Figure 16.11.

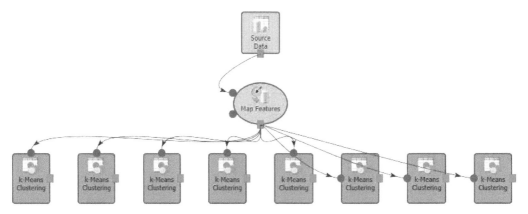

FIGURE 16.12   THE MACHINE LEARNING WORKFLOW FOR SINGLE LINKAGE AND AVERAGE LINKAGE FOR ALL 22 UTILITIES, USING ALL 8 MEASUREMENTS

PROBLEMS

16.1 **University Rankings.** The dataset `Universities.xlsx` contains information on 1302 American colleges and universities offering an undergraduate program. For each university there are 17 measurements, including continuous variables (e.g., tuition and graduation rate) and categorical variables (e.g., location by state and whether it is a private or public school). Three variables (Math, Verbal, ACT) from the original data were dropped because they had too many missing values.

Note that many observations are missing some measurements. Our first goal is to estimate these missing values from "similar" records. This will be done by clustering the complete records and then finding the closest cluster for each of the partial records. The missing values will be imputed from the information in that cluster.

a. Remove all observations with missing measurements from the dataset (by creating a new worksheet).

b. For all the continuous variables, run hierarchical clustering using complete linkage and Euclidean distance. Make sure to normalize the variables. Examine the dendrogram: How many clusters seem reasonable for describing these data?

c. Compare the summary statistics for each cluster and describe each cluster in this context (e.g., "Universities with high tuition, low acceptance rate…"). *Hint:* To obtain cluster statistics for hierarchical clustering, use Excel's Pivot Table on the "Predicted Clusters" table.

d. Use the categorical variables that were not used in the analysis (State and Private/Public) to characterize the different clusters. Is there any relationship between the clusters and the categorical information?

e. Can you think of other external information that explains the contents of some or all of these clusters?

f. Consider Tufts University, which is missing some information. Compute the Euclidean distance of this observation from each of the clusters that you found above (using only the measurements that you have). Which cluster is it closest to? Impute the missing values for Tufts by taking the average of the cluster on those variables.

16.2 **Pharmaceutical Industry.** An equities analyst is studying the pharmaceutical industry and would like your help in exploring and understanding the financial data collected by her firm. Her main objective is to understand the structure of the pharmaceutical industry using some basic financial measures.

Financial data gathered on 21 firms in the pharmaceutical industry are available in the file `Pharmaceuticals.xlsx`. For each firm, the following variables are recorded:

1. Market capitalization (in billions of dollars)

2. Beta

3. Price/earnings ratio

4. Return on equity

5. Return on assets

6. Asset turnover

7. Leverage

8. Estimated revenue growth

9. Net profit margin

10. Median recommendation (across major brokerages)

11. Location of firm's headquarters

12. Stock exchange on which the firm is listed.

Use cluster analysis to explore and analyze the given dataset as follows:

a. Use only the numerical variables (1–9) to cluster the 21 firms. Justify the various choices made in conducting the cluster analysis, such as weights accorded different variables, the specific clustering algorithm(s) used, the number of clusters formed, and so on.

b. Interpret the clusters with respect to the numerical variables that were used in forming the clusters.

c. Is there a pattern in the clusters with respect to the categorical variables (10–12) (those not used in forming the clusters)?

d. Provide an appropriate name for each cluster using any or all of the variables in the dataset.

16.3 **Customer Rating of Breakfast Cereals.** The dataset `Cereals.xlsx` includes nutritional information, store display, and consumer ratings for 77 breakfast cereals.

Data Preprocessing. Remove all cereals with missing values.

a. Apply hierarchical clustering to the data using Euclidean distance to the normalized variables. Compare the dendrograms from single linkage and complete linkage, and look at cluster centroids. Comment on the structure of the clusters and on their stability. *Hints:* (1) To obtain cluster centroids for hierarchical clustering, apply Excel's Pivot Table to the "Predicted Clusters" table. (2) Running hierarchical clustering in ASDM is an iterative process—run it once with a guess at the right number of clusters, then run it again after looking at the dendrogram, adjusting the number of clusters if needed.

b. Which method leads to the most insightful or meaningful clusters?

c. Choose one of the methods. How many clusters would you use? What distance is used for this cutoff? (Look at the dendrogram.)

d. The elementary public schools would like to choose a set of cereals to include in their daily cafeterias. Every day a different cereal is offered, but all cereals should support a healthy diet. For this goal, you are requested to find a cluster of "healthy cereals." Should the data be normalized? If not, how should they be used in the cluster analysis?

16.4 **Marketing to Frequent Fliers.** The file `EastWestAirlinesCluster.xlsx` contains information on 3999 passengers who belong to an airline's frequent flier program. For each passenger, the data include information on their mileage history and on different ways they accrued or spent miles in the last year. The goal is to try to identify clusters of passengers that have similar characteristics for the purpose of targeting different segments for different types of mileage offers.

a. Apply hierarchical clustering with Euclidean distance and Ward's method. Make sure to normalize the data first. How many clusters appear?

b. What would happen if the data were not normalized?

c. Compare the cluster centroid to characterize the different clusters, and try to give each cluster a label.

d. To check the stability of the clusters, remove a random 5% of the data (by taking a random sample of 95% of the records), and repeat the analysis. Does the same picture emerge?

e. Use k-means clustering with the number of clusters that you found above. Does the same picture emerge?

f. Which clusters would you target for offers, and what types of offers would you target to customers in that cluster?

## PART VII

Forecasting Time Series

## CHAPTER 17

Handling Time Series

In this chapter, we describe the context of business time series forecasting and introduce the main approaches that are detailed in the next chapters, and in particular regression-based forecasting and smoothing-based methods. Our focus is on forecasting future values of a single time series. This chapter and the next two chapters are meant as an introduction to the general forecasting approach and methods.

In this chapter, we start with a discussion of the difference between the predictive nature of time series forecasting vs. the descriptive or explanatory task of time series analysis. A general discussion of combining forecasting methods or results for added precision follows. Next we present a time series in terms of four components (level, trend, seasonality, and noise) and present methods for visualizing the different components and for exploring time series data. We close with a discussion of data partitioning (creating training and validation sets), which is performed differently from cross-sectional data partitioning.

17.1 INTRODUCTION[1]

Time series forecasting is performed in nearly every organization that works with quantifiable data. Retail stores use it to forecast sales. Energy companies use it to forecast reserves, production, demand, and prices. Educational institutions use it to forecast enrollment. Governments use it to forecast tax receipts and spending. International financial organizations like the World Bank and International Monetary Fund use it to forecast inflation and economic activity.

---

[1]This and subsequent sections in this chapter, copyright ©2019 Datastats, LLC, and Galit Shmueli. Used by permission.

Machine Learning for Business Analytics: Concepts, Techniques, and Applications with Analytic Solver® Data Mining, Fourth Edition. Galit Shmueli, Peter C. Bruce, Kuber R. Deokar, and Nitin R. Patel
© 2023 John Wiley & Sons, Inc. Published 2023 by John Wiley & Sons, Inc.

Transportation companies use time series forecasting to forecast future travel. Banks and lending institutions use it (sometimes badly!) to forecast new home purchases. And venture capital firms use it to forecast market potential and to evaluate business plans.

Previous chapters in this book deal with classifying and predicting data where time is not a factor, in the sense that it is not treated differently from other variables, and where the sequence of measurements over time does not matter. These are typically called cross-sectional data. In contrast, this chapter deals with a different type of data: time series.

With today's technology, many time series are recorded on very frequent time scales. Stock data are available at ticker-level. Purchases at online and offline stores are recorded in real time. Although data might be available at a very frequent scale, for the purpose of forecasting it is not always preferable to use this time scale. In considering the choice of time scale, one must consider the scale of the required forecasts and the level of noise in the data. For example, if the goal is to forecast next-day sales at a grocery store, using minute-by-minute sales data is likely to be less useful for forecasting than using daily aggregates. The minute-by-minute series will contain many sources of noise (e.g., variation by peak and nonpeak shopping hours) that degrade its forecasting power, and these noise errors, when the data are aggregated to a cruder level, are likely to average out.

The focus in this part of the book is on forecasting a single time series. In some cases, multiple time series are to be forecasted (e.g., the monthly sales of multiple products). Even when multiple series are being forecasted, the most popular forecasting practice is to forecast each series individually. The advantage of single-series forecasting is its simplicity. The disadvantage is that it does not take into account possible relationships between series. The statistics literature contains models for multivariate time series that directly model the cross-correlations between series. Such methods tend to make restrictive assumptions about the data and the cross-series structure. They also require statistical expertise for estimation and maintenance. Econometric models often include information from one or more series as inputs into another series. However, such models are based on assumptions of causality that are based on theoretical models. An alternative approach is to capture the associations between the series of interest and external information more heuristically. An example is using the sales of lipstick to forecast some measure of the economy, based on the observation by Ronald Lauder, chairman of Estee Lauder, that lipstick sales tend to increase before tough economic times (a phenomenon called the "leading lipstick indicator").

17.2 DESCRIPTIVE VS. PREDICTIVE MODELING

As with cross-sectional data, modeling time series data is done for either descriptive or predictive purposes. In descriptive modeling, or *time series analysis*, a time series is modeled to determine its components in terms of seasonal patterns, trends, relation to external factors, etc. These can then be used for decision making and policy formulation. In contrast, *time series forecasting* uses the information in a time series (and perhaps other information) to forecast future values of that series. The difference between the goals of time series analysis and time series forecasting leads to differences in the type of methods used and in the modeling process itself. For example, in selecting a method for describing a time series, priority is given to methods that produce understandable results (rather than "black-box" methods) and sometimes to models based on causal arguments (explanatory models). Furthermore describing can be done in retrospect, while forecasting is *prospective* in nature. This means that descriptive models might use "future" information (e.g., averaging the values of yesterday, today, and tomorrow to obtain a smooth representation of today's value) whereas forecasting models cannot.

In time series forecasting of this chapter, our goal is to predict future values of a time series. For information on time series analysis, see Chatfield (2003).

17.3 POPULAR FORECASTING METHODS IN BUSINESS

Two types of forecasting methods are popular in business applications. Both are versatile and powerful, yet relatively simple to understand and deploy. One type of forecasting tool is linear regression, where the user specifies a certain model and then estimates it from the time series. The other includes more data-driven methods, such as smoothing and deep learning, where the method learns patterns from the data. Each of the two types of tools has advantages and disadvantages, as detailed in Chapters 18 and 19. We also note that machine learning methods such as neural networks and others that are intended for cross-sectional data and are sometimes used for time series forecasting, especially for incorporating external information into the forecasts (see Shmueli, 2016).

Combining Methods

A popular approach for improving predictive performance is in fact to combine forecasting methods. This is similar to the ensembles approach described in Chapter 13. Combining forecasting methods can be done via two-level (or multi-level) forecasters, where the first method uses the original time series to generate forecasts of future values, and the second method uses the residuals from the first model to generate forecasts of future forecast errors, thereby "correcting" the first level forecasts. Another combination approach is via "ensembles," where multiple methods are applied to the time series, and their resulting forecasts are averaged in some way to produce the final forecast. Combining methods can take advantage of the strengths of different forecasting methods to capture different aspects of the time series (also true in cross-sectional data). The averaging across multiple methods can lead to forecasts that are more robust and of higher precision.

17.4 TIME SERIES COMPONENTS

In both types of forecasting methods, regression models and smoothing, and in general, it is customary to dissect a time series into four components: *level*, *trend*, *seasonality*, and *noise*. The first three components are assumed to be invisible, as they characterize the underlying series, which we only observe with added noise. Level describes the average value of the series, trend is the change in the series from one period to the next, and seasonality describes a short-term cyclical behavior of the series that can be observed several times within the given series. Last, noise is the random variation that results from measurement error or other causes not accounted for. It is always present in a time series to some degree.

In order to identify the components of a time series, the first step is to examine a time plot. In its simplest form, a time plot is a line chart of the series values over time, with temporal labels (e.g., calendar date) on the horizontal axis. To illustrate this, consider the following example.

Example: Ridership on Amtrak Trains

Amtrak, a US railway company, routinely collects data on ridership. We will forecast future ridership using the series of monthly ridership between January 1991 and March 2004.[2]

A time plot for the monthly Amtrak ridership series is shown in Figure 17.1. Note that the values are in thousands of riders. Looking at the time plot reveals the nature of the series components: the overall level is around 1,800,000 passengers per month. A slight U-shaped trend is discernible during this period, with pronounced annual seasonality, with peak travel during summer (July and August).

---

[2]Data from https://www.bts.gov/archive/publications/multimodal_transportation_indicators/june_2010/amtrak_ridership and available in `Amtrak.xlsx`.

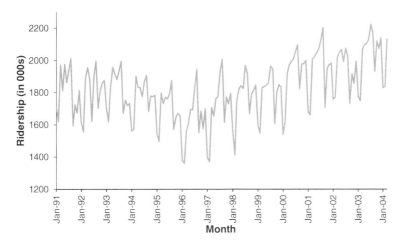

FIGURE 17.1   MONTHLY RIDERSHIP ON AMTRAK TRAINS (in thousands) FROM JANUARY 1991
TO MARCH 2004. CHART PRODUCED IN EXCEL

A second step in visualizing a time series is to examine it more carefully. A few tools are useful:

Zoom in: Zooming in to a shorter period within the series can reveal patterns that are hidden when viewing the entire series. This is especially important when the time series is long. Consider a series of the daily number of vehicles passing through the Baregg tunnel in Switzerland.[3] The series from November 1, 2003 to November 16, 2005 is shown in the top panel of Figure 17.2. Zooming in to a four-month period (bottom panel) reveals a strong day-of-week pattern that is not visible in the time plot of the complete time series.

Change scale of series: In order to better identify the shape of a trend, it is useful to change the scale of the series. One simple option, to check for an exponential trend, is to change the vertical scale to a logarithmic scale (in Excel,[4] Select Vertical Axis of chart > Format Tab > Vertical (Value) Axis > Format Selection > Format Axis > Axis Options, and check "Logarithmic scale"). If the trend on the new scale appears more linear, then the trend in the original series is closer to an exponential trend.

Add trend lines: Another possibility for better discerning the shape of the trend is to add a trend line (Select Chart > Chart Design tab > Add Chart Element > Trendline). By trying different trendlines, one can see what type of trend (e.g., linear, exponential, quadratic) best approximates the data.

---

[3]Data from http://neural-forecasting-competition.com/downloads/NNGC1/datasets/download.htm.
[4]Using Excel for Microsoft 365 MSO (Version 2205).

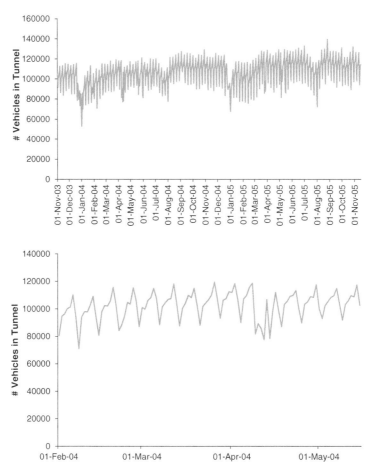

FIGURE 17.2   TIME PLOTS OF THE DAILY NUMBER OF VEHICLES PASSING THROUGH THE BAREGG TUNNEL, SWITZERLAND. (BOTTOM) ZOOMING IN TO A FOUR-MONTH PERIOD, REVEALING A DAY-OF-WEEK PATTERN. CHARTS PRODUCED IN EXCEL

Suppress seasonality: It is often easier to see trends in the data when seasonality is suppressed. Suppressing seasonality patterns can be done by plotting the series at a cruder time scale (e.g., aggregating monthly data into years) or creating separate lines or time plots for each season (e.g., separate lines for each day of week). Another popular option is to use moving average charts. We will discuss these in Chapter 19 (Section 19.2).

Continuing our example of Amtrak ridership, the charts in Figure 17.3 help make the series' components more visible.

Some forecasting methods directly model these components by making assumptions about their structure. For example, a popular assumption about trend is that it is linear or exponential over the given time period or part of

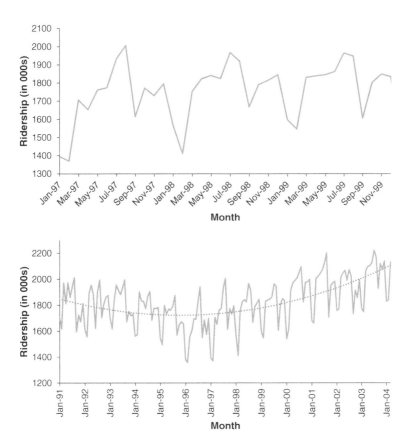

FIGURE 17.3   PLOTS THAT ENHANCE THE DIFFERENT COMPONENTS OF THE TIME SERIES. TOP: ZOOM-IN TO THREE YEARS OF DATA. BOTTOM: ORIGINAL SERIES WITH OVERLAID QUADRATIC TRENDLINE. CHARTS PRODUCED IN EXCEL

it. Another common assumption is about the noise structure: many statistical methods assume that the noise follows a normal distribution. The advantage of methods that rely on such assumptions is that when the assumptions are reasonably met, the resulting forecasts will be more robust and the models more understandable. Other forecasting methods that are data adaptive make fewer assumptions about the structure of these components, and instead try to estimate them only from the data. Data-adaptive methods are advantageous when such assumptions are likely to be violated, or when the structure of the time series changes over time. Another advantage of many data-adaptive methods is their simplicity and computational efficiency.

A key criterion for deciding between model-driven and data-driven forecasting methods is the nature of the series in terms of global vs. local patterns. A global pattern is one that is relatively constant throughout the series. An example is a linear trend throughout the entire series. In contrast, a local pattern is one that occurs only in a short period of the data, and then changes, for example, a trend that is approximately linear within four neighboring time points, but whose trend size (slope) changes slowly over time.

Model-driven methods are generally preferable for forecasting series with global patterns because they use all the data to estimate the global pattern. For a local pattern, a model-driven model would require specifying how and when the patterns change, which is usually impractical and often unknown. Therefore, data-driven methods are preferable for local patterns. Such methods "learn" patterns from the data and their memory length can be set to best adapt to the rate of change in the series. Patterns that change quickly warrant a "short memory," whereas patterns that change slowly warrant a "long memory." In short, the time plot should be used not only to identify the time series component but also the global/local nature of the trend and seasonality.

17.5 DATA PARTITIONING AND PERFORMANCE EVALUATION

As in the case of cross-sectional data, in order to avoid overfitting and to be able to assess the predictive performance of the model on new data, we first partition the data into a training set and a validation set (and perhaps an additional test set if the validation is used for model tuning and comparison). However, there is one important difference between data partitioning in cross-sectional and time series data. In cross-sectional data the partitioning is usually done randomly, with a random set of observations designated as training data and the remainder as validation data. However, in time series a random partition would create two time series with "holes." Most standard forecasting methods cannot handle time series with missing values. Therefore, we partition a time series into training and validation sets differently. The series is trimmed into two periods: the earlier period is set as the training data and the later period as the validation data. Methods are then trained on the earlier training period, and their predictive performance assessed on the later validation period. This approach also has the advantage of mimicking how the forecasting model will be used in practice: trained on existing data to forecast future values.

Evaluation measures typically use the same metrics used in cross-sectional evaluation (see Chapter 5) with *RMSE*, *MAE*, and *MAPE* being the most popular metrics in practice. In evaluating and comparing forecasting methods, another important tool is visualization: examining time plots of the actual and predicted series can shed light on performance and hint toward possible improvements.

Benchmark Performance: Naive Forecasts

While it is tempting to apply "sophisticated" forecasting methods, we must evaluate their value added compared to a very simple approach: the *naive forecast*. A naive forecast is simply the most recent value of the series. In other words, at time t, our forecast for any future period $t + k$ is simply the value of the series at time t. While simple, naive forecasts are sometimes surprisingly difficult to outperform with more sophisticated models. It is therefore important to benchmark against results from a naive forecasting approach.

When a time series has seasonality, a *seasonal naive forecast* can be generated. It is simply the value on the most recent similar season. For example, to forecast April 2001 for the Amtrak ridership, we use the ridership from the most recent April, which is April 2000. Similarly, to forecast April 2002, we also use April 2000 ridership.

Naive and seasonal naive forecasts are not available in ASDM but can be easily computed using Excel.

In Figure 17.4, we show naive (red horizontal line) and seasonal naive forecasts (blue line), as well as actual values (orange line), in a three-year validation set from April 2001 to March 2004. Performance on the validation set is more relevant than the performance on the training set because it is more indicative of how the models will perform in the future. Because Amtrak ridership has strong monthly seasonality, the seasonal naive forecast appears the clear winner. We can further compute and plot the forecast error series, as well as compute performance metrics such as *RMSE* and *MAPE* (these need to be calculated using Excel).

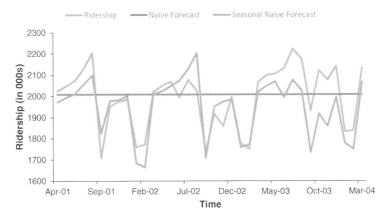

FIGURE 17.4   NAIVE AND SEASONAL NAIVE FORECASTS OF AMTRAK RIDERSHIP FOR A THREE-YEAR VALIDATION SET

Generating Future Forecasts

Another important difference between cross-sectional and time series partitioning occurs when creating the actual forecasts. Before attempting to forecast future values of the series, the training and validation sets are re-combined into one long series, and the chosen method/model is re-run on the complete data. This final model is then used to forecast future values. The three advantages in re-combining are (1) the validation set, which is the most recent period, usually contains the most valuable information in terms of being the closest in time to the forecast period; (2) with more data (the complete time series compared to only the training set), some models can be estimated more accurately; (3) if only the training set is used to generate forecasts, then it will require forecasting farther into the future (e.g., if the validation set contains four time points, forecasting the next observation will require a five-step-ahead forecast from the training set).

In ASDM, partitioning a time series is performed within the Time Series menu. Figure 17.5 shows a screenshot of the time series partitioning dialog box. After the final model is chosen, the same model should be re-run on the original, unpartitioned series in order to obtain forecasts. ASDM will only generate future forecasts if it is run on an unpartitioned series (see Figure 17.6).

FIGURE 17.5   PARTITIONING A TIME SERIES IN ASDM INTO TRAINING (123 VALUES) AND VALIDATION (36 VALUES) SETS

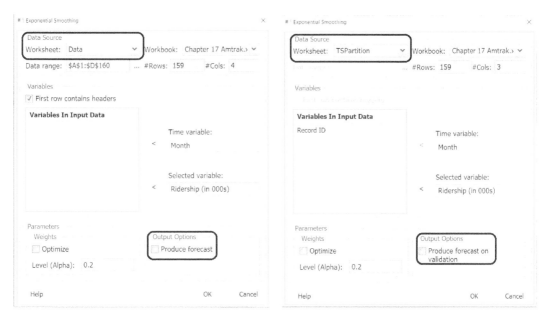

FIGURE 17.6   IN ASDM'S TIME SERIES FUNCTIONS, FUTURE FORECASTS CAN ONLY BE
GENERATED IF A FORECASTING METHOD IS APPLIED TO THE UNPARTITIONED
SERIES (LEFT PANEL). IF APPLIED TO THE PARTITIONED SERIES (RIGHT PANEL),
ONLY FORECASTS FOR THE VALIDATION SERIES WILL BE GENERATED

PROBLEMS

17.1 **Impact of September 11 on Air Travel in the United States.** The Research and Innovative Technology Administration's Bureau of Transportation Statistics conducted a study to evaluate the impact of the September 11, 2001 terrorist attack on US transportation. The 2006 study report and the data can be found at https://www.bts.gov/archive/publications/estimated_impacts_of_9_11_on_us_travel/index. The goal of the study was stated as follows:

> The purpose of this study is to provide a greater understanding of the passenger travel behavior patterns of persons making long distance trips before and after 9/11.

The report analyzes monthly passenger movement data between January 1990 and May 2004. Data on three monthly time series are given in file `Sept11Travel.xlsx` for this period:

    (1) Actual airline revenue passenger miles (Air),

    (2) Rail passenger miles (Rail), and

    (3) Vehicle miles traveled (Car).

    In order to assess the impact of September 11, BTS took the following approach: using data before September 11, they forecasted future data (under the assumption of no terrorist attack). Then, they compared the forecasted series with the actual data to assess the impact of the event. Our first step therefore is to split each of the time series into two parts: pre- and post-September 11. We now concentrate only on the earlier time series.

a. Is the goal of this study descriptive or predictive?

b. Plot each of the three pre-event time series (air, rail, car).

    i. What time series components appear from the plot?

    ii. What type of trend appears? Change the scale of the series, add trendlines, and suppress seasonality to better visualize the trend pattern.

17.2 **Performance on Training and Validation Data.** Two different models were fit to the same time series. The first 100 time periods were used for the training set and the last 12 periods were treated as a holdout set. Assume that both models make sense practically and fit the data pretty well. Below are the RMSE values for each of the models:

	Training set	Validation set
Model A	543	690
Model B	669	675

a. Which model appears more useful for explaining the different components of this time series? Why?

b. Which model appears to be more useful for forecasting purposes? Why?

17.3 Forecasting Department Store Sales. The file `DepartmentStoreSales.xlsx` contains data on the quarterly sales for a department store over a six-year period (data courtesy of Chris Albright).

    a. Create a well-formatted time plot of the data.

    b. Which of the four components (level, trend, seasonality, noise) seem to be present in this series?

17.4 Shipments of Household Appliances. The file `ApplianceShipments.xlsx` contains the series of quarterly shipments (in million $) of US household appliances between 1985 and 1989 (data courtesy of Ken Black).

    a. Create a well-formatted time plot of the data.

    b. Which of the four components (level, trend, seasonality, noise) seem to be present in this series?

17.5 Canadian Manufacturing Workers Workhours. The time plot in Figure 17.7 describes the average annual number of weekly hours spent by Canadian manufacturing workers (data are available in `CanadianWorkHours.xlsx`—thanks to Ken Black for the data).

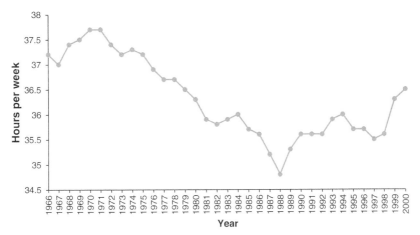

FIGURE 17.7   AVERAGE ANNUAL WEEKLY HOURS SPENT BY CANADIAN MANUFACTURING WORKERS. CHART PRODUCED IN EXCEL

    a. Reproduce the time plot.

    b. Which of the four components (level, trend, seasonality, noise) seem to be present in this series?

17.6 Souvenir Sales: The file `SouvenirSales.xlsx` contains monthly sales for a souvenir shop at a beach resort town in Queensland, Australia, between 1995 and 2001 [Source: Hyndman and Yang (2018)]. Back in 2001, the store wanted to use the data to forecast sales for the next 12 months (year 2002). They hired an analyst to generate forecasts. The analyst first partitioned the data into training and validation sets, with the validation set containing the last 12 months of data (year 2001). She then fit a regression model to sales, using the training set.

   a. Create a well-formatted time plot of the data.

   b. Change the scale on the x-axis, or on the y-axis, or on both to log-scale in order to achieve a linear relationship. Select the time plot that seems most linear.

   c. Comparing the two time plots, what can you say about the type of trend in the data?

   d. Why were the data partitioned? Partition the data into the training and validation set as explained above.

17.7 **Shampoo Sales.** The file `ShampooSales.xlsx` contains data on the monthly sales of a certain shampoo over a three-year period [Source: Hyndman and Yang (2018)].

   a. Create a well-formatted time plot of the data.

   b. Which of the four components (level, trend, seasonality, noise) seems to be present in this series?

   c. Do you expect to see seasonality in sales of shampoo? Why?

   d. If the goal is forecasting sales in future months, which of the following steps should be taken?

- Partition the data into training and validation sets.
- Tweak the model parameters to obtain good fit to the validation data.
- Look at MAPE and RMSE values for the training set.
- Look at MAPE and RMSE values for the validation set.

## CHAPTER 18

Regression-Based Forecasting

A popular forecasting tool is based on multiple linear regression models, using suitable predictors to capture trend and/or seasonality. In this chapter, we show how a linear regression model can be set up to capture a time series with a trend and/or seasonality. The model, which is estimated from the data, can produce future forecasts from the relevant predictor information that is inserted into the estimated regression equation. We describe different types of common trends (linear, exponential, polynomial), as well as two types of seasonality (additive and multiplicative). Next, we show how a regression model can be used to quantify the correlation between neighboring values in a time series (called autocorrelation). This type of model, called an autoregressive (AR) model, is useful for improving forecast precision by making use of the information contained in the autocorrelation (beyond trend and seasonality). It is also useful for evaluating the predictability of a series, by evaluating whether the series is a "random walk." The various steps of fitting linear regression and autoregressive models, using them to generate forecasts, and assessing their predictive accuracy, are illustrated using the Amtrak ridership series.

18.1 A MODEL WITH TREND[1]

Linear Trend

To create a linear regression model that captures a time series with a global linear trend, the output variable (Y) is set as the time series measurement or some function of it, and the predictor (X) is set as a time index. Let us consider a simple

---

[1] This and subsequent sections in this chapter copyright © 2019 Datastats, LLC, and Galit Shmueli. Used by permission.

Machine Learning for Business Analytics: Concepts, Techniques, and Applications with Analytic Solver® Data Mining, Fourth Edition. Galit Shmueli, Peter C. Bruce, Kuber R. Deokar, and Nitin R. Patel
© 2023 John Wiley & Sons, Inc. Published 2023 by John Wiley & Sons, Inc.

example: fitting a linear trend to the monthly Amtrak ridership data described in Chapter 17 and available in `Amtrak.xlsx`, where the series is partitioned into a training period of 123 months (January 1991 to March 2001), and a validation period of 36 months (April 2001 to March 2004).

A linear trend for the series is shown in Figure 18.1. From the time plot, it is obvious that the global trend is not linear. However, we use this example to illustrate how a linear trend is fitted, and later we consider more appropriate models for this series.

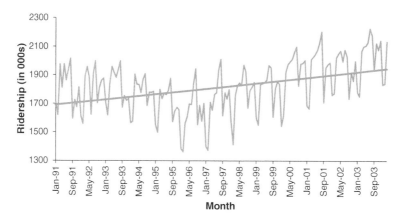

FIGURE 18.1   A LINEAR TREND FIT TO AMTRAK RIDERSHIP. CHART PRODUCED IN EXCEL

To obtain a linear relationship between Ridership and Time, we set the output variable Y as the Amtrak Ridership and create a new variable that is a time index $t = 1, 2, 3, \ldots$. This time index is then used as a single predictor in the regression model:

$$Y_t = \beta_0 + \beta_1 t + \epsilon,$$

where Y_t is the Ridership at time point t and ϵ is the standard noise term in a linear regression. Thus, we are modeling three of the four time series components: level (β_0), trend (β_1), and noise (ε). Seasonality is not modeled. A snapshot of the two corresponding columns (Y and t) for the first 14 months is shown in Table 18.1.

After partitioning the data into training and validation sets, the next step is to fit a linear regression model to the training set, with t as the single predictor. Applying this to the Amtrak ridership data (with a validation set consisting of the last 36 months) results in the estimated model shown in Figure 18.2. The actual and fitted values and the residuals are shown in the two lower panels in time plots. Note that examining only the estimated coefficients and their statistical significance can be very misleading! In this example, the statistically insignificant trend coefficient might indicate "no trend," although it is obvious from the plot that a trend does exist, albeit a quadratic one. The training RMSE

TABLE 18.1   OUTPUT VARIABLE (MIDDLE COLUMN) AND PREDICTOR
VARIABLE (RIGHT COLUMN) USED TO FIT A LINEAR
TREND. FIRST 14 ROWS SHOWN

Month	Ridership	t
Jan-91	1709	1
Feb-91	1621	2
Mar-91	1973	3
Apr-91	1812	4
May-91	1975	5
Jun-91	1862	6
Jul-91	1940	7
Aug-91	2013	8
Sep-91	1596	9
Oct-91	1725	10
Nov-91	1676	11
Dec-91	1814	12
Jan-92	1615	13
Feb-92	1557	14

Coefficients

Predictor	Estimate	Confidence Interval: Lower	Confidence Interval: Upper	Standard Error	T-Statistic	P-Value
Intercept	1750.3595	1692.8021	1807.9170	29.0729	60.2059	0.0000
t	0.3514	-0.4542	1.1570	0.4069	0.8635	0.3896

Training: Prediction Summary

Metric	Value
SSE	3106705.2435
MSE	25257.7662
RMSE	158.9269
MAD	129.6778
R2	0.0061

Validation: Prediction Summary

Metric	Value
SSE	2064731.9898
MSE	57353.6664
RMSE	239.4863
MAD	209.4371
R2	-1.8446

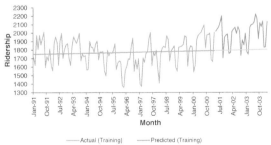

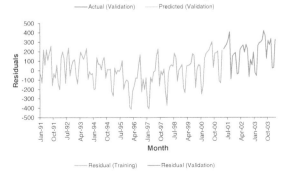

FIGURE 18.2   REGRESSION MODEL WITH LINEAR TREND FITTED TO TRAINING PERIOD.
REGRESSION OUTPUT (TOP), TIME PLOT OF ACTUAL AND FITTED SERIES
(MIDDLE), AND OF RESIDUALS (BOTTOM). CHARTS PRODUCED IN EXCEL

is 158.9 and the validation RMSE is 239.5. This discrepancy is indicative of an inadequate trend shape. However, an inadequate trend shape is easiest to detect by examining the time plot of the residuals.

Exponential Trend

Several alternative trend shapes are useful and easy to fit via a linear regression model. Recall Excel's *Trendline* and other plotting options that help assess the type of trend in the data. One such shape is an exponential trend. An exponential trend implies a multiplicative increase/decrease of the series over time ($Y_t = ce^{\beta_1 t + \varepsilon}$). To fit an exponential trend, simply replace the output variable Y with $\log Y$ (where log is the natural logarithm), and fit a linear regression ($\log Y_t = \beta_0 + \beta_1 t + \varepsilon$). In the Amtrak example, we would fit a linear regression of log(Ridership) on the index variable t. Exponential trends are popular in sales data, where they reflect percentage growth.

Note: As in the general case of linear regression, when comparing the predictive accuracy of models that have a different output variable, such as a linear trend model (with Y) and an exponential trend model (with $\log Y$), it is essential to compare forecasts or forecasts errors on the same scale. An exponential trend model will produce forecasts of $\log Y$, and the forecast errors reported by the software will therefore be $\log Y - \widehat{\log Y}$. To obtain forecasts in the original units, create a new column that takes an exponent of the model forecasts. Then use this column to create an additional column of forecast errors, by subtracting the original Y. An example is shown in Figures 18.3 and 18.4, where an exponential trend is fit to the Amtrak ridership data. Note that the performance measures for the training and validation data are not comparable to those from the linear trend model shown in Figure 18.2. Instead, we manually compute two new columns in Figure 18.4, one that gives forecasts of ridership (in thousands) and the other which gives the forecast errors in terms of ridership. To compare RMS Error or MAD, we would now proceed to the new forecast errors and compute their

Coefficients

Predictor	Estimate	Confidence Interval: Lower	Confidence Interval: Upper	Standard Error	T-Statistic	P-Value
Intercept	7.4647	7.4313	7.4981	0.0169	442.5354	0.0000
t	0.0002	-0.0003	0.0006	0.0002	0.7554	0.4515

Training: Prediction Summary

Metric	Value
SSE	1.0458
MSE	0.0085
RMSE	0.0922
MAD	0.0745
R2	0.0047

Validation: Prediction Summary

Metric	Value
SSE	0.5869
MSE	0.0163
RMSE	0.1277
MAD	0.1123
R2	-2.0676

FIGURE 18.3   OUTPUT FROM REGRESSION MODEL WITH EXPONENTIAL TREND, FIT TO TRAINING DATA

Record ID	logRidership	Prediction: logRidership	Residual	t	Predicted Ridership	Actual Ridership	Forecast Errors
Record 124	7.6127	7.4868	0.1259	124	1784.3561	2024	239.4359
Record 125	7.6241	7.4870	0.1371	125	1784.6743	2047	262.3337
Record 126	7.6367	7.4872	0.1495	126	1784.9926	2073	287.9204
Record 127	7.6623	7.4873	0.1750	127	1785.3110	2127	341.4060
Record 128	7.6974	7.4875	0.2099	128	1785.6295	2203	417.0085
Record 129	7.4429	7.4877	-0.0448	129	1785.9479	1708	-78.2549
Record 130	7.5760	7.4879	0.0881	130	1786.2665	1951	164.4495
Record 131	7.5876	7.4881	0.0996	131	1786.5851	1974	187.0289
Record 132	7.5932	7.4882	0.1050	132	1786.9038	1985	197.8252
Record 133	7.4729	7.4884	-0.0156	133	1787.2225	1760	-27.5935
Record 134	7.4791	7.4886	-0.0095	134	1787.5412	1771	-16.9462
Record 135	7.6108	7.4888	0.1220	135	1787.8601	2020	232.0519
Record 136	7.6248	7.4890	0.1359	136	1788.1790	2048	260.2190
Record 137	7.6347	7.4891	0.1456	137	1788.4979	2069	280.2651
Record 138	7.5980	7.4893	0.1087	138	1788.8169	1994	205.4501
Record 139	7.6378	7.4895	0.1484	139	1789.1360	2075	286.1220
Record 140	7.6141	7.4897	0.1244	140	1789.4551	2027	237.1049
Record 141	7.4583	7.4898	-0.0316	141	1789.7743	1734	-55.6193
Record 142	7.5584	7.4900	0.0684	142	1790.0935	1917	126.6775
Record 143	7.5274	7.4902	0.0372	143	1790.4128	1858	67.9322
Record 144	7.5991	7.4904	0.1087	144	1790.7321	1996	205.6199
Record 145	7.4833	7.4906	-0.0073	145	1791.0515	1778	-13.0185
Record 146	7.4671	7.4907	-0.0237	146	1791.3710	1749	-41.8820
Record 147	7.6336	7.4909	0.1427	147	1791.6905	2066	274.7755
Record 148	7.6492	7.4911	0.1581	148	1792.0101	2099	306.8889
Record 149	7.6520	7.4913	0.1608	149	1792.3297	2105	312.5813
Record 150	7.6637	7.4914	0.1723	150	1792.6494	2130	337.0216
Record 151	7.7068	7.4916	0.2151	151	1792.9691	2223	430.3799
Record 152	7.6845	7.4918	0.1927	152	1793.2889	2174	381.0711
Record 153	7.5660	7.4920	0.0740	153	1793.6088	1931	137.7972
Record 154	7.6599	7.4922	0.1677	154	1793.9287	2121	327.5413
Record 155	7.6382	7.4923	0.1459	155	1794.2487	2076	281.8053
Record 156	7.6689	7.4925	0.1764	156	1794.5687	2141	346.1083
Record 157	7.5129	7.4927	0.0202	157	1794.8888	1832	36.6192
Record 158	7.5164	7.4929	0.0236	158	1795.2089	1838	42.7971
Record 159	7.6650	7.4931	0.1720	159	1795.5291	2132	336.9169

FIGURE 18.4   ADJUSTING VALIDATION FORECASTS OF LOG(RIDERSHIP) TO THE ORIGINAL SCALE (SIXTH COLUMN), AND COMPUTING FORECAST ERRORS IN THE ORIGINAL SCALE (RIGHT COLUMN)

standard deviation (for RMS Error) or the average of their absolute values (for MAD). These would then be comparable to the numbers in Figure 18.2.

Polynomial Trend

Another nonlinear trend shape that is easy to fit via linear regression is a polynomial trend, and in particular, a quadratic relationship of the form $Y_t = \beta_0 + \beta_1 t + \beta_2 t^2 + \varepsilon$. This is done by creating an additional predictor t^2 (the square of t), and fitting a multiple linear regression with the two predictors t and t^2. For the Amtrak ridership data, we have already seen a U-shaped trend in the data. We therefore fit a quadratic model, concluding from the plots of model fit and residuals (Figure 18.5) that this shape adequately captures the trend during the training period. The training forecast errors are now devoid of trend

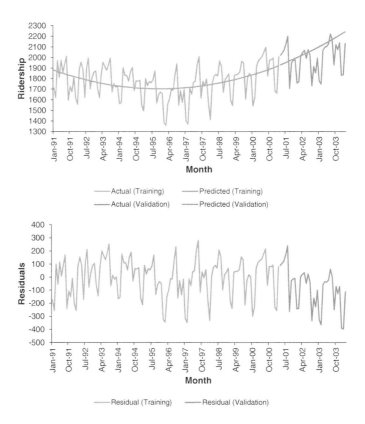

FIGURE 18.5   REGRESSION MODEL WITH QUADRATIC TREND FIT TO THE TRAINING DATA (TOP) AND MODEL RESIDUALS (BOTTOM). CHARTS PRODUCED IN EXCEL

and exhibit only seasonality. The forecast now overshoots for the test period, indicating that the quadratic trend that seemed to fit the training data well may not be useful for future data.

In general, any type of trend shape can be fit as long as it has a mathematical representation. However, the underlying assumption is that this shape is applicable throughout the period of data that we have and also during the period that we are going to forecast. Do not choose an overly complex shape. Although it will fit the training data well, it will in fact be overfitting them. To avoid overfitting, always examine performance on the validation set and refrain from choosing overly complex trend patterns.

18.2 A MODEL WITH SEASONALITY

A seasonal pattern in a time series means that observations that fall in some seasons have consistently higher or lower values than those that fall in other seasons. Examples are day-of-week patterns, monthly patterns, and quarterly patterns. The Amtrak ridership monthly time series, as can be seen in the time plot, exhibits strong monthly seasonality (with highest traffic during summer months).

Seasonality is modeled in a regression model by creating a new categorical variable that denotes the season for each observation. This categorical variable is then turned into dummies, which in turn are included as predictors in the regression model. To illustrate this, we created a new "Season" column for the Amtrak ridership data, as shown in Table 18.2.

TABLE 18.2   NEW CATEGORICAL VARIABLE (RIGHT) TO BE USED (VIA DUMMIES) AS PREDICTOR(S) IN A LINEAR REGRESSION MODEL. FIRST 17 MONTHS SHOWN

Month	Ridership	Season
Jan-91	1709	Jan
Feb-91	1621	Feb
Mar-91	1973	Mar
Apr-91	1812	Apr
May-91	1975	May
Jun-91	1862	Jun
Jul-91	1940	Jul
Aug-91	2013	Aug
Sep-91	1596	Sep
Oct-91	1725	Oct
Nov-91	1676	Nov
Dec-91	1814	Dec
Jan-92	1615	Jan
Feb-92	1557	Feb
Mar-92	1891	Mar
Apr-92	1956	Apr
May-92	1885	May

In order to include the season categorical variable as a predictor in a regression model for Y (e.g., Ridership), we turn it into dummies. For m seasons we create $m - 1$ dummies, which are binary variables that take on the value 1 if the record falls in that particular season and 0 otherwise.[2] We then partition the data into training and validation sets (see Section 17.5) and fit the regression model to the training data. The top panels of Figure 18.6 show the output of a linear regression fit to Ridership (Y) on 11 month dummies (using the training data). The fitted series and the residuals from this model are shown in the lower panels. The model appears to capture the seasonality in the data. However, since we have not included a trend component in the model (as shown in Section 18.1), the fitted values do not

---

[2]We use only $m - 1$ dummies because information about the $m - 1$ seasons is sufficient. If all $m - 1$ variables are zero, then the season must be the mth season. Including the mth variable would cause redundant information and multicollinearity errors.

Predictor	Estimate	Confidence Interval: Lower	Confidence Interval: Upper	Standard Error	T-Statistic	P-Value
Intercept	1819.0641	1755.5152	1882.6130	32.0700	56.7216	0.0000
season_Aug	151.5676	61.6959	241.4393	45.3539	3.3419	0.0011
season_Dec	-14.6768	-104.5485	75.1949	45.3539	-0.3236	0.7468
season_Feb	-288.0221	-375.8275	-200.2167	44.3111	-6.5000	0.0000
season_Jan	-245.0919	-332.8974	-157.2865	44.3111	-5.5312	0.0000
season_Jul	100.2346	10.3629	190.1063	45.3539	2.2101	0.0292
season_Jun	-11.6321	-101.5038	78.2396	45.3539	-0.2565	0.7981
season_Mar	15.6758	-72.1296	103.4812	44.3111	0.3538	0.7242
season_May	33.1303	-56.7414	123.0020	45.3539	0.7305	0.4666
season_Nov	-52.7367	-142.6084	37.1350	45.3539	-1.1628	0.2474
season_Oct	-44.4843	-134.3560	45.3874	45.3539	-0.9808	0.3288
season_Sep	-169.3304	-259.2021	-79.4587	45.3539	-3.7335	0.0003

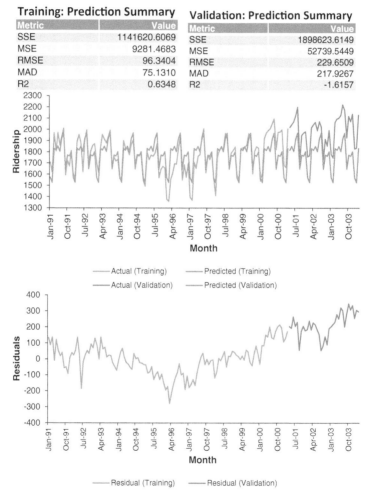

Training: Prediction Summary

Metric	Value
SSE	1141620.6069
MSE	9281.4683
RMSE	96.3404
MAD	75.1310
R2	0.6348

Validation: Prediction Summary

Metric	Value
SSE	1898623.6149
MSE	52739.5449
RMSE	229.6509
MAD	217.9267
R2	-1.6157

FIGURE 18.6   FITTED REGRESSION MODEL WITH SEASONALITY. REGRESSION OUTPUT (TOP), PLOTS OF FITTED AND ACTUAL SERIES (MIDDLE), AND MODEL RESIDUALS (BOTTOM). CHARTS PRODUCED IN EXCEL

capture the existing trend. Therefore the residuals, which are the difference between the actual and the fitted values, clearly display the remaining U-shaped trend.

When seasonality is added as described above (create categorical seasonal variable, create dummies from it, then regress on Y), it captures *additive seasonality*. This means that the average value of Y in a certain season is a fixed amount more or less than that in another season. For example, in the Amtrak ridership, the coefficient for August (151.568) indicates that the average number of passengers in August is higher by 151,568 passengers than the average in April (the reference category). In using regression models, we can also capture *multiplicative seasonality*, where values in a certain season are on average higher or lower by a percentage amount compared to another season. To fit multiplicative seasonality, we use the same model as above, except that we use $\log Y$ as the output variable.

18.3 A MODEL WITH TREND AND SEASONALITY

Last, we can create models that capture both trend and seasonality by including predictors of both types. For example, from our exploration of the Amtrak Ridership data, it appears that a quadratic trend and monthly seasonality are both warranted. We therefore fit a model to the training data with 13 predictors: 11 dummies for month, and t and t^2 for trend. The output and fit from this final model are shown in Figure 18.7. If we are satisfied with this model after evaluating its predictive performance on the validation data and comparing it against alternatives, we would re-fit it to the entire unpartitioned series. This re-fitted model can then be used to generate k-step-ahead forecasts (denoted by F_{t+k}) by plugging in the appropriate month and index terms. However, the predictions on the validation data are still missing the mark, indicating that the trend we have identified may not be so global, after all. More on this in the next chapter, where we allow a local trend component.

The machine learning workflow for the Amtrak regression example used in this chapter (Figures 18.2–18.7) is shown in Figure 18.8. The Create Dummies node is used to obtain seasonal dummies. This workflow can be modified to achieve the various trend and/or seasonal regression models mentioned thus far.

Predictor	Estimate	Confidence Interval: Lower	Confidence Interval: Upper	Standard Error	T-Statistic	P-Value
Intercept	1957.5968	1900.1941	2014.9995	28.9625	67.5908	0.0000
t	-7.1559	-8.6013	-5.7104	0.7293	-9.8122	0.0000
t^2	0.0607	0.0494	0.0720	0.0057	10.6598	0.0000
season_Aug	151.0339	88.1570	213.9107	31.7245	4.7608	0.0000
season_Dec	-17.6880	-80.6134	45.2374	31.7490	-0.5571	0.5786
season_Feb	-303.8633	-365.3528	-242.3738	31.0245	-9.7943	0.0000
season_Jan	-260.6175	-322.1002	-199.1347	31.0211	-8.4013	0.0000
season_Jul	100.0165	37.1469	162.8862	31.7208	3.1530	0.0021
season_Jun	-11.6560	-74.5205	51.2085	31.7182	-0.3675	0.7140
season_Mar	-0.6025	-62.1019	60.8968	31.0294	-0.0194	0.9845
season_May	33.1791	-29.6823	96.0405	31.7167	1.0461	0.2978
season_Nov	-54.9463	-117.8565	7.9639	31.7413	-1.7311	0.0863
season_Oct	-46.0138	-108.9109	16.8833	31.7347	-1.4500	0.1499
season_Sep	-170.3013	-233.1872	-107.4153	31.7291	-5.3674	0.0000

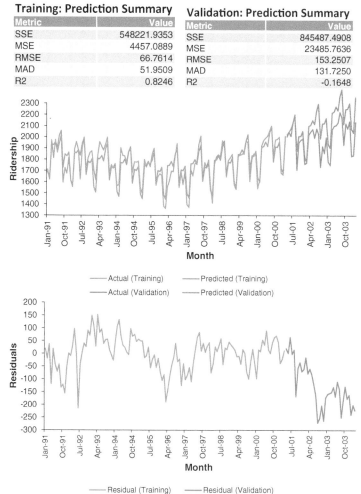

Training: Prediction Summary

Metric	Value
SSE	548221.9353
MSE	4457.0889
RMSE	66.7614
MAD	51.9509
R2	0.8246

Validation: Prediction Summary

Metric	Value
SSE	845487.4908
MSE	23485.7636
RMSE	153.2507
MAD	131.7250
R2	-0.1648

FIGURE 18.7   REGRESSION MODEL WITH MONTHLY (ADDITIVE) SEASONALITY AND QUADRATIC TREND, FIT TO AMTRAK RIDERSHIP TRAINING DATA. REGRESSION OUTPUT (TOP), PLOTS OF FITTED AND ACTUAL SERIES (MIDDLE), AND MODEL RESIDUALS (BOTTOM). CHARTS PRODUCED IN EXCEL

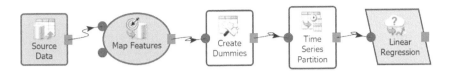

FIGURE 18.8   THE MACHINE LEARNING WORKFLOW FOR THE AMTRAK EXAMPLE (SEASONALITY MODEL)

18.4 AUTOCORRELATION AND ARIMA MODELS

When we use linear regression for time series forecasting, we are able to account for patterns such as trend and seasonality. However, ordinary regression models do not account for dependence between observations, which in cross-sectional data is assumed to be absent. Yet, in the time series context, observations in neighboring periods tend to be correlated. Such correlation, called *autocorrelation*, is informative and can help in improving forecasts. If we know that a high value tends to be followed by high values (positive autocorrelation), then we can use that to adjust forecasts. We will now discuss how to compute the autocorrelation of a series and how best to utilize the information for improving forecasts.

Computing Autocorrelation

Correlation between values of a time series in neighboring periods is called *autocorrelation* because it describes a relationship between the series and itself. To compute autocorrelation, we compute the correlation between the series and a lagged version of the series. A *lagged series* is a "copy" of the original series that is moved forward one or more time periods. A lagged series with lag-1 is the original series moved forward one time period, a lagged series with lag-2 is the original series moved forward two time periods, and so on. Table 18.3 shows the first 24 months of the Amtrak ridership series, the lag-1 series, and the lag-2 series.

Next, to compute the lag-1 autocorrelation, which measures the linear relationship between values in consecutive time periods, we compute the correlation between the original series and the lag-1 series (e.g., via the Excel function CORREL) to be 0.08. Note that although the original series shown above has 24 time periods, the lag-1 autocorrelation will only be based on 23 pairs (because the lag-1 series does not have a value for January 91). Similarly, the lag-2 autocorrelation, measuring the relationship between values that are two time periods apart, is the correlation between the original series and the lag-2 series (yielding −0.15).

TABLE 18.3   FIRST 24 MONTHS OF AMTRAK RIDERSHIP SERIES

Month	Ridership	Lag-1 Series	Lag-2 Series
Jan-91	1709		
Feb-91	1621	1709	
Mar-91	1973	1621	1709
Apr-91	1812	1973	1621
May-91	1975	1812	1973
Jun-91	1862	1975	1812
Jul-91	1940	1862	1975
Aug-91	2013	1940	1862
Sep-91	1596	2013	1940
Oct-91	1725	1596	2013
Nov-91	1676	1725	1596
Dec-91	1814	1676	1725
Jan-92	1615	1814	1676
Feb-92	1557	1615	1814
Mar-92	1891	1557	1615
Apr-92	1956	1891	1557
May-92	1885	1956	1891
Jun-92	1623	1885	1956
Jul-92	1903	1623	1885
Aug-92	1997	1903	1623
Sep-92	1704	1997	1903
Oct-92	1810	1704	1997
Nov-92	1862	1810	1704
Dec-92	1875	1862	1810

We can use ASDM's *ACF (autocorrelations)* utility within the *Time Series* menu to directly compute the autocorrelation of a series at different lags. For example, the output for the 24-month ridership is shown in Figure 18.9. To display a bar chart of the autocorrelation at different lags, check the *Plot ACF* option. ASDM automatically calculates and plots upper and lower confidence bounds, creating a 95% confidence interval.

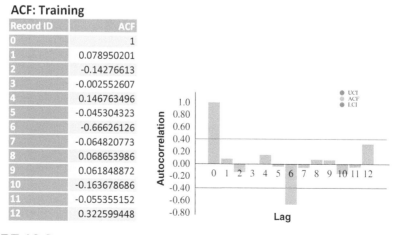

ACF: Training

Record ID	ACF
0	1
1	0.078950201
2	-0.14276613
3	-0.002552607
4	0.146763496
5	-0.045304323
6	-0.66626126
7	-0.064820773
8	0.068653986
9	0.061848872
10	-0.163678686
11	-0.055355152
12	0.322599448

FIGURE 18.9   ASDM OUTPUT SHOWING AUTOCORRELATION AT LAGS 1 TO 12 FOR THE FIRST 24 MONTHS OF AMTRAK RIDERSHIP

The typical autocorrelation behaviors that are useful to explore are the following three:

Strong autocorrelation (positive or negative) at a lag k larger than 1 and its multiples $(2k, 3k, \ldots)$ typically reflects a cyclical pattern. For example, strong positive lag-12 autocorrelation in monthly data will reflect an annual seasonality (where values during a given month each year are positively correlated).

Positive lag-1 autocorrelation (called "stickiness") describes a series where consecutive values move generally in the same direction. In the presence of a strong linear trend, we would expect to see a strong and positive lag-1 autocorrelation.

Negative lag-1 autocorrelation reflects swings in the series, where high values are immediately followed by low values, and vice versa.

Examining the autocorrelation of a series can therefore help detect seasonality patterns. In Figure 18.9, for example, we see that the strongest autocorrelation is at lag 6 and is negative. This indicates a bi-annual pattern in ridership, with six-month switches from high to low ridership. A look at the time plot confirms the high-summer low-winter pattern.

Besides looking at the autocorrelation of the raw series, it is useful to look at the autocorrelation of *residual series*. For example, after fitting a regression model (or using any other forecasting method), we can examine the autocorrelation of the series of residuals. If we have adequately modeled the seasonal pattern, then the residual series should show no autocorrelation at the season's lag. Figure 18.10 displays the autocorrelations for the residuals from the regression model with seasonality and quadratic trend shown in Figure 18.7. It is

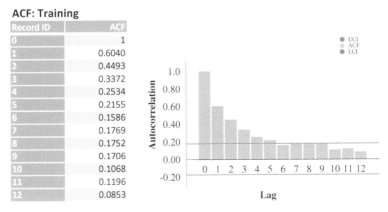

ACF: Training

Record ID	ACF
0	1
1	0.6040
2	0.4493
3	0.3372
4	0.2534
5	0.2155
6	0.1586
7	0.1769
8	0.1752
9	0.1706
10	0.1068
11	0.1196
12	0.0853

FIGURE 18.10   AMTRAK DATA: ASDM OUTPUT SHOWING AUTOCORRELATION OF RESIDUAL SERIES FROM FIGURE 18.7

clear that the 6-month (and 12-month) cyclical behavior no longer dominates the series of residuals, indicating that the regression model captured them adequately. However, we can also see a strong positive autocorrelation from lag 1 on, indicating a positive relationship between neighboring residuals. This is valuable information that can be used to improve forecasts.

Improving Forecasts by Integrating Autocorrelation Information

In general, there are two approaches to taking advantage of autocorrelation. One is by directly building the autocorrelation into the regression model, and the other is by constructing a second-level forecasting model on the residual series.

Among regression-type models that directly account for autocorrelation are *autoregressive* (AR) models, or the more general class of models called ARIMA models (autoregressive integrated moving average models). AR models are similar to linear regression models, except that the predictors are the past values of the series. For example, an AR model of order 2, denoted AR(2), can be written as

$$Y_t = \beta_0 + \beta_1 Y_{t-1} + \beta_2 Y_{t-2} + \varepsilon. \qquad (18.1)$$

Estimating such models is roughly equivalent to fitting a linear regression model with the series as the output, and the two lagged series (at lags 1 and 2 in this example) as the predictors. However, it is better to use designated ARIMA estimation methods (e.g., those available in ASDM's Time Series > ARIMA menu), over ordinary linear regression estimation, to produce more accurate results.[3] Moving from AR to ARIMA models creates a larger set of more flexible forecasting models, but also requires much more statistical expertise. Even with the simpler AR models, fitting them to raw time series that contain patterns such as trends and seasonality requires the user to perform several initial data transformations and to choose the order of the model. These are not straightforward tasks. Because ARIMA modeling is less robust and requires more experience and statistical expertise than other methods, the use of such models for forecasting raw series is generally less popular in practical forecasting. We therefore direct the interested reader to classic time series textbooks (e.g., see Chapter 4 in Chatfield, 2003).

However, we do discuss one particular use of AR models that is straightforward to apply in the context of forecasting and that can provide a significant improvement to short-term forecasts. This relates to the second approach for utilizing autocorrelation, which requires constructing a second-level forecasting model for the residuals, as follows:

1. Generate a k-step-ahead forecast of the series (F_{t+k}), using any forecasting method.

---

[3] ARIMA model estimation differs from ordinary regression estimation by accounting for the dependence between observations.

2. Generate a k-step-ahead forecast of the forecast error (residual) (E_{t+k}), using an AR (or other) model.

3. Improve the initial k-step-ahead forecast of the series by adjusting it according to its forecasted error: *Improved* $F_{t+k}^* = F_{t+k} + E_{t+k}$.

In particular, we can fit low-order AR models to series of residuals (or *forecast errors*) that can then be used to forecast future forecast errors. By fitting the series of residuals, rather than the raw series, we avoid the need for initial data transformations (because the residual series is not expected to contain any trends or cyclical behavior besides autocorrelation).

To fit an AR model to the series of residuals, we first examine the autocorrelations of the residual series. We then choose the order of the AR model according to the lags in which autocorrelation appears. Often, when autocorrelation exists at lag 1 and higher, it is sufficient to fit an AR(1) model of the form

$$E_t = \beta_0 + \beta_1 E_{t-1} + \varepsilon, \tag{18.2}$$

where E_t denotes the residual (or *forecast error*) at time t. For example, although the autocorrelations in Figure 18.10 appear large from lags 1 to 10 or so, it is likely that an AR(1) would capture all of these relationships. The reason is that if immediate neighboring values are correlated, then the relationship propagates to values that are two periods away, then three periods away, and so on.

The result of fitting an AR(1) model to the Amtrak ridership residual series is shown in Figure 18.11. The AR(1) coefficient (0.6) is close to the lag-1 autocorrelation that we found earlier (Figure 18.10). The forecasted residual for April 2003, given at the bottom, is computed by plugging in the most recent residual from March 2001 (equal to 12.1383) into the AR(1) model: $0 + (0.5997)(12.1383) = 7.279$. You can obtain this number directly from ASDM's ARIMA procedure, by requesting a forecast (see bottom table in Figure 18.11). The positive value tells us that the regression model will produce a ridership forecast for April 2001 that is too low, and that we should adjust it up by adding 7279 riders. In this example the regression model (with quadratic trend and seasonality) produced a forecast of 2,004,271 riders, and the improved two-stage model (regression + AR(1) correction) corrected it by increasing it to 2,011,550 riders. The actual value for April 2001 turned out to be 2,023,792 riders—much closer to the improved forecast.

From the plot of the actual vs. forecasted residual series, we can see that the AR(1) model fits the residual series quite well. However, the plot is based on the training data (until March 2001). To evaluate predictive performance of the two-level model (regression + AR(1)), we would have to examine performance (e.g., via MAPE or RMSE metrics) on the validation data in a fashion similar to the calculation that we performed for April 2001 above.

ARIMA Model

Record ID	Coeff	Std-Dev	p-value
Const	-3.69997E-15	2.408377442	1
AR 1	0.599693492	0.053995504	1.16825E-28
Mean	-9.24283E-15		
-2LogL	1326.969028		
Res. StdDev	53.39428888		
#Iterations	5		

Ljung-Box Test for Residuals

Record ID	p-value	chi-square	df
Lag 12	0.999663608	6.02558969	11
Lag 24	0.999999913	20.45688495	23
Lag 36	1	31.06335127	35
Lag 48	1	45.18382676	47

Forecast

Record ID	Forecast: Residual	StdDev	LCI	UCI
Forecast 1	7.279262074	53.1667216	-96.9255974	111.4841

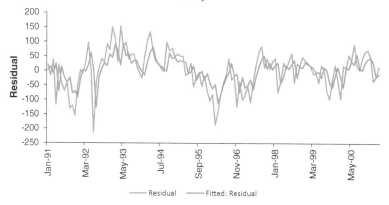

Time Plot of Actual Residuals vs Forecasted Residuals (Training Data)

—— Residual   —— Fitted: Residual

FIGURE 18.11   FITTING AN AR(1) MODEL TO THE RESIDUAL SERIES

To fit an AR (autoregression) model in ASDM, use ARIMA in the Time Series menu. In the "Nonseasonal Parameters," set *Autoregressive (p)* to the required order, and *Moving Average (q)* to 0. The *Advanced* menu will allow you to request forecasts and to display fitted values and residuals.

Last, to examine whether we have indeed accounted for the autocorrelation in the series and that no more information remains in the series, we examine the autocorrelations of the series of residuals-of-residuals (the residuals obtained after the AR(1) was applied to the regression residuals). This can be seen in Figure 18.12. It is clear that no more autocorrelation remains, and that the addition of the AR(1) model has captured the autocorrelation information adequately.

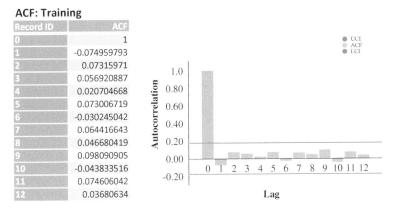

ACF: Training	
Record ID	ACF
0	1
1	-0.074959793
2	0.07315971
3	0.056920887
4	0.020704668
5	0.073006719
6	-0.030245042
7	0.064416643
8	0.046680419
9	0.098090905
10	-0.043833516
11	0.074606042
12	0.03680634

FIGURE 18.12   AUTOCORRELATIONS OF RESIDUALS-OF-RESIDUALS SERIES

We mentioned earlier that improving forecasts via an additional AR layer is useful for short-term forecasting. The reason is that an AR model of order k will usually only provide useful forecasts for the next k periods, and after that forecasts will rely on earlier forecasts rather than on actual data. For example, to forecast the residual of May 2001 when the time of prediction is March 2001, we would need the residual for April 2001. However, because that value is not available, it would be replaced by its forecast. Hence, the forecast for May 2001 would be based on the forecast for April 2001.

The machine learning workflow for obtaining the ACF plot for the Amtrak ridership residuals (Figure 18.10), the AR(1) model (Figure 18.11), and the residuals-of-residuals ACF (Figure 18.12) is shown in Figure 18.13.

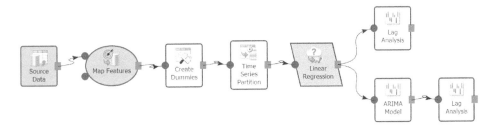

FIGURE 18.13   THE MACHINE LEARNING WORKFLOW FOR THE AMTRAK AUTOCORRELATION EXAMPLE USED IN THIS CHAPTER (FIGURES 18.10–18.12)

Evaluating Predictability

Before attempting to forecast a time series, it is important to determine whether it is predictable, in the sense that its past can be used to predict its future beyond the naive forecast. One useful way to assess predictability is to test whether the series is a *random walk*. A random walk is a series in which changes from one time period to the next are random. According to the Efficient Market Hypothesis in economics, asset prices are random walks, and therefore predicting stock prices is a game of chance.[4]

A random walk is a special case of an AR(1) model, where the slope coefficient is equal to 1:

$$Y_t = \beta_0 + Y_{t-1} + \varepsilon_t. \tag{18.3}$$

We can also write this as

$$Y_t - Y_{t-1} = \beta_0 + \varepsilon_t. \tag{18.4}$$

We see from the last equation that the difference between the values at periods $t-1$ and t is random, hence the term "random walk." Forecasts from such a model are basically equal to the most recent observed value (the naive forecast), reflecting the lack of any other information.

Testing whether a series is a random walk is equivalent to testing whether the lag-1 differenced series $Y_t - Y_{t-1}$ ($t = 2, 3, \ldots$) behaves like a random series. The latter can be done by examining the autocorrelations of the differenced series: if all autocorrelation values are close to zero, then the original series is likely a random walk.

As an example, consider the series of S&P500 monthly closing prices between May 1995 and August 2003 shown in Figure 18.14. The autocorrelations plot of the lag-1 differenced closing prices series is shown in Figure 18.15 (top). We see that all autocorrelation values are practically zero, indicating that the closing prices series is a random walk.

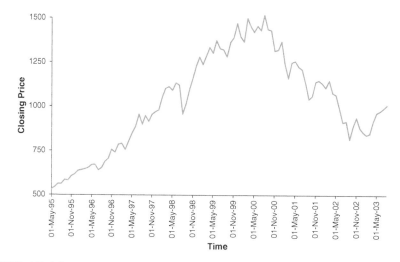

FIGURE 18.14   S&P500 MONTHLY CLOSING PRICES SERIES

---

[4]There is some controversy surrounding the Efficient Market Hypothesis, with claims that there is slight autocorrelation in asset prices, which does make them predictable to some extent. However, transaction costs and bid-ask spreads tend to offset any prediction benefits.

Another approach for evaluating whether the above S&P series is a random walk is to use an AR(1) model. The AR(1) model fitted to the series of S&P500 monthly closing prices is shown in the bottom panel of Figure 18.15. Here the slope coefficient is 0.985, with a standard error of 0.015. The coefficient is sufficiently close to 1 (around one standard error away), indicating—as we found by looking at the differenced series' ACF—that this is a random walk. Forecasting this series using any of the methods described earlier (aside from the naive forecast) is therefore futile.

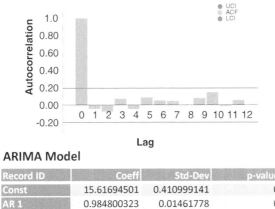

ARIMA Model

Record ID	Coeff	Std-Dev	p-value
Const	15.61694501	0.410999141	0
AR 1	0.984800323	0.01461778	0

FIGURE 18.15   TOP: ACF PLOT OF LAG-1 DIFFERENCED SERIES OF S&P500 MONTHLY CLOSING PRICES. BOTTOM: AR(1) MODEL FITTED TO S&P500 MONTHLY CLOSING PRICES. (NOTE: IGNORE THE P-VALUES REPORTED IN THE OUTPUT; THEY TEST A DIFFERENT HYPOTHESIS THAN THE ONE DISCUSSED IN THE TEXT)

PROBLEMS

18.1 **Impact of September 11 on Air Travel in the United States.** The Research and Innovative Technology Administration's Bureau of Transportation Statistics conducted a study to evaluate the impact of the September 11, 2001 terrorist attack on US transportation. The 2006 study report and the data can be found at https://www.bts.gov/archive/publications/estimated_impacts_of_9_11_on_us_travel/index. The goal of the study was stated as follows:

> The purpose of this study is to provide a greater understanding of the passenger travel behavior patterns of persons making long distance trips before and after 9/11.

The report analyzes monthly passenger movement data between January 1990 and May 2004. Data on three monthly time series are given in file Sept11Travel.xlsx for this period: (1) Actual airline revenue passenger miles (Air), (2) Rail passenger miles (Rail), and (3) Vehicle miles traveled (Car).

In order to assess the impact of September 11, BTS took the following approach: using data before September 11, they forecasted future data (under the assumption of no terrorist attack). Then, they compared the forecasted series with the actual data to assess the impact of the event. Our first step therefore is to split each of the time series into two parts: pre– and post–September 11. We now concentrate only on the earlier time series.

a. Plot the pre-event AIR time series. What time series components appear from the plot?

b. Figure 18.16 shows a time plot of the **seasonally adjusted** pre–September 11 AIR series. Which of the following methods would be adequate for forecasting the series shown in the figure?

- Linear regression model with dummies

- Linear regression model with trend

- Linear regression model with dummies and trend

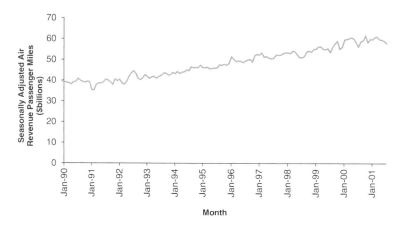

FIGURE 18.16   SEASONALLY ADJUSTED PRE–SEPTEMBER 11 AIR SERIES

c. Specify a linear regression model for the AIR series that would produce a seasonally adjusted series similar to the one shown in Figure 18.16, with multiplicative seasonality. What is the output variable? What are the predictors?

d. Run the regression model from (c). Remember to create dummy variables for the months (ASDM will create 12 dummies; use only 11 and drop the April dummy) and to use only pre-event data.

    i. What can we learn from the statistical insignificance of the coefficients for October and September?

    ii. The actual value of AIR (air revenue passenger miles) in January 1990 was 35.153577 billion. What is the residual for this month, using the regression model? Report the residual in terms of air revenue passenger miles.

e. Create an ACF (autocorrelation) plot of the regression residuals.

    i. What does the ACF plot tell us about the regression model's forecasts?

    ii. How can this information be used to improve the model?

f. Fit linear regression models to Air, Rail, and Auto with additive seasonality and an appropriate trend. For Air and Rail, fit a linear trend. For Rail, use a quadratic trend. Remember to use only pre-event data. Once the models are estimated, use them to forecast each of the three post-event series.

    i. For each series (Air, Rail, Auto), plot the complete pre-event and post-event actual series overlaid with the predicted series.

    ii. What can be said about the effect of the September 11 terrorist attack on the three modes of transportation? Discuss the magnitude of the effect, its time span, and any other relevant aspects.

18.2 **Analysis of Canadian Manufacturing Workers Workhours.** The time plot in Figure 18.17 describes the average annual number of weekly hours spent by Canadian manufacturing workers (data are available in CanadianWorkHours.xlsx, data courtesy of Ken Black).

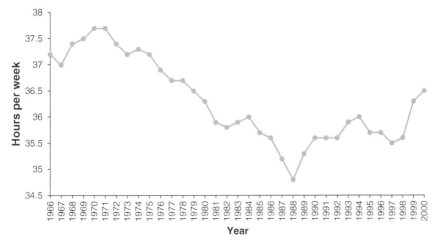

FIGURE 18.17   AVERAGE ANNUAL WEEKLY HOURS SPENT BY CANADIAN MANUFACTURING WORKERS

a. Which of the following regression-based models would fit the series best (choose one)?

- Linear trend model
- Linear trend model with seasonality
- Quadratic trend model
- Quadratic trend model with seasonality.

b. If we computed the autocorrelation of this series, would the lag-1 autocorrelation exhibit negative, positive, or no autocorrelation? How can you see this from the plot?

c. Compute the autocorrelation of the series and produce an ACF plot. Verify your answer to the previous question.

18.3 Toys "R" Us Revenues. Figure 18.18 is a time plot of the quarterly revenues of Toys "R" Us between 1992 and 1995 (thanks to Chris Albright for suggesting the use of these data, which are available in ToysRUsRevenues.xlsx).

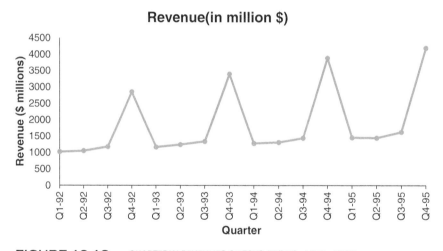

FIGURE 18.18   QUARTERLY REVENUES OF TOYS "R" US, 1992–1995

a. Fit a regression model with a linear trend and seasonal dummies. Use the entire series (excluding the last two quarters) as the training set.

b. A partial output of the regression model is shown in Figure 18.19 (where Quarter_2 is the Quarter 2 dummy, and Index is the trend). Use this output to answer the following questions:

   i. Which two statistics (and their values) measure how well this model fits the training data?

   ii. Which two statistics (and their values) measure the predictive accuracy of this model?

   iii. After adjusting for trend, what is the average difference between sales in Q3 and sales in Q1?

   iv. After adjusting for seasonality, which quarter (Q_1, Q_2, Q_3, or Q_4) has the highest average sales?

Coefficients

Predictor	Estimate	Confidence Interval: Lower	Confidence Interval: Upper	Standard Error	T-Statistic	P-Value
Intercept	906.75	645.8189506	1167.681049	115.3461191	7.861122744	2.54518E-05
Index	47.10714286	21.64287984	72.57140588	11.2566286	4.184835845	0.002359109
Quarter_Q2	-15.10714286	-285.7959718	255.581686	119.6596034	-0.126250986	0.90230871
Quarter_Q3	89.16666667	-201.914105	380.2474383	128.6739827	0.692965779	0.505817809
Quarter_Q4	2101.72619	1809.533712	2393.918669	129.1654192	16.27158572	5.55391E-08

Regression Summary

Metric	Value
Residual DF	9
R2	0.977372
Adjusted R2	0.967315111
Std. Error Estimate	168.4737902
RSS	255450.7619

Training: Prediction Summary

Metric	Value
SSE	255450.7619
MSE	18246.48299
RMSE	135.0795432
MAD	92.53061224
R2	0.977372

Validation: Prediction Summary

Metric	Value
SSE	196792.8345
MSE	98396.41723
RMSE	313.6820321
MAD	254.6666667
R2	0.940363648

FIGURE 18.19   OUTPUT FOR REGRESSION MODEL FITTED TO TOYS "R" US TIME SERIES

18.4 Walmart Stock. Figure 18.20 shows the series of Walmart daily closing prices between February 2001 and February 2002 (thanks to Chris Albright for suggesting the use of these data, which are publicly available, e.g., at http://finance.yahoo.com and are in the file WalMartStock.xlsx).

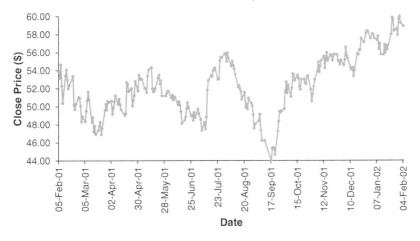

FIGURE 18.20   DAILY CLOSE PRICE OF WALMART STOCK, FEBUARY 2001–2002

a. Compute a lag-1 differenced series of the closing prices. Create a time plot of the differenced series. Note your observations by visually inspecting the differenced series.

b. Fit an AR(1) model to the close price series. Report the coefficient table.

c. Which of the following is/are relevant for testing whether this stock is a random walk?

- The autocorrelations of the close prices series
- The autocorrelations of the lag-1 differenced close prices series
- The AR(1) slope coefficient
- The AR(1) constant coefficient.

d. Use the relevant information from Figure 18.21 to decide whether this is a random walk. Explain how you reached your conclusion and based on which statistics and/or plots.

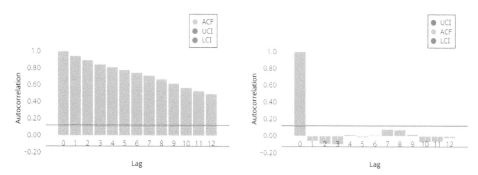

FIGURE 18.21   (TOP) AUTOCORRELATIONS OF WALMART STOCK PRICES AND (BOTTOM) AUTOCORRELATIONS OF LAG-1 DIFFERENCED WALMART STOCK PRICES

e. Does the AR model indicate that this is a random walk? Explain how you reached your conclusion.

f. What are the implications of finding that a time series is a random walk? Choose the correct statement(s) below.

- It is impossible to obtain forecasts that are more accurate than naive forecasts for the series.
- The series is random.
- The changes in the series from one period to the next are random.

18.5   Department Store Sales. The time plot in Figure 18.22 describes actual quarterly sales for a department store over a six-year period (data are available in DepartmentStoreSales.xlsx, data courtesy of Chris Albright).

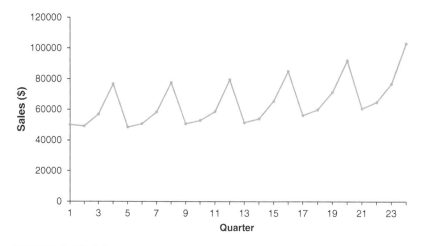

FIGURE 18.22   DEPARTMENT STORE QUARTERLY SALES SERIES

a. The forecaster decided that there is an exponential trend in the series. In order to fit a regression-based model that accounts for this trend, which of the following operations must be performed?

- Take log of quarter index.
- Take log of sales.
- Take an exponent of sales.
- Take an exponent of quarter index.

b. Fit a regression model with an exponential trend and seasonality, using the first 20 quarters as the training data (remember to first partition the series into training and validation series).

c. A partial output is shown in Figure 18.23. From the output, after adjusting for trend, are Q2 average sales higher, lower, or approximately equal to the average Q1 sales?

Coefficients

Predictor	Estimate	Confidence Interval: Lower	Confidence Interval: Upper	Standard Error	T-Statistic	P-Value
Intercept	10.7489	10.7090	10.7889	0.0187	574.0575	0.0000
Quarter	0.0111	0.0083	0.0138	0.0013	8.5607	0.0000
Q_2	0.0250	-0.0193	0.0692	0.0208	1.2019	0.2480
Q_3	0.1653	0.1208	0.2099	0.0209	7.9170	0.0000
Q_4	0.4337	0.3888	0.4787	0.0211	20.5719	0.0000

Regression Summary

Metric	Value
Residual DF	15
R2	0.979125113
Adjusted R2	0.973558476
Std. Error Estimate	0.032766293
RSS	0.016104449

FIGURE 18.23   OUTPUT FROM REGRESSION MODEL FIT TO DEPARTMENT STORE SALES TRAINING SERIES

d. Use this model to forecast sales in quarters 21 and 22.

e. The plots in Figure 18.24 describe the fit (top) and forecast errors (bottom) from this regression model.

  i. Recreate these plots.

  ii. Based on these plots, what can you say about your forecasts for quarters 21 and 22? Are they likely to over-forecast, under-forecast, or be reasonably close to the real sales values?

f. From the forecast errors plot, which of the following statements appear true?

- Seasonality is not captured well.
- The regression model fits the data well.
- The trend in the data is not captured well by the model.

g. Which of the following solutions is adequate *and* a parsimonious solution for improving model fit?

- Fit a quadratic trend model to the residuals (with Quarter and Quarter^2).
- Fit an AR model to the residuals.
- Fit a quadratic trend model to Sales (with Quarter and Quarter^2).

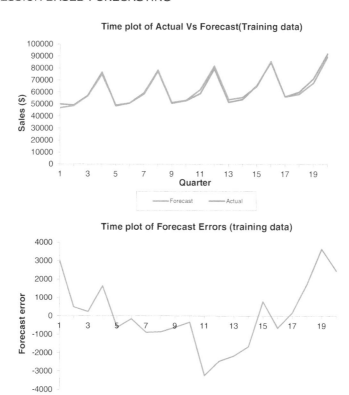

FIGURE 18.24   FIT OF REGRESSION MODEL FOR DEPARTMENT STORE SALES

18.6 **Souvenir Sales.** Figure 18.25 shows a time plot of monthly sales for a souvenir shop at a beach resort town in Queensland, Australia, between 1995 and 2001 (data are available in `SouvenirSales.xlsx`, Source: Hyndman and Yang (2018)]. The series is presented twice, in Australian dollars and in log-scale. Back in 2001, the store wanted to use the data to forecast sales for the next 12 months (year 2002). They hired an analyst to generate forecasts. The analyst first partitioned the data into training and validation sets, with the validation set containing the last 12 months of data (year 2001). She then fit a regression model to sales, using the training set.

a. Based on the two time plots, which predictors should be included in the regression model? What is the total number of predictors in the model?

b. Run a regression model with Sales (in Australian dollars) as the output variable, and with a linear trend and monthly predictors. Remember to fit only the training data. Call this model A.

   i. Examine the estimated coefficients. Which month tends to have the highest average sales during the year? Why is this reasonable?

   ii. The estimated trend coefficient is 245.36. What does this mean?

c. Run a regression model with log(Sales) as the output variable, and with a linear trend and monthly predictors. Remember to fit only the training data. Call this model B.

   i. Fitting a model to log(Sales) with a linear trend is equivalent to fitting a model to Sales (in dollars) with what type of trend?

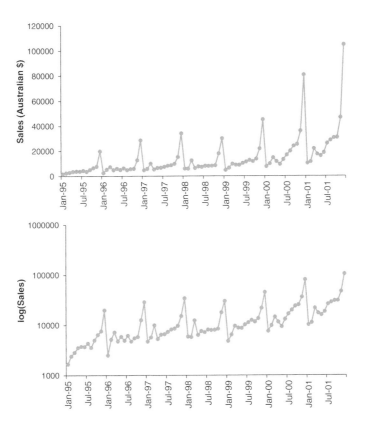

FIGURE 18.25   MONTHLY SALES AT AUSTRALIAN SOUVENIR SHOP IN DOLLARS (TOP) AND IN
LOG-SCALE (BOTTOM)

    ii. The estimated trend coefficient is 0.02. What does this mean?

    iii. Use this model to forecast the sales in February 2002. (Hint: Fit model B to
the entire series without partitioning.)

d. Compare the two regression models (A and B) in terms of forecast performance.
Which model is preferable for forecasting? Mention at least two reasons based on
the information in the outputs.

e. Continuing with model B (with log(Sales) as output), create an ACF plot until
lag 15 for the full series of forecast errors (without partitioning into training/
validation). Now fit an AR model with lag 2 [ARIMA(2, 0, 0)] to the forecast
errors. We will use this model to improve the forecast for January 2002.

    i. Examining the ACF plot and the estimated coefficients of the AR(2) model
(and their statistical significance), what can we learn about the forecasts that
result from model B?

    ii. Use the autocorrelation information to compute an improved forecast for Jan-
uary 2002, using model B and the AR(2) model above.

f. How would you model these data differently if the goal was to understand the different components of sales in the souvenir shop between 1995 and 2001? Mention
two differences.

18.7 **Shipments of Household Appliances.** The time plot in Figure 18.26 shows the series of quarterly shipments (in million dollars) of US household appliances between 1985 and 1989 (data are available in `ApplianceShipments.xlsx`, data courtesy of Ken Black).

If we compute the autocorrelation of the series, which lag (>0) is most likely to have the largest coefficient (in absolute value)? Create an ACF plot and compare with your answer.

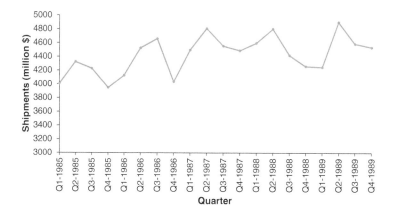

FIGURE 18.26   QUARTERLY SHIPMENTS OF US HOUSEHOLD APPLIANCES OVER FIVE YEARS

18.8 **Australian Wine Sales.** Figure 18.27 shows time plots of monthly sales of six types of Australian wines (red, rose, sweet white, dry white, sparkling, and fortified) for 1980–1994 (data are available in `AustralianWines.xlsx`, Source: Hyndman and Yang (2018)]. The units are thousands of liters. You are hired to obtain short-term forecasts (two to three months ahead) for each of the six series, and this task will be repeated every month.

a. Comment on the suitability of a regression-based forecaster for each wine type.

b. Fortified wine has the largest market share of the above six types of wine. You are asked to focus on fortified wine sales alone, and produce as accurate as possible forecasts for the next two months.

- Start by partitioning the data using the period until December 1993 as the training set.
- Fit a regression model to sales with a linear trend and seasonality.

i. Create the "actual vs. forecast" plot. What can you say about the model fit?

ii. Use the regression model to forecast sales in January and February 1994.

c. Create an ACF plot for the training residuals from the model above until lag 12. Examining this plot, which of the following statements are reasonable?

- Decembers (month 12) are not captured well by the model.
- There is a strong correlation between sales on the same calendar month.
- The model does not capture the seasonality well.
- We should try to fit an AR model with lag 12 to the residuals.

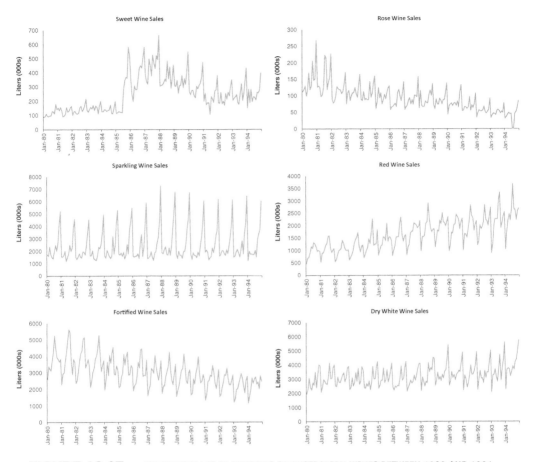

FIGURE 18.27   MONTHLY SALES OF SIX TYPES OF AUSTRALIAN WINES BETWEEN 1980 AND 1994

Smoothing Methods

In this chapter, we describe a set of popular and flexible methods for forecasting time series that rely on *smoothing*. Smoothing is based on averaging over multiple periods in order to reduce the noise. We start with two simple smoothers, the *moving average* and *simple exponential smoother*, which are suitable for forecasting series that contain no trend or seasonality. In both cases, forecasts are averages of previous values of the series (the length of the series history that is considered and the weights that are used in the averaging differ between the methods). We also show how a moving average can be used, with a slight adaptation, for data visualization. We then proceed to describe smoothing methods that are suitable for forecasting series with a trend and/or seasonality. Smoothing methods are data-driven, and are able to adapt to changes in the series over time. Although highly automated, the user must specify *smoothing constants*, which determine how fast the method adapts to new data. We discuss the choice of such constants and their meaning. The different methods are illustrated using the Amtrak ridership series.

19.1 INTRODUCTION[1]

A second class of methods for time series forecasting is *smoothing methods*. Unlike regression models, which rely on an underlying theoretical model for the components of a time series (e.g., linear trend or multiplicative seasonality), smoothing methods are data-driven, in the sense that they estimate time series components directly from the data without a predetermined structure.

---

[1] This and subsequent sections in this chapter copyright © 2019 Datastats, LLC, and Galit Shmueli. Used by permission.

Machine Learning for Business Analytics: Concepts, Techniques, and Applications with Analytic Solver® Data Mining, Fourth Edition. Galit Shmueli, Peter C. Bruce, Kuber R. Deokar, and Nitin R. Patel
© 2023 John Wiley & Sons, Inc. Published 2023 by John Wiley & Sons, Inc.

Data-driven methods are especially useful in series where patterns change over time. Smoothing methods "smooth" out the noise in a series in an attempt to uncover the patterns. Smoothing is done by averaging the series over multiple periods, where different smoothers differ by the number of periods averaged, how the average is computed, how many times averaging is performed, and so on. We now describe two types of smoothing methods that are popular in business applications due to their simplicity and adaptability. These are the moving average method and exponential smoothing.

19.2 MOVING AVERAGE

The moving average is a simple smoother: it consists of averaging across a window of consecutive observations, thereby generating a series of averages. A moving average with window width w means averaging across each set of w consecutive values, where w is determined by the user.

In general, there are two types of moving averages: a *centered moving average* and a *trailing moving average*. Centered moving averages are powerful for visualizing trends because the averaging operation can suppress seasonality and noise, thereby making the trend more visible. In contrast, trailing moving averages are useful for forecasting. The difference between the two is in terms of the window's location on the time series.

Centered Moving Average for Visualization

In a centered moving average, the value of the moving average at time t (MA_t) is computed by centering the window around time t and averaging across the w values within the window:

$$MA_t = \left(Y_{t-(w-1)/2} + \cdots + Y_{t-1} + Y_t + Y_{t+1} + \cdots + Y_{t+(w-1)/2}\right)/w.$$

For example, with a window of width $w = 5$, the moving average at time point $t = 3$ means averaging the values of the series at time points 1, 2, 3, 4, 5; at time point $t = 4$ the moving average is the average of the series at time points 2, 3, 4, 5, 6, and so on.[2] This is illustrated in the top panel of Figure 19.1. Choosing the window width in a seasonal series is straightforward: because the goal is to suppress seasonality for better visualizing the trend, the default choice should be the length of a seasonal cycle. Returning to the Amtrak ridership data (`Amtrak.xlsx`), the annual seasonality indicates a choice of $w = 12$. Figure 19.2 shows a centered moving average line (orange line) overlaid on the

---

[2]For an even window width, such as $w = 4$, we can obtain the moving average at time point $t = 3$ by averaging across two windows: across time points $1, 2, 3, 4$ and across time points $2, 3, 4, 5$. The average of the two averages is the final moving average.

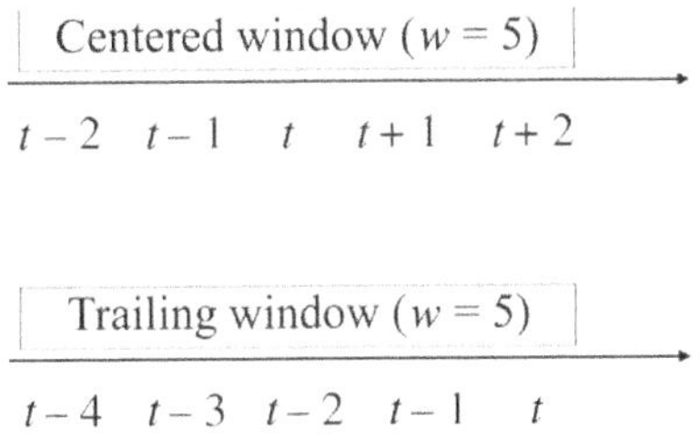

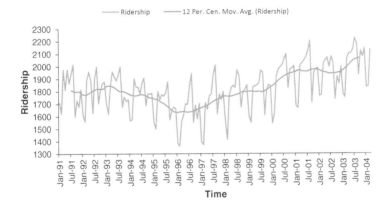

FIGURE 19.1   SCHEMATIC OF CENTERED MOVING AVERAGE (TOP) AND TRAILING MOVING AVERAGE (BOTTOM), BOTH WITH WINDOW WIDTH $W = 5$

FIGURE 19.2   CENTERED MOVING AVERAGE WITH WINDOW $W = 12$, OVERLAID ON AMTRAK RIDERSHIP SERIES. THIS HELPS VISUALIZE TRENDS. CREATED IN EXCEL

original series. We can see a global U-shape, but unlike the regression model that fits a strict U-shape, the moving average shows some deviation, such as the slight dip during the last year. This plot is created manually in Excel.[3]

Trailing Moving Average for Forecasting

Centered moving averages are computed by averaging across data in the past and the future of a given time point. In that sense, they cannot be used for forecasting because at the time of forecasting, the future is typically unknown. Hence, for purposes of forecasting, we use *trailing moving averages*, where the window of width w is set on the most recent available w values of the series. The k-step-ahead forecast F_{t+k} ($k = 1, 2, 3, \ldots$) is then the average of these w values (see also bottom plot in Figure 19.1):

$$F_{t+k} = (Y_t + Y_{t-1} + \cdots + Y_{t-w+1}) / w.$$

[3]In previous versions of Excel, a centered moving average could be obtained using Excel's *Trendline* menu (explained in Chapter 17.5) with the *Moving Average* option. However, the Excel version available at publication time (Microsoft 365 MSO Version 2205) produces only a trailing moving average chart.

For example, in the Amtrak ridership series, to forecast ridership in February 1992 or later months, given information until January 1992 and using a moving average with window width $w = 12$, we would take the average ridership during the most recent 12 months (February 1991 to January 1992).

> Computing a trailing moving average can be done via ASDM's *Moving Average* menu (within *Time Series > Smoothing*). This will yield forecasts and forecast errors for the training set, and if checked, for the validation set as well. The default window width (called *Interval* in the *Weights* box) is $w = 2$, which should be modified by the user.

Using ASDM, we illustrate a 12-month moving average forecaster for the Amtrak ridership. We partitioned once again the Amtrak ridership series, leaving the last 36 months as the validation set. Applying a moving average forecaster with window $w = 12$, we obtained the output partially shown in Figure 19.3. Note that for the first 12 records of the training set, there is no forecast because there are less than 12 past values to average. Computing forecasts for the validation period can be done in two ways: One option is to use the average of the final 12 months in the training period as the forecast for all future periods. In

Fitted

Month	Ridership	Fitted: Ridership	Residual
Jan-91	1708.917		
Feb-91	1620.586		
Mar-91	1972.715		
Apr-91	1811.665		
May-91	1974.964		
Jun-91	1862.356		
Jul-91	1939.86		
Aug-91	2013.264		
Sep-91	1595.657		
Oct-91	1724.924		
Nov-91	1675.667		
Dec-91	1813.863		
Jan-92	1614.827	1809.537	-194.710
Feb-92	1557.088	1801.696	-244.608
Mar-92	1891.223	1796.404	94.819

Forecast

Month	Ridership	Forecast: Ridership	StdDev	LCI	UCI	Residual
Apr-01	2023.792	1938.481	147.258	1649.860	2227.101	85.311
May-01	2047.008	1935.730	147.261	1647.102	2224.357	111.278
Jun-01	2072.913	1931.015	147.265	1642.381	2219.650	141.898
Jul-01	2126.717	1924.453	147.269	1635.812	2213.094	202.264
Aug-01	2202.638	1913.658	147.272	1625.010	2202.306	288.980
Sep-01	1707.693	1898.340	147.276	1609.685	2186.995	-190.647
Oct-01	1950.716	1904.560	147.279	1615.898	2193.222	46.156
Nov-01	1973.614	1898.523	147.283	1609.854	2187.192	75.091
Dec-01	1984.729	1891.616	147.286	1602.940	2180.292	93.113
Jan-02	1759.629	1882.571	147.290	1593.888	2171.254	-122.942
Feb-02	1770.595	1899.190	147.293	1610.500	2187.880	-128.595
Mar-02	2019.912	1918.839	147.297	1630.142	2207.535	101.073
Apr-02	2048.398	1911.415	147.301	1622.711	2200.118	136.983
May-02	2068.763	1909.159	147.304	1620.448	2197.870	159.604
Jun-02	1994.267	1906.945	147.308	1618.227	2195.663	87.322

FIGURE 19.3   PARTIAL OUTPUT FOR MOVING AVERAGE FORECASTER WITH $W = 12$ APPLIED TO AMTRAK RIDERSHIP SERIES

our example, that would produce a fixed forecast of 1,938,481 riders in each of the 36 validation months. A second option for computing validation forecasts is taking the average of the most recent 12 available values: if the actual value is not available, then we use its forecast. For example, the forecast for May 2001 would take an average of the 11 ridership values from May 2000 to March 2001 (in the training period) and the forecast for April 2001 (in the validation period), yielding a forecast of 1,935,730 riders. ASDM implements the second option. In both cases, the only the training ridership values are used.

In this example, it is clear that the moving average forecaster is inadequate for generating monthly forecasts because it does not capture the seasonality in the data. Hence seasons with high ridership are under-forecasted, and seasons with low ridership are over-forecasted. A similar issue arises when forecasting a series with a trend: the moving average "lags behind," thereby under-forecasting in the presence of an increasing trend, and over-forecasting in the presence of a decreasing trend.

In general, the moving average should be used for forecasting *only in series that lack seasonality and trend*. Such a limitation might seem impractical. However, there are a few popular methods for removing trends (de-trending) and removing seasonality (de-seasonalizing) from a series, such as regression models. The moving average can then be used to forecast such de-trended and de-seasonalized series, and then the trend and seasonality can be added back to the forecast. For example, consider the regression model shown in Figure 18.7 in Chapter 18, which yields residuals devoid of seasonality and trend (bottom plot). We can apply a moving average forecaster to that series of residuals (also called forecast errors), thereby creating a forecast for the next *forecast error*. For example, to forecast ridership in April 2001 (the first period in the validation set), assuming that we have information until March 2001, we use the regression model in Figure 18.7 to generate a forecast for April 2001 (which yields 2,004,162 riders). We then use a 12-month moving average (using the period April 2000 to March 2001) to forecast the *forecast error* for April 2001, which yields 30.71 (30,711 riders). This step can be done manually or using ASDM, as shown in Figure 19.4. The positive value implies that the regression model's forecast for April 2001 is too low, and therefore we should adjust it by adding 30,711 riders to the regression model's forecast of 2,004,162 riders.

Choosing Window Width (w)

With moving average forecasting or visualization, the only choice that the user must make is the width of the window (w). As with other methods such as k-nearest-neighbors, the choice of the smoothing parameter is a balance between under-smoothing and over-smoothing. For visualization (using a centered window), wider windows will expose more global trends, while narrow windows

Fitted

Month	Actual: Residual	Fitted: Residual	Residual
Apr-00	52.9448	-27.4866	80.4314
May-00	34.3874	-22.2883	56.6757
Jun-00	90.5299	-15.9615	106.4914
Jul-00	15.9725	-9.8394	25.8119
Aug-00	1.1150	-8.5888	9.7038
Sep-00	42.4576	-2.4596	44.9171
Oct-00	64.0001	9.2982	54.7019
Nov-00	69.8427	17.2678	52.5748
Dec-00	44.2852	21.6161	22.6691
Jan-01	-37.2896	28.5929	-65.8824
Feb-01	-21.8484	33.5315	-55.3799
Mar-01	12.1383	30.4321	-18.2938

Error Measures: Training

Record ID	Value
SSE	431967.9128
MSE	3891.6028
MAPE	266.8711
MAD	50.8853
CFE	643.9070
MFE	5.8010
TSE	12.6541

Forecast

Record ID	Forecast: Residual	StdDev	LCI	UCI
Forecast 1	30.7113	62.3827	-91.5566	152.9792

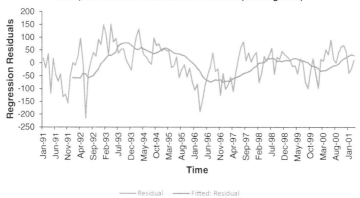

Time plot of Actual Residuals vs Forecast (training data)

FIGURE 19.4   APPLYING MOVING AVERAGE TO THE RESIDUALS FROM THE REGRESSION MODEL (WHICH LACK TREND AND SEASONALITY), TO FORECAST THE APRIL 2001 RESIDUAL

will reveal local trends. Hence, examining several window widths is useful for exploring trends of differing local/global nature. For forecasting (using a trailing window), the choice should incorporate domain knowledge in terms of relevance of past observations and how fast the series changes. Empirical predictive evaluation can also be done by experimenting with different values of w and comparing performance. However, care should be taken not to overfit!

19.3 SIMPLE EXPONENTIAL SMOOTHING

A popular forecasting method in business is exponential smoothing. Its popularity derives from its flexibility, ease of automation, cheap computation, and good performance. Simple exponential smoothing is similar to forecasting with a moving average, except that instead of taking a simple average over the w most recent values, we take a *weighted average* of *all* past values, such that the weights decrease exponentially into the past. The idea is to give more weight to recent information, yet not to completely ignore older information.

Like the moving average, simple exponential smoothing should only be used for forecasting *series that have no trend or seasonality*. As mentioned earlier, such series can be obtained by removing trend and/or seasonality from raw series, and then applying exponential smoothing to the series of residuals (which are assumed to contain no trend or seasonality).

The exponential smoother generates a forecast at time $t + 1$ (F_{t+1}) as follows:

$$F_{t+1} = \alpha Y_t + \alpha(1 - \alpha)Y_{t-1} + \alpha(1 - \alpha)^2 Y_{t-2} + \dots, \qquad (19.1)$$

where α is a constant between 0 and 1 called the *smoothing parameter*. This formulation displays the exponential smoother as a weighted average of all past observations, with exponentially decaying weights.

It turns out that we can write the exponential forecaster in another way, which is very useful in practice:

$$F_{t+1} = F_t + \alpha E_t, \qquad (19.2)$$

where E_t is the forecast error at time t. This formulation presents the exponential forecaster as an "active learner": It looks at the previous forecast (F_t) and how far it was from the actual value (E_t), and then corrects the next forecast based on that information. If in one period the forecast was too high, the next period is adjusted down. The amount of correction depends on the value of the smoothing parameter α. The formulation in (19.2) is also advantageous in terms of data storage and computation time: it means that we need to store and use only the forecast and forecast error from the most recent period, rather than the entire series. In applications where real-time forecasting is done, or many series are being forecasted in parallel and continuously, such savings are critical.

Note that forecasting further into the future yields the same forecast as a one-step-ahead forecast. Because the series is assumed to lack trend and seasonality, forecasts into the future rely only on information until the time of prediction. Hence, the k-step-ahead forecast is equal to

$$F_{t+k} = F_{t+1}.$$

Choosing Smoothing Parameter α

The smoothing parameter α, which is set by the user, determines the rate of learning. A value close to 1 indicates fast learning (i.e., only the most recent observations have influence on forecasts), whereas a value close to 0 indicates slow learning (past observations have a large influence on forecasts). This can be seen by plugging 0 or 1 into equation (19.1) or (19.2). Hence the choice of α depends on the required amount of smoothing, and on how relevant the history is for generating forecasts. Default values that have been shown to work well are around 0.1 and 0.2. Some trial and error can also help in the choice of α: examine the time plot of the actual and predicted series, as well as the predictive accuracy (e.g., MAPE or RMSE of the validation set). Finding the α value that optimizes predictive accuracy on the validation set can be used to determine the degree of local vs. global nature of the trend (e.g., by using "optimize" in ASDM's "Weights" box). However, beware of choosing the "best α" for forecasting purposes, as this will most likely lead to model overfitting and low predictive accuracy on future data.

> In ASDM, forecasting using simple exponential smoothing is done via the Exponential menu (within *Time Series > Smoothing*). This will yield forecasts and forecast errors for both the training and validation sets. You can use the default value of $\alpha = 0.2$, set it to another value, or choose to find the optimal α in terms of minimizing RMSE of the validation data.

To illustrate forecasting with simple exponential smoothing, we return to the residuals from the regression model, which are assumed to contain no trend or seasonality. To forecast the residual on April 2001, we apply exponential smoothing to the entire period until March 2001, and use the default $\alpha = 0.2$ value. The output is shown in Figure 19.5. We see that the forecast for the residual is 14.076 (in thousands of riders), implying that we should adjust the regression's forecast by adding 14,076 riders to that forecast.

Fitted

Record ID	Month	Actual: Residual	Fitted: Residual	Residual
Record 112	Apr-00	52.9448	-20.6636	73.6084
Record 113	May-00	34.3874	-5.9419	40.3293
Record 114	Jun-00	90.5299	2.1239	88.4060
Record 115	Jul-00	15.9725	19.8051	-3.8327
Record 116	Aug-00	1.1150	19.0386	-17.9236
Record 117	Sep-00	42.4576	15.4539	27.0037
Record 118	Oct-00	64.0001	20.8546	43.1455
Record 119	Nov-00	69.8427	29.4837	40.3589
Record 120	Dec-00	44.2852	37.5555	6.7297
Record 121	Jan-01	-37.2896	38.9014	-76.1910
Record 122	Feb-01	-21.8484	23.6632	-45.5116
Record 123	Mar-01	12.1383	14.5609	-2.4226

Error Measures: Training

Record ID	Value
SSE	420879.6143
MSE	3449.8329
MAPE	229.3703
MAD	46.3270
CFE	-25.4844
MFE	-0.2089
TSE	-0.5501

Forecast

Record ID	Forecast: Residual	StdDev	LCI	UCI
Forecast 1	14.0764	58.7353	-101.0426	129.1954

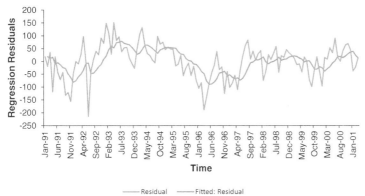

Time plot of Actual Residuals vs Forecast (training data)

——— Residual   ——— Fitted: Residual

FIGURE 19.5   PARTIAL OUTPUT FOR SIMPLE EXPONENTIAL SMOOTHING FORECASTER WITH $\alpha = 0.2$, APPLIED TO THE SERIES OF RESIDUALS FROM THE REGRESSION MODEL (WHICH LACK TREND AND SEASONALITY). THE FORECAST FOR APRIL 2001 RESIDUAL IS AT THE BOTTOM

Relation Between Moving Average and Simple Exponential Smoothing

In both smoothing methods, the user must specify a single parameter: in moving averages, the window width (w) must be set; in exponential smoothing, the smoothing parameter (α) must be set. In both cases, the parameter determines the importance of fresh information over older information. In fact, the two smoothers are approximately equal if the window width of the moving average is equal to $w = 2/\alpha - 1$.

19.4 ADVANCED EXPONENTIAL SMOOTHING

As mentioned earlier, both the moving average and simple exponential smoothing should only be used for forecasting series with no trend or seasonality, that is, series that have only a level and noise. One solution for forecasting series with trend and/or seasonality is first to remove those components (e.g., via regression models). Another solution is to use a more sophisticated version of exponential smoothing, which can capture trend and/or seasonality. In the following, we describe an extension of simple exponential smoothing that can capture a trend and/or seasonality.

Series with a Trend

For series that contain a trend, we can use "double exponential smoothing." Unlike in regression models, the trend shape is not assumed to be global, but rather, it can change over time. In double exponential smoothing, the local trend is estimated from the data and is updated as more data arrive. Similar to simple exponential smoothing, the level of the series is also estimated from the data and is updated as more data arrive. The k-step-ahead forecast is given by combining the level estimate at time t (L_t) and the trend estimate at time t (T_t):

$$F_{t+k} = L_t + kT_t. \tag{19.3}$$

Note that in the presence of a trend, one-, two-, three-step-ahead (etc.) forecasts are no longer identical. The level and trend are updated through a pair of updating equations:

$$L_t = \alpha Y_t + (1 - \alpha)(L_{t-1} + T_{t-1}), \tag{19.4}$$

$$T_t = \beta (L_t - L_{t-1}) + (1 - \beta)T_{t-1}. \tag{19.5}$$

The first equation means that the level at time t is a weighted average of the actual value at time t and the level in the previous period, adjusted for trend (in the presence of a trend, moving from one period to the next requires factoring in the trend). The second equation means that the trend at time t is a weighted average of the trend in the previous period and the more recent information on the change in level.[4] Here there are two smoothing parameters, α and β, that determine the rate of learning. As in simple exponential smoothing, they are both constants in the range [0, 1], set by the user, with higher values leading to faster learning (more weight to most recent information).

Series with a Trend and Seasonality

For series that contain both trend and seasonality, the "Holt–Winters exponential smoothing" method can be used. This is a further extension of double

---

[4]There are various ways to estimate the initial values L_1 and T_1, but the differences among these ways usually disappear after a few periods.

exponential smoothing, where the k-step-ahead forecast also takes into account the seasonality at period $t + k$. Assuming seasonality with M seasons (e.g., for weekly seasonality $M = 7$), the forecast is given by

$$F_{t+k} = (L_t + kT_t)\, S_{t+k-M}. \tag{19.6}$$

(Note that by the time of forecasting t, the series must have included at least one full cycle of seasons in order to produce forecasts using this formula, i.e., $t > M$.)

Being an adaptive method, Holt–Winters exponential smoothing allows the level, trend, and seasonality patterns to change over time. These three components are estimated and updated as more information arrives. The three updating equations are given by

$$L_t \;=\; \alpha Y_t / S_{t-M} + (1 - \alpha)(L_{t-1} + T_{t-1}), \tag{19.7}$$

$$T_t \;=\; \beta\,(L_t - L_{t-1}) + (1 - \beta)T_{t-1}, \tag{19.8}$$

$$S_t \;=\; \gamma Y_t / L_t + (1 - \gamma)S_{t-M}. \tag{19.9}$$

The first equation is similar to that in double exponential smoothing, except that it uses the seasonally adjusted value at time t rather than the raw value. This is done by dividing Y_t by its seasonal index, as estimated in the last cycle. The second equation is identical to double exponential smoothing. The third equation means that the seasonal index is updated by taking a weighted average of the seasonal index from the previous cycle and the current trend-adjusted value. Note that this formulation describes a multiplicative seasonal relationship, where values on different seasons differ by percentage amounts. There is also an additive seasonality version of Holt–Winters exponential smoothing, where seasons differ by a constant amount (also available in ASDM; see more in Shmueli, 2016).

To illustrate forecasting a series with the Holt–Winters method, we again consider the raw Amtrak ridership data. As we observed earlier, the data contain both a trend and monthly seasonality. Figure 19.6 shows part of ASDM's output. We see the values of the three smoothing parameters (left at their defaults), and the chosen 12-month cycle.

Series with Seasonality (No Trend)

Finally, for series that contain seasonality but no trend, we can use a Holt–Winters exponential smoothing formulation that lacks a trend term, by deleting the trend term in the forecasting equation and updating equations (in ASDM this is called Holt–Winters No Trend).

Parameters/Options	
Optimize Params	No
Period	12
Alpha (Level)	0.2
Beta (Trend)	0.15
Gamma (seasonality)	0.05
#Seasons	11
Forecast	TRUE
#Forecast	36
Confidence Level	0.95

Error Measures: Training

Record ID	Value
SSE	651240.6118
MSE	5294.6391
MAPE	3.3643
MAD	58.5577
CFE	392.1592
MFE	3.1883
TSE	6.6970

Error Measures: Validation

Record ID	Value
SSE	574301.3495
MSE	15952.8153
MAPE	5.4858
MAD	108.1237
CFE	-3759.7853
MFE	-104.4385
TSE	-34.7730

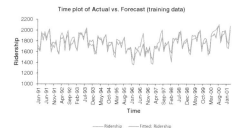

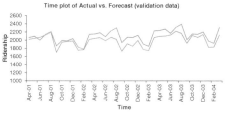

Fitted

Record ID	Month	Ridership	Fitted: Ridership	Residual
Record 1	Jan-91	1709	1656.2147	52.7023
Record 2	Feb-91	1621	1612.2176	8.3684
Record 3	Mar-91	1973	1928.3630	44.3520
Record 4	Apr-91	1812	1929.4274	-117.7624
Record 5	May-91	1975	1918.0254	56.9386
Record 6	Jun-91	1862	1813.3271	49.0289
Record 7	Jul-91	1940	1953.8984	-14.0384
Record 8	Aug-91	2013	2022.5987	-9.3347
Record 9	Sep-91	1596	1702.7120	-107.0550
Record 10	Oct-91	1725	1783.2454	-58.3214
Record 11	Nov-91	1676	1760.5866	-84.9196
Record 12	Dec-91	1814	1780.8041	33.0589
Record 13	Jan-92	1615	1627.4860	-12.6590
Record 14	Feb-92	1557	1564.2715	-7.1835
Record 15	Mar-92	1891	1861.1470	30.0760
Record 16	Apr-92	1956	1845.5102	110.4708

Forecast

Record ID	Month	Ridership	Forecast: Ridership	StdDev	LCI	UCI	Residual
Record 148	Apr-03	2099	2240.3558	81.7407	2080.1469	2400.5647	-141.4568
Record 149	May-03	2105	2274.0309	79.7067	2117.8087	2430.2531	-169.1199
Record 150	Jun-03	2130	2173.7176	95.7970	1985.9589	2361.4764	-44.0466
Record 151	Jul-03	2223	2320.2663	96.1084	2131.8973	2508.6353	-96.9173
Record 152	Aug-03	2174	2396.9981	97.5509	2205.8019	2588.1944	-222.6381
Record 153	Sep-03	1931	2017.9938	93.2458	1835.2355	2200.7522	-86.5878
Record 154	Oct-03	2121	2157.7034	99.5302	1962.6277	2352.7790	-36.2334
Record 155	Nov-03	2076	2151.0765	102.8197	1949.5536	2352.5995	-75.0225
Record 156	Dec-03	2141	2205.1208	86.5606	2035.4651	2374.7765	-64.4438
Record 157	Jan-04	1832	1979.7465	92.5517	1798.3485	2161.1445	-148.2385
Record 158	Feb-04	1838	1930.2921	92.2658	1749.4544	2111.1298	-92.2861
Record 159	Mar-04	2132	2319.7316	94.5824	2134.3535	2505.1096	-187.2856

FIGURE 19.6   PARTIAL OUTPUT FOR HOLT–WINTERS EXPONENTIAL SMOOTHING APPLIED TO AMTRAK RIDERSHIP SERIES (FITTED AND FORECAST VALUES SHOWN ONLY FOR A SUBSET OF RECORDS)

PROBLEMS

19.1 **Impact of September 11 on Air Travel in the United States.** The Research and Innovative Technology Administration's Bureau of Transportation Statistics conducted a study to evaluate the impact of the September 11, 2001, terrorist attack on US transportation. The 2006 study report and the data can be found at bts.gov/archive/publications/estimated_impacts_of_9_11_on_us_travel/index. The goal of the study was stated as follows:

> The purpose of this study is to provide a greater understanding of the passenger travel behavior patterns of persons making long distance trips before and after 9/11.

The report analyzes monthly passenger movement data between January 1990 and May 2004. Data on three monthly time series are given in file Sept11Travel.xlsx for this period: (1) actual airline revenue passenger miles (Air), (2) rail passenger miles (Rail), and (3) vehicle miles traveled (Car). In order to assess the impact of September 11, BTS took the following approach: using data before September 11, they forecasted future data (under the assumption of no terrorist attack). Then they compared the forecasted series with the actual data to assess the impact of the event. Our first step therefore is to split each of the time series into two parts: pre and post September 11. We now concentrate only on the earlier time series.

a. Create a time plot for the pre-event AIR time series.

b. What time series components appear from the plot?

c. Figure 19.7 shows a time plot of the **seasonally adjusted** pre September 11 AIR series. Which of the following smoothing methods would be adequate for forecasting this series?

- Moving average (with what window width?)
- Simple exponential smoothing
- Double exponential smoothing
- Holt–Winters exponential smoothing

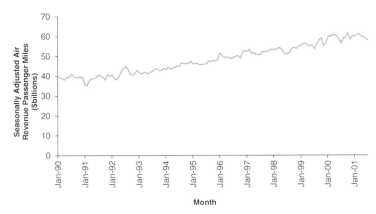

FIGURE 19.7   SEASONALLY ADJUSTED PRE–SEPTEMBER 11 AIR SERIES

19.2   Relation between Moving Average and Exponential Smoothing. Assume that we apply a moving average to a series, using a very short window span. If we wanted to achieve an equivalent result using simple exponential smoothing, what value should the smoothing coefficient take?

19.3   Forecasting with a Moving Average. For a given time series of sales, the training set consists of 50 months. The first five months' data are shown below:

Month	Sales
Sept 98	27
Oct 98	31
Nov 98	58
Dec 98	63
Jan 99	59

a. Compute the sales forecast for January 1999 based on a moving average with $w = 4$.

b. Compute the forecast error for the above forecast.

19.4   Optimizing Holt–Winters Exponential Smoothing. The output in Figure 19.8 shows the optimal smoothing constants from applying Holt–Winters exponential smoothing to data, using "optimal" smoothing constants.

a. The value of zero that is obtained for the trend smoothing constant means that (choose one of the following):

- There is no trend.
- The trend is estimated only from the first two periods.
- The trend is updated throughout the data.
- The trend is statistically insignificant.

b. What is the danger of using the optimal smoothing constant values?

Parameters/Options	
Alpha (Level)	1.000
Beta (Trend)	0.000
Gamma (seasonality)	0.246

FIGURE 19.8   OPTIMIZED SMOOTHING CONSTANTS

19.5   Department Store Sales.
The time plot in Figure 19.9 describes actual quarterly sales for a department store over a six-year period (data are available in `DepartmentStoreSales.xlsx`, data courtesy of Chris Albright).

a. Which of the following methods would **not** be suitable for forecasting this series?

- Moving average of raw series
- Moving average of deseasonalized series
- Simple exponential smoothing of the raw series
- Double exponential smoothing of the raw series
- Holt–Winters exponential smoothing of the raw series

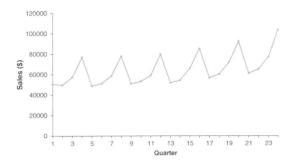

FIGURE 19.9   DEPARTMENT STORE QUARTERLY SALES SERIES

b. The forecaster was tasked to generate forecasts for four quarters ahead. He therefore partitioned the data such that the last four quarters were designated as the validation period. The forecaster approached the forecasting task by using multiplicative Holt–Winters exponential smoothing. The smoothing parameters used were $\alpha = 0.2, \beta = 0.15, \gamma = 0.05$.

  i. Run this method on the data.

  ii. The forecasts for the validation set are given in Figure 19.10. Compute the MAPE values for the forecasts of quarters 21 and 22 for each of the two models (regression and exponential smoothing).

Forecast

Quarter	Sales	Forecast: Sales	StdDev	LCI	UCI	Residual
21	60800	60847.9659	2675.8347	55603.4263	66092.5055	-47.9659
22	64900	62487.8728	2747.9508	57101.9882	67873.7575	2412.1272
23	76997	72125.2600	3171.7622	65908.7204	78341.7996	4871.7400
24	103337	95491.2588	4199.2995	87260.7830	103721.7347	7845.7412

FIGURE 19.10   FORECASTS FOR VALIDATION PERIOD USING EXPONENTIAL SMOOTHING

c. The fit and residuals from the exponential smoothing and regression models are compared in Figure 19.11. Using all the information thus far, is this model suitable for forecasting quarters 21 and 22?

19.6 **Shipments of Household Appliances.** The time plot in Figure 19.12 shows the series of quarterly shipments (in million dollars) of US household appliances between 1985 and 1989 (data are available in `ApplianceShipments.xlsx`, data courtesy of Ken Black).

  a. Which of the following methods would be suitable for forecasting this series if applied to the raw data?

   • Moving average

   • Simple exponential smoothing

   • Double exponential smoothing

   • Holt–Winters exponential smoothing

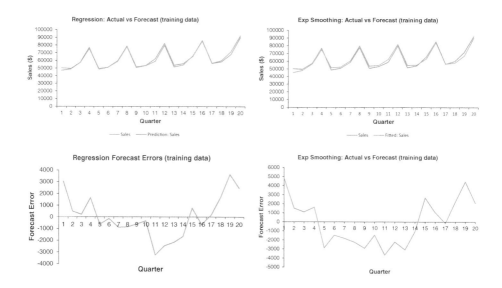

FIGURE 19.11   FORECASTS AND FORECAST ERRORS USING REGRESSION (LEFT) AND
EXPONENTIAL SMOOTHING (RIGHT)

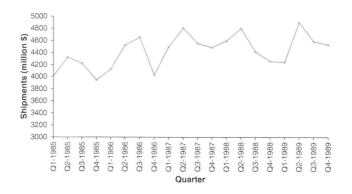

FIGURE 19.12   QUARTERLY SHIPMENTS OF US HOUSEHOLD APPLIANCES OVER FIVE YEARS

b. Apply a moving average with window span $w = 4$ to the data. Use all but the last
year as the training set. Create a time plot of the moving average series.

   i. What does the MA(4) chart reveal?

   ii. Use the MA(4) model to forecast appliance sales in Q1-1990.

   iii. Use the MA(4) model to forecast appliance sales in Q1-1991.

   iv. Is the forecast for Q1-1990 most likely to underestimate, overestimate, or accurately estimate the actual sales on Q1-1990? Explain.

   v. Management feels most comfortable with moving averages. The analyst therefore plans to use this method for forecasting future quarters. What else should
be considered before using the MA(4) to forecast future quarterly shipments of
household appliances?

c. We now focus on forecasting beyond 1989. In the following, continue to use all but the last year as the training set, and the last four quarters as the validation set. First, fit a regression model to sales with a linear trend and quarterly seasonality to the training data. Next, apply Holt–Winters exponential smoothing (with the default smoothing coefficient values) to the training data. Choose an adequate "season length."

    i. Compute the MAPE for the validation data using the regression model.

    ii. Compute the MAPE for the validation data using Holt–Winters exponential smoothing.

    iii. Which model would you prefer to use for forecasting Q1-1990? Give three reasons.

    iv. If we optimize the smoothing parameters in the Holt–Winters method, are the optimal parameters likely to get values that are close to zero? Why or why not?

19.7 **Shampoo Sales.** The time plot in Figure 19.13 describes monthly sales of a certain shampoo over a three-year period (data are available in `ShampooSales.xlsx`, Source: Hyndman and Yang (2018)]. Which of the following methods would be suitable for forecasting this series if applied to the raw data?

- Moving average
- Simple exponential smoothing
- Double exponential smoothing
- Holt–Winters exponential smoothing

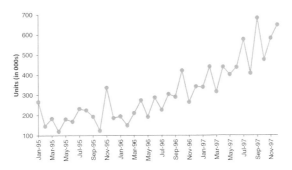

FIGURE 19.13   MONTHLY SALES OF A CERTAIN SHAMPOO

19.8 **Natural Gas Sales.** Figure 19.14 shows a time plot of quarterly natural gas sales (in billions of BTU) of a certain company, over a period of four years (data courtesy of George McCabe). The company's analyst is asked to use a moving average to forecast sales in Winter 2005.

a. Reproduce the time plot with the overlaying MA(4) line (use Excel's "trendline").

b. What can we learn about the series from the MA line?

c. Run a moving average forecaster with adequate season length. Are forecasts generated by this method expected to over-forecast, under-forecast, or accurately forecast actual sales? Why?

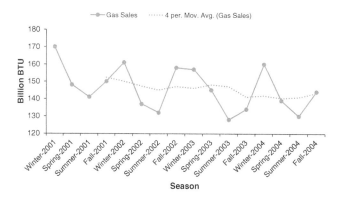

FIGURE 19.14   QUARTERLY SALES OF NATURAL GAS OVER FOUR YEARS

19.9 **Australian Wine Sales.** Figure 19.15 shows time plots of monthly sales of six types of Australian wines (red, rose, sweet white, dry white, sparkling, and fortified) for 1980–1994 (data are available in `AustralianWines.xlsx`, Source: Hyndman and Yang (2018)]. The units are thousands of liters. You are hired to obtain short-term forecasts (two to three months ahead) for each of the six series, and this task will be repeated every month.

a. Which forecasting method would you choose if you had to choose the same method for all series? Why?

b. Fortified wine has the largest market share of the six types of wine. You are asked to focus on fortified wine sales alone, and produce as accurate as possible forecasts for the next two months.

- Start by partitioning the data using the period until December 1993 as the training set.
- Apply Holt–Winters exponential smoothing to sales with an appropriate season length (use the default values for the smoothing constants).

c. Create an ACF plot for the training residuals from the Holt–Winters exponential smoothing until lag 12. Examining this plot, which of the following statements are reasonable?

- Decembers (month 12) are not captured well by the model.
- There is a strong correlation between sales on the same calendar month.
- The model does not capture the seasonality well.
- We should try to fit an autoregressive model with lag 12 to the residuals.
- We should first deseasonalize the data and then apply Holt–Winters exponential smoothing.

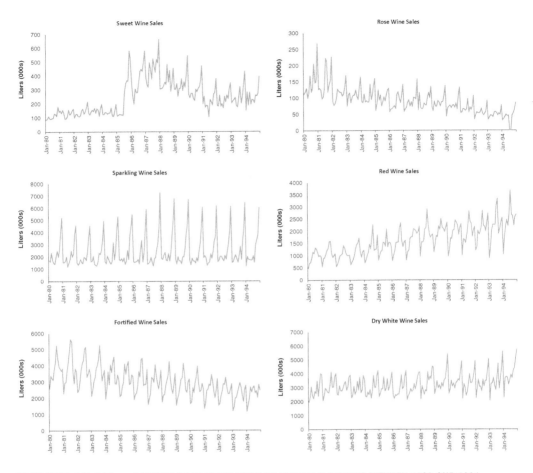

FIGURE 19.15 MONTHLY SALES OF SIX TYPES OF AUSTRALIAN WINES BETWEEN 1980 AND 1994

## PART VIII

Data Analytics

## CHAPTER 20

Social Network Analytics[1]

In this chapter, we will examine the basic ways to visualize and describe social networks, measure linkages, and analyze the network with both supervised and unsupervised techniques. The methods we will use long pre-date the Internet but gained widespread use with the explosion in social media data. Twitter, for example, makes its feed available for public analysis, and some other social media firms make some of their data available to programmers and developers via an application programming interface (API). Two powerful and free tools for network analysis and visualization are NodeXL (an Excel add-on) and Gephi. NodeXL is available for Windows at nodexl.com and Gephi at gephi.org.

20.1 INTRODUCTION[2]

The use of social media began its rapid growth in the early 2000s with the advent of Friendster and MySpace and, in 2004, Facebook. LinkedIn, catering to professionals, soon followed as did Twitter, Tumblr, Instagram, Yelp, TripAdvisor, and others. These information-based companies quickly began generating a deluge of data—especially data on links among people (friends, followers, connections, etc.).

For some companies, like Facebook, Twitter, and LinkedIn, nearly the entire value of the company lies in the analytic and predictive value of these data from their social networks. As of this writing (June 2022), Facebook was worth

---

[1] The organization of ideas in this chapter owes much to Jennifer Golbeck and her book *Analyzing the Social Web*. The contribution of Marc Smith, developer and shepherd of NodeXL, is also acknowledged.

[2] This and the subsequent sections in this chapter ©2023 Datastats, LLC, and Galit Shmueli. Used by permission.

Machine Learning for Business Analytics: Concepts, Techniques, and Applications with Analytic Solver® Data Mining, Fourth Edition. Galit Shmueli, Peter C. Bruce, Kuber R. Deokar, and Nitin R. Patel.
© 2023 John Wiley & Sons, Inc. Published 2023 by John Wiley & Sons, Inc.

more than double General Motors and Ford combined. Other companies, like Amazon and Spotify, use social network data as important components of predictive engines aimed at selling products and services.

Social networks are basically entities (e.g., people) and the connections among them. Let's look at the building blocks for describing, depicting, and analyzing networks. The basic elements of a network are:

- Nodes (also called vertices or vertexes)
- Edges (connections or links between nodes)

A very simple LinkedIn network might be depicted as shown in Figure 20.1. This network has six nodes depicting members, with edges connecting some, but not all, of the pairs of nodes.

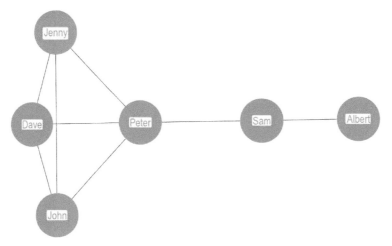

FIGURE 20.1   TINY HYPOTHETICAL LINKEDIN NETWORK. THE EDGES REPRESENT CONNECTIONS AMONG THE MEMBERS (CREATED IN NODEXL BASIC)

20.2 DIRECTED VS. UNDIRECTED NETWORKS

In the network plot shown in Figure 20.1, edges are bi-directional or undirected, meaning that if John is connected to Peter, then Peter must also be connected to John, and there is no difference in the nature of these connections. You can see from this plot that there is a group of well-connected members (Peter, John, Dave, and Jenny), plus two less-connected members (Sam and Albert).

Connections might also be directional, or directed. For example, on Twitter, Dave might follow Peter, but Peter might not follow Dave. A simple Twitter network (using the same members and connections) might be depicted using edges with arrows as shown in Figure 20.2.

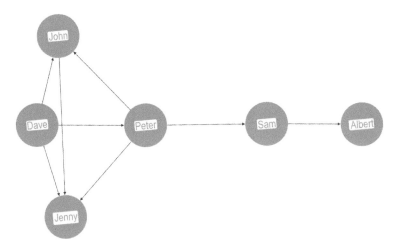

FIGURE 20.2   TINY HYPOTHETICAL TWITTER NETWORK WITH DIRECTED EDGES (ARROWS) SHOWING WHO FOLLOWS WHOM (CREATED IN NODEXL BASIC)

Edges can also be weighted to reflect attributes of the connection. For example, the thickness of the edge might represent the level of email traffic between two members in a network or the bandwidth capacity between two nodes in a digital network (as illustrated in Figure 20.3). The length of an edge can also be used to represent attributes like physical distance between two points on a map.

FIGURE 20.3   EDGE WEIGHTS REPRESENTED BY LINE THICKNESS (E.G., BANDWIDTH CAPACITY) BETWEEN NODES IN A DIGITAL NETWORK

20.3 VISUALIZING AND ANALYZING NETWORKS

You have probably seen network plots[3] used as a tool for visualizing and exploring networks; they are used widely in the news media. Jason Buch and Guillermo

---

[3]In the field of network analysis, the term *graph* refers to the data structure of networks (i.e., lists of edges and nodes). In a more general sense, and in other areas of statistics, the term is used synonymously with "chart" or "plot." Here, to avoid confusion, we will use the term *plot* or *network plot* to refer to the visualization and *network data* to refer to the data itself.

Contreras, reporters for the *San Antonio Express News*,[4] pored over law enforcement records and produced the network diagram shown in Figure 20.4 to understand and illustrate the connections used to launder drug money.[5] You can see that there is a well-connected central node; it is the address of an expensive residence in the gated Dominion community in San Antonio owned by accused launderers Mauricio and Alejandro Sanchez Garza. There are several entities in the lower left connected only to themselves and one singleton. Nodes are sized according to how central they are to the network (specifically, in proportion to their *eigenvector centrality*, which is discussed in Section 20.4).

FIGURE 20.4   DRUG MONEY LAUNDERING NETWORK IN SAN ANTONIO, TX (CREATED IN NODEXL BASIC)

Plot Layout

It is important to note that x–y coordinates usually carry no meaning in network plots; the meaning is conveyed in other elements such as node size, edge width, labels, and directional arrows. Consequently the same network may be depicted by two very different looking plots. For example, Figure 20.5 presents two different layouts of the hypothetical LinkedIn network.

As a result visualization tools face innumerable choices in plot layout. The first step in making a choice is to establish what principles should govern the

---

[4] *San Antonio Express News*, May 23, 2012, accessed May 3, 2022.
[5] The original visualization can be seen at www.google.com/fusiontables/DataSource?snapid= S457047pVkn, accessed May 3, 2022.

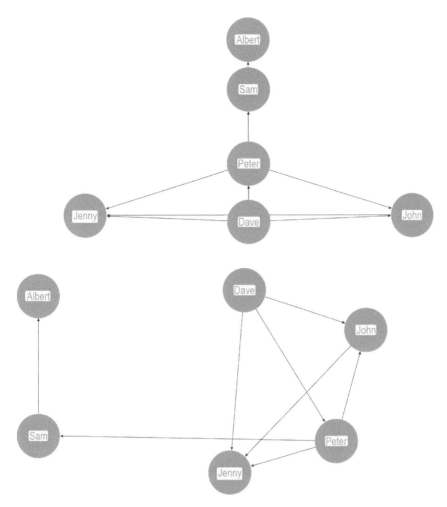

FIGURE 20.5   TWO DIFFERENT LAYOUTS OF THE SMALL LINKEDIN NETWORK PRESENTED
EARLIER (CREATED IN NODEXL BASIC)

layout. Dunne and Shneiderman (2009, cited in Golbeck, 2013) list these four
plot readability principles:

1. Every node should be visible.
2. For every node, you should be able to count its degree (explained below).
3. For every link, you should be able to follow it from source to destination.
4. Clusters and outliers should be identifiable.

These general principles are then translated into readability metrics by which
plots can be judged. Two simple layouts are *circular* (all nodes lie in a circle) and
grid (all nodes lie at the intersection of grid lines in a rectangular grid).

You can probably think of alternate layouts that more clearly reveal structures such as clusters and singletons, and so can computers using a variety of

algorithms. These algorithms typically use a combination of fixed arbitrary starting structures, random tweaking, analogues to physical properties (e.g., springs connecting nodes), and a sequence of iteration and measurement against the readability principles. A detailed discussion of layout algorithms is beyond the scope of this chapter; see Golbeck (2013, chapter 4) for an introduction to layout issues, including algorithms, the use of size, shape and color, scaling issues, and labeling.

Adjacency List

A network plot such as the one in Figure 20.4 is always tied to a data table called an *adjacency list* or an *edge list*. Table 20.1 shows an excerpt from the data table used to generate Figure 20.4.

TABLE 20.1   ADJACENCY LIST EXCERPT CORRESPONDING TO THE DRUG LAUNDERING NETWORK IN FIGURE 20.4

6451 Babcock Road	Q & M LLC
Q & M LLC	10 Kings Heath
Maurico Sanchez	Q & M LLC
Hilda Riebeling	Q & M LLC
Ponte Vedra Apartments	Q & M LLC
O S F STEAK HOUSE, LLC	Mauricio Sanchez
Arturo Madrigal	O S F STEAK HOUSE
HARBARD BAR, LLC	Arturo Madrigal
10223 Sahara Street	O S F STEAK HOUSE
HARBARD BAR, LLC	Maurico Sanchez
9510 Tioga Drive, Suite 206	Mauricio Sanchez
FDA FIBER, INC	Arturo Madrigal
10223 Sahara Street	O S F STEAK HOUSE
A G Q FULL SERVICE, LLC	Alvaro Garcia de Quevedo
19510 Gran Roble	Arturo Madrigal
Lorenza Madrigal Cristan	19519 Gran Roble
Laredo National Bank	19519 Gran Roble

In a typical network visualization tool, you can select a row from the data table and see its node and connections highlighted in the network plot. Likewise, in the plot, you can click on a node and see it highlighted in the data table.

All the entities in both columns are nodes, and each row represents a link between the two nodes. If the network is directional, the link is usually structured from the left column to the right column.

Adjacency Matrix

The same relationships can be presented in a matrix. The adjacency matrix for the small directed network for Twitter in Figure 20.2 is shown in Table 20.2.

Each cell in the matrix indicates an edge, with the originating node in the left header column and the destination node in the top row of headers. Reading the first row, we see that Dave is following three people—Peter, Jenny, and John.

TABLE 20.2   ADJACENCY MATRIX EXCERPT CORRESPONDING TO THE TWITTER DATA IN FIGURE 20.2

	Dave	Peter	Jenny	Sam	John	Albert
Dave	0	1	1	0	1	0
Peter	0	0	1	1	1	0
Jenny	0	0	0	0	0	0
Sam	0	0	0	0	0	1
John	0	1	1	0	0	0
Albert	0	0	0	0	0	0

Using Network Data in Classification and Prediction

In our discussion of classification and prediction, as well as clustering and data reduction, we were dealing mostly with highly structured data in the form of a matrix—columns were variables (features), and rows were records. We saw how to use ASDM to sample from relational databases to bring data into the form of a flat matrix.

Highly structured data like this can be used for network analysis, but network data often starts out in a more unstructured or semi-structured format. Twitter provides a public feed of a portion of its voluminous stream of tweets, which has captured researchers' attention and accelerated interest in the application of network analytics to social media data. Network analysis can take this unstructured data and turn it into structured data with usable metrics.

We now turn our attention to those metrics. These metrics can be used not only to describe the attributes of networks but also as inputs to more traditional machine learning methods.

20.4 SOCIAL DATA METRICS AND TAXONOMY

Several popular network metrics are used in network analysis. Before introducing them, we introduce some basic network terminology used for constructing the metrics:

Edge weight measures the strength of the relationship between the two connected nodes. For example, in an email network, there might be an edge weight that reflects the number of emails exchanged between two individuals linked by that edge.

Path and **path length** are important for measuring distance between nodes. A path is the route of nodes needed to go from node A to node B; path length is the number of edges in that route. Typically, these terms refer to the shortest route. In a weighted graph, the shortest path does not necessarily reflect the path with the fewest edges, but rather the path with the least weight. For example, if the weights reflect a cost factor, the shortest path would reflect the minimal cost.

A connected network is a network where each node in the network has a path, of any length, to all other nodes. A network may be unconnected in its entirety but consist of segments that are connected within themselves. In the money laundering visualization (Figure 20.4), the network as a whole is unconnected—the nodes are not all connected to one another. You can see three independent sub-networks: one large connected segment, a second small connected segment in the top left (with four nodes), and a singleton.

A clique is a network in which each node is directly connected by an edge to every other node. The connections must all be single edges—a connection via a multi-node path does not count.

A singleton is an unconnected node. It might arise when an individual signs up for a social network service (e.g., to read reviews) and does not participate in any networking activities.

Node-Level Centrality Metrics

Often we may be interested in the importance or influence of a particular individual or node, which is reflected in how central that node is in the network. One way to calculate this is by *degree*—how many edges are connected to the node. Nodes with many connections are more central. In Figure 20.1, the Albert node is of degree 1, Sam of degree 2, and Jenny of degree 3. In a directed network, we are interested in both indegree and outdegree—the number of incoming and outgoing connections of a node. In Figure 20.2, Peter has indegree of 2 and outdegree of 1.

Another metric for a node's centrality is *closeness*—how close the node is to the other nodes in the network. This is measured by finding the shortest path from that node to each of the other nodes and then taking reciprocal of the average path length. In the Figure 20.1 example, Albert's closeness centrality is $5/(1 + 2 + 3 + 3 + 3) = 0.417$.

Still another metric is *betweenness*—the extent to which a given node lies on the shortest path between pairs of nodes. The calculation starts with the given node, say, node A, and two other nodes, say, B and C, out of perhaps many nodes in a network. The shortest paths between B and C are listed, and the proportion of paths that include A is noted. This proportion is noted also for all other nodal pairs, and betweenness is the average proportion.

An aphorism relevant for social media networks is "it's not what you know, but who you know." A more accurate rendition would qualify it further—"it's who you know and who they know." A link to a member that has many other connections can be more valuable than a link to a member with few connections.

A metric that measures this connectivity aspect is *eigenvector centrality*, which factors in both the number of links from a node and the number of onward connections from those links. The mathematics of the calculation are not discussed here, but the result always lies between 0 (not central) and 1 (maximum centrality). The larger the value for a given node, the more central it is.

Centrality can be depicted on a network plot by the size of a node—the more central the node, the larger it is.

Egocentric Network

It is often important to gain information that comes only from the analysis of individuals and their connections. For example, an executive recruiting firm may be interested in individuals with certain job titles and the people those individuals are connected to.

An egocentric network is the network of connections centered around an individual node. A degree 1 egocentric network consists of all the edges connected to the individual node, plus their nodes. A degree 2 egocentric network is the network of all those nodes and edges, plus the edges and nodes connected to them.

The degree 1 and degree 2 egocentric networks for Peter in the LinkedIn network are shown in Figure 20.6. Note that the degree 2 egocentric network for Peter is the entire network shown in Figure 20.1.

Network Metrics

To this point we have discussed metrics and terms that apply to nodes and edges. We can also measure attributes of the network as a whole. Two main network metrics are *degree distribution* and *density*.

Degree distribution describes the range of *connectedness* of the nodes—how many nodes have (for example) five connections, how many have four connections, how many have three, and so on. In the tiny LinkedIn network (Figure 20.1), we see that Peter has four connections, Dave, John, and Jenny each have three, Sam has two, and Albert has one. A table of this degree distribution is shown in Table 20.3.

Density is another way to describe. the overall connectedness of network data is *density*, which focuses on the edges, not the nodes. The metric looks at the ratio of the actual number of edges to the maximum number of potential edges (i.e., if every node were connected to every other node) in a network with a fixed number of nodes. For a directed network with n nodes, there can be a maximum of $n(n-1)$ edges. For an undirected network, the number is $n(n-1)/2$. More formally, density calculations

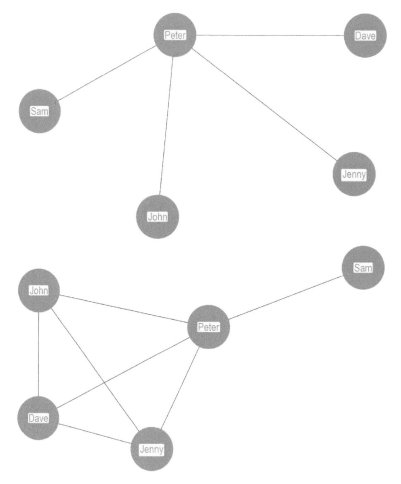

FIGURE 20.6   THE DEGREE 1 (TOP) AND DEGREE 2 (BOTTOM) EGOCENTRIC NETWORKS FOR
PETER, FROM THE LINKEDIN PLOT IN FIGURE 20.1. (CREATED IN NODEXL BASIC)

TABLE 20.3   DEGREE   DISTRIBUTION
OF THE TINY LINKEDIN
NETWORK

Degree	Frequency
Degree 0	0
Degree 1	1
Degree 2	1
Degree 3	3
Degree 4	1

for directed and undirected networks are as follows:

$$\text{Density (directed)} = \frac{e}{n(n-1)}, \qquad (20.1)$$

$$\text{Density (undirected)} = \frac{e}{n(n-1)/2}, \qquad (20.2)$$

where e = number of edges and n = number of nodes. This metric ranges between just above zero (not dense at all) and one (as dense as possible). Figure 20.7 illustrates a sparse and dense network.

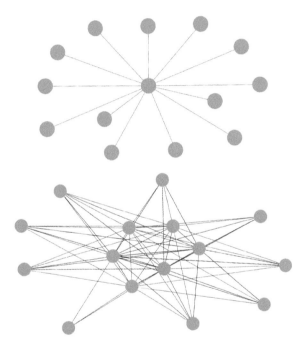

FIGURE 20.7   A RELATIVELY SPARSE NETWORK (TOP) AND DENSE NETWORK (BOTTOM) (CREATED IN NODEXL BASIC)

USING NODEXL FOR NETWORK PLOTTING AND ANALYSIS

In this chapter we used NodeXL, an Excel add-on, for creating the network plots. NodeXL Basic supports creating network plots, choosing a layout, setting the plot features [such as color, shape, and size of edges and nodes (called *vertices*)]. NodeXL Basic also allows computing basic node-level metrics (degree, indegree, and outdegree). Figure 20.8 shows a screenshot of NodeXL Basic. The data on the left are used to create the network plot on the right. The Graph Metrics menu provides various metrics, with the more advanced network metrics requiring the NodeXL Pro version.

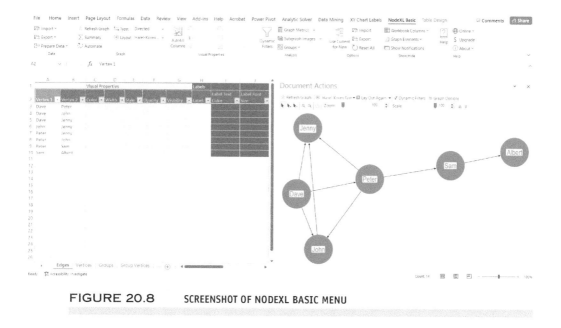

FIGURE 20.8   SCREENSHOT OF NODEXL BASIC MENU

20.5   USING NETWORK METRICS IN PREDICTION AND CLASSIFICATION

Network attributes can be used along with other predictors in standard classification and prediction procedures. The most common applications involve the
concept of *matching*. Online dating services, for example, will predict for their
members which other members might be potentially compatible. Their algorithms typically involve calculation of a distance measure between a member
seeking a relationship and candidate matches. It might also go beyond the members' self-reported features and incorporate information about links between the
member and candidate matches. A link might represent the action "viewed
candidate profile."

Link Prediction

Social networks such as Facebook and LinkedIn use network information to
recommend new connections. The translation of this goal into an analytics
problem is:

"If presented with a network, can you predict the next link to form?"

Prediction algorithms list all possible node pairs and then assign a score to
each pair that reflects the similarity of the two nodes. The pair that scores as most
similar (closest) is the next link predicted to form, if it does not already exist.
See Chapter 16 for a discussion of such distance measures. Some variables used
in calculating similarity measures are the same as those based on non-network

information (e.g., years of education, age, sex, location). Other metrics used in link prediction apply specifically to network data:

- Shortest path
- Number of common neighbors
- Edge weight

Link prediction is also used in targeting intelligence surveillance. "Collecting everything" may be technically, politically, or legally unfeasible, and an agency must therefore identify a priori a smaller set of individuals requiring surveillance. The agency will often start with known targets and then use link prediction to identify additional targets and prioritize collection efforts.

Entity Resolution

Governments use network analysis to track terrorist networks, and a key part of that effort is identification of individuals. The same individual may appear multiple times from different data sources, and the agencies want to know, for example, whether individual A identified by French surveillance in Tunisia is the same as individual AA identified by Israeli intelligence in Lebanon and individual AAA identified by US intelligence in Pakistan.

One way to evaluate whether an individual appears in multiple databases is to measure distances and use them in a similar fashion to nearest-neighbors or clustering. In Chapter 16, we looked in particular at Euclidean distance and discussed this metric not in terms of the network an individual belongs to but rather in terms of the profile (predictor values) of the individual. When basing entity resolution on these variables, it is useful to bring domain knowledge into the picture to weight the importance of each variable. For example, two variables in an individual's record might be street address and zip code. A match on street address is more definitive than a match on zip code, so we would probably want to give street address more weight in the scoring algorithm. For a more detailed discussion of automated weight calculation and assignment, see Golbeck (2013, p. 137).

In addition to measuring distance based on individual profiles, we can bring network attributes into the picture. Consider the simple networks for each individual in Figure 20.9, showing connections to known individuals: based on network connections, you would conclude that A and AA are likely the same person, while AAA is probably a different person. The metrics that can formalize this search and be used in automated fashion where human-intermediated visualization is not practical are the same ones that are used in link prediction.

Entity resolution is also used extensively in customer record management and search. For example, a customer might contact a company inquiring about

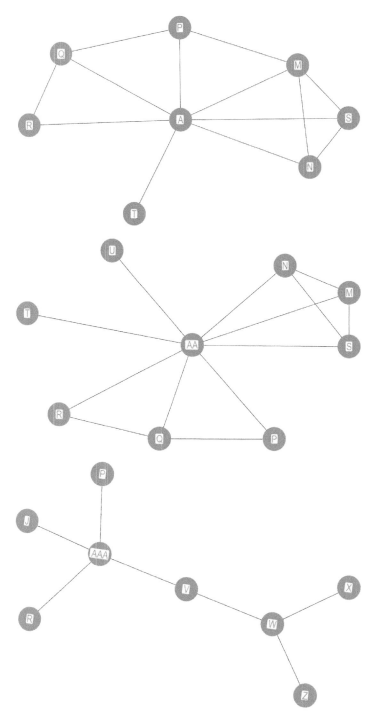

FIGURE 20.9   THE NETWORKS FOR SUSPECT A (TOP), SUSPECT AA (MIDDLE), AND SUSPECT
                AAA (BOTTOM)

a product or service, triggering the creation of a customer record. The same customer might later inquire again or purchase something. The customer database system should flag the second interaction as belonging to the first customer. Ideally, the customer will enter his or her information exactly the same way in each interaction, facilitating the match, but this does not necessarily happen. Failing an exact match, other customers may be proposed as matches based on proximity.

Another area where entity resolution is used is fraud detection. For example, a large telecom used link resolution to detect customers who "disappeared" after accumulating debt but then reappeared by opening a new account. The network of phone calls to and from such people tends to remain stable, assisting the company to identify them.

In traditional business operations, the match may be based on variables such as name, address, and postal code. In social media products, matches may also be calculated on the basis of network similarity.

Collaborative Filtering

We saw in Chapter 15 that collaborative filtering uses similarity metrics to identify similar individuals and thereby develop recommendations for a particular individual. Companies that have a social media component to their business can use information about network connections to augment other data in measuring similarity. For example, in a company where internet advertising revenue is important, a key question is what ads to show consumers.

Consider the following small illustration for a company whose business is centered around online users: user A has just logged on and is to be compared to users B–D. Table 20.4 shows some demographic and user data for each of the users.

TABLE 20.4   FOUR MEASUREMENTS FOR USERS A, B, C, AND D

User	Months as customer	Age	Spending	Education
A	7	23	0	3
B	3	45	0	2
C	5	29	100	3
D	11	59	0	3

Our initial step is to compute distances based on these values, to determine which user is closest to user A. First, we convert the raw data to normalized values to place all the measurements on the same scale (for education, 1 = high school, 2 = college, 3 = post-college degree). Normalizing means subtracting the mean and dividing by the standard deviation. The normalized data are shown in Table 20.5.

TABLE 20.5   NORMALIZED MEASUREMENTS FOR USERS A, B, C, AND D

User	Months as customer	Age	Spending	Education
A	0.17	−1.14	−0.58	0.58
B	−1.18	0.43	−0.58	−1.73
C	−0.51	−0.71	1.73	0.58
D	1.52	1.42	−0.58	0.58

Next we calculate the Euclidean distance between A and each of the other users (see Table 20.6). Based on these calculations, which only take into account the demographic and user data, user C is the closest one to the new user A.

TABLE 20.6   EUCLIDEAN DISTANCE BETWEEN EACH PAIR OF USERS

Pair	Months as customer	Age	Spending	Education	Euclidean distance
A–B	1.83	2.44	0	5.33	3.1
A–C	0.46	0.18	5.33	0	2.44
A–D	1.83	6.55	0	0	2.89

Let's now bring in network metrics, and suppose that the inter-user distances in terms of shortest path are A to B = 2, A to C = 4, and A to D = 3 (Table 20.7).

TABLE 20.7   NETWORK METRICS

Pair	Shortest path
A–B	2
A–C	4
A–D	3

Finally, we can combine this network metric with the other user measurement distances calculated earlier. There is no need to calculate and normalize differences, as we did with the other user measurements, since the shortest-path metric itself already measures distance between records. We therefore take a weighted average of the network and non-network metrics, using weights that reflect the relative importance we want to attach to each. Using equal weights (Table 20.8), user B is scored as the closest to A and could be recommended as a link for user A (in a social environment) or could be used as a source for

TABLE 20.8   COMBINING THE NETWORK AND NON-NETWORK METRICS

Pair	Shortest path	Weight	Non-network	Weight	Mean
A–B	2	0.5	3.1	0.5	2.55
A–C	4	0.5	2.44	0.5	3.22
A–D	3	0.5	2.89	0.5	2.95

product and service recommendations. With different weights it is possible to obtain different results. Choosing weights is not a scientific process; rather, it depends on the business judgment about the relative importance of the network metrics vs. the non-network user measurements.

In addition to recommending social media connections and providing data for recommendations, network analysis has been used for identifying clusters of similar individuals based on network data (e.g., for marketing purposes), identifying influential individuals (e.g., to target with promotions or outreach), and understanding—in some cases, controlling—the propagation of disease and information.

USING SOCIAL NETWORK DATA

The primary users of social network data are the social networks themselves, those who develop applications (apps) for the networks, and their advertisers. Facebook, Twitter, other networks, and associated app developers use the network data to customize each user's individual experience and increase engagement (that is, encourage more and longer use).

Social network data are also a powerful advertising tool. Facebook generates roughly $50 billion in advertising revenue annually, Twitter $2 billion, and LinkedIn about $5 billion, at this writing. Unlike traditional media, Internet social media platforms offer highly specific microtargeting of ads, the ability to experiment with different ads on a continuous basis to optimize performance, and the ability to measure response and charge advertisers only for the ads that people click on. Facebook gains its advantage from its large user base and the rich information portfolio it has on its regular users (including the identity of a user's connection, as well as information on those connected users).

Perhaps the most well-known example of this advantage was Donald Trump's 2016 campaign for President. Although Trump is most often associated with Twitter, Brad Parscale, Digital Director of the 2016 campaign, gives credit for the victory to Facebook, due to its ability to microtarget ads. He put it this way in a 2018 *60 Minutes* television interview:

> "Facebook now lets you get to places ... that you would never go with TV ads. Now, I can find, you know, 15 people in the Florida Panhandle that I would never buy a TV commercial for."

Parscale explained that he was able to generate 50,000–60,000 different ads per day, combining both microtargeting and continuous massive experimentation to see what ads worked best with what individuals. Although Trump lost the popular vote by 2.8 million votes overall, he was able to win the Electoral College by a razor thin margin of 77,744 votes in three key states—Pennsylvania, Wisconsin, and Michigan. The ability to surgically target voters where they would be most effective was crucial, and Facebook was instrumental in this effort. Facebook experts were embedded with the Trump campaign to implement the complex job, and Parscale credited the company with a key role in Trump's victory: "Donald Trump won, but I think Facebook was the method."

> Facebook and Twitter have in the past made data publicly available via Application Programming Interfaces (APIs). Controversial use of Facebook data via third-party apps has resulted in changes to Facebook procedures and significant limitations. Twitter requires that you register as an app developer to gain access to its API. Twitter data is especially popular with researchers for more than just its network data—it is used for analysis of social trends, political opinions, and consumer sentiment. Social media APIs are updated on a regular basis, as are the limits on what you can do with the data.
>
> As ethical issues in data science have come to the fore, social media has come in for increased scrutiny. Companies' command of huge amounts of detailed user data raises privacy concerns, heightened by the use of algorithms to microtarget advertising. Rapid sharing of user activity and opinion, coupled with powerful recommender systems, has the effect of magnifying and speeding up malignant social movements. These topics are covered in greater detail in Chapter 22.

20.6 Advantages and Disadvantages

The key value of social network data to businesses is the information it provides about individuals and their needs, desires, and tastes. This information can be used to improve targeted advertising—and perfectly targeted advertising is the Holy Grail of the advertising business. People often disdain or ignore traditional "broad spectrum" advertising, whereas they pay close attention when presented with information about something specific that they are interested in. The power of network data is that it allows capturing information on individual needs and tastes without measuring or collecting that data directly. Moreover network data are often user-provided rather than actively collected.

To see the power of social network data, one need look no further than the data-based social media giants of the 21st century—Facebook, LinkedIn, Twitter, Yelp, and others. They have built enormous value based almost exclusively on the information contained in their social data—they manufacture no products and sell no services (in the traditional sense) to their users. The main value they generate is the ability to generate real-time information at the level of the individual to better target ads.

It is important to distinguish between social network *engagement* and the use of social network *analytics*. Many organizations have social media policies and use social media as part of their communications and advertising strategies; however, this does not mean they have access to detailed social network data that they can use for analysis. Abrams Research, an Internet marketing agency, cited the edgy online retailer Zappos in 2009 for the best use of social media, but Zappos' orientation was engagement—use of social media for product support and customer service—rather than analytics.

Reliance on social network analytics comes with hazards and challenges. One major hazard is the dynamic, faddish, and somewhat ephemeral nature of social media use. In part this is because social media involvement is relatively new, and the landscape is changing with the arrival of new players and new technologies. In part it stems from the essential nature of social media. People use social media not to provide essential needs, like food and shelter, but as a voluntary avocation to provide entertainment and interaction with others. Tastes change, and what's in and out of fashion shifts rapidly in these spheres.

Facebook was a pioneer, and its initial appeal was to the college crowd and later to young adults. Eight years later, nearly half its users were age 45 or older, significantly higher than in the rest of the social media industry. These users spend more time per visit and are wealthier than college students, so Facebook may be benefiting from this demographic trend. However, this rapid shift shows how fast the essentials of their business model can shift.

Other challenges lie in the public and personal nature of the data involved. Although individuals nearly always engage with social media voluntarily, this does not mean they do so responsibly or with knowledge of the potential consequences. Information posted on Facebook became evidence in 33 percent of US divorce cases, and numerous cases have been cited of individuals being fired because of information they posted on Facebook.

One enterprising programmer created the website pleaserobme.com (since removed) that listed the real-time location of people who had "checked in" via FourSquare to a cafe or restaurant, thus letting the world know that they were not at home. FourSquare was not making this information easily available to hackers, but the check-ins were auto-posted to Twitter, where they could be harvested via an API. Thus information collected for the purpose of enriching the "targetability" of advertising to users ended up creating a liability for both FourSquare and Twitter. Twitter's liability came about indirectly, and it would have been easy for Twitter to overlook this risk in setting up their connection with FourSquare.

In summary, despite the potential for abuse and exposure to risk, the value provided by social network analytics seems large enough to ensure that the analytics methods outlined in this chapter will continue to be in demand.

PROBLEMS

20.1 **Describing a Network.** Consider an undirected network for individuals A, B, C, D, and E. A is connected to B and C. B is connected to A and C. C is connected to A, B, and D. D is connected to C and E. E is connected to D.

    a. Produce a network plot for this network.

    b. What node(s) would need to be removed from the network for the remaining nodes to constitute a clique?

    c. What is the degree for node A?

    d. Which node(s) have the lowest degree?

    e. Tabulate the degree distribution for this network.

    f. Is this network connected?

    g. Calculate the density of the network.

20.2 **Network Density and Size.** Imagine that two new nodes are added to the undirected network in the previous exercise.

    a. By what percentage has the number of nodes increased?

    b. By what percentage has the number of possible edges increased?

    c. Suppose the new node has a typical (median) number of connections. What will happen to network density?

    d. Comment on comparing densities in networks of different sizes.

    e. Now add those two nodes, connect them however you wish, and tabulate the degree distribution of the resulting network.

20.3 **Link Prediction.** Consider the network shown in Figure 20.10.

    a. Using the number of common neighbors score, predict the next link to form (i.e., suggest which new link has the best chance of success).

    b. Using the shortest path score, identify the link that is least likely to form.

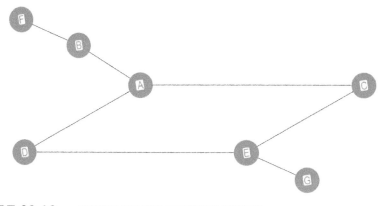

FIGURE 20.10   NETWORK FOR LINK PREDICTION EXERCISE

## CHAPTER 21

Text Mining

In this chapter, we introduce text as a form of data. First, we discuss a spreadsheet representation of text data in which each column is a word, each row is a document, and each cell is a 0 or 1, indicating whether that column's word is present in that row's document. Then, we consider how to move from unstructured documents to this structured matrix. Finally, we illustrate how to integrate this process into the standard machine learning procedures that we have already covered.

21.1 INTRODUCTION[1]

Up to this point, and in machine learning in general, we have been primarily dealing with three types of data:

- Numerical
- Binary (yes/no, true/false)
- Multicategory.

In some common predictive analytics applications, though, data come in text form. An Internet service provider, for example, might want to use an automated algorithm to classify support tickets as urgent or routine, so that the urgent ones can receive immediate human review. A law firm facing a massive discovery process (review of large numbers of documents) would benefit from a document review algorithm that could classify documents as relevant or irrelevant. In such cases, the input variables (features) are embedded as text in documents.

---

[1] This and subsequent sections in this chapter ©2022 Statistics.com and Galit Shmueli. Used by permission.

Machine Learning for Business Analytics: Concepts, Techniques, and Applications with Analytic Solver® Data Mining, Fourth Edition. Galit Shmueli, Peter C. Bruce, Kuber R. Deokar, and Nitin R. Patel
© 2023 John Wiley & Sons, Inc. Published 2023 by John Wiley & Sons, Inc.

Text mining methods have gotten a boost from the availability of social media data—the Twitter feed, for example, as well as blogs, online forums, review sites, and news articles. The public availability of web-based text has provided a huge repository of data on which researchers can hone text mining methods. One area of growth has been the application of text mining methods to notes and transcripts from contact centers and service centers.

21.2 THE SPREADSHEET REPRESENTATION OF TEXT: TERM-DOCUMENT MATRIX AND "BAG-OF-WORDS "

Consider the following three sentences:

```
S1. this is the first sentence.
S2. this is a second sentence.
S3. the third sentence is here.
```

We can represent the words (called *terms*) in these three sentences (called *documents*) in a spreadsheet called a *term-document matrix* (see Table 21.1), where each column is a word and each row is a sentence.

TABLE 21.1   SPREADSHEET REPRESENTATION OF WORDS IN SENTENCES S1—S3

	a	first	here	is	second	sentence	the	third	this
S1	1	1	0	1	0	1	0	0	1
S2	1	0	0	1	1	1	0	0	1
S3	0	0	1	1	0	1	1	1	0

Note that all the words in all three sentences are represented in the table and each word has one column. Although the words are listed in some form of order of appearance, order is not important—a "1" in a cell simply means that the word appeared at least once in the sentence for that row; a "0" means it did not appear. This is the *bag-of-words* approach, where the document is treated simply as a collection of words in which order, grammar, and syntax do not matter.

The three sentences have now been transformed into a data format just like those we have seen to this point. In a simple world, this binary matrix could be used in clustering, or, with the appending of a target variable, classification. However, the text mining world is not a simple one. Even confining our analysis to the bag-of-words approach, considerable thinking and preprocessing may be required. Some human review of the documents, beyond simply classifying them for training purposes, may be indispensable.

21.3 BAG-OF-WORDS VS. MEANING EXTRACTION AT DOCUMENT LEVEL

We can distinguish between two undertakings in text mining:

- Labeling a document as belonging to a class, or clustering similar documents.
- Extracting more detailed meaning from a document.

The first goal requires a sizable collection of documents, or a *corpus*,[2] the ability to extract predictor variables from documents, and for the classification task, lots of pre-labeled documents to train a model. The models that are used, though, are the standard statistical and machine learning predictive models that we have already dealt with for numerical and categorical data.

The second goal might involve a single document and is much more ambitious. The computer must learn at least some version of the complex "algorithms" that make up human language comprehension: grammar, syntax, punctuation, and so on. In other words, it must undertake the processing of a natural (i.e., noncomputer) language to *understand* documents in that language. Understanding the meaning of one document on its own is a far more formidable task than probabilistically assigning a class to a document based on rules derived from hundreds or thousands of similar documents.

For one thing, text comprehension requires maintenance and consideration of word order. "San Francisco beat Boston in last night's baseball game" is very different from "Boston beat San Francisco in last night's baseball game."

Even identical words in the same order can carry different meanings, depending on the cultural and social context: "Hitchcock shot The Birds in Bodega Bay," to an avid outdoors person indifferent to capitalization and unfamiliar with Alfred Hitchcock's films, might be about bird hunting. Ambiguity resolution is a major challenge in text comprehension—does "bot" mean "bought," or does it refer to robots?

Our focus will remain with the overall focus of the book and the easier goal—probabilistically assigning a class to a document, or clustering similar documents. The second goal—deriving understanding from documents—is the subject of the field of natural language processing (NLP).

---

[2]The term "corpus" is often used to refer to a large, fixed standard set of documents that can be used by text preprocessing algorithms, often to train algorithms for a specific type of text, or to compare the results of different algorithms. A specific text mining setting may rely on algorithms trained on a corpus specially suited to that task. One early general-purpose standard corpus was the Brown corpus of 500 English language documents of varying types (named Brown because it was compiled at Brown University in the early 1960s). These days many corpora rely on web-based sources such as Wikipedia and Twitter, which provide huge amounts of documents.

21.4 PREPROCESSING THE TEXT

The simple example we presented had ordinary words separated by spaces, and a period to denote the end of the each sentence. A fairly simple algorithm could break the sentences up into the word matrix with a few rules about spaces and periods. It should be evident that the rules required to parse data from real world sources will need to be more complex. It should also be evident that the preparation of data for text mining is a more involved undertaking than the preparation of numerical or categorical data for predictive models.

For example, consider the following four sentences:

```
S1.   this is the first     sentence!!
S2.   this is a second Sentence :)
S3.   the third sentence, is here
S4.   forth of all sentences
```

This set of sentences has extra spaces, non-alpha characters, incorrect capitalization, and a misspelling of "fourth."

> While Excel was not designed as a text processing tool, it has native facilities that can be used for this purpose. ASDM's Text Miner tool substantially expands those capabilities. Some projects, though, will inevitably require the flexibility and power of a standard programming language.

Tokenization

Our simple data set was composed entirely of words found in the dictionary. A real set of documents will have more variety—it will contain numbers, alphanumeric strings like date stamps or part numbers, web and email addresses, abbreviations, slang, proper nouns, misspellings, and more.

Tokenization is the process of taking a text and, in an automated fashion, dividing it into separate "tokens" or terms. A token (term) is the basic unit of analysis. A word separated by spaces is a token. 2 + 3 would need to be separated into three tokens, while 23 would remain as one token. Punctuation might also stand as its own token (e.g., the @ symbol). These tokens become the column headers in the data matrix. Each text mining software program will have its own list of delimiters (spaces, commas, colons, etc.) that it uses to divide up the text into tokens. ASDM uses a wide variety of characters for delimiting, but defines certain sequence types as being exempt from splitting (e.g., email addresses, urls, monetary amounts). In some programs the delimiters themselves are retained as tokens, while in others (ASDM included) they are immediately removed from the document.

The results of tokenization are cumulative from document to document, in the sense that a master term matrix is built up in which a new column is added each time a new term (not previously encountered in the current document or prior documents) is found.

Figure 21.1 shows the output of tokenization where ASDM removes white space and punctuation marks from the four sentences shown earlier. There is no separate process/menu for tokenization in ASDM and rather it is an operation that happens in the background prior to data preprocessing. For purposes of illustration, we show the result of applying tokenization to the four sentences.[3] We can see that the punctuation marks and white spaces are gone.

Term-Document Matrix

Doc ID	all	first	forth	here	is	of	second	sentence	sentences	the	third	this
Text_Doc1	0	1	0	0	1	0	0	1	0	1	0	1
Text_Doc2	0	0	0	0	1	0	1	1	0	0	0	1
Text_Doc3	0	0	0	1	1	0	0	1	0	1	1	0
Text_Doc4	1	0	1	0	0	1	0	0	1	0	0	0

FIGURE 21.1   ASDM OUTPUT FOR TOKENIZATION OF SENTENCES S1–S4

Text Reduction

For a sizable corpus, tokenization will result in a huge number of predictor variables—the English language has over a million words, let alone the non-word terms that will be encountered in typical documents. Anything that can be done in the preprocessing stage to reduce the number of terms will aid in the analysis. The initial focus is on eliminating terms that simply add bulk and noise.

Some of the terms that result from the initial parsing of the corpus may not be useful in prediction and can be eliminated in the preprocessing stage. For example, in a legal discovery case, one corpus of documents might be emails, all of which have company information and some boilerplate as part of the signature. These terms might be added to a *stopword list* of terms that are to be automatically eliminated in the preprocessing stage (*stopwords*).

Most text-processing software (ASDM included) come with a generic *stopword* list of frequently occurring terms to be removed. If you review the ASDM stopword list during preprocessing stages, you will see that it contains a large number of terms to be removed (the "a's" contain, for example, "a," "about," "actually," "again," "after," etc.; see Figure 21.2). You can add additional terms or remove existing terms from the generic list.[4]

---

[3]This is done with the Text Miner tool, by unchecking the default options *Stopword removal*, *Perform stemming*, and all *Term Filtering* options in the Pre-Processing menu, and checking the option *Presence/Absence* in the *Representation* menu. (Keep all other options at their default).

[4]ASDM actually has two term-removal facilities. The stopword list identifies terms to be removed when they appear in the document exactly in the form in which they appear in the list. The *exclusion list* removes all the variants of the term that stem from the same core (see "stemming").

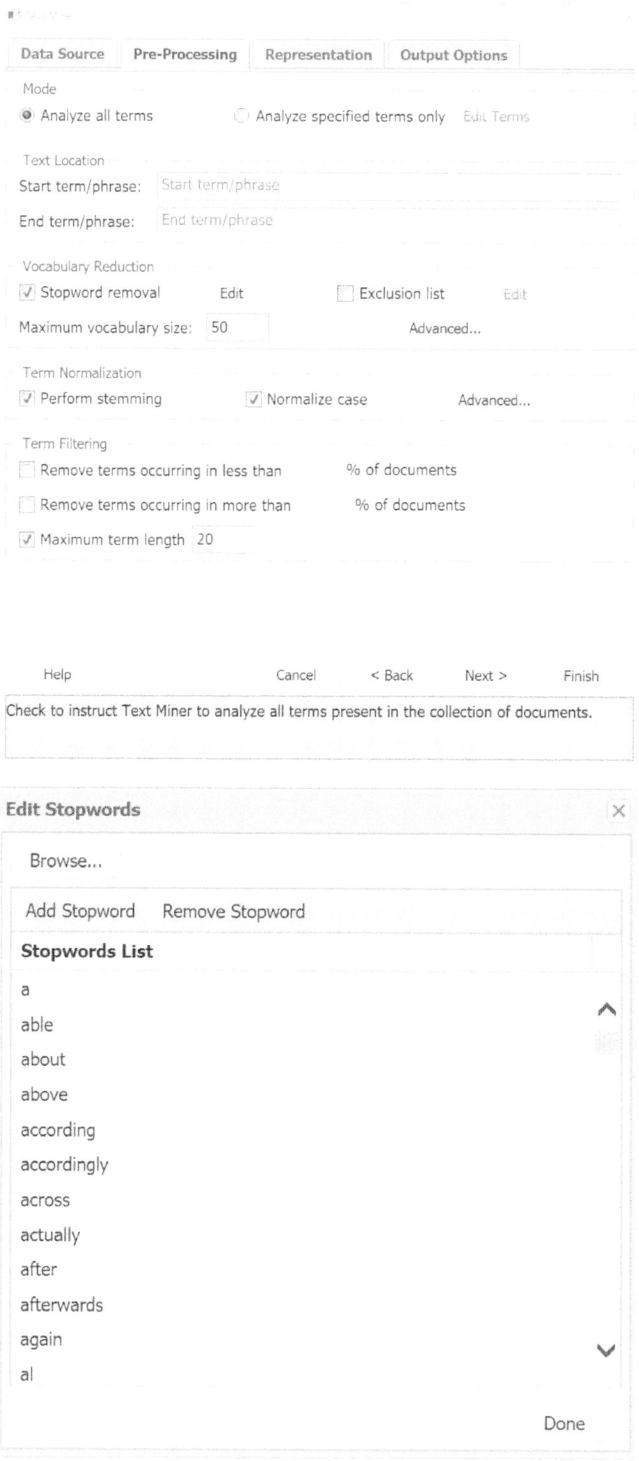

FIGURE 21.2   STOPWORD LIST IN ASDM (BOTTOM), REACHED FROM STOPWORD REMOVAL
OPTION IN PREPROCESSING MENU (TOP)

Another approach is to specify the terms that you want the analysis to focus on, rather than the terms you want it to ignore (the "specified terms only" option in ASDM). This is useful when there is accurate and informative domain knowledge about the documents. For example, in a forensic review of voluminous company communications, those heading the investigation might supply a list of individual and company names to focus on.

Additional techniques to reduce the volume of text ("vocabulary reduction") and focus on the most meaningful text include:

- *Stemming*, a linguistic method that reduces different variants of words to a common core.

- Frequency filters can be used to eliminate either terms that occur in a great majority of documents or very rare terms. They can also be used to limit the vocabulary to the *n* most frequent terms.

- Synonyms or synonymous phrases may be consolidated.

- Letter case uppercase/lowercase can be ignored.

- *Normalization*: A variety of specific terms in a category can be replaced with the category name. This is called *normalization*. Normalization is a general term that does not have a single, specific definition; we need to either consult documentation or specify the rules for normalization. In ASDM, normalization of case means converting everything to lower case. Normalization of certain terms and characters in ASDM means replacing all unique occurrences in a category (e.g., email addresses) with a single user-specified token that represents that category. For example, different email addresses or different numbers might all be replaced with "emailtoken" or "numbertoken." Figure 21.3 shows the different normalization options in ASDM.

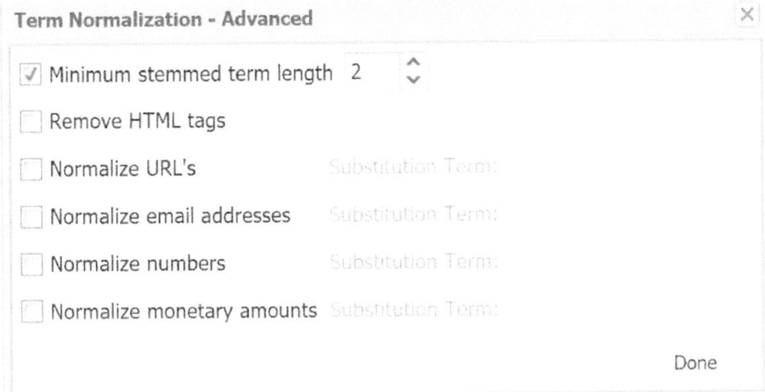

FIGURE 21.3   NORMALIZATION OPTIONS IN ASDM

All these data reduction options can be achieved through the *PreProcessing* menu in ASDM (see Figure 21.2, top).

Presence/Absence vs. Frequency

The bag-of-words approach can be implemented in terms of either *frequency* or *presence/absence* of terms. The latter might be appropriate in some circumstances—in a forensic accounting model, for example, the presence or absence of a particular vendor name may be a key predictor variable, without regard to how often it appears in a given document. *Frequency* can be important in other circumstances, however. For example, in processing support tickets, a single mention of "IP address" may be non-meaningful—all support tickets might involve a user's IP address as part of the submission. Repetition of the phrase multiple times, however, might provide useful information that IP address is part of the problem (e.g., DNS resolution). In ASDM's Text Miner tool, we can select either *Presence/Absence* in the Representation menu, or *Term Frequency* (see Figure 21.5).

Term Frequency—Inverse Document Frequency (TF-IDF)

There are additional popular options that factor in both the frequency of a term in a document and the frequency of documents with that term. One such popular option is Term Frequency—Inverse Document Frequency (TF-IDF). For a given document d and term t, the term frequency (TF) is the number of times term t appears in document d:

$$\text{TF}(t, d) = \# \text{ times term } t \text{ appears in document } d.$$

To account for terms that appear frequently in the domain of interest, we compute the *Inverse Document Frequency* (IDF) of term t, calculated over the entire corpus and defined as

$$\text{IDF}(t) = \frac{\text{total number of documents}}{\# \text{ documents containing term } t}.$$

TF-IDF(t, d) for a specific term–document pair is the product of TF(t, d) and IDF(t):

$$\text{TF-IDF}(t, d) = \text{TF}(t, d) \times \text{IDF}(t). \tag{21.1}$$

The above definition of TF-IDF is a common one; however, there are multiple ways to define and weight both TF and IDF, so there are a variety of possible definitions of TF-IDF. ASDM's default for TF-IDF uses the formula

$$\text{TF-IDF}(t, d) = \\ \log(1 + \text{TF}(t, d)) \times \log\left(\frac{\text{total number of documents}}{1 + \# \text{ documents containing term } t}\right). \tag{21.2}$$

For example, the TF-IDF value for the term "first" in document 1, computed using Eq. (21.2), is

$$\text{TF-IDF(first, 1)} = \log(1 + 1) \times \left[\log \left(\frac{4}{1 + 1} \right) \right] = 0.4805.$$

The other TF-IDF values in document 1 are: TF-IDF(this, 1) = 0.1994, TF-IDF(is, 1) = 0, TF-IDF(the, 1) = 0.1994, TF-IDF(sentence, 1) = -0.1547, and the remaining TF-IDF values for document 1 are 0 (because $\log(1) = 0$).

The TF-IDF matrix contains the value for each term-document combination. Figure 21.4 presents the result of the text reduction step applied to the four sentences example using TF-IDF, after a slight modification. If we use ASDM's data reduction defaults, the result is a single term ("sentenc"). This happens because most of the words ("first", "second", "third", "forth", "is", "here", "of", "the", "this") are on ASDM's stopword list. To get more terms (for the purpose of this illustration), we excluded the terms "first", "second", "third", and "forth" from the stopword list (using the *Stopword removal* option). The resulting term-document matrix is shown in Figure 21.4. We see that the number of terms has reduced to five. The cells contain the TF-IDF values computed using equation (21.1).

Term-Document Matrix

Doc ID	first	forth	second	sentenc	third
Var1_Doc1	0.4805	0	0	-0.1547	0
Var1_Doc2	0	0	0.4805	-0.1547	0
Var1_Doc3	0	0	0	-0.1547	0.4805
Var1_Doc4	0	0.4805	0	-0.1547	0

FIGURE 21.4   ASDM OUTPUT SHOWING TF-IDF MATRIX FOR TEXT REDUCTION OF SENTENCES S1–S4 USING ASDM'S DEFAULT FORMULA (EQUATION (21.2))

The general idea of TF-IDF is that it identifies documents with frequent occurrences of rare terms. TF-IDF yields high values for documents with a relatively high frequency for terms that are relatively rare overall, and near-zero values for terms that are absent from a document, or present in most documents.

In ASDM, choosing between the two bag-of-words approaches (presence/absence or frequency) or one of the TF-IDF options is done through the Representation menu (see Figure 21.5).

From Terms to Concepts: Latent Semantic Indexing

In Chapter 4, we showed how numerous continuous numeric predictor variables can be reduced to a small number of "principal components" that explain most of the variation in a set of variables. The principal components are linear combinations of the original (typically, correlated) variables, and a subset of them serve as new variables to replace the numerous original variables.

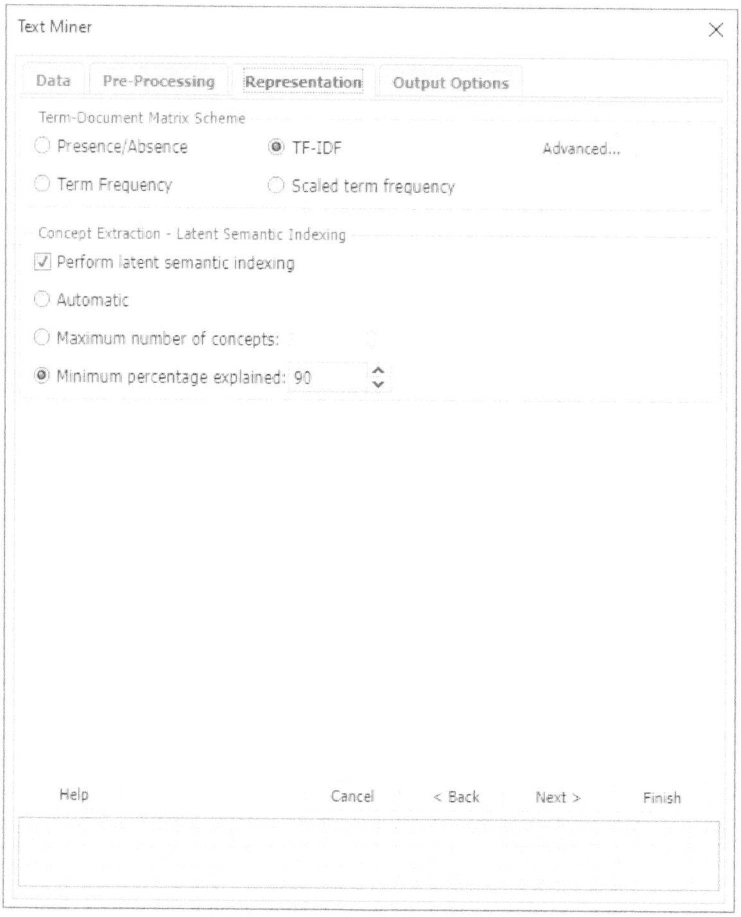

FIGURE 21.5   ASDM'S TEXT MINER REPRESENTATION MENU

An analogous dimension reduction method—latent semantic indexing—can be applied to text data. The mathematics of the algorithm are beyond the scope of this book, but a good intuitive explanation comes from Frontline Solver's Analytic Solver Data Mining User Guide[5]:

> For example: if we inspected our document collection, we might find that each time the term "alternator" appeared in an automobile document, the document also included the terms "battery" and "headlights." Or each time the term "brake" appeared in an automobile document, the terms "pads" and "squeaky" also appeared. However there is no detectable pattern regarding the use of the terms "alternator" and "brake" together. Documents including "alternator" might or might not include "brake" and documents including "brake" might or might not include "alternator." Our four terms, battery, headlights, pads, and squeaky describe two different automobile repair issues: failing brakes and a bad alternator.

---

[5]https://www.solver.com/text-mining-example

So, in this case, latent semantic indexing would reduce the four terms to two concepts:

- Brake failure
- Alternator failure

We illustrate latent semantic indexing using ASDM in the example in Section 21.6.

Extracting Meaning

In this simple example, the concepts to which the terms map (failing brakes, bad alternator) are clear and understandable. In many cases, unfortunately, this will not be true—the concepts to which the terms map will not be obvious. In such cases, latent semantic indexing will greatly enhance the manageability of the text for model-building purposes and sharpen its predictive power by reducing noise, but it will turn the model into a black-box device for prediction, not so useful for understanding the roles that terms and concepts play. This is OK for our purposes—as noted earlier, we are focusing on text mining to classify or cluster new documents, not to extract meaning.

From Terms to High Dimensional Word Vectors: Word2Vec

Word embedding is a form of text representation technique in which each word is represented in the form of a multi-dimensional vector (called word vector) so that words that are closer to one another in this vector space would also be similar in meaning. Latent semantic indexing discussed earlier is one such word embedding that considers occurrences of terms at a document level. Yet another form of word embedding approaches is Word2Vec, which considers occurrences of terms at a context level and uses prediction-based models to arrive at the word vector representations. The Word2Vec technique uses a neural network model and trains words against other words in its neighborhood within the corpus. This technique is not implemented in ASDM, but for a more complete discussion see either the RapidMiner or second R edition of this text.

21.5 IMPLEMENTING MACHINE LEARNING METHODS

After the text has gone through the preprocessing stage, it is in a numeric matrix format; then you can apply the various machine learning methods discussed earlier in this book. Clustering methods can be used to identify clusters of documents—for example, large numbers of medical reports can be mined to identify clusters of symptoms. Prediction methods could be used with tech support tickets to predict how long it will take to resolve an issue. Perhaps the most popular application of text mining is for classification—also termed *labeling*—of documents.

21.6 EXAMPLE: ONLINE DISCUSSIONS ON AUTOS AND ELECTRONICS

This example (from the ASDM user guide, with minor modifications) illustrates a classification task—to classify Internet discussion posts as either auto-related or electronics-related. One post looks like this:

> From: smith@logos.asd.sgi.com (Tom Smith) Subject: Ford Explorer 4WD – do I need performance axle?
> We're considering getting a Ford Explorer XLT with 4WD and we have the following questions (All we would do is go skiing - no off-roading):
> 1. With 4WD, do we need the "performance axle" - (limited slip axle). Its purpose is to allow the tires to act independently when the tires are on different terrain.
> 2. Do we need the all-terrain tires (P235/75X15) or will the all-season (P225/70X15) be good enough for us at Lake Tahoe?
> Thanks,
> Tom
> –
> ==
> Tom Smith Silicon Graphics smith@asd.sgi.com 2011 N. Shoreline Rd. MS 8U-815 415-962-0494 (fax) Mountain View, CA 94043
> ==

The posts are taken from Internet groups that are devoted to autos and electronics, so are pre-labeled. This one, clearly, is auto-related. A related organizational scenario might involve messages received by a medical office that must be classified as medical or non-medical (the messages in such a real scenario would probably have to be labeled by humans as part of the preprocessing). The posts are in the form of small files whose names are numbers—all the auto posts start with "1" and all the electronics posts start with "5." In the following, we describe the main steps from preprocessing to building a classification model using a sample of 80 posts. Note that we are using just 80 documents (or posts) because the education edition of ASDM allows a maximum of 100 documents and a maximum of 5000 characters.

Importing and Labeling the Records

Importing and preprocessing text data in ASDM involves more steps and decisions than opening the other datasets used in this book. Here is a schematic of the whole classification process in ASDM:

1. Import data via the *Get Data* menu. In this example format, each document is a file, and the files are to be imported from a folder (in ASDM either use the "write file contents" option at import, or, if you write file

paths, you can use the option "Text variables contain file paths" at a later stage). Another possible import format is one in which all the documents are in a single text file, one document per row.

2. From the *Text* menu, use "Pre-Processing" and "Representation" for the various preprocessing steps discussed here.

3. At some point after tokenization, add or restore labels.

4. From the *Text* menu, use "Output Options" to produce the matrix that is needed to build a predictive model. You will need to add the target variable.

5. Using the matrix thus produced, use the *Classify* menu to select and configure various classification models.

IMPORTANT: This is just a schematic, covering only the major phases of analysis, using ASDM V2021. The ASDM user guide section on Text Mining should be consulted in detail, as the process is more complex than with analyzing numeric data, and the user interface is not a sufficient guide by itself.

Note that prior to preprocessing, each document is treated as a single row in Excel, or a single variable. It has not yet been split up into tokens. How will we handle the document labels? If they are part of the document itself, they will be subsumed, and perhaps lost, as part of the preprocessing.

It is best to add, or restore, the labels after the automated preprocessing that ASDM does. In this example, the labels correspond to the first character in the file names—1's for autos and 5's for electronics. We can add labels later, as long as we know which documents (rows in Excel) come from which source.

Tokenization

The first preprocessing step is *tokenization*, which includes the removal of white space, punctuation, and numbers. ASDM will split the document into tokens or terms (words, or non-word character strings). For example, the term "4WD" is isolated as a term because, in two instances, it has spaces on either side and, in one instance, it has a space on one side and a comma (another delimiter) on the other. Recall that ASDM uses a wide variety of characters for delimiting, but defines certain sequence types as being exempt from splitting (e.g., email addresses, urls, monetary amounts). Hence, here the full email address is treated as a single term and not split up.

Text Reduction

The next step is *stemming*, or the consolidation of multiple forms of a word into a single core. For example, "road" and "Rd." might stem to "road." After stemming, ASDM's default is set to discard tokens that stem to two or fewer characters. The user can modify this. As mentioned earlier, other options include removal of words (tokens) on a stopword list (see Figure 21.2) and normalization.

Figure 21.6 shows part of the Term-Document matrix for the autos-electronics data, after tokenization and text reduction. These operations are achieved using the Pre-Processing menu in ASDM's Text Miner tool.

Term-Document Matrix

Doc ID	appreci	articl	back	better	buy	call	car	comput	design	doesn
52810	1	0	0	1	0	0	0	0	0	0
102875	0	0	1	0	0	0	1	0	0	0
102818	0	0	1	0	1	0	1	0	0	0
102808	0	1	0	0	0	0	0	1	0	0
53693	0	1	0	0	0	0	0	0	1	0
53673	1	0	1	0	0	0	0	1	0	1
53771	1	0	0	0	1	0	0	1	1	0
102967	0	1	1	1	0	0	1	0	0	0
101610	0	0	0	0	0	0	1	0	0	0
101635	0	1	0	0	0	1	1	0	0	0

FIGURE 21.6   TERM-DOCUMENT MATRIX FOR AUTOS-ELECTRONICS DATA AFTER TOKENIZATION AND TEXT REDUCTION (FIRST 10 TERMS SHOWN FOR 10 DOCUMENTS)

Producing a Concept Matrix

The tokenization and text reduction term-document matrix like the one shown in Figure 21.6 if we choose presence/absence. Alternatively, we can get the TF-IDF matrix (select that option in the Representation menu). This measure will incorporate both the frequency of a term and the frequency with which documents containing that term appear in the overall corpus. The resulting TF-IDF matrix is probably too large to efficiently analyze in a predictive model, so we will have ASDM use *latent semantic indexing* to extract a reduced set of columns, termed "concepts." For manageability, we will limit the number of concepts to 20.

Figure 21.7 shows 10 of the 20 resulting "concepts" for a sample of 10 documents. We will use this reduced set of concepts simply to facilitate the processing of a predictive model. We will not attempt to interpret the concepts for meaning (although ASDM has tools to do so, this lies more properly in the realm of natural language processing than text mining).

Labeling the Documents

Now we have a compact numerical matrix to work with—80 rows and just 20 columns. At this point, we can add the labels—we will use "1" for autos and "0" for electronics. Recall that document names beginning with "5" are electronics and those beginning with "1" are autos. We need to add a new column for the

Class	Doc ID	Concept 1	Concept 2	Concept 3	Concept 4	Concept 5	Concept 6	Concept 7	Concept 8	Concept 9	Concept 10
0	53867	-0.601103	-0.127793	-0.172709	-0.005314	0.24842	-0.123263	-0.022751	-0.184413	-0.039814	0.3063533
0	53854	-0.391326	-0.30248	0.324835	-0.189966	0.02678	-0.20242	0.54401	-0.15201	0.244892	-0.0857365
0	53843	-0.5682	0.108949	-0.163039	-0.395603	0.051274	-0.286588	-0.198094	0.426656	-0.102343	0.1099064
0	53837	-0.411392	-0.263571	0.449727	-0.141866	-0.096729	-0.09606	0.272247	0.094724	-0.311274	-0.0862991
0	53815	-0.154632	-0.091113	0.195876	0.129567	0.042071	-0.195075	0.36677	0.131703	0.158432	0.0649704
0	53809	-0.466386	-0.261281	0.075137	0.230874	-0.327696	0.230032	-0.319836	-0.248514	0.269048	-0.0158134
0	53788	-0.459857	-0.047296	-0.200117	0.212025	0.23317	-0.220519	0.068941	0.165423	0.302612	0.2961424
0	53777	-0.411222	-0.088878	0.285553	-0.296208	-0.202719	-0.043069	0.458534	0.102572	-0.136371	-0.1141986
0	53776	-0.47814	-0.388738	0.016464	-0.022211	0.065635	-0.15932	-0.073727	0.070336	0.555988	0.0945037
0	53771	-0.394122	-0.292414	0.197202	-0.085314	-0.050913	-0.201698	0.120805	0.369089	0.00608	-0.5317915

FIGURE 21.7   A SMALL PORTION OF THE CONCEPT MATRIX (USING LATENT SEMANTIC INDEXING) FOR THE AUTOS-ELECTRONICS EXAMPLE; THE FULL MATRIX HAS 20 CONCEPTS AND 80 DOCUMENTS

document class, and looking at the document names we see that the first 39 rows should be classified as "0" and the remaining 41 rows "1."

Fitting a Model

At this point, we have transformed the original text data into a familiar form needed for predictive modeling—a single target variable (1 = autos, 0 = electronics) and 20 predictor variables (the concepts).

We can now partition the data (60% training, 40% validation), and try applying several classification models. Here are the results of a logistic regression model, with "class" as the target and the 20 concept variables as the predictors, using the default values for ASDM (2020 release).

The confusion matrix (Figure 21.8, left) shows poor accuracy in separating the two classes of documents—an error rate of 31.25%. The poor performance of

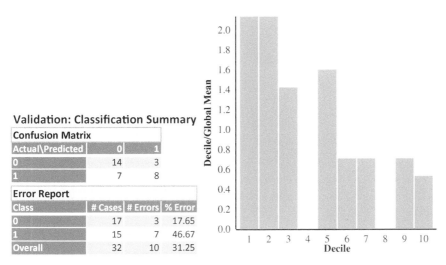

Validation: Classification Summary

Confusion Matrix

Actual\Predicted	0	1
0	14	3
1	7	8

Error Report

Class	# Cases	# Errors	% Error
0	17	3	17.65
1	15	7	46.67
Overall	32	10	31.25

FIGURE 21.8   VALIDATION DATA CONFUSION MATRIX (LEFT) AND LIFT DECILE CHART (RIGHT), FOR AUTOS-ELECTRONICS DOCUMENT CLASSIFICATION

the logistic regression model is probably because the sample is so small. However, in terms of ranking, the decile lift chart (Figure 21.8, right) shows reasonable performance of the model in capturing autos ("1"s), especially if we select the top 20% of documents most likely to be classified as autos. For this two-class dataset with a nearly 50/50 split between the classes, the maximum lift per decile is 2.13, and the lift shown here is slightly above 2 for the first 20% of the cases, 1.4 for the next 10% of the cases and mostly unstable thereafter. In a decision making process, human review could be concentrated on the middle ranked 40% where the classification error is most likely to occur.

Next, we would also try other models to see how they compare; this is left as an exercise.

Prediction

The most prevalent application of text mining is classification ("labeling"), but it can also be used for prediction of numerical values. For example, maintenance or support tickets could be used to predict length or cost of repair. The only step that would be different in the process above would be that the label applied after the preprocessing would be a numeric value rather than a class.

The machine learning workflow for the Online Discussions on Autos and Electronics documents classification example is shown in Figure 21.9.

FIGURE 21.9   THE MACHINE LEARNING WORKFLOW FOR THE ONLINE DISCUSSIONS ON AUTOS AND ELECTRONICS DOCUMENTS CLASSIFICATION EXAMPLE

21.7 SUMMARY

In this chapter, we drew a distinction between text processing for the purpose of extracting meaning from documents (natural language processing) and classifying or labeling numerous documents in probabilistic fashion (text mining). We concentrated on the latter and examined the preprocessing steps that need to occur before text can be mined. Those steps are more varied and involved than those used in preparing numerical data. The ultimate goal is to produce a matrix in which columns are terms and rows are documents. The nature of language is such that the number of terms is excessive for effective model building, so the preprocessing steps include vocabulary reduction. A final major reduction takes place if we use, instead of the terms, a limited set of concepts that represents most of the variation in the documents, in the same way that principal components capture most of the variation in quantitative data. Finally, we end up with a quantitative matrix in which the cells represent the frequency or presence of terms and the rows represent documents. To this we append document labels (classes), and then we are ready to use this matrix for classifying documents using classification methods.

PROBLEMS

21.1 **Tokenization.** Consider the following text version of a post to an online learning forum in a statistics course:

```
Thanks John!<br /><br /><font size="3">
&quot;Illustrations and demos will be
provided for students to work through on
their own&quot;</font>.
Do we need that to finish project? If yes,
where to find the illustration and demos?
Thanks for your help.\<img title="smile"
alt="smile" src="\url{http://lms.statistics.
com/pix/smartpix.php/statistics_com_1/s/smil
ey.gif}" \><br /> <br />
```

a. Identify 10 non-word tokens in the passage.

b. Suppose that this passage constitutes a document to be classified, but you are not certain of the business goal of the classification task. Identify material (at least 20% of the terms) that, in your judgment, could be discarded fairly safely without knowing that goal.

c. Suppose that the classification task is to predict whether this post requires the attention of the instructor, or whether a teaching assistant might suffice. Identify the 20% of the terms that you think might be most helpful in that task.

d. What aspect of the passage is most problematic from the standpoint of simply using a bag-of-words approach, as opposed to an approach in which meaning is extracted?

21.2 **Classifying Internet Discussion Posts.** In this problem you will use the data and scenario described in this chapter's example, in which the task is to develop a model to classify documents as either auto-related or electronics-related.

a. From the folder autos-electronics, import the files into ASDM using the *Get Data* menu and the option to read the file contents into individual rows during import. Use *Sample from selected files* with *Simple random sampling* and *Desired sample size of 80*. *Set seed* to 12345. Which row IDs correspond to the autos class? To the electronics class?

b. Proceed in ASDM to the preprocessing of the text, accepting defaults except as noted. Explain what would be different if you unchecked the "perform stemming" box (but leave it checked).

c. Continue to the Representation options in ASDM, and change the maximum number of concepts to 20. Explain what is different about the Term-Frequency matrix, as opposed to the TF-IDF matrix.

d. Continue to the Output Options section, without changing defaults.

i. Explain very briefly how the different matrix options differ.

ii. Restate the goal of the text mining project, and why we are not using the Concept Extraction options.

e. Going back to your notes about which rows correspond to which class of documents, add class identifications to the concept document matrix. Using this matrix, fit a predictive model (different from the model presented in the chapter illustration) to classify documents (rows) as autos or electronics. Compare its performance to that of the model presented in the chapter illustration.

21.3 **Classifying Classified Ads Submitted Online.** Consider the case of a website that caters to the needs of a specific farming community and carries classified ads intended for that community. Anyone, including robots, can post an ad via a web interface, and the site owners have problems with ads that are fraudulent, spam, or simply not relevant to the community. They have provided a file with 4143 ads, each ad in a row, and each ad labeled as either −1 (not relevant) or 1 (relevant). An additional 0/1 column has been added with −1 mapping to 0, and 1 mapping to 1, to be used as the outcome variable. The goal is to develop a predictive model that can classify ads automatically.

- Open the file `Farm-ads.xlsx`, and briefly review some of the relevant and irrelevant ads to get a flavor for their contents. In ASDM, use the *Get Data > Worksheet* option to take a sample of ads. In the *Sample From Worksheet* dialog, move the variable *Var2* to *Variables in Sampled Data*. Use *Simple random sampling* and *Desired sample size* of 100. *Set seed* to 12345.

- Preprocess the data in ASDM, using the defaults, except limit the vocabulary size to 50 and number of concepts to 20. Since all the documents have been consolidated in a single file, one document per row, the option "Text variables contain file paths" should NOT be checked in ASDM.

a. Examine the term-document matrix.

 i. Is it sparse or dense?

 ii. Find two non-zero entries and briefly interpret their meaning, in words (you do not need to derive their calculation).

 iii. Had you chosen the presence/absence option for the term-document matrix, what would those two non-zero entries be?

b. Briefly explain the difference between the term-document matrix and the concept-document matrix. Relate the latter to what you learned in the principal components chapter (Chapter 4).

c. To start the process of building a predictive model, add a final column of 0's and 1's to the concept-document matrix, to label the −1's as 0's, and the 1's as 1's. To do this, make a note in the original data of where (which row) the −1's stop and the 1's begin. Then consult the first column in the concept-document matrix, which contains this row (document) number. You should also add a name for this first column, say "docnum," so that all columns have names.

d. Using logistic regression, partition the data (60% training, 40% validation), and develop a model to classify the documents as 1's or 0's. Comment on its efficacy.

e. Why use the concept-document matrix, and not the term-document matrix, to provide the predictor variables?

## CHAPTER 22

Responsible Data Science

In this chapter, we go beyond technical considerations of model fitting, selection, and performance and discuss the potentially harmful effects of machine learning. The catalog of harms is now extensive, including a host of cases where AI has deliberately been put to ill purposes in service of big brother surveillance and state suppression of minorities. Our focus, however, is on cases where the intentions of the model developer are good and the resulting bias or unfairness has been unintentional. We review the principles of responsible data science (RDS), and discuss a concrete framework that can govern data science work to put those principles into practice. We discuss some key elements of that framework: datasheets, model cards, and model audits.

22.1 INTRODUCTION[1]

Machine learning and AI bring the promise of seemingly unlimited good. After all, the ability to ingest any set of arbitrarily sized, minimally structured data and produce predictions or explanations for these data is applicable to almost every domain. Our societal attention often focuses on the revolutionary future applications of this potential: cars that drive themselves, computers that can hold natural conversations with humans, precision medications tailored to our specific genomes, cameras that can instantly recognize any object, and software that can automatically generate new images or videos. Conversations about these benefits, though, too often ignore the harms that machine learning models can cause.

---

[1] This chapter draws *Responsible Data Science*, Wiley 2021, by Grant Fleming and Peter Bruce, for its organization of ideas. This chapter copyright ©2021 Datastats, LLC. Used by permission.

Machine Learning for Business Analytics: Concepts, Techniques, and Applications with Analytic Solver® Data Mining, Fourth Edition. Galit Shmueli, Peter C. Bruce, Kuber R. Deokar, and Nitin R. Patel
© 2023 John Wiley & Sons, Inc. Published 2023 by John Wiley & Sons, Inc.

Example: Predicting Recidivism

Decisions about criminal defendants in the US justice system are based on the weight of probabilistic evidence at multiple stages: whether to arrest, whether to go to trial, arrival at a verdict, and sentencing. At the sentencing phase, judges determine the length and terms of sentences, in part, by assessing the likelihood that a convicted defendant will commit another crime (recidivate). Courts have started relying increasingly on machine learning recidivism algorithms to inform decisions on sentencing. The COMPAS algorithm,[2] sold by Equivant (originally Northpointe), is among the most prominent of these, and critics have charged that it is biased against African-Americans. The algorithm is not public, and involves more than 170 predictors. Its advocates retort that COMPAS has good overall predictive performance, and that its accuracy, as measured by the area under the ROC curve (Receiver Operating Characteristics curve), is similar for African-American and White defendants. The trouble is that the errors made are quite different:

- African-American defendants are over-predicted to re-offend (leading to tougher sentences).
- White defendants are under-predicted to re-offend (leading to lighter sentences).

The over-prediction errors (penalizing African-Americans) balance out the under-prediction errors (favoring Whites), so the overall error rate is the same for both. A single-minded focus on one overall accuracy metric obscures this bias against African-Americans. We will work through this example in greater detail below.

22.2 UNINTENTIONAL HARM

The COMPAS algorithm did not set out to penalize African-Americans. Its goal was to make sentencing decisions overall more consistent and "scientific." The bias against African-Americans was unintended and unwanted.

Another stark example of unintentional harm was the Optum healthcare algorithm. In 2001, the healthcare company Optum launched Impact-Pro, a predictive modeling tool that purported to predict patients' future need for followup care and assign a risk score, based on a variety of predictor inputs. The result would be better healthcare for patients, as followup interventions could be better timed and calibrated. Hospitals could use the tool to better manage resources, and insurers could use it to better set insurance rates. Unfortunately,

---

[2]COMPAS stands for "Correctional Offender Management Profiling for Alternative Sanctions"; a good summary by the public interest group ProPublica can be found at https://www.propublica. org/article/how-we-analyzed-the-compas-recidivism-algorithm

experience proved that the algorithm was biased against African-Americans: a research team led by Ziad Obermeyer studied these algorithms and found that, for any given risk score, African-American patients consistently experienced more chronic health conditions than did White patients.

It turned out that a key predictor for "future health care need" is "prior healthcare spending." African-American spending on healthcare was, on average, less than that for whites, but not because of better health. Rather, it was due to lower income levels and less access to health insurance and costly medical facilities. Hence, an African-American individual would be predicted to need less followup care than a White individual with similar health.

There are numerous other examples of well-intentioned algorithms going wrong.[3] The algorithms that power social media and internet ads foster connections among people and with things they are interested in, "bringing the world closer together" in Facebook's words. Those same algorithms can also nurture communities of hate and facilitate the spread of false news and conspiracy theories.

22.3 LEGAL CONSIDERATIONS

Many treatments of the ethical aspects of data science focus on legal issues. This is understandable, as avoiding legal jeopardy is a strong motivator. Legal compliance is ultimately a matter for attorneys more than data scientists. The latter may contribute best by pursuing a general framework for responsible data science, so our legal discussion will be brief and focused on two points: the European Union's GDPR, and the concept of "protected groups."

The General Data Protection Regulation (GDPR)

The most recognized legal environment for machine learning is the General Data Protection Regulations (GDPR) of the European Union (EU), which went into effect in August 2018. The GDPR provides sweeping protections to those in the EU (whether citizens of EU countries or not) including a "right to be forgotten" (a requirement that technology companies provide mechanisms by which individuals can have their data removed from online platforms), as well as the right to data portability and the right to object to automated decision-making and profiling. The GDPR's focus is strongly on empowering the individual, educated citizen with greater leverage to enforce the privacy of their data. Because the GDPR was the first comprehensive regulatory framework for big data services, it set the pattern for other legal initiatives that followed, including the California

---

[3]The popular author Cathy O'Neil coined the catchphrase "Weapons of Math Destruction" in recounting such examples in her book of the same name (O'Neil, 2016).

Consumer Protection Act (CCPA) and Canada's Personal Information Protection and Electronic Documents Act (PIPEDA). Given the size of the EU market and the global nature of internet activity, the GDPR has become, in effect, a global regulatory regime.

INTENDED HARM

Not all damage from machine learning algorithms is unintentional. In some cases, bad actors "weaponize" algorithms for purposes that are malicious. In other cases, seemingly legitimate law enforcement practices creep into the realm of "big brother:"

- Facial recognition and identification technology, combined with the widespread presence of security cameras, enable police departments to track down criminal suspects who would have gone undetected in the pre-technology age. A good thing!

- Those same technologies, though, have enabled U.S. immigration authorities to track down and deport undocumented individuals who may have been living and working peacefully for years or decades. Not so clearly a good thing—the technology empowered bureaucrats (not legislators) to shift the terms of a highly contentious political debate that was broadly agreed on only one thing: authorities should not be sweeping the country to round up and deport long-term residents who are undocumented.

- These technologies have also aided Chinese police authorities in their surveillance and suppression of Uighur and Tibetan communities. A bad thing, by the standards of most pluralistic societies that honor the rule of law.

Some might also consider that knowing about damage caused by algorithms and proceeding anyway ("turning a blind eye") constitutes intentional harm. In late 2021, a disaffected employee at Facebook released a trove of internal Facebook research showing that ML-enabled algorithms harmed teenagers (for teen girls with mental health and body-image issues, Instagram exacerbated those issues) and fostered civil discord (2018 algorithm changes for the Facebook newsfeed boosted angry and contentious content). Top executives knew about the internal research, but were reluctant to make significant changes in highly profitable platforms.

The framework and process we discuss in this chapter will do little to counter the individual or entity that is determined to develop or repurpose algorithms for harmful purposes. However, the framework outlined below does have an important message for data scientists involved in developing algorithms: anticipate and be mindful of potentially harmful uses to which their work might be put.

Protected Groups

Regulations and laws that address not simply consumer privacy, but also issues of algorithmic discrimination and bias, are less well developed. However, one guiding principle is that laws that restrict behavior by individuals or corporations do not disappear merely because the decisions are made by algorithms. Decisions or actions that are illegal for a human in a company (discrimination in lending based on gender or age, for example) are also illegal for an algorithm to do in automated fashion. In US law (and in other countries as well), there are various "protected groups" where such restrictions apply.

Protected groups may be identified on the basis of race, gender, age, sexual orientation, medical disability, or other factors. Although there may be no AI-specific or big data-specific laws in this area, there is ample and long-standing legal history that must be considered in the deployment of algorithms.

To evaluate fairness and calculate fairness metrics, a "privileged group" is designated. Often this reflects actual societal advantage enjoyed by the group (terminology coinciding with the social justice movement), but it is also a technical requirement. Fairness metrics must be calculated relative to some base group, so the term by itself does not imply privilege in the lay meaning.

22.4 PRINCIPLES OF RESPONSIBLE DATA SCIENCE

Legal statutes and regulations are typically lengthy, detailed, and difficult to understand. Moreover, legal compliance alone is not sufficient to avoid some of the harm caused by machine learning. The potential for reputational harm may be just as great as that for legal jeopardy. In late 2021, Facebook began conducting "reputational reviews" of its services and products. The publicly stated purpose was to avoid harm to children, but news stories also cited Facebook's desire to anticipate how its algorithms might be criticized. A significant movement has arisen in the data science community to focus greater attention on this potential for harm, and how to avoid it. A number of commentators have suggested that data scientists should adhere to a framework for responsible data science: a set of best practices. Common to most suggested frameworks are five principles:

- Non-maleficence (avoiding harm)
- Fairness
- Transparency
- Accountability
- Privacy

Non-maleficence

Non-maleficence covers concepts associated with causing or avoiding harm. At a high level, following this principle requires that data scientists ensure that their models do not cause foreseeable harms or harms of negligence. While unforeseen harms are sometimes unavoidable, they should be accounted for as much as reasonably possible. Harms that ought to be avoided include risks of physical harm, legal risks, reductions in future opportunities, privacy violations, emotional distress, facilitating illegal activities, and other results which could negatively impact individuals.

Non-maleficence is the hardest principle to guarantee in practice, and we recommend thinking of it as more of a goal to strive for than a necessary box to check for every data science project. A model can be fair, transparent, accountable to users, and respecting of privacy, yet still make predictions that advantage some people while causing harm for others. Medical triaging algorithms for prioritizing scarce medical resources necessarily place some individuals further back in the queue, or out of the queue entirely. Credit scoring algorithms make life difficult for those receiving low credit scores. In such cases, non-maleficence must be considered in the context of other principles.

Fairness

Fairness covers concepts associated with equal representation, anti-discrimination, dignity, and just outcomes. Dimensions of interest for fairness evaluations typically involve human-specific factors like ethnicity, gender, sexual orientation, age, socioeconomic status, education, disability status, presence of preexisting conditions (healthcare), and history of adverse events. Model fairness is primarily a function of whether the model produces fair outcomes, with input factors (how the model uses certain features, how the features were created, etc.) being less relevant. Like non-maleficence, fairness is a difficult concept to pin down. What is fair for one person or context might be unfair for another. One person might consider it fair for everyone to pay the same absolute amount in taxes. Another person might think everyone should pay the same share of their income in taxes. Another might think the wealthy should pay a higher share of their income in taxes. Yet another might think that the wealthy should pay all the taxes. There is no universally agreed definition, in this case, of what constitutes fairness. Because fairness relies primarily on ensuring fair outcomes, it is easier to translate into practice than the other four principles. However, fairness-improving methods are still very underused. Fairness is almost always talked about exclusively in the context of models that make predictions for individual people, like whether a person should be provided a loan. In actuality, fairness is relevant for any modeling task where the goal is either to minimize differences between groups or maximize predictive performance with respect to specific groups. For example, in a spam email classification task, it might make sense to use fairness interventions to make the spam classification model more balanced in how well it classifies spam across different identified topics. While this is not a use case that deals directly with people, it can still be beneficial to consider fairness.

Transparency

Transparency covers concepts associated with user consent, model interpretability, and explanations for other modeling choices made by the creators of a model. Typically, this communication is conveyed via clear documentation about the data or model.[4] Transparency as a concept is as simple as it appears: where possible, decisions about the modeling process should be recorded and available for inspection. However, transparency quickly becomes complex when trying to move it from principle to practice. For example, the modeling team, regulators, users, and clients all might require mutually exclusive forms of transparency due to their different needs and technical abilities. Documentation about the datasets used, explanations for choices made within the modeling process, and interpretations for individual predictions made for one group might need to be completely revamped for another.

An important related term is the *interpretability* of a model. Some of the greatest advances in machine learning have come with so-called uninterpretable, black-box models—models where the learned relationships between predictors and outcomes are so complex that humans cannot discern how one affects the other. Neural nets are one example, and they have become ubiquitous now with the power and popularity of deep learning. Random forests and boosted trees are also examples of black-box methods: single trees can easily be translated into decision rules, but when the predictions from many different trees are simply averaged or otherwise aggregated, that interpretability disappears.

Classical statistical models like linear and logistic regression are "intrinsically interpretable." Their coefficients provide clear and direct estimates of the effects of individual predictors.

Without interpretability, we are handicapped in reviewing the ethical impact of our models. If a model is producing biased predictions, how would we know which predictors are instrumental in generating the biased predictions, so that we might make corrections? In seeking interpretability, we can follow a two-pronged approach:

- Where possible, include an interpretable model among the final candidates to serve as a benchmark. If we ultimately choose a better-performing black-box model, we'd like to know how much, in terms of performance, we would have to give up if we went with an intrinsically interpretable model.

- Apply interpretability methods, ex-post, to a black box model. Some examples of these methods are illustrated in the COMPAS example in Section 22.7.

---

[4]Under Basel II banking regulations, for example, deployed credit scoring models should be repeatable, transparent, and auditable (Saddiqi, 2017).

Accountability

Accountability covers concepts associated with legal compliance, acting with integrity, responding to the concerns of individuals who use or are affected by machine learning algorithms, and allowing for individual recourse for harmful modeling decisions. For example, people who receive a loan denial ideally ought to be entitled to not just an explanation for why that decision was made, but also the ability to appeal the decision and an indication of the minimum set of differences that would have resulted in a change in the decision. In practice, accountability typically does not go beyond ensuring that a model achieves legal compliance (which itself has gotten more difficult because of regulation like the GDPR), or, in a few cases, adherence to company or industry standards.

Data Privacy and Security

Privacy covers concepts associated with only gathering necessary information, storing data securely, ensuring that data is de-identified once it is used in a model, and ensuring that other aspects of user data cannot be inferred from the model results. Fortunately, there are already several well-understood approaches for maintaining the privacy of systems (via preventing hacks, unintentional disclosures, physical attacks, etc.). Making data available for analysis in models circumvents some of these protections, and it may be necessary to use differential privacy methods (for example, adding randomization to the underlying data.) Unfortunately, differential privacy methods are not yet built into many popular modeling packages.

22.5 A RESPONSIBLE DATA SCIENCE FRAMEWORK

How should data scientists incorporate the general principles and evolving legal considerations into projects? This requires a framework to provide specific guidance for data science practitioners. Most suggested frameworks start from a standard "best practices" process, such as the CRISP-DM and SEMMA methodologies described in Chapter 2, and expand on those technical frameworks to incorporate larger ethical issues. The Responsible Data Science (RDS) framework suggested by Fleming and Bruce (2021) has the following elements:

Justification

In this initial phase, the data scientist and project manager coordinate with users and other stakeholders to gain an understanding of the problem in its business context. Questions such as the following should be addressed:

- Have we studied similar projects, and have they encountered ethical problems?

- Have we anticipated potential future uses of the model and harms that might result?
- Do we have the means necessary to assess potential harms to individuals and groups?

Assembly

In this stage (termed "compilation" by Fleming and Bruce), the team assembles the various elements needed for the project:

- The raw data
- Software tools and environments
- Datasheets, documents that go beyond descriptions of the data features to include explanations of how the data was gathered, pre-processed, and intended to be used
- Identification of any protected groups

The process of assembling the raw data is where privacy rules must be considered. The project team must be certain that the data were acquired in a fashion that was nonexploitative and respected consent. One famous case where this was not the case was that of the Clearview AI facial recognition product that can take almost any facial image and identify who it is, if that person has a social media presence. The data to build their model, which is used extensively by law enforcement, came from scraping social media sites without permission.

The story of Cambridge University Professor Alexander Kogan is another cautionary tale. Kogan helped develop a Facebook app, "This is Your Digital Life," which collected the answers to quiz questions, as well as user data from Facebook. The purported purpose was a research project on online personality. Although fewer than 270,000 people downloaded the app, it was able to access (via friend connections) data on 87 million users. This feature was of great value to the political consulting company Cambridge Analytica, which used data from the app in its political targeting efforts, and ended up doing work for the Trump 2016 campaign, as well as the 2016 Brexit campaign in the UK.[5] Facebook later said this further sharing of its user data violated its rules for apps, and it banned Kogan's app.

Great controversy ensued: Facebook's CEO Mark Zuckerberg was called to account before the US Congress, and Cambridge Analytica was eventually forced into bankruptcy. In an interview with Lesley Stahl on the *60 Minutes*

---

[5]Read more about the efficacy of psychological manipulation via the internet in the paper "Psychological targeting as an effective approach to digital mass persuasion" by Matz et al. (2017).

television program, Kogan contended that he was an innocent researcher who had fallen into deep water, ethically:

> "You know, I was kinda acting, honestly, quite naively. I thought we were doing everything okay…. I ran this lab that studied happiness and kindness."

How did machine learning play a role? Facebook's sophisticated algorithms on network relationships (Chapter 20) allowed the Kogan app to reach beyond its user base and get data from millions of users who had never used the app.[6]

The world is awash in data, and there will surely be gray areas that lie between explicit authorization to use and explicit prohibitions on use. Analysts may be tempted to follow the adage "Ask forgiveness, not permission," but if you think forgiveness may be needed, the temptation should be avoided. Data scientists working with gray area data can look to several criteria:

- *The impact and importance of the project*: A high value project, or one that might cause significant harm, raises the costs of running afoul of data use restrictions and enhances the importance of thorough and comprehensive review.

- *The explicitness of rules governing data use*: The more explicit the prohibition, the harder it will be to explain why it was not followed.

- *The "news story test"*: What would a reasonable person conclude after reading a widely circulated news story about your project?

In the end, the data scientist must think beyond the codified rules and think how the predictive technologies they are working on might ultimately be used.

Data Preparation

This stage incorporates the standard data exploration and preparation that we discussed in Chapters 1–4. A couple of additional points not covered there are worth noting:

- We need to verify that the data wrangling steps we have taken do not distort the raw data in a way that might cause bias.

- Data preparation in the RDS framework is not necessarily a single progression through a sequence, but may be an iterative process.

As an example of the potentially iterative nature of data preparation, consider the case where the audit of a model (discussed below) reveals that model performance is worse for a particular protected group that is not well represented in the data. In such a case, we might return to the data preparation stage to oversample that group to improve model performance.

---

[6]www.cbsnews.com/news/aleksandr-kogan-the-link-between-cambridge-analytica-and-facebook-60-minutes/

Modeling

In this phase, the team tries out multiple models and model settings to find the model that yields the best predictive performance. Most of this book is about this process, so we need to add little here, with one exception. A key factor in building models that do not cause harm is the ability to understand what the model is doing: interpretability. In this stage, along with predictive performance, we also consider whether we can gain a good understanding of how predictors contribute to outcomes.

Auditing

This final stage is the key one. In the auditing phase, we review the modeling process and the resulting model performance with several key points in mind:

- Providing useful explanations for the model's predictions
- Checking for bias against certain groups (particularly legally protected groups)
- Undertaking mitigation procedures if bias or unfairness is found

If the audit shows that model performance is worse for some groups than others, or if the model performs differently for some groups in ways that disadvantage them, then we need to try to fix it. Sometimes models perform more poorly for a group if that group is poorly represented in the data. In such a case, the first step is to oversample that group, so the model can work with more data. The COMPAS example in Section 22.7 illustrates this approach. Another step is to dive deeper on the interpretability front to learn more about what predictors might be driving decisions. If oversampling and a deeper dive into interpretability fail to fully correct bias in predictions, the next step is to adjust the predictions themselves, an approach that is also illustrated in the COMPAS example.

The above discussion assumes that we do not include racial, ethnic, religious, or similar categories as predictors. This is typically, but not always, the case. Structuring a model that could be construed as denying a loan to someone because they are Hispanic, for example, would be illegal in the US, whether the decision is based on a human review or a machine learning model. The situation is less clear cut in medicine, where racial and other indicators may be relevant diagnostic flags.

Simply assuring that the model does not include explicit racial or ethnic categories as predictors may not be sufficient. There may be other variables that serve as proxies: membership in an African-American fraternity, for example. The risk of including such variables increases with the use of massive black-box models where huge numbers of variables are available. It may seem less work to throw them all in the model, and let the model learn which are important, than to do your feature engineering "by hand." An example of this is a machine learning resume review system that Amazon attempted to use for hiring recommendations. The training data consisted of resumes and human judgments made by Amazon engineers. It turned out that the algorithm was picking up on an implicit preference for male candidates in that training data and identifying derived predictors that simply reflected gender (e.g., participation in the Women's Chess Club).

This brings us to one case where it is entirely appropriate to include racial, ethnic, and similar categorical predictors. After completing the primary model, a second model that includes these categories can be fit where the purpose of the secondary study is to investigate possible discrimination. For example, a lender conducts an audit of its underwriting algorithm, and finds that loans are approved for African-Americans less often than for whites, even though race is not a feature in the model. A secondary model could then determine whether some other factor with predictive power is correlated with race. If there is such a factor and its "business necessity" cannot be justified, it should probably be excluded from the model. Rules and regulations governing discriminatory practices constitute a rich legal field beyond the scope of this book; you can get a flavor by doing a web search for "FDIC policy on discrimination in lending" (FDIC is the Federal Deposit Insurance Corporation, an important financial regulator in the US).

22.6 Documentation Tools

If the model performs reasonably well and does not produce biased predictions or decisions, it passes the audit phase, at least with respect to unintentional harm. Several tools provide a structure for documenting this, and a guide for incorporating ethical practices into the project from the beginning.

Impact Statements

One such tool is a prospective statement of the project's impact. Impact statements for data science became popular, or, more accurately, infamous, when the prestigious Neural Information Processing Systems (NeurIPS) Conference required the inclusion of a "Broader Impact Statement" for submissions to the 2020 conference. NeurIPS provided the following guidance for the statement:

> "In order to provide a balanced perspective, authors are required to include a statement of the potential broader impact of their work, including its ethical aspects and future societal consequences. Authors should take care to discuss both positive and negative outcomes."

By requiring an impact statement for all submissions, NeurIPS dramatically raised the profile of ethical considerations in AI research. For their work to be deemed credible, researchers now had to contend with the ethical implications of their work. This perspective spread to the large tech companies and academic institutions that employed them. Leading AI companies like OpenAI, Google, Microsoft, and IBM have since begun leveraging variants of impact statements to make their own models and software products more transparent. Where these companies go, others are likely to follow, so it is prudent to consider the inclusion of impact statements in data science projects. Such an impact statement should address the following questions:

1. What is the goal of our project?
2. What are the expected benefits of our project?
3. What ethical concerns do we consider as relevant to our project?
4. Have other groups attempted similar projects in the past, and, if so, what were the outcomes of those projects?
5. How have we anticipated and accounted for future uses of our project beyond its current use?

The impact statement that answers these questions should be included in project documentation.

Model Cards

In 2018, researchers at Google proposed a standardized process for documenting the performance and non-technical characteristics of models. The idea of model cards has caught on quickly across the industry. Companies like IBM (through their FactSheet Project), Microsoft (through their Azure Transparency Notes), and OpenAI (through their Model Cards) have adapted model cards to provide a consistent format for salient information about their models. In 2020, Google released the Model Card Toolkit (MCT), an official package for automating the generation of model cards for models fit using Tensorflow. A sample model card generated by MCT can be seen at github.com/tensorflow/model-card-toolkit. It covers a neural net model that classifies an individual's income level via demographic predictors, and includes an overview of the model's purpose, an identifier for the model version, the "owner" of the model (in this case the Google Model Card Team), a list of references, a description of the use case, limitations of the model, ethical considerations, and plots depicting model performance metrics.

Datasheets

Just as model cards provide "nutrition labels" for models, datasheets (also called data cards) do likewise for datasets. "Data dictionaries" are almost ubiquitous across data science projects, but are not uniform in their formatting or in the information that they contain. Where one team might use a simple .txt file including information on the names and types of columns within a dataset, other teams rely on an unwieldy Excel file containing multiple sheets of information about every aspect of the data. Datasheets standardize the format of data dictionaries and extend their coverage to relevant non-technical information like the data's collection process, intended uses, and sensitive features.

Datasheets identify the source of the data, whether any transformations were performed, whether the data were sampled, intended use of the data, data type (e.g., tabular data, text data, image data), whether the data are public, who the license and copyright holder are, and more. Data collection, preparation, and documentation is sometimes regarded as a tedious aspect of machine learning, compared to the building of predictive models. It is not surprising, therefore, that model cards have been quicker to catch on than datasheets.

Audit Reports

Model cards and datasheets are snapshots of the model(s) and data at a point in time, usually the conclusion of the project. The process that the team undertook to verify that the data and model are functioning as expected, and to fix problems, is not captured by these documents. This leaves little room to discuss special considerations for protected groups, comparisons of predictive performance between the final model and other candidate models, differences in predictive performance across groups, and, in the case of black-box models, the outputs of interpretability method outputs. These issues should be addressed in audit reports, which consist of:

- A summary page for general model performance information
- Detailed performance pages for each sensitive group within the data, showing:
  - Comparisons of final model and candidate model performance across groups within the data
  - Visualizations of interpretability method outputs for the final model to show how the model is using its features when creating predictions
  - Descriptive text for findings from the plots/metrics and other relevant considerations

UNSTRUCTURED DATA

Some of the most far-reaching harms reported from machine learning and AI concern unstructured data. Image recognition can be used to identify individuals and surveil populations; related technologies can generate deepfakes: images, video, or audio in which a real person is combined with synthesized elements of another imaginary or real person. In one case, the face of Adolf Hitler was substituted onto the image of the president of Brazil. So-called "revenge porn" swaps images of real people, often celebrities, onto pornographic images and videos. There are similar examples in natural language processing:

- Creation of fake personas on social media to corrupt or drown out legitimate content.
- Text classification models that discriminate against certain groups or viewpoints.

With unstructured data, deep neural nets predominate. Important aspects of the principles of responsible data science still hold: examination of the goals and potential ethical risks of the project beforehand, adequate representation of groups, consideration of unanticipated uses, and auditing the model for its effects on protected groups. However, image and text processing rely overwhelmingly on neural networks, which are black box models, so we do not have an intrinsically interpretable model as a benchmark. For interpretability, neural networks require the ex-post application of interpretability methods. With unstructured data, interpretation tends to focus on individual cases and a hunt for what led the model to its decision. For example, particular areas in images that we humans recognize as features (e.g., eyes) might surface as important. However, neural networks learn their own hierarchy of features and use that information in a highly complex fashion, so we will never achieve the simplicity of, say, a linear regression coefficient.

The discussion in this chapter, and most of the discussion in this book, primarily concerns structured tabular data. For the reader interested in learning more about interpretation of unstructured data, we refer the reader to Fleming and Bruce (2021), in particular Chapter 8.

Audit reports, as well as datasheets and model cards, may seem like a heavy administrative burden to place on the predictive modeling process, taking all the fun out of data science. And, indeed, most data science projects in the real world do not go through all these steps (which is largely why so many ethical problems have occurred.) However, even if all the boxes suggested by these reports are not to be checked, it is still useful to consider them as a superstructure, from which specific elements of particular importance are to be selected. In illustrating Analytic Solver Data Mining, we will use this pick and choose approach, focusing on areas of interest.[7] We return now to the COMPAS example to illustrate selected aspects of the principles, procedures and documentation steps for responsible data science.

---

[7]Machine learning communities have developed more automated and comprehensive approaches to reporting bias and fairness metrics in R and Python; see Fleming and Bruce (2021) for more details.

22.7   EXAMPLE: APPLYING THE RDS FRAMEWORK TO THE COMPAS EXAMPLE

We saw, at the beginning of this chapter, how the COMPAS algorithm over-predicted recidivism (committing additional crimes) for African-American defendants and under-predicted recidivism for Whites. In doing so, we jumped ahead to the interesting puzzle in the story. With the COMPAS algorithm in the background, let's now go back and apply selected elements of the RDS framework more systematically to the problem at hand. Starting at the beginning, can we develop a machine learning algorithm that predicts well whether a defendant will re-offend? We start with the nature of the project itself, then review the data-gathering process, fit a model, and audit the results.

Unanticipated Uses

Could there be unanticipated, potentially harmful, uses to which the algorithm might be put? Two possibilities are:

- The system could "migrate down" in the justice system, and be used *prior* to conviction, so that "who you are" (i.e., the essence of the model) might affect whether you are determined to be a criminal in the first place.
- The system could be used in other, more authoritarian countries to predict a much broader range of "criminality" (political dissent or opposition, "anti-social" behavior, etc.).

Ethical Concerns

Are there any ethical issues that we should flag apriori? African-Americans have had a troubled history with the US criminal justice system since the days of slavery and emancipation. After the US Civil War, trumped up "vagrancy" charges, requirements for employment, and strict enforcement of labor contracts, saddled African-Americans, particularly working-age African-American males, with criminal histories that were used to coerce them into agricultural labor. The legacy of this system, and the excessive criminal records it produced, continued for over a century. For this reason, we will want to be particularly alert for any discriminatory effect of the recividism algorithm with respect to African-Americans.

Protected Groups

Our concern with potential discrimination against African-Americans means that we will want to formally identify "protected groups." To do this, we include categorical variables to identify each individual's racial status. Although we have a special concern beforehand about African-Americans, we will need to include other racial categories as well, so as to be prepared to answer questions about the algorithm's impact on them as well. Of course, these racial category variables will not be used as predictors, but rather in the audit phase. Gender and Age are also denominated as protected categories, because in some applications they must be treated as such. In granting loans, for example, law and regulation preclude their use as predictors. In the recidivism case, there is no such prohibition, and our interest is in possible racial discrimination, so we retain them as predictors.

Data Issues

Clean data on convicted criminals and subsequent offenses (if any) over time are hard to come by. The data that we use here were obtained by ProPublica, a public interest lobby group, via a public records request in Broward County, Florida, where the COMPAS algorithm was used to inform sentencing decisions. The data consisted of demographic and recidivism information for 7214 defendants, 51% of whom were African-American and 34% White. We end up with 5304 records after taking the following steps to clean the data:

1. Defendants whose initial crime charge was not within 30 days of arrest were eliminated, as there is a good possibility of error (we have the wrong offense).

2. Traffic offenses were removed.

3. Data were limited to those meeting our study's definition of recidivist (another offense within two years) or non-recidivist (spending two years outside a correctional facility).

Note that there are multiple possible definitions of recidivism: what type of crime qualifies, does mere arrest qualify, over what time period. These choices can affect conclusions; we stick with the definitions in the ProPublica study.[8]

Fitting the Model

After splitting the data into a training partition (70%) and a validation partition (30%), we fit two models, logistic regression and random forest, using the following predictors: Age greater than 45, age 25–45, charge is misdemeanor, sex, and number of prior crimes. The random forest model produces only predictions, but the logistic regression model for the training data, shown in Figure 22.1, yields coefficients that are informative about the roles played by different predictors.

The logistic regression is intrinsically interpretable; the coefficients provide clear estimates of the effects of individual predictors. We see that sex and age

---

[8]https://www.propublica.org/article/how-we-analyzed-the-compas-recidivism-algorithm

Coefficients

Predictor	Estimate	Confidence Interval: Lower	Confidence Interval: Upper	Odds	Standard Error	Chi2-Statistic	P-Value
Intercept	-0.7268	-0.9490	-0.5045	0.4835	0.1134	41.0822	0.0000
c_charge_degree	-0.2310	-0.3842	-0.0777	0.7938	0.0782	8.7259	0.0031
sex	0.4538	0.2586	0.6490	1.5743	0.0996	20.7631	0.0000
priors_count	0.1637	0.1442	0.1833	1.1779	0.0100	268.9839	0.0000
age_cat_25 - 45	-0.6291	-0.8081	-0.4501	0.5331	0.0913	47.4504	0.0000
age_cat_Greater than 45	-1.3575	-1.5927	-1.1222	0.2573	0.1200	127.9166	0.0000

FIGURE 22.1   LOGISTIC REGRESSION MODEL FOR COMPAS DATA

are the most powerful predictors (we can compare the magnitudes because, after age is transformed to dummies, they are binary variables). Being male raises the odds of recidivism by a factor of 1.57. Being in the oldest group (older than 45) lowers the odds by a factor of $1/0.26 = 3.9$, and being in the middle group lowers them by a factor of $1/0.53 = 1.9$. The youngest group is the reference group (not included as an explicit predictor, to avoid multicollinearity), so being young, by elimination, increases the odds of recidivism. The predictor c_charge_degree ("is the charge a misdemeanor, as opposed to a felony") decreases the odds of recidivism by a factor of $1/0.79 = 1.3$. The predictor priors_count is a count variable, and its odds of 1.18 indicate an increasing chance of recidivism as the number of prior crimes increases. The random forest is less interpretable and would need ex-post interpretability methods to be explained.

In terms of predictive performance, the logistic regression and random forest achieved comparable accuracy (calculations are left as an exercise), and thus far, we see no performance advantage to the black-box model.

Auditing the Model

In the audit of the model, we focus first on overall accuracy. The metrics of 69% (random forest) and 69.5% (logistic) provide a modest improvement over the naive model, in which we can achieve about 63% accuracy by predicting all cases as non-recidivist. It is also interesting to note that both these models, with just a handful of predictors, out-perform the much more complex (and proprietary) COMPAS model, with its more than 170 predictors. (Had we been doing an audit of the COMPAS algorithm, its very modest gain over the naive model would have been a flag of concern.)

Next we look at per-group performance for both the logistic regression and the random forest. As shown in Figure 22.2 the accuracy is lowest for African-Americans and Hispanics. There is considerable range in model accuracy over models and groups: from 66% for the random forest for African-Americans to 74% for the logistic model for "Other.")

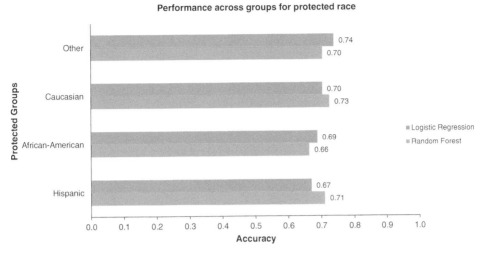

FIGURE 22.2   MODEL ACCURACY FOR DIFFERENT GROUPS (PRODUCED IN EXCEL)

However, overall accuracy is not a sufficient measure of model performance. There are two possible types of error:

- Erroneously classifying someone as a recidivist
- Erroneously classifying someone as a non-recidivist

These carry dramatically different consequences. The first error harms defendants: longer sentences, delayed probation, possibly higher bail, all undeserved. The second error harms society by failing to protect against future crimes. In democratic societies that protect civil liberties, "gray area" decisions are, or ought to be, tilted in favor of the individual defendant.

Fairness Metrics   We capture these errors with two metrics:

- *The False Positive Rate (FPR)*: The proportion of non-recidivists (0's) falsely classified as recidivists (1's)
- *The False Negative Rate (FNR)*: The proportion of recidivists (1's) falsely classified as non-recidivists (0's)

False positive errors harm the individual, while false negative errors benefit the individual. Figures 22.3 and 22.4 reveal a dramatic picture of discrimination. No matter which of the two models we choose, the FPR for African-Americans is by far the highest, compared to any other group, while their FNR is the lowest.

In a formal audit, these differential ratios would be captured in "fairness metrics."[9]

---

[9]For more on fairness metrics, see *Responsible Data Science* by Fleming and Bruce (2021).

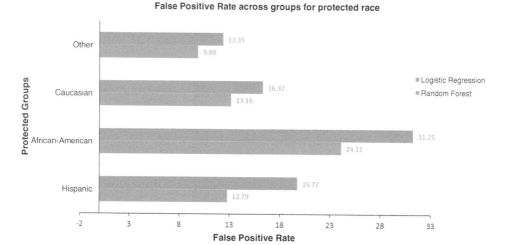

FIGURE 22.3   FALSE POSITIVE RATES FOR DIFFERENT GROUPS (PRODUCED IN EXCEL)

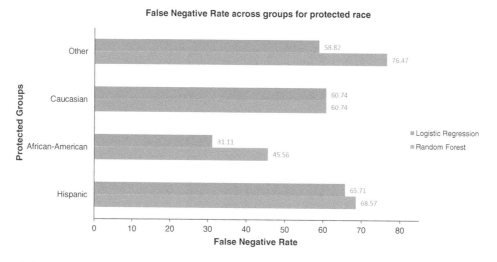

FIGURE 22.4   FALSE NEGATIVE RATES FOR DIFFERENT GROUPS (PRODUCED IN EXCEL)

Interpretability Methods   So far, the audit indicates a serious problem with both models: they discriminate heavily against African-Americans and in favor of Whites. Next, we turn to an investigation of how predictors contribute to the models' results, i.e., interpretability methods. We discussed above the coefficients of the logistic regression model. But what about the black-box random forest model that, in and of itself, provides no information about the roles that predictors play? Random forest models can produce *variable importance scores* that tell us how big a role individual predictors play (see Figure 22.5).

Features Importance

Feature	Importance
c_charge_degree	1.8945
sex	1.6604
priors_count	1.3012
age_cat_25 - 45	0.6003
age_cat_Greater than 45	0.6447
age_cat_Less than 25	0.6578

FIGURE 22.5   FEATURE IMPORTANCE SCORES FOR RANDOM FOREST MODEL FOR COMPAS DATA

As mentioned in Chapter 9, the variable importance score for X is computed by averaging some predictive measure improvement that comes from splitting on X across the trees in the forest.[10] For example, we see that whether the charge was misdemeanor (*c_charge_degree*) is the most important predictor of recidivism in the random forest, followed by sex, and the number of prior convictions.

Another interpretability method, the Partial Dependence Plot (PDP), provides information about *how* a predictor affects the outcome. In Figure 22.6, we see how the predicted probability of recidivism increases as the number of prior convictions increases.[11] See the companion box for a summary of interpretability methods that can be applied to any model after the model has been specified and run.

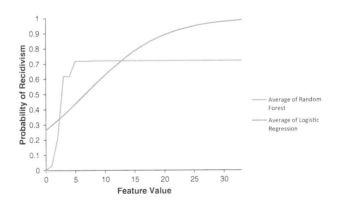

FIGURE 22.6   PARTIAL DEPENDENCE PLOT (PDP) FOR PREDICTOR PRIORS_COUNT (PRODUCED IN EXCEL)

---

[10]ASDM uses the reduction in Gini impurity for classification trees and reduction in variance (MSE) for regression trees. These reductions are computed for each predictor and averaged across the trees in the forest.

[11]We obtained this plot by using the logistic regression and the random forest to score the 1591 validation records 34 times, each time modifying *priors_count* between 0 and 33. The lines are averages across the 1591 records.

INTERPRETABILITY METHODS

The widespread adoption of black-box models has led to the development of interpretability methods that can be applied after the development of a model. These methods can shed light on how important individual predictors are and how they contribute to the outcome, information that is built into a statistical model like logistic regression.

Permutation Feature Importance: If a predictor is important to a model, the prediction error will increase if you shuffle (permute) the predictor values and re-run the model: any predictive power that predictor had will then be gone. Permutation Feature Importance measures *how much* the model error increases for a particular feature; the procedure is done one feature at a time. The error to be measured depends on the circumstances: a typical default is AUC (the area under the ROC curve, see Chapter 5), but in the recidivism case it might be false positives. Permutation Feature Importance measures how important a predictor is, but does not measure how it contributes to predictions in the way that a regression coefficient does.

Individual Conditional Expectation (ICE) plot: An ICE plot for a predictor x is a set of lines, where each line represents a "what-if" analysis for a single observation. Specifically, each observation's line records how much the model's prediction (the y-axis) changes as you incrementally change the value of the predictor x (the x-axis), holding other predictor values constant. This results in a single line for each observation. Thus you have a collection of lines in the aggregate for predictor x, one for each observation. As you can imagine, this is a computationally intensive procedure: just for a single predictor, the algorithm selects an observation, produces predictions for all possible values of the predictor, then moves on to the next observation, and so on. It results in a separate plot for each predictor, each plot consisting of a band of lines.

Partial Dependence Plot (PDP): An ICE plot has a lot of information displayed; of more interest is the PDP, which is the average of the band of lines in an ICE plot. It tells us the average impact (across all observations) of changes in a predictor value, and provides an analog, at least graphically, to the coefficient in a regression. The PDP in Figure 22.6 shows how the probability of recidivism changes as the number of prior convictions increases.

The smooth logistic regression curve, shown for illustrative purposes, reveals the same information that is compactly embodied in the logistic regression model coefficient for priors_count. The random forest curve shows analogous information, gathered through "brute force" repeated runs of the model with changed predictor values.

The above interpretability methods are at the model level—they highlight contributions of predictors to the overall model and provide global explanations that cover the entire dataset. A different kind of interpretability methods is aimed at individual records. Such methods highlight how different predictors affect the predicted values. This is especially important in applications where predicted values must be justified, such as in loan and judicial decisions. Uncovering the effect of predictors on the predicted values is called *explainability*. "Explaining" predictions provides insight on (1) how the predicted score (e.g., predicted value, class, or probability) is affected by the values of the predictor attributes, and (2) how changes to the values of predictors might change the predicted score. The first is a descriptive question, while the second is a causal question. There are different "explainability" methods, each with its strengths and weaknesses. In the following, we briefly describe three approaches for explaining individual record predictions: Shapley values, Local Interpretable Model-agnostic Explanations (LIME), and counterfactual explanations.

Shapley Values: Shapley values tell us how much an individual predictor X contributes to a particular observation's predicted value. Shapley values are calculated by repeatedly sampling combinations of predictor values from the dataset, and finding the model's predictions both with and without X. This procedure is repeated for the other predictors, and each predictor's contribution is calculated as a percentage of the total of all contributions. Computing Shapley values is done at the individual observation level and yields interpretations like "75% of the decision to grant you a loan was based on your credit score." Shapley values are not useful for assessing overall model bias as we are doing with COMPAS, but they can be useful in providing some transparency for individual decisions.

LIME: Similarly, the originators of the LIME (Local Interpretable Model-agnostic Explanations) approach described their goal of explaining a prediction as "presenting textual or visual artifacts that provide qualitative understanding of the relationship between the [features ...] and the model's prediction" (Ribeiro et al., 2016). The LIME algorithm generates additional training data around the record to be explained, then generates predicted values for these synthetic data, and subsequently builds a linear regression model on the newly created dataset. Because the linear regression model is trained only on the record and its created "neighbors," it is called a *local* model. We note that even if the overall global relationship between the predictors and the predictions is nonlinear, the *local* linear relationship is useful when the objective is to explain the predictions. While LIME is primarily a local method, it is possible to compute "global" model-specific weights by computing the averages of the local attribute weights on the validation set. While these weights give us a good idea of important predictors and can be computed for any modeling algorithm, it is important to recognize their dependency on the validation set in terms of considering their generalizability.

Counterfactual Explanations of Predictions: *What-If Scenarios* Given a record's predicted score and its predictor values, another important question for decision makers and the scored individuals is "what predictor values would have led to a better predicted score?" This causal question asks a counterfactual (what-if) question. Counterfactual explanations of predictions use a "what-if" approach to answer the questions such as "what changes to the predictor value(s) would have led to a different classification?". Stated formally, "a counterfactual explanation of a prediction describes the smallest change to the feature values that changes the prediction to a predefined output." (Molnar, 2022).[12] Counterfactual explanations are also used in recommender systems to help explain why a user has received a particular recommendation (e.g., "you received this restaurant's ad because you often click on photos of food"), and what might have led to a different recommendation (e.g., "had you 'liked' more posts about pets, you would have received an ad for pet accessories").

The machine learning workflow applying logistic regression and a random forest to COMPAS data is shown in Figure 22.7.

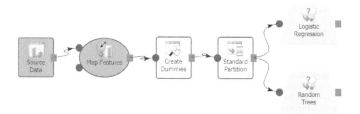

FIGURE 22.7   MACHINE LEARNING WORKFLOW FOR LOGISTIC REGRESSION AND RANDOM FOREST APPLIED TO COMPAS DATA

Bias Mitigation

Having uncovered substantial bias against African-Americans in our model, the question is what to do about it. In our examination of the roles of different predictors, we see that there are only two that have substantial predictive power, so there is little scope for exploring different combinations of predictor variables to see if doing so can lessen the bias. Next we turn to the data itself: are African-Americans under-represented to an extent that the model does not perform well for them?

Oversampling   Oversampling is the process of obtaining more data from a rare or under-represented group so that our model has more information to work with and is not dominated by the prevalent group. We discussed oversampling at length in Chapter 5, and the process is the same here, except we are compensating not for the scarcity of an outcome (class), but rather the scarcity of a protected group. In the COMPAS data, African-Americans are as plentiful as other groups, so oversampling is unlikely to be helpful, and, indeed, it is not: even after augmenting the number of African-Americans by 85% (through bootstrap oversampling) false positive rates remain above 20% (compared to 11% for Whites).[13]

Cutoff Adjustment   In the COMPAS case, it appears the true structure of the data (with just two predictors predominating) suggests that further tinkering with the model itself, in hopes that an improved understanding of complex data will result, is ruled out. So is oversampling. In this case, we must conclude that,

---

[13] Oversampling can sometimes be helpful even if the group to be oversampled is not especially rare; the poor performance of some facial recognition algorithms with dark-skinned faces can be improved incrementally by substantial oversampling, even when the original number of dark-skinned faces was large.

given the existing data, the model itself cannot be sufficiently corrected. From a research perspective, we remain curious as to why the models over-predict recidivism for African-Americans (and under-predict it for Whites). Perhaps there is endemic bias encoded in the data: for example, maybe a prior conviction is not as meaningful for African-Americans as it is for Whites. This would accord with what we know of racial history in the US—since the Civil War, African-Americans have been over-policed, and are, in fact, less prone to future crimes than their conviction rate would suggest.

From a prediction perspective, the only course of action is to adjust the cutoff level for deciding if an individual will recidivate for African-Americans and Whites differently, so that the model predictions accord with reality. This means creating one model for African-Americans and one for Whites. The degree of bias built into the model is reflected in the difference in the cutoff probabilities required to bring false positives into balance:

- African-American cutoff for classifying as recidivist: 0.625
- White cutoff for classifying as recidivist: 0.45

22.8 SUMMARY

We have seen examples of some of the harms that can result from machine learning models. Models can aid authoritarian governments in the squelching of dissent and suppression of minority groups that are out of favor, and enhance the power of autocratically minded agents even in pluralistic, democratic societies. But even the best-intentioned models, models built to help people and reduce suffering, can also result in unintentional bias and unfairness, especially when they encode or amplify biases that are built into training data. The framework provided in this chapter offers a process by which data science practitioners and project managers can minimize the probability of such harm, though not completely guarantee against it. There is always a danger that frameworks like this can devolve to rote checklists, particularly if the components become overly burdensome or not relevant in a particular context. Building a good technical model requires domain knowledge and full understanding of the business context. Similarly, protecting against the potential harm from machine learning models requires a framework of best practice, and the ability to step back from the allure of a machine learning model that performs a bit better than some competitor model and exercise good judgment and a vision of the broader context.

PROBLEMS

22.1 **Criminal Recidivism.** In this exercise, you will recreate some of the analysis done in the chapter for the COMPAS recidivism case, using the data `COMPAS-clean.xlsx`. After partitioning the data into training and validation sets, fit a logistic regression model, a single decision tree, and a Random Forest model.

    a. Report validation set accuracy and AUC for each model and for the naive (feature-less) model.

    b. Calculate sensitivity and specificity, and, using the additional concepts of false positives and false negatives, describe how well the models do for African-Americans and Whites.

    c. Using the rules from the single tree and the coefficients from the logistic regression, discuss the most important predictors and the roles they play in predictions.

    d. Run separate models for African-Americans and Whites with separate cutoffs, with the goal of eliminating or reducing bias.

22.2 **Classifying Phrases as Toxic.** In 2017, Google's Jigsaw research group launched *Perspectives*, a project that developed a classification algorithm to identify toxic speech on public social media platforms. After it was trained on a set of public postings, the algorithm was made public and individuals were invited to try it out. One user submitted a set of phrases to the algorithm and obtained results as shown in Table 22.1 (posted on Twitter by Jessamyn West, August. 24, 2017).

TABLE 22.1   JIGSAW TOXICITY SCORES FOR CERTAIN PHRASES

Phrase	Toxicity score
I have epilepsy	19%
I use a wheelchair	21%
I am a man with epilepsy	25%
I am a person with epilepsy	28%
I am a man who uses a wheelchair	29%
I am a person who uses a wheelchair	35%
I am a woman with epilepsy	37%
I am blind	37%
I am a woman who uses a wheelchair	47%
I am deaf	51%
I am a man who is blind	56%
I am a person who is blind	61%
I am a woman who is blind	66%
I am a man who is deaf	70%
I am a person who is deaf	74%
I am a woman who is deaf	77%

    a. Can you identify two problems suggested by these results?

    b. What do you think accounts for these problems?

22.3 **Predictive Policing.** *Predpol* is an algorithm that predicts crime occurrence by location in nearly real time, using historical data on crime type, crime location, and crime date/time as predictors. Police use the service to deploy patrols efficiently.

    a. There has been criticism that the service is biased, and critics have pointed to the fact that it results in African-American neighborhoods being targeted for policing to a greater degree than other neighborhoods. Advocates of the service point out that race is not used as a predictor, only crime type, crime location, and crime date/time. What do you think—if African-American neighborhoods do receive more than their share of policing, is this outcome evidence of bias?

b. Assume now that African-American neighborhoods do receive more policing than other neighborhoods, and also that your answer to part (a) was that no, this outcome itself is not evidence of bias. Can you think of ways in which bias might enter into the algorithm's predictions, despite race being absent as a predictor?

22.4 **Bank Product Marketing** This problem uses the dataset `bank-bias.xlsx`.[14] A bank with operations in the US and Europe is seeking to promote a new term deposit product with a direct marketing campaign to its customers (primarily via telemarketing). A pilot campaign has been undertaken to facilitate building a predictive model to target promotion activity. Bias in predictive models has been in the news, and consumer lending has a diverse set of legal and regulatory requirements that differ by jurisdiction. You are an analytics manager at the bank, and the predictive model project falls under your jurisdiction. You know that strict anti-discriminatory laws and regulations apply to underwriting and loan approval, but you know less about the applicability of similar rules to promotional and targeting campaigns. Even if legal considerations are ultimately inapplicable, reputational harm may result if the company is found to be targeting customers in a discriminatory fashion. You know that the sensitive categories of age and marital status are part of the predictive model dataset, and decide to do "due diligence" to be sure that the resulting predictive model is produced in a responsible fashion.

a. Explore the data to assess any imbalance in the target outcome, "deposit," across sensitive categories (age and marital status).

b. Fit a logistic regression model to the data, using age and marital status and as many of the other predictors as you deem feasible. Report the regression equation.

c. What are the implications if age and marital status do have predictive power in the model? What are the implications if they do not?

d. Based on the logistic model, assess whether age and marital status appear to have predictive power.

e. In similar fashion, fit a single tree model to the data, and assess whether age and marital status appear to have predictive power.

f. Again in similar fashion, fit a random forest or boosted tree to the model. Use a permutation feature importance test to assess whether age and marital status have predictive power. (*Hint*: In Excel, to permute a column, create a separate column of random values, then sort the two columns by the order of the random values.)

g. Compare the three models' performance in terms of lift, and sum up your findings about the roles played by the sensitive predictors.

---

[14]For the data dictionary, see https://archive.ics.uci.edu/ml/datasets/bank+marketing

## PART IX

Cases

## CHAPTER 23

Cases

23.1 CHARLES BOOK CLUB[1]

`CharlesBookClub.xlsx` is the dataset for this case study.

The Book Industry

Approximately 50,000 new titles, including new editions, are published each year in the United States, giving rise to a $25 billion industry in 2001. In terms of percentage of sales, this industry may be segmented as follows:

16%	Textbooks
16%	Trade books sold in bookstores
21%	Technical, scientific, and professional books
10%	Book clubs and other mail-order books
17%	Mass-market paperbound books
20%	All other books

Book retailing in the United States in the 1970s was characterized by the growth of bookstore chains located in shopping malls. The 1980s saw increased purchases in bookstores stimulated through the widespread practice of discounting. By the 1990s, the superstore concept of book retailing gained acceptance and contributed to double-digit growth of the book industry. Conveniently situated near large shopping centers, superstores maintain large inventories of 30,000 80,000 titles and employ well-informed sales personnel. Book retailing changed fundamentally with the arrival of Amazon, which started out as an online bookseller and went on to become the world's largest online retailer

[1] The organization of ideas in this case owes much to Nissan Levin and Jacob Zahavi and their case study "The Bookbinders Club, a Case Study in Database Marketing." The assistance of Ms. Vinni Bhandari is also gratefully acknowledged.

Machine Learning for Business Analytics: Concepts, Techniques, and Applications with Analytic Solver® Data Mining, Fourth Edition. Galit Shmueli, Peter C. Bruce, Kuber R. Deokar, and Nitin R. Patel
© 2023 John Wiley & Sons, Inc. Published 2023 by John Wiley & Sons, Inc.

of any kind. Amazon's margins were small and the convenience factor high, putting intense competitive pressure on all other book retailers. Borders, one of the two major superstore chains, discontinued operations in 2011.

Subscription-based book clubs offer an alternative model that has persisted, though it too has suffered from the dominance of Amazon.

Historically, book clubs offered their readers different types of membership programs. Two common membership programs are the continuity and negative option programs, which are both extended contractual relationships between the club and its members. Under a *continuity program*, a reader signs up by accepting an offer of several books for just a few dollars (plus shipping and handling) and an agreement to receive a shipment of one or two books each month thereafter at more-standard pricing. The continuity program is most common in the children's book market, where parents are willing to delegate the rights to the book club to make a selection, and much of the club's prestige depends on the quality of its selections.

In a *negative option program*, readers get to select how many and which additional books they would like to receive. However, the club's selection of the month is delivered to them automatically unless they specifically mark "no" on their order form by a deadline date. Negative option programs sometimes result in customer dissatisfaction and always give rise to significant mailing and processing costs.

In an attempt to combat these trends, some book clubs have begun to offer books on a *positive option basis* but only to specific segments of their customer base that are likely to be receptive to specific offers. Rather than expanding the volume and coverage of mailings, some book clubs are beginning to use database-marketing techniques to target customers more accurately. Information contained in their databases is used to identify who is most likely to be interested in a specific offer. This information enables clubs to design special programs carefully tailored to meet their customer segments' varying needs.

Database Marketing at Charles

The Club   The Charles Book Club (CBC) was established in December 1986 on the premise that a book club could differentiate itself through a deep understanding of its customer base and by delivering uniquely tailored offerings. CBC focused on selling specialty books by direct marketing through a variety of channels, including media advertising (TV, magazines, newspapers) and mailing. CBC is strictly a distributor and does not publish any of the books that it sells. In line with its commitment to understanding its customer base, CBC built and maintained a detailed database about its club members. Upon enrollment, readers were required to fill out an insert and mail it to CBC. Through this process, CBC created an active database of 500,000 readers; most were acquired through advertising in specialty magazines.

The Problem   CBC sent mailings to its club members each month containing the latest offerings. On the surface, CBC appeared very successful: mailing volume was increasing, book selection was diversifying and growing, and their customer database was increasing. However, their bottom-line profits were falling. The decreasing profits led CBC to revisit their original plan of using database marketing to improve mailing yields and to stay profitable.

A Possible Solution   CBC embraced the idea of deriving intelligence from their data to allow them to know their customers better and enable multiple targeted campaigns where each target audience would receive appropriate mailings. CBC's management decided to focus its efforts on the most profitable customers and prospects and to design targeted marketing strategies to best reach them. The two processes they had in place were:

1. Customer acquisition:

    ○ New members would be acquired by advertising in specialty magazines, newspapers, and on TV.

    ○ Direct mailing and telemarketing would contact existing club members.

    ○ Every new book would be offered to club members before general advertising.

2. Data collection:

    ○ All customer responses would be recorded and maintained in the database.

    ○ Any information not being collected that is critical would be requested from the customer.

For each new title, they decided to use a two-step approach:

1. Conduct a market test involving a random sample of 4000 customers from the database to enable analysis of customer responses. The analysis would create and calibrate response models for the current book offering.

2. Based on the response models, compute a score for each customer in the database. Use this score and a cutoff value to extract a target customer list for direct-mail promotion.

Targeting promotions was considered to be of prime importance. Other opportunities to create successful marketing campaigns based on customer behavior data (returns, inactivity, complaints, compliments, etc.) would be addressed by CBC at a later stage.

Art History of Florence   A new title, *The Art History of Florence*, is ready for release. CBC sent a test mailing to a random sample of 4000 customers from its customer base. The customer responses have been collated with past purchase data. The dataset was randomly partitioned into three parts: *Training Data* (1800 customers), initial data to be used to fit models; *Validation Data* (1400 customers), validation data used to compare the performance of different models; and *Test Data* (800 customers), data to be used only after a final model has been selected to estimate the probable performance of the model when it is deployed. Each row (or case) in the spreadsheet (other than the header) corresponds to one market test customer. Each column is a variable, with the header row giving the name of the variable. The variable names and descriptions are given in Table 23.1.

TABLE 23.1   LIST OF VARIABLES IN CHARLES BOOK CLUB DATASET

Variable name	Description
Seq#	Sequence number in the partition
ID#	Identification number in the full (unpartitioned) market test dataset
Gender	0 = male 1 = female
M	Monetary—total money spent on books
R	Recency—months since last purchase
F	Frequency—total number of purchases
FirstPurch	Months since first purchase
ChildBks	Number of purchases from the category child books
YouthBks	Number of purchases from the category youth books
CookBks	Number of purchases from the category cookbooks
DoItYBks	Number of purchases from the category do-it-yourself books
RefBks	Number of purchases from the category reference books (atlases, encyclopedias, dictionaries)
ArtBks	Number of purchases from the category art books
GeoBks	Number of purchases from the category geography books
ItalCook	Number of purchases of book title *Secrets of Italian Cooking*
ItalAtlas	Number of purchases of book title *Historical Atlas of Italy*
ItalArt	Number of purchases of book title *Italian Art*
florence	= 1 if *The Art History of Florence* was bought; = 0 if not
Related Purchase	Number of related books purchased

Machine Learning Techniques

Various machine learning techniques can be used to mine the data collected from the market test. No one technique is universally better than another. The particular context and the particular characteristics of the data are the major factors in determining which techniques perform better in an application. For this assignment we focus on two fundamental techniques: k-nearest neighbors and logistic regression. We compare them with each other as well as with a standard industry practice known as *RFM (recency, frequency, monetary) segmentation*.

RFM Segmentation   The segmentation process in database marketing aims to partition customers in a list of prospects into homogeneous groups (segments) that are similar with respect to buying behavior.   The homogeneity criterion we need for segmentation is the propensity to purchase the offering. However, since we cannot measure this variable, we use variables that are plausible indicators of this propensity.

In the direct marketing business, the most commonly used variables are the *RFM variables*:

R = *recency*, time since last purchase

F = *frequency*, number of previous purchases from the company over a period

M = *monetary*, amount of money spent on the company's products over a period

The assumption is that the more recent the last purchase, the more products bought from the company in the past, and the more money spent in the past buying the company's products, the more likely the customer is to purchase the product offered.

The 1800 observations in the training data and the 1400 observations in the validation data were divided into recency, frequency, and monetary categories as follows:

Recency:

0–2 months (Rcode = 1)
3–6 months (Rcode = 2)
7–12 months (Rcode = 3)
13 months and up (Rcode = 4)

Frequency:

1 book (Fcode = 1)
2 books (Fcode = 2)
3 books and up (Fcode = 3)

Monetary:

$0–$25 (Mcode = 1)
$26–$50 (Mcode = 2)
$51–$100 (Mcode = 3)
$101–$200 (Mcode = 4)
$201 and up (Mcode = 5)

Tables 23.2 and 23.3 display the 1800 customers in the training data cross-tabulated by these categories. Both buyers and nonbuyers are summarized. These tables are available for Excel computations in the RFM spreadsheet in the data file.

TABLE 23.2   RFM COUNTS FOR BUYERS

Rcode = all Sum of Florence	Mcode					
Fcode	1	2	3	4	5	Grand Total
1	2	2	10	7	17	38
2		3	5	9	17	34
3		1	1	15	62	79
Grand Total	2	6	16	31	96	151

Rcode = 1 Sum of Florence	Mcode					
Fcode	1	2	3	4	5	Grand Total
1	0	0	0	2	1	3
2		1	0	0	1	2
3		1	0	0	5	6
Grand Total	0	2	0	2	7	11

Rcode = 2 Sum of Florence	Mcode					
Fcode	1	2	3	4	5	Grand Total
1	1	0	1	1	5	8
2		0	3	5	5	13
3			0	4	10	14
Grand Total	1	0	4	10	20	35

Rcode = 3 Sum of Florence	Mcode					
Fcode	1	2	3	4	5	Grand Total
1	1	0	1	2	5	9
2		1	1	2	4	8
3		0	0	4	31	35
Grand Total	1	1	2	8	40	52

Rcode = 4 Sum of Florence	Mcode					
Fcode	1	2	3	4	5	Grand Total
1	0	2	8	2	6	18
2		1	1	2	7	11
3			1	7	16	24
Grand Total	0	3	10	11	29	53

TABLE 23.3   RFM COUNTS FOR ALL CUSTOMERS (BUYERS AND NONBUYERS)

Rcode = all

Count of Florence	Mcode					
Fcode	1	2	3	4	5	Grand Total
1	20	40	93	166	219	538
2		32	91	180	247	550
3		2	33	179	498	712
Grand Total	20	74	217	525	964	1800

Rcode = 1

Count of Florence	Mcode					
Fcode	1	2	3	4	5	Grand Total
1	2	2	6	10	15	35
2		3	4	12	16	35
3		1	2	11	45	59
Grand Total	2	6	12	33	76	129

Rcode = 2

Count of Florence	Mcode					
Fcode	1	2	3	4	5	Grand Total
1	3	5	17	28	26	79
2		2	17	30	31	80
3			3	34	66	103
Grand Total	3	7	37	92	123	262

Rcode = 3

Count of Florence	Mcode					
Fcode	1	2	3	4	5	Grand Total
1	7	15	24	51	86	183
2		12	29	55	85	181
3		1	17	53	165	236
Grand Total	7	28	70	159	336	600

Rcode = 4

Count of Florence	Mcode					
Fcode	1	2	3	4	5	Grand Total
1	8	18	46	77	92	241
2		15	41	83	115	254
3			11	81	222	314
Grand Total	8	33	98	241	429	809

Assignment

Partition the data into training (45%), validation (35%), and holdout (20%). Use random seed = 12345.

1. What is the response rate for the training data customers taken as a whole? What is the response rate for each of the $4 \times 5 \times 3 = 60$ combinations of RFM categories? Which combinations have response rates in the training data that are above the overall response in the training data?

2. Suppose that we decide to send promotional mail only to the "above-average" RFM combinations identified in part 1. Compute the response rate in the validation data using these combinations.

3. Rework parts 1 and 2 with three segments:

   Segment 1:   RFM combinations that have response rates that exceed twice the overall response rate

   Segment 2:   RFM combinations that exceed the overall response rate but do not exceed twice that rate

   Segment 3:   remaining RFM combinations

   Draw the lift chart (consisting of three points for these three segments) showing the number of customers in the validation dataset on the x-axis and cumulative number of buyers in the validation dataset on the y-axis.

k-Nearest Neighbors   The k-nearest neighbors technique can be used to create segments based on product proximity to products similar to the products offered as well as the propensity to purchase (as measured by the RFM variables). For *The Art History of Florence*, a possible segmentation by product proximity could be created using the following variables:

   R: recency—months since last purchase

   F: frequency—total number of past purchases

   M: monetary—total money (in dollars) spent on books

   FirstPurch: months since first purchase

   RelatedPurch: total number of past purchases of relatedbooks (i.e., sum of purchases from the art and geography categories and of titles *Secrets of Italian Cooking*, *Historical Atlas of Italy*, and *Italian Art*)

4. Use the k-nearest neighbor option under Classify in ASDM to classify cases with $k = 1$, $k = 3$, and $k = 11$, using "Florence" as the target variable. Also use ASDM's automated function to find the best k. Use normalized data (using "Rescale Data" in the dialog box) and all five variables. Create a lift chart for the best k model for the validation data. How many customers should be targeted in a sample of a size equal to the validation set size?

5. Use the k-nearest neighbor option under Predict in ASDM to compute a lift chart for the validation data for the best k calculated above. Use normalized data (note the checkbox "Rescale Data" in the dialog box) and all five variables. The k-NN prediction algorithm gives a numerical value, which is a weighted average of the values of the Florence variable for the k-nearest neighbors with weights that are inversely proportional to distance. What is the range within which a prediction will fall? How does it compare to the output you get with the k-NN classification option?

Logistic Regression   The logistic regression model offers a powerful method for modeling response because it yields well-defined purchase probabilities. The model is especially attractive in consumer-choice settings because it can be derived from the random utility theory of consumer behavior.

Use the training set data of 1800 observations to construct three logistic regression models with "Florence" as the target variable and each of the following sets of predictors:

- The full set of 15 predictors in the dataset
- A subset of predictors that you judge to be the best
- Only the R, F, and M variables

6. Create lift charts for the validation set, summarizing the results from the three logistic regression models created above. For each model, report how many customers should be targeted in a test set of the same size.

7. If the cutoff criterion for a campaign is a 30% likelihood of a purchase, find the customers in the validation data that would be targeted, and count the number of buyers in this set.

Final Model Selection   Now that multiple models have been trained and assessed, it is time to select the final model and measure its performance before deployment.

8. Based on the above analysis, which model would you select for targeting customers with Florence as the outcome? Why?

9. Test the "best" model on the holdout set. Create a lift chart, and comment on how this chart compares to the analysis done earlier with the validation set in terms of how many customers to target.

23.2 GERMAN CREDIT

`GermanCredit.xlsx` is the dataset for this case study.

Background

Money lending has been around since the advent of money; it is perhaps the world's second-oldest profession. The systematic evaluation of credit risk, though, is a relatively recent arrival, and lending was largely based on reputation and very incomplete data. Thomas Jefferson, the third President of the United States, was in debt throughout his life and unreliable in his debt payments, yet people continued to lend him money. It wasn't until the beginning of the 20th century that the Retail Credit Company was founded to share information about credit. That company is now Equifax, one of the big three credit-scoring agencies (the other two are Transunion and Experion).

Individual and local human judgment are now largely irrelevant to the credit-reporting process. Credit agencies and other big financial institutions extending credit at the retail level collect huge amounts of data to predict whether defaults or other adverse events will occur, based on numerous customer and transaction information.

Data

This case deals with an early stage of the historical transition to predictive modeling, in which humans were employed to label records as either good or poor credit. The German Credit dataset[2] has 30 variables and 1000 records, each record being a prior applicant for credit. Each applicant was rated as "good credit" (700 cases) or "bad credit" (300 cases). All the variables are explained in Table 23.4. Table 23.5 shows the values of these variables for the first four records. New applicants for credit can also be evaluated on these 30 predictor variables and classified as a good or a bad credit risk based on the predictor variables.

The consequences of misclassification have been assessed as follows: the costs of a false positive (incorrectly saying that an applicant is a good credit risk) outweigh the benefits of a true positive (correctly saying that an applicant is a good credit risk) by a factor of 5. This is summarized in Table 23.6. The opportunity cost table was derived from the average net profit per loan as shown in Table 23.7.

Because decision makers are used to thinking of their decision in terms of net profits, we use these tables in assessing the performance of the various models.

---

[2] This dataset is available from https://archive.ics.uci.edu/ml/datasets/statlog+(german+credit+data)

TABLE 23.4   VARIABLES FOR THE GERMAN CREDIT DATASET

Var.	Variable name	Description	Variable type	Code description
1	OBS#	Observation numbers	Categorical	Sequence number in dataset
2	CHK_ACCT	Checking account status	Categorical	0: < 0 DM (Deutsch Marks)
				1: 0 — 200 DM
				2 : >200 DM
				3: No checking account
3	DURATION	Duration of credit in months	Numerical	
4	HISTORY	Credit history	Categorical	0: No credits taken
				1: All credits at this bank paid back duly
				2: Existing credits paid back duly until now
				3: Delay in paying off in the past
				4: Critical account
5	NEW_CAR	Purpose of credit	Binary	Car (new) 0: No, 1: Yes
6	USED_CAR	Purpose of credit	Binary	Car (used) 0: No, 1: Yes
7	FURNITURE	Purpose of credit	Binary	Furniture/equipment 0: No, 1: Yes
8	RADIO/TV	Purpose of credit	Binary	Radio/television 0: No, 1: Yes
9	EDUCATION	Purpose of credit	Binary	Education 0: No, 1: Yes
10	RETRAINING	Purpose of credit	Binary	Retraining 0: No, 1: Yes
11	AMOUNT	Credit amount	Numerical	
12	SAV_ACCT	Average balance in savings account	Categorical	0: < 100 DM
				1 : 101 — 500 DM
				2 : 501 — 1000 DM
				3 : > 1000 DM
				4 : Unknown/ no savings account
13	EMPLOYMENT	Present employment since	Categorical	0 : Unemployed
				1: < 1 year
				2: 1 — 3 years
				3: 4 — 6 years
				4: ≥ 7 years
14	INSTALL_RATE	Installment rate as % of disposable income	Numerical	
15	MALE_DIV	Applicant is male and divorced	Binary	0: No, 1:Yes

(continued)

TABLE 23.4   *(CONTINUED)*

Var.	Variable name	Description	Variable type	Code description
16	MALE_SINGLE	Applicant is male and single	Binary	0: No, 1:Yes
17	MALE_MAR_WID	Applicant is male and married or a widower	Binary	0: No, 1:Yes
18	CO-APPLICANT	Application has a coapplicant	Binary	0: No, 1:Yes
19	GUARANTOR	Applicant has a guarantor	Binary	0: No, 1:Yes
20	PRESENT_RESIDENT	Present resident since (years)	Categorical	0: ≤ 1 year 1: $1 - 2$ years 2: $2 - 3$ years 3: ≥ 3 years
21	REAL_ESTATE	Applicant owns real estate	Binary	0: No, 1:Yes
22	PROP_UNKN_NONE	Applicant owns no property (or unknown)	Binary	0: No, 1:Yes
23	AGE	Age in years	Numerical	
24	OTHER_INSTALL	Applicant has other installment plan credit	Binary	0: No, 1:Yes
25	RENT	Applicant rents	Binary	0: No, 1:Yes
26	OWN_RES	Applicant owns residence	Binary	0: No, 1:Yes
27	NUM_CREDITS	Number of existing credits at this bank	Numerical	
28	JOB	Nature of job	Categorical	0 : Unemployed/ unskilled— non-resident 1 : Unskilled— resident 2 : Skilled employee/ official 3 : Management/ self-employed/ highly qualified employee/officer
29	NUM_DEPENDENTS	Number of people for whom liable to provide maintenance	Numerical	
30	TELEPHONE	Applicant has phone in his or her name	Binary	0: No, 1:Yes
31	FOREIGN	Foreign worker	Binary	0: No, 1:Yes
32	RESPONSE	Credit rating is good	Binary	0: No, 1:Yes

Note: The original dataset had a number of categorical variables, some of which were transformed into a series of binary variables so that they can be handled appropriately by ASDM. Several ordered categorical variables were left as is, to be treated by ASDM as numerical.
Source: Data adapted from German Credit

TABLE 23.5 FIRST FOUR RECORDS FROM GERMAN CREDIT DATASET

OBS	CHK_ACCT	DURATION	HISTORY	NEW_CAR	USED_CAR	FURNITURE	RADIO/TV	EDUCATION	RETRAINING	AMOUNT	SAV_ACCT	EMPLOYMENT	INSTALL_RATE	MALE_DIV	MALE_SINGLE	MALE_MAR_WID	CO-APPLICANT	GUARANTOR
1	0	6	4	0	0	0	1	0	0	1169	4	4	4	0	1	0	0	0
2	1	48	2	0	0	0	1	0	0	5951	0	2	2	0	0	0	0	0
3	3	12	4	0	0	0	0	1	0	2096	0	3	2	0	1	0	0	0
4	0	42	2	0	0	1	0	0	0	7882	0	3	2	0	1	0	0	1

PRESENT_RESIDENT	REAL_ESTATE	PROP_UNKN_NONE	AGE	OTHER_INSTALL	RENT	OWN_RES	NUM_CREDITS	JOB	NUM_DEPENDENTS	TELEPHONE	FOREIGN	RESPONSE
4	1	0	67	0	0	1	2	2	1	1	0	1
2	1	0	22	0	0	1	1	2	1	0	0	0
3	1	0	49	0	0	1	1	1	2	0	0	1
4	0	0	45	0	0	0	1	2	2	0	0	1

Source: Data adapted from German Credit

TABLE 23.6 OPPORTUNITY COST TABLE (DEUTSCHE MARKS)

Actual	Predicted (decision)	
	Good (accept)	Bad (reject)
Good	0	100
Bad	500	0

TABLE 23.7 AVERAGE NET PROFIT (DEUTSCHE MARKS)

Actual	Predicted (decision)	
	Good (accept)	Bad (reject)
Good	100	0
Bad	−500	0

Assignment

1. Review the predictor variables, and guess what their role in a credit decision might be. Are there any surprises in the data?

2. Divide the data into training and validation partitions, and develop classification models using the following machine learning techniques in ASDM: logistic regression, classification trees, and neural networks.

3. Choose one model from each technique, and report the confusion matrix and the cost/gain matrix for the validation data. Which technique has the highest net profit?

4. Let us try and improve our performance. Rather than accepting ASDM's initial classification of all applicants' credit status, use the "predicted probability of success" in logistic regression (where *success* means 1) as a basis for selecting the best credit risks first, followed by poorer-risk applicants.

   - Sort the validation on "predicted probability of success."

   - For each case, calculate the net profit of extending credit.

   - Add another column for cumulative net profit.

   a. How far into the validation data should you go to get maximum net profit? (Often this is specified as a percentile or rounded to deciles.)

   b. If this logistic regression model is used to score to future applicants, what "probability of success" cutoff should be used in extending credit?

23.3 Tayko Software Cataloger[3]

Tayko.xlsx is the dataset for this case study.

Background

Tayko is a software catalog firm that sells games and educational software. It started out as a software manufacturer and later added third-party titles to its offerings. It has recently put together a revised collection of items in a new catalog, which it is preparing to roll out in a mailing.

In addition to its own software titles, Tayko's customer list is a key asset. In an attempt to expand its customer base, it has recently joined a consortium of catalog firms that specialize in computer and software products. The consortium affords members the opportunity to mail catalogs to names drawn from a pooled list of customers. Members supply their own customer lists to the pool and can "withdraw" an equivalent number of names in each quarter. Members are allowed to do predictive modeling on the records in the pool so they can do a better job of selecting names from the pool.

The Mailing Experiment

Tayko has supplied its customer list of 200,000 names to the pool, which totals over 5,000,000 names, so it is now entitled to draw 200,000 names for a mailing. Tayko would like to select the names that have the best chance of performing well, so it conducts a test—it draws 20,000 names from the pool and does a test mailing of the new catalog.

This mailing yielded 1065 purchasers, a response rate of 0.053. To optimize the performance of the machine learning techniques, it was decided to work with a stratified sample that contained equal numbers of purchasers and nonpurchasers. For ease of presentation, the dataset for this case includes just 1000 purchasers and 1000 nonpurchasers, an apparent response rate of 0.5. Therefore, after using the dataset to predict who will be a purchaser, we must adjust the purchase rate back down by multiplying each case's "probability of purchase" by 0.053/0.5, or 0.107.

Data

There are two response variables in this case. *Purchase* indicates whether or not a prospect responded to the test mailing and purchased something. *Spending* indicates, for those who made a purchase, how much they spent. The overall procedure in this case will be to develop two models. One will be used to classify records as *purchase* or *no purchase*. The second will be used for those cases that are classified as *purchase* and will predict the amount they will spend.

---

[3]Copyright ©Datastats, LLC 2019 used with permission.

Table 23.8 shows the first few rows of data. Table 23.9 provides a description of the variables available in this case. A partition variable is used because we will develop two different models and want to preserve the same partition structure for assessing each model.

TABLE 23.8   **FIRST 10 RECORDS FROM TAYKO DATASET**

sequence_number	US	source_a	source_c	source_b	source_d	source_e	source_m	source_o	source_h	source_r	source_s	source_t	source_u	source_p	source_x	source_w	Freq	last_update_days_ago	1st_update_days_ago	Web order	Gender=male	Address_is_res	Purchase	Spending	Partition
1	1	0	0	1	0	0	0	0	0	0	0	0	0	0	0	0	2	3662	3662	1	0	1	1	127.87	s
2	1	0	0	0	0	1	0	0	0	0	0	0	0	0	0	0	0	2900	2900	1	1	0	0	0	s
3	1	0	0	0	0	0	0	0	0	0	0	1	0	0	0	0	2	3883	3914	0	0	0	1	127.48	t
4	1	0	1	0	0	0	0	0	0	0	0	0	0	0	0	0	1	829	829	0	1	0	0	0	s
5	1	0	1	0	0	0	0	0	0	0	0	0	0	0	0	0	1	869	869	0	0	0	0	0	t
6	1	0	0	0	0	0	0	0	1	0	0	0	0	0	0	0	1	1995	2002	0	0	1	0	0.06	s
7	1	0	0	0	0	0	0	0	0	0	0	0	0	0	0	1	2	1498	1529	0	0	1	0	0.06	s
8	1	0	0	1	0	0	0	0	0	0	0	0	0	0	0	0	1	3397	3397	0	1	0	0	0.08	t
9	1	1	0	0	0	0	0	0	0	0	0	0	0	0	0	0	4	525	2914	1	1	0	1	488.5	t
10	1	1	0	0	0	0	0	0	0	0	0	0	0	0	0	0	1	3215	3215	0	0	0	1	173.5	v

TABLE 23.9   **DESCRIPTION OF VARIABLES FOR TAYKO DATASET**

Var.	Variable name	Description	Variable type	Code description
1	US	Is it a US address?	Binary	1: Yes 0: No
2–16	Source_ *	Source catalog for the record (15 possible sources)	Binary	1: Yes 0: No
17	Freq.	Number of transactions in last year at source catalog	Numerical	
18	last_update_days_ago	How many days ago last update was made to customer record	Numerical	
19	1st_update_days_ago	How many days ago first update to customer record was made	Numerical	
20	RFM%	Recency-frequency-monetary percentile, as reported by source catalog (see Section 23.1)	Numerical	
21	Web_order	Customer placed at least one order via Web	Binary	1: Yes 0: No
22	Gender=mal	Customer is male	Binary	1: Yes 0: No
23	Address_is_res	Address is a residence	Binary	1: Yes 0: No
24	Purchase	Person made purchase in test mailing	Binary	1: Yes 0: No
25	Spending	Amount (dollars) spent by customer in test mailing	Numerical	
26	Partition	Variable indicating which partition the record will be assigned to	Alphabetical	t: Training v: Validation s: Test

Assignment

1. Each catalog costs approximately $2 to mail (including printing, postage, and mailing costs). Estimate the gross profit that the firm could expect from the remaining 180,000 names if it selects them randomly from the pool.

2. Develop a model for classifying a customer as a purchaser or nonpurchaser.

   a. Partition the data into training data on the basis of the partition variable, which has 800 t's, 700 v's, and 500 s's (training data, validation data, and test data, respectively) assigned randomly to cases.

   b. Using the "Best Subsets" option in logistic regression's Feature Selection menu, implement the full logistic regression model, select the best subset of variables, and then implement a regression model with just those variables to classify the data into purchasers and nonpurchasers. (Logistic regression is used because it yields an estimated "probability of purchase," which is required later in the analysis.)

3. Develop a model for predicting spending among the purchasers.

   a. Make a copy of the data sheet (call it data2), sort by the "Purchase" variable, and remove the records where Purchase = 0 (the resulting spreadsheet will contain only purchasers).

   b. Partition this dataset into training and validation partitions on the basis of the partition variable.

   c. Develop models for predicting spending, using:

      i. Multiple linear regression (use Best Subsets in Feature Selection)

      ii. Regression trees

   d. Choose one model on the basis of its performance with the validation data.

4. Return to the original test data partition. Note that this test data partition includes both purchasers and nonpurchasers. Note also that although it contains the scoring of the chosen classification model, we have not used this partition in our analysis up to this point, so it will give an unbiased estimate of the performance of our models. It is best to make a copy of the test data portion of this sheet to work with, since we will be adding analyses to it. This copy is called *Score Analysis*.

   a. Copy to this sheet the "predicted probability of success" (*success = purchase*) column from the classification of test data.

   b. Score to this data sheet the prediction model chosen.

    c. Arrange the following columns so that they are adjacent:

        i. Predicted probability of purchase (*success*)

        ii. Actual spending (dollars)

        iii. Predicted spending (dollars)

    d. Add a column for "adjusted probability of purchase" by multiplying "predicted probability of purchase" by 0.107. *This is to adjust for over-sampling the purchasers* (see earlier description).

    e. Add a column for expected spending: adjusted probability of purchase × predicted spending.

    f. Sort all records on the "expected spending" column.

    g. Calculate cumulative lift [this is the cumulative "actual spending" divided by the average spending that would result from random selection (each adjusted by 0.107)].

    h. Plot the lift curve using the calculated cumulative lift. Using this lift curve, estimate the gross profit that would result from mailing to the 180,000 names on the basis of your machine learning models.

Note: Although Tayko is a hypothetical company, the data in this case (modified slightly for illustrative purposes) were supplied by a real company that sells software through direct sales. The concept of a catalog consortium is based on the Abacus Catalog Alliance.

23.4 POLITICAL PERSUASION[4]

`Voter-Persuasion.xlsx` is the dataset for this case study.

Note: Our thanks to Ken Strasma, President of HaystaqDNA and director of targeting for the 2004 Kerry campaign and the 2008 Obama campaign, for the data used in this case and for sharing the information in the following writeup.

Background

When you think of political persuasion, you may think of the efforts that political campaigns undertake to persuade you that their candidate is better than the other candidate. In truth, campaigns are less about persuading people to change their minds, and more about persuading those who agree with you to actually go out and vote. Predictive analytics now plays a big role in this effort, but in 2004 it was a new arrival in the political toolbox.

Predictive Analytics Arrives in US Politics

In January of 2004, candidates in the US presidential campaign were competing in the Iowa caucuses, part of a lengthy state-by-state primary campaign that culminates in the selection of the Republican and Democratic candidates for president. Among the Democrats, Howard Dean was leading in national polls. The Iowa caucuses, however, are a complex and intensive process attracting only the most committed and interested voters. Those participating are not a representative sample of voters nationwide. Surveys of those planning to take part showed a close race between Dean and three other candidates, including John Kerry.

Kerry ended up winning by a surprisingly large margin, and the better than expected performance was due to his campaign's innovative and successful use of predictive analytics to learn more about the likely actions of individual voters. This allowed the campaign to target voters in such a way as to optimize performance in the caucuses. For example, once the model showed sufficient support in a precinct to win that precinct's delegate to the caucus, money and time could be redirected to other precincts where the race was closer.

Political Targeting

Targeting of voters is not new in politics. It has traditionally taken three forms:

- Geographic
- Demographic
- Individual

In geographic targeting, resources are directed to a geographic unit—state, city, county, and so on—on the basis of prior voting patterns or surveys that reveal the political tendency in that geographic unit. This has significant limitations, though. If a county is only, say, 52% in your favor, it may be in the greatest need of attention, but if messaging is directed to everyone in the county, nearly half of it is reaching the wrong people.

In demographic targeting, the messaging is intended for demographic groups—for example, older voters, younger women voters, Hispanic voters, an so on. The limitation of this method is that it is often not easy to implement because messaging is hard to deliver just to single demographic groups.

Traditional individual targeting, the most effective form of targeting, was done on the basis of surveys asking voters how they plan to vote. The big limitation of this method is, of course, the cost. The expense of reaching all voters in a phone or door-to-door survey can be prohibitive.

The use of predictive analytics adds power to the individual targeting method, and reduces cost. A model allows prediction to be rolled out to the entire voter base, not just those surveyed, and brings to bear a wealth of information. Geographic and demographic data remain part of the picture, but they are used at an individual level.

Uplift

In a classical predictive modeling application for marketing, a sample of data is selected and an offer is made (e.g., on the web) or a message is sent (e.g., by mail), and a predictive model is developed to classify individuals as responding or not-responding. The model is then applied to new data, propensities to respond are calculated, individuals are ranked by their propensity to respond, and the marketer can then select those most likely to respond to mailings or offers.

Some key information is missing from this classical approach: how would the individual respond in the absence of the offer or mailing? Might a high propensity customer be inclined to purchase regardless of the offer? Might a person's propensity to buy actually be diminished by the offer? Uplift modeling (see Chapter 14) allows us to estimate the effect of "offer vs. no offer" or "mailing vs. no mailing" at the individual level.

In this case, we will apply uplift modeling to actual voter data that were augmented with the results of a hypothetical experiment. The experiment consisted of the following steps:

1. Conduct a pre-survey of the voters to determine their inclination to vote Democratic.
2. Randomly split the voters into two samples—control and treatment.
3. Send a flyer promoting the Democratic candidate to the treatment group.
4. Conduct another survey of the voters to determine their inclination to vote Democratic.

Data

The data in this case are in the file `Voter-Persuasion.xlsx`. The target variable is MOVED_AD, where a 1 = "opinion moved in favor of the Democratic candidate" and 0 = "opinion did not move in favor of the Democratic candidate." This variable encapsulates the information from the pre- and post-surveys. The important predictor variable is *Flyer*, a binary variable that indicates whether or not a voter received the flyer. In addition there are numerous other predictor variables from these sources:

1. Government voter files
2. Political party data
3. Commercial consumer and demographic data
4. Census neighborhood data

Government voter files are maintained, and made public, to assure the integrity of the voting process. They contain essential data for identification purposes such as name, address, and date of birth. The file used in this case also contains party identification (needed if a state limits participation in party primaries to voters in that party). Parties also staff elections with their own poll watchers, who record whether an individual votes in an election. These data (termed "derived" in the case data) are maintained and curated by each party and can be readily matched to the voter data by name. Demographic data at the neighborhood level are available from the census and can be appended to the voter data by address matching. Consumer and additional demographic data (buying habits, education) can be purchased from marketing firms and appended to the voter data (matching by name and address).

Assignment

The task in this case is to develop an uplift model that predicts the uplift for each voter. Uplift is defined as the increase in propensity to move one's opinion in a Democratic direction. First, review the variables in `Voter-Persuasion.xlsx`, and understand which data source they are probably coming from. Then, answer the following questions and perform the tasks indicated:

1. Overall, how well did the flyer do in moving voters in a Democratic direction? (Look at the target variable among those who got the flyer, compared to those who did not.)
2. Explore the data to learn more about the relationships between the predictor variables and MOVED_AD (visualization can be helpful). Which of the predictors seem to have good predictive potential? Show supporting charts and/or tables.
3. Partition the data using the partition variable that is in the dataset, make decisions about predictor inclusion, and fit three predictive models accordingly. For each model, give sufficient detail about the method

used, its parameters, and the predictors used, so that your results can be replicated.

4. Among your three models, choose the best one in terms of predictive power. Which one is it? Why did you choose it?

5. Using your chosen model, report the propensities for the first three records in the validation set.

6. Create a derived variable that is the opposite of *Flyer*. Call it *Flyer-reversed*. Using your chosen model, re-score the validation data using the *Flyer-reversed* variable as a predictor, instead of *Flyer*. You can do this either by using the stored model utility in ASDM or by creating a second copy of the validation data with the *Flyer-reversed* variable as a predictor and repeating the model with that copy as "new data" to be scored. Report the propensities for the first three records in the validation set.

7. For each record, uplift is computed based on the following difference:

$$P(\text{success} \mid \text{Flyer} = 1) - P(\text{success} \mid \text{Flyer} = 0)$$

Compute the uplift for each of the voters in the validation set, and report the uplift for the first three records.

8. If a campaign has the resources to mail the flyer only to 10% of the voters, what uplift cutoff should be used?

23.5 TAXI CANCELLATIONS[5]

`Taxi-cancellation-case.xlsx` is the dataset for this case study.

Business Situation

In late 2013, the taxi company Yourcabs.com in Bangalore, India, was facing a problem with the drivers using their platform—not all drivers were showing up for their scheduled calls. Drivers would cancel their acceptance of a call and, if the cancellation did not occur with adequate notice, the customer would be delayed or even left high and dry.

Bangalore is a key tech center in India, and technology was transforming the taxi industry. Yourcabs.com featured an online booking system (though customers could phone in as well) and presented itself as a taxi booking portal. The Uber ride sharing service would start its Bangalore operations in mid-2014. Yourcabs.com had collected data on its bookings from 2011 to through 2013 and posted a contest on Kaggle, in coordination with the Indian School of Business, to see what it could learn about the problem of cab cancellations.

The data presented for this case are a randomly selected subset of the original data, with 10,000 rows, one row for each booking. There are 17 input variables, including user (customer) ID, vehicle model, whether the booking was made online or via a mobile app, type of travel, type of booking package, geographic information, and the date and time of the scheduled trip. The target variable of interest is the binary indicator of whether a ride was canceled. The overall cancellation rate is between 7% and 8%.

Assignment

1. How can a predictive model based on these data be used by Yourcabs.com?

2. How can a profiling model (identifying predictors that distinguish canceled/uncanceled trips) be used by Yourcabs.com?

3. Explore, prepare, and transform the data to facilitate predictive modeling. Here are some hints:

   - In exploratory modeling it is useful to move fairly soon to at least an initial model without solving *all* data preparation issues. One example is the GPS information—other geographic information is available, so you could defer the challenge of how to interpret/use the GPS information.

   - How will you deal with missing data, such as cases where NULL is indicated?

- Think about what useful information might be held within the date and time fields (the booking timestamp and the trip timestamp).

- Think also about the categorical variables and how to deal with them. Should we turn them all into dummies? Use only some?

4. Fit several predictive models of your choice. Do they provide information on how the predictor variables relate to cancellations?

5. Report the predictive performance of your model in terms of error rates (the confusion matrix). How well does the model perform? Can the model be used in practice?

6. Examine the predictive performance of your model in terms of ranking (lift). How well does the model perform? Can the model be used in practice?

23.6 SEGMENTING CONSUMERS OF BATH SOAP[6]

BathSoap.xlsx is the dataset for this case study.

Business Situation

CRISA is an Asian market research agency that specializes in tracking consumer purchase behavior in consumer goods (both durable and nondurable). In one major research project, CRISA tracks numerous consumer product categories (e.g., "detergents") and, within each category, perhaps dozens of brands. To track purchase behavior, CRISA constituted household panels in over 100 cities and towns in India, covering most of the Indian urban market. The households were carefully selected using stratified sampling to ensure a representative sample; a subset of 600 records is analyzed here. The strata were defined on the basis of socioeconomic status and the market (a collection of cities).

CRISA has both transaction data (each row is a transaction) and household data (each row is a household), and for the household data, it maintains the following information:

- Demographics of the households (updated annually)
- Possession of durable goods (car, washing machine, etc., updated annually; an "affluence index" is computed from this information)
- Purchase data of product categories and brands (updated monthly)

CRISA has two categories of clients: (1) advertising agencies that subscribe to the database services, obtain updated data every month, and use the data to advise their clients on advertising and promotion strategies; (2) consumer goods manufacturers that monitor their market share using the CRISA database.

Key Problems

CRISA has traditionally segmented markets on the basis of purchaser demographics. They would now like to segment the market based on two key sets of variables more directly related to the purchase process and to brand loyalty:

1. Purchase behavior (volume, frequency, susceptibility to discounts, and brand loyalty)
2. Basis of purchase (price, selling proposition)

Doing so would allow CRISA to gain information about what demographic attributes are associated with different purchase behaviors and degrees of brand loyalty and thus deploy promotion budgets more effectively. More effective

---

[6]Copyright ©Cytel, Inc. and Datastats, LLC 2019; used with permission.

market segmentation would enable CRISA's clients (in this case, a firm called IMRB) to design more cost-effective promotions targeted at appropriate segments. Thus multiple promotions could be launched, each targeted at different market segments at different times of the year. This would result in a more cost-effective allocation of the promotion budget to different market segments. It would also enable IMRB to design more effective customer reward systems and thereby increase brand loyalty.

Data

The data in Table 23.10 profile each household, each row containing the data for one household.

Measuring Brand Loyalty

Several variables in this case measure aspects of brand loyalty. The number of different brands purchased by the customer is one measure of loyalty. However, a consumer who purchases one or two brands in quick succession and then settles on a third for a long streak is different from a consumer who constantly switches back and forth among three brands. Therefore how often customers switch from one brand to another is another measure of loyalty. Yet a third perspective on the same issue is the proportion of purchases that go to different brands—a consumer who spends 90% of his or her purchase money on one brand is more loyal than a consumer who spends more equally among several brands.

All three of these components can be measured with the data in the purchase summary worksheet.

Assignment

1. Use k-means clustering to identify clusters of households based on:

   a. The variables that describe purchase behavior (including brand loyalty)

   b. The variables that describe the basis for purchase

   c. The variables that describe both purchase behavior and basis of purchase

   Note 1: How should k be chosen? Think about how the clusters would be used. It is likely that the marketing efforts would support two to five different promotional approaches.

   Note 2: How should the percentages of total purchases accounted for by various brands be treated? Isn't a customer who buys all brand A just as loyal as a customer who buys all brand B? What will be the effect on any distance measure of using the brand share variables as is? Consider using a single derived variable.

TABLE 23.10   DESCRIPTION OF VARIABLES FOR EACH HOUSEHOLD

Variable type	Variable name	Description
Member ID	Member id	Unique identifier for each household
Demographics	SEC	Socioeconomic class (1 = high, 5 = low)
	FEH	Eating habits(1 = vegetarian, 2 = vegetarian but eat eggs, 3 = nonvegetarian, 0 = not specified)
	MT	Native language (see table in worksheet)
	SEX	Gender of homemaker (1 = male, 2 = female)
	AGE	Age of homemaker
	EDU	Education of homemaker (1 = minimum, 9 = maximum)
	HS	Number of members in household
	CHILD	Presence of children in household (4 categories)
	CS	Television availability (1 = available, 2 = unavailable)
	Affluence Index	Weighted value of durables possessed
Purchase summary over the period	No. of Brands	Number of brands purchased
	Brand Runs	Number of instances of consecutive purchase of brands
	Total Volume	Sum of volume
	No. of Trans	Number of purchase transactions (multiple brands purchased in a month are counted as separate transactions
	Value	Sum of value
	Trans/ Brand Runs	Average transactions per brand run
	Vol/Trans	Average volume per transaction
	Avg. Price	Average price of purchase
Purchase within promotion	Pur Vol	Percent of volume purchased
	No Promo - %	Percent of volume purchased under no promotion
	Pur Vol Promo 6%	Percent of volume purchased under promotion code 6
	Pur Vol Other Promo %	Percent of volume purchased under other promotions
Brandwise purchase	Br. Cd. (57, 144), 55, 272, 286, 24, 481, 352, 5, and 999 (others)	Percent of volume purchased of the brand
Price categorywise purchase	Price Cat 1 to 4	Percent of volume purchased under the price category
Selling propositionwise purchase	Proposition Cat 5 to 15	Percent of volume purchased under the product proposition category

2. Select what you think is the best segmentation, and comment on the characteristics (demographic, brand loyalty, and basis for purchase) of these clusters. (This information would be used to guide the development of advertising and promotional campaigns.)

3. Develop a model that classifies the data into these segments. Since this information would most likely be used in targeting direct-mail promotions, it would be useful to select a market segment that would be defined as a *success* in the classification model.

23.7 DIRECT-MAIL FUNDRAISING

`Fundraising.xlsx` and `FutureFundraising.xlsx` are the datasets used for this case study.

Background

Note: Be sure to read the information about oversampling and adjustment in Chapter 5 before starting to work on this case.

A national veterans' organization wishes to develop a predictive model to improve the cost-effectiveness of their direct marketing campaign. The organization, with its in-house database of over 13 million donors, is one of the largest direct-mail fundraisers in the United States. According to their recent mailing records, the overall response rate is 5.1%. Out of those who responded (donated), the average donation is $13.00. Each mailing, which includes a gift of personalized address labels and assortments of cards and envelopes, costs $0.68 to produce and send. Using these facts, we take a sample of this dataset to develop a classification model that can effectively capture donors so that the expected net profit is maximized. Weighted sampling is used, underrepresenting the nonresponders so that the sample has equal numbers of donors and nondonors.

Data

The file `Fundraising.xlsx` contains 3120 records with 50% donors (TARGET_B = 1) and 50% nondonors (TARGET_B = 0). The amount of donation (TARGET_D) is also included but is not used in this case. The descriptions for the 22 variables (including two target variables) are listed in Table 23.11.

Assignment

Step 1: *Partitioning*: Partition the dataset into 60% training and 40% validation (set the seed to 12345).

Step 2: *Model Building*: Follow the following steps to build, evaluate, and choose a model.

    1. *Select classification tool and parameters*: Run at least two classification models of your choosing. Be sure NOT to use TARGET_D in your analysis. Describe the two models that you chose, with sufficient detail (method, parameters, variables, etc.) so that it can be replicated.

    2. *Classification under asymmetric response and cost*: What is the reasoning behind using weighted sampling to produce a training set with equal numbers of donors and non-donors? Why not use a simple random sample from the original dataset?

TABLE 23.11   DESCRIPTION OF VARIABLES FOR THE FUNDRAISING DATASET

Variable	Description
ZIP	Zip code group (Zip codes were grouped into five groups; 1 = the potential donor belongs to this zip group.)
	00000–19999 $\Rightarrow$ zipconvert_1
	20000–39999 $\Rightarrow$ zipconvert_2
	40000–59999 $\Rightarrow$ zipconvert_3
	60000–79999 $\Rightarrow$ zipconvert_4
	80000–99999 $\Rightarrow$ zipconvert_5
HOMEOWNER	1 = homeowner, 0 = not a homeowner
NUMCHLD	Number of children
INCOME	Household income
GENDER	0 = male, 1 = female
WEALTH	Wealth rating uses median family income and population statistics from each area to index relative wealth within each state The segments are denoted 0 to 9, with 9 being the highest wealth group and zero the lowest. Each rating has a different meaning within each state.
HV	Average home value in potential donor's neighborhood in hundreds of dollars
ICmed	Median family income in potential donor's neighborhood in hundreds of dollars
ICavg	Average family income in potential donor's neighborhood in hundreds
IC15	Percent earning less than $15K in potential donor's neighborhood
NUMPROM	Lifetime number of promotions received to date
RAMNTALL	Dollar amount of lifetime gifts to date
MAXRAMNT	Dollar amount of largest gift to date
LASTGIFT	Dollar amount of most recent gift
TOTALMONTHS	Number of months from last donation to July 1998 (the last time the case was updated)
TIMELAG	Number of months between first and second gift
AVGGIFT	Average dollar amount of gifts to date
TARGET_B	Target variable: binary indicator for response
	1 = donor, 0 = nondonor
TARGET_D	Target variable: donation amount (in dollars). We will NOT be using this variable for this case

3. *Calculate net profit*: For each method, calculate the lift of net profit for both the training and validation sets based on the actual response rate (5.1%). Again, the expected donation, given that they are donors, is $13.00, and the total cost of each mailing is $0.68. (*Hint*: To calculate estimated net profit, we will need to undo the effects of the weighted sampling and calculate the net profit that would reflect the actual response distribution of 5.1% donors and 94.9% nondonors. To do this, divide each row's net profit by the oversampling weights applicable to the actual status of that row. The oversampling weight for actual donors is 50%/5.1% = 9.8. The oversampling weight for actual nondonors is 50%/94.9% = 0.53.)

4. *Draw lift curves*: Draw each model's net profit lift curve for the validation set onto a single graph (net profit on the y-axis, proportion of list or number mailed on the x-axis). Is there a model that dominates?

5. *Select best model*: From your answer in (4), what do you think is the "best" model?

Step 3: Testing: The file `FutureFundraising.xlsx` contains the attributes for future mailing candidates.

6. Using your "best" model from step 2 (number 5), which of these candidates do you predict as donors and non-donors? List them in descending order of the probability of being a donor. Starting at the top of this sorted list, roughly how far down would you go in a mailing campaign?

23.8 CATALOG CROSS-SELLING[7]

CatalogCrossSell.xlsx is the dataset for this case study.

Background

Exeter, Inc., is a catalog firm that sells products in a number of different catalogs that it owns. The catalogs number in the dozens but fall into nine basic categories:

1. Clothing
2. Housewares
3. Health
4. Automotive
5. Personal electronics
6. Computers
7. Garden
8. Novelty gift
9. Jewelry

The costs of printing and distributing catalogs are high. By far, the biggest cost of operation is the cost of promoting products to people who buy nothing. Having invested so much in the production of artwork and printing of catalogs, Exeter wants to take every opportunity to use them effectively. One such opportunity is in cross-selling—once a customer has "taken the bait" and purchases one product, try to sell them another while you have their attention.

Such cross-promotion might take the form of enclosing a catalog in the shipment of a purchased product, together with a discount coupon to induce a purchase from that catalog. Or, it might take the form of a similar coupon sent by email, with a link to the web version of that catalog.

But which catalog should be enclosed in the box or included as a link in the email with the discount coupon? Exeter would like it to be an informed choice—a catalog that has a higher probability of inducing a purchase than simply choosing a catalog at random.

Assignment

Using the dataset CatalogCrossSell.xlsx, perform an association rules analysis, and comment on the results. Your discussion should provide interpretations in English of the meanings of the various output statistics (lift ratio, confidence,

---

[7]Copyright ©Datastats, LLC 2019; used with permission.

support) and include a very rough estimate (precise calculations are not necessary) of the extent to which this will help Exeter make an informed choice about which catalog to cross-promote to a purchaser.

Acknowledgment The data for this case have been adapted from the data in a set of cases provided for educational purposes by the Direct Marketing Education Foundation ("DMEF Academic Data Set Two, Multi Division Catalog Company, Code: 02DMEF"), used with permission.

23.9   Time Series Case: Forecasting Public Transportation Demand

`bicup2006.xlsx` is the dataset for this case study.

Background

Forecasting transportation demand is important for multiple purposes such as staffing, planning, and inventory control. The public transportation system in Santiago de Chile has gone through a major effort of reconstruction. In this context, a business intelligence competition took place in October 2006 that focused on forecasting demand for public transportation. This case is based on the competition, with some modifications.

Problem Description

A public transportation company is expecting an increase in demand for its services and is planning to acquire new buses and to extend its terminals. These investments require a reliable forecast of future demand. To create such forecasts, one can use data on historic demand. The company's data warehouse has data for each 15-minute interval between 6:30 and 22:00, on the number of passengers arriving at the terminal. As a forecasting consultant, you have been asked to create a forecasting method that can generate forecasts for the number of passengers arriving at the terminal.

Available Data

Part of the historic information is available in the file `bicup2006.xlsx`. The file contains the worksheet "Historic Information" with known demand for a 3-week period, separated into 15-minute intervals. The second worksheet ("Future") contains dates and times for a future 3-day period, for which forecasts should be generated (as part of the 2006 competition).

Assignment Goal

Your goal is to create a model/method that produces accurate forecasts. To evaluate your accuracy, partition the given historic data into two periods: a training period (the first two weeks) and a validation period (the last week). Models should be fitted only to the training data and evaluated on the validation data.

Although the competition winning criterion was the lowest mean absolute error (MAE) on the future 3-day data, this is *not* the goal for this assignment. Instead, if we consider a more realistic business context, our goal is to create a model that generates reasonably good forecasts on any time/day of the week. Consider not only predictive metrics such as MAE, MAPE, and RMSE but also look at actual and forecasted values, overlaid on a time plot, as well as a time plot of the forecast errors.

Assignment

For your final model, present the following summary:

1. Name of the method/combination of methods.

2. A brief description of the method/combination.

3. All estimated equations associated with constructing forecasts from this method.

4. The MAPE and MAE for the training period and the validation period.

5. Forecasts for the future period (March 22–24), in 15-minute bins.

6. A single chart showing the fit of the final version of the model to the entire period (including training, validation, and future). Note that this model should be fitted using the combined training + validation data.

Tips and Suggested Steps

1. Use exploratory analysis to identify the components of this time series. Is there a trend? Is there seasonality? If so, how many "seasons" are there? Are there any other visible patterns? Are the patterns global (the same throughout the series) or local?

2. Consider the frequency of the data from a practical and technical point of view. What are some options?

3. Compare the weekdays and weekends. How do they differ? Consider how these differences can be captured by different methods.

4. Examine the series for missing values or unusual values. Think of solutions.

5. Based on the patterns that you found in the data, which models or methods should be considered?

6. Consider how to handle actual counts of zero within the computation of MAPE.

23.10 LOAN APPROVAL[8]

Universal-Bank-Case.xlsx is the dataset for this case study.

Background

You are a data scientist recently hired by Universal Bank, a mid-sized bank in the southern United States. Most of your work to this point has involved pulling reports from databases, but now you have been given a more interesting task. The bank is facing competition from online lenders that can offer rapid automated loan approvals, and it wants to develop its own predictive model so that it can do likewise. Before building the web infrastructure, which could be costly, the bank wants to pilot a prototype loan approval model, developed by you.

The bank wants to launch its model with the approval process for personal loans extended to existing customers. The bank has only been offering these loans for a relatively short time, so has little data on default rates. It does have data on prior loan applications and whether they were approved or disapproved. You have done some preliminary data prep and feature selection work, resulting in the dataset of 5000 records for this project. Each record is for a customer, and consists of feature values for that customer and a record of the human decision on their loan application. Your end goal is to develop a model to predict that human decision, and an accompanying report to the bank's chief lending officer.

Regulatory Requirements

You are somewhat familiar with regulatory requirements with respect to discrimination (do a web search for the US Department of Justice Equal Credit Opportunity Act or ECOA). Bank attorneys have told you that the ECOA requirements pertain to the basis for credit decisions and do not mean that the proportion of approved loans must be the same for all groups.

Getting Started

You have the RDS framework in hand (see Chapter 22). You recognize that some aspects of the framework may take more time (e.g., consulting with other stakeholders and learning more about how the data were produced), but you want to get started with at least a draft so that you can discuss next steps with your superiors.

---

[8]Copyright ©2022 Datastats, LLC, and Galit Shmueli. Used by permission.

Assignment

1. Identify any features that might need to be excluded from the modeling task, per the ECOA.

2. Should you simply eliminate these features from the data?

3. Explore the data, with a focus on loan approval rates for different groups.

4. Split the data into training and validation data, and fit several models of your choice to predict whether a personal loan should be approved, using only permitted features. There are a number of possible performance measures; evaluate the model performance by the metric(s) you consider useful.

5. Assess the usefulness of the model from a pure model performance stand-point.

6. Considering the "protected" categories per the ECOA, evaluate whether the model is fair.

7. Describe steps that might be taken to improve the model fairness. Implement any measures that can be taken without going beyond the dataset at hand. (*Hint*: If you did not calculate a correlation matrix earlier, you should do one now.)

8. Write a very short report summarizing your findings.

References

Agrawal, R., Imielinski, T., and Swami, A. (1993). Mining associations between sets of items in massive databases. In: *Proceedings of the 1993 ACM-SIGMOD International Conference on Management of Data*, pp. 207–216. New York: ACM Press.

Anderson, D. R., Sweeney, D. J., Williams, T. A., Cam, J. D., Cochran, J. J., Fry, M. J., and Ohlmann, J. W. (2021). *Modern Business Statistics with Microsoft Excel*, 7th ed. Boston: Cengage Learning.

Berry, M. J. A., and Linoff, G. S. (1997). *Data Mining Techniques*. New York: Wiley.

Berry, M. J. A., and Linoff, G. S. (2000). *Mastering Data Mining*. New York: Wiley.

Breiman, L., Friedman, J., Olshen, R., and Stone, C. (1984). *Classification and Regression Trees*. Boca Raton, FL: Chapman Hall/CRC (orig. published by Wadsworth).

Chatfield, C. (2003). *The Analysis of Time Series: An Introduction*, 6th ed. Boca Raton, FL: Chapman Hall/CRC.

Delmaster, R., and Hancock, M. (2001). *Data Mining Explained*. Boston: Digital Press.

Efron, B. (1975). The efficiency of logistic regression compared to normal discriminant analysis. *Journal of the American Statistical Association*, vol. 70, number 352, pp. 892–898.

Few, S. (2009) *Now You See It*. Oakland, CA: Analytics Press.

Few, S. (2012). *Show Me the Numbers*, 2nd ed. Oakland, CA: Analytics Press.

Few, S. (2021). *Now You See It*, 2nd ed. Oakland, CA: Analytics Press

Fleming, G., and Bruce, P. C. (2021). *Responsible Data Science*. Hoboken, NJ: Wiley.

Golbeck, J. (2013). *Analyzing the Social Web*. Waltham, MA: Morgan Kaufmann.

Han, J., and Kamber, M. (2001). *Data Mining: Concepts and Techniques*. San Diego, CA: Academic Press.

Hand, D. J. (2009). Measuring classifier performance: a coherent alternative to the area under the ROC curve. *Machine Learning*, vol. 77, number 1, pp. 103–123.

Harris, H., Murphy, S., and Vaisman, M. (2013). *Analyzing the Analyzers: An Introspective Survey of Data Scientists and Their Work*. Cambridge, MA: O'Reilly Media.

Hastie, T., Tibshirani, R., and Friedman, J. (2001). *The Elements of Statistical Learning*. New York: Springer.

Hosmer, D. W., and Lemeshow, S. (2000). *Applied Logistic Regression*, 2nd ed. New York: Wiley-Interscience.

Hothorn, T., Hornik K., and Zeileis, A. (2006). Unbiased recursive partitioning: a conditional inference framework. *Journal of Computational and Graphical Statistics*, vol. 15, number 3, pp. 651–674.

Hyndman, R., and Yang, Y. Z. (2018). tsdl: Time Series Data Library. v0.1.0. https://pkg.yangzhuoranyang.com/tsdl/.

Jank, W., and Yahav, I. (2010). E-Loyalty networks in online auctions. *The Annals of Applied Statistics*, vol. 4, number 1, pp. 151-178.

Johnson, W., and Wichern, D. (2002). *Applied Multivariate Statistics*. Upper Saddle River, NJ: Prentice Hall.

Kohavi, R., Tang, D., and Xu, Y. (2020). *Trustworthy Online Controlled Experiments: A Practical Guide to A/B Testing*. Cambridge: Cambridge University Press.

Larsen, K. (2005). Generalized naive Bayes classifiers. *SIGKDD Explorations*, vol. 7, number 1, pp. 76–81.

Le, Q. V., Ranzato, M. A., Monga, R., Devin, M., Chen, K., Corrado, G. S., Dean, J., and Ng, A.Y. (2012). Building high-level features using large scale unsupervised learning. In *Proceedings of the Twenty-Ninth International Conference on Machine Learning*. Editors: John Langford and Joelle Pineau. Edinburgh: Omnipress.

Lobo, J. M., Jiménez-Valverde, A., and Real, R. (2008). AUC: a misleading measure of the performance of predictive distribution models. *Global ecology and Biogeography*, vol. 17, number 2, pp. 145–151.

Loh, W. -Y., and Shih, Y. -S. (1997), Split selection methods for classification trees. *Statistica Sinica*. vol. 7, number 4, pp. 815-840.

Matz, S. C., Kosinski, S. C., Nave, G., and Stillwell, D. J. (2017). Psychological targeting in digital mass persuasion. *Proceedings of the National Academy of Sciences*, vol. 114, number 48, pp. 12714–12719.

McCullugh, C. E., Paal, B., and Ashdown, S. P. (1998). An optimisation approach to apparel sizing. *Journal of the Operational Research Society*, vol. 49, number 5, pp. 492–499.

Molnar, C. (2022). Interpretable Machine Learning: A Guide for Making Black Box Models Explainable, 2nd ed. https://christophm.github.io/interpretable-ml-book/.

O'Neil, C. (2016). *Weapons of Math Destruction*. New York: Crown Publishers.

Pregibon, D. (1999). 2001: a statistical odyssey. Invited talk at *The Fifth ACM SIGKDD International Conference on Knowledge Discovery and Data Mining*. New York: ACM Press, p. 4.

Ribeiro, M. T., Singh, S., and Guestrin, C. (2016). Why should I trust you?: explaining the predictions of any classifier. In: Proceedings of the 22nd ACM SIGKDD International Conference on Knowledge Discovery and Data Mining. San Francisco, CA: ACM, pp. 1135–1144. DOI: 10.1145/2939672.2939778.

Russell, S. (2019). *Human Compatible: Artificial Intelligence and the Problem of Control*. New York: Penguin Books.

Saddiqi, N. (2017). *Intelligent Credit Scoring: Building and Implementing Better Credit Risk Scorecards*, 2nd ed. Hoboken, NJ: Wiley.

Shmueli, G. (2016). *Practical Time Series Forecasting: A Hands-On Guide*, 3rd ed. Green Cove Springs, FL: Axelrod-Schnall Publishers.

Siegel, E. (2013). *Predictive Analytics*. New York: Wiley.

Sutton, R. S., and Barto, A. G. (2018). *Reinforcement Learning: An Introduction*, 2nd ed. Cambridge, MA: The MIT Press.

Data Files Used in the Book

1. Accidents.xlsx
2. Airfares.xlsx
3. Amtrak.xlsx
4. ApplianceShipments.xlsx
5. AustralianWines.xlsx
6. Autos-electronics.zip
7. Banks.xlsx
8. Banks-adj.xlsx
9. bank-bias.xlsx
10. BareggTunnel.xlsx
11. BathSoap.xlsx
12. bicup2006.xlsx
13. Book Purchases.xlsx
14. BostonHousing.xlsx
15. CanadianWorkHours.xlsx
16. CatalogCrossSell.xlsx
17. Cereals.xlsx
18. CharlesBookClub.xlsx
19. COMPAS-clean.xlsx
20. Cosmetics.xlsx
21. Cosmetics-small.xlsx
22. Coursetopics.xlsx
23. DepartmentStoreSales.xlsx
24. drug.xlsx
25. EastWestAirlines.xlsx
26. EastWestAirlinesCluster.xlsx
27. EastWestAirlinesNN.xlsx
28. eBayAuctions.xlsx
29. eBayNetwork.xlsx
30. EbayTreemap.xlsx
31. EuropeanJobs.xlsx
32. email-A-B-test.xlsx
33. Faceplate.xlsx
34. Farm-ads.xlsx
35. FlightDelays.xlsx
36. Fundraising.xlsx
37. FutureFundraising.xlsx
38. gdp.xlsx
39. GermanCredit.xlsx
40. Hair-Care-Product.xlsx
41. LaptopSales.zip
42. LaptopSalesJanuary2008.xlsx
43. liftExample.xlsx
44. MortgageDefaulters.xlsx

Machine Learning for Business Analytics: Concepts, Techniques, and Applications with Analytic Solver® Data Mining,
Fourth Edition. Galit Shmueli, Peter C. Bruce, Kuber R. Deokar, and Nitin R. Patel
© 2023 John Wiley & Sons, Inc. Published 2023 by John Wiley & Sons, Inc.

Index

A/B testing, 319
accident data
    discriminant analysis, 293
    naive Bayes, 195
    neural nets, 269
accountability, 514
activation function, 261
additive seasonality, 423
adjacency list, 472
adjusted-R^2, 160, 162
affinity analysis, 16, 341
agglomerative, 372, 380
agglomerative algorithm, 380
aggregation, 71, 73, 75, 78
airfare data
    multiple linear regression, 166
algorithm, 10
ALVINN, 258
Amtrak data
    time series, 404, 416
    visualization, 62
Amtrak ridership example, 404
analytics, 3
antecedent, 343
appliance shipments data
    time series, 413, 442, 459
    visualization, 88
Apriori algorithm, 341, 345
AR models, 428
area under the curve, 129
ARIMA models, 428
artificial intelligence, 5, 9, 92, 257
artificial neural networks, 257

association rules, 16, 18, 341, 342
    confidence, 345, 350
    cutoff, 348
    data format, 347
    itemset, 343
    lift ratio, 345, 347
    random selection, 350
    statistical significance, 352
    support, 344
asymmetric cost, 22, 139, 565
asymmetric response, 565
attribute, 10
AUC, 129
audit report, 520
Australian wine sales data
    time series, 442, 462
Auto posts example, 498
autocorrelation, 415, 425
automatic machine learning, 310
AutoML, 303, 309, 310
    advantages and weaknesses, 313
average error, 117
average linkage, 385, 389
average squared errors, 154

back propagation, 264
backward elimination, 162, 241
bag-of-words, 488, 494
bagging, 222, 307
balanced portfolios, 370
bandit, 331
    contextual, 332
bar chart, 62

Machine Learning for Business Analytics: Concepts, Techniques, and Applications with Analytic Solver® Data Mining,
Fourth Edition. Galit Shmueli, Peter C. Bruce, Kuber R. Deokar, and Nitin R. Patel.
© 2023 John Wiley & Sons, Inc. Published 2023 by John Wiley & Sons, Inc.